T0418908

PALMYRA

THE OXFORD HANDBOOK OF

PALMYRA

Edited by

RUBINA RAJA

OXFORD

UNIVERSITY PRESS

OXFORD
UNIVERSITY PRESS

Oxford University Press is a department of the University of Oxford. It furthers the University's objective of excellence in research, scholarship, and education by publishing worldwide. Oxford is a registered trade mark of Oxford University Press in the UK and certain other countries.

Published in the United States of America by Oxford University Press
198 Madison Avenue, New York, NY 10016, United States of America.

Library of Congress Cataloging-in-Publication Data
Names: Raja, Rubina, 1975– author.
Title: The Oxford handbook of Palmyra / Rubina Raja.
Description: New York, NY : Oxford University Press, 2024. |
Series: Oxford handbooks series | Includes bibliographical references and index.
Identifiers: LCCN 2023017833 (print) | LCCN 2023017834 (ebook) |
ISBN 9780190858117 (hardback) | ISBN 9780190858131 (epub) | ISBN 9780190858148
Subjects: LCSH: Tadmur (Syria)—Civilization. | Tadmur
(Syria)—Antiquities. | Inscriptions—Syria—Tadmur.
Classification: LCC DS99.P17 R348 2024 (print) | LCC DS99.P17 (ebook) |
DDC 939.4/3—dc23/eng/20230419
LC record available at https://lccn.loc.gov/2023017833
LC ebook record available at https://lccn.loc.gov/2023017834

DOI: 10.1093/oxfordhb/9780190858117.001.0001

Printed by Sheridan Books, Inc., United States of America

CONTENTS

PART FIVE PALMYRA AND ITS MONUMENTS

PART SIX PALMYRA AND ITS ART

CONTRIBUTORS

Nathanael Andrade received his PhD in Greek and Roman history from the University of Michigan and is currently a professor in the history department at Binghamton University (SUNY). He has published extensively on the Roman and later Roman Near East, the social connections between the Roman Empire and various societies of Asia, and on the city of Palmyra. His books include *Syrian Identity in the Greco-Roman World* (Cambridge University Press, 2013); *The Journey of Christianity to India in Late Antiquity: Networks and the Movement of Culture* (Cambridge University Press, 2018); and *Zenobia: Shooting Star of Palmyra* (Oxford University Press, 2018).

Nicole Blanc is a CNRS archaeologist, Emeritus Director of research in the AOROC at the Ecole normale supérieure of Paris (France). Her work relates especially to wall decoration in the Roman world, focusing on stuccowork as a specific form of Roman artistic language and paying special attention to its contribution in the development of funeral rites. She took part in several archaeological missions, mainly in Italy (Rome and Vesuvian sites) and more recently in Syria (Palmyra), investigating new discoveries as well as formerly unearthed but neglected stucco reliefs. She has devoted several articles to the Palmyrene stuccoes discovered near the Efqa spring.

Olympia Bobou was born in Greece, where she studied history and archaeology; she received her MPhil in classical archaeology at the Aristotle University of Thessaloniki. She continued her studies at Oxford, where she completed a doctoral thesis on statues of children in the Hellenistic period, under the supervision of Professor Bert Smith. She worked as a research assistant and lecturer at various institutions in the United Kingdom, including the Universities of Oxford and Cambridge. She has published a monograph and various articles on the representations of children, as well as articles on emotions in ancient art. She is now working at the Circular Economy and Urban Sustainability in Antiquity Project, UrbNet, Aarhus University, as an assistant professor.

Eleonora Cussini PhD (1993) in Near Eastern Studies, Johns Hopkins University, Baltimore, MD (USA), studied and defended her dissertation 'The Aramaic Law of Sale and the Cuneiform Legal Tradition' under the direction of Delbert R. Hillers and Raymond Westbrook. From 1986 to 1996, she participated in the research project *The Comprehensive Aramaic Lexicon*, co-directed by Delbert R. Hillers, working on the lexical analysis of Palmyrene Aramaic dialect and preparing a comprehensive text edition of Palmyrene epigraphs. Since 1999, she has taught Semitic Philology at the Ca' Foscari University of Venice. Together with Delbert R. Hillers, she published *Palmyrene Aramaic*

Texts (Johns Hopkins University Press, 1996). After his untimely passing, she edited the memorial volume *A Journey to Palmyra: Collected Essays to Remember Delbert R. Hillers* (Brill, 2005). She has published extensively on Aramaic legal language, Palmyrene epigraphy, the role and representation of Palmyrene women, and Jewish identity in first- to third-century Syria.

Lucinda Dirven studied History of Art and Theology at the University of Leiden, where she obtained her PhD in 1999 with *The Palmyrenes of Dura-Europos: A Case Study of Religious Interaction* (Brill). Since then, she has taught at the departments of archaeology and history of the Universities of Utrecht and Amsterdam. Currently she is Professor of Antique Religions at Radboud University in Nijmegen. Her research concentrates on the Roman Near East in general and Dura, Hatra, and Palmyra in particular. Her hallmark is the use of a combination of literary and archaeological sources to reconstruct the religious history in the region.

Peter Edwell is Senior Lecturer in the Department of History and Archaeology at Macquarie University, Sydney in Australia. He teaches subjects on Late Antiquity, Palmyra, and the relationship between Rome and Parthia/Persia. Dr Edwell also works on the numismatics of the imperial and late Roman periods and is currently Deputy Director of the Australian Centre for Ancient Numismatic Studies. He recently published *Rome and Persia at War: Imperial Competition and Contact, 193–363 CE* (Routledge), which focuses on the relationship between Rome and Parthia/Persia from the second to fourth centuries AD.

Eugenia Equini Schneider is Professor Emeritus of Archaeology of the Roman Provinces, Teacher at the School for specialization in Archaeological Heritage and at the School for the Doctorate in Archaeology at the University of Rome La Sapienza, and a corresponding member of the German Archaeological Institute. Her areas of research and publication mainly concern the provincial sculpture in Rome and northern Africa, through field missions in Libya and the Eastern provinces during the Roman Age with surveys, research, and studies in Syria, Jordan, Israel, and Turkey. Presently, she is Director Emeritus of the Italian Archaeological Mission at Elaiussa Sebaste (Turkey), which she directed since 1995.

Her most significant publications on Asia Minor, Syria, and Arabia during the Roman Age concern the necropolis of Hierapolis and Elaiussa Sebaste and the funerary and honorary portraits, divinities, and religious traditions in the city of Palmyra, as well as a monographic publication on the Palmyrene Queen Zenobia and a volume on the city of Petra.

Hélène Eristov is a CNRS archaeologist. Her research focuses on Hellenistic and Roman wall painting in Italy, Gaul, and the Middle East. In particular, she studied material from the excavations of Beirut's city centre and painted decorations from Jerash (Jordan). She directed the Syro-French mission in Palmyra between 2004 and 2009.

Michał Gawlikowski is Professor Emeritus of the University of Warsaw, where he spent his entire career teaching archaeology and history of the Ancient Near East. He is particularly interested in Palmyra, having excavated there for over forty years. He also excavated in Jordan, Iraq, and, most recently, in Saudi Arabia. His main interests lay in the Graeco-Roman period in the Near East, in particular art, architecture, and epigraphy. He has recently published *Le sanctuaire d'Allat à Palmyre* (University of Warsaw, 2017) and in 2021 published a monograph entitled *Tadmor-Palmyra: A Caravan City Between East and West*.

Udo Hartmann studied history and philosophy in Leipzig and Berlin, received his PhD in ancient history at the Free University of Berlin ('Das palmyrenische Teilreich', 2001) and his habilitation in ancient history at the University of Jena (*Der spätantike Philosoph*, Habelt, 2018). Since 2012, he has been Lecturer in Ancient History at the University of Jena. His main research interests are the history of the Roman Empire in the third century, the Roman Near East, the history of Late Antiquity, and the relations between the Iranian and the Greek and Roman worlds in antiquity.

John F. Healey is Professor Emeritus of the University of Manchester since 2014, he completed his undergraduate and MA studies (Semitic Languages) in Dublin in 1972 and his doctorate (on Ugaritic) at the University of London in 1977. He went on to teach in universities in Cardiff and Durham, becoming Professor of Semitic Studies in Manchester in 1997. His publications have been mainly concerned with Nabataean Aramaic inscriptions and early Syriac inscriptions (*The Nabataean Tomb Inscriptions of Mada'in Salih*, Oxford University Press, 1993; *The Religion of the Nabataeans*, Brill, 2001; *The Old Syriac Inscriptions of Edessa and Osrhoene*, Brill, 1999, this last written with Han J. W. Drijvers). He also published *Aramaic Inscriptions and Documents of the Roman Period* (Oxford University Press, 2009), which contains a substantial section on Palmyrene inscriptions. He was for many years one of the editors of the *Journal of Semitic Studies* and is a Fellow of the British Academy.

Agnes Henning came to Palmyra for the first time as a student of classical archaeology during an excursion in 1996. She decided to write her master's thesis at Freie Universität Berlin and her PhD thesis at Köln University on the tower tombs of the Syrian oasis town, in close collaboration with the German Archaeological Institute in Damascus. After receiving her PhD in 2001, she was involved in the project of 'A New City Map of Palmyra.' In the following years, Dr Henning held several positions at universities and research institutions in Kiel, Berlin, Heidelberg, and Rome, focusing her research and fieldwork mainly on ancient south Italy and Sicily. Since 2015, she has been permanent scientific collaborator at Winckelmann-Institut of Humboldt University of Berlin and curator of the institute's collection of antiquities. In 2020, she completed her habilitation thesis on fortification architecture in pre-Roman south Italy. Despite this scientific reorientation, she continues to publish on Palmyra and its tombs.

Maura K. Heyn is Professor and Associate Dean at the University of North Carolina at Greensboro. She earned her PhD in Archaeology at the University of Southern California Los Angeles (2002), where she studied the art and archaeology of the Eastern Roman provinces under Dr Susan B. Downey. Maura's main research focus is the funerary sculpture of Palmyra, with particular attention to the ways in which the sculpture was used in the negotiation of social identities in the aftermath of Roman conquest. In addition to her work on the significance of hand gestures in Palmyrene funerary art, Maura has also published and presented on depictions of women in Palmyra and the meaning of the different styles of dress in the funerary portraiture. More recently, she has collaborated with Rubina Raja on several projects related to the attributes displayed in the Palmyrene funerary portraits.

Emanuele E. Intagliata is Assistant Professor at the University of Education in Milan, where he teaches Christian and Medieval Archaeology. His research interests lie primarily in the transformation of the townscape during the long Late Antiquity in the Roman East. He authored *Palmyra After Zenobia* (Oxbow, 2018), which was the first attempt to reassess the history of this site between the fourth and eighth centuries at monograph length. He has also worked extensively on late antique military history and frontier studies in northeastern Anatolia and present-day western Georgia.

Karol Juchniewicz was a member of the Polish Archaeological Mission in Palmyra in 2004–2011. He graduated in 2006 with the dissertation 'The Iconography of Victoria in Palmyra.' His PhD, obtained in 2011 at the University of Warsaw, was dedicated to the architecture and chronology of the late Roman fortifications of the city. In addition to long-lasting research on Palmyra, he was also a member of Polish archaeological projects in Lebanon, Egypt, Sudan, Kuwait, and Saudi Arabia. In 2009 and 2012, he took part in the Islamic Jerash Project. In 2013, he was a field director of the Danish archaeological project on Failaka Island. From 2014 until 2019, he was a field director of the Saudi-Polish archaeological project in Aynuna, Saudi Arabia. Currently he is conducting research projects in Lebanon, the United Arab Emirates, and Saudi Arabia under the auspices of the Institute of the Mediterranean and Oriental Cultures, Polish Academy of Sciences, Warsaw.

Sławomir P. Kowalski is Director at the Department of Cooperation with Polish Community Abroad, Ministry of Foreign Affairs of the Republic of Poland, Warsaw, Poland. Dr Kowalski joined the Ministry of Foreign Affairs of the Republic of Poland in 1998, served in embassies in Canada, Lebanon, Kenya, Albania, and Norway. Dr Kowalski holds a PhD in Classical Archaeology from the University of Warsaw, where he was an academic teacher and researcher for ten years. As an archaeologist he participated in research projects in Syria and Lebanon, as well as in Italy, France, Germany, Switzerland, Austria, and Bulgaria. In the 1990s, he was a member of the Polish archaeological excavations team in Palmyra headed by M. Gawlikowski.

Nathalia Breintoft Kristensen is a PhD student at the Department of Classics and Ancient History at the University of Warwick. She has a BA and MA in Classical

Archaeology from Aarhus University. She has previously worked on the Palmyra Portrait Project based at Aarhus University. Her PhD project investigates the circulation and economic patterns of small change in Roman Syria through the Palmyrene coinage. She has also worked on the iconography of Palmyrene coins and how they reflected civic Palmyrene identity.

Robyn L. Le Blanc is Assistant Professor of Classical Studies at the University of North Carolina at Greensboro. Her research and fieldwork focus on communities in the Roman provinces and, in particular, on the development and transformation of public space and civic coinage. She has excavated in Israel, Montenegro, and Britain and has recently published on the Forum Marsyas on coins of Roman Mesopotamia for *The Numismatic Chronicle* (2020) and co-authored an article on the Roman bouleuterion from Ascalon/Ashkelon for *AJA* (2016).

Jørgen Christian Meyer is Professor emeritus of Ancient History at the University of Bergen, where he taught from 1983 to 2020. He studied history and classical archaeology at the University of Aarhus, Denmark. Dr Meyer conducted fieldwork in a village in the south-eastern part of Turkey from 1985 to 1990, to make a comparative analysis with ancient agriculture and friendship and family structures. From 2001 to 2004, he was a member of the research project Trade, Migration and Cultural Change in the Indian Ocean (The Norwegian Research Council), and he conducted fieldwork in Oman and in the desert between the Nile and the Red Sea, following the old Roman caravan route. He started to work in Syria in 2004, and, from 2008 to 2013, he was head of the joint Syrian-Norwegian project 'Palmyrena: City, Hinterland and Caravan Trade Between Orient and Occident with Surveys North of Palmyra' in 2008, 2009, and 2011. The results of the surveys were published in *Palmyrena: Palmyra and the Surrounding Territory from the Roman to the Early Islamic Period* (Archaeopress, 2017). Meyer is currently working on nomadic networks on the Arabian Peninsula from antiquity up into the Ottoman period.

Rubina Raja (DPhil 2005, University of Oxford) is Professor of Classical Art and Archaeology at Aarhus University, Denmark, and Centre Director of the Danish National Research Foundation's Centre of Excellence for Urban Network Evolutions. Dr Raja has published widely on the Mediterranean region and the East from the Hellenistic to the medieval periods, high-definition archaeology, and the intersection between archaeology and natural sciences, iconography, and portrait studies, as well as the history of religion in the Roman world. Among her monographs about Palmyrene archaeology and history are *Pearl of the Desert. A History of Palmyra* (OUP, 2022) and co-authored together with Olympia Bobou, *Palmyrene Sarcophagi* (Brepols, 2023). She has headed the Palmyra Portrait Project since 2012.

Annie Sartre-Fauriat is Emeritus Professor of Ancient History at Artois University (France). She has published many books and articles about Syria, especially on architecture, society, and culture in Syria (first century BC–seventeenth century AD); she edited and commented a volume on William John Bankes's account of his journeys in Syria

(1816 and 1818). She works on the corpus of Greek and Latin inscriptions in the Hawran (south Syria), and she has also published many books and articles about Palmyra. She is associated with the Center for Research and Study of History and Society (CREHS), in Artois, France, and the Histoire et Sources des Mondes antiques (HiSoMa), Maison de l'Orient et de la Méditerranée Université Lyon-2, Lyon.

Andreas Schmidt-Colinet completed his dissertation in Classical Archaeology at Cologne University in 1974. He was Assistant at Frankfurt University from 1975 to 1980 and earned a travel scholarship from the German Archaeological Institute for 1975–1976. He was Scientific Assistant at the German Archaeological Institute in Damascus from 1980 to 1984. Since then (until 2010), he has served as Director of the Syro-German Archaeological Mission at Palmyra and as Assistant Professor at Bern University from 1980 to 1984. He received his 1972 habilitation in Classical Archaeology in 1972. He was Visiting Professor at the Universities of Warsaw, Berlin, Frankfurt, Mainz, Besançon, Neuchâtel, Paris, and Vienna from 1980 to 1996, and Professor of Classical Archaeology at Vienna University from 1996 to 2010. His main field of research and publication is art and architecture of the Hellenistic-Roman Near East, especially the Nabatean architecture at Petra and Madain Saleh; the Nymphaeum at Apamea; and the funerary art and architecture, textiles, quarries, and early urbanism of Palmyra.

Katia Schörle is Researcher in Ancient History and Archaeology at Université Côte d'Azur, CNRS, CEPAM. Her research and publications focus on the Roman Mediterranean in terms of its economy, maritime connections, and long-distance trade. Some of her recent publications include research on Roman Palmyra and its trading patterns, in particular its maritime trade.

Eivind Heldaas Seland is Professor of Ancient History and Premodern Global History at the University of Bergen. His research interest is in the interaction between environment, economy, ideology, and political power in shaping complex societies and early states in the ancient world. He has worked extensively within the Indian Ocean/Red Sea region and the Near East, but is also interested in the Mediterranean and Central Asia. Seland is the author of *Ships of the Desert and Ships of the Sea: Palmyra in the World Trade of the First Three Centuries CE* (Harrassowitz, 2016).

Andrew M. Smith II is Associate Professor of Classics and History at George Washington University. Smith specializes in the history and archaeology of the Hellenistic, Roman, and Byzantine Near East. His research focuses on processes of community formation and urbanism in the Near East, with an emphasis on Arab communities. His most recent book, *Roman Palmyra: Identity, Community, and State Formation* (Oxford University Press, 2014), examines the 'making' of Palmyrenes and the development of Palmyra (Syria) into a classical Mediterranean city. Smith also has a long-term interest in Nabataean, Roman, and Byzantine Petra (Jordan), where his research interests target social and economic activity in rural settings as well as the integration of cities with their hinterlands. Smith has worked in Jordan since 1989, and he has been involved with and directed numerous archaeological surveys and excavations. Currently, he directs the Bir Madhkur Project and the Bir Madhkur Incense Route Project in southern Jordan, in the hinterland of Petra.

Julia Steding is a postdoctoral researcher at the Centre for Urban Network Evolutions, Aarhus University. From 2016 to 2019 she wrote her PhD on the production economy of Palmyrene funerary portraiture at Aarhus University. Her main interest is funerary portraiture, including its iconography as well as aspects of production and economy.

Claude Vibert-Guigue is an archaeologist; in 1976, he specialized in the field of Roman wall paintings. He was trained at the Centre d'Etude des Peintures Murales Romaines (Soissons). A stay at the French Institute of Archaeology of the Near East in Jordan allowed him to work in various contexts, including rock or monumental structures in Petra and painted hypogea in the necropolis of the Decapolis. A second stay in Jordan allowed him to document the Umayyad bathhouse of Qusayr 'Amra. His thesis on Umayyad paintings was defended in 1997. He joined the CNRS in 1999, as a research engineer. He developed the 'Décor *in situ*' programme and contributed to the study of a decorated reservoir in Azraq (Jordan). In 2004, a Franco-Syrian programme including the Three Brothers Tomb began. In 2016, he collaborated on Jordan's Bayt Ras Tomb Project. His many works are regularly the subject of lectures, articles, and monographs.

Dagmara Wielgosz-Rondolino is an archaeologist and Assistant Professor at the Institute of Archaeology of the University of Warsaw. Since 1993, she has been working in Palmyra as a member of the Polish Archaeological Mission headed by Michał Gawlikowski. She obtained her PhD in Near Eastern Archaeology from the University 'La Sapienza' in Rome for dissertation 'Scultura di tradizione occidentale a Palmira' (Western Tradition Sculpture in Palmyra). She was employed as Adjunct Professor in Archaeology and Art History of Ancient Greece and Rome at the University Ca' Foscari in Venice from 2002 to 2007, and was appointed as a research fellow in KU Leuven in 2007–2009. Her major interests and research projects concern Palmyra and the Roman East, as well as archaeometry and research on ancient marbles (the project *Marmora Asiatica*). In addition to Syria, she took part in excavations in Cyprus, Lebanon, and Turkey, and she led an excavation project in Egypt (Marea, Mareotis region).

Jean-Baptiste Yon is Senior Researcher at the French CNRS, French Institute for the Near East in Beirut, Ifpo, and Laboratoire Hisoma, Lyon (PhD, Tours 1999, 'Les notables de Palmyre'; Habilitation, Paris 2014). He is now Director of the French archaeological mission at Tyre (Lebanon), as well as part of the IGLS team (Inscriptions grecques et latines de la Syric) working in Lebanon and Jordan and a member of the Palmyra Portrait Project. He has worked extensively on the history and the epigraphy of the Hellenistic and Roman Near East. Among his recent publications are the corpus of the Greek and Latin inscriptions of Palmyra (*IGLS* XVII), the catalogue of the Greek and Latin inscriptions in the national museum of Beirut (*IGLMusBey*), and an edited volume on the ports of the ancient Indian Ocean.

Gioia Zenoni (PhD in Classical Archaeology) has been Vice-Director of the Syro-Italian Archaeological Mission in Palmyra PAL.M.A.I.S., directed by Maria Teresa Grassi (Università degli Studi di Milano). Her research there focused on domestic architecture and the development of building techniques over time. She is involved both in excavation projects in Italy and in the Middle East and in research programmes on public archaeology, collaborating with many universities, museums, and institutions. She is Lecturer at IULM University and Project Manager of the research centre HumanLab, dealing with archaeological films, communication plans, and digital tools for archaeology.

Maps

....

MAP 0.1 City plan of Palmyra and its four necropoleis.

Courtesy of Katarína Mokránová and Rubina Raja. Vector data were based on extended
Topographia Palmyrena (Schnädelbach 2008) data, provided courtesy of Deutsches
Archäologisches Institut (Orient-Abteilung, AS Damaskus).

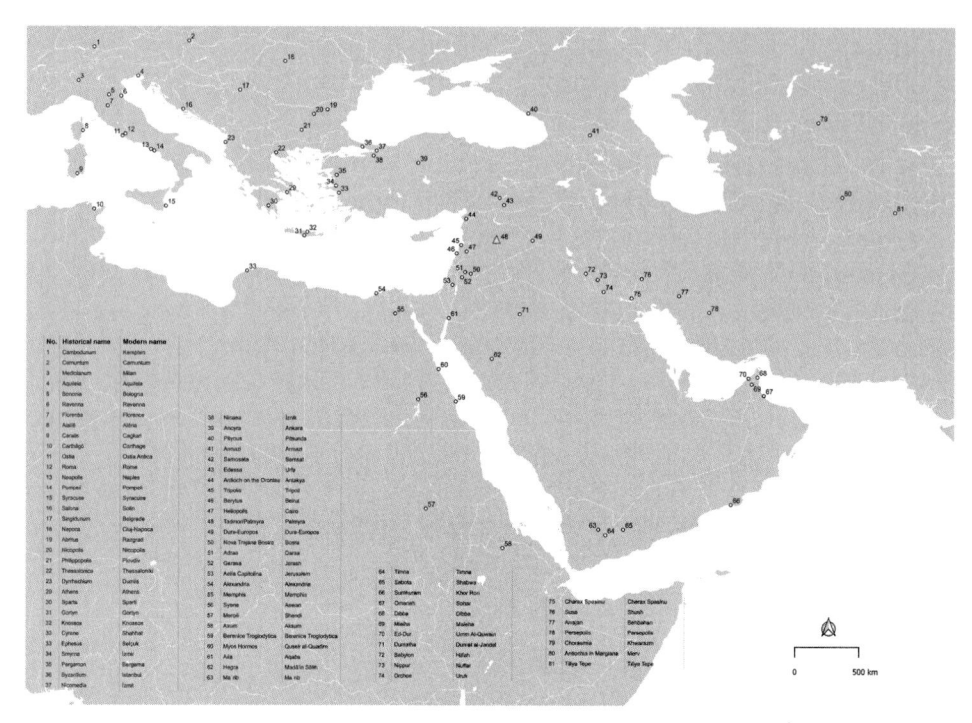

MAP 0.2 Map of the regions surrounding Palmyra, showing notable (but not exhaustive) Roman sites within the area.

Courtesy of Katarína Mokránová and Rubina Raja.

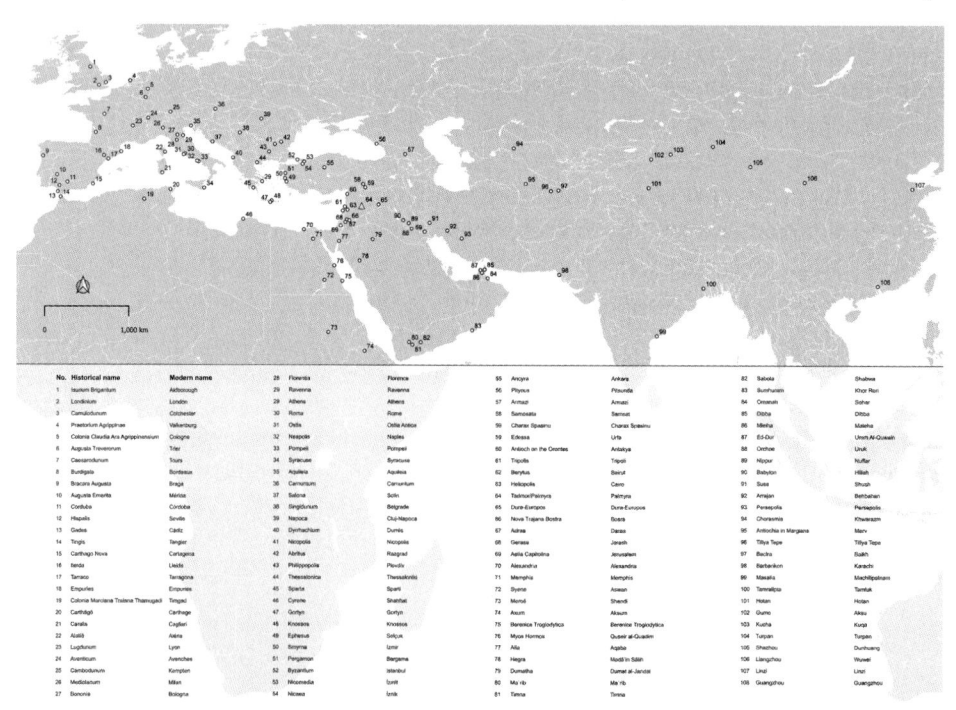

MAP 0.3 Map showing Palmyra's broader embedment in the Eastern Hemisphere and a range of ancient sites (not exhaustive).

Courtesy of Katarína Mokránová and Rubina Raja.

CHAPTER 1

PALMYRA–TADMOR IN THE SYRIAN DESERT

An Introduction to the Handbook of Palmyra

RUBINA RAJA

PALMYRA: AN OASIS CITY IN THE SYRIAN DESERT

PALMYRA, in antiquity and today also known as Tadmor, is a famed oasis city in the Syrian Desert (Map 1.1). It is mentioned as early as the time of the Amarna letters in the second millennium BC, and Pliny the Elder also wrote about the site in the first century AD. His passages are still being quoted by many scholars, although there is agreement that the man did not visit the site himself (Plin., *NH* 5.88). It is a site spun in legends and about which numerous narratives and fairytale-like accounts have been written and told in the Western world after its (re)discovery in the seventeenth century, when an entourage of British merchants tried to reach the site but were taken hostage by Bedouins. They succeeded in reaching Palmyra a few years later. But it was only in the eighteenth century, with visits by French and British travellers and their descriptions and drawings that were successively published, that the site entered the European cultural sphere and took the Europeans by storm (Wood 1753). Among that entourage was its funder, James Dawkins, drawing on his family's plantation wealth. The engravings in the published volume were based on the drawings of Giovanni Battista Borra, who was also a member of the expedition (Hutton 1927; Dardanello 2013).[1] However, it is also a site which has suffered excruciating devastation several times and at the hands of many: the Roman

---

[1] Also see, e.g., Sartre-Fauriat 2021, as well as Sartre-Fauriat 2019. Orientalist and philosopher Constantin-François de Chasseboeuf, comte de Volney, published on the decline of great civilizations: Volney 1791.

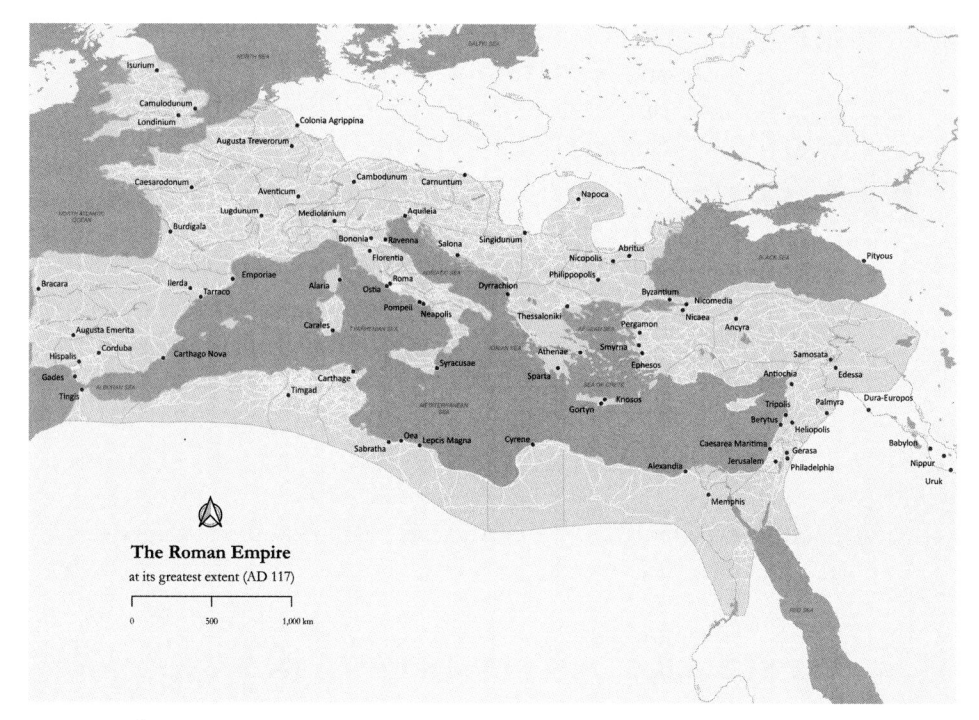

MAP. 1.1 The Roman Empire.

© Katarina Mokránová and Rubina Raja.

army during the reign of Aurelian, Arab invaders, Ottoman rulers, the colonial powers during the Mandate period, the Assad regime, and, last but not least, the ongoing conflict in Syria. Before and during the Assad regime Tadmor was known for its local prison, one of the most notorious in the country, a place where one did not want to go (Amnesty International, 2001; Haugbølle 2008; Cooke 2011).[2] To many Syrians, Tadmor, or Palmyra, was not the romantic site it was to tourists who began to visit there in the thousands in the years before civil war broke out, when Syria became one of the very attractive countries for European as well as American and Asian tourists to visit. Syria was, of course, already at this point in time a heaven for Arabs from other countries who visited the country to enjoy both the more relaxed unofficial regulations related to alcohol and prostitution as well as to see the country's rich cultural heritage. In the early 2000s, the country was flourishing in a way it had not for many decades and the future promised to be a bit brighter than it had looked in a long time—at least on the surface. The conflict in Syria broke out in 2011, which is the last time that many scholars who did fieldwork or research in the country went there. Only recently have people begun to

---

[2] Much has been written on the destruction of the site, its reconstruction, and digital initiatives which aim to preserve Palmyrene heritage. For understanding the destruction itself and the number of actors, ASOR's reporting is valuable: https://www.asor.org/chi/reports/weekly-monthly. The prison at the site was already in use during the 1920s: Moubayed 2018, 28.

return, but only to take part in survey work concerning reconstruction projects as well as preservation and conservation initiatives.[3]

Despite this, enough has survived for scholars, archaeologists, and historians alike— as well as visitors and the interested public—to stay fascinated with this site and want to know it better. While one must first and foremost face up to the fact that the devastation of Palmyra and all of Syria is one of the largest humanitarian catastrophes since World War II, we must also realize that the only way to move forward in the hope of a better future is to learn from the past. This can be understood in a twofold way: we must learn from things which have happened in the past in order to make sure that they do not happen again, and, to learn from the past, we need scholars of the past to communicate this knowledge to us in a way so that it can be incorporated into and penetrate ongoing discourses—including outside its own narrow field of scholarship. That is what this handbook aims to do through thirty-six chapters written by experts on various aspects of Palmyra's archaeology and history.

The focus in this handbook is on exactly that: the archaeology and history of Palmyra—our hard evidence for what this location was before, during, and after the Roman period. However, it is not a handbook on the historiography of research on Palmyra or the profound destruction which the site has undergone in the past decade. Only one chapter is dedicated to the modern period. For the research history of the site, other resources are available that give good overviews and provide the necessary literature to do further research (Sartre-Fauriat 2019; Sartre 2016).[4] In the nineteenth century the export of antiquities from Palmyra took off, and it was in the later part of that century that today's largest collections outside of Syria were founded containing Palmyrene objects, including the collection in the Ny Carlsberg Glyptotek in Copenhagen (Figure 1.1) and Musée de Louvre in Paris (Raja 2018; 2019; Simiot 1978).[5]

While numerous travellers, tourists, and scholars alike had visited Palmyra since the eighteenth century, it was only with the German expedition headed by Theodor Wiegand that systematic archaeological exploration of the site began. This took place during Ottoman rule and was one of numerous German expeditions to the Near East. Others included that at Baalbek, another monumental site today located in modern Lebanon (Wiegand 1932).[6] It was, however, from the very early years of the French Mandate that large-scale archaeological excavations at the site began (Figure 1.2).

---

[3] For the conflict and its implications for archaeology, see, e.g., Ali 2013; Guidetti and Perini 2015.

[4] Also see the exhibition catalogue Charles-Gaffiot et al. 2001, as well as Baird and Kamash 2019, esp. 11; Baird et al. 2023.

[5] For writing on the antiquities' laws during the Ottoman and later Mandate period, see Goode 2007, esp. 25, 33–34; Griswold 2020; Bahrani et al. 2011; Bobou and Thomsen 2021.

[6] On the creation of the Mandate's antiquities service by René Dussaud, see Gelin 2002, esp. 280. On Dussaud and his archaeological policies in the antiquities service, see Al-Maqdissi 2019. For the context of French archaeology in the Middle East, see Chevalier 2002; see especially 460ff. On the French financing of archaeological service, see Neep 2012.

FIGURE 1.1 Exhibition of Palmyrene funerary sculptures during the special exhibition 'The Road to Palmyra', 2019–2020.

© Courtesy of Ny Carlsberg Glyptotek, photographer Anders Sune Berg.

FIGURE 1.2 Workers in Palmyra at an excavation led by the Danish archaeologist Harald Ingholt during the French Mandate.

© Rubina Raja and Palmyra Portrait Project, courtesy of Mary Ebba Underdown.

These focused on both the graves around the city as well as monuments within the urban landscape. One of the most prominent, which today must be regarded as a dubious undertaking, was the clearing of the entire local village (Figure 1.3) situated in the approximately 200 by 200m temenos of Bēl sprawling around the Roman-period temple, which had been turned into a mosque.

One of the first things that the French archaeological mission to the site initiated was a dismantling of the village and displacement of the entire population to newly built constructions in the new village (Baird and Kamesh 2019, esp. 13, with further references). They did so in order to restore the complex to its Roman-period heyday and make it more attractive to tourists. Many of the locals who worked with the archaeological missions must have been living in the village and been employed while they were being actively displaced.[7] However, to this day, we know very little about this entire process (however, see Baird et al. 2023). World War II put a halt to archaeological work at the site for a while, and it was only in the second half of the twentieth century that research at the site resumed, despite the fact that numerous scholars in the meantime had published results from their work at the site (Bobou et al. 2021; Bobou et al. 2022).

In recent years, numerous works on the archaeology and history of the site have appeared, most recently by Michal Gawlikowski (2021) and Rubina Raja (2022).

FIGURE 1.3 The local village in the temenos of the Temple of Bēl, before its clearing.

© Rubina Raja and Palmyra Portrait Project.

[7] On local archaeological knowledge in Middle Eastern expeditions, see Mickel 2019; 2021. On the disinheritance of Syrian archaeological labourers through archaeological photography, see Baird 2011.

However, earlier works such as those by Sommer, Smith, and Kaizer have also greatly contributed to our knowledge about the site (Kaizer 2002; Smith 2013; Sommer 2018). In these books, one finds further literature and solid overviews of the site's development, with a point of departure in very different approaches ranging from personal experiences during fieldwork at the site, to new research on the city's sculptural corpus, or with a focus on the integration of the site into the Roman Empire with a point of departure in the local community and its local heritage. Other important works have also appeared and add to our perspectives on the city (Sartre-Fauriat and Sartre 2008; Smith 2013; Sartre and Sartre-Fauriat 2016; Sommer 2017).[8]

However, one cannot ignore that Palmyra was part of a greater whole, very rightly as Pliny wrote.

> Palmyra is a city famous for the beauty of its site, the riches of its soil, and the delicious quality and abundance of its water. Its fields are surrounded by sands on every side, and are thus separated, as it were, by nature from the rest of the world. Though placed between the two great empires of Rome and Parthia, it still maintains its independence; never failing, at the very first moment that a rupture between them is threatened, to attract the careful attention of both. It is distant 337 miles from Seleucia of the Parthians, generally known as Seleucia on the Tigris, 203 from the nearest part of the Syrian coast, and twenty-seven less from Damascus. (Plin., *NH* 5.88)

Indeed, the city was part of a more or less global network, with all its terminological complications, and when it comes to the ancient world we must acknowledge this when studying the site. Therefore, Palmyra must also be seen within its local regional context, that of the Near East as well as its surrounding neighbours, the empires of Rome and Parthia (see, e.g., Blömer and Raja 2019; Seland 2016). When considering the fact that Palmyra was not an empire as such, did not found cities across vast territories, and did not export its language and religion to numerous other places, it is profoundly interesting to see just how the city succeeded in positioning itself as a major player—at one point having extended its reign far into Asia Minor and incorporating all of Egypt into its territory—although only for a short time. Such a relatively small site must have had an immense amount of wealth and economic resources as well as political power to pull off such stunts in times when strong powers around it, despite having been weakened, were watching it closely. So, to understand that framework, one must go to the broader scholarship on the Near East. In this handbook, this broader outlook comes only from a Palmyrene perspective and is covered in the regional chapters; for broader basic literature one must go to other sources, such as the standard works on the Roman Near East including those of Butcher, Millar, and Sartre (Butcher 2003; Millar 1993; Sartre 2001; 2005), as well Edwell and the somewhat more disputed accounts by Ball (Edwell 2008; Ball 2016; see also, e.g., Fowlkes and Seymour 2019).

---

[8] Also see the recent edited volume by Nielsen and Raja (2019), which contains a number of up-to-date contributions on various aspects of the city's archaeology and history.

In general, research on Palmyra has yielded an enormous amount of scholarly publications in a number of languages, and the current handbook can in no way be entirely exhaustive when it comes to the literature published on the site. However, it provides a very thorough and well-researched point of departure, offering the opinions of experts on the topics covered and with a great wealth of further literature to be found in the notes and bibliographies at the end of each chapter. The interested reader is encouraged to explore these sources for an expanded view on the subject of Palmyra. The handbook will most certainly stand as the most comprehensive and wide-ranging standard work on the site, its archaeology, and history for many years to come.

So, if this handbook pulls together the status quo, where is there to go for newcomers, students, scholars looking for comparative angles or hoping to work on Palmyra? I believe that there are many paths to take from here, many angles from which to do research, and while this handbook shows the way through updated and stellar researched chapters, it also opens up questions. How can we understand even better Palmyra as an integrated part of the region within which it was located? How can we understand the Roman Near East in a new light through the most current research undertaken on the site? How can we understand it as part of a broader global scope? Recently the series Studies on Palmyrene Archaeology and History published a number of volumes concerning a string of topics ranging from research history, historiography, the religious life of Palmyra, the role of attributes, production economy, and Palmyra and the East, as well as the coins and banqueting tesserae from the site (Bobou et al. 2021; Heyn and Raja 2021; Raja and Steding 2021; Lapatin and Raja 2022; Raja 2022; Raja, Steding, and Yon 2021; Steding 2022). The seven volumes so far have shown that there still are immense amounts of research topics which need to be tackled, and, when seen together with the three earlier volumes in the series Palmyrenske Studier (Palmyrene Studies) (Kropp and Raja 2016; Long and Sørensen 2017; Krag and Raja 2019), it is clear to everyone that research topics pertaining to the archaeology and history of Palmyra are far from exhausted. New contributions with expanded overviews of Palmyra's location in a broader setting include those pulled together by Graf (2017; 2019), which contain useful summaries of the evidence and plentiful bibliographies. Interested readers, students, scholars, and the lay public can, however, begin here to explore Palmyra and its local, regional, and global relations by delving into the thirty-six chapters of this handbook.

The handbook is structured according to a set of topics which cover the site and its immediate hinterland, starting out with Chapters 1 and 2 on the climate and environment as well as the hinterland and sedentarization processes. These chapters are written by two scholars who undertook surveys in the hinterland of Palmyra and have first-hand experience with the site and the region.

Part Two, consisting of nine chapters, tackles various aspects of the site which together gives the reader a longue durée perspective on the site from the pre-Roman period up to the medieval period. (Not many publications can boast such chronological coverage of the site through chapters written by experts on exactly these topics.) The three chapters in Part Three are all dedicated to the languages of Palmyra, the local Aramaic dialect as well as the evidence for Greek and Latin, which are found at the site.

Furthermore, the famous Tax Tariff text, today in the Hermitage in Saint Petersburg is tackled, and we are also given insight into the legal language used in Palmyra. Part Four, consisting of five chapters, deals with the contacts that the Palmyrenes had outside of Palmyra. These chapters cover the city's connections to the East and the West and investigate the lives of Palmyrenes living abroad, both fairly close to home in Dura-Europos on the Euphrates as well as much further away in the Gulf region, Egypt, Rome, and other places where evidence for their presence has been found. Part Five covers the monuments of Palmyra from the Roman period until Late Antiquity in a set of five chapters. Both urban monuments as well as funerary buildings are covered in this section. In Part Six, 11 chapters delve into various aspects of the art of Palmyra in the Roman period. The site is extremely rich in both architectural decoration and sculptural material, and the experts on various aspects of the city's rich cultural heritage address these topics through fresh research. The very last chapter of the book is a postludium written by one of the most experienced researchers on the site's history and its current state. While there is undoubtedly more to be said about the site, this handbook most certainly presents a solid attempt to present the site from a variety of angles through entirely new research undertaken by experts.

ACKNOWLEDGEMENTS

The editor acknowledges the funding received by the Danish National Research Foundation's Centre for Urban Network Evolutions (grant no. 119) as well as the funding received from the Carlsberg Foundation for the various Palmyra projects based at Aarhus University, first and foremost the Palmyra Portrait Project. Furthermore, I thank the ALIPH Foundation as well as the Augustinus Foundation for funding for further Palmyra-related projects.

BIBLIOGRAPHY

Ali, Cheikhmous. 2013. 'Syrian Heritage Under Threat'. *Journal of Eastern Mediterranean Archaeology & Heritage Studies* 1(4): 361–366.

Al-Maqdissi, Michel. 2019. 'Les fouilles de Ras Shamra- Ougarit dans le contexte de la 'question archéologique syrienne' durant la première décennie du mandat français (1919–1929)'. *Semitica* 61: 163–183.

Amnesty International. 2001. 'Syria: Torture, Despair and Dehumanisation in Tadmur Military Prison'. https://www.amnesty.org/en/documents/mde24/014/2001/en/.

Bahrani, Zainab, Zeynep Çelik, and Edhem Eldem, eds. 2011. *Scramble for the Past: A Story of Archaeology in the Ottoman Empire, 1753–1914*. Istanbul: SALT.

Baird, J. A., and Zena Kamash. 2019. 'Remembering Roman Syria: Valuing Tadmor-Palmyra, from "Discovery" to Destruction'. *Bulletin of the Institute of Classical Studies* 62: 1–29.

Baird, J., Zena Kamash, and Rubina Raja. 2023. 'Knowing Palmyra. Mandatory Production of Archaeological Knowledge'. *Journal of Social Archaeology*: 1–23. doi.org/10.1177/14696053221144013

Ball, Warwick. 2016. *Rome in the East: The Transformation of an Empire*. New York: Routledge.

Blömer, Michael, and Rubina Raja, eds. 2019. *Funerary Portraiture in Greater Roman Syria*. Studies in Classical Archaeology 6. Turnhout: Brepols.

Bobou, Olympia, Jesper V. Jensen, Nathalia B. Kristensen, Rubina Raja, and Rikke Randeris Thomsen, eds. 2021. *Studies on Palmyrene Sculpture: A Translation of Harald Ingholt's Studier over Palmyrensk Skulptur, Edited and with Commentary*. Studies in Palmyrene Archaeology and History 1. Turnhout: Brepols.

Bobou, Olympia, Amy C. Miranda, and Rubina Raja. 2022. 'Harald Ingholt's Twentieth-Century Archive of Palmyrene Sculptures: "Unleashing" Archived Archaeological Material of Modern Conflict Zones'. *Journal of Eastern Mediterranean Archaeology and Heritage Studies* 10(1): 74–101. https://10.5325/jeasmedarcherstu.10.1.0074.

Bobou, Olympia, and Rikke Randeris Thomsen. 2021. 'Collecting Then and Now'. In *Studies on Palmyrene Sculpture: A Translation of Harald Ingholt's Studier over Palmyrensk Skulptur, Edited and with Commentary*, edited by Olympia Bobou, Jesper V. Jensen, Nathalia B. Kristensen, Rubina Raja, and Rikke Randeris Thomsen, 533–535 Turnhout: Brepols.

Butcher, Kevin. 2003. *Roman Syria and the Near East*. Los Angeles: The J. Paul Getty Museum.

Charles-Gaffiot, Jacques, Henri Lavagne, and Jean-Marc Hofman, eds. 2001. *Moi, Zénobie, reine de Palmyre*. Paris: Seuil.

Chevalier, Nicole. 2002. *La recherche archéologique française au Moyen-Orient 1842–1947*. Editions Recherche sur les Civilisations 11. Paris: Éditions Recherche sur les civilisations.

Cooke, Miriam. 2011. 'The Cell Story: Syrian Prison Stories After Hafiz Asad'. *Middle East Critique* 20: 169–187.

Dardanello, Giuseppe, ed. 2013. *Giovanni Battista Borra: Da Palmira a Racconigi*. Turin: Editris Duemila.

Edwell, Peter M. 2008. *Between Rome and Persia: The Middle Euphrates, Mesopotamia and Palmyra under Roman Control*. London: Routledge.

Fowlkes, Blair, and Michael Seymour. 2019. *The World Between Empires: Art and Identity in the Ancient Middle East*. New York: The Metropolitan Museum of Art.

Gawlikowski, Michal. 2021. *Tadmor – Palmyra: A Caravan City Between East and West*. Krakow: Irsa.

Gelin, Mathilde. 2002. *L'archéologie en Syrie et au Liban à l'époque du Mandat 1919–1946: Histoire et organisation*. Paris: Geuthner.

Goode, James F. 2007. *Negotiating for the Past: Archaeology, Nationalism, and Diplomacy in the Middle East, 1919–1941*. Austin: University of Texas Press.

Graf, David F. 2017. 'The Silk Road Between Syria and China'. In *Trade, Commerce, and the State in the Roman World*, edited by Andrew Wilson and Alan K. Bowman, 443–530. Oxford: Oxford University Press.

Graf, David F. 2019. 'Palmyra: The Indigenous Factor'. In *Ancient Cities*. Vol. 1, *Roman Imperial Cities in the East and in Central-Southern Italy*, edited by Nathanael Andrade, Carlo Marcaccini, Giulia Marconi, and Donata Violante, 295–318. Rome: 'L'Erma' di Bretschneider.

Griswold, Sarah. 2020. 'Locating Archaeological Expertise: Debating Antiquities Norms in the A Mandates, 1918–1926'. In *Experts et expertise dans les Mandats de la société des nations: Figures, champs, outils*, edited by Philippe Bourmaud, Norig Neveu, and Chantal Verdeil, 141–158. Paris: Presses de l'Inalco.

Guidetti, Mattia, and Silvia Perini. 2015. 'Civil War and Cultural Heritage in Syria, 2011–2015'. *Syrian Studies Association Bulletin* 20(1): 1–42.

Haugbølle, Sune. 2008. 'Imprisonment, Truth Telling and Historical Memory in Syria'. *Mediterranean Politics* 13 (2008), 261–276.

Heyn, Maura K., and Rubina Raja, eds. 2021. *Individualizing the Dead: Attributes in Palmyrene Funerary Sculpture*. Studies in Palmyrene Archaeology and History 3. Turnhout: Brepols.

Hutton, C. A. 1927. 'The Travels of "Palmyra" Wood in 1750–51'. *The Journal of Hellenic Studies* 47: 102–128.

Kaizer, Ted. 2002. *The Religious Life of Palmyra: A Study of the Social Patterns of Worship in the Roman Period*. Stuttgart: Steiner.

Krag, Signe, and Rubina Raja, eds. 2019. *Women, Children and the Family in Palmyra*. Palmyrene Studies 3. Copenhagen: Royal Danish Academy of Sciences and Letters.

Kropp, Andreas, and Rubina Raja, eds. 2016. *The World of Palmyra*. Palmyrene Studies. Copenhagen: Royal Danish Academy of Sciences and Letters.

Lapatin, Kenneth, and Rubina Raja. 2022. *Palmyra and the East*. Studies in Palmyrene Archaeology and History 6 Brepols: Turnhout.

Long, Tracey, and Annette H. Sørensen, eds. 2017. *Positions and Professions in Palmyra*. Palmyrene Studies. Copenhagen: Royal Danish Academy of Sciences and Letters.

Mickel, Allison. 2019. 'Essential Excavation Experts: Alienation and Agency in the History of Archaeological Labor'. *Archaeologies: Journal of the World Archaeological Congress* 15(2): 181–205.

Mickel, Allison. 2021. *Why Those Who Shovel Are Silent: A History of Local Archaeological Knowledge and Labor*. Louisville: University Press of Colorado.

Millar, Fergus. 1993. *The Roman Near East, 31 BC–AD 337*. Cambridge, MA: Harvard University Press.

Moubayed, Sami. 2018. *The Makers of Modern Syria: The Rise and Fall of Syrian Democracy 1918–1958*. London: Bloomsbury.

Neep, Daniel. 2012. *Occupying Syria Under the French Mandate: Insurgency, Space and State Formation*. Cambridge: Cambridge University Press.

Nielsen, Anne M., and Rubina Raja, eds. 2019. *The Road to Palmyra*. Copenhagen: Ny Carlsberg Glyptotek.

Raja, Rubina. 2018. 'Palmyrene Funerary Portraits: Collection Histories and Current Research'. In *Palmyra: Mirage in the Desert*, edited by Joan Aruz, 100–109. New York: Metropolitan Museum.

Raja, Rubina. 2019. *The Palmyra Collection*. Copenhagen: Ny Carlsberg Glyptotek.

Raja, Rubina, ed. 2022. *The Small Stuff of the Palmyrenes: The Coins and Tesserae from Palmyra*. Studies in Palmyrene Archaeology and History 5. Turnhout: Brepols.

Raja, Rubina, and Julia Steding. 2021. *Production Economy in Greater Roman Syria: Trade Networks and Production Processes*. Studies in Palmyrene Archaeology and History 2. Turnhout: Brepols.

Raja, Rubina, Julia Steding, and Jean-Baptiste Yon. 2021. *Excavating Palmyra: Harald Ingholt's Excavation Diaries; A Transcript, Translation, and Commentary*. Studies in Palmyrene Archaeology and History 4, 2 vols. Turnhout: Brepols.

Sartre, Maurice. 2001. *D'Alexandre à Zénobie: Histoire du Levant antique, IVe siècle avant J.-C.-IIIe siècle après J.-C*. Paris: Fayard.

Sartre, Maurice. 2005. *The Middle East under Rome*. Cambridge, MA: Harvard University Press.

Sartre, Maurice. 2016. 'Zénobie dans l'imaginaire occidental'. In *The World of Palmyra*, edited by Andreas Kropp and Rubina Raja, 207–221. Copenhagen: Royal Danish Academy of Sciences and Letters.

Sartre, Maurice, and Annie Sartre-Fauriat. 2016. *Palmyre: Vérités et légendes*. Paris: Perrin.

Sartre-Fauriat, Annie. 2019. 'The Discovery and Reception of Palmyra'. In *The Road to Palmyra*, edited by Anne M. Nielsen and Rubina Raja, 65–76. Copenhagen: Ny Carlsberg Glyptotek.

Sartre-Fauriat, Annie. 2021. *Aventuriers, voyageurs et savants à la découverte archéologique de la Syrie (xviie – xxie siècle)*. Paris: CNRS.

Sartre-Fauriat, Annie, and Maurice Sartre. 2008. *Palmyre: La cité des caravanes*. Paris: Gallimard.

Seland, Eivind Heldaas. 2016. *Ships of the Desert and Ships of the Sea: Palmyra in the World Trade of the First Three Centuries CE*. Wiesbaden: Harrassowitz.

Simiot, Bernard. 1978. *Moi, Zénobie, reine de Palmyre*. Paris: Albin Michel.

Smith, Andrew M. I. 2013. *Roman Palmyra: Identity, Community, and State Formation*. Oxford: Oxford University Press.

Sommer, Michael. 2017. *Palmyra: Biographie einer verlorenen Stadt*. Darmstadt: von Zabern.

Sommer, Michael. 2018. *Palmyra: A History*. New York: Routledge.

Steding, Julia. 2022. *Carvers and Customers in Roman Palmyra: The Production Economy of Limestone Loculus Reliefs*. Brepols: Turnhout.

Volney, Constantin-Francois. 1791. *The Ruins, or Meditation on the Revolutions of Empires*. Paris.

Wiegand, Theodor. 1932. *Palmyra: Ergebnisse der Expeditionen von 1902 und 1917*. Berlin: Keller.

Wood, Robert. 1753. *The Ruins of Palmyra, Otherwise Tedmor in the Desart*. London.

PART ONE

SETTING AND LANDSCAPE

CHAPTER 2

CLIMATE AND ENVIRONMENT OF PALMYRA AND THE SYRIAN DESERT

EIVIND HELDAAS SELAND

THE BRIDE OF THE DESERT?

IN his famous *Natural History* (5.88), dedicated to Emperor Titus in AD 79, the Roman naturalist Pliny the Elder described Palmyra as a fertile and well-watered island in a vast sea of sand. His contemporary, Flavius Josephus, attributed the location of the city to the presence of wells and springs in an otherwise arid landscape (*Jewish Antiquities*, 8.153–4). Although any visitor to the region will notice that the surface of the Syrian Desert consists more of gravel, rocks, and dirt than sand, the evocative image of a desert city has continued to inspire outside observers, ranging from authors of academic scholarship to those writing romances and tourist brochures. However, the notion of Palmyra as 'the bride of the desert', goes beyond worn orientalist clichés. Like any settlement, Palmyra depended on, and thus was also formed by her hinterland. The natural environment of the region defined a scope of action that arguably came to define both sociopolitical and socioeconomic aspects of Palmyrene society. Below, the climate and geography of the Palmyrene region, in the wider sense of the Syrian Desert and in the narrower sense of the immediate Palmyrene hinterland, are discussed with this in mind. This topic borders on and partially overlaps those addressed in the chapters of this volume on hinterland and sedentarization, and on trade networks (Chapter 3 [Meyer] and Chapter 17 [Seland], this volume) and may usefully be read in conjunction with these.

Location and Historical Terminology

Palmyra is situated in the northern Syrian Desert, some 215 km from Damascus to the southwest and 135 km from Homs to the west. To the north, the distance to Raqqa and the Euphrates is about 150 km, whereas Dura-Europos, also on the Euphrates, is reached 225 km to the east. To the south, the closest permanent habitation of historical significance is Tayma, in present-day Saudi Arabia, some 750 km away (Map 2.1).

On the evidence of the Palmyrene Tax Tariff (*PAT* 0259: Chapter 4 [Healey], this volume), the Palmyrenes themselves seem to have distinguished between the city, its territory, and the hinterland. Boundary stones fixed the limits of the territory towards the north-west-west at Khirbet al-Bilas, 75 km from Palmyra, and to the west at Qasr al-Heir al-Gharbi, 65 km away (*IGLS* V, 2550, 2552; Schlumberger 1939), whereas the delimitation of the territory towards the Euphrates and the south is unknown.

To outsiders in the Roman period, Palmyra was situated in 'the Syrian wilderness [*solitudines*] of Palmyra', said to go from Petra to the Euphrates and to extend southwards all the way to present-day Yemen (Pliny, *NH* 5.87), or in 'the Arabia of the tent-dwellers' (*skenitai*) (Strabo, *Geo.* 16.1.8, 28). In Ptolemy's *Geography* (5.14), Palmyra is described as a town in the territory of the Palmyrena, being a part of Syria, and bordering on the regions of Arabia Petrae and Arabia Deserta.

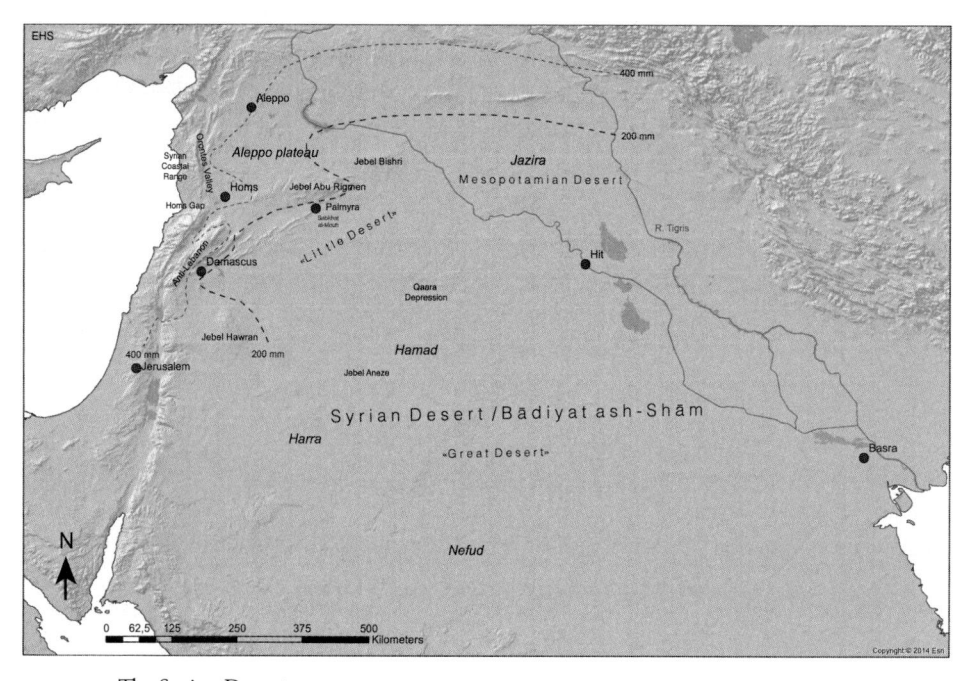

MAP 2.1 The Syrian Desert.

Basemap © ESRI 2014.

The ancient, and admittedly vague notions of Palmyra's geographical situation are of interest for two reasons: first, because they describe the marginality and remoteness of the Palmyrene region in terms that remained valid until the introduction of modern communication and direct government control in the 1920s, and second, because they formed the basis of later Western geographical knowledge of the region, which was subsequently reimposed on the region by travellers, explorers, and orientalists in the seventeenth to twentieth centuries. The lands they visited were called the Badya as-Sham by the people who lived there. *Sham*, 'left', was the term designated for Greater Syria by the Islamic conquerors because their worldview was based in the Hejaz and oriented towards the east. *Badya* is untilled country without permanent habitations (Grant 1937, 11), not very different from the notions reflected in the terminology employed by outside observers in the ancient world, and above all, signifying that this region was primarily the domain of pastoralists, thus underlining the anomaly of Palmyra as a major settlement in the first three centuries AD (Raja and Seland 2022).

Two works of historical geography remain particularly useful for the modern student of Palmyra despite their venerable age. Alois Musil's *Palmyrena: A Topographical Itinerary* (1928) consists of edited diaries from extensive journeys by camel, horse, and (occasionally and involuntarily) on foot, undertaken in the period between 1908 and 1915. As hinted at by the paraphrase of Ptolemy's *Geography* in the title, an important aim of the journeys was to survey the traces of the Roman presence in the region. The relative lack of success of this part of the endeavour was more than compensated for by Musil's keen ethnographic interest in the nomadic communities still dominating the region and the minute measurements he made for the benefit of Austrian-Hungarian intelligence-gathering before and during the early phases of World War I. Christina Phelps Grant's (later Harris) *The Syrian Desert* (Grant 1937) combines the much greater geographical detail available during the French and British mandates twenty years later with extensive historical and ethnographic information on travel and communication in the premodern period.

Geography, Vegetation, and Fauna

The Syrian Desert, in the modern and Roman-period usage of the term, corresponds to a stretch of land shaped like a right-angled triangle (Map 2.1). The baseline extends from the head of the Gulf of Aqaba to the head of the Persian Gulf. The apex is south of Aleppo, and the hypotenuse is formed by the Euphrates River (Grant 1937, 8–9). Geologically it is constituted by the top of the Arabian plate, bordered by the Levantine rift system to the west and the Anti-Taurus Mountains of the Eurasian plate to the north and east (Held 1989, 31–33, Mart, Ryan, and Lunina 2005). The upper part of this triangle was the region that Ptolemy called Palmyrena. Early modern travellers called it 'the Little Desert' and its Bedouin inhabitants 'Shamyia'. The lower part of the triangle is the Arabia Deserta and parts of the Arabia Petrae of Ptolemy, and was later known as 'the Great Desert' or

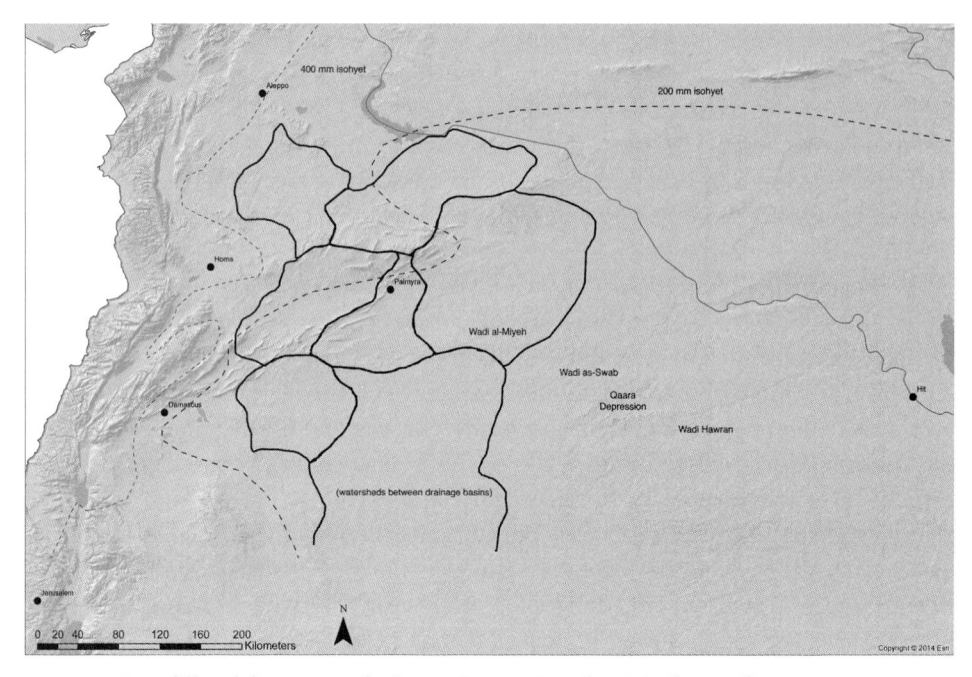

MAP 2.2   Rainfall and drainage in the Syrian Desert. Based on Wirth 1971, fig. 10.

Basemap © ESRI 2014.

'as-Samawa' (Grant 1937, 11–12). As discussed below, this division is based on ecological grounds and has important implications for our understanding of Palmyrene society.

Topographically, the Syrian Desert is a plateau, declining gently from an elevation of 400 m to 800 m above mean sea level at the foothills of the northern and western mountain chains respectively, to 30 m to 40 m above mean sea level at the escarpment of the Euphrates Valley. The plain is broken by a chain of low, but steep mountains, known as the Palmyrides, starting just north-east of Damascus and extending north-west to Palmyra, which it skirts on the north side. From Palmyra the mountains continue towards the Euphrates, but in the form of the taller, although gentler, limestone massifs of Jebel Chaar, Jebel Abyat, Jebel Abu Rigmen, and Jebel Bishri, reaching the river just north of Deir es Zor (Wirth 1971, 52–55). The limestone mountains, with their rich soil, plentiful opportunities for water harvesting, and occasional perennial springs (Meyer 2017; Meyer 2020; Seland 2019; see Chapter 3 [Meyer], this volume) have remained important pastures for sheep and goats until today. South and east of Palmyra the landscape is almost level, cut only by a series of deep wadis (seasonal watercourses), draining eastwards towards the Euphrates. This rock-strewn and arid landscape, known to the Bedouin as the Hamad, is the traditional winter pasture of camel pastoralists. It is bordered to the west by the rough lava plateau of al-Harra (Betts 1999, 1–4), to the east by the Euphrates, and gives way in the south to the sandy Nefud Desert in present-day Saudi Arabia.

Commentators have been quick to point out that the 'desert' part of the Syrian Desert name is a misnomer and that the region would be better described as a dry steppe, due to regular winter rains and lush vegetation, if, unlike today, left undisturbed (Oppenheim 1899, 319; Millar 1994, xi–xii; Lewis 1987, 1–2; Meyer 2017, 17). This is especially true of the northern 'Little Desert', and particularly to the north and north-west of Palmyra, which is indeed categorized as dry steppe (BS) in the Köppen-Geiger climate classification (Beck et al. 2018). Early travellers described this region in terms of open parkland with scattered vegetation of terebinth and pistachio (Betts 1999, 2–4; Wilkinson 2003, 18–19; Oppenheim 1899; Meyer 2017, 17–22; Musil 1928, *passim*). On the other hand, the southern 'Great Desert' is considerably less verdant and is also classified as a true desert (Köppen-Geiger BW) (Held 1989, 45–55; Wirth 1971, 88–93; Beck et al. 2018).

Today, most of the Syrian Desert appears to be badlands. In part this is deceptive, in part it is a result of human activity. Overgrazing, logging for fuel and charcoal, strip mining, geological prospection, and extensive motorized transport over the past century have heavily degraded the terrain. On the other hand, vegetation in protected landscape reserves and remote mountain areas attests to potential for recovery, and even today the hard topsoil shelters grass roots that turn the landscape light green within hours after rains. A telling example is that local social media users posted videos of water returning in force to the Efqa spring in Palmyra in early 2019. The spring had been dry since the 1990s due to a receding groundwater table. The return of water, likely due to a combination of an unusually moist winter and the tragic circumstances of the Syrian civil war, which led to a near depopulation of the city and cessation of agriculture in the oasis, nevertheless attests to the robustness and potential of the landscape. Historically, the region was home to gazelle, onyx, ibex, wild sheep and goats, ostriches, lions, wild boar, onagers, jackals, wolves, hyenas, and foxes, but most of these are now extinct or severely endangered due to hunting (Held 1989, 66–67). We cannot, however, extrapolate directly from this to Palmyrene history, as environmental degradation of the hinterland was probably also a problem during the peak of Palmyrene urbanism. However, no studies have been made of this thus far.

COMMUNICATION

The Syrian Desert south of Palmyra is mostly flat. The problem is that a direct crossing, for example, from Damascus to middle Mesopotamia, leads through areas almost void of perennial water sources and thus is impractical for larger groups (Grant 1937, 39; Seland 2019; see also Map 2.3). Palmyra, with its location at a major water source, and by the lowest and easiest passage through the mountain chain running across the northern Syrian Desert, was well situated to control regional communication on both a north–south and an east–west axis (Grant 1937, 13–14). Until the twentieth century, communication in the Syrian Desert was accomplished by horse, camel, donkey, mule, or on foot. The 20 miles/32 km a day recommended for pack camels in the British army may be taken as an approximate measure of travel time (Leonard 1894, 186), keeping in mind that messengers and mounted soldiers could travel much faster. The surviving infrastructure along the Strata Diocletiana, going from Damascus (ca. 7 days' travel)

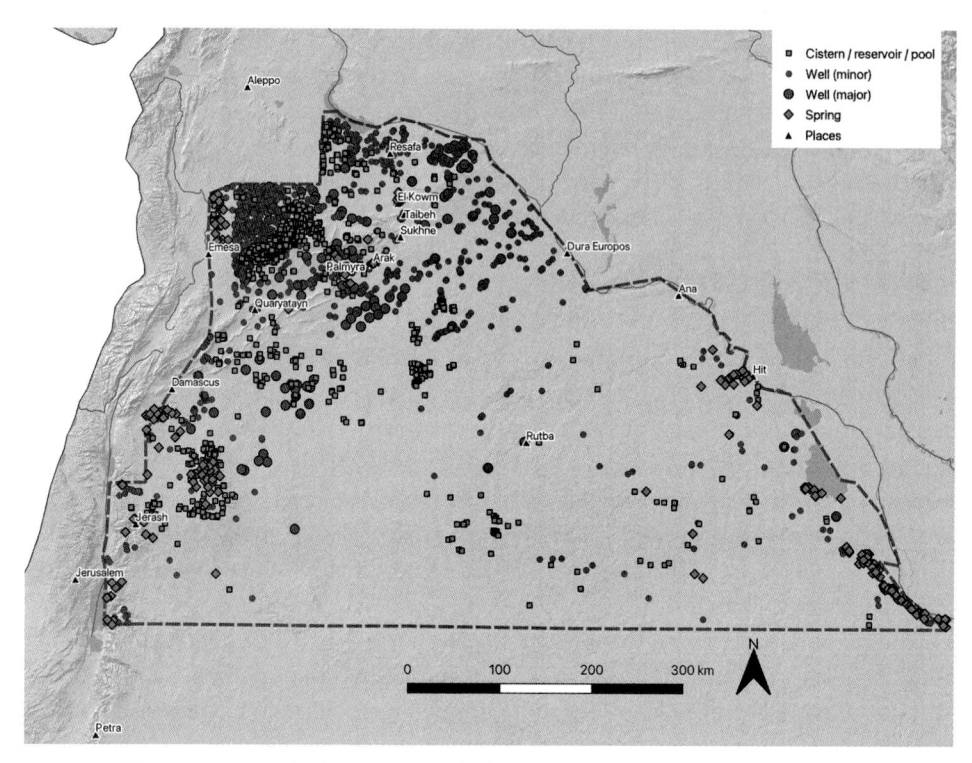

MAP 2.3   Water sources in the Syrian Desert (Seland 2019), Palmyra, and the Euphrates.

Basemap © ESRI 2014.

along the southern edge of the mountains to Sura at the Euphrates (5–6 days) by way of Palmyra, postdates the Roman sack and occupation of Palmyra, but certainly follows an older track (Mior 2016). Such routes, although less fortified, are also evident from the boundary stones mentioned, probably marking passage to the territories of Emesa (Homs) (5 days) and Apamea (ca. 8 days) and placed on the tracks leading there. A secondary route that may be pieced together from late Roman itineraries and the remains of military strongholds also seems to have led to the town of Seriana/Isryeh, and from there to Chalkis, Beroa (Aleppo), and Antioch (Meyer 2017, 60–62) (ca. 10 days). The crossing to Dura-Europos on the Euphrates (ca. 7 days), which was home to a sizeable Palmyrene community, has not yet been adequately tracked (Poidebard 1934, 115–116), whereas the caravan road south-east to Hit on the Euphrates (ca. 14 days) is well documented (Poidebard 1934; Gregory and Kennedy 1985; Meyer and Seland 2016).

Climate

Two major atmospheric systems influence precipitation and temperature in the region of Palmyra. The first is the subtropical high-pressure belt, which contributes to arid weather and high temperatures in the summer months (Held 1989, 46–48; Roberts and Wright 1993, 194). In the winter, this system shifts to the south, and a second phenomenon takes prominence. This is a series of low-pressure systems that travel from the Atlantic through the Mediterranean, most of them hitting the Levantine coast in northern Syria, providing precipitation all the way eastwards to present-day Afghanistan, mostly as rain, occasionally as sleet and snow.

The rainfall pattern in the Syrian Desert is also heavily influenced by the parallel mountain ranges running along the coast, at their tallest in the Lebanon and Anti-Lebanon Mountains. To some extent, these funnel cyclones northwards along the coast before they head inland, but, more importantly, they relieve passing clouds of the greater part of their moisture, creating a partial rain shadow (Karmon 1983, 27; Wirth 1971, 80–87). Together, the mountains and the storm paths are responsible for the semicircular shape of the isohyet known as 'the Fertile Crescent'. The Syrian Desert is on the barren side of that imaginary line, which is in fact not a line at all but a wide and shifting frontier between agricultural and pastoral lands famously described by Gertrude Bell as 'between the Desert and the Sown' (Bell 1907). To illustrate, the minimum annual precipitation necessary for the cultivation of barley, Syria's staple crop in antiquity and today, is 200 mm. The 1961–1990 average for Aleppo was 335 mm, Palmyra received 133 mm, and Kuwait, at the south-eastern extreme of the Syrian Desert, 107 mm (World Meteorological Organization 2017). Thus the region north-west of Palmyra is a transitional zone between stable Mediterranean (Aleppo) and stable desert (Palmyra) climates. Almost all rain falls from October to March. Also, rainfall varies, with drought years occurring at irregular intervals, and these are up to 50 percent drier than the mean (Wirth 1971, 88–93). It follows that the limits of cultivation are not static and fluctuate not only with climate change but also with sociopolitical and socioeconomic factors, such as market access and security (Lewis 1987, 1–2; Wirth 1969, 45). Changes in precipitation influence not only agricultural production, but also have an impact on pasturelands and thus the pastoral economy (Wirth 1969).

Has the Palmyrene regional climate changed since antiquity? The question is critical, as the archaeological record of permanent habitation in the Roman and early Islamic periods is far more extensive than of more recent periods. Although regional data from the Syrian Desert are lacking, much work has been done elsewhere in the Near East. Collocated palaeoclimatological data series from the Soreq caves in Jerusalem, Lake Van in eastern Turkey, the Dead Sea, the Nile, and elsewhere provide relatively robust time series for meso-regional climate change (Roberts and Wright 1993; Wilkinson 2003, 17–22; Rosen 2007, 50–71, 165–169; Issar and Zohar 2007, 11–37; Witakowski 2010; Orland et al. 2009; Finné et al. 2011; McCormick et al. 2013; Izdebski et al. 2016; Harper and McCormick 2018).

As a point of departure, we might underline that the regional climate in the Near East in antiquity broadly resembled modern conditions. For example, this is clear from Pliny's, Josephus's, and Strabo's descriptions of the Syrian Desert as desert/wilderness and nomad's land, cited above. However, this does not imply that the climate was similar. As the discussion above made clear, minor changes in precipitation have potentially significant consequences for agricultural and pastoral production, especially so in the transition zone between desert and agricultural land. If such changes were long-term, they were also likely to have had lasting consequences for marginal regions such as that of the Palmyrene hinterland.

From the palaeoclimatological record, it seems that the onset of the Hellenistic period coincided with a period of a moister climate, which lasted until approximately AD 200 (Enzel et al. 2003; Issar and Zohar 2007, 194, 205; Finné et al. 2011, 3186). In the third century, the climate became more variable, and, by the mid-fourth century, it had become considerably drier than the historical average (Issar and Zohar 2007, 214; Izdebski et al. 2016, 196–198, 205; Harper and McCormick 2018, 36–37). The dry period lasted until the latter half of the fifth century, when a comparatively moist climate returned until the late seventh century (Enzel et al. 2003; Issar and Zohar 2007, 215–216; Finné et al. 2011, 3186; Izdebski et al. 2016, 196–198, 205). After this, a long period of difficult climatic conditions commenced (Enzel et al. 2003; Issar and Zohar 2007, 217; Büntgen et al 2016; Izdebski et al. 2016, 196–198, 205; Harper 2017, 249–259).

Although both the paleoclimatological and historical/archaeological time resolution is currently insufficient for discussion of possible causal relationships between climate change and Palmyrene history, some general observations may be made: the urbanization and growth of Palmyra coincided with the period of favourable conditions known as the 'Roman Climate Optimum' (Lamb 1997, 14–24; Harper 2017, 23–64). More humid conditions in the Syrian Desert would have strengthened the pastoral economy from which Palmyra evolved and facilitated the agricultural economy it had to develop in order to flourish (Raja and Seland 2022). Drier conditions in the third century, however, seem to have not had a strong negative impact on Palmyra (contra: Issar and Zohar 2007, 213–214), which by that period evidently had political and economic means to compensate for lower productivity in the hinterland. Even if the return of more humid conditions from the late fifth century must have facilitated the continued settlement of the northern and western Palmyrena into the late Roman and early Islamic periods (Raja and Seland 2022), drier conditions from the mid–late seventh century onwards cannot alone explain their gradual abandonment, which happened subsequently, although it may have contributed to that development.

DRAINAGE, WATER, AND SUBSISTENCE

Next to rainfall, drainage has a large role in explaining settlement and subsistence patterns in the Syrian Desert, including the favourable situation of Palmyra and the significant differences between the northern and southern 'Little' and 'Great' deserts. Topography divides the northern Syrian Desert into a number of drainage basins (Wirth 1971, 63–64) (Map 2.2). The topsoil in the Syrian Desert is too hard to be penetrated by the infrequent and short showers that bring most of the winter rain. Most water drains along the surface, gathering in wadis and natural depressions. Although evaporation is too high and rainfall too low for the formation of permanent lakes, the wadis and also the fissures in the limestone bedrock and mountains north of Palmyra funnel underground water towards the lowest points of the drainage basins, providing the basis for numerous springs and wells. Palmyra is situated at the lowest point of one of these basins, explaining not only the presence of rich springs, but also the seasonal lake just south of the city, which turns into the economically important salt flats of Sabkhat al-Mouh during the summer. The varied topography of the mountains north of Palmyra also facilitates the artificial funnelling of water into cisterns or the construction of small-scale irrigation walls (Meyer 2017), whereas the pools gathering in natural depressions (*khabras*) may be used for animal consumption.

South of the present-day border with Iraq the situation is different. The terrain slopes towards the Euphrates. Groundwater and surface water follow three major wadis—Swab, Helqum, and Hauran—and the only permanent wells are found in these, in some cases up to 150 km apart (Map 2.3). Thus, water supply is severely limited outside the winter months, when pools of rainwater gather here, as well (Seland 2019).

The varying access to water resulting from the rainfall and drainage patterns had a strong bearing on subsistence, which is likely to have influenced the nature of Palmyrene society and the dynamics between the city and its hinterland. The exploitation of the Syrian Desert by sheep and goat pastoralists goes back to at least the late third millennium, for which the Mari archives offer insight into an already fully developed, semi-nomadic economy (Prag 1985; Pappi 2005; Schou 2015, 260–322). The Mari texts describe societies where segments of the population followed the herds into the desert in the winter months, returning to the river settlement in the dry season to let the animals graze on—and thus fertilize—the recently harvested fields. Other segments of the same groups would stay permanently in the city. This lifestyle, famously described as 'dimorphic' by Rowton (1973a; 1973b), has also been applied as a model for Palmyrene society (Stoneman 1992, 25–26; Yon 2002, 95–98, 148; Sommer 2005, 95–97; Smith 2013, 53). The Little Desert, with short distances between water sources, is indeed well suited to this kind of nomadism. Ethnographic studies show how such groups cover distances of 50–200 km over the course of a season, returning to agricultural land in the period from May to November. However, by the time of Palmyra, the one-humped camel had been introduced to the Syrian Desert. These animals make do with the moisture in their fodder and cover 600–800 km in their annual treks between summer and winter pastures, also utilizing the less verdant Great Desert, which is mostly off limits for sheep nomads, who camp in the northern part of this region only in the winter (Wirth 1969; 1971, 255; Raswan 1930). Thus Palmyrene society must have been trimorphic, integrating an urban segment, a semi-nomadic segment under way in the well-watered surroundings of Palmyra, and a fully nomadic population following the camels through most of the year (Seland 2016, 19–24). It was the reliance on camel nomadism that also enabled the Palmyrenes to operate caravans to the Euphrates and southern Mesopotamia, through the arid and inaccessible Great Desert. This model arguably reconciles the archaeological evidence of an intensively utilized immediate territory (Meyer 2017; Chapter 3 [Meyer], this volume), contrasted with only scattered inscriptions and archaeological traces in the southern outer periphery, with the three-layer structure of city, territory, and hinterland evident in the regulations laid down in the tax law (*PAT* 0259; Matthews 1984; Chapter 4 [Healey], this volume).

CONCLUSION

Although the orientalist clichés of Palmyra as 'the queen of the desert' or 'the bride of the desert' carry some truth, the union between urban centre and desert hinterland was one of necessity rather than romance. Palmyra is situated at a natural communication hub and at the ecotone between the dry steppe, with good possibilities for sheep and goat pastoralism and even agriculture (Meyer 2020; Chapter 3 [Meyer], this volume) and the true desert, which was the domain of camel nomads. The physical location in this transitional zone enabled the Palmyrenes to not only establish and maintain a major city in an arid environment, but also to engage in long-distance trade. However, Palmyra's history is not an example of environmental determinism. This is clear from the fact that, although Palmyra has an urban history spanning more than a millennium (Hammad 2010), it was never a place of more than regional (Syrian Desert) importance, except during the first three centuries AD, when it grew into a major geopolitical player. The long-term success of Palmyrene urbanism and trade depended on each other, but each rested on the willingness and ability of the Palmyrenes to actively utilize the possibilities offered by the marginal landscape.

ABBREVIATIONS

PAT   Hillers, Delbert R., and Eleonora Cussini, eds. 1996. *Palmyrene Aramaic texts*. Baltimore: Johns Hopkins University Press.

IGLS   Yon, Jean-Baptiste, ed. 2012. *Inscriptions grecques et latines de la Syrie*. Vol. 1, *Palmyre*. Beirut: Institut français du Proche-Orient.

BIBLIOGRAPHY

Beck, Hylke E., Niklaus E. Zimmermann, Tim R. McVicar, Noemi Vergopolan, Alexis Berg, and Eric F. Wood. 2018. 'Present and Future Köppen-Geiger Climate Classification Maps at 1-km Resolution'. *Scientific Data* 5: 1–12.

Bell, Gertrude Lowthian. 1907. *The Desert and the Sown*. London: Heinemann.

Betts, Alison V. G., ed. 1999. *The Harra and the Hamad: Excavations and Explorations in Eastern Jordan*. London: Bloomsbury Academic.

Büntgen, Ulf, Vladimir S. Myglan, Fredrik Charpentier Ljungqvist, Michael McCormick, Nicola Di Cosmo, Michael Sigl, Johann Jungclaus, et al. 2016. 'Cooling and Societal Change

During the Late Antique Little Ice Age from 536 to Around 660 AD'. *Nature Geoscience* 9(3): 231–236.

Enzel, Yehouda, Revital Bookman, David Sharon, Haim Gvirtzman, Uri Dayan, Baruch Ziv, and Mordechai Stein. 2003. 'Late Holocene Climates of the Near East Deduced from Dead Sea Level Variations and Modern Regional Winter Rainfall'. *Quaternary Research* 60(3): 263–273.

Finné, Martin, Karin Holmgren, Hanna S. Sundqvist, Erika Weiberg, and Michael Lindblom. 2011. 'Climate in the Eastern Mediterranean, and Adjacent Regions, During the Past 6000 Years: A Review'. *Journal of Archaeological Science* 38(12): 3153–3173. doi:10.1016/j.jas.2011.05.007.

Grant, Christina Phelps. 1937. *The Syrian Desert*. London: A & C Black.

Gregory, Shelagh, and David Kennedy. 1985. *Sir Aurel Stein's Limes Report*. British Archaeological Reports, International Series 272. Oxford: Archaeopress.

Hammad, Manar. 2010. *Palmyre: Transformations urbaines: Développement d'une ville antique de la marge aride syrienne*. Paris: Geuthner.

Harper, Kyle. 2017. *The Fate of Rome: Climate, Disease, and the End of an Empire*. Princeton, NJ: Princeton University Press.

Harper, Kyle and McCormick, Michael. 2018. 'Reconstructing Roman Climate'. In *The Science of Roman History: Biology, Climate, and the Future of the Past*, edited by Walter Scheidel, 11–52. Princeton, NJ: Princeton University Press.

Held, Colbert C. 1989. *Middle East Patterns: Places, Peoples, and Politics*. Boulder: Westview.

Issar, Arie S., and Mattanyah Zohar. 2007. *Climate Change: Environment and History of the Near East*. Berlin: Springer.

Izdebski, Adam, Jordan Pickett, Neil Roberts, and Tomasz Waliszewski. 2016. 'The Environmental, Archaeological and Historical Evidence for Regional Climatic Changes and Their Societal Impacts in the Eastern Mediterranean in Late Antiquity'. *Quaternary Science Reviews* 136: 189–208. doi.org/10.1016/j.quascirev.2015.07.022.

Karmon, Yehuda. 1983. *Israel: Eine geographische Landeskunde*. Vol. 22, *Wissenschaftliche Länderkunden*. Darmstadt: Wissenschaftliche Buchgesellschaft.

Lamb, Hubert H. 1997. *Climate, History and the Modern World*. London: Routledge.

Leonard, Arthur Glyn. 1894. *The Camel: Its Uses and Management*. London: Longman, Greens.

Lewis, Norman N. 1987. *Nomads and Settlers in Syria and Jordan, 1800–1980*. Cambridge: Cambridge University Press.

Mart, Yossi, William B. F. Ryan, and Oxana V. Lunina. 2005. 'Review of the Tectonics of the Levant Rift System: The Structural Significance of Oblique Continental Breakup'. *Tectonophysics* 395(3): 209–232. doi:10.1016/j.tecto.2004.09.007.

Matthews, John F. 1984. 'The Tax Law of Palmyra: Evidence for Economic History in a City of the Roman East'. *Journal of Roman Studies* 74: 157–80.

McCormick, Michael, Kyle Harper, Alex M. More, and Kelly Gibson. 2013. 'Geodatabase of Historical Evidence on Roman and Post-Roman Climate'. In Digital Atlas of Roman and Medieval Civilization Dataverse, Harvard Dataverse. Volume 4. doi:10.7910/DVN/TVXATE.

Meyer, Jørgen Christian. 2017. *Palmyrena: Palmyra and the Surrounding Territory from the Roman to the Early Islamic Period*. Oxford: Archaeopress.

Meyer, Jørgen Christian. 2020. 'Palmyra: Marginal Agriculture in a Marginal Landscape?' In *Inter duo imperia: Palmyra Between East and West*, edited by Michael Sommer, 47–63. Stuttgart: Steiner.

Meyer, Jørgen Christian and Eivind Heldaas Seland. 2016. 'Palmyra and the Trade Route to the Euphrates'. *ARAM* 28: 497–523.

Millar, Fergus. 1994. *The Roman Near East, 31 BC–AD 337*. Cambridge, MA: Harvard University Press.

Mior, Paola. 2016. 'The Road from Palmyra to Damascus in the Tabula Peutingeriana'. In *Palmyrena: City, Hinterland and Caravan Trade between Orient and Occident. Proceedings of the Conference Held in Athens, December 1–3, 2012*, edited by Jørgen Christian Meyer, Eivind Heldaas Seland, and Nils Anfinset, 49–58. Archaeopress: Oxford.

Musil, Alois. 1928. *Palmyrena: A Topographical Itinerary*. New York: American Geographical Society.

Orland, Ian J., Miryam Bar-Matthews, Noriko T. Kita, Avner Ayalon, Alan Matthews, and John W. Valley. 2009. 'Climate Deterioration in the Eastern Mediterranean as Revealed by Ion Microprobe Analysis of a Speleothem that Grew from 2.2 to 0.9 ka in Soreq Cave, Israel'. *Quaternary Research* 71(1): 27–35.

Pappi, Cinzia. 2005. 'The Jebel Bišri in the Physical and Cultural Landscape of the Ancient Near East'. *KASKAL: Rivista di storia, ambienti e culture del Vicino Oriente Antico* 3: 241–256.

Poidebard, Antoine. 1934. *La trace de Rome dans le désert de Syrie*. Paris: Geuthner.

Prag, Kay. 1985. 'Ancient and Modern Pastoral Migration in the Levant'. *Levant* 17: 81–88.

Raja, Rubina, and Eivind Heldaas Seland. 2002. 'The Paradox of Palmyra: An Ancient *anomalopolis* in the Desert'. *Journal of Urban Archaeology* 5: 177–189. doi:10.1484/J.JUA.5.129848

Raswan, Carl R. 1930. 'Tribal Areas and Migration Lines of the North Arabian Bedouins'. *Geographical Journal* 20(3): 494–502.

Roberts, Neil, and H. E. Wright, Jr., eds. 1993. *Vegetational, Lake-Level, and Climatic History of the Near East and Southwest Asia*. Minneapolis: University of Minnesota Press.

Rosen, Arlene Miller. 2007. *Civilizing Climate: Social Responses to Climate Change in the Ancient Near East*. Lanham: Altamira.

Rowton, Michael B. 1973a. 'Autonomy and Nomadism in Western Asia'. *Orientalia* 42(1): 247–258.

Rowton, Michael B. 1973b. 'Urban Autonomy in a Nomadic Environment'. *Journal of Near Eastern Studies* 42: 201–215.

Schlumberger, Daniel. 1939. 'Bornes frontières de la Palmyrène'. *Syria* 20(1): 43–73.

Schou, Torbjørn P. 2015. 'Mobile Pastoralist Groups and the Palmyrene in the Late Early to Middle Bronze Age (c. 2400–1700 BCE): An Archaeological Synthesis Based on a Multidisciplinary Approach Focusing on Satellite Imagery Studies, Environmental Data, and Textual Sources'. Unpublished doctoral thesis, University of Bergen.

Seland, Eivind Heldaas. 2016. *Ships of the Desert and Ships of the Sea: Palmyra in the World Trade of the First Three Centuries CE*. Wiesbaden: Harrassowitz.

Seland, Eivind Heldaas. 2019. 'Water Sources in the Syrian Desert' [dataset]. *DataverseNO*. doi.org/10.18710/CEY9QR.

Smith, Andrew M., II. 2013. *Roman Palmyra: Identity, Community, and State Formation*. Oxford: Oxford University Press.

Sommer, Michael. 2005. *Roms orientalische Steppengrenze: Palmyra, Edessa, Dura-Europos, Hatra: Eine Kulturgeschichte von Pompeius bis Diocletian*. Oriens et Occidens. Stuttgart: Steiner.

Stoneman, Richard. 1992. *Palmyra and Its Empire: Zenobia's Revolt Against Rome*. Ann Arbor: University of Michigan Press.

von Oppenheim, Max Adrian, and Simon Freiherr. 1899. *Vom Mittelmeer zum Persischen Golf durch den Haurān, die syrische Wüste und Mesopotamien*. Berlin: Dietrich Reimer.

Wilkinson, Tony J. 2003. *Archaeological Landscapes of the Near East*. Tucson: University of Arizona Press.

Wirth, Eugen. 1969. 'Das Problem der Nomaden im heutigen Orient'. *Geographische Rundschau* 21: 41–51.

Wirth, Eugen. 1971. *Syrien: Eine geographische Landeskunde*. Wissenschaftliche Länderkunden 4/5. Darmstadt: Wissenschaftliche Buchgesellschaft.

Witakowski, Witold. 2010. 'Why Are the So-Called Dead Cities of Northern Syria Dead?' In *The Urban Mind: Cultural and Environmental Dynamics*, edited by Paul Sinclair, Gullög Nordquist, Frands Herschend, and Christian Isendahl, 295–310. Uppsala: Department of Archaeology and Ancient History, Uppsala University.

World Meteorological Organization. 2017. 'World Weather Information Service'. World Meteorological Organization. http://worldweather.wmo.int/en/home.html.

Yon, Jean-Baptiste. 2002. *Les notables de Palmyre*. Beirut: Institut français d'archéologie du Proche-Orient.

CHAPTER 3

THE PALMYRENE
Hinterland and Sedentarization

JØRGEN CHRISTIAN MEYER

THE CLIMATIC AND ENVIRONMENTAL SETTING

THE Palmyrene hinterland is often labelled a 'desert', but the locals call it *bādiya*, which means a territory suitable for pasture, more precisely 'dry steppe' or 'arid land'. The *bādiya* receives rain every winter and the surface turns green with sprouting grass and blossoming shrubs. However, there are great differences between the northern and southern parts of the *bādiya*. The landscape of the northern part of the Arabian Peninsula, al-Hamad, is undulating and relatively level. The yearly precipitation ranges from 100 to 200 mm. In the hot summer months, the vegetation wilts, turning the *bādiya* into a dusty and desolate place. The landscape north of Palmyra is dominated by mountain ranges and broader valleys, and, up to the second half of the twentieth century, the mountains were covered by a large population of slow-growing terebinth trees (*Pistacia Atlantica*), which have now been almost entirely depleted by logging due to the growing demand for charcoal. The mountainous area receives between 200 and 250 mm of rain, and the local climate is cooler and moister, which preserves the vegetation until late autumn (Musil 1928a, 149), though all the hinterland may experience drought years, with precipitation of less than 100 mm (Wirth 1971, 88–92). The differences between the northern and southern parts of the *bādiya* have determined the yearly migration patterns not only of animals such as gazelles, but also of some Bedouin with their flocks of sheep and goats, who take refuge in the more inviting mountain pastures in late May. Nothing seems to indicate that the climatic conditions changed fundamentally between ca. BC 3000 and the present (Wirth 1971, 98; Rosen 2007, 150–171). It has been 'arid land', though there have been fluctuations between cooler and warmer periods. Overexploitation of the pastures during the past 50 years has also changed the environments of the *bādiya* dramatically, reducing the normal regeneration of forage plants, and other species unsuitable for grazing have gained ground (Wirth 1971, 131–134).

THE HINTERLAND IN THE BRONZE AGE AND IRON AGE

The first more intensive exploitation of the Palmyrene hinterland can be dated to the Bronze Age. Over eight thousand cairns, distributed over an area of 3,800 km², have been identified in the mountains north and north-east of Palmyra (Schou 2015, 130–175) (Figure 3.1). They are difficult to date exactly, but many of them seem to belong to EBA IV and MBA, ca. BC 2400 to 1700. There are no major Bronze Age settlements in the area, and habitation in the oasis was insignificant, so these cairns must have been constructed by pastoral nomadic groups. These groups are frequently mentioned in the Mari archives, and they interacted with the settled population of the river valleys during their seasonal migrations. Most of the cairns are situated on mountain ridges visible from long distances, along communication lines and crossroads, and they probably marked the territorial rights of specific groups and control over pasture and water resources (Schou 2015, 336–345). No finds can be reliably dated to the later part of the Bronze Age. In the Iron Age and the Hellenistic period, we see the introduction of

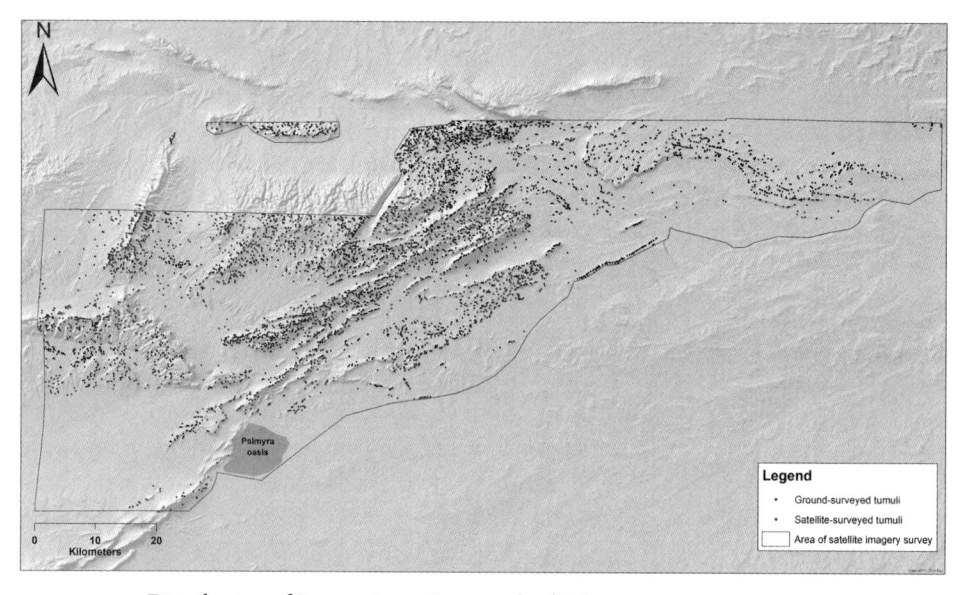

FIGURE 3.1 Distribution of Bronze Age cairns north of Palmyra.

Torbjørn Preus Schou 2015.

the camel in the Middle East (Magee 2015), which must have changed the migration patterns and increased access to pasture in the more arid lands of the northern part of the Arabian Peninsula, but the nomadic groups have left no visible traces today. The Aramaic-speaking population in Palmyra descended from those groups.

Settlements in the Hinterland in the Roman Period

Beginning in the first century AD, there was a dramatic change in the exploitation of Palmyrene territory. Numerous villages and estates now occupied the northern hinterland (Figure 3.2). Our knowledge of these settlements derives partly from

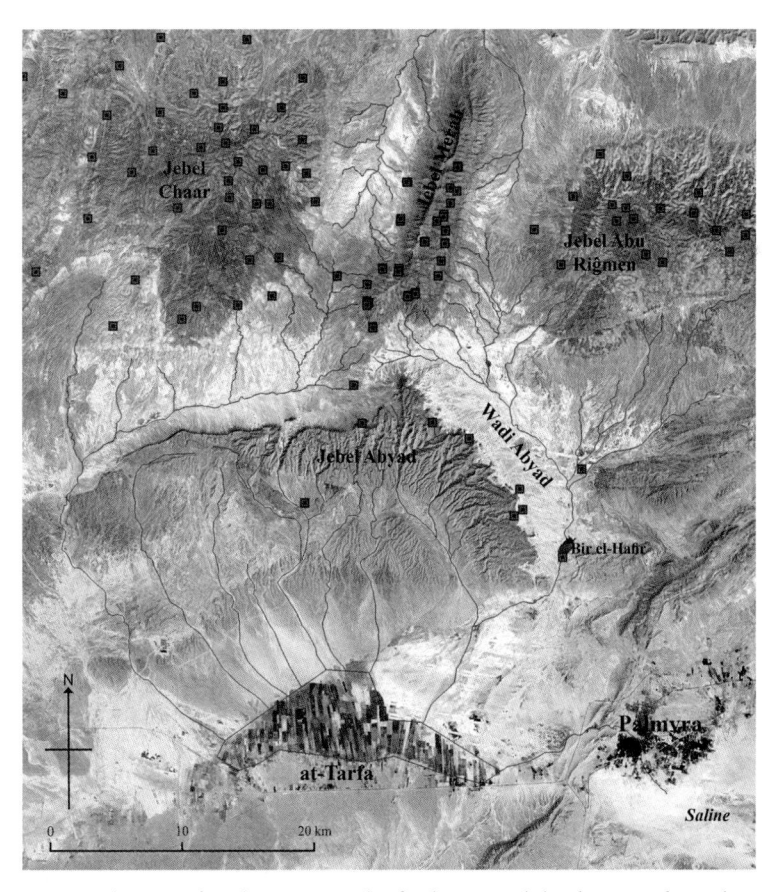

FIGURE 3.2 Distribution of settlements north of Palmyra and the drainage from the mountains towards the at-Tarfa depression and Palmyra.

Jørgen Christian Meyer, based on Google Earth 2019.

excavations on the Jebel Chaar tableland 50 km north-west of Palmyra, carried out by the great French archaeologist Daniel Schlumberger in the 1930s (Schlumberger 1951), and partly from a Syrian-Norwegian surface survey from 2008 to 2011 (Meyer 2017). Schlumberger excavated fifteen villages with buildings, shrines, and cisterns. The buildings had a square or rectangular layout, some measuring up to 50×50 m, with small rooms facing an internal courtyard. The walls were constructed with larger stones on the faces and a filling of smaller stones and clay in the middle, a technique widely used in the modern oasis of Palmyra for both enclosure walls and buildings. The shrines were more solidly built of stone blocks (Schlumberger 1951, 93–105). The smaller ones were simple structures, measuring only about 6×4 m, but in some settlements the shrines contained several rooms, including banquet halls, with courtyards in front and monumental doorposts decorated with floral designs. Many of the shrines and altars were adorned with dedicatory inscriptions and reliefs depicting lions, mounted horsemen, and deities (Schlumberger 1951, 114–116). On the basis of reliefs, finer artefacts, inscriptions, and coins, Schlumberger dated the occupation of the northern territory to the first three centuries of the Christian era, contemporary with the heyday of Palmyra as an important metropolis on the caravan route between the Mediterranean and the Arabian Gulf. According to Schlumberger, the villages were abandoned after the fall of Zenobia and the subsequent conversion of Palmyra into a military and administrative stronghold along the Strata Diocletiana (Schlumberger 1951, 132–133).

The Syrian–Norwegian surface survey, combined with the study of high-resolution satellite imagery, has shown that villages or estates were not confined to the Jebel Chaar tableland, where many new sites have been registered, and that there was a dense settlement pattern over all the mountains. On Jebel Chaar, the villages are spaced some 3,000 to 6,000 m apart. On Jebel Merah, some of the settlements consisted of only a few buildings, but the distance between them is less, between 500 and 2,000 m. The surface survey has also revealed that Schlumberger's chronology of the occupation of the hinterland should be revised (Meyer 2017, 13–16). Nothing can be dated to the Hellenistic period, as noted by Schlumberger, but the majority of the datable surface finds of pottery, mostly common ware, and some coins, in fact belong to the period after AD 300. Sites covered with thick layers of windblown material display a predominance of late finds, whereas sites exposed to heavy erosion show a much earlier chronology. It is evident that the chronological distribution of the surface finds cannot be used to determine the exact chronology of the individual sites and whether there have been changes in the settlement patterns (Walmsley 2012, 108–109). These questions can be answered only by excavating the sites, but the trend is clear. The occupation of the hinterland continued long after the fall of Zenobia, up into the Umayyad period. There is a sharp decline after the Umayyads, but a few sites were occupied as late as the thirteenth century. There are almost no finds from the Ottoman period apart from a few clay pipe bowls.

THE ECONOMIC BASIS OF THE SETTLEMENTS

What was the economic basis of the Palmyrene settlements and the relationship between the hinterland and the city in the oasis? According to Schlumberger, the villages
had two functions. First, they were founded by the elite in Palmyra as centres for
breeding horses, which were vital to Palmyra's military strength. Second, they also
became part of a larger nomadic network with seasonal movements from the winter
pastures on the southern dry steppe, al-Hamad, to the mountains north of the oasis
with more precipitation and better pastures, in the hot summer months. The construction of cisterns increased the amount of water available for human and animal
consumption. Some of the nomadic groups may have used the villages as more permanent bases, and Schlumberger did not exclude the possibility of some rain-fed agriculture in connection with the settlements, as the mountains lie within the 200-250 mm
isohyet. This allows the cultivation of barley, which needs a minimum of 200 mm of
precipitation.

An analysis of a mud brick at a site datable to the first half of the seventh century AD
(Krzywinski and Krzywinski 2016) shows high concentrations of pollen from domesticated barley, and a crushing basin for olive production that was found (Meyer 2017, 40)
confirms that agriculture and horticulture were practised in the settlements. According
to the Palmyrene Tariff, foodstuffs imported from or exported to villages or the countryside were not liable to taxation (Aramaic version: 109-113; Greek version: 187-191;
Fox et al. 2005, 45, 52; Healey 2009, 182–183), but the tariff does not specify the kinds
of provisions and the exact location of villages. The high density of settlements also
suggests a more intensive exploitation of the territory than that of a pastoral economy.
However, all this evidence fails to inform us about the importance of agriculture and
horticulture for the existence of the villages compared to pastoralism. The layout of
the buildings in the settlements is multifunctional and can be related both to a pastoral
economy and to agriculture/horticulture.

FOOD SUPPLIES TO PALMYRA

It is an often overlooked fact that the oasis itself cannot sustain a larger population
(Meyer 2017, 1), despite Pliny the Elder's claim that Palmyra was famous for its agree-
able springs and the richness of its soil (Plin., *NH* 5.88). The Efqa spring and some
other minor springs created a fertile green oasis on the Syrian dry steppe, but they
could not supply water to areas large enough to produce foodstuffs for a metropolis
of perhaps thirty thousand individuals (Crouch 1972). When the Czech explorer and

orientalist Alois Musil visited Tadmur in 1912, the population of the oasis numbered only three hundred fifty families within the precinct of the ancient temple of Bēl and its immediate surroundings. Still, the inhabitants had to import wheat and barley from the Homs and Hama area, which they exchanged for salt from the *salina* south-east of the oasis (Musil 1928a, 145-146). The ancient settlements north of Palmyra un-doubtedly played a role in providing Palmyra with food supplies. These settlements emerged in parallel with the growth of the city in the oasis and the opening of the caravan route across the dry steppe to Hit, on the Euphrates (Seland 2016, 75–83), and they disappeared with the drastic decline of the population after the Umayyad period.

TRADITIONAL AGRICULTURE AROUND PALMYRA

Agriculture in the Palmyrene countryside cannot have been based on traditional rain-fed farming. There are numerous traces of old fields in the landscape, and local Bedouin tribes and the population of Tadmur have practised some agriculture north of Palmyra in the past century, but this was abandoned (Meyer 2017, 35–36). Agriculture was risky because of recurrent years with insufficient precipitation for the cultiva-tion of barley and wheat or rainfall in the wrong months (Musil 1928a, 147; Sanlaville 2000). Very often, the seed was wasted. This type of opportunistic, rain-fed agri-culture certainly could not have provided Palmyra with sufficient foodstuffs. Stable cultivation of barley requires an annual average of 400 mm of precipitation (Wirth 1971, 92; Rosen 2007, 7–8). There are only a few natural springs in the Palmyrene area (Meyer 2017, 24–25) that may have been utilized by constructing *qanats*, underground aqueducts, leading water from aquifers to fields. This is a widespread technique since antiquity in Iran, the oases on the Arabian Peninsula, and the Tarim depres-sion in north-west China (English 1968). The only instance in the Palmyrene area is at the village of Arak, the ancient Aracha, 33 km east-north-east of Palmyra (Meyer 2017, 41). Another 15 km-long *qanat* was constructed from the Abu Fawares spring 15 km west of the oasis, but the water was intended primarily for human consump-tion in Palmyra (Barański 1997; Hammad 2010, 25–30), as was that from the 11 km-long Abar al-Amy *qanat* (Hammad 2010, 34–35) coming from the north of the city. There are some concentrations of wells in the northern territory (Meyer 2017, 24), but the settlements relied primarily on underground cisterns harvesting the runoff from mountainsides and smaller wadis by means of long supply channels. The water from wells and cisterns is primarily for animal and human consumption and to some extent for watering small gardens, not for the large-scale cultivation of cereals (Lancaster and Lancaster 1999, 142–145).

Floodwater Farming

For large-scale agriculture, the ancients relied on another technique, well documented from other arid lands such as the Negev Desert and North Africa, so-called *floodwater farming* (Rosen 2007, 161–167; Gilbertson and Hunt 1996, 191–226). The surface of the dry steppe, the *bādiya*, is generally very hard and impervious and during even short rain showers with only a few millimetres of precipitation, much of the water is soon collected in the wadis, where it can develop tremendous momentum, rather than penetrate the surface. Thus the natural environment concentrates the water, and if the floods can be controlled, stable agriculture is possible even in regions with an annual precipitation as low as 100 mm. There may be variations from year to year, but winter rainfalls in the cool season are a recurrent phenomenon, and there are no years of absolute drought, as may occur in other regions in the southern Arabian Peninsula.

The simplest way to control the floods is to construct a series of walls across the wadi beds, not for the purpose of storing water, but to slow the torrents and create turbulent flows, which settle deep, moist sediments between the walls, ready for cultivation after the water has passed (Meyer 2017, 37–38). This type of agriculture was practised until recently by Bedouin, close to their camps on the dry steppe south of Palmyra and in some modern villages north-west of Palmyra. Another technique is to divert some of the water in the wadis through open canals and into adjoining fields and gardens (Gilbertson and Hunt 1996, 192–193). There is not yet any archaeological evidence of diverting canals, but at several sites cross-wadi walls have been registered (Musil 1928a, 134–135; Meyer 2017, 40).

Floodwater agriculture has several advantages compared to traditional farming. In arid lands, agriculture and horticulture based on proper water management are much more resistant to variations in annual precipitation (Wilkinson 2003, 172; Rosen 2007, 45), which may have catastrophic consequences in other regions with rain-fed agriculture if it falls significantly below the required 200 mm for barley or 250 mm for wheat. There is no need to store water behind dams, exposing the body of water to evaporation during the hot season. The rainfall normally comes in the cool winter months, when it is needed in the fields, for example, when sowing spring cereals to be harvested in May. The floods also bring fresh fine-grained nutritious material from the frequent dust storms in the open landscape. Therefore, there is no exhaustion or salinization of the soil, and in modern times the Palmyrene area is known to be extremely fertile if the fields get enough water (Jabbur 1995, 63; Wirth 1971, 441). The yield far surpasses regions with traditional farming and can be compared to the output of irrigated fields in other parts of Syria.

The problem with agriculture in the Palmyrene hinterland is not the lack of water or the fertility of the soil, but other challenges. In larger wadis, the floods are too strong to be controlled with cross-wadi walls and only smaller side wadis can be sown. This imposes limits on the size of the areas put under cultivation. If the showers come at the wrong time, the ensuing torrents will wash away the growing plants. Heavy showers in May, which may occur, will have disastrous consequences for the harvest. The ancient farmers tried to minimize the risks by constructing smaller dams across the wadis above the fields (Gilbertson and Hunt 1996; Wilkinson 2003, 170–172; Rosen 2007, 161–167; Meyer 2020, 60–61). The purpose was not primarily to store the water for use in the hot season, but to retain the floods and control the torrents as check dams. In the mountains north of Palmyra, only one dam of this type has been preserved (Meyer 2017, 199–200), but most of them have probably been washed away by the torrents.

AGRICULTURE WEST OF PALMYRA

The settlements north of Palmyra are not the only potential agricultural districts in the Palmyrene hinterland. There are *qanats* at Arak, mentioned above, but by far the most important district was the at-Tarfa depression, about 20 km west of Palmyra (Figure 3.2). Today, the depression is cultivated as fields that produce wheat, barley, and cotton of a very high quality by pumping up groundwater, but the depression receives the runoff from all the mountains north and north-west of Palmyra and from the Palmyra Range south of the depression before it flows towards Palmyra and Wadi al-Qubur through the city. When Alois Musil travelled through the area in 1912, the depression was a marsh covered with sorrel, but he made some very important observations. He registered several old dams across the wadis leading towards the depression, foundation walls of demolished farms, and an olive press (Musil 1928a, 134-135). The depression was not inhabited in the Ottoman period, and the dams and the farms must be dated to the ancient period. This is confirmed by three monumental altars in the middle of the modern fields, with inscriptions in both Aramaic and Greek (Meyer 2017, 45–46; Pillet 1941) Figure 3.3). In AD 114 they were dedicated by the city and the treasurers of Palmyra to Baʿal Šâmîn, Lord of the Heavens and the bringer of rain and fertility at the spring equinox. Reliefs show a hand holding ears of corn and a hand holding a tree, stressing the aspects of agricultural fertility. There are ruins of a small fort (Musil 1928a, 134-135; Meyer 2017, 43–44) and a late Roman bath (al-Asʿad 2014), all testifying to the importance of the district after the fall of Zenobia, but other traces of habitation, apart from those mentioned by Musil, have been destroyed by modern deep ploughing.

AN ANCIENT DAM NORTH OF PALMYRA?

Agriculture in the at-Tarfa depression was also vulnerable to flash floods, especially in the late spring, even though the flat landscape reduces the force of the torrents. Heavy rain in the mountains has occasionally caused flooding as far as the city of Palmyra. In the second half of the twentieth century, a small dam was constructed across Wadi al-Qubur,

FIGURE 3.3 Ba'al Šâmîn altars in the at-Tarfa depression.

Jørgen Christian Meyer 2005.

just west of the Valley of the Tombs, to reduce the momentum of the currents. It is difficult to protect the fields from all the floods, even with the small dams mentioned by Musil, but the depression receives much of its water from the huge Wadi Abyad basin, north of the oasis, which even in years of low precipitation (100 mm) catches about 60 million cubic metres of water (Figure 3.2). In the 1980s, a dam was constructed across the narrow opening to the basin at the southern end of Wadi Abyad. The reservoir floods a natural depression in the landscape, which, before the construction, was called Bir el-Hafir (Musil 1928a, 148; Meyer 2017, 92). (In Arabic, *hafir* means 'water reservoir'.) In the Wadi Abyad basin, there are several remains of old channels diverting water from the western mountainsides and from tributary wadis into the Bir el-Hafir depression before it entered the plain leading to at-Tarfa (Meyer 2017, 91–93). Everything indicates that there was an ancient forerunner at the site, but all possible traces have now been destroyed by the modern construction. The primary function of the ancient dam was probably not to store water for the hot season but to regulate the flow during the rainy season as a check dam.

THE HARBAQAH DAM

Well-preserved remains of a dam are found 70 km south-east of Palmyra—the Harbaqah dam, at the edge of Palmyrene territory (Figure 3.4). It is one of the largest

FIGURE 3.4 The Harbaqah dam.

Jørgen Christian Meyer 2004.

dams in the Roman world, 365 m long and 20.5 m high, and it controlled all the runoff and drainage from a catchment area in the Palmyra Range covering 600 km^2, which is comparable with the Wadi Abyad basin. The original capacity of the reservoir was about 5 million cubic metres. In the 1930s Schlumberger investigated the dam (Schlumberger 1986; Meyer 2017, 46–54), along with the Umayyad castle, Qasr al-Heir al-Gharbi, 15 km north of the dam. He differentiated between two construction phases of the dam. The first dam was built in the first century AD, where it fed a larger settlement on the plain of ad-Daw, north of the mountains. After the fall of Zenobia, it fell out of use, but the Umayyads rebuilt and enlarged the dam in the seventh century AD to supply Qasr al-Heir al-Gharbi and the adjacent garden with water via a long aqueduct, which is partly preserved. Schlumberger's dating of the first phase to the Roman period was based on a comparison of the construction technique with the funerary towers in Palmyra, and it was recently contested by Denis Genequand (Genequand 2006; Genequand 2012, 255–259). He rightly points out that the dating evidence for the first phase is inconclusive and that there are no traces of any larger settlements on the plain from the Roman period. Instead, he relates the first construction of the dam to the Umayyad castle, and he compares it with other Umayyad hydraulic constructions in Syria and Jordan (Genequand 2012, 259–280). He does not deny the existence of two building phases but dates them both to the Umayyad period, as a response to heavy silting. The chronology of the two phases of the dam is now an open question, but dating it uniquely to the Umayyad period is also problematic. The amount of water controlled by the dam from the catchment area, and also that retained behind the dam, is totally out of proportion to the needs of the castle and the adjacent garden (Meyer 2017, 52–53). It makes much more sense if viewed in relation to agricultural activity on the plain. The absence of any traces of settlements or farms is not conclusive. The plain is covered with thick layers of accumulated windblown material, and only monumental buildings such as the castle are visible in the landscape. The dam needs to be reinvestigated.

Semi-Nomadism in the Villages
North of Palmyra

The villages north of Palmyra also played an important role in the seasonal migrations of sheep and goats. This is reflected in the religious cults of the villages (Schlumberger 1951, 124–128; Drijvers 1976, 20–22; Teixidor 1979, 80–85). Baʿal Šâmîn, the god of thunder and lightning, ʿAglibôl, the sun god, Malakbêl, the moon god, and ʾAllât, equivalent to the Greek Athena, are represented, but otherwise the divine universe differs from the cults in the city of Palmyra. The Arabian god Abgal, mounted on a horse on the reliefs, was the most popular, and a sanctuary on Jebel Chaar was dedicated to him (Schlumberger 1951, 13–22, 51–62). We also find a large group of other Arabian deities, Maʿanû, Saʿadû, or Ašar, mounted on a camel, and Šalmân, together with the local gods of the villages and gardens. All inscriptions on altars, reliefs, and architectural fragments are in Aramaic, not bilingual Greek-Aramaic, which was common in the public sphere in Palmyra and on the altars in the at-Tarfa agricultural district mentioned above. The composition of the divine universe and the absence of bilingual inscriptions show that the settlements obviously belonged to another social sphere than the official one in the city, similar to the dominance of Aramaic in the Palmyrene sepulchral culture. The shrines cannot be compared to the shrines in Palmyra, but the reliefs bear witness to surprisingly good workmanship, comparable to many other works of art in the city, and they belong to the same artistic tradition.

Unfortunately, we have no sources indicating who owned the land and founded the villages, but some of the larger estates probably belonged to the Palmyrene elite (Meyer 2017, 76, 140). The cultural duality in the villages, with strong connections to the Arab divinities of the dry steppe, may be explained by the possibility that semi-nomadic groups inhabited the northern territory (Musil 1928b, 44–45; Salzman 1980; Haiman 1995; Meyer 2020, 49–50). They were not isolated from the city but integrated into Palmyra's social and political life. They were insiders, not outsiders. Part of the family, or clan, lived permanently in the villages, where they practised agriculture and horticulture, and they sent their surplus to the market in Palmyra and contributed to the city's food supply. Some family members may have lived in Palmyra itself. Other members followed the seasonal migrations to and from the pastures of the southern dry steppe. The herds probably also included animals owned by other families in the city, a system that is well documented in the Middle East in modern times (Naval Intelligence Division 1943, 270; Wirth 1971, 264; Lancaster and Lancaster 1999, 212–214; Métral 2000, 127).

Safaitic Nomads in Palmyrene
Territory

Among the inscriptions found in the settlements north of Palmyra there are several graffiti written in the Safaitic language (Schlumberger 1951, 143–176; Meyer 2017, 66–68), spoken by the nomadic population in southern Syria, north-western Jordan, and north-western Saudi Arabia (MacDonald 1993), where forty thousand graffiti have been registered in the black basalt region so far (*OCIANA*). A graffito from one of the villages mentions journey and pasture (Meyer 2017, 171–172), and many of the graffiti mention an affiliation to a larger group. This occurs relatively seldom in Safaitic graffiti and indicates that the author was far from home. Some graffiti from the Safaitic core area also mention travel to and from Tadmur (Meyer 2017, 210–211). The nomadic groups spent the winter season on the southern dry steppe, al-Hamad. With the approach of the hot season, most of them returned to the well-watered region in the west and south-west around Hawran (MacDonald 2014, 149), but some migrated to the mountainous area north of Palmyra, where pasture was still available during the hot summer months. The construction of cisterns increased the pasture capacity, and the flocks could also feed on stubble fields after the harvest in May. In return, the animals fertilized gardens and fields with their manure. This kind of relationship between 'the desert and the sown' is well attested in modern times (Naval Intelligence Division 1943, 270; Lancaster and Lancaster 1999, 195, 207). These Safaitic-speaking groups are undoubtedly those mentioned in a section in the Palmyrene Tariff. According to the tariff, animals brought into the Palmyrene territory were liable to a special tax, whereas animals belonging to the territory were not (Greek: 233–237, Aramaic 145–149; Fox et al. 2005, 46, 54; Healey 2009, 184–185, 204–205). The last category refers to sheep and goats owned by the Palmyrene families, both in the villages and the city. We find no proper Safaitic inscriptions in the shrines, only graffiti, and the Safaitic-speaking nomads were not integrated into the social life of the villages but were occasional visitors.

PALMYRENE CONTROL OF ITS TERRITORY

Pastoralism and agriculture are two complementary economic systems (MacDonald 2014), but they are dependent on some kind of control over the seasonal migrations, especially in the case of groups coming from outside Palmyrene territory. Sheep, and goats in particular, can inflict heavy damage on gardens. If there was insufficient rain on the southern dry steppe in winter and spring, the nomads were compelled to move to the summer pastures before the harvest was finished. There may also have been competition and conflict between the various nomadic groups concerning access to pasture and water resources. To solve these problems, Palmyra built several forts and stations in the immediate hinterland, some of them even staffed by Roman military personnel (Schlumberger 1951, 44–50, 85–88; Meyer 2017, 58–69). They controlled the main lines of communication through the mountain ranges from the south to the north, the landscape, and important water resources, and they probably also functioned as centres for tax farming related to the various grazing rights mentioned in the tariff.

From Zenobia to the Umayyad Dynasty

The transformation of Palmyra into a military and administrative stronghold after AD 300 fundamentally changed the political and social landscape (Sommer 2018, 211–212; Intagliata 2018, 99–100). Old networks between the population of the city and the nomads of the southern dry steppe disappeared. However, these changes do not seem to have altered the general settlement pattern north of the city, and the at-Tarfa depression continued to be occupied at least into the late Roman period, as mentioned above. The population of Palmyra and the Roman military garrison still needed provisions from the hinterland. The forts and stations continued to be operational, controlling the immediate hinterland. Also, the construction of a series of forts along the Strata Diocletiana tightened control towards the southern dry steppe (Gawlikowski 1997, 41–45; Butcher 2003, 416–421). This indicates that nomadic groups from outside were still entering Palmyrene territory during their seasonal migrations.

We do not know who populated the villages in the Palmyrene hinterland, who owned the land, and who was responsible for the agricultural production in the at-Tarfa depression. Aramaic inscriptions disappear, as they did in Palmyra itself. It is noteworthy that Schlumberger did not register any finds datable to the period after AD 300, apart from a few coins. In the fourth century, Palmyra became a Christian city and a bishopric, but there are no traces of any Christian shrines on Jebel Chaar. Schlumberger may have neglected potsherds of common ware, as there was no reliable chronology for this type of pottery in the 1930s, but it is extremely unlikely that he would have overlooked finer artefacts, reliefs, altars, or Greek inscriptions. We have no reason to doubt that the excavated villages on Jebel Chaar are representative of at least the majority of the other sites. Did the villages lose their importance as centres of a strong social life? Were they still part of a semi-nomadic network? At present, these remain open questions.

In the later part of sixth century, the Palmyrene area became dominated by the powerful Banu Kalb tribe (Genequand 2012, 30–31; Donner 1981, 106–107), and they controlled the city, the northern hinterland with the villages, and the southern pasture grounds, which secured a close relationship between the desert and the sown. This continued into the Umayyad period, where we see the construction of 'desert castles' such as Qasr al-Heir al-Gharbi and Qasr al-Heir al-Sharki (Genequand 2012, 95-174) and also a new estate on Jebel Chaar (Schlumberger 1951, 44–46; Genequand 2012, 184–186). However, the city of Palmyra changed (Genequand 2012, 45-66; Gawlikowsky 2008; Intagliata 2018). The former colonnaded street was transformed into a *suq*, or bazaar (al-As'ad and Stępniowski 1989), and olive oil production took place within the city (Waliszewski 2014, 405–416), which became a regional centre and a market for the surrounding territory, a process that Hugh Kennedy has described as 'from *polis* to *madina*', the traditional Islamic town (Kennedy 1985). We do not know how this affected the settlement pattern north of Palmyra, but it is possible that there was a decline in the demand for provisions from the hinterland.

The Palmyrene Territory in the Islamic and Ottoman Periods

After the Umayyads, Palmyra began to dwindle, and the villages and estates disappeared. In the northern hinterland, there are only a few finds from the subsequent centuries. By the tenth century, the population of the oasis had probably already moved behind the protective walls of the precinct of the ancient temple of Bēl (Intagliata 2018, 107–108), which was converted into a fortress. These changes were not due to climatic deterioration (Rosen 2000; Rosen 2009). From a political standpoint, the Palmyrene area became a marginal region in the Middle East, and, in the Ottoman period, a Bedouin strategy of survival with a very low degree of sedentarization had entirely taken over, with occasional conflicts between the desert and the sown (Musil 1928a, 85–86; Marcus 1989, 140-141; Lewis 2000; Reilly 2015), although the Bedouin benefited from the cisterns constructed during the Roman period, which they have maintained up to the present.

Conclusion

Palmyra's growth as a metropolis depended on extensive expansion into the hinterland, not only in the mountains north of Palmyra, but also to other areas where it was possible to exploit the runoff during the rainy season to establish stable agriculture and horticulture to feed the population. The at-Tarfa depression, and possibly also the plain north of the Harbaqah dam, were typical agricultural districts, but the villages in the mountains north of Palmyra also played an important role in nomadic migrations to and from al-Hamad. The exploitation of the Syrian dry steppe and the relationship between Palmyra and the hinterland can be divided into the following phases:

1. Bronze Age: Pastoral nomads in the northern hinterland interact with the settled populations in the river valleys.
2. Iron Age and Hellenistic Periods: Pastoral nomads migrate to and from southern pastures to the northern hinterland.
3. Roman Period: Expansion of settlements with agriculture and horticulture in the hinterland. Semi-nomadic population in the settlements. Safaitic-speaking nomads include the northern hinterland in their seasonal migrations.
4. Late Roman Period: New relations between city, hinterland, and southern pastures. Strengthened control over the nomadic migrations.
5. Byzantine Period: Tribal control of the city, hinterland, and southern pastures.
6. Umayyad Period: Castles built in the hinterland. Palmyra becomes a regional centre for the surrounding territory. Decline in the settlements in the northern hinterland?

7. ISLAMIC AND OTTOMAN PERIODS: The settlements in the hinterland disappear. The Palmyrene area becomes a politically marginal area, and Bedouin take over the territory.

The changing settlement pattern in the Palmyrene territory cannot be explained in terms of climatic fluctuations. Agriculture and horticulture were relatively resistant to variations in the annual precipitation if the farmers and the community invested time and resources on the construction and maintenance of retaining walls and large and small dams, but it presupposed a well-organized society and peaceful relations between the city and the nomadic groups. The Palmyrenes had close social and economic ties to these groups, and, in late antiquity and the early Islamic period, the tribes of the dry steppe were an integrated part of the political landscape. In the Ottoman period, however, the Palmyrene area became a marginal zone from a political point of view and the conditions for a high degree of sedentarization disappeared.

BIBLIOGRAPHY

al-As'ad, Khaled, and Franciszek M. Stępniowski. 1989. 'The Umayyad Sūq in Palmyra'. *Damaszener Mitteilungen* 4: 205–223.

al-As'ad, Waleed. 2014. 'Les bains d'al-Kilibiyya'. In *25 siècles de bain collectif en Orient: Proche-Orient, Égypte et péninsule Arabique; Βαλανεῖα – Thermae –* حمامات, edited by Marie-Françoise Boussac, Sylvie Denoix, Thibaud Fournet, and Bérangère Redon, 453–464. Cairo: Institut français d'archéologie orientale.

Barański, Marek. 1997. 'Western Aqueduct in Palmyra'. *Studia Palmyreńskie* 10: 7–18.

Butcher, Kevin. 2003. *Roman Syria and the Near East*. London: The British Museum Press.

Crouch, Dora P. 1972. 'A Note on the Population and the Area of Palmyra'. *Mélanges de l'Université Saint-Joseph, Beyrouth* 47: 241–250.

Donner, Fred M. 1981. *The Early Islamic Conquests*. Princeton, NJ: Princeton University Press.

Drijvers, H. J. W. 1976. *The Religion of Palmyra*. Leiden: Brill.

English, Paul Ward. 1968. 'The Origin and Spread of Qanats in the Old World'. *Proceedings of the American Philosophical Society* 112: 170–181.

Fox, Greg, Sam Lieu, and Norman Ricklefs. 2005. 'Select Palmyrene Inscriptions'. In *From Palmyra to Zayton: Epigraphy and Iconography*, edited by Iain Gardner, Sam Lieu, and Ken Parry, 27–188. Silk Road Studies 10. Turnhout: Brepols.

Gawlikowski, Michał. 1995. 'Les arabes en Palmyrène'. In *Présence arabe dans le croissant fertile avant l'Hégire*, edited by Hélène Lozachmeur, 103–108. Paris: Éditions Recherche sur les civilisations.

Gawlikowski, Michał. 1997. 'The Syrian Desert under the Romans'. In *The Early Roman Empire in the East*, edited by Susan E. Alcock, 37–54. Oxford: Oxbow.

Gawlikowski, Michał. 2008. 'Palmyra in Early Islamic Times'. In *Residences, Castles, Settlements: Transformation Processes from Late Antiquity to Early Islam in Bilad al-Sham: Proceedings of the International Conference Held in Damascus, 5–9 November 2006*, edited by Karin Bartl and Abd al-Razzaq Moaz, 89–96. Rahden: Leidorf.

Genequand, Denis. 2006. 'Some Thoughts on Qasr al-Hayr al-Gharbi, Its Dam, Its Monastery and the Ghassanids'. *Levant* 38: 63–83.

Genequand, Denis. 2012. *Les établissements des élites omeyyades en Palmyrène et au Proche-Orient*. Beirut: Institut français du Proche-Orient.

Gilbertson, David D., and Chris Hunt. 1996. 'Romano-Libyan Agriculture: Walls and Floodwater Farming'. In *Farming the Desert: The Unesco Libyan Valleys Archaeological Survey*, vol. 1, edited by Graeme Barker, David D. Gilbertson, Barri Jones, and David Mattingly, 191–225. Tripoli: Unesco Publishing.

Haiman, Mordechai. 1995. 'Agriculture and Nomad–State Relations in the Negev Desert in the Byzantine and Early Islamic Periods'. *Bulletin of the American Schools of Oriental Research* 297: 29–53.

Hammad, Manar. 2010. *Palmyre: Transformations urbaines; Développement d'une ville antique de la marge aride syrienne*. Paris: Geuthner.

Healey, John F. 2009. *Aramaic Inscriptions and Documents of the Roman Period*. Textbook of Syrian Semitic Inscriptions 4. Oxford: Oxford University Press.

Intagliata, Emanuele E. 2018. *Palmyra after Zenobia, AD 273–750: An Archaeological and Historical Reappraisal*. Oxford: Oxbow.

Jabbur, Jibrail S. 1995. *The Bedouins and the Desert: Aspects of Nomadic Life in the Arab East*. New York: State University of New York Press.

Kennedy, Hugh. 1985. 'From *Polis* to *Madina*: Urban Change in Late Antique and Early Islamic Syria'. *Past and Present* 106: 3–27.

Krzywinski, Knut, and Jonatan Krzywinski. 2016. 'Agriculture in Byzantine Palmyrena'. In *Palmyrena: City, Hinterland and Caravan Trade between Orient and Occident* (Proceedings of the Conference held in Athens, December 1–3, 2012), edited by Jørgen Christian Meyer, Eivind Heldaas Seland, and Nils Anfinset, 171–183. Oxford: Archeopress.

Lancaster, William, and Fidelity Lancaster. 1999. *People, Land and Water in the Arab Middle East: Environment and Landscapes in Bilâd ash-Shâm*. Amsterdam: Harwood.

Lewis, Norman. 2000. 'The Syrian Steppe During the Last Century of Ottoman Rule: Hawran and the Palmyrena'. In *The Transformation of Nomadic Society in the Arab East*, edited by Martha Mundy and Bassim Musallam, 33–43. Cambridge: Cambridge University Press.

MacDonald, Michael C. A. 1993. 'Nomads and the Hawran in the Late Hellenistic and Roman Periods: A Reassessment of the Epigraphic Evidence'. *Syria revue d'art oriental et d'archéologie* 70(3–4): 303–403.

MacDonald, Michael C. A. 2014. '"Romans Go Home"? Rome and Other "Outsiders" as Viewed from the Syro-Arabian Desert'. In *Inside and Out: Interactions Between Rome and the Peoples on the Arabian and Egyptian Frontiers in Late Antiquity*, edited by Jitse H. F. Dijkstra and Greg Fisher, 145–164. Leuven: Peeters.

Magee, Peter. 2015. 'When Was the Dromedary Domesticated in the Ancient Near East'? *Zeitschrift für Orient-Archäologie* 8: 253–277.

Marcus, Abraham. 1989. *The Middle East on the Eve of Modernity: Aleppo in the Eighteenth Century*. New York: Columbia University Press.

Métral, Françoise. 2000. 'Managing Risk: Sheep-Rearing and Agriculture'. In *The Transformation of Nomadic Society in the Arab East*, edited by Martha Mundy and Basim Musallam, 123–144. Cambridge: Cambridge University Press.

Meyer, Jørgen C. 2017. *Palmyrena: Palmyra and the Surrounding Territory from the Roman to the Early Islamic Period*. Oxford: Archaeopress.

Meyer, Jørgen C. 2020. 'Palmyra. Marginal Agriculture in a Marginal Landscape'. In *Inter duo Imperia: Palmyra Between East and West*, edited by Michael Sommer, 47–63. Stuttgart: Steiner.

Musil, Alois. 1928a. *The Manners and Customs of the Rwala Bedouins*. New York: American Geographical Society.

Musil, Alois. 1928b. *Palmyrena: A Topographical Itinerary*. New York: American Geographical Society.

Naval Intelligence Division. 1943. *Syria*. Geographical Handbook Series, B. R. 513. London: Naval Intelligence Division.

OCIANA: Online Corpus of the Inscriptions of Ancient North Arabia. Oxford: University of Oxford. http://krc.orient.ox.ac.uk/ociana/index.php/database.

Pillet, Maurice. 1941. 'Les autels de l' 'el-Karassi' (Syrie centrale)'. *Revue archéologique* 17: 5–17.

Reilly, James A. 2015. 'Town and Steppe in Ottoman Syria'. *Der Islam* 92(1): 148–160.

Rosen, Arlene M. 2007. *Civilizing Climate: Social Responses to Climate Change in the Near East*. Plymouth: Altamira.

Rosen, Steven A. 2000. 'The Decline of Desert Agriculture: A View from Classical Period Negev'. In *Archaeology of Drylands: Living at the Margin*, edited by Graeme Barker and David Gilbertson, 45–62. London: Routledge.

Rosen, Steven A. 2009. 'History Does Not Repeat Itself: Cyclicity and Particularism in Nomad-Sedentary Relations in the Negev in the Long Term'. In *Nomads, Tribes, and State in the Ancient Near East: Cross-Disciplinary Perspective*, edited by Jeffrey Szuchman, 1–13. Chicago: Oriental Institute, University of Chicago.

Salzman, Phillip C. 1980. 'Introduction'. In *When Nomads Settle: Processes of Sedentarization as Adaptation and Response*, edited by Phillip C. Salzman and Edward Sadala, 1–22. New York: Praeger.

Sanlaville, Paul. 2000. 'Environment and Development'. In *The Transformation of Nomadic Society in the Arab East*, edited by Martha Mundy and Basim Musallam, 6–16. Cambridge: Cambridge University Press.

Schlumberger, Daniel. 1951. *La Palmyrène du nord-ouest: Villages et lieux de culte de l'époque impériale; Recherches archéologiques sur la mise en valeur d'une région du désert par les palmyréniens*. Paris: Geuthner.

Schlumberger, Daniel. 1986. *Qasr el-Heir el Gharbi*. Paris: Geuthner.

Schou, Torbjørn P. 2015. 'Mobile Pastoralist Groups and the Palmyrene in the Late Early to Middle Bronze Age (c. 2400–1700 BCE): An Archaeological Synthesis Based on a Multidisciplinary Approach Focusing on Satellite Imagery Studies, Environmental Data, and Textual Sources'. Unpublished doctoral thesis, University of Bergen. http://bora.uib.no/handle/1956/10808.

Seland, Eivind H. 2016. *Ships of the Desert and Ships of the Sea: Palmyra in the World Trade of the First–Third Centuries CE*. Munich: Harrassowitz.

Sommer, Michael. 2018. *Palmyra: A History*. London: Routledge.

Teixidor, Javier. 1979. *The Pantheon of Palmyra*. Leiden: Brill.

Waliszewski, Tomasz. 2014. *Elaion: Olive Oil Production in Roman Byzantine Syria-Palestine*. PAM Monograph Series 6. Warsaw: Warsaw University Press.

Walmsley, Alan. 2012. *Early Islamic Syria: An Archaeological Assessment*. London: Bristol Classical Press.

Wilkinson, Tony J. 2003. *Archaeological Landscapes of the Near East*. Tucson: University of Arizona Press.

Wirth, Eugen. 1971. *Syrien: Eine geographische Landeskunde*. Darmstadt: Wissenschaftliche Buchgesellschaft.

PART TWO

TADMOR/PALMYRA IN A LONGUE DURÉE PERSPECTIVE

....

CHAPTER 4

GLIMPSES OF TADMŪR
BEFORE ALEXANDER

The Pre-Hellenistic Evidence

....

JOHN F. HEALEY

INTRODUCTION

....

THERE are two fundamental problems about attempting to say anything about Tadmūr/ Palmyra in the pre-Hellenistic period. First, there is a lack of evidence: the archaeological evidence is meagre and the textual evidence is both slight and sporadic (being scattered thinly over almost two millennia). Second, there is an almost irresistible inclination in the scholarly tradition to see pre-Hellenistic Palmyra through the lens of the much better-known Roman period (with its abundance of archaeology and texts in both Greek and Aramaic). This anachronistic perspective conjures up the image of the caravan trade, through 'caravan cities', and leads us to seek in ancient Tadmūr an earlier centre of such trade. Indeed, it is emblematic of this inclination that we speak of 'Palmyra' in, for example, the second millennium BC, when the little we know is about an entity called Tadmūr which must have borne little resemblance, economically, politically, or culturally (let alone architecturally and artistically) to the Palmyra of later times.

ARCHAEOLOGICAL EVIDENCE

....

Detail on the prehistoric evidence of the Palmyra oasis and especially the region around it is beyond the scope of this contribution (see Cremaschi and Zerboni 2016, who conclude that the oasis became more important as the climate became less favourable because of reduced rainfall; in brief, Sommer 2018, 20–21), but such evidence as exists for the earliest period in Palmyra itself amounts to little more than that arising from the excavations of R. du Mesnil du Buisson in the area of the Efqa spring (du Mesnil du Buisson 1966, 163–164) and below the visible levels of the Bēl temple in 1965 and 1967 (du Mesnil du Buisson 1966; 1967). It is widely held that the site of the temple corresponds to 'l'ancien tell de la ville' (du Mesnil du Buisson 1967, 21), what al-Maqdissi (al-Maqdissi 2000, 148) calls 'le site primitif de Palmyre' (see also al-Maqdissi 2009, 23 on earlier soundings at the temple), though other, much earlier material (early Neolithic) was found at the Efqa spring.

Immediately below the Hellenistic foundations of the Bēl temple, du Mesnil du Buisson found strata which he dated to the Late Bronze period (their location so close to the surface being explicable if the site was levelled before the building of the later temple). At a much deeper level he found lithic artefacts and ceramics which suggested to the excavator a date in the late third millennium BC (2200–2100 BC by his dating). He ascribed the foundation of the city to this period and connected it with the Amorites, believing it to have been built by West Semitic peoples. Among the arguments for a West Semitic origin were the names of the ancient spring at Palmyra, Efqa, and of the deity Yarḥibōl, both known at Palmyra from much later sources but having antecedents in the Ugaritic literature (Ugaritic 'apq and yrḫ). Whatever the details of this interpretation (and we need to bear in mind that the Ugaritic material is Late Bronze Age in date and that, as noted by Shifman [2014, 14], Ugaritic Yariḫ is a moon deity, unlike the Palmyrene sun deity, Yarḥibōl), this evidence archaeologically confirms the existence of a settlement at Tadmūr in the third millennium BC. When combined with the written sources for the slightly later period (below), this suggests continuous occupation during the Bronze Age (Sommer 2018, 21).

A more recent re-evaluation of du Mesnil du Buisson's work by M. al-Maqdissi (al-Maqdissi 2000, cf. also al-Maqdissi and Ishaq 2023), who struggled with the inadequate records left by the excavator, distinguished four phases of activity on the site of the Bēl temple. An early phase (Phase I) may be of ceramic Neolithic date, though al-Maqdissi also allows for the possibility that it may belong to a much later period (mid-third millennium). Ceramic material from the Early Bronze IVA and IVB periods (Phase II: 2400–2000 BC) includes fragments of Syrian-type goblets which suggest that Tadmūr was on the eastern fringe of the Syrian regional tradition. Phase II pottery suggests distinct links to the Orontes area from the mid-third millennium onwards (al-Maqdissi 2000, 148; cf. also al-Maqdissi 2009 summarizing the archaeological work of Adnan Bounni from 1981 at the Bēl temple, which produced pottery sherds dated to the third millennium). Thus, at this point, Tadmūr is seen as participating in the socioeconomic system of western Syria. The debris from Phase III, 4 m in depth in some places (first half of the second millennium BC), is noteworthy. Of mixed character, it corresponds in date to the period of the most extensive textual material on ancient Tadmūr. Artefacts of Babylonian style suggest contact with Mesopotamian culture. This fits well with the textual evidence, which shows Tadmūr's role in the long-distance routes across the Syrian Desert during the period of the dominance of Mari in the east and Qaṭna in the west. Material from the Iron Age (first millennium BC) remains elusive: Phase IV belongs to the Hellenistic period, and the absence of evidence from earlier in the Iron Age may be explained by the levelling of this part of the site prior to the building of the Bēl temple.

The limited archaeological evidence for this earlier period suggests a founding of the settlement in the middle of the third millennium BC, after some earlier activity in the Neolithic and continuous occupation thereafter until at least the Late Bronze period. The general absence of evidence of the pre-Hellenistic Iron Age should not, however, lead to the conclusion that Tadmūr was abandoned during this 'dark age'.

Turning now to textual evidence, we can draw a rough distinction in it between the circumstances of the major part of the second millennium BC and the period of the Assyrian Empire. Textual allusions to Tadmūr and Tadmūrians are rare, and they are scattered over five or six hundred years. They are also mostly obscure in their significance and tell us rather little. There is a fuller treatment of these texts in the wider geographical and social context in Ulf Scharrer (2002; see also Sommer 2018, 14–20).

THE SECOND MILLENNIUM BC

Kültepe/Kaniš

Tadmūrians are mentioned in the Cappadocian archives associated with the great trading centre (*kārum*) of Kültepe/Kaniš, which flourished in the first three centuries of the second millennium BC.

(i) In one such text Puzur-Ištar, a Tadmūrian, is the witness to a debt-repayment document:

> . . . in the presence of Mērali and of Puzur-Ištar the Tadmūrian.
> Seal of Mērali son of Šallim-Aššur and of Puzur-Ištar the Tadmūrian. (Eisser and Lewy 1935, 18–21, no. 303 A15–17, B1–3)

It is possible that the descriptor 'Tadmūrian' (*ta/tá-ad-mu-ri-im*) here refers also to Mērali (see Eisser and Lewy 1935, 21, n. a; Scharrer 2002, 302), though in the second reference to him he is identified mainly through his father's name, so the matter remains in doubt.

There is a danger of reading too much into the personal name Puzur-Ištar (and the names of Mērali and his father, if we include them as Tadmūrians): the name Puzur-Ištar is known fairly widely, for example, at Mari (Scharrer 2002, 302), and it occurs elsewhere at Kaniš without any known connection with Tadmūr (Dercksen 1996, 102, 119, 122; Kienast 1960, no. 59: 5, 25). Hence, we cannot rely here on the name Puzur-Ištar as suggesting the worship of Ištar in Tadmūr in this period. The style of the seal on the tablet may show Assyrian influence, though we have no way of knowing whether it was made in Tadmūr (Scharrer 2002, 303).

(ii) There is also an obscure reference to Tadmūr in another text from Kaniš:

⅓ of a *mina* of silver from a Tadmūrian. (Larsen and Møller 1991, 231; Lewy 1936, no. 82: 17)

According to Dercksen (1996, 164), the Tadmūrian owed this amount of silver. This may point to a trading relationship between some merchants at Kaniš and others in Tadmūr. It is also possible that Puzur-Ištar the Tadmūrian is again involved (Scharrer 2002, 304, n. 99).

(iii) Scharrer (2002, 304) also refers to an unpublished text which is reported to contain a reference to 'Pilaḫ-Adad, son of a Tadmūrian' (see Dercksen 1996, 164, n. 514), and (iv) another in which a Tadmūrian owes payment for copper:

⅓ of a *mina* of silver for 31 *minas* of copper—according to our weight-stones—is owed by the man from Tadmūr (*da-ad-mu-ri-im*). (Larsen and Møller 1991, 231, 239 [copy], F. de la Grange = F. T. 4: 8–10)

The presence of Tadmūrians at Kaniš is unsurprising given the intensity of the long-distance trade documented in the archive. None of the occurrences is very informative, though they do show that Tadmūr was a known place in the first centuries of the second millennium BC and that people of Tadmūrian origin regarded themselves as having a distinct identity. At least it is clear that there was an identifiable settlement at the oasis.

The fact that in two of the four texts cited above the Tadmūrians are in possession of, or entrusted with, valuable material suggests that these individuals were involved in commercial transactions. We know from other evidence (below) that Tadmūr was small, but it is not unlikely that it had some merchant families who had contacts with Anatolia.

Attempts to draw conclusions on the basis of Puzur-Ištar's name about stronger connections with Mesopotamia than with the West seem hazardous, as does the conclusion that there was a cult of Ištar in the settlement.

The Mari Archives

A small number of Mari texts also mention Tadmūr and Tadmūrians.

ARM V, 23 is a long-discussed letter to Yasmaḫ-Addu, son and western viceroy of Šamši-Adad I of Assyria, which had control of Mari around 1750 BC (Sommer 2018, 22).

Say to my Lord Yasmaḫ-Addu: thus says Tarīm-Šakim, your servant. Gâzizânum, Abî-sarê, Hammi-talû the Sutaeans, as well as two thousand Sutaeans, met together. They went to attack the flocks in the pastures of the land of Qaṭna. Even before that, a second band, of sixty Sutaeans, went to pillage Tadmūr (*ta-ad-mé-er*[ki]) and Našalâ. They returned empty-handed and the Tadmūrians even killed one of them. This news about the Sutaeans came to me and I have written about it to my lord. (Joannès

1997, 408; Durand 1998, 507–508, no. 745; Scharrer 2002, 307–308. Note *ARM* XV, 135, n. 2 for correction of the original reading in *ARM* V)

Despite the defenders' relative success, the implication is that the attack on Tadmūr was a minor sideshow, requiring only a handful of Sutaean attackers. Tadmūr was obviously not under Sutaean control, and the impression is created that Tadmūr was not regarded as part of the Sutaean and Benjaminite 'problem' (but rather on the side of Mari and the bigger powers). This impression is confirmed by other Mari evidence cited below and it continues into the reign of Tiglath-Pileser I with respect to the *aḫlamû*-Aramaeans (also below).

It is notable that *ARM* V, 23 mentions Tadmūr and Našalâ as being under attack by Sutaeans. The Tadmūrians fight back, and the letter sending a report to Yasmaḫ-Addu, governor of Mari, appears to be pleased to report that one of the Sutaeans was killed. This may be viewed as indicating a close connection between Mari and Tadmūr, perhaps even with Mari acting as overlord (Shifman 2014, 15).

Našalâ/Nazalâ, identified with modern Qaryatain, is located west of Tadmūr, though it belonged to Qaṭna (Joannès 1997, 402–408). It is probable that Tadmūr's cooperation (or its dependence on Mari) would have been essential for the exploitation of Qaṭna's timber resources by the rulers of Mari, as suggested by a report about the obtaining of timber from Ḥabdu-Ami, probably sent to Yasmaḫ-Addu (Joannès 1997, 402–404, A.2080). There can be little doubt that the Sutaeans presented a disruptive threat to an already established trade route between the Euphrates and Qaṭna (Klengel 1977; 1996; Joannès 1997, 299: 'un relais pour les relations entre Mari et l'ouest'; see broader discussion in Sommer 2018, 22–23).

The same impression is given by a second report on the misdeeds of the Sutaeans. The report indicates that a Sutaean attack was carried out against a mission comprising Babylonians, Qaṭnans, and Mariotes (plus livestock) while its members were encamped, evidently in separate encampments, near the Euphrates. Five Sutaeans were killed and the Qaṭnans and Mariotes escaped safely to Tadmūr.

> But during the night, Sutaeans came to attack the Babylonians. They killed a high-ranking Babylonian called Lidnuša and wounded a second. In response to the clamour our men [the Mariotes] took up arms . . . they killed five of the enemy. Our messengers, the Qaṭnans and the tablets are safe. An escort has escorted them as far as Tadmūr (*ta-ad-mi-ir*[ki]). (Joannès 1997, 400–402, M.6159; Scharrer 2002, 311–315)

Although the name of the recipient of this report is missing, it has been ascribed to the reign of Zimrilim (ca. 1775–1761 BC), during a period of frequent Babylonian contacts with the West. It is not clear what was going on between the Mariotes, Qaṭnans, and Babylonians, but, again, the implication is that Tadmūr is at least a close ally of Mari and regarded as less vulnerable to attack by predatory desert dwellers for those taking refuge there. It might even have been a vassal of Mari.

In a third Mari text, it appears that Tadmūrians are conveying diplomatic messages from Qaṭna to Mari. This letter, addressed by Lā'ûm (an administrator) to Yasmah-Addu, refers to a letter from the king of Qaṭna to the Assyrian king Šamši-Adad I, which is being conveyed by two Tadmūrians via Mari.

> On another matter: two Tadmūrians have brought a tablet of Išḥi-Addu from Qaṭna for the king. Now I have sent them to my lord: let my lord question them and then send them to the king. (Joannès 1997, 399–400, M.11516; Scharrer 2002, 314–315)

Clearly, these Tadmūrians are trusted intermediaries: it is hard to avoid the conclusion that Tadmūr is part of an alliance with, or even under the overlordship of Mari. The Tadmūrians appear to have been acting as postmen in the service of Mari (and Qaṭna). A rather similar situation of Tadmūrians acting as intermediaries or postmen is reflected in another unpublished Mari text in which four Tadmūrians arrive in Mari from Qaṭna (Scharrer 2002, 314–315).

Up to this point we have evidence of Tadmūrians, and the name of Tadmūr is accompanied by the determinative KI (= *erṣetu*, 'land, territory') rather than URU (= *ālu*, 'city'), which might have suggested at least an established township of significant size. This in itself may suggest that it was not a very important place. But with the next text we move on to a different level, one in which the 'city' determinative appears. As we have seen, the idea that Tadmūr was quite small in the early second millennium BC is reinforced by *ARM* V, 23, which describes an incident in which a small band of Sutaeans was thought sufficient to overcome it.

Emar

A single text from Emar, from ca. 1300 BC, that is, 500 years after the events described above involving Mari (Arnaud 1986, no. 21, 32–33; Scharrer 2002, 315–316; Sommer 2018, 24), is a legal document recording the receipt of a payment, apparently a ransom or a loan repayment, from Imlik-Dagan to Atteu (via a servant called Kalbiu). Two Tadmūrians witness the document.

> Witness: Gīrī, a Tadmūrian ($^{\text{lú.uru}}$*ta-ad-mir*)
> Witness: Šakniu
> also a Tadmūrian ($^{\text{lú.uru}}$*ta-ad-mi-ir-ma*). (Msk 7234; Arnaud 1985, 34 [copy]; 1986, 32–33, no. 21; Scharrer 2002, 315–316)

Arnaud initially implied that Atteu, too, was a Tadmūrian (Arnaud 1975, 90), but this detail does not appear in the final publication (Arnaud 1986; see also Arnaud 1982). This is very meagre evidence, but it does contain one detail worthy of note: the name of Tadmūr (the gentilic) is qualified with the determinative URU, normally indicating a city (*ālu*). At least we can be confident in concluding that Tadmūr continued to be an important settlement at this time, and it seems to have had some contact with Emar to its north. It might be unwise to conclude too much, however, since *ālu* sometimes refers to a settlement which would not amount to a city in any normal sense (*CAD* A/1, 379–387, 'city, village, fort').

THE AGE OF EMPIRE: TIGLATH-PILESER I (1114–1076 BC)

The name Tadmūr appears much more regularly in a series of campaign inscriptions of Tiglath-Pileser I. Tadmūr is mentioned in almost identical contexts as marking one of the boundaries of the king's successful campaign against the *aḥlamû*-Aramaeans. The anti-Aramaean campaigns have been studied in detail by Younger (2016, 167–177). Four of these accounts identify Tadmūr in the following fashion:

> I have crossed the Euphrates . . . times, twice in one year, in pursuit of the *aḥlamû*-Aramaeans, to the land Ḫatti. I brought about their defeat from the foot of Mount Lebanon, the city Tadmar (^uru^*ta-ad-mar*) of the land Amurru, Anat of the land of Suḫu, as far as Rapiqu of Karduniaš. I brought their booty (and) possessions to my city Aššur. (Grayson 1991, 37–38 = A.0.87.3, lines 29–35)

In this text and in A.0.87.4 (Grayson 1991, 43), Tadmūr is again qualified by the determinative URU = *ālu*, 'city'. As noted above, its precise significance is not entirely clear: also, it is omitted in other inscriptions of this series referring to Tadmūr (so in A.0.8713, Grayson 1991, 59–60 lines 4′–9′). As at Emar, the determinative does appear at least to indicate a permanent settlement, possibly fortified. Tadmūr was a key site in the Assyrian military 'map' of the West, reflecting its key geopolitical and strategic position, as discussed by Scharrer (2002, 279–301) and Younger (2016, 22–23; also Sommer 2018, 24). It seems very doubtful that Tadmūr was a very substantial 'city' at this time, especially in view of the fact that it then disappears from the written record for the rest of the Assyrian, Neo-Assyrian, and Neo-Babylonian eras (below).

Nor do the Tiglath-Pileser accounts throw any real light on the ethnic character of Tadmūr or its founders (Scharrer 2002, 317). Specifically they do not clarify the relationship of Tadmūr with the *aḥlamû*-Aramaeans (despite Starcky 1952, 28; Shifman 2014, 16). Since these were such a prominent feature of this region, there may well have been *aḥlamû*-Aramaeans in Tadmūr, though nothing suggests that it was specifically Aramaean in this period. Rather, it is associated with Amurru, and it is partly for this reason, as well as archaeological and textual evidence cited earlier, that some commentators have assumed that Tadmūr could be regarded as an originally Amorite city.

In any case, all the mentions of Tadmūr in the inscriptions of Tiglath-Pileser I involve Tadmūr rather marginally, as a geographical marker of the territory where the *aḥlamû*-Aramaeans were being confronted (Scharrer 2002, 317). There is no direct confrontation with Tadmūr itself as part of the anti-Aramaean campaign, though it was clearly well known on the Syrian trade and military route.

Palmyra in the Early Period: Nomads and Settled Populations

It is interesting that in both the Mari period and that of Tiglath-Pileser I, Tadmūr was regarded as being of some (minor) importance in areas which were subject to nomad depredations. Recent discussions of Tadmūr in the second millennium BC (Joannès 1997; Scharrer 2002; Sommer 2018, 14–20) have usefully discussed it in the context of the issues of nomadism and the infringement of nomads or semi-nomads on settled centres. Detailed discussion of these questions reaches far beyond the scope of this discussion of early sources of evidence for Palmyra, but it is clear from all the second-millennium BC evidence that Tadmūr was a minor centre probably of trade and, in some sense, of political power during the centuries-long period of conflict between, on the one hand, the settled populations of towns and cities and, on the other, the mobile nomadic or semi-nomadic pastoralists who frequently, as it appears, impinged on the settlement centres to steal animals and other goods. In the Mari period, the preoccupation was with the Sutaeans and Benjaminites; in the Assyrian period, the preoccupation was with the *aḥlamû*-Aramaeans.

Although the Sutaeans attacked Tadmūr on at least one occasion (*ARM* V, 23 above), it is also likely that there was an element of symbiosis between the 'city' and the nomads, with Tadmūr, located on a major route and with known connections to the east and to the west, introducing some goods to the nomads which they needed for everyday life. To judge from later evidence (see Teixidor 1984, 78–82), Tadmūr may have produced salt. It certainly had things which the Sutaeans and Aramaeans wanted to obtain: they may have obtained them by peaceful exchange most of the time.

A Dark Age

With the end of Tiglath-Pileser's campaigns, Tadmūr disappears from the record and even the archaeological evidence is minimal until we reach the Hellenistic period: we have already mentioned du Mesnil du Buisson's evidence of the clearance of earlier material prior to the building of the later temple of Bēl.

As Sommer points out (Sommer 2018, 24–25), even when other, apparently minor towns or villages near Tadmūr are referred to in later annals, Tadmūr itself does not even merit a mention. Thus in one of Ashurbanipal's campaigns against the Arabs in the mid-seventh century BC, he traversed the Syrian Desert towards Damascus, and there is mention of Yarki (= Arki), just to the east of Tadmūr, but not of Tadmūr itself (*RINAP* 5: Ashurbanipal Prism A (text 011) viii 108: ^{uru}*ia-ar-ki*; see Eph'al 1984, 160–161). Tadmūr might simply have been too insignificant to mention in the period after Tiglath-Pileser I. It is tempting to fill this lacuna with speculation on what *might* have happened in the 'dark age' before Palmyra's resurgence. Such speculation is hazardous, but any reconstruction of events would have to take account of the facts which had undoubtedly changed in the intervening period.

First, even if (though it is far from certain) Tadmūr may have been originally Amorite and not part of the *aḫlamû*-Aramaean problem experienced by Tiglath-Pileser I and his successors, it is abundantly clear that during the Roman period it had a strong Aramaean character: Aramaic was the vernacular, and typically Aramaean gods were worshipped (among others). How this change came about is unknown: it may have involved a dramatic *aḫlamû*-Aramaean takeover soon after the time of Tiglath-Pileser, with Aramaean cultural hegemony taking root to such an extent that the older Amorite traditions were barely perceptible by the time of the Romans. On the other hand, Aramaic became predominant in wide swathes of the Assyrian west, and Tadmūr could have been Aramaized slowly and painlessly, like other regions and like Assyria itself.

Second, by the end of the dark age, Tadmūr/Palmyra was emerging as a major trading centre with a commercial role and a geopolitical position which gave it a new importance in an era which saw the blossoming of a 'globalized' economy. It is reasonable to assume that this role developed slowly during the Achaemenid and Seleucid periods. Whether either regime promoted or gave special attention to Tadmūr/Palmyra remains unknown.

There are other glimmers of light. It is clear that the Aramaic used later in Palmyra is ultimately derived from Achaemenid Aramaic. Also, as noted by Shifman (2014, 18), the evidence we have of Palmyrene legal tradition suggests that it originated in or was transmitted through the Achaemenid period. Continuity in legal forms and formularies implies continuity, at least in this aspect of life, in the dark age (Shifman 2014, 17–18; see Shifman 1965; Cussini 2015). In the sphere of religion, it is probable that the impact of Mesopotamian tradition on the later Tadmūr/Palmyra (worship and mythology of Bēl, Nabû, etc.) had its origins in this dark age, though it is not provable. The 'dark age' is one of Stygian gloom. Nothing is certain.

THE HEBREW BIBLE AND JEWISH TRADITIONS

After disappearing from the cuneiform record, then, Tadmūr remained in obscurity also during the Achaemenid period. There may, however, be faint glimmers of light in the biblical and Jewish traditions.

The Hebrew Bible as it comes down to us through Jewish tradition dates from long after the events it purports to describe. We cannot be sure of the date particular 'historical' reports were compiled and must also allow for later interpolations and tendentious adjustments in the extant texts. Since the Hebrew Bible was originally transmitted in a consonants-only text, sometimes such adjustments consist simply of alterations of the vowels of particular words, leading to a different interpretation. With this in mind, we may note the main biblical tradition about Tadmūr, found in 2 Chronicles 8:3–5, where we are told that Tadmūr was built by Solomon in the tenth century BC.

> And Solomon went to Ḥamāth-Ṣōbāh and took it. He built Tadmōr [*tadmōr*] in the wilderness and all the store-cities [which] he built in Ḥamath. He also built Upper Bēth-Ḥōrōn and Lower Bēth-Ḥōrōn, fortified cities with walls, gates and bars.

The context in 2 Chronicles is that of Solomon's putative campaigns in Syria, and the other places mentioned suggest that we are dealing with Syrian Tadmūr.

However, like much of the material in 1–2 Chronicles, this appears to be a later, post-exilic (post 537 BC) rewriting of a report which was created earlier (probably before 587 BC) and appears in 1 Kings 9:17–18.

> so Solomon rebuilt Gezer and Lower Bēth-Ḥōrōn and Baʿalath and Tamōr in the wilderness in the land.

Here, the reference in the Hebrew text is to 'TMR', with the vowels added much later to give *tamōr*. Although this text does not refer to Tadmōr, later Jewish scholarship was aware of the discrepancy between 2 Chronicles and 1 Kings and so suggested a correction of the 1 Kings reading to *Tadmōr*. Through this late correction the two versions of events are harmonized. However, it is noteworthy that the phrase 'in the land' in 1 Kings suggests that the Tamōr being referred to is within the land of Israel (and translations reflect this: RSV 'the land of Judah'; Jerusalem Bible 'inside the country'). This would point clearly to the Tāmār which is mentioned in Ezekiel 47:19 and 48:28 as part of the description of the southern borders of the restored state:

> On the south side it will run from Tāmār as far as the waters of Merībath-Qādesh, thence along the Brook of Egypt to the Great Sea. This shall be the south side. (Ezekiel 47:19)

This Tāmār is located at the southern end of the Dead Sea and it is likely, therefore, that the transmitters of the Hebrew Bible have put the cart before the horse here: Tadmūr/Palmyra was becoming well known in the Persian, Hellenistic, and Roman periods for its splendour and wealth, and this probably encouraged the copyists of 2 Chronicles to assume that *it* was the desert city built by Solomon, rather than Tāmār (or Tāmōr), a more obscure settlement in southern Palestine (see, e.g., Février 1931,

3–4; Starcky 1952, 28–29). However, this idea of a Solomonic foundation of Tadmūr/ Palmyra became fixed in Jewish tradition and led to the pseudo-correction of 1 Kings. From a historian's point of view, it should have been 2 Chronicles, not 1 Kings, which was corrected!

Some modern scholars, however, have concluded that Solomon really *did* rebuild Tadmūr after its destruction by the Assyrians, though this is an implausible scenario which is not supported by any other evidence. It was accepted by Malamat (1963, 4) and Gichon (1963, 116–119), the latter noting the implied geographical position of the place in the 2 Chronicles account, beyond Ḥamāth-Ṣōbāh. Gichon speculated that both names, Tāmōr *and* Tadmōr, stood in the original report of these events (in the *Urtext*). Shifman, too (2014, 17), was inclined to accept the accuracy of the claim to Solomonic rebuilding of Tadmūr, noting a later Jewish polemic against Palmyra because of the supposed Palmyrene involvement in the destruction of Jerusalem in 586 BC *and* in AD 70. This is found in the ca. fourth-century AD text *Genesis Rabbah* 56:11, where the city is called *Tarmōd* (Février 1931, 4 and Shifman 2014, 17). According to John Malalas (*Chr.* 18.2), Nebuchadnezzar captured Palmyra on his way to attack Jerusalem. If there were any truth in these traditions, they would provide another faint glimmer of light on Tadmūr in the dark age.

The presence of Jews in Roman-period Palmyra is in any case clear (Moss 1928). Palmyrene Jews visited Jerusalem, where they are mentioned in burial inscriptions (Noy and Bloedhorn 2004, 227–232). A late reflection of this Jewish Palmyra is found in the account of Benjamin of Tudela (d. 1173) of his visit to Palmyra in 1172. He calls it *Tarmōd*, like *Genesis Rabbah* above, and regards Solomon as its builder (Adler 1907, 31 [Hebrew 31–32]). Clearly, Jews knew about Palmyra, and this knowledge gives the simplest and most plausible explanation of why Tamār/Tamōr was changed to Tadmōr in 2 Chronicles: to add it to the glory of Solomon's great achievements.

THE SEPTUAGINT AND JOSEPHUS

In passing, we may note that there is no direct parallel to 1 Kings 9:17–18 in the Greek Septuagint translation, but in 2 Chronicles (in the Septuagint: 2 Paralipomena) 8:4 we are told that Solomon built τήν θεδμὸρ ἐν τῇ ἐρήμῳ. The variability of the spelling of the city's name is notable and is also reflected in Josephus, who was aware of this tradition (*Antiquities* 8.6.1) and calls the Solomonic city Θαμαδορα, while identifying it explicitly with Palmyra, which was, of course, flourishing in Josephus's time. It must have seemed plausible enough to ascribe it to Solomon.

> He [Solomon] also advanced into the desert of Upper Syria and, having taken possession of it, founded there a very great city at a distance of two days' journey from Upper Syria and one day's journey from the Euphrates, while from the great Babylon the distance was a journey of six days. . . . And so, when he had built this city and

surrounded it with very strong walls, he named it Thamadora, as it is still called by the Syrians, while the Greeks call it Palmyra. (trans. Ralph Marcus in Thackeray and Marcus 1934, 652–655)

Thus the Solomonic foundation of Palmyra came to be an established 'fact' of biblical history by the first century AD and was accepted by Christians (John Malalas, *Chr.* 5.69).

CONCLUSION

Palmyra underwent a remarkable development and flourished during the Hellenistic/ Roman periods. It is even more remarkable in the light of the fact that it appears almost ex nihilo at this time. Earlier we find a small settlement cooperating in minor matters with the major powers, from Mari to Assyria. But this period in the second millennium BC was followed by a descent into a dark age which lasted almost a thousand years.

ABBREVIATIONS

ARM   *Archives royales de Mari*

CAD   *Chicago Assyrian Dictionary*

RINAP   The Royal Inscriptions of the Neo-Assyrian Period (oracc.museum.upenn.edu)

BIBLIOGRAPHY

Adler, Marcus N. 1907. *The Itinerary of Benjamin of Tudela: Critical Text, Translation and Commentary.* London: Henry Frowde. Reprinted Whitefish, MT: Kessinger, 2010.

al-Maqdissi, Michel. 2000. 'Note sur les sondages réalisés par Robert du Mesnil du Buisson dans la cour du sanctuaire de Bêl à Palmyre'. *Syria* 77: 137–158.

al-Maqdissi, Michel. 2009. 'Notes d'archéologie Levantine XV: Le bronze ancien à Palmyre'. *al-Rāfidān* 30: 23–33.

al-Maqdissi, Michel, and Eva Ishaq. 2023. 'Note d'Archéologie Levantine LXVII: les phases anciennes de Palmyre d'après les données des archives de R. du Mesnil du Buisson et de la mission syrienne de 2011'. In *Style and Society in the Prehistory of West Asia: Essays in Honour of Olivier P. Nieuwenhuyse* (Papers on Archaeology of the Leiden Museum of Antiquities 29), edited by Bleda S. Düring and Peter M. M. G. Akkermans, 207–221. Leiden: Sidestone Press.

Arnaud, Daniel. 1975. 'Catalogue des textes cunéiformes trouvés au cours des trois premières campagnes à Meskéné Qadimé Ouest'. *Les annales archéologiques arabes syriennes* 25: 87–93.

Arnaud, Daniel. 1982. 'Emar et Palmyre'. *Les annales archéologiques arabes syriennes* 32: 83–88.

Arnaud, Daniel. 1985. *Recherches au pays d'Aštata: Emar.* Vol. 6.1, *Textes sumériens et accadiens: Planches.* Paris: Éditions Recherche sur les civilisations.

Arnaud, Daniel. 1986. *Recherches au pays d'Aštata: Emar.* Vol. 6.3, *Textes sumériens et accadiens: Texte.* Paris: Éditions Recherche sur les civilisations.

Cremaschi, Mauro, and Andrea Zerboni. 2016. 'The Oasis of Palmyra in Prehistory: Late Pleistocene and Early Holocene Paleoclimate and Human Occupation in the Region of Palmyra/Tadmor (Central Syria)'. In *Climate and Cultural Change in Prehistoric Europe and the Near East*, edited by Peter F. Biehl and Olivier Nieuwenhuyse, 13–35. Albany: State University of New York Press.

Cussini, Eleonora. 2015. 'Reconstructing Palmyrene Legal Language'. In *The World of Palmyra*, edited by Andreas Kropp and Rubina Raja, 42–52. Palmyrene Studies 1. Copenhagen: Det Kongelige Danske Videnskabernes Selskab.

Dercksen, Jan G. 1996. *The Old Assyrian Copper Trade in Anatolia*. Istanbul: Nederlands Historisch-Archaeologisch Instituut te Istanbul.

du Mesnil du Buisson, Robert. 1966. 'Première campagne de fouilles à Palmyre'. *Comptes rendus des séances de l'Académie des inscriptions et belles-lettres* 110: 158–190.

du Mesnil du Buisson, Robert. 1967. 'La découverte de la plus ancienne Palmyre'. *Bibliotheca Orientalis* 24: 20–21.

Durand, Jean-Marie. 1998. *Les documents épistolaires du palais de Mari*. Vol. 2. Littéraires anciennes du Proche-Orient 17. Paris: du Cerf.

Eisser, Georg, and Julius Lewy. 1935. *Die altassyrischen Rechtsurkunden von Kültepe*. Parts 3 and 4, *Urkunden 291–341; Register zu Teil 1–4*. Mitteilungen der Vorderasiatisch-Aegyptischen Gesellschaft, vol. 35, part 3. Leipzig: Hinrichs.

Eph'al, Israel. 1984. *The Ancient Arabs: Nomads on the Borders of the Fertile Crescent, 9th–5th Centuries B.C.* Jerusalem: Magnes.

Février, James G. 1931. *Essai sur l'histoire politique et économique de Palmyre*. Paris: Vrin.

Gichon, Mordechai. 1963. 'The Defences of the Salomonic Kingdom'. *Palestine Exploration Quarterly* 95: 113–126.

Grayson, A. Kirk. 1991. *Assyrian Rulers of the Early First Millennium BC*. Vol. 1, *1114–859 BC*. The Royal Inscriptions of Mesopotamia, Assyrian Periods 2. Toronto: University of Toronto Press.

Joannès, Francis. 1997. 'Palmyre et les routes du désert au début du deuxième millénaire av. J.-C'. *Mari: Annales de recherches interdisciplinaires* 8: 393–415.

Kienast, Burkhardt. 1960. *Die altassyrischen Texte des orientalischen Seminars der Universität Heidelberg und der Sammlung Erlenmeyer-Basel*. Untersuchungen zur Assyriologie und vorderasiatischen Archäologie 1. Berlin: de Gruyter.

Klengel, Horst. 1977. 'Nomaden und Handel'. *Iraq* 39: 163–169.

Klengel, Horst. 1996. 'Palmyra and International Trade in the Bronze Age: The Historical Background'. *Les annales archéologiques arabes syriennes* 42: 159–163.

Larsen, Mogens T., and Eva Møller. 1991. 'Five Old Assyrian Texts'. In *Marchands, diplomates et empereurs: Études sur la civilisation mésopotamienne offertes à Paul Garelli*, edited by Dominique Charpin and Francis Joannès, 227–252. Paris: Éditions Recherche sur les civilisations.

Lewy, Julius. 1936. *Tablettes cappadociennes: Troisième série, deuxième partie; Textes cunéiformes du Louvre XX*. Paris: Geuthner.

Malamat, Avraham. 1963. 'Aspects of the Foreign Policies of David and Solomon'. *Journal of Near Eastern Studies* 22: 1–17.

Moss, Cyril. 1928. 'Jews and Judaism in Palmyra'. *Palestine Exploration Quarterly* 60: 100–107.

Noy, David, and Hanswulf Bloedhorn. 2004. *Inscriptiones Judaicae Orientis*. Vol. 3, *Syria and Cyprus*. Texts and Studies in Ancient Judaism 102. Tübingen: Mohr Siebeck.

Scharrer, Ulf. 2002. 'Nomaden und Sesshafte in Tadmor im 2. Jahrtausend v. Chr'. In *Grenzüberschreitungen: Formen des Kontakts zwischen Orient und Okzident im Altertum*, edited by Monika Schuol, Udo Hartmann, and Andreas Luther, 279–330. Oriens et Occidens 3. Stuttgart: Steiner.

Shifman, Il'ia Sholeĭmovich. 1965. 'Property and Agrarian Relationships in Palmyra in the 1st–3rd Centuries A.D. According to the Epigraphic Data'. *Palestinskiĭ Sbornik* 13: 100–113. In Russian.

Shifman, Il'ia Sholeĭmovich. 2014. *The Palmyrene Tax Tariff*. Journal of Semitic Studies Supplement 33. Oxford: Oxford University Press. Russian original 1980.

Sommer, Michael. 2018. *Palmyra: A History*. Cities of the Ancient World. London: Routledge.

Starcky, Jean. 1952. *Palmyre*. L'Orient ancien illustré 7. Paris: Maisonneuve.

Teixidor, Javier. 1984. *Un port romain du désert: Palmyre et son commerce d'Auguste à Caracalla*. Semitica 34. Paris: Maisonneuve.

Thackeray, Henry St J., and Ralph Marcus. 1934. *Josephus*. Vol. 5, *Jewish Antiquities, Books V–VIII*. Loeb Classical Library. Cambridge, MA: Harvard University Press.

Younger, K. Lawson. 2016. *A Political History of the Arameans: From Their Origins to the End of Their Polities*. Archaeology and Biblical Studies 13. Atlanta: SBL Press.

CHAPTER 5

HELLENISTIC PALMYRA

A Fata Morgana?

ANDREAS SCHMIDT-COLINET

INTRODUCTION

THERE is no doubt that there was a Greek influence on Palmyra (Schlumberger 1969; 1970; Sartre 1996; *contra* Kaizer 2007). Usually, this process is called 'Hellenization'. The best-known example of this influence is the ground plan of the temple of Bēl constructed in the first century AD (Seyrig et al. 1968/1975; Gawlikowski 1973, 67–86; Pietrzykowski 1997; Delplace 2017, 15–37; Gros 2017, 99, n. 17). This plan is an exact copy of the ground plan of the temple of Artemis at Magnesia in Asia Minor, constructed in about 200 BC by the Greek architect Hermogenes. Even the Ionic capitals of the small sides of the cella of the temple of Bēl are copies of the capitals of the Hellenistic temple in Magnesia.

Here, we do not use 'Hellenistic' to generally indicate 'influenced by Graeco-Roman culture' but only as a chronological term for the period between the third century BC and the first century AD. Thus, the question, 'Hellenistic Palmyra—a Fata Morgana?' is: Did there already exist a settlement at Palmyra in this early period, and, if so, how and where? Until recently, some literary and epigraphic sources and some small archaeological artefacts provided the only hints of the existence of such a settlement.

SUMMARY OF THE ARCHAEOLOGICAL EVIDENCE

Excavations within the sanctuary of Bēl prove that by the third to the first centuries BC, building structures existed there, now beneath the later temple of Bēl (Seyrig

1939, 322–323, fig. 11, no. 28; 1940a; du Mesnil du Buisson 1966, esp. 179–185, fig. 5–6; Gawlikowski 1973, 53–66, esp. 54–56; Will 1992, 37–38; al-Maqdissi 2000; Bounni and al-Maqdissi 2001; Delplace and Dentzer-Feydy 2017, 73–74; Sommer 2017, 61–62; Graf 2018, 483–489). The underground tomb near the later temple of Baalshamin can be dated to the second century BC (Fellmann 1970; 1975; 1976; Gawlikowski 1973, 17–19; Kaizer 2017b, 35; Sommer 2017, 62). A coffin tomb of a young man in the south-east necropolis, recently discovered by a Japanese mission, may also be dated to the second century BC (Saito 2002; 2005, 34, figs. 42–44; 2016, 351, fig. 4). The earliest primitive shrine (*hamana*) in the area of the sanctuary of Allat existed in the mid-second century BC (Gawlikowski 1983, 61; 1990; 1997; 2004, 84–89, figs. 3–4; 2012, 779, fig. 11; Delplace 2017, 55–58; Kaizer 2017b, 35; Gawlikowski 2018, 29, fig. 1; 33–64). Also, the first constructions in the sanctuary of Nabu (Bounni et al. 1992/2004; Delplace 2017, 49–54) and of the temple of Arsu (Will 1983, 76–78 with n. 17 and fig. 3; al-Asʻad and Teixidor 1985; Delplace 2017, 59; Kaizer 2017b, 37) may be traced back to the first century BC. The tower tomb of Atenatan (tomb no. 7 = Q 279)—the earliest monumental tomb dated by a foundation inscription—was built in 9 BC (Cantineau 1930, 28; *PAT* 0457; Gawlikowski 1970, 45, no. 1; 52–55; 184, no. 1; 1993, 112–115; Henning 2013a, 145f., no. 7, plates 7–8; 2013b, 161, 169, fig. 3; Delplace and Dentzer-Feydy 2017, 80). Other tombs may be dated to even earlier periods by typological approaches (Gawlikowski 1970, 54–60; Henning 2013b, 160). A Chinese silk fragment found in the tomb of Atenatan (Schmidt-Colinet et al. 2000, 107, no. 15, fig. 65, plate 81; Stauffer 2005, 76, 80, fig. 121) proves that Palmyra's Far East connections were already established at this early period.

SUMMARY OF THE LITERARY SOURCES

Appian's report (*Bell. Civ.* 5.9) is the most famous literary source that mentions an early settlement at Palmyra. Appian refers to Marcus Antonius's abortive cavalry raid of the *polis* Palmyra in 41 BC. This report proves the existence of an important settlement at Palmyra at that time, even if one can doubt this report completely (Hekster and Kaizer 2004; Kaizer 2017b, 34–35; differently, Will 1992, 35–36; Sommer 2005, 152, n. 39; Delplace 2017, 11; Sommer 2017, 78–80; Graf 2018, 481).[1]

---

[1] On the other hand, this Roman attack may have been the reason for the construction of a city wall.

Chronological Summary of the Data Concerning Palmyra in the Hellenistic Period

Post ca. 300 BC	Construction work on the terrace of the tell of the sanctuary of Bēl; construction of a building; pottery of the second century BC (see above)
217 BC	A Palmyrene detachment fights for the Seleucid army at the battle of Raphia (Polybios 5.79.8; Seyrig 1940b, 331; Gawlikowski 1973, 54; Fellmann 1976, 214; the critics of Kaizer 2017b, 33, n. 20)*
Second century BC	Palmyrene proper names and a Palmyrene tribe are attested in connection with trade (Fellmann 1970, 118–119; 1976a, 213–214; Milik 1972, 173; Gawlikowski 1973, 54; Will 1992, 34–35)
ca. 90/80 BC	Seleucid (?) King Ephiphanes in Palmyra (Seyrig 1939, 322–323, fig. 11, no. 28; Grainger 1990, 182, n. 52)
82 BC (?)	Building activities in the sanctuary of Bēl (Teixidor 1965, no. 87; *PAT* 1511 'no date'; for the date see Milik 1972, 172–173; Gawlikowski 1973, 59–60, no. 22)
44 BC	The existence of a congregation of the priests of Bēl confirms the existence of a building for the cult of Bēl and of the Bene Kahennabu tribe (Teixidor 1965, no. 100; *PAT* 1524 with wrong date 'AD 44'; Milik 1972, 31, plate II, 3; Gawlikowski 1973, 59, no. 18, fig. 6; Starcky and Gawlikowski 1985, 28, 37, fig. 6; Will 1992, 35 with fig.; Delplace 2017, 12; Delplace and Dentzer-Feydy 2017, 76; Kaizer 2017a, 70–71, n. 38; 2017b, 33; Sommer 2017, 61)
41 BC	Roman cavalry attack led by Marcus Antonius (see above)
33 BC	Construction of a sanctuary for Bēl and Yarhibol in Dura-Europos by the two Palmyrenes Zabdibol and Maliku (du Mesnil du Buisson 1939, 3–4, no. 1; *PAT* 1067; Milik 1972, 17, 38; Dirven 1996, 47–49; Delplace and Dentzer-Feydy 2017, 76–77, 81; Kaizer 2017a, 71; 2017b, 45, n. 65)
31/30 BC	Construction of a *hamana* in the sanctuary of Allat attested (Gawlikowski 2018, 243, no. 11, fig. 215)
18 BC	Oldest inscription from the colonnaded street attesting the Bene Zmr tribe (Bounni and Teixidor 1975, no. 22; *PAT* 1539 with wrong date, 'AD 18'; Delplace 2017, 12; Delplace and Dentzer-Feydy 2017, 76)
17 BC	Offering of a statue by the Bene Komara tribe (Teixidor 1965, no. 84; *PAT* 0315; Delplace 2017, 12; Delplace and Dentzer-Feydy 2017, 76)
9 BC	Construction of the tower tomb of Atenatan from the Bene Mitha tribe (see above)
6 BC	Building activities in the sanctuary of Bēl (Cantineau 1936, 271, no. 17; Milik 1972, 38; Gawlikowski 1973, 60, no. 24)

6/5 BC	An altar for Allat/Artemis attested in the sanctuary of Allat (Gawlikowski 1977, 271; 1983, 66; Will 1983, 78, n. 24; Gawlikowski 2018, 249, no. 20, fig. 219)
Before AD 8/9 (or 24?)	Construction of the tower tomb of Moqimo (Cantineau 1930, no. 26; *PAT* 1150 with the date AD 24; for the date see Gawlikowski 1970, 45, no. 2, n. 14)
AD 9	Construction of a tomb for a member of the Bene Matabol (Milik 1972, 16)
AD 11	Caravan trade and a city wall (?) mentioned (Gawlikowski and al-As'ad 1991–1992)
AD 11	Dismantling of the tomb near the temple of Baalshamin, and reuse of the area as a sanctuary (Dunant 1971, 72–74, no. 60; Gawlikowski 1973, 17–19; 1974, 238)
AD 17/19	Greek and Palmyrene merchants from Seleucia honour a Palmyrene who contributed to the construction of the temple (Cantineau 1933, no. 6; *PAT*, 0270–0271; *CIS* 3924–3925; Gawlikowski 1973, 68, no. 4; 1974, 239; Sommer 2017, 81, n. 57; Graf 2018, 484, n. 213)
AD 19	Latin inscription honouring Tiberius, Drusus, and Germanicus in the sanctuary of Bēl (Cantineau 1933, no. 2; Gawlikowski 1973, 68, no. 2; Will 1992, 40 with fig.; Sommer 2017, 81, n. 61; Graf 2018, 489, n. 231)
AD 19	Tiberius sends Germanicus and the Palmyrene, Alexandros, as ambassadors to Characene and Emesa (Cantineau 1931, 139–141, no. 18; *PAT* 2754; Gawlikowski 1973, 68–69, no. 3, fig. 11; Dirven 1996, 50–51, n. 58; Kaizer 2017a, 72, n. 45; Sommer 2017, 81–82, n. 59–60; Graf 2018, 484, n. 216); a visit from Germanicus in Palmyra may be the reason for further construction activities at the temple (Will 1992, 36, 39–40; Sartre 2001, 318, n. 4)
AD 21	Honorific inscription attests construction activities at the sanctuary of Bēl (Cantineau 1933, no. 13; *CIS* 3915; *PAT* 0261, Gawlikowski 1973, 69, no. 6)
AD 24	Palmyrene merchants from Babylon again honour a Palmyrene who contributed to the construction of the temple of Bēl (Cantineau 1933, no. 11; *PAT* 1352; Milik 1972, 39; Dirven 1996, 51, n. 58; Gawlikowski 1973, 69, nos. 7–9; Graf 2018, 434, n. 214)
6 April AD 32	Inauguration of the cult at the temple of Bēl (Cantineau 1933, no. 1; *PAT* 1347; Milik 1972, 39, 222; Gawlikowski 1973, 68, no. 1; Will 1992, 39)

*Kaizer 2017b, 33, n. 21, for an inscription from Laghman (south of Ai Khanoum), which may be connected with Palmyra in the mid-third century BC.

In general, from the foregoing evidence one may conclude that Palmyra was an important trade station by the Seleucid period, during the third century BC. In the second and first centuries BC, one may suppose an increased settling of individual tribes and urbanization with a more complex civic organization. Evidently, several extensive sanctuaries of various tribes were the starting points for the city's later urban development (Schlumberger 1935; Seyrig 1940b, 334–336; Gawlikowski 1973, 9–12, 26–41; 1974, 231–233; van Berchem 1976; Frézouls 1976b; Starcky and Gawlikowski 1985, 33–37; Grainger 1990, 182; Will 1983, 75–79, n. 19, fig. 3; 1992, 29–38; al-As'ad and Yon 2001, 54, fig. 1; Hartmann 2001, 45–50; Edwell 2008, 31–62, 217–227; Hammad 2010, 8–25; Delplace 2017, 11–12; Sommer 2017, 81–86; Kaizer 2017a; 2017b, 33–39, 45–51; Delplace and Dentzer-Feydy 2017).

Until recently, there was no archaeological evidence of any pre-Roman settlement in Palmyra. According to several hypotheses, the location of the earlier settlement was supposed to be located outside the Roman town, south of the wadi. This area stretches between the so-called Hellenistic wall to the west (van Berchem 1954, 254–257; Gawlikowski 1973, 11–19 plan I; 1974, 231–235 with fig.; 1986; Delplace 2017, 186–190; Kaizer 2017b, 36, n. 39), the wadi in the north, and the modern asphalt road to the south. It is located near the Efqa spring (Gawlikowski 1973, 112–120) and the gardens of Palmyra, and between the sanctuary of Bēl-Hammon (Gawlikowski 1973, 11–14 plan I–II) and that of Bēl. The sanctuaries of Bēl and Nabu and the agora and the basilica originally faced this area (Delplace and Dentzer-Feydy 2005; Delplace 2017, 64–75; Kaizer 1917b, 37). The temple of Arsu is located to the north of the area, south of the wadi. Several mud brick walls are still visible at the southern border of the wadi (Schmidt-Colinet 2005, 83, fig. 132), and underground building structures may be observed at the surface under certain weather conditions (Schmidt-Colinet and al-As'ad 2013, 76, fig. 12). Above ground, only a few remains of antique building activity may be seen. Finally, this area evidently was never built over by late antique or modern structures. It is approximately triangular and covers about 20 ha.

Thus, in 1992, Ernest Will imagined the existence of the 'Hellenistic' town of Palmyra in this area.

> La ville hellénistique est toujours là sous les sables; la catastrophe de 273 lui fut fatale et c'est la ville impériale qui survécut. Il faudra attendre de nouvelles fouilles dans cette zone pour se faire une idée plus précise de ce que fut la ville à cette date; elle a des chances d'avoir rassemblé à une ville orientale aux maisons serrées dans des ruelles étroites et irrégulières dépourvues de plan systématique. (Will 1992, 38)

The 'new excavations' suggested by Will were carried out between 1997 and 2010, by a joint Syro-German/Austrian archaeological mission. The final publication was published in 2013 (Schmidt-Colinet and al-As'ad 2013. Reviews: Kaizer 2015; Yon 2015. Preliminary reports: Schmidt-Colinet and al-As'ad 2000; al-As'ad and Schmidt-Colinet 2002; Schmidt-Colinet et al. 2016, 345–348, figs. 12–17. See also Sartre-Fauriat and Sartre 2008, 28–29, 56; Hammad 2010, 22–23, fig. 47; Schnädelbach 2010, 51–52, 92; Sommer 2017, 62–66; Graf 2018, 481–483). First, building structures hidden under the sand were revealed by a photogrammetric and topographic survey and geophysical prospection (Becker and Fassbinder 1999; Becker 2000; Stephani 2000; Schmidt-Colinet and Plattner 2001; Fassbinder and Linck 2013; Linck 2016). The magnetogram (Figures 5.1 and 5.2)—result

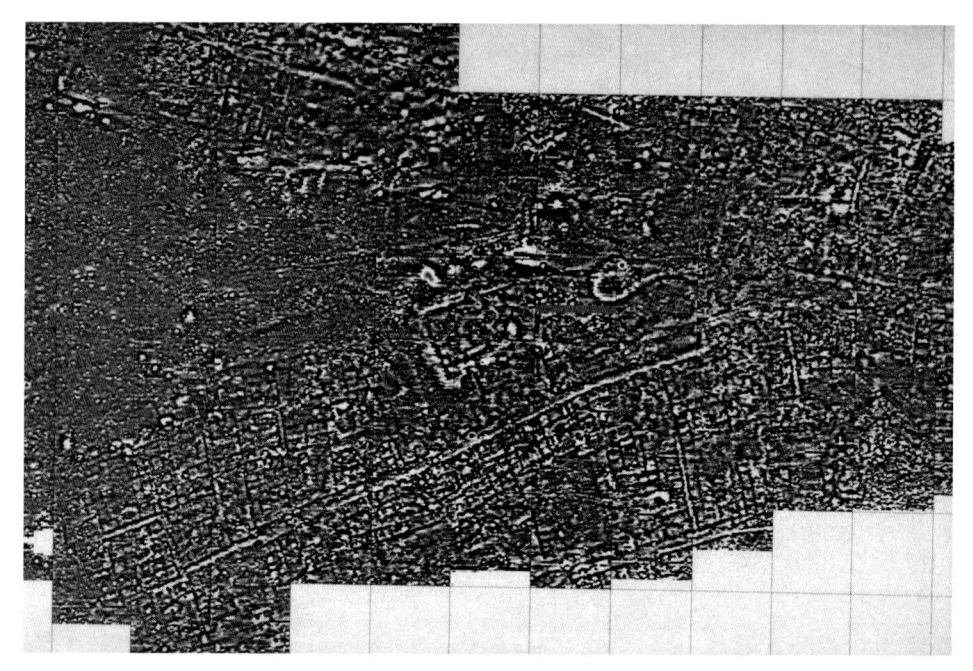

FIGURE 5.1 Palmyra, area south of the wadi. Magnetogram, after Schmidt-Colinet and al-As'ad 2013, 316, fig. 13.

Processing by H. Becker and J. Fassbinder.

FIGURE 5.2 Palmyra. Satellite picture with interpretation of the magnetogram, after Schmidt-Colinet and al-As'ad 2013, 288, fig. 260.

© Digital Globe/European Space Imaging Space Agency.

of the geophysical prospection—shows a system of main and secondary streets with adjacent building structures. One main street to the south, running from south-west to north-east, is joined by secondary roads at more or less right angles. Another main road to the north runs from north-west to south-east, parallel to the wadi. Here the adjacent houses seem to be larger than in the southern area. Between these two main roads there is an area without any buildings.

Two trenches (I and II) proved that at least some of the structures visible on the magnetogram do date back to the Hellenistic period. In trench I (Plattner and Schmidt-Colinet 2010; Plattner 2013), the following early construction phases may be distinguished according to the stratigraphic correlation between the small finds and the architectural remains: Phase 1, ca. 220–175 BC (plastered mud brick walls based on foundations built of rubble stones); Phase 2, ca. 180–150 BC (construction of a deep well); Phase 3, ca. 150–100 BC (construction of a mud brick pavement on the main road and of a first water pipe); Phase 4, ca. 100–30 BC (little building activity); Phase 5, ca. 30 BC–AD 50 (monumental structures during Augustan times); later building activity, up to the end of the third century AD.

The stratigraphic units contain pottery finds from the end of the third century BC up to the third century AD (Römer-Strehl 2000; 2013, 7–18 tab. 1 diagr. 1–6; p. 33–41). Imported objects (e.g., Rhodian amphora handles) and local wares from the third up to the middle of the second century BC show a high affinity with the central and eastern Mediterranean area (Figures 5.3 and 5.4). From ca. 150 BC onwards, south Mesopotamian

FIGURE 5.3 Bottom of a skyphos with palmette stamp, from trench I, ca. 225–175 BC, Museum, Palmyra, inv. no. PA 99/83/6, after Römer-Strehl 2013, 334, no. K 6, fig. 1.

Photograph by A. Schmidt-Colinet.

FIGURE 5.4 Rhodian amphora stamp of Damokrateus, from trench I, ca. 205–175 BC, Museum, Palmyra, inv. no. PA 99/79/1, after Römer-Strehl 2013, 106–107, no. 2, fig. 83.

Photograph by A. Schmidt-Colinet.

influences are visible. Forms produced in the eastern Mediterranean area (fish plates, 'Megarian Bowls', red glazed pottery, Eastern Sigillata A [ESA]) and in Mesopotamia (Parthian glazed pottery) and pieces imitating these forms were used simultaneously in Palmyra. Amphorae were also produced locally as well as being imported from as far away as Rhodes and Italy (Laubenheimer et al. 2007; Laubenheimer 2013; Laubenheimer and Römer-Strehl 2013).

All in all, trench I revealed a stratigraphic sequence of construction activities and daily life, including long-distance trade, from the pre-Roman Hellenistic period to the end of the third century AD. It seems quite possible that the destruction or the surrendering of the area can be connected with Aurelian's destruction of Palmyra in AD 272, and/or with the construction of Diocletian's wall at the beginning of the fourth century.

In trench II (Ertel and Ployer 2013, especially 118–121, figs. 90–93; 158; 162–164 plans A–C; Delplace 2017, 141–142), a monumental square stone building was excavated. It was interpreted as the residence ('*khan*') of a noble Palmyrene family. The following construction phases may be distinguished according to the stratigraphic correlation between the small finds and the architectural remains: Phase 1, ca. 50 BC (layout and construction of a large square stone building with a quadrangular courtyard over an older mud brick structure, oriented diagonally to the later stone walls); Phases 2a–b, ca. 30 BC–AD 20 (modifications, enlargements, and a monumentalizing of the building during Augustan times); Phase 3, ca. AD 140–160 (rebuilding and restoration following destruction by fire); later building activity up to the end of the third century AD.

The stratigraphic units contain pottery (Römer-Strehl 2013a 21–25 tab. 2 diagr. 8–10; p. 42–45) and small finds, especially glass (Ployer 2010; 2012; 2013) from the first century BC up to the late third century AD: in contrast to the pottery from trench I, in the pottery from trench II the local ware predominates over the fine imported ware. Nevertheless, this fine imported ware documents Palmyra's worldwide economic and cultural connections to the west and with the Parthian east, and with Saudi Arabia, from the first century BC onwards.

All in all, trench II revealed a stratigraphic sequence of construction from the middle of the first century BC to the end of the third century AD. It seems possible that the construction of the '*khan*' may be connected with the founding of the Roman province of Syria in 64 BC or with Marcus Antonius's Roman cavalry attack in 41/40 BC. The destruction or abandonment of the building—as in trench I—may be connected with Aurelian's destruction of Palmyra in AD 272 and/or with the construction of the Diocletian's wall at the beginning of the fourth century.

The research in the area of the so-called Hellenistic town did prove that construction activities occurred in this area from at least the second half of the third century BC onwards. One may debate the label 'Hellenistic city' based on only slight archaeological evidence. The label 'pre-central colonnade Tadmor-Palmyra' was proposed as an alternative (Kaizer 2017a, 71–72 with n. 41; 2017b, 37). In any case, one cannot deny the existence of such an early settlement (as did Raja 2017a, 117, n. 8; 2017b, 322, n. 13). The scant archaeological evidence for 'Hellenistic' Palmyra fits into 'The problem of Hellenistic Syria' (Millar 1987; Kaizer 2017b, 29–30). Very little archaeological evidence exists for the Hellenistic period of other Syrian cities, such as Apamea (Balty 1994; 2000, 167–175) and Dura-Europos (summarizing Kaizer 2017a, 65, n. 13; 2017b, 40–51), with very few exceptions, such as Jebel Khaled (summarizing Clark and Jackson 2002/2003; 2016). Several recent historical proposals attempt to explain this 'gap', and the sudden appearance of Palmyra in the historical and archaeological documents of the first century BC (Kaizer 2017b, esp. 48–50; Sommer 2017, 81–86).

Many questions about Hellenistic Palmyra are still open. Recently, the locations of the 'tariff' and the small sanctuary of Rabaseire were discovered south of the agora. This section of the wadi was paved, demonstrating that, by the first century BC, the wadi itself was the main route from the west (Gawlikowski 2012; 2013; 2014; Kaizer 2017b, 37, n. 41; also Żuchowska 2008).

Further large-scale excavations in the wadi, especially in the area south of it, will enlarge our knowledge about the urban development of early Palmyra from the third to the first centuries BC. As we said elsewhere,

> The hypogeum near the later temple of Baalshamin must have been situated outside the walls. But who knows how far north Palmyra extended in the second and first centuries BC? Furthermore, who knows whether our principles of never burying the dead inside a settlement were held at that time, at this place? In trench I, dwellings were excavated that date from the third century BC to the third century AD. They are situated immediately proximate to a tower tomb. To what period does this tomb date? Is it possible that the Palmyrenes constructed tombs within an inhabited area? We do not know. It is up to others in the future to answer these questions. (Stucky 2018, 5; translation by the author)

BIBLIOGRAPHY

al-As'ad, Khaled, and Andreas Schmidt-Colinet. 2002. 'Archaeological News from Hellenistic Palmyra'. *Parthica* 4: 157–166.

al-As'ad, Khaled, and Javier Teixidor. 1985. 'Un culte arabe préislamique à Palmyre d'après une inscription inedite'. *Comptes rendus des séances de l'Académie des inscriptions et belles-lettres*: 286–293.

al-As'ad, Khaled, and Jean-Baptiste Yon. 2001. *Inscriptions de Palmyre: Promenades épigraphiques dans la ville antique de Palmyre*. Guide archéologique de l'Institut français d'archéologie du Proche-Orient 3. Beirut: Institut français d'archéologie du Proche-Orient.

al-Maqdissi, Michel. 2000. 'Note sur les sondages réalisés par Robert du Mesnil du Buisson dans la cour du sanctuaire de Bêl à Palmyre'. *Syria* 77: 137–158.

Balty, Jean-Charles. 1994. 'Grande colonnade et quartiers nord d'Apamée à la fin de l'époque hellénistique'. *Comptes rendus des séances de l'Académie des inscriptions et belles-lettres* 138(1): 77–101.

Balty, Jean-Charles. 2000. 'Apamée: Mutations et permanences de l'espace urbain, de la fondation hellénistique à la ville romano byzantine'. In *La ville en Syrie et ses territoires: Héritages et mutation*, edited by Jean-Claude David and Mohamed al-Dbiyat, 167–185. Bulletin d'études orientales 52. Damascus: Institut français du Proche-Orient.

Becker, Helmut. 2000. 'Geophysikalische Prospektion in Palmyra und ihre Auswertung'. In Andreas Schmidt-Colinet and Khaled al-As'ad, 'Zur Urbanistik des hellenistischen Palmyra. Ein Vorbericht'. *Damaszener Miteilungen* 12: 77–81, plates 9–12.

Becker, Helmut, and Jörg W. E. Fassbinder. 2001. 'Combined Caesium Magnetometry and Resistivity Survey in Palmyra (Syria) 1997 and 1998'. In *Magnetic Prospecting in Archaeological Sites*, edited by Jörg W. E. Fassbinder and Walter E. Irlinger, 76–80. Monuments and Sites 6. Munich: International Council on Monuments and Sites (ICOMOS) = https://www.geophysik.uni-muenchen.de/research/archaeologicalprospection/publicationdetails/1482

Bounni, Adnan, and Javier Teixidor, eds. 1975. *Inventaire des inscriptions de Palmyre*. Vol. 12. Damascus: Direction Général des Antiquités et des Musées de la République Arabe Syrienne.

Bounni, Adnan, and Michel al-Maqdissi. 2001. 'Note sur un sondage dans la cour du sanctuaire de Bêl à Palmyre'. *Topoi* 11: 17–34.

Bounni, Adnan, Jacques Seigne, and Nassib Saliby. 1992/2004. *Le sanctuaire de Nabu à Palmyre. Planches*, 1992; *Texte*, 2004. Bibliothèque archéologique et historique 131. Paris: Geuthner.

Cantineau, Jean, ed. 1930. *Inventaire des inscriptions de Palmyre*. Vol. 4, *La vallée des tombeaux*. Beirut: Imprimerie catholique.

Cantineau, Jean. 1931. 'Textes palmyréniens provenant de la fouille du temple de Bêl'. *Syria* 12: 116–142.

Cantineau, Jean, ed. 1933. *Inventaire des inscriptions de Palmyre*. Vol. 11, *Le sanctuaire de Bèl*. Beirut: Imprimerie catholique.

Cantineau, Jean. 1936. 'Tadmorea'. *Syria* 17: 267–282.

Clarke, Graeme, and Heather Jackson. 2002/2003. 'Jebel Khalid on the Euphrates: An Overview'. *Annales Archéologique arabes Syriennes* 45/46: 189–206.

Clarke, Graeme, and Heather Jackson. 2016. 'Jebel Khalid (Aleppo)'. In *A History of Syria in One Hundred Sites*, edited by Youssef Kanjou and Akira Tsuneki, 335–338. Oxford: Archaeopress.

Delplace, Christiane. 2017. *Palmyre: Histoire et archéologie d'une cité caravanière à la croisée des cultures*. Collection l'esprit des lieux. Paris: CNRS.

Delplace, Christiane, and Jacqueline Dentzer-Feydy. 2005. *L'agora de Palmyre, sur la base des travaux de Henri Seyrig, Raymond Duru et Edmond Frézouls*. Bibliothèque archéologique et historique 175. Bordeaux: Institut français du Proche-Orient.

Delplace, Christiane, and Jacqueline Dentzer-Feydy. 2017. 'Topographie cultuelle et urbanisation à Palmyre'. In *Les archives au secours des temples détruits de Palmyre*, edited by Paul Ducrey, Pierre Gros, and Stephan Zink, 73–91. Paris: de Boccard.

Dentzer, Jean-Marie, and René Saupin. 1996. 'L'espace urbain à Palmyre. Remarques sur des photographies aériennes anciennes'. *Palmyra and the Silk Road: International Colloquium; Palmyra, 7–11 April 1992, Les annales archéologiques arabes syriennes* 42: 297–318.

Dirven, Lucinda. 1996. 'The Nature of the Trade Between Palmyra and Dura'. *ARAM* 8: 39–54.

du Mesnil du Buisson, Robert. 1939. *Inventaire des Inscriptions palmyréniennes de Doura-Europos*. Paris: Geuthner.

du Mesnil du Buisson, Robert. 1966. 'Première campagne de fouilles à Palmyre'. *Comptes rendus des séances de l'Académie des inscriptions et belles-lettres* 110: 158–190.

Dunant, Christiane. 1971. *Le sanctuaire de Baalshamin à Palmyre*. Vol. 3, *Les inscriptions*. Biblioteca Helvetica Romana, vol. 10, part 3. Rome: Institut suisse de Rome.

Edwell, Peter M. 2008. *Between Rome and Persia: The Middle Euphrates, Mesopotamia and Palmyra Under Roman Control*. London: Routledge.

Ertel, Christine, and René Ployer. 2013. 'Sondage II: Ein späthellenistisch-römisches Hofhaus. Baubefund, Architektur, Chronologie'. In *Palmyras Reichtum durch weltweiten Handel: Archäologische Untersuchungen im Bereich der hellenistischen Stadt*. Vol. 1, *Architektur und ihre Ausstattung*, edited by Andreas Schmidt-Colinet and Waleed al-As'ad, 118–169. Vienna: Verlag Holzhausen.

Fassbinder, Jörg W. E., and Roland Linck. 2013. 'Geophysikalische Prospektion'. In *Palmyras Reichtum durch weltweiten Handel: Archäologische Untersuchungen im Bereich der hellenistischen Stadt*. Vol. 1, *Architektur und ihre Ausstattung*, edited by Andreas Schmidt-Colinet and Waleed al-As'ad, 79–88. Vienna: Verlag Holzhausen.

Fellmann, Rudolf. 1970. *Le sanctuaire de Baalshamin à Palmyre*. Vol. 5, *Die Grabanlage*. Neuchâtel: Attinger.

Fellmann, Rudolf. 1975. 'Die Lampen'. In *Le sanctuaire de Baalshamin à Palmyre*. Vol. 6, *Die Kleinfunde: Objets divers*, edited by Rudolf Fellmann and Christiane Dunant, 9–59. Biblioteca Helvetica Romana, vol. 10, part 6. Rome: Institut suisse de Rome.

Fellmann, Rudolf. 1976. 'Le tombeau près du temple de Baalsamen, temoin de deux siècles d'histoire palmyrénienne'. In *Palmyre: Bilan et perspectives; Colloque de Strasbourg, 18–20 octobre 1973*, edited by Edmund Frézouls, 213–231. Travaux du Centre de recherche sur le Proche-Orient et la Grèce antique 3. Strasbourg: Centre de recherches sur le Proche-Orient et la Grèce.

Finlayson, Cynthia. 2010. *Syro-American Expedition to Palmyra 2010: Preliminary Report*. Unpublished Excavation Report, 30 May 2010.

Frézouls, Edmund, ed. 1976a. *Palmyre: Bilan et perspectives; Colloque de Strasbourg, 18–20 octobre 1973*. Travaux du Centre de recherche sur le Proche-Orient et la Grèce antique 3. Strasbourg: Centre de recherches sur le Proche-Orient et la Grèce.

Frézouls, Edmund. 1976b. 'Questions d'urbanisme palmyrénien'. In *Palmyre: Bilan et perspectives; Colloque de Strasbourg, 18–20 octobre 1973*, edited by Edmund Frézouls, 191–207. Strasbourg: Centre de recherches sur le Proche-Orient et la Grèce.

Gawlikowski, Michał. 1970. *Monuments funéraires de Palmyre*. Travaux du Centre d'archéologie méditeranéenne de l'Académie polonaise des sciences 9. Warsaw: Państwowe Wydawnictwo Naukowe.

Gawlikowski, Michał. 1973. *Le temple palmyrénien: Etude d'épigraphie et de topographie historique*. Palmyre 6. Warsaw: Państwowe Wydawnictwo Naukowe.

Gawlikowski, Michał. 1974. 'Les défenses de Palmyre'. *Syria* 51: 231–242, plates 9–14. In *Palmyre: Bilan et perspectives: Colloque de Strasbourg, 18–20 octobre 1973*, edited by Edmund Frézouls, 209–211. Travaux du Centre de recherche sur le Proche-Orient et la Grèce antique 3. Strasbourg: Centre de recherches sur le Proche-Orient et la Grèce).

Gawlikowski, Michał. 1977. 'Le temple d'Allat à Palmyre'. *Revue archéologique* 2: 253–274.

Gawlikowski, Michał. 1983. 'Reflexions sur la chronologie du sanctuaire d'Allat à Palmyre'. *Damaszener Mitteilungen* 1: 59–67, plates 13–14.

Gawlikowski, Michał. 1986. 'La première enceinte de Palmyre'. In *La fortification dans l'histoire du monde grec*, edited by Pierre Leriche and Henri Tréziny, 51–54. Paris: Centre national de la recherche scientifique.

Gawlikowski, Michał. 1990. 'Le premier temple d'Allat'. In *Resurrecting the Past: A Joint Tribute to Adnan Bounni*, edited by Paolo Matthiae, Maurits van Loon, and Harvey Weiss, 101–108. Leiden: Nederlands Instituut voor het Nabije Oosten.

Gawlikowski, Michał. 1991. 'L'Hellénisme et les dieux de Palmyre'. In *Ho Hellēnismos stēn Anatolē: International Meeting of History and Archaeology Delphi, 6–9 November 1986*, edited by European Cultural Centre of Delphi, 245–256. Athens: European Cultural Centre of Delphi.

Gawlikowski, Michał. 1993. 'Palmyre 1992'. *Polish Archaeology in the Mediterranean* 4: 111–118.

Gawlikowski, Michał. 1997. 'Du *hamana* au *naos*. Le temple palmyrénien hellénisé'. *Topoi* 7: 837–849.

Gawlikowski, Michał. 2004. 'L'architecture sacrée en Syrie romaine'. In *Lokale Identitäten in Randgebieten des Römischen Reiches: Akten des Internationalen Symposiums in Wiener Neustadt, 24–26 April 2003*, edited by Andreas Schmidt-Colinet, 83–90. Wiener Forschungen zur Archäologie 7. Vienna: Phoibos.

Gawlikowski, Michał. 2012. 'Le Tarif de Palmyre et le temple de Rab'asirê'. *Comptes rendus des séances de l'Académie des inscriptions et belles-lettres* 156(2): 765–780.

Gawlikowski, Michał. 2013. 'In the Footsteps of Prince Abamelek'. *Studia Palmyreńskie* 12: 87–96.

Gawlikowski, Michał. 2014. 'Palmyra: Reexcavating the Site of the Tariff. Fieldwork in 2010 and 2011'. *Polish Archaeology in the Mediterranean* 23(1): 415–430.

Gawlikowski, Michał. 2018. *Le sanctuaire d'Allat à Palmyra*. PAM Monograph Series 8. Warsaw: Uniwersytet Warszawski.

Gawlikowski, Michał, and Khaled al-As'ad. 1991–1992. 'Le péage à Palmyre en 11 après J.-C'. *Semitica* 41–42: 163–172.

Gawlikowski, Michał, and Grzegorz Majcherek, eds. 2013. *Fifty Years of Polish Excavations in Palmyra 1959–2009: International Conference Warsaw, 6–8 December 2010*. Studia Palmyreńskie 12. Warsaw: Wydawnictwa Uniwersytetu Warszawskiego.

Graf, David F. 2018. 'The Silk Road Between Syria and China'. In *Trade, Commerce, and the State in the Roman World*, edited by Andrew Wilson and Alan Bowman, 443–530. Oxford: Oxford University Press.

Grainger, John D. 1990. *The Cities of Seleucid Syria*. Oxford: Clarendon Press.

Gros, Pierre. 2017. 'Les chois formels et ornementaux des concepteurs du temple de Bêl: Une relecture à partir des recherches récentes'. In *Actes du colloque international organisé par l'Académie des inscriptions et belles-lettres, à l'Académie des inscriptions et belles-lettres (Palais de l'Institut) le 19 Mai 2017*, edited by Pierre Ducrey, Pierre Gros, and Michel Zink, 95–133. Paris: Académie des inscriptions et belles-lettres.

Hammad, Manar. 2010. *Palmyre: Transformations urbaines; Développement d'une ville antique de la marge aride syrienne*. Paris: Geuthner.

Hartmann, Udo. 2001. *Das palmyrenische Teilreich*. Oriens et Occidens 2. Stuttgart: Steiner.

Hekster, Olivier, and Ted Kaizer. 2004. 'Marc Antony and the Raid on Palmyra: Reflections on Appian, *Bella civilia* V 9'. *Latomus* 63: 70–80.

Henning, Agnes. 2013a. *Die Turmgräber von Palmyra: Eine lokale Bauform im kaiserzeitlichen Syrien als Ausdruck kultureller Identität*. Orient-Archäologie 29. Rahden: Leidorf.

Henning, Agnes. 2013b. 'The Tower Tombs of Palmyra: Chronology, Architecture and Decoration'. In *Fifty Years of Polish Excavations in Palmyra, 1959–2009: International Conference, Warsaw, 6–8 December 2010*, edited by Michał Gawlikowski and Grzegorz Majcherek, 159–176. Studia Palmyrenskie 12. Warsaw: Wydawnictwa Uniwersytetu Warszawskiego.

Kaizer, Ted. 2007. '"Palmyre, cite grecque"? A Question of Coinage'. *Klio* 89: 39–60.

Kaizer, Ted. 2015. 'On the Origins of Palmyra and Its Trade'. *Journal of Roman Archaeology* 28: 881–888.

Kaizer, Ted. 2017a. 'Empire, Community, and Culture on the Middle Euphrates. Durenes, Palmyrenes, Villagers, and Soldiers'. In *Roman History: Six Studies for Fergus Millar*, edited by Nicholas Purcell. *Bulletin of the Institute of Classical Studies of the University of London* 60(1): 63–95.

Kaizer, Ted. 2017b. 'Trajectories of Hellenism at Tadmor-Palmyra and Dura-Europos'. In *Hellenism and the Local Communities of the Eastern Mediterranean, 400 BCE–250 CE*, edited by Boris Chrubasik and Daniel King, 29–51. Oxford: Oxford University Press.

Kanjou, Youssef, and Akira Tsuneki, eds. 2016. *A History of Syria in One Hundred Sites*. Oxford: Archaeopress.

Laubenheimer, Fanette. 2013. 'Les amphores'. In *Palmyras Reichtum durch weltweiten Handel: Archäologische Untersuchungen im Bereich der hellenistischen Stadt*. Vol. 2, *Kleinfunde*, edited by Andreas Schmidt-Colinet and Waleed al-As'ad, 93–105. Vienna: Verlag Holzhausen.

Laubenheimer, Fanette, and Christiane Römer-Strehl. 2013. 'Hellenistische Amphorenstempel'. In *Palmyras Reichtum durch weltweiten Handel: Archäologische Untersuchungen im Bereich der hellenistischen Stadt*. Vol. 2, *Kleinfunde*, edited by Andreas Schmidt-Colinet and Waleed al-As'ad, 106–108. Vienna: Verlag Holzhausen.

Laubenheimer, Fanette, Khaled al-As'ad, and Andreas Schmidt-Colinet. 2007. 'Des amphores à Palmyre: Le matériel des fouilles récentes de la mission syro-allemande'. In *Productions et échanges dans la Syrie grecque et romaine: Actes du colloque de Tours, juin 2003*, edited by Maurice Sartre, 329–355. Topoi Suppl. 8. Lyon: de Boccard.

Linck, Roland. 2016. 'Geophysical Prospection by Ground- and Space-Based Methods of the Ancient Town of Palmyra (Syria)'. In *Palmyrena: City, Hinterland and Caravan Trade Between Orient and Occident; Proceedings of the Conference Held in Athens, December 1–3, 2012*, edited by Jørgen Christian Meyer, Eivind E. Seland, and Nils Anfinset, 77–86. Oxford: Archaeopress.

Maschek, Dominik. 2017. 'Die etruskische Spätzeit zwischen 'Hellenismus', 'Hellenisierung' und 'Romanisierung'. Eine forschungsgeschichtliche Skizze'. In *L'étruscologie dans l'Europe d'après-guerre: Actes des journées d'études internationales des 14 au 16 septembre 2015 (Amiens et Saint-Valéry-sur-Somme)*, edited by Marie-Laurence Haack and Martin Miller, 33–46. Scripta receptoria 10. Bordeaux: Ausonius.

Meyer, Jørgen Christian, Eivind E. Seland, and Nils Anfinset, eds. 2016. *Palmyrena: City, Hinterland and Caravan Trade Between Orient and Occident; Proceedings of the Conference Held in Athens, December 1–3, 2012*. Oxford: Archaeopress.

Milik, Józef Tadeusz. 1972. *Dédicaces faites par des dieux (Palmyre, Hatra, Tyre) et des thiases sémitiques à l'époque romaine*. Bibliothèque archéologique et historique 92. Recherches d'épigraphie Proche-Orientale 1. Paris: Geuthner.

Millar, Fergus. 1987. 'The Problem of Hellenistic Syria'. In *Hellenism in the East*, edited by Amelie Kuhrt and Susan M. Sherwin-White, 110–133. Berkeley: University of California Press.

PAT Palmyrene Aramaic Texts, edited by Delbert R. Hillers and Eleonora Cussini, 1996. Publications of the Comprehensive Aramaic Lexicon Project. Baltimore: Johns Hopkins University Press.

Pietrzykowski, Michał. 1997. *Les adytons des temples palmyréniens*. Warsaw: Uniwersytet Warszawski, Instytut Archeologii. Polish text with French summary.

Plattner, Georg A. 2013. 'Sondage I: Eine hellenistisch-römische Straßenkreuzung und angrenzende Wohnbebauung Baubefund, Architektur, Chronologie'. In *Palmyras Reichtum durch weltweiten Handel: Archäologische Untersuchungen im Bereich der hellenistischen Stadt*. Vol. 1, *Architektur und ihre Ausstattung*, edited by Andreas Schmidt-Colinet and Waleed al-As'ad, 89–117. Vienna: Verlag Holzhausen.

Plattner, Georg A., and Andreas Schmidt-Colinet. 2010. 'Untersuchungen im hellenistisch-kaiserzeitlichen Palmyra'. In *Städtisches Wohnen im östlichen Mittelmeerraum 4. Jh. v. Chr. – 1. Jh. n. Chr.: Akten des Kolloquiums vom 24–27. Oktober 2007 an der Österreichischen Akademie der Wissenschaften*, edited by Sabine Ladstätter and Veronika Scheibelreiter, 417–427. Vienna: Verlag der Österreichischen Akademie der Wissenschaften.

Ployer, René. 2010. 'Glas aus Palmyra. Funde aus den Grabungen im Areal der 'hellenistischen' Stadt – Ein Zwischenbericht'. In *Standortbestimmung: Akten des 12. Österreichischen Archäologentages vom 28. 2. bis 1. 3. 2008 in Wien*, edited by Marion Meyer and Verena Gassner, 313–320, figs. 1–12. Wiener Forschungen zur Archäologie 13. Vienna: Phoibos.

Ployer, René. 2012. 'Glass from the Excavations in the So-Called "Hellenistic" Town of Palmyra. A Preliminary Report'. In *Annales du 18ᵉ congrès de l'association international pour l'histoire du verre, Thessaloniki 2009*, edited by Despina Ignatiadou and Anastassios Antonaras, 104–108. Thessaloniki: ZITI.

Ployer, René. 2013. 'Gläser'. In *Palmyras Reichtum durch weltweiten Handel: Archäologische Untersuchungen im Bereich der hellenistischen Stadt*. Vol. 1, *Architektur und ihre Ausstattung*, edited by Andreas Schmidt-Colinet and Waleed al-As'ad, 127–205. Vienna: Verlag Holzhausen.

Raja, Rubina. 2017a. 'To Be or Not to Be Depicted as a Priest in Palmyra: A Matter of Representational Spheres and Societal Values'. In *Positions and Professions in Palmyra*, edited by Tracey Long and Annette Højen Sørensen, 115–130. Scientia Danica. Series H, Humanistica 4, vol. 9, Palmyrene Studies 2. Copenhagen: Det Kongelige Danske Videnskabernes Selskab.

Raja, Rubina. 2017b. 'Powerful Images of the Deceased: Palmyrene Funerary Portrait Culture between Local, Greek and Roman Representations'. In *Bilder der Macht: Das griechische Porträt und seine Verwendung in der antiken Welt*, edited by Dieter Boschung and François Queyrel, 319–348. Morphomata 34. Paderborn: Fink.

Römer-Strehl, Christiane. 2000. 'Die Keramik'. In Andreas Schmidt-Colinet and Khaled al-As'ad, 'Zur Urbanistik des hellenistischen Palmyra. Ein Vorbericht'. *Damaszener Miteilungen* 12: 81–93, pls. 12b–d.

Römer-Strehl, Christiane. 2013. 'Keramik'. In *Palmyras Reichtum durch weltweiten Handel: Archäologische Untersuchungen im Bereich der hellenistischen Stadt*. Vol. 2, *Kleinfunde*, edited by Andreas Schmidt-Colinet and Waleed al-As'ad, 7–80. Vienna: Verlag Holzhausen.

Saito, Kiyohide. 2002. 'New Discovery at the Southeast Necropolis in Palmyra, 2001'. In *Proceedings of the International Conference Homs on Zenobia and Palmyra, During 19–21/10/2002 in Al-Bath University and Palmyra*, edited by Al-Baath University, Ministry of Culture, and Directorate General of Antiquities and Museums, 131–143. Homs: Al-Baath University.

Saito, Kiyohide. 2005. 'Die Arbeiten der japanischen Mission in der Südost-Nekropole'. In *Palmyra: Kulturbegegnung im Grenzbereich*, edited by Andreas Schmidt-Colinet, 32–35. 3rd ed. Mainz am Rhein: von Zabern.

Saito, Kiyohide. 2016. 'Palmyra. Japanese Archaeological Mission (Homs)'. In *A History of Syria in One Hundred Sites*, edited by Youssef Kanjou and Akira Tsuneki, 349–354. Oxford: Archaeopress.

Sartre, Maurice. 1996. 'Palmyre, cité grecque'. *Palmyra and the Silk Road: International Colloquium; Palmyra, 7–11 April 1992, Les annales archéologiques arabes syriennes* 42: 385–405.

Sartre, Maurice. 2001. *D'Alexandre à Zénobie: Histoire du Levant antique, IVe siècle avant J.-C. – IIIe siècle après J.-C.* Paris: Fayard.

Sartre-Fauriat, Annie, and Maurice Sartre. 2008. *Palmyre: La cité des caravanes*. Paris: Gallimard.

Schlumberger, Daniel. 1935. 'Études sur Palmyre I. Le développement urbain de Palmyre'. *Berytus* 2: 149–162.

Schlumberger, Daniel. 1969. *Der hellenisierte Orient: Die griechische und nachgriechische Kunst außerhalb des Mittelmeerraumes*. Baden-Baden: Holle.

Schlumberger, Daniel. 1970. *L'Orient hellénisé: L'art grec et ses héritiers dans l'Asie non méditerranéenne*. Paris: Albin Michel.

Schmidt-Colinet, Andreas. 1991. 'Aspects of "Hellenism" in Nabataean and Palmyrene Funerary Architecture'. In *Ho Hellēnismos stēn Anatolē: International Meeting of History and*

Archaeology Delphi, 6–9 November 1986, edited by European Cultural Centre of Delphi, 141–144. Athens: European Cultural Centre of Delphi.

Schmidt-Colinet, Andreas, ed. 2005. *Palmyra: Kulturbegegnung im Grenzbereich*. 3rd ed. Mainz am Rhein: von Zabern.

Schmidt-Colinet, Andreas, and Khaled al-As'ad. 2000. 'Zur Urbanistik des hellenistischen Palmyra. Ein Vorbericht'. *Damaszener Miteilungen* 12: 61–93, plates 7–16.

Schmidt-Colinet, Andreas, Khaled al-As'ad, and Waleed al-As'ad. 2008. 'Untersuchungen im Areal der hellenistischen Stadt von Palmyra. Zweiter Vorbericht'. *Zeitschrift für Orient-Archäologie* 1: 452–478.

Schmidt-Colinet, Andreas, Khaled al-As'ad, and Waleed al-As'ad. 2013. 'Thirty Years of Syro-German/Austrian Archaeological Research at Palmyra'. In *Fifty Years of Polish Excavations in Palmyra, 1959–2009: International Conference Warsaw, 6–8 December 2010*, edited by Michał Gawlikowski and Grzegorz Majcherek, 299–318. Studia Palmyreńskie 12. Warsaw: Wydawnictwa Uniwersytetu Warszawskiego.

Schmidt-Colinet, Andreas, Khaled al-As'ad, and Waleed al-As'ad. 2016. 'Palmyra: 30 Years of Syro-German/Austrian Archaeological Research (Homs)'. In *A History of Syria in One Hundred Sites*, edited by Youssef Kanjou and Akira Tsuneki, 339–348. Oxford: Archaeopress.

Schmidt-Colinet, Andreas, and Waleed al-As'ad, eds. 2013. *Palmyras Reichtum durch weltweiten Handel: Archäologische Untersuchungen im Bereich der hellenistischen Stadt*. Vol. 1: *Architektur und ihre Ausstattung*; vol. 2: *Kleinfunde* (with English and Arabic summaries). Vienna: Verlag Holzhausen. Vol. 1, https://e-book.fwf.ac.at/detail_object/o:382; vol. 2, https://e-book.fwf.ac.at/detail_object/o:384.

Schmidt-Colinet, Andreas, and Georg A. Plattner. 2001. 'Geophysical Survey and Excavation in the "Hellenistic Town" of Palmyra'. In *Archaeological Prospection: Fourth International Conference on Archaeological Prospection, Vienna, 2001*, edited by Michael Doneus, Alois Eder-Hinterleitner, and Wolfgang Neubauer, 175–177. Vienna: Verlag der Österreichischen Akademie der Wissenschaften.

Schmidt-Colinet, Andreas, Annemarie Stauffer, and Khaled al-As'ad. 2000. *Die Textilien aus Palmyra: Neue und alte Funde*. Damaszener Forschungen 8. Mainz: von Zabern.

Schnädelbach, Klaus. 2010. *Topographia Palmyrena*. Vol. 1, *Topography*. Documents d'archéologie syrienne 18. Bonn: Habelt.

Seyrig, Henri. 1939. 'Antiquités Syriennes 29: À propos du culte de Zeus à Séleucie'. *Syria* 20: 296–323.

Seyrig, Henri. 1940a. 'Antiquités Syriennes 32: *Ornamenta palmyrena antiquiora*'. *Syria* 21: 277–328, plates 29–35.

Seyrig, Henri. 1940b. 'Antiquités Syriennes 33: Remarques sur la civilisation de Palmyre'. *Syria* 21: 328–337.

Seyrig, Henri, Robert Amy, and Ernest Will. 1968/1975. *Le temple de Bêl à Palmyre*. *Album*, 1968; *Texte et Planches*, 1975. Bibliothèque archéologique et historique 83. Paris: Geuthner.

Sommer, Michael. 2005. *Roms orientalische Steppengrenze: Palmyra – Edessa – Dura-Europos – Hatra; Eine Kulturgeschichte von Pompeius bis Diocletian*. Oriens et Occidens 9. Stuttgart: Steiner.

Sommer, Michael. 2017. *Palmyra: Biographie einer verlorenen Stadt*. Darmstadt: von Zabern.

Starcky, Jean, and Michel Gawlikowski. 1985. *Palmyre*. Paris: Librarie d'Amérique et d'Orient.

Stauffer, Annemarie. 2005. 'Kleider, Kissen, bunte Tücher. Einheimische Textilproduktion und weltweiter Handel'. In *Palmyra: Kulturbegegnung im Grenzbereich*, 3rd ed., edited by Andreas Schmidt-Colinet, 67–81. Mainz am Rhein: von Zabern.

Stephani, Manfred. 2000. 'Geodätische und photogrammetrische Datenerfassung in Palmyra und ihre Auswertung'. In Andreas Schmidt-Colinet and Khaled al-As'ad, 'Zur Urbanistik des hellenistischen Palmyra. Ein Vorbericht'. *Damaszener Miteilungen* 12: 74–76, figs. 7–8.

Stucky, Rolf A. 2018. 'Fouille suisses du Sanctuaire de Baalshamîn à Palmyre: Le passé confronté au présent et à l'avenir'. *Antike Kunst* 61: 100–105.

Teixidor, Javier, ed. 1965. *Inventaire des inscriptions de Palmyre*. Vol. 11. Beirut: Institut français d'archéologie de Beyrouth.

van Berchem, Denis. 1954. 'Recherches sur la chronologie des enceintes de Syrie et de Mésopotamie'. *Syria* 31: 254–270.

van Berchem, Denis. 1976. 'Le plan de Palmyre'. In *Palmyre: Bilan et perspectives; Colloque de Strasbourg, 18–20 october 1973*, edited by Edmond Frézouls, 165–173. Strasbourg: Centre de recherches sur le Proche-Orient et la Grèce.

Will, Ernest. 1983. 'Le développement urbain de Palmyre: Témoignages épigraphiques anciens et nouveaux'. *Syria* 60: 69–81 [Will, Ernest. 1995. *De l'Euphrate au Rhin: Aspects de l'hellénisation et de la romanisation du Proche-Orient*, 511–523. Bibliothèque archéologique et historique 135. Beirut: Institut français d'archéologie du Proche-Orient.]

Will, Ernest. 1992. *Les palmyréniens: La Venise des sables (Ier siècle avant – IIIème siècle après J.C.)*. Paris: Colin.

Yon, Jean-Baptiste. 2002. *Les notables de Palmyre*. Bibliothèque archéologique et historique 163. Beirut: Institut français d'archéologie du Proche-Orient.

Yon, Jean-Baptiste. 2015. 'Review of *Palmyras Reichtum durch weltweiten Handel: Archäologische Untersuchungen im Bereich der hellenistischen Stadt*', edited by Andreas Schmidt-Colinet and Waleed al-As'ad, *Revue archéologique*: 422–424.

Żuchowska, Marta. 2008. 'Wadi al Qubur and Its Interrelations with the Development of Urban Space of the City of Palmyra in the Hellenistic and Roman Period'. In *Proceedings of the 4th International Congress of the Archaeology of the Ancient Near East, 29 March–3 April 2004, Freie Universität Berlin*. Vol. 1, *The Reconstruction of Environment: Natural Resources and Human Interrelation through Time; Art History; Visual Communication*, edited by Hartmut Kühne, Rainer M. Czichon, and Florian J. Kreppner, 229–234. Wiesbaden: Harrassowitz.

....

CHAPTER 6

PALMYRA

The Development of an Ancient City

....

MICHAŁ GAWLIKOWSKI

INTRODUCTION: STATE OF RESEARCH

THE first precise plan of Palmyra (Gabriel 1926) has progressively been supplemented by the results of later excavations to the point where full coverage, using all the available material, has finally provided an up-to-date reference (Schnädelbach 2010). In the meantime, several studies have attempted to explain the shape of the ancient city (Schlumberger 1935; van Berchem 1976; Frézouls 1976; Will 1983; Hammad 2010). In the years 1930 to 1940, and again from 1956 to 2011, various excavation projects uncovered and recorded particular monuments, as described below. Needless to say, general books on Palmyra and its history have also often included relevant observations on topography and urban development (Starcky and Gawlikowski 1985; Will 1992; Delplace 2017).

NATURAL CONDITIONS AND PREHISTORY

The oasis of Tadmor, known by this name for at least four thousand years and to this day, lies on an easy pass through a chain of hills branching north-east from the Anti-Lebanon Range (Hammad 2013). The track leading through this pass goes west to Homs and proceeds on to the Mediterranean coast. To the east, at roughly the same distance across a flat desert, flows the Euphrates River. Another track follows the eastern foot of the hills in the direction of Damascus. Close to the pass there gushed out from a grotto an abundant spring of tepid and sulphurous water, called Efqa in antiquity and still today (Figure 6.1.1). The stream issuing from it fed a small oasis. The recent, as yet unpublished Syrian excavations at Tell ez-Zor not far from the spring have uncovered the ruins of a Pre-Pottery Neolithic village, apparently as old as the seventh millennium BC. The place

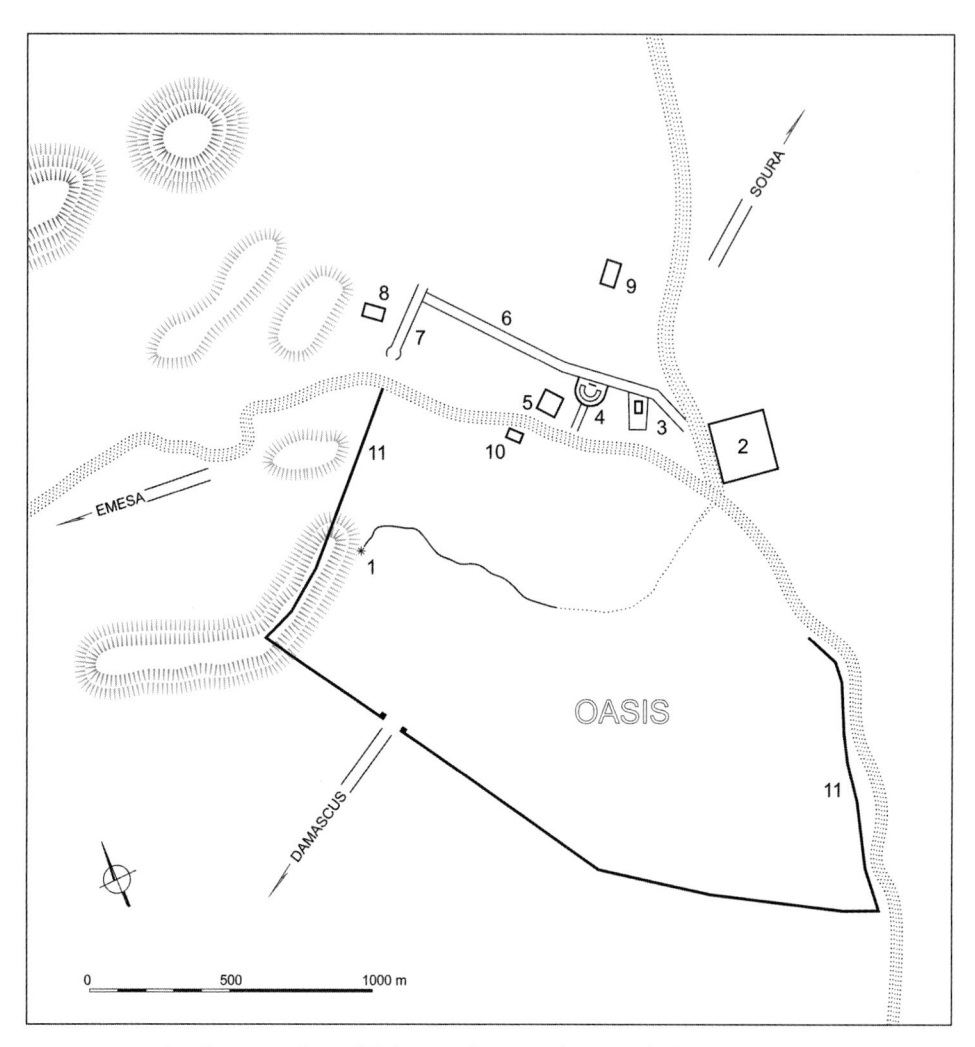

FIGURE 6.1 A schematic plan of Palmyra showing the principal monuments mentioned in the text.
1. Efqa source; 2. Bēl sanctuary; 3. Nabu sanctuary; 4. Theatre; 5. Agora; 6. Great Colonnade; 7. Transverse Colonnade; 8. Allat sanctuary; 9. Baalshamin sanctuary; 10. Arsu sanctuary and the southern town; 11. First-century rampart.

remained an all-important attraction point until the spring dried out in 1993, as a result of the overexploitation of deep water deposits. Reportedly it is flowing again as a result of the stoppage of pumping due to the destruction and depopulation of Tadmor in 2015.

To the north of the oasis extends a higher desert plateau intersected by two wadis, dry stream beds that fill only after a heavy rain and this only for a few hours. These violent swells are rare, but destructive (Seigne 2022a). The two wadis, called today Wadi as-Suraysir and Wadi al-ʿEid, met some 1.3 km east from Efqa and were rejoined by the permanent rivulet that issued from the spring, before disappearing in a salty depression

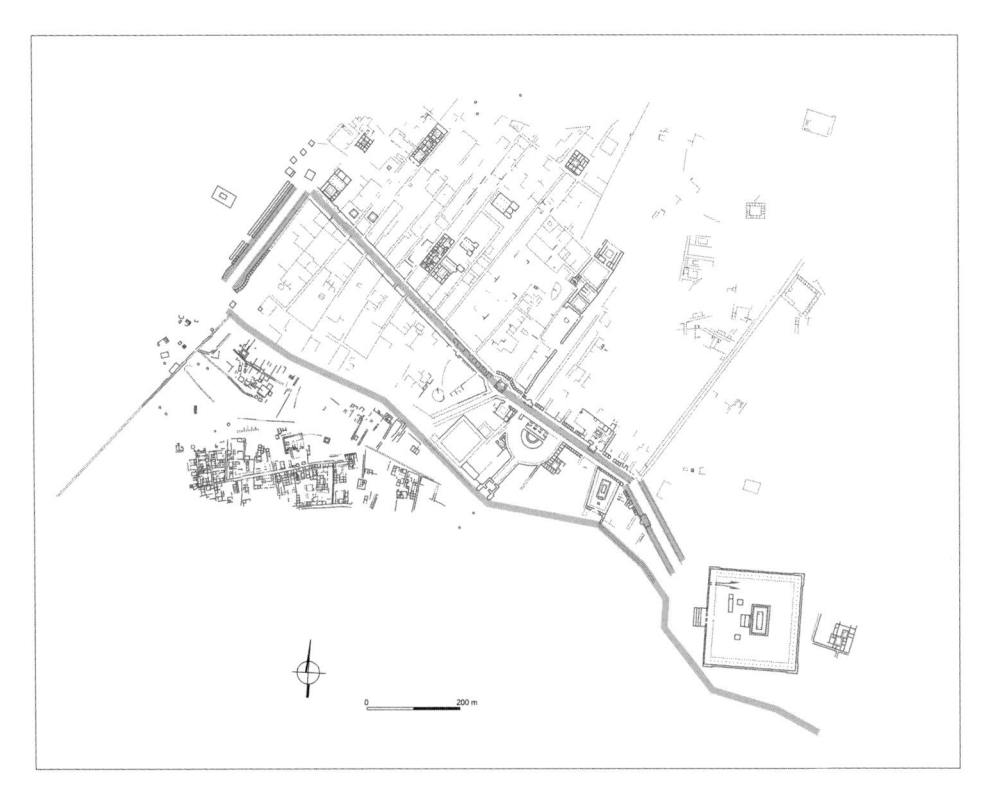

FIGURE 6.2 Palmyra in the third century, showing the principal axes of circulation.

to the south-east, which is all that remains of a prehistoric lake. Close to their conflu-ence, traces of human activity from the Neolithic and Bronze Ages (sixth to third mil-lennium BC) have been detected (al-Maqdissi 2000; al-Maqdissi and Ishaq 2018). Over the centuries the remains of buildings accumulated to form a tell which today is about 7 m in height. It could be tackled only in a very limited way, as the top of the hillock is occupied by the great temple of Bēl (Figure 6.1.2). It is very likely that a cult place has existed there since time immemorial.

The First Urban Settlement

Between these two locations, the spring and the tell, there progressively grew a recently discovered settlement. A remote sensing programme has revealed a dense cluster of buildings along a street that ran north-east from the neighbourhood of the Efqa source (Figure 6.1.2 and Figure 6.2). The built area was naturally limited by the gardens of the oasis to the south and Wadi as-Suraysir to the north. It was there that the first township formed in the Hellenistic period (Will 1983; Hammad 2010). A small part of it could be excavated (Schmidt-Colinet and al-As'ad 2013). Only short segments of mud brick walls of the oldest buildings were found, dated to the late third century BC and later. A mansion of the Augustan age replaced them, consisting of rooms aligned around a quadrilateral courtyard. The excavators suppose the existence of porticoes fronting the rooms, but no trace of columns remains. Many fragments of the lavish painted and stuccoed decoration found there are of the second century, when the house was rebuilt after a fire. This part of ancient Tadmor deserves further investigation, which could bring a renewed picture of the city in its heyday, even if the Hellenistic levels prove difficult to attain.

The Recently Discovered Early Main Street

Wadi as-Suraysir comes through the pass in the hills known as Valley of the Tombs (Wadi al-Qubur). In ancient times, it coincided with the track joining the oasis from the west. At some point it became necessary to bar the wadi at the head of the valley in order to avoid flooding and at the same time to create a reserve of water; a dam was recently built for this purpose, not far from the ancient one. Within the limits of the settlement, the wadi bed was paved with flagstones 3 to 4 m beneath the present level of the plain on either side (Gawlikowski 2013). The main artery of the growing city, 12 m wide, came thus into being. It was silted over in later centuries and could be uncovered, in 2011, only in two short stretches, one in front of the agora (Figure 6.1.5) and the other in front of the Nabu sanctuary (Figure 6.1.3). There are no wheel grooves in the pavement, and the slippery flagstones are not convenient for camels, so it seems that the paved road had become the main pedestrian artery in the city, no doubt a kind of *corso* where people could walk, meet, and see others. The higher ground to left and right along this street was, of course, the best location in the city. It is not a coincidence that several temples opened facing onto this street, as did the first agora, the only known civil monument of the early city, all of them arising in the course of the first century AD. The paved road separated the earliest township on its southern side from the plateau to the north. The public monuments on the other side are a sure sign of development in this area, too, a development that resulted from Palmyra becoming a city.

The Sanctuary of Bēl

The Roman annexation of Syria in BC 63 did not at first reach the oasis, which remained insignificant until the peace on the eastern frontier made possible the development of international trade. The track from the Mediterranean to the Euphrates became safe thanks to the Palmyrenes, who controlled large swathes of the desert and pushed their caravans to the head of the Arabian Gulf, where they could acquire the exotic goods brought by sea from India and coveted in the Roman Empire at large. The opening of this traffic coincided in time with the formal annexation of the oasis to the Roman province (probably in AD 18/19). The building of the new Bēl temple started about this time (Seyrig et al. 1975).

The site of the temple (Figure 6.1.2) was certainly a sacred ground in the preceding century, as attested by many sculptural, architectonic, and epigraphic fragments of that period found around the standing building (Seyrig 1941). The actual shrine or shrines to which these fragments belonged was probably destroyed by the foundations of the new temple, but three columns which stood in a row east of it show that an auxiliary building, interpreted as a banquet room, existed some 2 m lower than the new temple (Maqdissi and Ishaq 2018). There is also a stretch of oval enclosure around the northeast corner of the great temple, of uncertain date. No trace is as yet known of the still earlier religious monuments on the tell; soundings have revealed only domestic architecture from the early Hellenistic period. Perhaps it will become possible one day to further explore the temple surroundings as a collateral bonus of the present tragedy of destruction.

The building process of the temple we know was extended for a century as it depended on contributions from private donors. It was conceived by a Greek architect, an imitator of Hermogenes of Magnesia, and executed by hired master builders helped by local hands (Seyrig et al. 1975, 170). The unsurpassed precision of the stone fitting and its sheer size made the temple not only the paramount building of the city, but also the clearest sign of its joining the Hellenistic world. Yet the very classical *pseudodipteros*, probably designed to resemble some lost temple of Antioch, was transformed in the course of its realization in a very idiosyncratic way. Both the short sides were closed, while Ionic half-columns were retained where originally there should have been open passages. Instead, a grandiose gateway on a long side interrupted the colonnade and led into the cella, where two raised rooms filled the closed short sides. Their architectural form is entirely alien to the classical model. These *adyton*s, as they are called, are typical features of Syrian temples of the age, but only here are there two of them in one temple at opposite ends, perhaps mirroring the location of earlier shrines.

Contrary to what is stated in the official publication (Seyrig et al. 1975, 149), the temple was not completed in AD 32. Only the northern *adyton* was consecrated that year, while the cella was not finished until the end of the first century (Pietrzykowski 1997). In the meantime, the square temenos, measuring 200 m to a side, was laid out around the temple about AD 80. This involved a great deal of levelling and resulted in the foundations of the new temple becoming exposed. To conceal them, a podium was built over the original steps all around the temple and a ramp was added in front of the monumental gateway. The Corinthian colonnades of this huge courtyard rose at a slow pace, and the western, higher portico opposite the temple's entrance was never completed (Schlumberger 1933, 114–132; cf. Seigne 2022b, 125–137).

The sanctuary of Bēl was the major monument of the city and the centre of the civic cult. It towered over all other monuments throughout history. In time, the cella became a church, and then, for more than a thousand years, a mosque, surrounded by the medieval fortified settlement and then the modern village. Cleared in the 1930s, it became the main archaeological monument of the site, and so it still remains after the destruction of 2015.

OTHER TEMPLES AND SANCTUARIES

Two much smaller sanctuaries were founded outside the built area, in the close vicinity of tombs, by members of the same tribe, probably recently settled nomads. The sanctuary of Allat (Figure 6.1.8) grew around a modest shrine founded not later than about 50 BC on the settlement's western outskirts. The original building was just big enough to contain the seated statue of the Arab goddess but provided with excessively thick stone walls. It was called *hamana*, the name apparently used for similar shrines of the nomads, marking the fixed points of their yearly movements (Gawlikowski 2017, 33–64). A colonnaded courtyard was laid around the Allat shrine early in the first century AD, progressively surrounded by columns, though it was probably never completed before the fall of the city in 272.

Another excavated sanctuary was dedicated to Baalshamin (Figure 6.1.9) and was apparently founded after AD 11, when a neighbouring tomb was put out of use. The earliest shrine did not survive, but we do have several dedicatory inscriptions of columns, starting in AD 23 and culminating in AD 67, with porticoes disposed on all four sides of a spacious courtyard to the north (Collart and Vicari 1969). We have no idea what the southern part of the sanctuary looked like in the first century. At any rate, there is no reason to agree with the excavators in seeing the plan of the Baalshamin sanctuary as a copy of that at Si'a in the Hawran nor to consider an auxiliary building with a peristyle, partly excavated under the front yard of the modern Hotel Zenobia, as the main cult site. The primitive shrine probably stood on the site of the later temple.

Two small archaic shrines stood on the northern bank of Wadi as-Suraysir, one devoted to the gods Shadrafa and Du'Anat, known by its foundation inscription only, and the other, a small square building preserved at great pains among the later structures on the southern front of the agora, to Rab'asire (Gawlikowski 2013; Jakubiak 2022). Opposite, on the southern bank of the wadi, the Arsu temple (Figure 6.1.10) was utterly destroyed and its form cannot be defined.

The last excavated sanctuary was that of Nabu (Figure 6.1.3), a god borrowed from Babylonia who was identified with Apollo (Bounni et al. 1992; Bounni 2004; Seigne 2022b, 139–162). It existed already about the turn of the millennium, but the surviving ruins go back only to the late first century and later. Its irregular courtyard opened to the south into the wadi. It was surrounded by colonnades in the so-called Tuscan order and boasted a cella which featured a Roman-style podium carrying a Corinthian peristasis. Rows of crow steps and a probably flat roof, on the other hand, recalled the local tradition.

The colonnaded courtyards are a common feature of Palmyra's sanctuaries. They have served, no doubt, as the background of religious gatherings and banquets following sacrifice. The porticoes provided shelter, but at the same time bore a powerful message—the columns, mostly Corinthian, expressed the sense of belonging to the world of Graeco-Roman civilization. While true to their ancestral traditions, the Palmyrenes wished to mark by this means their newly won status. It was in the course of the first century AD that the federation of tribes became a full-fledged city, endowed with the typical institutions of a *polis* as part of the Roman province. There is no reason to speak of a semi-independent merchant republic or a balancing act between the Roman and Parthian empires. Palmyra had no more autonomy than any other provincial city; it aspired to look like them (Sartre 1996).

THE FIRST PUBLIC BUILDINGS

The only public building of the first century we know of other than temples was the early agora, probably somewhat smaller than the successor monument and known only from two limited soundings (Delplace and Dentzer-Feydy 2005, 34). Its stone pavement is apparently contemporary with the paved street in the wadi, barely 1 m higher, and was connected with it by three steps.

The first-century city was protected by a wall which also enclosed the gardens and the spring (Figure 6.1.11) but excluded the sanctuaries of Allat and of Baalshamin. The surviving sections on the plain were built in mud brick and may date back to the first century BC. The defensive value of this work was rather limited, but it could protect the oasis from nomad incursions and also serve as a customs barrier. Indeed, the southern section, which had survived longer and is clearly visible on the ground, was known in modern times as the 'customs wall' (*sūr al-jamārek*); a part of the western section was excavated (Gawlikowski 1974). Only as a second thought was the circuit completed by joining these two separate sections with a stone rampart climbing the hill of Jebel Muntar. The northern course of the enclosure has left no visible trace, but, to the east, beyond the gardens and along the Wadi al-'Eid, a short stretch in mud brick is still standing (Hammad 2013). It seems that the Bēl sanctuary was situated in the north-east corner of this enclosure.

The western section, which crossed the plain in a straight line between the Jebel Muntar and the wadi, continued further north, excluding the necropolis and the Allat sanctuary; but it was abandoned in the late first century AD. Instead, a spacious street was laid outside along its course, known as the Transverse Colonnade (Figure 6.1.7); this was 230 m long and 35 m wide and consisted of two rows of shops, fronted by colonnades erected progressively over a period of at least one hundred years. It was clearly the main marketplace, conveniently situated at the edge of the inhabited area and allowing the passage of caravans and general traffic between the track from Emesa and the empty space to the north of the city (Schlumberger 1935). This market ended to the south with an oval plaza and a triple ornamental gate opening into the thus enlarged city space. Interestingly, at least six columns were erected there in honour of the gods Shamash, Allat, and Rahim, suggesting some sort of bequest to their sanctuaries; Rahim might be associated with Allat, and the temple of the solar god must have been close to that of the goddess.

THE AGORA AND THE GREAT COLONNADE

The agora (Figure 6.1.5) goes back in its present form to the beginning of the second century. It is a rectangular plaza 83 m × 71 m, laid about 1.60 m above the old one but, unlike its predecessor, not paved. The change could possibly have resulted from a disastrous flood, such as happens there from time to time. The square is lined on all four sides with eighty columns, carrying brackets for statues which were set up one by one in the course of the second and third centuries, transforming the plaza into a local hall of fame (Delplace and Dentzer-Feydy 2005). The five oldest inscriptions date from 75 to 86, but they are clearly later copies of the original inscriptions, likely made in the reigns of Trajan or Hadrian.

The agora has two annexed buildings: a meeting room opening in the south-east corner, which is interpreted as the seat of the council (*boule*) and, along the opposite wall, a large open space with a monumental entrance from the wadi, sharing a common wall with the agora. This was explained by Delplace and Dentzer-Feydy as an unfinished basilica, never covered or equipped with columns. If so, the whole complex resembled the civic centres of the Roman West, though conspicuously lacking a temple. At any rate, this was the civic centre of Palmyra, adapted to the usual administrative and social functions of a Graeco-Roman city (Seigne 2022b, 37–64).

In the same period, another major project was launched: the colonnaded street known as the Great Colonnade (Figure 6.1.6). This has never been published and was mapped with some precision only recently (Ostrasz 1969; Schnädelbach 2010). It was not built, or even planned, as it appears now. In the first stage, only the western section was designed, starting at the northern end of the Transverse Colonnade and ending level with and parallel to the agora (Żuchowska 2000). It makes sense to suppose that the street followed the course of the early rampart, though no material traces of this have yet been found. If so, it would be a kind of outer boulevard, inviting the development of the area to the north. The surveyors limited themselves to putting in place cornerstones at every planned side-street corner, leaving the building job to the owners of plots. Along this large avenue, 26 m wide wall to wall, columns, forming porticoes 7 m wide, were progressively erected in sections corresponding to each block. Some column alignments cannot be earlier than the mid-second century (Barański 1991). The colonnade opened with the western gate, with one large passage and two smaller lateral ones corresponding to the porticoes (Żuchowska 2010). It ended some 630 m further on with a huge foundation in the middle, later levelled, which left clear traces on the ground discovered recently by Jacques Seigne (Seigne 2022b, 77–85). Turning right from this, one could reach in a few paces an entrance to the open building flanking the agora. It makes sense to suppose that the agora and the street formed a functional complex.

PALMYRA AND THE EMPEROR HADRIAN

The orderly plan of the newly opened north-west quarter (Figure 6.2), with its parallel streets (though for some reason these are not perpendicular to the colonnade), indicates an initiative from above, perhaps suggested by the Roman administration. In 131, Palmyra was visited by the Emperor Hadrian, and this event called for some grandiose building enterprise. At Athens, Hadrian had founded a 'new city'—why not do the same in Palmyra? He did allow the city to bear his name, Hadriana Palmyra. The colonnade, the agora, and the new residential quarter to the north-west could well have been laid out on this occasion, making the oasis city more like many Greek cities in the province and elsewhere. It must be admitted, however, that there is no positive proof of the imperial connection.

It should be observed, on the other hand, that the aqueducts providing water to the city were in 137 referred to as 'the water sources of Aelius Caesar', that is, of Hadrian. We cannot be sure that the channels were laid under Hadrian and not just renamed in his honour. Indeed, it would be surprising if the rich caravan city relied exclusively on the sulphurous stream gushing from the Efqa spring. One of the aqueducts comes from the west, first underground, then on the surface. Its course began some 10 km from Palmyra with a system of underground channels (*qanat*) under the hill of Ruwaysat, marked by a lonely column bearing a statue of Herakles and showing characteristics of the first century (Seigne 2022a). It entered Palmyra by the Valley of the Tombs and the future Diocletian's Camp (Juchniewicz and Żuchowska 2012). Another, northern aqueduct is called Biyar al-Amye ('Blind Wells'); it is poorly known, having remained for many years off limits within a military area.

It is certain that the imperial visit was also marked by a smaller, private initiative. A secretary of the council, Male Agrippa, distinguished himself by generous donations during the visit and also commissioned the temple of Baalshamin in 130/131, according to the inscription of his statue on one of the porch columns. It was a small cella with a colonnaded porch that stood nearly complete until destroyed in 2015 (Collart and Vicari 1969). It was squeezed between the earlier colonnades standing on three sides of it and probably replaced the primitive shrine in the same place. The courtyard to the south was provided with columns slightly later, in the mid-second century. The cella of Allat was built around the preserved first shrine, in or shortly after 148 (Gawlikowski 2017, 127–154). It was so similar in design to the temple of Baalshamin that both were quite possibly the work of the same architect.

THE EXTENSION OF THE COLONNADE

The western section of the Great Colonnade was originally conceived as a complete monument, closed at both ends. Shops of merchants and artisans along each side of the street catered to the needs of the townspeople, just as those of the Transverse Colonnade can be supposed to have been more attuned to the far-flung caravans and suppliers from the countryside.

At some point, the colonnade was extended to the east (Figure 6.3.1). The square monument that had marked its end was razed to the ground and an oval plaza was designed, shortening the western section, while new columns were raised beyond it towards the east (Ostrasz 1969). One of the first columns east of the oval plaza bears an inscription dated 242/243, while the earliest text in the western section dates from 158. We do not know whether there were any columns around the plaza, nor whether the row of columns branching from the plaza and passing obliquely behind the agora towards the Arsu temple is contemporary with these changes. How long the extension of the colonnade was planned to be remains uncertain. It could not have been intended to go in a straight line to the Propylaea of Bēl because this would imply the destruction of the Nabu temple standing right in the way. Instead, the street was bent slightly (9 degrees) to the north, perhaps to accommodate some other existing buildings.

THE BATHS AND THE THEATRE

Two major monuments stand along this section of the colonnade. Both are excavated, but unfortunately no certain dating was acquired in either case. One of them is the baths (Figure 6.3.5). Their lavish sculptural decoration (of which only discarded remnants have been found) belongs to the Antonine and Severan periods, that is, to the second and early third century. The baths were fronted by a long portico, and one column on the opposite side of the street bears an honorific inscription dated in 224/225. It follows that this section of the street was in place at least as early as that. However, it could not have continued much further east because the way was blocked by the temenos of Nabu (Figure 6.3.3). The facade of the theatre (Figure 6.3.4) also follows the direction of the bent section of the colonnade. As a result, the short colonnaded passage behind the theatre ending with a decorative gate allowing access from the southern quarter is not on the theatre's axis, but parallel to the neighbouring annex of the agora. Of the arches opening at each end of the front portico, one introduced the slanting street leading to the agora and the other, dated 260 or 263, to a perpendicular portico which further on curved to follow the projected outline of the monument that was actually never completed. Indeed, while the stage building rose to the projected height, only the lower tier of seats (*ima cavea*) was put in place. Behind the *cavea*, a semicircular space was

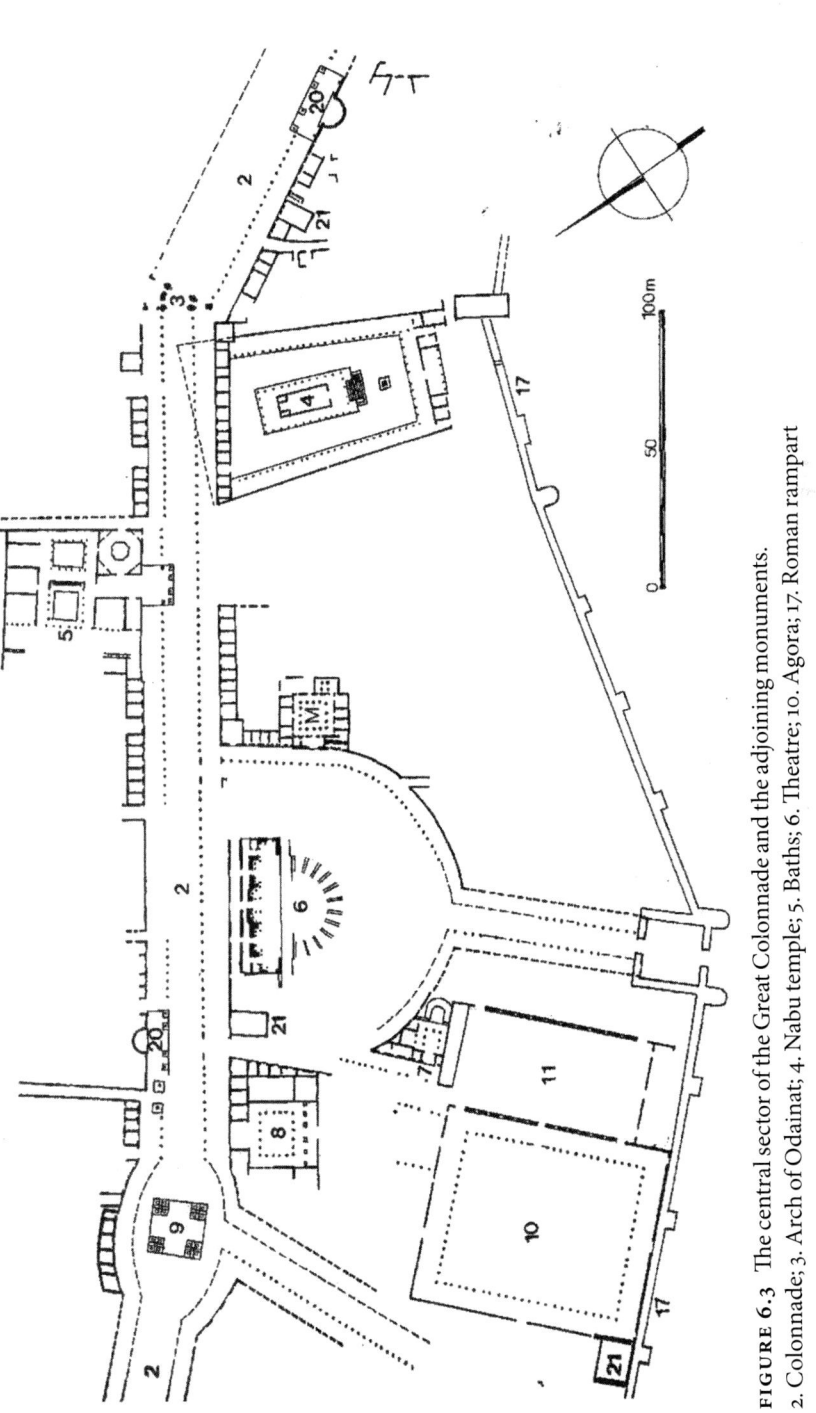

FIGURE 6.3 The central sector of the Great Colonnade and the adjoining monuments.
2. Colonnade; 3. Arch of Odainat; 4. Nabu temple; 5. Baths; 6. Theatre; 10. Agora; 17. Roman rampart

reserved for the two missing tiers, and the exposed innards of the structure were left apparent, clearly in expectation of a follow-up. The building process was halted halfway (Fourdrin 2009).

The date of the theatre is usually given as about 200, but there is no compelling reason for this estimation. It is hard to imagine that it remained unfinished for seventy years in the very centre of the city. Moreover, the honorific inscriptions on the twenty-six columns in the front, integrated into the Great Colonnade, were addressed to the greatest personalities: Odainat and his son Hairan, from 251 to 259, and the *argapet* (city governor) Worod between 256 and 267, and finally Queen Zenobia. Their statues would hardly have been put up in front of a neglected building, but it is conceivable if the work was in progress. Work on the theatre would therefore have begun shortly before 250 and could coincide with the elevation of Odainat and his son to the paramount position in the city.

THE FINAL STAGE OF THE COLONNADE

The third, eastern section of the Great Colonnade is only partially excavated. Nevertheless, it is clear that it was conceived as an independent structure. It was a large avenue, nearly 40 m from wall to wall, with porticoes on each side. Only a few columns remain standing or were restored. An inscription dates the erection of a portico of eight columns in front of a building as early as 219. It is not clear how long this section was. The distance to the Propylaea of Bēl is about 300 m, but the street could not have reached the portico directly at such a sharp angle. Apparently, one should envisage a plaza in front of the sanctuary where both the colonnade and the paved wadi street should converge, close to each other. Such a plaza would make the proportions of this section of the colonnade similar to those of the Transverse Colonnade at the other end of the town (Plate 2). There was a monumental fountain, fronted by four high columns, and the entrance to a probably much older shrine, but the main function of this complex must have been commercial. As we are there at the confluence of two wadis, Saraysir and ʿEid, it is just possible that a marketplace in front of the sanctuary might have a long tradition, but the laying out of the colonnade became possible only after the wadi al-ʿEid was barred to prevent flooding. A massive dam has indeed been found in a sounding executed in the courtyard of the Ottoman *konak*, recently the Ethnographic Museum (Scholl and Taha 1997).

The wide colonnaded street and the central section passing between the baths and the theatre could not meet directly until a corner of the Nabu sanctuary had been removed by obliquely cutting the northern wall of the sacred precinct (Figure 6.3.3). Not only was the sanctuary sensibly reduced in this way, but the whole northern portico of the courtyard has also disappeared, as well as the hypothetical outside porch of ten columns. The foundations of the condemned corner were found beneath the level of the extended street (Bounni et al. 1992, plates xxvi–xxviii).

The angle between the two sections was about 30 degrees, and the difference in width made it difficult to make them meet harmoniously. The problem was solved by erecting a monumental triple arch of a particular form, that of a pie section of a circle. The eastern face, turned towards the Bēl sanctuary, was adjusted to the wide street on this side, while the western face had to accommodate the narrower span between the porticoes (Seigne 2022b, 107–123). As a result, to the east the arch presented all three bays between the two rows of columns, while on the western side the lateral bays opened within the porticoes. The adjustment is manifest: immediately after the facade of the baths, the extended colonnade becomes narrower. The nests of architraves on both sides of the arch are clearly an afterthought, interfering with the sculpted decoration.

Within the main passage of the arch there are the remains of two inscriptions referring to the statues of Odainat and his son, here called Herodianus. The inscription for the son preserved the title 'king of kings' and is dated to 260 (or alternatively, less probably, 263); that for the father was no doubt termed likewise. These honours were awarded after their victory over the invading Persians in 260. It seems very likely that this was also the occasion of erecting the arch (Gawlikowski 2007). Such a major event could easily have made more acceptable the encroachment on the space of the Nabu sanctuary.

There is perhaps more. In the middle of the oval plaza close to the agora, the bend of the street was marked and yet at the same time concealed by a square monument of sixteen granite columns, set four by four in the corners. This so-called Tetrapylon (an inaccurate name that is in common use) had no practical purpose, and yet the founder did not hesitate to employ columns of red Aswan granite brought at great expense from the imperial quarries in Egypt (even before the recent destruction, none had remained complete). Four more such columns were added as a porch to the entrance of the baths; they seem to have similar diameters, though the same height for both sets cannot be proven. The extravaganza is best explained as a result of Zenobia's short-lived conquest of Egypt. The central section of the colonnade, 300 m long from the arch to the Tetrapylon, thus became a kind of royal mall celebrating Odainat and his family, beginning in the 250s with the statues in front of the theatre, completed with the arch in 260 or 263, and adorned with precious columns of the royal red.

THE LATER PALMYRA

The Palmyra of Odainat and Zenobia was an open city (van Berchem 1976). The original mud brick barrier (which never formed a complete circuit anyway) was mostly overbuilt. The burial grounds, interspersed with *khans* serving the caravans, were immediately adjacent to the inhabited area. Palmyra could not offer any meaningful resistance to the Roman army and was taken in 272, probably without attempting any. The destruction appears to have been limited (Figure 6.4). A Roman legion was established in the oasis in the following year, and no doubt the building of fortifications started without delay (Juchniewicz 2013). The rampart surrounded only the monumental centre on both

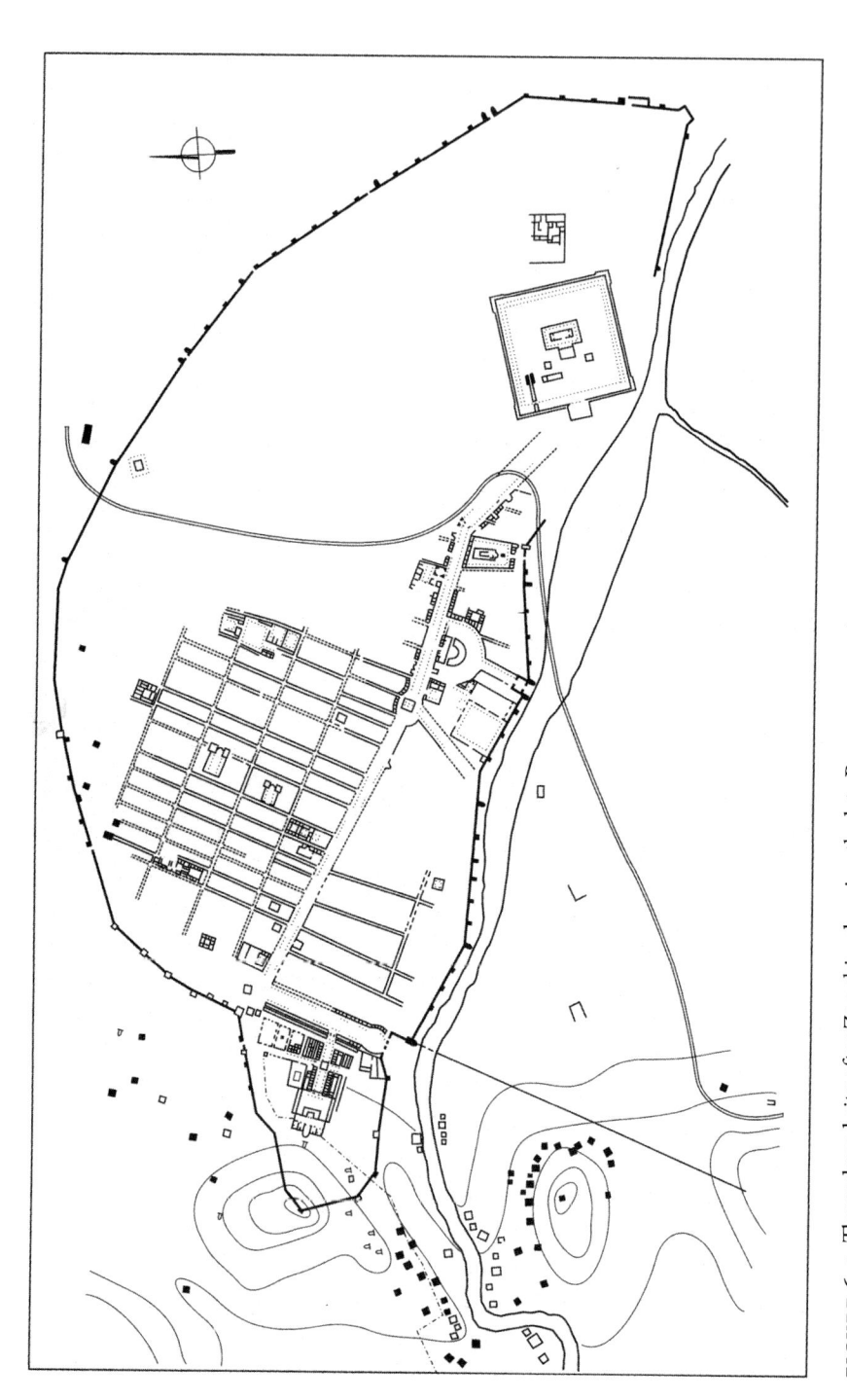

FIGURE 6.4 The reduced city after Zenobia, showing the late Roman rampart.

sides of the Great Colonnade (Plate 4). The key position was the western quarter, around the hastily rebuilt sanctuary of Allat, where the headquarters and barracks were planted (Gawlikowski 1984). The often quoted inscription of the Tetrarchs marked the completion of the works in the years 293–303 and gave to these buildings their modern name, Diocletian's Camp. They were surrounded by a rampart which continued around the city centre, incorporating on its way many tombs as bastions (Juchniewicz 2013). The Great Colonnade, the agora, the theatre, the Bēl and Baalshamin temples, and more were included. The baths were restored and renamed after Diocletian. The southern part of the city, on the contrary, was left outside the enclosure and probably razed to the ground to clear the field in the immediate vicinity of the fortifications. The paved road in the wadi became a dry moat.

Impoverished and diminished, Palmyra survived within its rampart for several centuries. It was still a densely built city, now an important fortress of the Syrian *limes*. Soon Christianized, it possessed several churches fitted into the urban fabric. Even the temple of Bēl was converted into a church.

The Islamic conquest at first brought little change. While the military facilities were taken over by squatters, the churches remained in service (Gawlikowski 2009). The Great Colonnade was overgrown by rows of shops, at least in its western section, suggesting a degree of economic growth (al-As'ad and Stępniowski 1989). A mosque was installed by the agora to serve this *suq*, which is the prime example of the development of an ancient *polis* into an Islamic city (Genequand 2013). The decline, however, came in the ninth century: churches and houses were abandoned, and the remaining population moved for safety to the Bēl precinct behind the ancient walls of the temenos. The temple became a mosque, probably already in the eighth century. For centuries, Tadmor was again an insignificant village, at times harbouring just a few families. This settlement survived until it was removed in 1930 by archaeologists eager to uncover the ancient remains.

CONCLUSION

The spontaneous development of the first century AD resulted in a city very different from the orderly Hellenistic foundations of the Roman East. Several temples, of which the great Bēl temple stood out as the major feature, seem to have been surrounded by irregular clusters of houses. The first attempt at imposing a monumental character on the urban fabric occurred in the early second century, with the laying out of the western section of the Great Colonnade and of the new agora. The civic centre was thus created, imitating Hellenistic and Roman models. Continuing the colonnade eastwards, and building along it the baths and the theatre, was a long process, extended over the course of the second and third centuries. Eventually, the Great Colonnade became the main artery linking the Bēl sanctuary with the other end of the city. This happened late, only after the erection of the arch in honour of Odainat transformed the central section into a royal avenue between the arch and the Tetrapylon.

The colonnade replaced the first-century paved road in the wadi as the main thoroughfare of the city. Both were linked at each end by two wide commercial malls: the Transverse Colonnade in the west and a later marketplace in the east (Plate 2). The civic centre of the city became accessible from two directions: from the southern city, as originally planned, and from the Great Colonnade and the new quarters to the north. This frame was irregular, resulting from its slow formation without a preconceived plan. It functioned as a complete whole for a few years only under Zenobia.

PLANS

See Figures 6.1–6.4.

BIBLIOGRAPHY

al-As'ad, Khaled, and Franciszek M. Stępniowski. 1989. 'The Umayyad *suq* in Palmyra'. *Damaszener Mitteilungen* 4: 205–225.

al-Maqdissi, Michel. 2000. 'Note sur les sondages réalisés par Robert du Mesnil du Buisson dans la cour du sanctuaire de Bêl à Palmyre'. *Syria* 77: 137–158.

al-Maqdissi, Michel, and Eva Ishaq. 2022. 'Les phases anciennes du temple de Bêl d'après les archives de R. du Mesnil du Buisson et les travaux de la Mission syrienne'. In *Life in Palmyra, Life for Palmyra*, edited by Dagmara Wielgosz-Rondolino and Michał Gawlikowski, 21–54. Warsaw: Uniwersytet Warszawski.

Barański, Marek. 1991. 'Opus Palmyrenum'. *Damaszener Mitteilungen* 5: 59–63.

Barański, Marek. 1995. 'The Great Colonnade of Palmyra Reconsidered'. *ARAM* 7: 37–46.

Bounni, Adnan. 2004. *Le sanctuaire de Nabū à Palmyre: Planches*.Texte. Bibliothèque archéologique et historique 131. Paris: Geuthner.

Bounni, Adnan, Jacques Seigne, and Nassib Saliby. 1992. *Le sanctuaire de Nabū à Palmyre: Planches*. Bibliothèque archéologique et historique 131. Paris: Geuthner.

Collart, Paul, and Jacques Vicari. 1969. *Le sanctuaire de Baalshamîn à Palmyre*. Vols. 1–2, *Topographie et architecture*. Rome: École suisse de Rome.

Delplace, Christiane. 2017. *Palmyre: Histoire et archéologie d'une cité caravanière à la croisée des cultures*. Paris: CNRS.

Delplace, Christine, and Jacqueline Dentzer-Feydy. 2005. *L'agora de Palmyre*. Beirut: Institut français du Proche-Orient.

Fourdrin, Jean-Pascal. 2009. 'Le front de scène du théâtre de Palmyre'. In *Fronts de scène et lieux de culte dans le théâtre antique*, edited by Jean-Charles Moretti, 189–234. Travaux de la Maison de l'Orient 52. Lyon: Maison de l'Orient et de la Méditerranée.

Frézouls, Edmond. 1976. 'Questions d'urbanisme palmyrénien'. In *Palmyre: Bilan et perspectives; Colloque de Strasbourg, 18–20 Octobre 1973, à la mémoire de Daniel Schlumberger et de Henri Seyrig*, edited by Edmond Frézouls, 191–207. Strasbourg: Centre de recherches sur le Proche-Orient et la Grèce.

Gabriel, Albert. 1926. 'Recherches archéologiques à Palmyre'. *Syria* 7: 71–92.

Gawlikowski, Michał. 1974. 'Les défenses de Palmyre'. *Syria* 51: 231–242.

Gawlikowski, Michał. 1984. *Palmyre.* Vol. 8, *Les principia de Dioclétien: Temple des Enseignes.* Warsaw: Państwowe Wydawnictwo Naukowe.

Gawlikowski, Michał. 2007. 'Odainat et Hérodien, rois des rois'. *Mélanges de l'Université Saint-Joseph* 60: 289–311.

Gawlikowski, Michał. 2009. 'Palmyra in Early Islamic Times'. In *Residences, Castles, Settlements: Transformation Processes from Late Antiquity to Early Islam in Bilad al-Sham,* edited by Karin Bartl and Abd al-Razzaq Moaz, 89–96. Rahden: Leidorf.

Gawlikowski, Michał. 2013. 'Le Tarif de Palmyre et le temple de Rab'asirê'. *Comptes rendus des séances de l'Académie des inscriptions et belles-lettres* 156(2): 765–780.

Gawlikowski, Michał. 2017. *Le sanctuaire d'Allat à Palmyre.* PAM Monograph Series 8. Warsaw: Uniwersytet Warszawski.

Genequand, Denis. 2013. 'Between Rome and Islam: Recent Research on the So-Called Caesareum of Palmyra'. *Studia Palmyreńskie* 12: 97–114.

Hammad, Manar. 2010. *Palmyre: Transformations urbaines; Développement d'une ville antique de la marge aride syrienne.* Paris: Geuthner.

Hammad, Manar. 2013. 'Morphologie des environs de Palmyre: relief, enceintes, pistes'. *Studia palmyreńskie* 12: 129–148.

Jakubiak, Krzysztof. 2022. 'Distribution of Sanctuaries Within the City of Palmyra and Their Role in the City's Sacred Life'. In *Life in Palmyra, Life for Palmyra,* edited by Dagmara Wielgosz-Rondolino and Michał Gawlikowski, 225–238. Warsaw: Uniwersytet Warszawski.

Juchniewicz, Karol. 2013. 'Late Roman Fortifications in Palmyra'. *Studia Palmyreńskie* 12: 193–202.

Juchniewicz, Karol, and Marta Żuchowska. 2012. 'Water Supply in Palmyra: A Chronological Approach'. In *The Archaeology of Water Supply,* edited by Marta Żuchowska, 61–73. British Archaeological Reports, International Series 2414. Oxford: Archaeopress.

Ostrasz, Antoni. 1969. 'Note sur le plan de la partie médiane de la rue principale à Palmyre'. *Annales archéologiques arabes syriennes* 19: 109–120.

Pietrzykowski, Michał. 1997. *Adyta świątyń palmyreńskich,* edited by Michał Gawlikowski. Warsaw: Uniwersytet Warszawski. In Polish with a French summary.

Sartre, Maurice. 1996. 'Palmyre, cité grecque'. *Annales archéologiques arabes syriennes* 43: 385–405.

Schlumberger, Daniel. 1933. 'Les formes anciennes du chapiteau corinthien en Syrie, en Palestine et en Arabie'. *Syria* 14: 283–317.

Schlumberger, Daniel. 1935. 'Études sur Palmyre: I, le développement urbain de Palmyre'. *Berytus* 2: 149–162.

Schmidt-Colinet, Andreas, and Walid al-As'ad, eds. 2013. *Palmyras Reichtum durch weltweiten Handel: Archäologische Untersuchungen im Bereich der hellenistischen Stadt.* Vienna: Verlag Holzhausen.

Schnädelbach, Klaus. 2010. *Topographia Palmyrena.* Vol. 1, *Topography.* Documents d'archéologie Syrienne 18. Bonn: Habelt.

Scholl, Tomasz, and Ahmed Taha. 1997. 'Sounding in the Courtyard of the Saray in Palmyra 1986'. *Studia palmyreńskie* 10: 63–68.

Seigne, Jacques. 2022a. 'Palmyre: De l'eau dans la steppe syrienne'. In *Life in Palmyra, Life for Palmyra,* edited by Dagmara Wielgosz-Rondolino and Michał Gawlikowski, 381–465. Warsaw: Wydawnictwa Uniwersytetu Warszawskiego.

Seigne, Jacques. 2022b. *Observations sur la topographie de Palmyre*. Studia palmyreńskie 14. Warsaw: Wydawnictwa Uniwersytetu Warszawskiego.

Seyrig, Henri. 1941. 'Antiquités Syriennes 32: *Ornamenta palmyrena antiquiora*'. *Syria* 21: 277–328, plates 29–35.

Seyrig, Henri, Robert Amy, and Ernest Will. 1975. *Le temple de Bêl à Palmyre*. Bibliothèque archéologique et historique 33. Paris: Institut français d'archéologie du Proche-Orient.

Starcky, Jean, and Michał Gawlikowski. 1985. *Palmyre*. Paris: Librairie d'Amérique et d'Orient.

van Berchem, Denis. 1976. 'Le plan de Palmyre'. In *Palmyre: Bilan et perspectives, Colloque de Strasbourg, 18–20 Octobre 1973, à la mémoire de Daniel Schlumberger et de Henri Seyrig*, edited by Edmond Frézouls, 165–173. Strasbourg: Centre de recherches sur le Proche-Orient et la Grèce.

Will, Ernest. 1983. 'Le développement urbain de Palmyre: Témoignages épigraphiques anciens et nouveaux'. *Syria* 60: 69–81.

Will, Ernest. 1992. *Les Palmyréniens: La Venise des sables*. Paris: Armand Colin.

Żuchowska, Marta. 2000. 'Quelques remarques sur la Grande Colonnade à Palmyre'. *Bulletin d'études orientales* 52: 187–193.

Żuchowska, Marta. 2010. 'The Western Gate at Palmyra'. *Studia palmyreńskie* 11: 107–114.

ADDENDUM

Completing Schnädelbach 2010: Delplace, Christiane, 2023. *Topographia Palmyrena, 2. Le centre urbain*. Mémoires de l'Académie des Inscriptions et Belles-Lettres 61. Paris.

....

CHAPTER 7

PALMYRENE IDENTITY AND COMMUNITY

Continuity and Change

....

ANDREW M. SMITH II

INTRODUCTION

....

MANY transitions took place in the third century AD, but few had such a profound impact on the social, economic, and political landscapes of the Roman Near East as the demise of Parthian rule and the rise of a militant Persian state. At its head was Ardashir, king of kings, who sought to reclaim the former glory and landholdings held by the Persians in the past (Herodian 6.2.1–2). Perhaps as early as 230, Ardashir campaigned in Roman Mesopotamia, eventually capturing Nisibis and Carrhae in 238 and Hatra in 240. Shapur succeeded his father Ardashir and campaigned against the Romans in the 240s. In 252 or 253, Shapur took Antioch; he captured Dura-Europos in 256.

The city of Palmyra seems to have been spared during this turbulent period, but, as the city's economic lifelines abroad were severed, its communal foundations were shaken. Earlier, the Palmyrenes had flourished because of their isolated location. In the first century AD, Pliny (*NH* 5.21.88) described the city succinctly.

> Palmyra, a city famous for its position, the richness of its soil, and its pleasant waters, incorporates fields encircled on all sides by a vast circuit of sand; and, as though removed by the natural order from other lands, and enjoying a separate lot between two supreme empires, that of the Romans and that of the Parthians, in times of discord, it is always the first concern on both sides.

While Palmyra may have been seen as removed from other lands due to its location, the Palmyrenes themselves were not. They travelled extensively abroad, serving in such capacities as ambassadors, diplomats, and soldiers beyond their home territory.

They also established communities of merchants in both Roman and Parthian empires. The source material is fragmentary, but these individuals are visible to us because they maintained their cultural identities and communal connections abroad by expressing themselves in their native language and by worshipping their native gods. This does not mean that every Palmyrene expat did so. Some probably travelled abroad and acculturated themselves into other communities and so disappeared from our records. But for those who did not, questions arise about how and why they maintained their attachments to their unique Palmyrene identities (Smith 2013). There is also the question about whether the expression of their distinctive group identity reflected any primordial sentiments or distant support for the communal structures that shaped Palmyra itself.

Those who maintained the strongest connection to their home city were the Palmyrene merchants, who also excelled as middlemen in the long-distance trade of exotic goods between empires. Their activities, in terms of servicing and equipping the caravans, epitomized the significant role played by Palmyra, their home emporium, in the economies of both empires. And the profits from the caravan trade helped to finance the monumental rise of Palmyra as a preeminent Graeco-Roman city in the Near East, as it grew institutionally from being a Greek *polis* in the first century BC to a Roman *colonia* in the third century AD. While Shapur had been campaigning in the Roman East, Palmyra had attained the status of *metrocolonia*, and the city itself could claim as one of its own a member of the Roman senatorial order (*vir clarissimus*), Septimius Odenathus (Millar 1993, 157).

Odenathus, like many before him, was a great patron of his community. He may have had Palmyrene trade interests in mind when he, according to a fragmentary Greek text,

> paid [much] court to Shapur as one who had greatly surpassed the Romans. Wanting to lead him on, he sent magnificent gifts and other goods which Persia was not rich in, conveying them by camels. He also sent letters expressing entreaty and saying that he had done nothing against the Persians. Shapur, however, instructed the slaves who received the gifts to throw them into the river and tore up and crushed the letters. 'Who is he,' he declared, 'and how has he dared to write letters to his master? If then he wants to obtain a lighter punishment, let him know that I shall destroy him and his people and his land'. (Peter the Patrician, frag. 10, *FHG* IV 4, 187)

There is little reason to doubt that this exchange occurred, although dating it is problematic (Hartmann 2001, 135–137). Odenathus had many reasons to reach out to Shapur. On the one hand, as a *vir clarissimus*, he may have had Roman interests in mind, or, concurrently, he may have courted Shapur's favour in his capacity as a leading citizen of Palmyra with the goal of protecting his community's vested interests in what was formerly Parthian territory. Wanting to see the caravan trade resume would have been a strong motivator since this trade fuelled Palmyra's economy. Unfortunately, Shapur was not interested in restoring the state of affairs as previously constituted under the Parthians. His reaction to Odenathus's entreaties was decisive.

We may never know Odenathus's true motivation. In the context of all of the social groupings at Palmyra, he was many things to many different people. Selectively labelled, he was a Roman, a Palmyrene, a member of the tribal elite, a military leader, a patron, and a father. These various social identities overlapped one another, each competing for his attention and each with its own set of motivations. In terms of his indigenous persona as a Palmyrene, therefore, we might consider how embedded were the memories of his forefathers within the various manifestations of his social self. More generally, for the community of the Palmyrenes, how connected were they to their collective past?

The purpose of this chapter is to examine what it meant to be a Palmyrene in the first century BC, when we see the distinctive origins of the Palmyrene community, compared with what it meant to be a Palmyrene in the third century AD, as the community faced a crisis that challenged their communal existence. Since this is a matter of identity and our sources are not as explicit as we would like, the issue of what it meant to be a Palmyrene, or how the Palmyrenes perceived themselves and their community, is naturally elusive and debatable. Identity is, in and of itself, hard to pin down because it is always in flux and changing in response to external influences, in addition to the fact that individuals support a plurality of identities at any given moment (Tajfel 1982). In other words, as our experiences accumulate over time, perceptions of self and others evolve, and change takes place. There are, however, more conservative elements in our cultural expressions that tend to change less, religious practices being among them (Kaizer 2002). Also, more conservative are the social formations framed and supported by religious expressions (such as tribalism); and, to the extent to which these practices are preserved in the archaeological and epigraphic record, we are that much closer to understanding expressions of identity. The focus of this chapter, therefore, is on the creation, structure, and maintenance of Palmyrene identity and the evolution of this communal identity over two centuries in an isolated, at times volatile frontier zone.

INSTITUTIONAL DEVELOPMENTS AND THE TEMPLE OF BĒL

The earliest attestation of a Palmyrene community comes from an inscription of AD 10 (*PAT* 2636). It references a tax on camels due upon crossing a wall of the city and to be paid to the 'funds of the people of Palmyra' (*blw* / *gbl tdmry'*). Any amount in excess of that duty was to be paid to a certain 'Atenatan Khaffatût, son of Bar'â, and to Yamlikû his son, of the tribe of the *bny myt'*. The *gbl tdmry'* reappear in a bilingual, honorific inscription of AD 25, when they decide to honour a certain Malkû, son of Neshâ, a member of the *bny kmr'*, with a statue in the temple of Bēl (*PAT* 1353). Here the *gbl tdmry'* is rendered in the Greek as the Παλμυρηνῶν ὁ δῆμος. Similarly, 'all the people of Palmyra' (*gbl tdmry' klhn*) honour a certain Moqîmû, son of Ogeîlû, in AD 51 (*PAT* 0269). In the bilingual inscription honouring Moqîmû, *gbl tdmry' klhn* is rendered as 'the city of the Palmyrenes' ([Παλμυρη]νῶν ἡ [π]ό[λις]). It should be emphasized that both Malkû and Moqîmû are honoured for their contributions to the construction of the temple of Bēl, referred to as the 'house of the gods' (*bt 'lhyn*). Malkû himself had already received honours in AD 24 because 'he had helped them in everything and he helped with the construction of the temple of Bēl and he gave from his own funds more than anyone before him' (*PAT* 1352). Honouring Malkû were 'all the merchants who are in the city of Babylon' (*t[g]ry' klhwn dy bmdynt bbl*), identified in the Greek text as the *demos* of the Palmyrenes, Παλμυρηνῶν ὁ δῆμος.

The evidence cited above of the declarations made by 'the council and the people' of Palmyra (*bwl' wdms*) indicates the nature of the political community that the tribal confederation was aiming to form at the outset. The goal, it seems, was to follow the institutional development of a Greek city state (*polis*). Appian (*Bell. Civ.* 5.9) comments that Palmyra was already a *polis* in 41 BC when Mark Antony raided the city, but his account has been shown to be anachronistic (Hekster and Kaizer 2004). When we imagine a *polis*, what we see is a council or *boule*, an assembly, and a group of magistrates (Jones 1940). It seems therefore that the Palmyrenes had reached their goal by AD 74, when a trilingual inscription was cut that references the *boule* for the first time. The Greek text reads ἡ [βουλ]ὴ καὶ ὁ [δῆμος], which appears in Palmyrene as *bwl' wdms*. The Latin text transliterates the Greek *boule*, but identifies the *demos* as the '*civitas* of the Palmyrenes' (Cantineau 1933, 174–176).

The evidence suggests that Palmyra in the early first century AD was in the developmental stages of a long process of becoming a more consolidated, more urban, political community. The inspiration is clear. The Peace of Augustus, confirmed in 27 BC, motivated many groups in the Near East to promote urbanization, and the tribes in and around Palmyra were industrious enough not to miss an opportunity. Various familial groups with tribal associations attached themselves to the oasis (Smith 2013). Many may have migrated from the surrounding countryside, while others may have remained at large in the vast territory that constituted the hinterland of Palmyra, nonetheless recognizing the centrality of Palmyra as a place of power and authority (Meyer 2017). Some were probably long-standing inhabitants of the oasis, while all promoted Palmyra as the locus of a new communal formation. The city itself was becoming a major economic and religious centre. Even the merchants in Babylon could feel as though they constituted the Palmyrene *demos*.

During these formative years, the focal point for the congregation of tribal groups near and afar was the temple of Bēl, which went through many phases of construction and took nearly a century to complete. Malkû and Moqîmû made their contributions and were duly honoured. Others contributed as well. In AD 19, for example, Palmyrene and Greek merchants in Seleucia on the Tigris made a dedication to a certain Yedîbêl, son of Azîzû, a Palmyrene of the *bny mtbwl*, because of his contributions to the construction of the temple of Bēl (*PAT* 0270). Yedîbêl himself dedicated a statue of his father, Azîzû (*PAT* 0271). In AD 21, both the *bny mtbwl* and the *bny kmr'* set up a statue to Hashash 'because he was their leader and made peace between them and assisted them in everything, great and small' (*PAT* 0261). This Hashash was the brother of Malkû, son of Neshâ, and so a member of the *bny kmr'*. Other members of the *bny kmr'* honoured for their contributions to the temple include a certain Ogeîlû, son of Taîmaî (*PAT* 0268), and Lishamsh, son of Taîbbôl, who consecrated the completion of the cella of the temple in AD 32, which was dedicated to the divine triad of Bēl, Yarhibol, and Aglibol (*PAT* 1347). In addition to the *bny mtbwl* and the *bny kmr'*, the *bny myt'* (*PAT* 1356 and *PAT* 2762), the *bny zbdbwl* (*PAT* 0269), and the *bny šm'r* or *šm'd* (*PAT* 1355) are also associated with the temple of Bēl. Construction of the temple complex continued into the second century. In AD 108, for example, the Gaddeibōlioi, or *bny gdybwl*, honoured a benefactor because he had made for them the gate and doors of the cella (*PAT* 0263), and, in AD 175, the council and the people (*bwl' wdms*) honoured a certain Yarhibôlâ and his cousin Awîdâ with statues for their having paid for six brazen doors for the 'great portico of the house of Bēl' (*PAT* 0260).

Shared religious observance was the glue that bonded the tribal confederation uniting at the oasis as a political community, and it was central to the process of becoming and the state of being a Palmyrene. Indeed, many brought with them their native gods, and the different backgrounds of these gods reflect the mixed nature of the tribal confederation that assembled at Palmyra (Teixidor 1979; Kaizer 2002). The deities' origins were Babylonian (Bēl, Belti, Nebu, Nergal, and Nanai), Phoenician (Baalshamin and Belhammon), and Aramaean (Ishtar and Atargatis). There were even Canaanite deities (Shadrafa and Elqonera) and Arab ones (Shamash, Allat, Abgal, Manawat), in addition to many others. Those attested in inscriptions from the foundation trenches of the early sanctuary include Herta, Nanai, Reshef, Yarhibol, Belhammon, Manawat, the 'daughter of Bēl' (*brt bl*), Ashtart, Bolastor, 'the demons' (*šdy'*), and Baaltak (for references, see Smith 2013, 61). As we have seen above in the inscription of AD 25, the temple of Bēl could be referred to as the 'house of the gods' (*bt 'lhyn*). In AD 48/49, for example, the *bny myt'* honour their god Bolastor with a portico in the *bt 'lhyn* (*PAT* 2749).

Other sanctuaries were constructed at Palmyra to service the religious associations of particular tribes. For example, while the temple of Bēl was under construction, a temple precinct was laid out for the god Baalshamin (Collart and Vicari 1969). Three women are recorded as having dedicated two columns to the god in AD 23 (*PAT* 0167), and by 67 an early sanctuary had appeared (*PAT* 0158), although the existing sanctuary was not dedicated until 132. Nevertheless, despite the rise of tribal sanctuaries across the city, it was at the temple of Bēl where those from different backgrounds and tribal affiliations could congregate as one community: as Palmyrenes.

THE PALMYRENE ECONOMY

In addition to becoming a major religious centre, another key factor that drove Palmyra's communal development was economic. The city became a commercial hub in the Near East. Appian (*Bell. Civ.* 5.9) states that the Palmyrenes conveyed the products of India and Arabia into Roman territory. The caravan trade was particularly lucrative, and colonies of Palmyrene traders established in communities down the Tigris and Euphrates Rivers, well into Parthian territory, supported it. This was apparent throughout the city of Palmyra, where inscriptions were placed and statues erected to honour Palmyrene notables for their public munificence. These were financed by Palmyrenes, expats, and others. For example, it was the Palmyrene merchants in Seleucia on the Tigris, alongside their Greek colleagues, who honoured Yedîbêl, son of Azîzû, in AD 19 for contributions to the construction of the temple of Bēl (*PAT* 0270). Malkû, son of Neshâ, was likewise honoured in AD 24, but it was Palmyrene merchants in Babylon who sponsored his dedication (*PAT* 1352). In AD 50 (or 70), Palmyrene merchants in the port of Spasinou Charax in Mesene honoured a certain Zabdibôl, son of Obayhan, of the tribe of the *bny mtbwl*, with a statue at Palmyra (*PAT* 1584). Upon their return from Spasinou Charax in AD 81, Palmyrene merchants sponsored a statue for another Zabdibôl, a member of the *bny m'zyn* (*PAT* 1376). In the second century, Marcus Ulpius Yarhai looms prominent as a Palmyrene notable involved with the caravan trade and with strong connections to Spasinou Charax, having received dedications in his honour in AD 156 (*PAT* 1411), AD 157 (*PAT* 1399), and AD 159 (*PAT* 1409). He was also recognized by merchants in the Parthian city of Choumana in AD 157 (*PAT* 0306), and again in the same year by merchants who had returned from Scythia by sea in the boat of Honainô, son of Haddûdân (*PAT* 1403). Palmyrene merchants associated with Spasinou Charax dedicated other statues in the agora at Palmyra to Palmyrene notables in AD 88 (or 28; *PAT* 1366), AD 89 (or 189; *PAT* 0309), AD 131 (*PAT* 1374), AD 135 (*PAT* 1397), AD 140 (*PAT* 1412, when the merchants passed through the remote emporium of Vologesias), AD 161 (*PAT* 1373), and in AD 193 (*PAT* 0294).

There are also several inscriptions attesting trade relations with Vologesias, a Parthian city south of Babylon and a commercial hub for Palmyrene traders (Maricq 1959). One prominent notable who supported this connection was Soados (or Shoadû), son of Bōliados. In fact, the earliest reference to Vologesias is in an inscription of AD 132, once displayed in the courtyard of the temple of Baalshamin. It records the erection of four statues at Palmyra to Soados, sponsored by Hagegû, son of Yarhibôlâ, and Taîmarsû, son of Taîmarsû, chiefs of the caravan. Soados had given assistance to the merchants, the caravans, and the citizens of Vologesias and had saved the caravan from a 'great risky endeavour' (*qdns rb*; *PAT* 0197). Soados was similarly honoured with four statues in AD 144 (Drijvers 1995). Another Palmyrene who played a prominent role in the caravan trade with Vologesias was Neshâ, son of Halâ. Neshâ was twice honoured for his role leading the caravans: in AD 142, when a statue was set up in his honour in the temple of Bēl (*PAT* 0262), and again in AD 150 (*PAT* 1419). This trade relationship with Vologesias lasted into the third century. For example, an inscription of AD 210 associates a certain Yaddai with Vologesias (*PAT* 0295), and, in AD 247, merchants whom Julius Aurelius Zebîdâ had accompanied to Vologesias honoured him with a statue along the Great Colonnade (*PAT* 0279).

When we imagine the significance of Palmyra as a religious and economic centre, our attention navigates to the temple of Bēl and other monumental structures within the city, including the agora (Delplace and Dentzer-Feydy 2005). As mentioned, however,

Palmyra developed institutionally as a *polis*, which means that there was much more to Palmyra than its increasingly urbanized core. As a *polis*, Palmyra also included a vast hinterland, with a rural population engaged in an array of economic pursuits and subsistence strategies. This is evident from the Palmyrene tariff inscription of AD 137, which highlights the significance of boundaries, both civic and territorial, in the regulation of regional and interregional trade. The pronouncement by the Roman governor, the *legatus pro praetore*, which is preserved in the tariff inscription, reads:

> As for provisions, I decree that a tax of one *denarius* should be exacted according to the law for each load imported from outside the borders of Palmyra or exported there; but those who convey provisions to the villages or from them should be exempt, according to the concession made to them. . . . As for camels, if they are brought in from outside the borders whether loaded or unloaded, one *denarius* is due for each camel according to the law. (*PAT* 0259 [tariff]: Greek 187–197; cf. *PAT* 0259 [tariff]: Palmyrene II.109–113 and 118–123; see Matthews 1984)

Care was thus taken for the welfare of the villages, but it should be stressed that those in the villages were no less Palmyrene than those in the city. Similarly, mention of those native to the region as exempt from payments due from grazing rights shows concern for the pastoralists in the countryside, who also were no less Palmyrene than those in the city. Those who brought animals into the city's territory for the purpose of grazing, meanwhile, paid the duty (*PAT* 0259). By exercising power and authority within established territorial boundaries, therefore, the Palmyrene community prospered, and, collectively, the activities of those in the city together with those in the countryside facilitated communal formation at and fostered the urbanization of Palmyra. Understanding the boundaries that defined the city state in its broadest sense, therefore, helps us to understand better what being a Palmyrene meant and how that communal identity was maintained over time. Both urban and rural groups self-identified as Palmyrenes, a community that comprised many subgroups or tribal entities engaged in a range of subsistence strategies and economic pursuits, from farming to pastoralism and mining to mercantilism. Another aspect of these territorial boundaries was that they defined the community of the Palmyrenes in relation to 'others' who identified with population groups and urban communities elsewhere.

ROMAN, PARTHIAN, AND PALMYRENE INTERACTIONS

The aforementioned period of institutional and economic growth, alongside the appearance of the 'people of Palmyra' as a unique community, coincides with our earliest evidence of the Romans taking an active role in defining the regional limits of Palmyrene territory. A column from Khirbet el-Bilaas, ca. 75 km north-west of Palmyra, bears three inscriptions, one of which refers to a rescript by Creticus Silanus, the *legatus pro praetore* of Syria in AD 11–17, establishing the 'limits of Palmyrene territory' (*AÉ* 1939, no. 179: *fines regionis Palmyrenae*). At Qasr el-Heir el-Gharbi, roughly 60 km southwest of Palmyra, a boundary marker defines the border with Emesa (*AÉ* 1939, no. 180). Soon after establishing their territorial boundaries to the west, the Emperor Tiberius sent his adopted son, Germanicus, to the region for diplomatic reasons. At that time, the Parthian king, Atabanus III, dispatched a diplomatic mission of his own to meet with Germanicus while the latter was in Syria (see Tacitus *Annales* 2.43–58; Edwell 2007, 36–41), just as Germanicus himself dispatched a diplomatic mission to the Parthian vassal state of Mesene using a Palmyrene envoy. A poorly preserved inscription recording the event identifies a Palmyrene surnamed Alexandros, whom Germanicus sent to a certain Orabzes of Mesene (*PAT* 2754). It seems that this Alexandros also visited Sampsigeramus, king of Emesa—his purpose is unclear but may have dealt with boundary disputes. Territorial boundaries east of Palmyra are more difficult to define, and it is unclear to what extent the Romans were involved in this region. An inscription found south of Dura-Europos identifies a certain Abgar, son of Shalman, 'who came to the end of the boundaries when Yarhai was *stratēgos*' (*PAT* 2810). Another inscription (*PAT* 2730) found 200 km south-east of Palmyra in the Qa'ara depression identifies a group of 'harvesters' (*ḥṣdy'*) with a certain Abgar, son of Haîran, at the 'border' (*qṣt'*; Smith 2013, 72). The tariff inscription may give some grounds for inferring that the Romans were interested in Palmyra's eastern boundaries for tax reasons, when it refers to a letter addressed by Germanicus to Statilius that fixed the requirement that taxes were to be collected in Italic asses (*PAT* 0259: Palmyrene, II.102–105, Greek 181–184). There is also a trilingual inscription dating to AD 58 that identifies L. Spedius Chrysanthus as a tax collector (*mks'*: *PAT* 0591). The Roman presence at Palmyra is further attested in AD 19 when the legate of the Legio X Fretensis, Minucius Rufus had statues set up in the temple of Bēl to honour Tiberius, his son Drusus, and Germanicus (*Inventaire* IX, 2). All this evidence, though fragmentary, highlights direct Roman involvement in the affairs of Palmyra, including the establishment of territorial boundaries west and perhaps east of the city—it also suggests that Palmyrene identity was maintained from within community and through their interactions with others. Meanwhile, Roman involvement in Palmyrene affairs does not confirm that Palmyra was officially annexed in the first century AD because the city may simply have attained special status as a Roman client. One privilege, it seems, that the Romans granted the Palmyrenes was the power to maintain their own military.

While Palmyra became more urban and prosperous over the course of the first century, the necessities of exercising administrative control, policing the desert, and providing security and assurances to the residents of the countryside became significant. This burden probably fell upon Palmyrene tribal leaders, who maintained their connections between city and countryside and may have had residences in both (Yon 2002). It almost certainly fell upon the Palmyrene military, the nature of which is obscure. For example, we know nothing about recruitment or length of service. What is clear is that the military was led by a *stratēgos* ('*sṭrtg*). In AD 98, for example, Zebîdâ, son of Haumal, served as a *stratēgos* when he led a small group into the distant Wadi Rijelat Umm-Kubar near Wadi Hauran, some 50 km south-west of Hadita on the Euphrates (*PAT* 2732; see Safar 1964, 13, no. 1; *PAT* 2810). In AD 144, the aforementioned Soados, son of Bōliados, received honours from a caravan of all the Palmyrenes for having taken the initiative to assemble a large force and protect them from a certain Abdallat and his band of robbers who were waiting in ambush to attack (*PAT* 0197). Later in AD 198, Aelius Bôra, son of Titus Aelius Ogeîlû, is identified in a bilingual inscription found east of the temple of Bēl as a *stratēgos* 'who made peace in the territory of the city' (*PAT* 1063). He was most likely suppressing banditry, as was Ogeîlû, son of Maqqai, at about the same time. According to a bilingual inscription found outside the agora, Ogeîlû received a statue set up by the council and the people of Palmyra for his dutiful service, which included not only his support of the merchants and caravans, but his many military commands against 'nomads' in the region (*PAT* 1378). What is interesting here is that these *stratēgoi* seem more active in the second and third centuries than in the first century AD.

The Palmyrene military also maintained units abroad. Palmyrene soldiers were based at Dura-Europos from AD 117 to at least AD 162, and perhaps after the Romans occupied the city in AD 164/165 (Dirven 1999). In AD 169, a certain Atpanaî, son of Zabda'eh, is identified in a Mithraic relief as a *stratēgos* of the archers at Dura-Europos (*PAT* 1085). Another relief of AD 170/171 identifies a certain Zenobios as *stratēgos* of the archers (Dirven 1999, 264–265, no. 29). Presumably both were Palmyrenes. Further south, a garrison may be found as early as AD 132 on the island of Ana in the Euphrates, based on a dedication that a Nabataean horseman made to his patron and friend, Zebîdâ, son of Shimeôn (*PAT* 0319). Further, an inscription of AD 188 refers to the horsemen of Ana and Gamla, who had erected a statue in Palmyra to a certain Zebâ, son of Maqqai (*PAT* 0200), and an inscription of AD 225 refers to someone as the *stratēgos* of Ana and Gamla (*PAT* 2757). There may also have been Palmyrene units at Bijan and Kifrin, two forts in the Middle Euphrates near to Ana (Smith 2013, 145).

Over the course of the second and third centuries, the Roman presence at Palmyra increased, but how this affected the community of the Palmyrenes is less clear, although the city did adopt the civic name of Hadriana Palmyra and may have been granted the status of a *civitas libera* under Hadrian (*PAT* 1374). A Roman *ala* arrived in the mid-second century. *Inventaire* IX, 23, for instance, mentions a certain Vibius Celer, identified as prefect of the *ala* based in the city, being honoured by the council and the people of Palmyra as a citizen and colleague. This may have been the Ala I Thracum Herculiana, whose commander is honoured in AD 167 (*Inventaire* IX, 22; *ILS* 8869). In the third century, the Cohors I Flavia *chalcidenorum* replaced the *ala* stationed in the city (Seyrig 1933). This Roman military presence coincides with Rome's many wars fought against the Parthians between AD 167 and 217, when the Romans twice sacked the Parthian capitol of Ctesiphon, the last occasion being in AD 197 under Septimius Severus. Moreover, the local commander probably had some involvement in the administration of the city as well as the collection of tolls (*portoria*) on the caravan trade. No doubt he would have supported the activities of Marcus Aemilius Marcianus Asclepiades. A town councillor of Antioch and a 'quarter-collector' (*tetartōnēs*) of caravan revenues, Marcus was honoured in AD 161 with a statue in the agora of Palmyra (*PAT* 1373), as was Lucius Antonius Callistratus, another collector of the 'fourth' honoured in AD 174 (*PAT* 1413). That Roman interest in the city was largely economic is further suggested by the fact that the Palmyrene *stratēgoi*, like others who gave protection or leadership to the caravans, the *synodiarchs* or the *archemporoi*, were frequently honoured by the governor of the province.

FOUR TRIBES, FOUR SANCTUARIES

Concurrently with the Roman military presence at Palmyra, new social and economic developments seem to have impacted the city's institutional and communal structures. Specifically, there are three inscriptions from the late second century AD that refer to the 'four tribes' of the city. These suggest that there may have been a consolidation of tribal groupings within the city. The first inscription, dated AD 171, identifies a certain Yarihibol, who was honoured with several equestrian statues—one in the Kaisareion, one in the temple of Bēl, and one in each of four sanctuaries by the four tribes of the city (*PAT* 2769). Similarly, in AD 198, by decree of the council and the people (or by decree of the fatherland [*patris*] as it appears in the Greek text), the *stratēgos* Aelius Bôra, who had made peace in the territory of the city, was honoured with an equestrian statue in addition to four other statues by the four tribes of the city, each in their own sanctuaries and at their own expense (*PAT* 1063). A year later, Ogeîlû, son of Maqqai, received four statues from the four tribes of the city, also by command of the council and the people, specifically for the assistance he had provided them on the caravans he had escorted (*PAT* 1378).

The three inscriptions referring to the four tribes of the city do not identify the tribal sanctuaries themselves, and only the inscription of AD 198 states the name of one of the four tribes, the Khōneitoi (φυλὴ Χωνειτῶν), who may be the same as the *bny kmr'* (Kaizer 2002, 126). The four sanctuaries can be presumed to be identified in two bilingual inscriptions from AD 132 and 144, both of which record that statues were set up in honour of a Soados, son of Bōliados, in four separate sanctuaries. The inscription of AD 132 identifies the four sanctuaries as the temple of Arsu, the Sacred Grove, the temple of Atargatis, and the temple of Allat. Although unspecified, it seems safe to assume that these were tribal sanctuaries. The correlation between tribe and sanctuary, therefore, would be that the *bny kmr'* (φυλὴ Χομαρηνῶν = φυλὴ Χωνειτῶν/*bny kmr'*) were patrons of the Sacred Grove (of Aglibol and Malakbel), the *bny myt'* φυλὴ Μιθηνῶν/*bny myt'*) of the temple of Atargatis, the *bny mtbwl* (φυλὴ Μαθθαβωλίων = φυλὴ Μανθ(α)βωλείων/*bny mtbwl*) of the temple of Arsu, and the *bny m'zyn* (φυλὴ Μαγερηνῶν/*bny m'zyn*) of the temple of Allat (Kaizer 2002, 64–66). However, simply correlating the four sanctuaries mentioned in earlier inscriptions with four known Palmyrene tribes does not mean that these four comprised the 'four tribes' of the city mentioned in later inscriptions (Smith 2013, 132–143).

Perhaps a more relevant question concerns the nature of the community represented by the four tribes as a subset of the Palmyrene population. It has been argued that they comprised the civic body of Palmyra (Schlumberger 1971). This seems doubtful, given that the inscriptions referencing the four tribes clearly distinguish them from the council and the people (*bwl' wdms*). We should also not presume that the tribes of Palmyra in the late second and early third century AD were any less tribal than they were in the first century, although much has been written about the loss of tribal identities (based, as it were, on extended kinship networks) as civic identities strengthened over time (Smith 2013). Moreover, the people of Palmyra (*gbl tdmry'*) who emerge in the first century are not coterminous with the four tribes who appear later as an institutional body, although each of the four tribes probably did have an ancestry that linked them to the early formative period of the *polis*. To understand the nature of the four tribes as an institutional body, therefore, we need to examine the political, social, and economic contexts from which they emerged.

The 'four tribes' first appeared in the Antonine period, during the reigns of Lucius Verus and Marcus Aurelius. As noted, this coincides with the earliest evidence we have of a Roman garrison in the city, the Ala Herculiana of Thracians, commanded by its *praefectus*, Julius Julianus (*Inventaire* IX, 22), and it was just the beginning of a long period of Roman involvement in Palmyra's civic affairs. It was probably at this time, too, that the imperial cult was introduced into the city (*PAT* 2769). Nor should we neglect the impact that the Antonine Plague may have had on the population, both urban and rural (Duncan-Jones 1996). Meanwhile, as the city was undergoing transformations in light of the Roman military presence, banditry in the countryside increased. There was also a decline in the caravan trade. Between the years AD 161 and 193, for example, there are no caravan inscriptions (Smith 2013). Regional insecurity was clearly associated with the decline of the caravan trade, which was concurrent with the Parthian war of Lucius Verus and the plague that followed. During this time, Palmyrene communities along the Tigris and Euphrates would have been impacted. What we can conclude from all of this is that the 'four tribes' appear in our sources in a period of intense regional stress that would have challenged the social, economic, and political institutions of Palmyra. One Palmyrene response, at least for those more directly involved in the caravan trade, may have been to consolidate resources and refocus attention on revitalizing the trade routes. It is noteworthy, for example, that all the inscriptions referencing the 'four tribes,' and even those that identify the four sanctuaries earlier, honour individuals for the care they took to protect the caravans by campaigning against bandits and maintaining peace in the territory of the city. These individuals also received testimonies from imperial officials, which highlight Roman interests in Palmyrene affairs as well as the role played by certain individuals among the elite in keeping the Palmyrene economy afloat through the revival of the caravan trade and through the maintenance of regional security. In terms of the caravan trade, it may be that the 'four tribes' represented a *collegium* of sorts, or some other corporate group who pooled their resources to finance trade ventures in very challenging and dangerous times. It may also have been a practical way to divide their financial obligations to the Romans who were there to collect the *tetarte*, the 25 percent tax on goods brought into the empire.

Conclusion

The Roman wars against Parthia and Persia in the late second and early third centuries placed Palmyra in a perilous predicament between two empires. These wars were disruptive to both the local and the regional economy of the city. The caravan trade, in particular, was adversely affected because it depended on peaceful and more or less fluid borders between the two empires so that Palmyrene merchants could go about their business. And everyone stood to benefit. Real change came with the arrival of the Persians. Their attitude towards the Palmyrenes was one of hostility—that is, if Shapur's reaction to Odenathus's embassy can be trusted. What is clear is that these external relationships between the Palmyrenes and the many 'others' whom they encountered helped to structure the boundary (one of many) that defined their communal identity, and the stresses of the late second and early third centuries complicated the maintenance of this boundary. This brings us back to the central issue of this chapter: what it meant to be a Palmyrene in the first century AD versus what it meant to be a Palmyrene in the third century.

In broad strokes, because the social, political, economic, and cultural landscapes had changed drastically between the first and third centuries AD, it seems hard to imagine that the boundaries defining Palmyrene identity had not morphed in some manner. Indeed, there are some areas of identity expression that would suggest that they had—or rather, that the boundaries within which a unique Palmyrene identity could be expressed had extended over time and had embraced associative identities that made the social practice of being a Palmyrene more complicated and diverse. For example, in the first two centuries AD, we can observe Roman citizenship status seep into the social matrix of the city as some families advanced higher in rank than others. How this affected social relationships within the Palmyrene community itself is difficult to assess, although it would have made those in the elite who promoted their Roman identities yet still served as patrons of their city all the more distinctive, while some of their social peers leaned more towards Parthia in their cultural preferences. This was lost after AD 212, however, when Caracalla issued his famous edict granting Roman citizenship status to all free inhabitants of the empire. By then, the city was garrisoned by Roman troops. This meant that the freedom the Palmyrenes had enjoyed in the first century to grow their communal identities had diminished by the third century. Now there was more direct oversight, and their freedom of expression would have been more constrained to fit within Roman expectations. Moreover, the social and economic hardships of successive Roman–Parthian wars in the region and the aftermath of the Antonine Plague would have tested communal foundations. On the one hand, there was the potential to abandon a sense of shared community; on the other, the Palmyrenes could reinforce their communal foundations and move forward through the volatile world of the third century with a greater sense of themselves as Palmyrenes.

The argument presented here is that the latter was the case. The Palmyrenes reinforced their communal foundations and reasserted their communal expression of themselves in a world that grew increasingly chaotic and economically depressed. The Palmyrenes of the third century became who they were through the accretion of the memories and experiences of those who preceded them. These memories surrounded them in the monuments and tombs that they built, and the narrative of their communal foundations echoed through their inscriptions and art. The conservatism visible in their religious life also suggests a thread of continuity with the past, which was strained as the Roman presence in the city grew, as the frontier grew more unstable, and as the local and regional economy faltered. To weather the storm of the late second and early third centuries, the Palmyrenes, it seems, turned to their religious institutions, which may account for the activities of the four tribes of the city and their role in reviving the caravan trade. By the third century, as their community became more Romanized, the Palmyrenes (Odenathus included) remained, at their core, politically, socially, culturally, and uniquely Palmyrene.

BIBLIOGRAPHY

Cantineau, Jean. 1933. 'Tadmorea'. *Syria* 14: 169–202.

Collart, Paul, and Jacques Vicari. 1969. *Le sanctuaire de Baalshamin à Palmyre*. Vols. 1–2, *Topographie et architecture*. Rome: Institut suisse de Rome.

Delplace, Christiane, and Jacqueline Dentzer-Feydy. 2005. *L'agora de Palmyre*. Beirut: Institut français du Proche-Orient.

Dirven, Lucinda. 1999. *The Palmyrenes of Dura-Europos: A Study of Religious Interaction in Roman Syria*. Leiden: Brill.

Drijvers, H. J. W. 1995. 'Greek and Aramaic in Palmyrene Inscriptions'. In *Studia Aramaica: New Sources and New Approaches*, edited by Markham J. Geller, Jonas C. Greenfield, and Michael Weitzman, 31–42. Oxford: Oxford University Press.

Duncan-Jones, Richard P. 1996. 'The Impact of the Antonine Plague'. *Journal of Roman Archaeology* 9: 108–136.

Edwell, Peter M. 2007. *Between Rome and Persia: The Middle Euphrates, Mesopotamia and Palmyra under Roman Control*. London: Routledge.

Hartmann, Udo. 2001. *Das palmyrenische Teilreich*. Stuttgart: Steiner.

Hekster, Olivier, and Ted Kaizer. 2004. 'Mark Antony and the Raid on Palmyra: Reflections on Appian, "Bella civilian" V, 9'. *Latomus* 63: 70–80.

Jones, A. H. M. 1940. *The Greek City from Alexander to Justinian*. Oxford: Oxford University Press.

Kaizer, Ted. 2002. *The Religious Life of Palmyra: A Study of the Social Patterns of Worship in the Roman Period*. Stuttgart: Steiner.

Maricq, Andre. 1959. 'Vologesias, Le Emporium de Ctésiphon'. *Syria* 36: 264–276.

Matthews, John F. 1984. 'The Tax Law of Palmyra: Evidence for Economic History in a City of the Roman East'. *Journal of Roman Studies* 74: 157–180.

Meyer, Jørgen Christian. 2017. *Palmyrena: Palmyra and the Surrounding Territory from the Roman to the Early Islamic Period*. Oxford: Archaeopress.

Millar, Fergus. 1993. *The Roman Near East, 31 BC–AD 337*. Cambridge, MA: Harvard University Press.

Safar, Fuad. 1964. 'Inscriptions from Wadi Hauran'. *Sumer* 20: 9–27.

Schlumberger, Daniel. 1971. 'Les quatre tribus de Palmyre'. *Syria* 48: 121–133.

Seyrig, Henri. 1933. 'Textes relatifs à la garnison romaine de Palmyre'. *Syria* 14: 152–168.

Smith, Andrew M. 2013. *Roman Palmyra: Identity, Community, and State Formation*. Oxford: Oxford University Press.

Tajfel, Henri. 1982. *Social Identity and Intergroup Relations*. Cambridge: Cambridge University Press.

Teixidor, Javier. 1979. *The Pantheon of Palmyra*. Leiden: Brill.

Yon, Jean-Baptiste. 2002. *Les notables de Palmyre*. Beirut: Institut français d'archéologie du Proche-Orient.

CHAPTER 8

PALMYRA AND ITS 'DARK AGES' (273–750)

An Archaeological and Historical Reassessment

EMANUELE E. INTAGLIATA

OUR knowledge of the late antique and early Islamic history of Palmyra is dramatically lacunose compared to its Roman counterpart. Such a gap is mostly the result of the nature of the evidence: archaeological remains are comparatively few and less monumental, written sources are sporadic, and the epigraphic record diminishes considerably after the late third century. However, the data available seem to clearly define the downfall of Zenobia and the second Palmyrene revolt (272–273) as a watershed in the history of the site. In the last quarter of the third century, Palmyra lost its role as caravan hub, to become a strongly militarized fortress city on the eastern Roman frontier. Gradually, the urban aesthetic of 'classical' Palmyra gave way to a more practical approach to urban life, which was characterized by the gradual privatization of public space. Christianity, which spread within the city early compared to other urban centres in central Syria, was one of the key factors that contributed to late antique urbanism and promoted the destruction or abandonment of pagan shrines and the construction of churches over previously existing buildings (see Gawlikowski 2021, 189–204; Genequand 2012, 17–37, 45–67; Kowalski 1997; Chapter 9 [Kowalski], this volume; Intagliata 2015; 2018a).

The scope of this chapter is to explore how these two components—the military and religion—were responsible for the urban transformations that unfolded in Palmyra over the course of late antiquity. It will do so by also shortly presenting to the reader the history of this site from the end of the second Palmyrene revolt to the fall of the Umayyad caliphate (273–750). The picture that emerges from an analysis of written sources and archaeological evidence is that of a resilient urban settlement that survived the dramatic end of the third century to become a new city shaped by the historical circumstances of its time.

Urban Continuity After 273

The events that brought about Zenobia's defeat in 272 and the second Palmyrene revolt in 273 have been extensively explored by modern scholarship (Stoneman 1992; Equini Schneider 1993; Chapter 11 [Andrade], this volume, with further references). The two writers that describe the aftermath of these events, namely the author of the *Historia Augusta Vita Aureliani* (31.5–9) and Zosimus (*Hist. Nov.* 1.61–62), mention destruction in the city and the massacre of the population by Aurelian's troops and their allies. The archaeological evidence does not support the theory of the complete devastation of Palmyra reported by Zosimus, but evidence of general disruption does exist. The urban surface shrank considerably, and the so-called Hellenistic quarter, to the south of Wādī al-Qubūr, appears to have been abandoned. Half-finished columns were abandoned in the quarries surrounding the site, and important building projects, such as the Great Colonnade and the theatre, were discontinued (Barański 1994, 9; Żuchowska 2000, 191, 192, fig. 7). Traces of destruction, possibly associated with the Aurelianic event, have been uncovered in the Hellenistic quarter (Schmidt-Colinet et al. 2013, 303), the north-west quarter (Gawlikowski 2004, 323), the Great Colonnade (Żuchowska 2000, 187), the sanctuary of Allat (Gawlikowski 1983, 61; Gawlikowski 2017, 155), the agora (Seyrig 1940, 242), and, possibly, the theatre (Will 1966, 1413–1414; Kowalski 1997, 44) (see Figure 8.1).

However, such disruptions did not mark the end of urban life. Renovations are shown epigraphically along the Great Colonnade. One of the inscriptions dedicated to such restorations is dated to 328; it records the reconstruction of a portico in the north-west quarter and the name of its benefactor, the λογιστής (*logistes*) Flavius Diogenes. The presence of a λογιστής, a civic dignitary appointed by the *curia*, suggests that the administrative heart of the city still functioned. A second inscription reports the roofing of a 'Basilica of Arṣū' by some members of the tribe of the Maththabōlioi in 279–280. This proves also that the Palmyrene tribal system was still in place (al-Asʿad and Gawlikowski 1986–1987, 167–168, n. 7–8; *IGLS* XVII.1, 101). The city also retained its juridical status. Numerous milestones found on the Palmyra–Homs road define the settlement as a *colonia* (for evidence, see Hartmann 2001, 59).

The continuity of Palmyrene life is also evident in the religious sphere. The last recorded inscription to a pagan god is dated 302, and was found in the courtyard of the sanctuary of Baalshamin. It was dedicated to Zeus the Highest by the *princeps* Avitus, probably a soldier of the newly established garrison in town (*IGLS* XVII.1, 154). In the first half of the fourth century, the lavish mosaic of the Bellerophon Hall, a banqueting chamber in a private residential building situated in the north-west quarter, received modest additions. These consisted of two black-and-white mosaic panels, each featuring a pair of open hands. The presence of this motif, which is linked to the cult of the Anonymous God, has been interpreted as the result of the conversion of the Bellerophon Hall into a place for the cult of the homonymous deity (Gawlikowski 2004, 318).

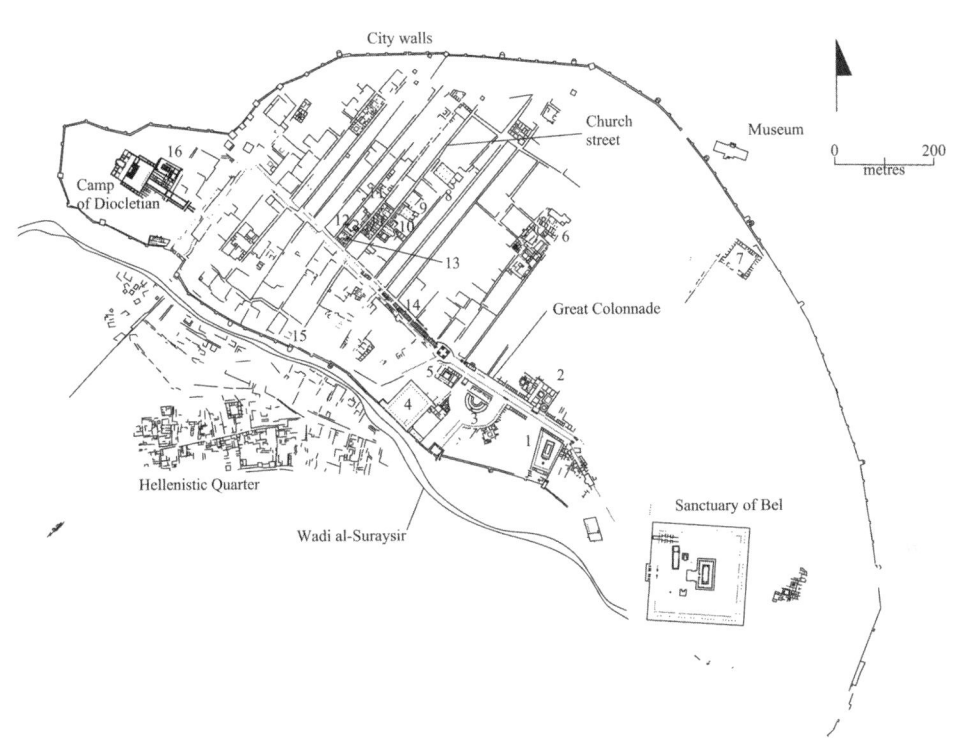

FIGURE 8.1 Map of Palmyra. 1. Sanctuary of Nabu; 2. Baths of Diocletian; 3. Theatre; 4. Agora; 5. Mosque; 6. Sanctuary of Baalshamin; 7. Marché Suburbain; 8. Church 4; 9. Church 3; 10. Church 2; 11. Block house; 12. Church 1; 13. Bellerophon hall; 14. Suq; 15 Peristyle Building; 16. Sanctuary of Allath.

Redrawn after Schnädelbach 2010.

THE ROLE PLAYED BY THE MILITARY

Although the continuity of Palmyrene life in the aftermath of the Aurelianic event is demonstrated archaeologically, there is evidence of a complete change in the nature and role of the site. The end of the Palmyrene Empire had significant economic and geopolitical repercussions that can be reconstructed only with difficulty from the available data. As far as trade is concerned, the collapse of Palmyrene power coincided with the end of the Palmyrene caravan links through the Syrian steppe. The last inscription reporting Palmyrene caravan activity in the city is dated to the 260s and was dedicated to a certain Worod, who brought back to Palmyra several caravans, unharmed, at his own expense (*CIS* II, 3942). Eventually, the treaty reached at Nisibis (298 or 299) between Rome and the Sassanians established that city as the sole trading point between the two superpowers; this put an end to any ambition Palmyra may have had with respect to reviving its caravan trade (Seland 2016, 86).

The collapse of the Palmyrene Empire, and, therefore, its army, shocked the fragile balance among local nomadic tribes, also known as *Sarakēnoi* in primary sources, and left the eastern borderlands in a state of internal and external turmoil. Palmyra's military role in late antiquity is addressed in detail in another contribution to this volume but cannot be ignored in this discussion, as it was the main contributing factor that shaped the 'new Palmyra' after 273. Here, it suffices to say that Emperor Diocletian considerably strengthened the military presence on the border with Persia along a *via militaris*—a military road—protected by fortified posts mainly garrisoned by auxiliary units. Modern scholars have argued at length about the causes behind the imperial decision to strengthen this border area, which may have ranged from defending the frontier from the Saracen threat to patrolling its roads (see Lewin 2007, 243–244). Palmyra was chosen as the base for a legion, the *Legio I Illyricorum*, as recorded in the *Notitia dignitatum* (*Or.* 32.30).

The need to garrison new troops in the late third/beginning of the fourth century led to the construction of a military camp, the Camp of Diocletian, between 293 and 303 (Chapter 25 [Juchniewicz], this volume, with further references). The camp, whose founding is recorded in an inscription on the lintel of the Temple of the Standards (*IGLS* XVII.1, 121), occupies the western appendix of the city, lying on the eastern slope of a hill. For its construction, an entire quarter had to be rearranged and most of its buildings razed to the ground, with the exception of a pagan sanctuary, the sanctuary of Allat. The Camp of Diocletian is by far the most monumental fortress of its kind in the whole of the Syrian stretch of the eastern frontier as well as one of the most ambitious and articulated building projects the site would ever see in the last phases of its occupation.

Dated to the same time is the restoration of the bathhouse in the city centre—the so-called 'Baths of Diocletian'. An inscription records its 'construction', although presumably it was a renovation, ordered by Sossianus Hierocles, governor of the province of Phoenicia Libanensis and also the person responsible for the construction of the Camp of Diocletian (*IGLS* XVII.1, 100). It is also likely that, under Emperor Diocletian, the city walls were restored and strengthened to include monumental, U-shaped, projecting towers (Chapter 25 [Juchniewicz], this volume; Juchniewicz 2013; Intagliata 2017).

The fate of the *Legio I Illyricorum* after the late fourth century is obscure, but it is unlikely that the unit remained garrisoned in the city throughout the fifth and sixth centuries. In discussing the changes brought about by the renovations ordered by Emperor Justinian, Malalas (*Chr.* 17.2) writes that Justinian 'ordered a *numerus* of soldiers to be stationed there [Palmyra] with the *limitanei* [frontier troops], and also the *dux* of Emesa, to protect the Roman territories and Jerusalem' (transl. Jeffreys et al. 1986, 245). The necessity of providing Palmyra with fresh troops reported by Malalas may come after a drastic reduction of the settlement's military strength in the fifth century (Intagliata 2015, 172; Intagliata 2018a, 100–102), a time of relatively peaceful relations between the Romans and Persians (Greatrex and Lieu 2002, 31–61). The decision to move the *dux* of Emesa and, probably, his large retinue to Palmyra also indicates the increased strategic role conferred to the settlement at the time of Justinian.

The troops stationed along the eastern *limes* were not the sole defence of the Syrian borderland. Considerable help was also assured by local nomadic confederations of tribes with which Rome was allied by a *foedus* ('agreement', 'treaty'—hence, the term *foederati*). These were the Tanukhids, who helped to break the Zenobian revolt, in the fourth century, the Salihids in the fifth century, and the Jafnids, in the sixth century. The last of these *foederati* has left significant evidence of their presence in Palmyra and its surroundings in written sources. Procopius (*De Bel.* 2.1.6) records a dispute that arose between the Jafnids and the philo-Persian Nasrids in the first half of the sixth century over the control of a territory to the south of Palmyra named 'Strata'. Furthermore, a Syriac codex, now at the British Museum and said to have belonged to a monastery near Palmyra, mentions King Abokarib, the brother of al-Ḥārith b. Jabala (Wright 1872, 2, 468, n. 585; Millar 2013, 24–25). In addition, Ḥamza al-Hiṣfahānī (*Ṭāʾrīkh* 121) and Abū al-Fidāʾ (*Taqwīm al-Buldān*, 128–130), report that al-Ayham b. Jabala b. al-Ḥārith ruled Palmyra in the early seventh century. Finally, of the six inscriptions mentioning Jafnid phylarchs, one is at Qasr al-Hayr al-Gharbi, some 80 km south-west of Palmyra (Schlumberger 1939; 1986, 26–28; Jalabert and Mouterde 1959, 240–243; Genequand 2006, 69–70). However, despite these clues, the full extent of the Jafnid involvement in Roman military operations remains unknown.

CHRISTIANITY IN LATE ANTIQUE PALMYRA: A BRIEF HISTORY

The Church played a major role in shaping Palmyra after 273. In the fourth century, Christianity consolidated its position in the city. The first bishop of Palmyra mentioned by the conciliar records is Marinus, who took part in the Council of Nicaea in 325 (Le Quien 1740, 845; Devreesse 1945, 206). The presence of a bishop of Palmyra and his participation in the council indicates the important religious role attributed to the city at such an early stage. In the late fourth century, the city appears to have experienced a violent wave of anti-paganism. Probably as a consequence of this, the sanctuary of Allat underwent significant destruction. The cult statue of Athena located in its cella was knocked off its base and its facial features deliberately mutilated (Gąssowska 1982; Gawlikowski 2017, 162–166). In the north-west quarter, the mosaics of the Bellerophon Hall were covered with a more practical mortar floor (Żuchowska 2006, 447), perhaps suggesting that the function of the whole building changed, to the detriment of the pagan worship of the Anonymous God.

The violent destruction and repurposing of Palmyrene pagan sanctuaries might not have necessarily translated into the complete demise of paganism in the city. Although evidence from Palmyra is lacking, we know that paganism was particularly resilient in the Near East and survived long after the Theodosian anti-pagan edicts (Drijvers 1982, esp. 36). John of Ephesus (*Eccl. Hist.* 3.27), for example, reports the eradication of paganism in Baʿalbak, ancient Heliopolis, as late as 597, and, in discussing the persistence of paganism, he would write that 'numerous persons in every district and city in their land [practice paganism], and in almost every town in the East'.

The fifth century was marked by the events triggered by the Council of Chalcedon (451), the sixth canon of which was signed by Theodorus, bishop of Damascus, on behalf of John, bishop of Palmyra (Le Quien 1740, 845–846; *ACO* 2.12, 154; 2.3.2, 174). The council marked a significant turning point for the Christological debates of the time, postulating the existence of two distinct natures in Christ—human and divine. The Monophysites, who supported the teaching of Dioscuros and believed in the presence of a single nature in Christ (*fusis*—a union between human and divine), opposed this doctrine. In some cases, this Christological controversy sparked violent reactions. In 457, Proterius was murdered and his body burnt in Alexandria by Timothy Aelurus (Sellers 1953, 274, n. 4). This action was condemned in a letter signed by twelve bishops of Phoenicia Libanensis, including John, bishop of Palmyra, and sent to Emperor Leo. Therein, the bishops rejected the Chalcedonian creed but distanced themselves from Timothy Aelurus's action (*ACO* 2.5, 46).

There were attempts to eradicate Monophysitism in the East. The Emperor Justin was particularly concerned about the diffusion of this heresy and promoted a veritable purge within the ecclesiastical ranks that lasted for a couple of years (518–519) and resulted in the incarceration and exile of many members of the Monophysite movement. According to Michael the Syrian (*Chr.* 9.13) and the author of the *Chronicle of Zuqnīn* (3.19), Bishop John of Palmyra was one of them, and he died in exile.

According to written sources, the Justinianic period was a turning point for the city. Procopius (*Aed.* 2.11, 10–12), Malalas (*Chr.* 17.2), and, much later, Theophanes (*Chr.* 1.174), saw in Justinian the promoter of the construction of a number of churches in Palmyra. The existence of a *xenodokos/hospitalarius* at that time, the deacon Julian, suggests that in the city there also existed charitable institutions controlled by the Church (Mansi 1759–1798, 921; *ACO* 3.151). In the *Notitia Antiochena*, which lists cities based on their religious importance, the site is recorded as being under the jurisdiction of Damascus in the sixth century. It is ranked in third place after only Eliopolis and Abila (Honigmann 1925, 75; Vailhé 1907, 145).

THE ROLE OF THE CHURCH IN TRANSFORMING THE TOWNSCAPE

The religious history of Palmyra between the early fourth and sixth centuries reveals the site's early attachment to Christianity, which would later permeate the history of the settlement even after the Islamic conquest. The urban space was also affected by the new religion. It was noted above how pagan places of worship were sometimes the object of Christian hatred. The sanctuaries that lost their religious nature were often repurposed as private residential buildings or productive areas, as in the case of the sanctuary of Nabū (Bounni et al. 1992, plate 8, fig. 12; Bounni 2004, 6) and the sanctuary of Baalshamin (Kowalski 1996; Intagliata 2017).

Churches became the most frequent type of public building. At least eight churches are known to have been constructed *intra muros* in late antiquity—nine, if we count the problematic structures uncovered in and around the cella of the sanctuary of Baalshamin (Kowalski 1996). Four of them (Churches 1–4), were built in the north-west quarter of the city, forming a veritable Christian hub (Gawlikowski 2001; Majcherek 2013 with further references). Church 1 opens onto the Great Colonnade with a 50 m-long *atrium* (Żuchowska 2006, 448–450), whereas all the others are accessed from a street perpendicular to this, known as 'Church Street'. Save for Church 1, which has a transversal plan dictated by a previously existing civic building on top of which it sits (Gawlikowski 1990, 40–43), all the others share a basilica plan and adhere to an architectural form strongly linked to northern Syrian building traditions (Intagliata 2015, 144–151; Intagliata 2018a, 61–63). Also, four churches are situated along, or in close proximity to, the Great Colonnade. These include three small chapels (Majcherek 2005) and the church dedicated to the Virgin Mary in the cella of the temple of Bēl, the inner arrangement of which remains mostly unknown (Jastrzębowska 2013, with further references). The presence of five churches (including Church 1) along the main axis of the city highlights the importance of the Great Colonnade as one of the city's main religious arteries, probably the processional road.

Another way in which Christianity considerably shaped Palmyrene urban space has to do with a reevaluation of death. After the first relics of saints were moved into cities in the late fourth century, more people wanted to be buried *ad sanctos* (literally, 'close to saints'), to seek salvation for eternal life (Dagron 1977, 11–19; Saradi 2008, 321). Cemeteries were moved into towns, and Palmyra was no exception to this trend. A graveyard consisting of seven graves orientated east to west between Churches II and III in the north-west quarter has been excavated by the Polish team (Gawlikowski 1999, 192–194; 2000, 254–255). The burial ground exposed within the suburban market close to the Dura Gate probably belongs to a later period (seventh–eighth centuries) (Delplace 2013, 40). However, one should note that the largest late antique and early Islamic graveyard is situated *extra muros*. It was accidentally discovered during renovations in the garden of the archaeological museum, and partly excavated to reveal seventy-eight graves (al-As'ad and Ruprechtsberger 1987, 137–146).

LIFE UNDER THE CALIPHATE (634–750)

The nature of the evidence available for tracing a history of Palmyra ('Tadmor' in Arabic written sources) under early Islam is radically different from that of earlier centuries. Published data from the archaeological record are rather sporadic, as we shall see, but written sources abound, allowing us to outline the fate of the site between the seventh and eighth centuries from a more historical perspective. After a brief Persian occupation, of which no traces are left on the site, and another short Byzantine hiatus, the city fell into the hands of the Muslims in 634. The conquest of Palmyra by the Islamic general

Khālid b. al-Walīd is abundantly recorded in written sources. However, all the writers who recount the capitulation of Palmyra wrote some centuries after the event, the closest being al-Wāqidī (*al-Maghāzī* 1.44), and therefore should be taken *cum grano salis*.

Khālid b. al-Walīd entered Syria from Iraq and marched to Palmyra, but some sources report he took a different route through Dūmat al-Jandal (Donner 1981, 121, 124). Although the sources seem to contradict each other, two recurring elements often emerge in the account of the city's capitulation. First is the impregnability of the circuit wall. Palmyra is said to have been well fortified when Khālid b. al-Walīd's army reached the settlement, a theme that will also recur in later incidents involving the city (e.g., al-Ṭabarī, *Ta'rikh*, 9.1796; b. 'Asakir, *Ta'rikh*, 63.337). B. A'tham al-Kufi (*Kitab*, 1.140–142), to cite one example, reports the general's irritation at the impossibility of penetrating the city's fortifications: 'when the next day came, he [Khālid b. al-Walid] rode out leading some of his companions, and moved around the city [trying to find a weak point], but Khālid could not find any stratagem against them owing to the strength of the walls'. The reason for the difficulty in penetrating the city's defence may also lie in the fact that Khālid b. al-Walīd's army is likely to have been very small, numbering, according to al-Balādhurī (*Futūḥ*, 110) and al-Ṭabarī (*Tā'rīkh* 4.2108–2110) just some five hundred to eight hundred soldiers (Donner 1981, 126, 314, n. 185 provides sources with larger numbers).

The second frequently recurring element of the nature of Palmyra's capitulation is that most sources state that it was taken by treaty and not by force. To cite an example, when describing the event, al-Balādhurī (*Futūḥ*, 111–112) writes how, after an initial battle, the Palmyrenes asked for a guarantee of safety and Khālid b. al-Walīd 'granted it to them on condition that they would be *dhimma* people, accept Muslims' authority, and be subordinate to them'. Therefore, Palmyra's capitulation may have been a simple takeover agreed to by both parties, rather than the result of a bloody fight. The archaeological record, which so far has yielded no traces of destruction associated with this event, points decidedly to a smooth transition of power, in contrast to Aurelian's disruptive conquest about three centuries earlier. Thus conquered, the city was included in the *jund* (province) of Homs (al-Muqaddasī, *Aḥsan*, 159).Besides the conquest of 634, the early Islamic history of Palmyra, as seen through the lens of written sources, is marked by two critical events. The first concerns the conflict between the Umayyad caliph 'Abd al-Malik b. Marwān, and the usurper 'Abd Allāh b. al-Zubayr, who was supported by al-Ḍaḥḥāk b. Qays. According to Abū Mikhnaf, as cited by al-Ṭabarī, who presents the most detailed report of the event, during these clashes the caliph had found refuge in Tadmor. It was there that 'Abd al-Malik b. Marwān decided to move against the usurper and, after having received an oath of allegiance from the people of Tadmor, fought and defeated al-Ḍaḥḥāk b. Qays at Marj Rāhiṭ, near Damascus, in 684 (al-Ṭabarī, *Tā'rīkh* 7.482; also see Ibn 'Asākir, *Tā'rīkh* 55.261).

After the battle at Marj Rāhiṭ, a conflict broke out between the Qays, who supported b. al-Zubayr during the conflict, and the pro-Umayyad Yemenites, among whom were the powerful members of the tribe of the Kalb in Palmyra. The feud broke out when Zufar b. al-Ḥārith, leader of the Qaysi Banū 'Amir attacked al-Muṣayyakh and massacred twenty Kalbites. To avenge the killing, the Banū Kalb murdered sixty members of the Banū Numayr who were living in Tadmor. One of the written sources to recount the event is al-Iṣfahānī (897–967). In two places in his *al-Aghānī* (17.112–113; 20.120–121), al-Iṣfahānī recounts how Ḥumayd b. Ḥurayth b. Baḥdal, who led the Kalbites, went to Tadmor, imprisoned the members of the Banū Numayr, and, in a moment of anger, ordered the prisoners to be killed, only to regret his action later. The reliability of al-Iṣfahānī's words cannot be proven with the archaeological data available; however, the discovery of two hoards in the heart of the ancient city would suggest at least that the city was going through a troubling period at that time, whether for these events or other causes (see Intagliata 2018b). The first metal hoard in order of discovery was brought to light in the Camp of Diocletian by the Polish team led by Michałowski in 1960. The assemblage consisted of six pieces of jewellery and twenty-seven gold coins, the latest dating to the mid-seventh century (Michałowski 1962, 60–66, 223–236; Skowronek, in Krzyżanowska 2014, 60–64). The second was found while excavating Church Street in the north-west quarter. It consists of two coin assemblages containing a total of over seven hundred issues, the latest being Islamic-Sassanian dirhams minted between 683 and 695 (Skowronek, in Krzyżanowska 2014, 71–120; Gawlikowski 2014).

The second event that saw Tadmor playing an important role in the political events of the time was a two-year rebellion that broke out in 745, and was led by Thābit b. Nuʿaym, the governor of Palestine, against Marwān. The caliph subdued the rebel cities one by one, including Homs, which had been reinforced by a contingent of Kalbites from Palmyra led by Dhuʾāla b. al-Aṣbagh b. Dhuʾāla al-Kalbī (al-Ṭabarī, *Taʾrīkh* 9.1892–1893), leaving Tadmor until last. According to al-Ṭabarī, the capitulation of Palmyra was achieved by treaty, thanks to the intercession of a Kalbite, a certain al-Abrash b. al-Walīd; al-Ṭabarī also reports that the caliph's first order was to raze the city walls to the ground. In contrast, Yāqūt (*Kitāb*, 1.829) reports that the city was taken by force and its inhabitants massacred. The archaeological record, which is extremely lacunose for this period, does not shed light on the fate of the city at that time. However, it is worth mentioning that no destruction layers associated with this event have been uncovered in the city centre so far and that the urban circuit wall still stands for most of its length.

As noted above, so far, archaeology has contributed relatively little to our understanding of Palmyra's history in the early Islamic period. The most representative compounds from this period are a mosque and a *suq*, an open market. The mosque was installed within the limits of a preexisting building—a *Caesareum?*—which had its south wall reorientated towards Mecca (Genequand 2008; 2012, 52–57; 2013). What is left of the early medieval *suq* of Palmyra, built between the end of the seventh century and the beginning of the eighth, is situated to the west of the *Tetrakionion* and includes forty-seven shops situated along the middle of the carriageway (al-Asʿad and Stępniowski 1989). The presence of a *suq* and a mosque in close topographical proximity is not new in the panorama of early Islamic cities and has important parallels in numerous cities in the East, such as at Jerash, Resafa, Anjar, and Amman (Genequand 2012, 64).

The establishment of the *suq*, and the consequent narrowing of the carriageway of the Great Colonnade, is one of the many clues suggesting that, in the early Islamic period, the gradual disintegration of the street grid and the privatization of urban space accelerated drastically. The Camp of Diocletian, which lost its military role, had its spaces invaded by squatters. Its *via Praetoria* narrowed considerably, but the traffic was not completely blocked, and the *Groma* was restructured to include at least four new dwellings (Michałowski 1960, 62–78; 1962, 64–77; 1963, 41–60). It was also at that time that new structures intruded into the northern courtyard of the sanctuary of Baalshamin (Intagliata 2016 with extensive bibliography). Existing private residential buildings were being partitioned into more, smaller rooms to accommodate more families. Rather than being a sign of the decline of the city's fortunes, such phenomena reflect a growing population's need to find space in which to settle and grow within the urban perimeter.

Epilogue: Life After the Umayyads in Palmyra

The collapse of the Umayyad dynasty was likely the primary cause of Palmyra's demise. The reason behind this may be found in the relations between the Umayyad dynasty and the Banū Kalb who, except for the Marwānid parenthesis, had always been strong supporters of the former. The Abbasid takeover coincided with the beginning of a bloody purge that saw most of the members of the Umayyad family and their allies brutally removed from the political scene. There were pro-Umayyad rebellions after the mid-eighth century, such as that of Abū al-Ward al-Kilābī and Abū Muḥammad al-Sufyānī in 750–751, in which the Kalbites of Tadmur took part (Cobb 2001, 46–48), but these did not help to revive the Umayyad prestige, which collapsed, together with that of the Banū Kalb. As it had supported the Umayyad dynasty, Palmyra's urban community may have been affected by this turmoil. However, the city centre seems to have been occupied until the early ninth century (Genequand 2008, 13), after which the settlement shrank into the precinct of the sanctuary of Bēl. There, it would mostly remain until the early 1930s, when French authorities ordered its relocation to a new town, modern Tadmor, beside the ancient site.

Abbreviations

ACO	Schwartz, Eduard, ed. 1914–1940. *Acta conciliorum oecumenicorum.* 4 vols. Strasbourg, de Gruyter.
CIS	*Corpus inscriptionum Semiticarum.* Paris: Reipublicæ Typographeo, 1881–1962.
IGLS XVII.1	Yon, Jean-Baptiste, ed. 2012. *Inscriptions grecques et latines de la Syrie: Palmyre.* Beirut: Presses de l'Institut français du Proche-Orient.

BIBLIOGRAPHY

Written Sources

Abū al-Fidā, *Taqwīm al-Buldān*, edited by Heinrich O. Fleischer. Leipzig: Vogel, 1831.

al-Balādhurī, *Futūḥ al-Buldān*, edited by Michael J. de Goeje. Leiden: Brill, 1866.

al-Iṣfahānī, *Kitāb al-Aghānī*, edited by Nasr al-Hurini. Cairo: Bulaq, 1867–1869.

al-Muqaddasī, *Aḥsan al-taqāsīm fī maʿrifat al-aqālīm*, edited by Michael J. de Goeje. Leiden: Brill, 1906.

al-Ṭabarī, *Tāʾrīkh al-rusul wa-al-mulūk*, edited by Michael J. de Goeje et al. Leiden: Brill, 1879–1901.

al-Wāqidī, *Kitāb al-Maghāzī*, edited by William Nassau Lees. Calcutta: F. Carbery, Bengal Military Orphan Press, 1854.

Ibn ʿAsākir, *Tāʾrīkh madīnat Dimashq*, edited by ʿUmar G. al-ʿAmrawi. Beirut: Dar al-Fikr, 1995–2000.

Chronicle of Zuqnīn, edited by Jean-Baptiste Chabot. Paris: Peeters, 1933.

Ḥamza al-Iṣfahānī, *Tāʾrīkh sinī mulūk al-arḍ waʾl-anbiyaʾ*, edited by and trans. Joseph M. E. Gottwald. Leipzig: Leopoldum Voss, 1844–1848.

Historia Augusta Vita Aureliani, edited and translated by François Pashoud. Paris: Les belles lettres, 1996.

John of Ephesus, *Ecclesiastical History*, edited by William Cureton. Oxford: Oxford University Press, 1853; *The Third Part of the Ecclesiastical History of John, Bishop of Ephesus*, translated by Payne R. Smith. Oxford: Oxford University Press, 1860.

John Malalas, *Chronographia*, edited by Ludwig A. Dindorf. Bonn: Weber, 1831; *The Chronicle of John Malalas: A Translation*, translated by Elizabeth Jeffreys, Michael Jeffreys, and Roger Scott. Melbourne: Australian Association for Byzantine Studies, 1986.

Michael the Syrian, *Chronicle*, edited and translated by Jean-Baptiste Chabot. Paris: Ernest Leroux, 1899–1910. Reprinted 2010.

Procopius, *De bellis*, edited by Jakob Haury. Leipzig: Teubner, 1963–1964.

Procopius, *De aedificiis*, edited and translated by Henry B. Dewing. London: William, 1961. Also see the more recent translation by Denis Roques. *Constructions de Justinien Ier: Peri ktismaton = De aedificiis*. Alessandria: Edizioni dell'Orso, 2011.

Theophanes, *Chronographia*, edited by Carolus de Boor. Leipzig: Teubner, 1884; *The Chronicle of Theophanes Confessor: Byzantine and Near Eastern History, A.D. 284–813*, translated by Cyril Mango and Roger Scott. Oxford: Clarendon Press, 1997.

Yāqūt, *Kitāb muʿjam al-buldān*, edited by Ferdinand Wüstenfeld. Leipzig: Brokhaus, 1866–1873.

Zosimus, *Historia nova*, edited and translated by François Paschoud. Paris: Les belles lettres, 2000.

Secondary Literature

al-Asʿad, Khaled, and Michał Gawlikowski. 1986–1987. 'New Honorific Inscriptions in the Great Colonnade of Palmyra'. *Annales archéologiques arabes syriennes* 36–37: 164–171.

al-Asʿad, Khaled, and Franciszek Stępniowski. 1989. 'The Umayyad Suq in Palmyra'. *Damaszener Mitteilungen* 4: 205–223.

al-As'ad, Khaled, and Erwin M. Ruprechtsberger. 1987. 'Palmyra in spätantiker, oströmischer (byzantinischer) und frühislamischer Zeit'. In *Palmyra: Geschichte, Kunst und Kultur der syrischen Oasenstadt*, edited by Erwin M. Ruprechtsberger, 137–148. Linz: Gutenberg.

Barański, Marek. 1994. 'The Roman Army in Palmyra: A Case of Adaptation of a Pre-existing City'. In *The Roman and Byzantine Army in the East: Proceedings of a Colloquium Held at the Jagiellonian University, Kraków in September 1992*, edited by Edward Dąbrowa, 9–17. Krakow: Drukarnia Uniwersytetu Jagiellońskiego.

Bounni, Adnan. 2004. *Le sanctuaire de Nabu: Texte*. Beirut: Institut d'archéologie du Proche-Orient.

Bounni, Adnan, Jacques Seigne, and Nassib Saliby. 1992/2004. *Le sanctuaire de Nabū à Palmyre. Planches* (1992); *Texte* (2004). Bibliothèque archéologique et historique 131. Paris: Geuthner.

Cobb, Paul M. 2001. *White Banners: Contention in 'Abbāsid Syria, 750–880*. Albany: State University of New York Press.

Dagron, Gilbert. 1977. 'Le christianisme dans la ville Byzantin'. *Dumbarton Oaks Papers* 51: 1–25.

Delplace, Christiane. 2013. 'Les recherches de la mission archéologique Française à Palmyre'. In *Fifty Years of Polish Excavations in Palmyra (1959–2009)*, edited by Michał Gawlikowski and Grzegorz Majcherek, 37–48. Studia Palmyreńskie 12. Warsaw: Wydawnictwa Uniwersytetu Warszawskiego.

Devreesse, Robert. 1945. *Le patriarcat d'Antioche: Depuis la paix de l'Eglise jusqu' à la conquête arabe*. Paris: Gabalda.

Donner, Fred M. 1981. *The Early Islamic Conquest*. Princeton, NJ: Princeton University Press.

Drijvers, Hendrik Jan Willem. 1982. 'The Persistence of Pagan Cults and Practices in Christian Syria'. In *East of Byzantium: Syria and Armenia in the Formative Period*, edited by Nina G. Garsoïan, Thomas F. Mathews, and Robert W. Thomson, 35–43. Washington, DC: Dumbarton Oaks, Center for Byzantine Studies.

Equini Schneider, Eugenia. 1993. *Septimia Zenobia Sebaste*. Rome: 'l'Erma' di Bretschneider.

Gąssowska, Barbara. 1982. 'Maternus Cynegius, Praefectus Praetorio Orientis and the Destruction of the Allat Temple in Palmyra'. *Archeologia: Rocznik Instytutu historii kultury materialnej Polskiej akademii nauk* 22: 107–123.

Gawlikowski, Michał. 1983. 'Réflexions sur la chronologie du sanctuaire d'Allat à Palmyre'. *Damaszener Mitteilungen* 1: 59–67.

Gawlikowski, Michał. 1990. 'Palmyra'. *Polish Archaeology in the Mediterranean* 1: 38–44.

Gawlikowski, Michał. 1999. 'Palmyra, Excavations 1998'. *Polish Archaeology in the Mediterranean* 10: 189–196.

Gawlikowski, Michał. 2000. 'Palmyra, Season 1999'. *Polish Archaeology in the Mediterranean* 11: 249–260.

Gawlikowski, Michal. 2001. 'Le groupe épiscopal de Palmyre'. In *Rome et ses province: genèse et diffusion d'une image du pouvoir: hommages à Jean-Charles Balty*, edited by Cécile Evers and Athéna Tsingarida, 119–127. Bruxelles: Le Livre Timperman.

Gawlikowski, Michał. 2004. 'Palmyra. Season 2003. Preliminary Report'. *Polish Archaeology in the Mediterranean* 15: 313–324.

Gawlikowski, Michał. 2014. 'Le trésor Sasanide'. In *Monnaies des fouilles Polonaises à Palmyre*, edited by Aleksandra Krzyżanowska and Michał Gawlikowski, 61–120. Studia Palmyreńskie 13. Warsaw: Wydawnictwa Uniwersytetu Warszawskiego.

Gawlikowski, Michał. 2017. *Le Sanctuaire d'Allat à Palmyre*. PAM Monograph Series 8. Warsaw: Polish Centre of Mediterranean Archaeology, University of Warsaw.

Gawlikowski, Michał. 2021. *Tadmor–Palmyra: A Caravan City Between East and West*. Bibliotheca artibus et historiae. Krakow: IRSA.

Genequand, Denis. 2006. 'Some Thoughts on Qasr al-Hayr al Gharbi, Its Dam, Its Monastery and the Ghassanids'. *Levant* 38: 63–84.

Genequand, Denis. 2008. 'An Early Islamic Mosque in Palmyra'. *Levant* 60: 3–15.

Genequand, Denis. 2012. *Les établissements des élites omeyyades en Palmyène et au Proche-Orient*. Beirut: Institut français du Proche-Orient.

Genequand, D. 2013. 'Between Rome and Islam: Recent Research on the So-Called Caesareum of Palmyra'. *Studia Palmireńskie* 12: 97–114.

Greatrex, Geoffrey, and Samuel N. C. Lieu. 2002. *The Roman Eastern Frontier and the Persian Wars*. Part 2, AD 363–630: *A Narrative Sourcebook*. London: Routledge.

Hartmann, Udo. 2001. *Das Palmyrenische Teilreich*. Stuttgart: Steiner.

Honigmann, Ernst. 1925. 'Studien zur Notitia Antiochena'. *Byzantinische Zeitschrift* 25: 60–88.

Intagliata, Emanuele E. 2015. 'Palmyra/Tadmur in Late Antiquity and Early Islam: An Archaeological and Historical Reassessment'. Unpublished doctoral thesis, University of Edinburgh.

Intagliata, Emanuele E. 2016. 'The Post-Roman Occupation of the Northern Courtyard of the Sanctuary of Baalshamin in Palmyra: A Reassessment of the Evidence Based on the Documents in the Fonds d'Archives Paul Collart, Université de Lausanne'. *Zeitschrift für Orientarchäologie* 9: 180–199.

Intagliata, Emanuele E. 2017. 'Palmyra and Its Ramparts During the Tetrarchy'. In *New Cities in Late Antiquity: Documents and Archaeology*, edited by Efthymios Rizos, 71–83. Turnhout: Brepols.

Intagliata, Emanuele E. 2018a. *Palmyra After Zenobia: An Archaeological and Historical Reappraisal*. Oxford: Oxbow.

Intagliata, Emanuele E. 2018b. 'Pinpointing Unrest at Palmyra in the Early Islamic Period: The Evidence from Coin Hoards and Written Sources'. *Études et travaux* 31: 183–196.

Jalabert, Louis, and René Mouterde, eds. 1959. *Inscriptions grecques et latines de la Syrie*. Vol. 5, *Emésène*. Paris: Geuthner.

Jastrzębowska, Elżbieta. 2013. 'La christianisation de Palmyre: L'exemple du temple de Bel'. *Studia Palmireńskie* 12: 177–192.

Juchniewicz, Karol. 2013. 'Late Roman Fortifications in Palmyra'. *Studia Palmireńskie* 12: 193–202.

Kowalski, Sławomir P. 1996. 'Doubtful Christian Reutilization of the Baalshamin Temple in Palmyra'. *Damaszener Mitteilungen* 9: 217–226.

Kowalski, Sławomir P. 1997. 'Late Roman Palmyra in Literature and Epigraphy'. *Studia Palmireńskie* 10: 39–62.

Krzyżanowska, Aleksandra. 2014. 'Monnaies grecques et romaines'. In *Monnaies des fouilles Polonaises à Palmyre*, edited by Aleksandra Krzyżanowska and Michał Gawlikowski, 13–70. Studia Palmireńskie 13. Warsaw: Wydawnictwa Uniwersytetu Warszawskiego.

Le Quien, Michel. 1740. *Oriens christianus, in quatuor patriarchatus digestus quo exhibentur ecclesiae, patriarchae, caeterique praesules totius orientis*. Paris: Ex typographia regia.

Lewin, Ariel S. 2007. 'Amr ibn 'Adi, Mavia, the Phylarchs and the Late Roman Army: Peace and War in the Near East'. In *The Late Roman Army in the Near East from Diocletian to the Arab*

Conquest: Proceedings of a Colloquium Held at Potenza, Acerenza and Matera, Italy (May 2005), edited by Ariel S. Lewin and Pietrina Pellegrini, 243–262. Oxford: Archaeopress.

Majcherek, Grzegorz. 2005. 'More Churches from Palmyra: An Inkling of the Late Antique City'. In *Aux pays d'Allat: Mélanges offerts à Michal Gawlikowski*, edited by Piotr Bieliński and Franciszek M. Stępniowski, 141–150. Warsaw: Instytut Archeologii Uniwersytet.

Majcherek, Grzegorz. 2013. 'Excavating the Basilicas'. *Studia Palmyreńskie* 12: 251–268.

Mansi, Gian Domenico. 1759–1798. *Sacrorum conciliorum nova et amplissima collectio*. Florence, Venice: Apud Antonii Zatta.

Michałowski, Kazimierz. 1960. *Palmyre*. Vol. 1, *Fouilles Polonaises, 1959*. Warsaw: Państwowe Wydawnictwo Naukowe.

Michałowski, Kazimierz. 1962. *Palmyre*. Vol. 2, *Fouilles Polonaises, 1960*. Warsaw: Państwowe Wydawnictwo Naukowe.

Michałowski, Kazimierz. 1963. *Palmyre*. Vol. 3, *Fouilles Polonaises, 1961*. Warsaw: Państwowe Wydawnictwo Naukowe.

Millar, Fergus. 2013. 'A Syriac Codex from Near Palmyra and the 'Ghassanid' Abokarib'. *Hugoye: Journal of Syriac Studies* 16(1): 15–35.

Saradi, Hélène. 2008. 'Towns and Cities'. In *The Oxford Handbook of Byzantine Studies*, edited by Elizabeth Jeffreys, John Haldon, and Robin Cormack, 317–327. Oxford: Oxford University Press.

Seland, Eivind Heldaas. 2016. *Ships of the Desert and Ships of the Sea: Palmyra in the World Trade of the First Three Centuries CE*. Philippika 101. Wiesbaden: Harrassowitz.

Schlumberger, Daniel. 1939. 'Les fouilles de Qasr el-Heir el-Gharbi (1936–1938): Rapport préliminaire'. *Syria* 20: 197–238, 325–373.

Schlumberger, Daniel. 1986. *Qasr el-Heir el Gharbi*. Paris: P.Geuthner.

Schmidt-Colinet, Andreas, Khaled al-As'ad, and Waleed al-As'ad. 2013. 'Thirty Years of Syro-German/Austrian Archaeological Research at Palmyra'. In *Fifty Years of Polish Excavations in Palmyra, 1959–2009: International Conference Warsaw, 6–8 December 2010*, edited by Michał Gawlikowski and Grzegorz Majcherek, 299–318. Studia Palmyreńskie 12. Warsaw: Wydawnictwa Uniwersytetu Warszawskiego.

Schnädelbach, Klaus. 2010. *Topographia Palmyrena*. Vol. 1, *Topography*. Documents d'archéologie syrienne 18. Bonn: Habelt.

Sellers, Robert V. 1953. *The Council of Chalcedon: A Historical and Doctrinal Survey*. London: Society for Promoting Christian Knowledge.

Seyrig, Henri. 1940. 'Rapport sommaire sur les fouilles de l'agora de Palmyre'. *Comptes rendus des séances de l'Académie des inscriptions et belles-lettres* 84: 237–249.

Skowronek, Stefan. 1962. 'Un trésor byzantin'. In *Monnaies des fouilles Polonaises à Palmyre*, edited by Aleksandra Krzyżanowska and Michał Gawlikowski, 60–64. Studia Palmyreńskie 13. Warsaw: Wydawnictwa Uniwersytetu Warszawskiego.

Stoneman, Richard. 1992. *Palmyra and Its Empire: Zenobia's Revolt Against Rome*. Ann Arbor: University of Michigan Press.

Vailhé, Simeon. 1907. 'La 'Notitia episcopatuum' d'Antioche du patriarche Anastase, VIᵉ siècle'. *Échos d'Orient* 10: 139–145, 363–368.

Will, Ernest. 1966. 'Le sac de Palmyre'. In *Mélanges d'archéologie et d'histoire offerts á André Piganiol*, edited by Raymond Chevallier, 1409–1416. Ecole pratique des Hautes études, VIᵉ section. Paris: SEVPEN

Wright, William. 1872. *Catalogue of the Syriac Manuscripts in the British Museum*. London: Order of the Trustees of the British Museum.

Żuchowska, Marta. 2000. 'Quelques remarques sur la grande colonnade á Palmyre'. *Bulletin d'études orientales* 52: 187–193.

Żuchowska, Marta. 2006. 'Palmyra. Excavations 2002–2005 (insula E by the Great Colonnade). Preliminary report'. *Polish Archaeology in the Mediterranean* 17: 439–450.

CHAPTER 9

PALMYRA IN LATE ANTIQUE AND MEDIEVAL TIMES

SŁAWOMIR P. KOWALSKI

FALL OF A TRADE CENTRE, RISE OF A FORTRESS

THE defeat of Zenobia by Aurelian marked a decline for the flourishing municipality that Palmyra had been. Indeed, the army of Aurelian captured the city twice, in 272 (Février 1931, 132–135) and in 273 (Février 1931, 140–141) as reported in the *Life of Aurelian* (*HA Aurel*. 31.5–9; Dodgeon and Lieu 1991, 102) and in the *Historia nova* by Zosimus (Zos. 1.61; Dodgeon and Lieu 1991, 103, 107). Both sources recount a pillage of the temple of the Sun by the soldiers of the Legio III Cyrenaica. The spoils, according to Zosimus, were placed in the temple of the Sun (*sol invictus*) erected in Rome (Watson 1999, 191–192).

The identification of the temple of the Sun in Palmyra, mentioned in the texts, is not obvious (Kaizer 2002, 154–155; Dirven 1999, 169, n. 49). It could have been the temple of Bēl, as the most eminent (Will 1992, 196), or the temple of Malakbel and Aglibol, solar and lunar companions of Baalshamin (Will 1966, 1410), as an altar in the Capitoline Museum in Rome depicting Malakbel with an inscription in Latin and Aramaic and referring to the god as *sol sanctissimus*, might suggest (Dirven 1999, 176–179; Teixidor 1979, 47–48). The temple of Malakbel and Aglibol has not yet been found, but some inscriptions mention it as 'the Sacred Garden': in Aramaic, GNT' 'LYM, or in Greek, ἱερὸν ἄλσος (Gawlikowski 1973, 49; Kaizer 2002, 124–143). Texts also allude to the cult of the sun in Palmyra, possibly with a temple in the western quarter. (Hillers and Cussini 1996, 75: *PAT* 0325; Gawlikowski 1973, 100; Yon 2012, 130, inscr. 120, 269–270, inscr. 320, 300, inscr. 376; Kaizer 2002, 154–157). Thus, in Palmyra the cult of the sun seemed to be associated with more than one god, and therefore it remains difficult to identify the pillaged temple beyond doubt (Teixidor 1979, 29–52).

The cult of Malakbel, whose name means the 'angel of Bēl' (Kaizer 2002, 140), became known in the Roman military milieu through soldiers who originated from or had served in Palmyra (Watson 1999, 193–196; Dirven 1999, 181–183; Turcan 2004, 172). Thus the troops of Legio III Cyrenaica were more likely to recognize Sol in Malakbel (Kaizer 2002, 140), and the attribution must have been driven by Aurelian's religious policy and the cult's familiarity in the Roman army (Watson 1999, 188–196). Two fourth-century inscriptions from Egypt indicate that, among the Syrian soldiers of Legio III Gallica and Legio I Illyricorum, Malakbel and Aglibol were venerated as angels (i.e., mediators between the human and divine worlds in private and personal piety; Kowalski 1998, 192–194; Cline 2011, 59–60; Cumont 1915, 161). Cumont explains the inscriptions' invocation of Tyche of angels in the context of astrology and the belief that fortune is determined by stars (Cumont 1915, 175, n. 2). Malakbel and Aglibol were also linked with the Anonymous God, probably an aspect of Baalshamin, who, in accordance with epigraphic evidence, was accompanied by two angels (Kaizer 2002, 140–142; Teixidor 1979, 34–52; Dirven 1999, 166–169; Hillers and Cussini 1996, 87; *PAT* 0406; Milik 1972, 195–200). The cult of the Anonymous God, very private and personal, was associated with that of Zeus *hypsistos*, characterized by affinities to Jewish traditions and the veneration of angels (Teixidor 1979, 115–116; Dirven 1999, 171–174; Kaizer 2010, 118–120; Mitchell 1999, 102–104; Cline 2011, 53–56).

In 302, Avitus, an officer of the otherwise unknown rank of *optio princeps* (Fellmann 1995, 240) offered an altar with a dedication to Zeus *hypsistos* and *epekoos* which was found in the temple of Baalshamin (Kowalski 1997, 45; Kowalski 1998, 191–192; Yon 2012, 163–164, inscr. 154). His name could be a Latin or a Greek adaptation of a Semitic name 'WYDW. It is reasonable to assume that he served in the Legio I Illyricorum, if at the time the unit was stationed in Palmyra, as later sources indicate (*Not. Dign. Or.* 32.30). Fellmann suggested that the dedication could have been made in relation to Diocletian's prosecution of Christian army officers (Fellmann 1995, 240). It is also possible that Avitus truly venerated Zeus *hypsistos* and his angels, as did his colleagues in the legion's detachment in Upper Egypt. The cult of Malakbel and Aglibol had a tradition in the Roman military milieu of oriental descent (Turcan 2004, 171–173) and was further strengthened by Aurelian's religious policies, which were intended to incorporate the defeated Palmyra into his unified empire (Watson 1999, 188–196)—a reasonable policy if Aurelian is to be credited with garrisoning the Legio I Illyricorum in Palmyra. Many followers of Zeus *hypsistos* linked their cult with the worship of the sun (Mitchell 1999, 124).

Whichever temple in Palmyra was looted by Aurelian's soldiers, according to Aurelian's letter to Cerrenius Bassus (*HA Aurel.* 31.5–9), it was to be restored. This source is doubtful and rhetorical. The author might well have confused the restoration of the temple in Palmyra with the erection of the temple of the Sun in Rome (Kowalski 1997, 41).

Some objects discovered during archaeological excavations by the Polish team in 2003 could be related to the plunder (Gawlikowski 2004, 232). The destruction, however, might have been less extensive than generally thought. The priestly confraternity of Bēl continued to function, presided over by Septimius Ḥaddudan, a Roman senator, mentioned in two inscriptions dated to March 272 and March 273 (Hillers and Cussini 1996, 200: *PAT* 1358, 328: *PAT* 2812; Milik 1972, 270; Gawlikowski 1973, 76–78; Kaizer 2002, 232–233). According to the later inscription, in Gawlikowski's restoration, he provided assistance to Aurelian (Gawlikowski 1973, 78; Watson 1999, 81). Funerary customs continued as well. An inscription of 274 in the tomb of Malku in the south-western necropolis records the cession of five niches (Hillers and Cussini 1996, 31: *PAT* 0055). In the same area, the hypogeum of Dionysos was opened in 333, as a Greek inscription informs us (Yon 2012, 394, inscr. 527). Two column consoles inscribed in Greek and Aramaic refer to a reconstruction of the great basilica of Ares/Arsu, probably a portico of the colonnaded street leading from the city centre towards the temple of Arsu across the Wadi as-Suraysir (al-Asʿad and Gawlikowski 1986, 167–168, inscr. 7–8; Yon 2012, 95–97, inscr. 80–81). One of these is dated to 279/280 according to Gawlikowski. Yon, however, argued for 179/180.

About half a century later, Flavius Diogenes covered a portico of eight columns of the Great Colonnade with a roof, as recorded in the inscription on a column shaft dated to September 328 (Cantineau 1930, 34–35, inscr. 27; Kowalski 1997, 45–46; Yon 2012, 116–117, inscr. 103). The portico, as the text affirms, had been in ruins for a long time. Traces of the restoration were identified during the archaeological excavations near a basilica, transformed into a church in the course of the sixth century (Gawlikowski 1998, 209–210). The inscription also provides important information about the status of the city, since Flavius Diogenes, son of Uranios, is presented as λογιστής, that is, *curator rei publicae* or *curator civitatis* (Jones 1964, 726), an imperial government official initially responsible for regulating city finances but, by the fourth century, administrating practically all aspects of municipal activity. Thus Palmyra maintained the status of a city (Yon 2012, 117).

The portico restoration was a municipal contribution to a project begun some thirty years earlier under the Tetrarchy, one that is essential to understand the new role of Palmyra (Kowalski 1997, 44–47). It resulted in the construction of a military camp to the west of the city, the restoration of an earlier bathhouse in the centre, the erection of the walls or the strengthening of the existing fortifications, and, outside Palmyra, the creation of a military infrastructure along the route network known as Strata Diocletiana (Dunand 1931; Mouterde 1930; Bauzou 1993; Bauzou 2000). This project caused many earlier buildings in Palmyra to be robbed of their architectural elements, which were dismantled and reassembled as parts of entirely new buildings.

The Tetrarchy project either resulted in the reduction of the city space or represents an accommodation to a city space which had already been reduced. The dating of the inner city walls is crucial for determining when the area across the wadi was abandoned and the ramparts along the riverbed erected. The inner walls of Palmyra, studied by von Gerkan, Crouch, and, recently, Syrian archaeologists, were protected by ninety-eight towers, including twenty-three rounded towers as well as nine tombs adapted for defence and incorporated into the ramparts, the most recent of the tombs dated by an inscription of 215 (von Gerkan 1935; Crouch 1975, 12, 30; Juchniewicz et al. 2010; Hammad 2010,

115–117; Yon 2012, 342, inscr. 445). Some rounded towers were added to the rectangular fortifications, and some covered the earlier buttress towers (Crouch 1975, 13). The inner walls are generally attributed to the reign of Diocletian (Seyrig 1950; van Berchem 1954; Gawlikowski 1974; Crouch 1975), although dating to the reign of Zenobia was also advanced (von Gerkan 1935). Seyrig suggested that the rounded towers should be credited to Justinian, based on Procopius's report (Seyrig 1950, 242; Procop., *Aed.* 2.11 and 5.1). This was questioned by Juchniewicz who, on the basis of analysing masonry styles and parallels, proposed attributing the defences with rectangular towers to Aurelian (whom he also credited with the installation of the Legio I Illyricorum in Palmyra) and those with rounded towers to Diocletian (Juchniewicz 2013, 194–195; *Not. Dign. Or.* 32.30). Intagliata distinguished two or three types of interventions based on the Italian archaeological documentation and the study of construction techniques (Intagliata 2017a). He also upheld the dating of the rounded towers to the Tetrarchy, suggesting that this was a strengthening of the earlier fortifications which had suffered considerable destruction prior to the 290s/300s, presumably during the siege by Aurelian's army (Intagliata 2017a, 78–79). Intagliata rejects Juchniewicz's attribution of the defences and the camp to Aurelian, citing in particular the construction techniques of the northern gate of the camp in line with the Via Principalis (Kowalski 1998, 195–199), the gate that must have been planned from the very beginning of this military project and whose opening was pierced through the earlier wall (Intagliata 2017a, 79–80). The dating of the inner ramparts to 215–272 means that the southern part of the city across the wadi must have been abandoned before the fall of Palmyra to Aurelian, probably because it was too difficult to defend it effectively.

Two inscriptions, one in Latin and the other in Greek, credit Sossianus Hierocles, governor of the province and known for his anti-Christian sentiments (Barnes 1976), with construction of the military camp and the completion of the baths, named in the Greek text 'Diocletian's bath'—τὸ Διοκλητιανὸν βαλανῖον (Cantineau 1931, 7–8, inscr. 2; Seyrig 1931, 321–323; Kowalski 1997, 44–45; Yon 2012, 112–114, inscr. 100). Both are dated to 293–303, after the proclamation of Tetrarchy and before Hierocles became governor of Bithynia (Cantineau 1931, 8; Yon 2012, 114; Barnes 1976, 243–245). The camp was founded to the west of the Transverse Colonnade, where the temple of Allat was located, which was incorporated into the new military installation but remained in use (Gawlikowski 1977). The camp was separated from the city by the Transverse Colonnade and was accessed through a monumental gate (Porta Praetoria) leading, through a porticoed street (Via Praetoria), to the headquarters (the Principia), a large edifice with a court (Gawlikowski 1984; Kowalski 1998, 195–207). The enclosure of the temple of Allat was adjusted to the line of the Via Principalis, which crossed the Via Praetoria at a right angle, and the crossing was marked with a monumental *groma* (Gawlikowski 1983, 65; Kowalski 1998, 199–200). There were barracks on the sides of both streets (Kowalski 1998, 204–205) and a granary (*horreum*) adjoining the ramparts to the south (Gawlikowski 1986; Kowalski 1998, 203–204). When the temple of Allat was destroyed shortly after 380 (Gawlikowski 1983, 60), a house was built in the south-eastern corner of the temple enclosure to serve as a residence for the commanding officer (the

Praetorium), manifestly a Christian at the time since the lintel of the residence's main door, made of a reused column shaft, had a cross chiselled out of it (Kowalski 1994, 48, 52–53, plate XIX.2).

Contemporaneously, Sossianus Hierocles carried out a restoration of an earlier bathhouse in the centre, constructed probably at the end of the second century (Vannesse 2015, 115–117; Yon 2012, 112–114, inscr. 100). Yon, after Barnes, notes that the inscription mentioned two names of the officials, one of them missing, probably *vicarius orientis* (Barnes 1976, 243; Yon 2012, 114). The bath was an edifice of imperial style, emphasized by the addition of a monumental portico with granite columns (Vannesse 2015, 117).

Seyrig noted that the governor chose the language of his inscriptions carefully: Latin for that in the military camp and Greek for the other in a civilian context, as the bath served the local population (Seyrig 1931, 323). Interestingly, the last inscriptions in Aramaic date to shortly after the capture of the city by Aurelian. Later inscriptions are very few: one in Latin in the military milieu, the rest in Greek. Palmyra was no longer the creation of local elites, but a frontier garrison town with little to honour in the form of inscriptions. The texts that remained were mostly funerary dedications or expressions of religious sentiments (Kowalski 1997, 45–57; Yon 2012, 55–56, 118, 374–382, inscr. 47–48, 106–108, 494–511). Municipal institutions were overshadowed by the imperial government, interested in a fortified zone along the route linking the Euphrates with Palestine and Arabia and known as Strata Diocletiana (Ioannes Malalas, *Chr.* 12.40; van Berchem 1952, 10–24; Bauzou 2000; Lewin 2015, 159–166). This programme also included a reform of the army and a new allocation of military units, begun by Diocletian and completed under Constantine (van Berchem 1952). *Notitia dignitatum*, a list of government and military institutions whose section on the Eastern Empire was compiled at the end of the fourth century (Ward 1974, 414), generally reflects the disposition of the troops of the eastern frontier after Jovian's treaty with the Persians of 363 (Dodgeon and Lieu 1991, 340). Palmyra is mentioned there as the seat of *praefectus legionis primae Illyricorum* (*Not. Dign. Or.* 32.30), subordinate in the chain of command to *dux Foenicis* (*Not. Dign. Or.* 32.17). Two units probably formed by Palmyrenes are also listed: a mobile army unit (*vexillatio comitatensis*) of heavy cavalry (Cuneus equitum secundum clibanariorum Palmirenorum) under *magister militum per Orientem* (*Not. Dign. Or.* 7.34) and a cavalry squadron (Ala octava equitum Palmyrenorum) stationed in Laqeita/Phoinikon (*Phoenicionis*) under *dux Thebaidos* (*Not. Dign. Or.* 31.49) in Upper Egypt, where two fourth-century inscriptions mentioning soldiers of Legio I Illyricorum were found, in Aswan and in Koptos (Kowalski 1998, 192–194). A fragmentary inscription in Greek, stored in the Museum of Palmyra, in tufa stone from outside Palmyra, mentions Flavius Platanius Serenianus, *vir perfectissimus, dux orientis*, and is dated between 325 and the reign of emperor Valentinian I (Kowalski 1997, 46; Yon 2012, 297, inscr. 366). It could refer to Serenianus, native of Pannonia, mentioned by Ammianus Marcellinus as *dux Phoenicis* before 354 (Amm. Marc. 14.7.7–8; Kowalski 1997, 46; Lewin 2015, 165–166). This inscription could be linked to an unknown military project under the supervision of Serenianus.

As Cantineau explained, scholars named the military base in Palmyra the 'Camp of Diocletian' because of the inscription commemorating its foundation (Cantineau 1931, 3). The name is not attested in any of the ancient sources. It does however follow a trend exemplified by the bath's name—Diocletian's bath—mentioned in the inscription from Palmyra and also by the name given to a contemporary bathhouse in Antioch (Yon 2012, 114; Ioannes Malalas, *Chr.* 12.38). The Tetrarchic fortified network of desert routes passing through Palmyra is marked by a number of milestones bearing varied names and spelling: Strata Diocletiana, Istra(ta) Diocletiani et Maximiani, Ctrata Diocletiani, suggesting that, rather than the proper name of the road, 'Strata Diocletiana' is a common noun denoting the infrastructure (Bauzou 2000, 81–83). Thus crediting Diocletian with various constructions must have been common already in the early fourth century, in particular in relation to the frontier reorganized under the supervision of Sossianus Hierocles.

The development of the city in the fourth century as a military stronghold follows the lines in urban development traced in the preceding period. The restorations along the Great Colonnade were carried out in continuity with the project started in the second century and carried on in the third, which moved the main axis of the town from the riverbed to the new artery traced along the ancient city wall (Gawlikowski 1974, 235–236; Will 1983, 79–81). Palmyra, under state management, became a typical provincial town among many of late Roman Syria or Phoenicia. The ascent of Christianity strengthened this drift.

Throughout the fifth and the sixth centuries, Palmyra continued to play its role. Its municipal status is confirmed by an inscription of 469 mentioning Maranios, son of Maneos ἐκδικός, that is, *defensor civitatis* (Kowalski 1997, 49–50; Yon 2012, 375–376, inscr. 496). This magistrate, in the fourth century responsible for protecting the townspeople against fiscal extortion and oppression by the powerful, as well as having some judicial duties, by the fifth century came to perform the tasks of the *decuriones* (Jones 1964, 726–727).

Palmyra's military importance was crucial in Justinian's reorganization of the frontier defences in view of the new threats posed by the conflict with Persia (Kowalski 1997, 50–52; Lewin 2015, 170; Greatrex and Lieu 2002, 85). In 527, the emperor sent *comes orientis* Patricius with funds to restore Palmyra and settled the *dux* or provincial commander from Emesa there with a *numerus* or company of soldiers in addition to the frontier troops that had already been stationed there (Ioannes Malalas, *Chr.* 18.2; Theophanes, *Chronographia I*, edited by Carl de Boor, Leipzig: Teubner 1883, 174; Procop., *Aed.* 2.11 and 5.1). Malalas informs us that churches and public buildings were restored, and Procopius adds to this restoration programme a water supply (Juchniewicz and Żuchowska 2012, 67) and fortifications. The transfer of the seat of *dux Phoenicis* from Emesa to Palmyra, also recorded by Theophanes, together with a mobile unit (*comitatenses*), was certainly connected with new security arrangements where, in the context of threat of Persian invasions, every provincial commander (*dux*) was assisted by Arab allies led by a phylarch (Lewin 2015, 169–170). Stein, interpreting a note by Malalas, argued that, in 527, the command of *dux Phoenicis* had been divided between two *duces*, one in Emesa transferred to Palmyra and the other in Damascus (Stein 1949, 289; Ioannes Malalas, *Chr.* 18.26). According to Shahid, Justinian was concerned to protect Palestine and Jerusalem, especially after the Persian ally Mundhir the Nasrid raided Emesa and Apamea in 527, moving his troops by the route from Palmyra (Shahid 1995, 79–80, 172–174). The emperor wanted his units to be able to intercept Mundhir's forces at Palmyra in order to prevent any further penetrations. Therefore, two years later, Harith the Jafnid became *archiphylarchos* and was vested with supreme command over all the Byzantine Arab allies (Edwell et al. 2015, 233; Lewin 2015, 169–174; Greatrex 2015, 123). It is not clear whether the new arrangement lasted longer than Justinian's wars against the Persians, but it certainly contributed to strengthening of the influence of the Arab allies around Palmyra. The division of powers between the Arab allies and the state military government remains unclear. Indeed, in reference to the events of 541, Procopius reported two *duces* from Phoenicia Libanensis: Recithancus and Theoctistus (Procop., *Pers.* 2.16.17), one of them possibly still residing in Palmyra. Later, during the campaign of the Emperor Maurice and the battle of Solachon in 586, the Byzantine generals included Eiliphredas, *dux Phoenicis* from Emesa (Theophylactus Simocatta, *Historiae*, 2.3, edited by Carl de Boor, Leipzig: Teubner, 1887, 73). Thus Palmyra might have no longer been the seat of the provincial military command. The battle, however, occurred after the disintegration of the Jafnid federation and the arrest of Nu'man the Jafnid, as ordered by the Emperor Maurice in 582 (Greatrex 2015, 132–141), which could have resulted in a change of the provincial command structure.

After the peace treaty of 532, Mundhir the Nasrid showed his discontent with the Jafnids' control of the land south of Palmyra as described by Procopius in what is often referred to as the 'Strata dispute' (Procop., *Pers.* 2.1.1–15; Shahid 1995, 209–218). The area, called 'Strata' by Procopius in clear reference to the network of routes and forts set up under the Tetrarchy, was a boundary land claimed by the Arab allies of both competing empires. In Procopius's opinion, this stretch of land was useless for agriculture and fit only for pasture (Procop., *Pers.* 2.I.6). The Persian king Chosroes used this conflict as a pretext to begin the war in 540.

Archaeological research confirms that the Principia in the Camp of Diocletian underwent some rebuilding in the course of the sixth century, probably after a fire (Gawlikowski 1984, 43–45; Kowalski 1998, 201). The *horreum* was also destroyed and rebuilt in the sixth century, as the archaeological finds suggest (Gawlikowski 1986, 399). Perhaps both these rebuilding initiatives should be credited to *comes* Patricius. At the end of the sixth century or the beginning of the seventh, Palmyra must have been affected by an earthquake, which destroyed the Praetorium (Kowalski 1994, 57–58). The last stage of occupation of the granary, not related to its initial function, is dated by the finds of coins of the Emperor Heraclius (Gawlikowski 1986, 399). When the Muslim army of Khalid b. al-Walid arrived at Palmyra in 634, the city surrendered, although some Arab sources, namely al-Kufi and al-Baladhuri, related the story of a siege and fierce opposition by the Byzantine garrison (Genequand 2012, 40). The conquest by the Muslim army ended Palmyra's role as a garrison frontier town.

CHRISTIANITY IN PALMYRA

The Christian community in Palmyra must have been established by 325, when the local bishop participated in the Council of Nicaea (Kowalski 1997, 45). The earliest dated Christian funerary inscription was executed in 442; others followed in 463 and 469 (Kowalski 1997, 49–50). After 380, in the Camp of Diocletian, a limestone lintel with a chiselled cross was placed over the entrance to the Praetorium (Kowalski 1994, 48, 52–53, plate XIX.2), built upon the ruins of the temple of Allat. The policy of the destruction of pagan temples, supported by Maternus Cynegius, praetorian prefect of the East, in execution of the anti-pagan laws of 381 and 385 (Jones 1964, 167) was certainly carried out inside the military base without any public disorder. The temple inside the camp could not have been accessed without restrictions. Some soldiers, in particular of Palmyrene origin, could have been observants of the local cults, especially that of the Anonymous God, identified with Zeus *hypsistos* and his angels. Allat, possibly perceived as Minerva (Kaizer 2010, 121, n. 46), might have fit into the military religious context before the anti-pagan laws were enforced.

The cult of the Anonymous God, in the opinion of Ted Kaizer (Kaizer 2010, 119), might help to explain a comment in the *Life of Alexander the Acoemete* (*Vie d'Alexandre l'Acémète* 1911). The biography of the saint, who lived in Syria in 397/398–427/428, was written towards the end of the fifth century (Gatier 1995, 439; Kaizer 2010, 115). He stayed with a number of monks in the desert, where for three years he was assisted by Roman soldiers, probably in Rasafa or Oriza, modern Tayyibe (Gatier 1995, 453; Kowalski 1997, 48). After three years of drought, the camp was destroyed by nomads in search of food and the saint, together with his company, travelled on to Palmyra, where the inhabitants did not receive him since they were not willing to share their resources to feed such a large group. The saint and his company then had to remain in the desert outside the city, where they were aided by nomads. The author of the hagiography comments on the lack of hospitality of the inhabitants of Palmyra, who, in his opinion, were Jews who called themselves Christians (*Vie d'Alexandre l'Acémète*, 685–686). He also notes that the city was mentioned in the Book of Kings as founded by King Solomon (1 Kgs 9:15–19; Starcky and Gawlikowski 1985, 34–35). The foundation of Palmyra by King Solomon, a myth resulting from a misinterpretation, might be a reason enough to perceive the Palmyrenes as Jews, probably not a compliment in the context of uneasy relations between Christians and Jews at the time (Millar 2006, 392). Kaizer's hypothesis that the comment might also be related to the cult of Zeus *hypsistos* due to its affinities with Jewish traditions and, in a wider context, of hints at a Jewish community in Palmyra is certainly interesting (Kaizer 2010; Mitchell 1999, 110–121). It is also worth noting that the inhospitable inhabitants of Palmyra are contrasted with compassionate nomads, a rhetorical figure of religious value. Thus the biography confirms the role of monks in spreading Christianity among the nomads and might give some insight into the complex relations between nomadic and settled peoples, also reflected in the division of military power between Roman duces and Arab phylarchs in the fifth and sixth centuries (Charles 2012, 35–50; Hoyland 2001, 96–102; Lewin 2015, 167–174).

John, bishop of Palmyra, is mentioned in two documents of 451 and 457 (Kowalski 1997, 48). In 518, Emperor Justin exiled John II, bishop of Palmyra, a supporter of Severus, patriarch of Antioch and his criticism of the Council of Chalcedon (Kowalski 1997, 50). The bishops of Palmyra at the end of the sixth century and in the seventh century were 'Monophysites' (Millar 2013b, 51–52; Fischer et al. 2015, 279) whose patrons were the Jafnids (Kowalski 1997, 52–53; Millar 2013; Fischer et al. 2015, 281). Bishops Simeon and John III were ordained in 793 and 818, respectively (Charles 2012, 79, 81).

Four large churches, forming an episcopal complex, were located north of the nearby portico of the Great Colonnade, restored in 328 by Flavius Diogenes (Gawlikowski 1998; 2001; 2002; 2003; Majcherek 2005; 2013). One of these was an adaptation of a second-century public building poorly suited to the purpose. Three other churches have a standard basilican plan with a central nave and two aisles, though one of them (Basilica II) was also an adaptation of an earlier structure. Basilica III, founded in the fifth century and restored under the Emperor Justinian, was probably the cathedral (Gawlikowski 2002, 263; 2003, 284). Basilica IV, the largest, was erected as part of Justinian's project (Majcherek 2012, 468). Basilica II was modified in Umayyad times, which proves the continuity of the cult after the advent of Islam (Gawlikowski 1998, 205–206).

In the sixth century, the cella of Bēl was turned into a church, probably dedicated to the Virgin Mary, who is depicted on a fresco partly preserved and referred to in an invocation by Lazaros painted on the wall (Jastrzębowska 2013, 181; Kowalski 1997, 57, inscr. 14). St. Sergius was also honoured in the church. The church went out of use before 729, as an Arabic graffito on the wall of the cella indicates (Cantineau 1933, 51, inscr. 39). The transformation of the cella of Baalshamin into a church as suggested by Paul Collart, who excavated the temple, has been questioned (Kowalski 1996); late habitations in the main court of the temple have been thoroughly reanalysed (Intagliata 2017b).

Three more churches have been identified in Palmyra, two in the city centre and one at the western extremity of the Great Colonnade (Majcherek 2005). The latter, due to its proximity to a side entrance to the military base, might have served the needs of the army.

Churches certainly constituted the most impressive, if not the only, public buildings constructed in Byzantine Palmyra.

PALMYRA IN THE TIMES OF ISLAM

The city's capture by the Muslim army in 634 marked a significant change (Genequand 2012, 45–46; Gawlikowski 2008). In the succession conflict following the death of the Caliph Yazid, the inhabitants of Palmyra rallied behind Marwan b. al-Hakam against the Qays confederation. The inquietude is confirmed by two treasures of coins found in the Camp of Diocletian and the episcopal complex (Michałowski 1962, 222–236;

Gawlikowski 2002, 266–269). Palmyra's defences were partly destroyed in 744–745, as a result of the city's support for Sulayman b. Hisham against the caliph Marwan b. Muhammad (Genequand 2012, 46). In 750, the town was besieged for giving shelter to the leader of the pro-Umayyad revolt, Abu Muhammad al-Sufyani.

In Umayyad Palmyra, in addition to the churches, new public buildings appear: a mosque and an oriental market or *suq* (Genequand 2012, 52–63; Genequand 2013; al-As'ad and Stępniowski 1989). The *suq* of Palmyra was located in the course of the Great Colonnade, where a section of forty-seven shops erected in the seventh/eighth century was unearthed west of the Tetrapylon without reaching the western extremity of the complex (al-As'ad and Stępniowski 1989, 206). The earlier shops of the northern side of the colonnaded street were reoccupied (al-As'ad and Stępniowski 1989, 222). The structure was in use up to the Abbasid period.

The mosque was built to the west of the theatre as an adaptation of an edifice of the Severan period (Genequand 2012, 52–63; 2013). The earlier hypostyle room was used as a prayer hall, with the *qibla* wall adjusted to the orientation towards Mecca. The court of the earlier peristyle served as a yard to the north of the prayer hall. The northern limit of the mosque was not determined. A smaller mosque adjoined the building at the southeast corner. The relation between the two is, however, difficult to determine since no physical link between them has been preserved. In the abandonment layer, medieval pottery of the twelfth to fourteenth centuries was discovered. The mosque was erected not far from the *suq*, and the two certainly remained in relation.

Some modest houses of the Umayyad and Abbasid period were found in the Camp of Diocletian, the agora, the temples of Nebo and Baalshamin, and next to the Christian basilicas, installed as modifications of earlier structures. They often contained industrial elements, pithoi, and mangers. Most of them had no upper storey (Gawlikowski 2001, 165; Intagliata 2017b; Kowalski 1994, 57–59; Genequand 2012, 49–50).

The settlement inside the temenos of the temple of Bēl certainly was the *qasaba* described in 985 by al-Muqaddasi (*Kitāb aḥsan al-taqasīm*, 156; Gawlikowski 2008, 91). After the earthquake of 1040, the enclosure walls were strengthened in 1132–1133 by Yusuf b. Firuz and later in 1177 (Sauvaget 1931, 147–150; Gawlikowski 2008, 91). The cella of Bēl was turned into a mosque in 1180. The mosque was restored by al-Malik al-Mujahid b. Shirquh, ruler of Hims in 1237–1239 and later in 1300–1301. The same prince was also patron of the construction of the castle dominating Palmyra and commonly referred to as Qalaat Ibn Maan (Byliński 1999; Hammad 2010, fig. 15).

CONCLUSION

After the defeat of Zenobia, Palmyra became a garrison city on the eastern frontier of the empire. With no more revenues from trade, the new projects were mostly state-financed. As a consequence Palmyra was unable to maintain its distinct character of a gateway to the eastern neighbours of the Roman Empire. Inscriptions in Aramaic disappeared. Greek continued to be the language of official texts, with the exception of the military sphere, reserved for Latin. In Islamic times, the city, no longer a frontier military base, became dominated by local merchants and a middle class who turned the relatively luxurious houses of previous times into modest habitations with extensive sections for storage, animal keeping, and industry. In the twelfth and thirteenth centuries, the settlement was reduced to the enclosure of the temple of Bēl and became a fort, later accompanied by a castle on top of the hill dominating Palmyra.

BIBLIOGRAPHY

al-As'ad, Khaled, and Michal Gawlikowski. 1986. 'New Honorific Inscriptions in the Great Colonnade of Palmyra'. *Annales archéologiques arabes syriennes* 36: 164–171.

al-As'ad, Khaled, and Franciszek M. Stępniowski. 1989. 'The Umayyad Suq in Palmyra'. *Damaszener Mitteilungen* 4: 205–223.

Barnes, Timothy D. 1976. 'Sossianus Hierocles and the Antecedents of the Great Persecution'. *Harvard Studies in Classical Philology* 80: 239–252.

Bauzou, Thomas. 1993. 'Épigraphie et toponymie: Le cas de la Palmyrène du sud-ouest'. *Syria* 70: 27–50.

Bauzou, Thomas. 2000. 'La "Strata Diocletiana"'. In *Aux origines de l'archéologie aérienne: A. Poidebard (1878–1955)*, edited by Lévon Nordiguian and Jean-François Salles, 79–91. Beirut: Presses de l'Université Saint-Joseph.

Byliński, Janusz. 1999. 'Qal'at Shirkuh at Palmyra: A Medieval Fortress Reinterpreted'. *Bulletin d'études orientales* 51: 151–208.

Cantineau, Jean, ed. 1930. *Inventaire des inscriptions de Palmyre.* Fasc. 3, *La Grande Colonnade*. Beirut: Imprimerie catholique.

Cantineau, Jean, ed. 1931. *Inventaire des inscriptions de Palmyre.* Fasc. 6, *Le Camp de Dioclétien*. Beirut: Imprimerie catholique.

Cantineau, Jean, ed. 1933. *Inventaire des inscriptions de Palmyre.* Fasc. 9, *Le sanctuaire de Bèl*. Beirut: Imprimerie catholique.

Charles, Henri. 2012. *Le Christianisme des arabes nomades sur le limes et dans le désert syro-mésopotamien aux alentours de l'hégire.* Piscataway: Gorgias. Reprinted from the 1936 Paris edition.

Cline, Rangar. 2011. *Ancient Angels: Conceptualizing Angeloi in the Roman Empire.* Leiden: Brill.

Crouch, Dora. 1975. 'The Ramparts of Palmyra'. *Studia Palmyreńskie* 6: 6–44.

Cumont, Franz. 1915. 'Les anges du paganisme'. *Revue de l'histoire des religions* 72: 159–182.

Dirven, Lucinda. 1999. *The Palmyrenes of Dura-Europos: A Study of Religious Interaction in Roman Syria.* Leiden: Brill.

Dodgeon, Michael H., and Samuel N. C. Lieu. 1991. *The Roman Eastern Frontier and the Persian Wars, AD 226–363: A Documentary History.* London: Routledge.

Dunand, Maurice. 1931. 'La Strata Diocletiana'. *Revue biblique* 40: 227–248.

Edwell, Peter, Greg Fisher, Geoffrey Greatrex, Conor Whately, and Philip Wood. 2015. 'Arabs in the Conflict Between Rome and Persia, AD 491–630'. In *Arabs and Empires Before Islam*, edited by Greg Fisher, 214–275. Oxford: Clarendon Press.

Fellmann, Rudolf. 1995. 'L'inscription d'un 'optio princeps' au temple de Ba'alshamîn à Palmyre'. In *Actes du Colloque de Lyon 1994: La hiérarchie de l'armée romaine sous le haut-empire*, edited by Yan Le Bohec, 239–240. Paris: de Boccard.

Février, James Germain. 1931. *Essai sur l'histoire politique et économique de Palmyre*. Paris: Vrin.

Fischer, Greg, Philip Wood, George Bevan, Geoffrey Greatrex, Basema Hamarneh, Peter Schadler, and Walter Ward. 2015. 'Arabs and Christianity'. In *Arabs and Empires Before Islam*, edited by Greg Fisher, 276–372. Oxford: Clarendon Press.

Gatier, Pierre-Louis. 1995. 'Un moine sur la frontière, Alexandre l'Acémète en Syrie'. In *Frontières terrestres, frontières célestes dans l'antiquité*, edited by Aline Rousselle, 435–457. Paris: de Boccard.

Gawlikowski, Michał. 1973. *Palmyre*. Vol. 4, *Le temple palmyrénien*. Warsaw: Państwowe Wydawnictwo Naukowe.

Gawlikowski, Michał. 1974. 'Les défenses de Palmyre'. *Syria* 51: 231–242.

Gawlikowski, Michał. 1977. 'Le temple d'Allat à Palmyre'. *Revue archéologique* 2: 253–274.

Gawlikowski, Michał. 1983. 'Réflections sur la chronologie du sanctuaire d'Allat à Palmyre'. *Damaszener Mitteilungen* 1: 59–67.

Gawlikowski, Michał. 1984. *Palmyre*. Vol. 8, *Les principia de Dioclétien: Temple des Enseignes*. Warsaw: Państwowe Wydawnictwo Naukowe.

Gawlikowski, Michał. 1986. 'Palmyre (Mission polonaise)'. In 'Chronique archéologique', edited by Olivier Aurenche. *Syria* 63: 397–399.

Gawlikowski, Michał. 1997. 'L'habitat à Palmyre de l'antiquité au moyen-age'. In *Les maisons dans la Syrie antique du IIIe millénaire au début de L'Islam: Practiques et représentations de l'espace domestique*, edited by Corinne Castel, Michel al-Maqdissi, and François Villeneuve, 161–166. Beirut: Institut français d'archéologie du Proche-Orient.

Gawlikowski, Michał. 1998. 'Palmyra 1997'. *Polish Archaeology in the Mediterranean* 9: 197–211.

Gawlikowski, Michał. 2001. 'Le groupe épiscopal de Palmyre'. In *Rome et ses provinces: Genèse & diffusion d'une image du pouvoir; Hommages à Jean-Charles Balty*, edited by Cécile Evers and Athéna Tsingarida, 119–127. Brussels: Timperman.

Gawlikowski, Michał. 2002. 'Palmyra: Season 2001'. *Polish Archaeology in the Mediterranean* 13: 257–269.

Gawlikowski, Michał. 2003. 'Palmyra: Season 2002'. *Polish Archaeology in the Mediterranean* 14: 279–290.

Gawlikowski, Michał. 2004. 'Palmyra: Season 2003 Preliminary Report'. *Polish Archaeology in the Mediterranean* 15: 313–324.

Gawlikowski, Michał. 2008. 'Palmyra in Early Islamic Times'. In *Residences, Castles, Settlements: Transformation Processes from Late Antiquity to Early Islam in Bilad al-Sham*, edited by Karin Bartl and Abd al-Razzaq Moaz, 89–96. Rahden: Leidorf.

Genequand, Denis. 2012. *Les établissements des élites omeyyades en Palmyrène et au Proche-Orient*. Beirut: Presses de l'Institut français du Proche-Orient.

Genequand, Denis. 2013. 'Between Rome and Islam: Recent Research on the So-Called Caesareum of Palmyra'. *Studia Palmyreńskie* 12: 97–114

Greatrex, Geoffrey, and Samuel N. C. Lieu. 2002. *The Roman Eastern Frontier and the Persian Wars*. Part 2, *AD 363–630*. London: Routledge.

Greatrex, Geoffrey. 2015. 'Les Jafnides et le défense de l'Empire au VIe siècle'. In *Les Jafnides: Des rois arabes au service de Byzance*, edited by Denis Genequand and Christian Julien Robin, 121–154. Paris: de Boccard.

Hammad, Manar. 2010. *Palmyre: Transformations urbaines*. Paris: Geuthner.

Hillers, Delbert R., and Eleonora Cussini, eds. 1996. *Palmyrene Aramaic Texts*. Baltimore: Johns Hopkins University Press.

Hoyland, Robert G. 2001. *Arabia and the Arabs from the Bronze Age to the Coming of Islam*. London: Routledge.

Intagliata, Emanuele E. 2017a. 'Palmyra and Its Ramparts During the Tetrarchy'. In *New Cities in Late Antiquity: Documents and Archaeology*, edited by Efthymios Rizos, 71–83. Turnhout: Brepols.

Intagliata, Emanuele E. 2017b. 'The Post-Roman Occupation of the Northern Courtyard of the Sanctuary of Baalshamin in Palmyra: A Reassessment of the Evidence Based on the Documents in the Fonds d'Archives Paul Collart, Université de Lausanne'. *Zeitschrift für Orient-Archäologie* 9: 180–199.

Jastrzębowska, Elżbieta. 2013. 'Christianisation of Palmyra: Early Byzantine Church in the Temple of Bel'. *Studia Palmyreńskie* 12: 177–191.

Jones, A. H. M. 1964. *The Later Roman Empire, 284–602: A Social, Economic, and Administrative Survey*. Oxford: Blackwell.

Juchniewicz, Karol. 2013. 'Late Roman Fortifications in Palmyra'. *Studia Palmyreńskie* 12: 193–202.

Juchniewicz, Karol, Khalid al-Asʿad, and Khalil Al-Hariri. 2010. 'The Defence Wall in Palmyra after Recent Syrian Excavations'. *Studia Palmyreńskie* 11: 55–73.

Juchniewicz, Karol, and Marta Żuchowska. 2012. 'Water Supply in Palmyra: A Chronological Approach'. In *The Archaeology of Water Supply*, edited by Marta Żuchowska, 61–73. British Archaeological Reports, International Series 2414. Oxford: Archaeopress.

Kaizer, Ted. 2002. *The Religious Life of Palmyra*. Stuttgart: Steiner.

Kaizer, Ted. 2010. 'From Zenobia to Alexander the Sleepless: Paganism, Judaism and Christianity at Late Roman Palmyra'. In *Zeitreisen: Syrien–Palmyra: Rom; Festschrift für Andreas Schmidt-Colinet zum 65. Geburtstag*, edited by Beatrix Bastl, Verena Gassner, and Ulrike Muss, 113–123. Vienna: Phoibos Verlag.

Kowalski, Sławomir. 1994. 'The Praetorium of the Camp of Diocletian in Palmyra'. *Studia Palmyreńskie* 9: 39–70.

Kowalski, Sławomir. 1996. 'Doubtful Christian Reutilisation of the Baalshamin Temple in Palmyra'. *Damaszener Mitteilungen* 9: 217–226.

Kowalski, Sławomir. 1997. 'Late Roman Palmyra in Literature and Epigraphy'. *Studia Palmyreńskie* 10: 39–62.

Kowalski, Sławomir. 1998. 'The Camp of Legio I Illyricorum in Palmyra'. *Novensia* 10: 189–209.

Lewin, Ariel. 2015. 'Did the Roman Empire Have a Military Strategy and Were the Jafnids Part of It'? In *Les Jafnides: Des rois arabes au service de Byzance*, edited by Denis Genequand and Christian Julien Robin, 155–192. Paris: de Boccard.

Majcherek, Grzegorz. 2005. 'More Churches from Palmyra: An Inkling of the Late Antique City'. In *Au pays d'Allat: Mélanges offerts à Michał Gawlikowski*, edited by Piotr Bieliński and Franciszek M. Stępniowski, 141–150. Warsaw: Instytut Archeologii, Uniwersytet Warszawski.

Majcherek, Grzegorz. 2012. 'Polish Archaeological Mission to Palmyra: Seasons 2008 and 2009'. *Polish Archaeology in the Mediterranean* 21: 459–479.

Majcherek, Grzegorz. 2013. 'Excavating the Basilicas'. *Studia Palmyreńskie* 12: 251–268.

Michałowski, Kazimierz. 1962. *Palmyre: Fouilles polonaises, 1960*. Warsaw: Państwowe Wydawnictwo Naukowe.

Milik, Józef Tadeusz. 1972. *Dédicaces faites par des dieux*. Paris: Geuthner.

Millar, Fergus. 2006. 'Ethnic Identity in the Roman Near East AD 325–450: Language, Religion, and Culture'. In *Rome, the Greek World, and the East*. Vol. 3, *The Greek World, the Jews, and the East*, edited by Hannah M. Cotton and Guy M. Rogers, 378–405. Chapel Hill: University of North Carolina Press. First published in *Mediterranean Archaeology* 11 (1998): 159–176.

Millar, Fergus. 2013. 'A Syriac Codex from Near Palmyra and the 'Ghassanid' Abokarib'. *Hugoye: Journal of Syriac Studies* 16(1): 15–35.

Millar, Fergus. 2013b. 'The Evolution of the Syrian Orthodox Church in the pre-Islamic Period. From Greek to Syriac'. *Journal of Early Christian Studies* 21(1): 43–92.

Mitchell, Stephen. 1999. 'The Cult of Theos Hypsistos Between Pagans, Jews and Christians'. In *Pagan Monotheism in Late Antiquity*, edited by Polymnia Athanassiadi and Michael Frede, 81-148. Oxford: Clarendon Press.

Mouterde, René. 1930. 'La Strata Diocletiana et ses bornes milliaires'. *Mélanges de l'Université Saint-Joseph* 15: 221–233.

Sauvaget, Jean. 1931. 'Inscriptions arabes du temple de Bel à Palmyre'. *Syria* 12: 143–153.

Seyrig, Henri. 1931. 'Antiquités syriennes'. *Syria* 12: 316–325.

Seyrig, Henri. 1950. 'Antiquités syriennes'. *Syria* 27: 229–252.

Shahîd, Irfan. 1995. *Byzantium and the Arabs in the Sixth Century*. Vol. 1.1, *Political and Military History*. Washington, DC: Dumbarton Oaks Research Library and Collection.

Starcky, Jean, and Michał Gawlikowski. 1985. *Palmyre: Civilisations d'hier ou d'aujourd'hui*. Paris: Librairie d'Amérique et d'Orient.

Stein, Ernest. 1949. *Histoire du Bas-Empire*. Vol. 2. Paris: Desclée de Brouwer.

Teixidor, Javier. 1979. *The Pantheon of Palmyra*. Leiden: Brill.

Turcan, Robert. 2004. *Les cultes orientaux dans le monde romain*. Paris: Les belles lettres.

van Berchem, Denis. 1952. *L'armée de Dioclétien et la réforme constantinienne*. Paris: Geuthner.

van Berchem, Denis. 1954. 'Recherches sur la chronologie des enceintes de Syrie et Mésopotamie'. *Syria* 31: 254–270.

Vannesse, Michaël. 2015. 'L'architecture balnéaire dans la province romaine de Syrie: quelques cas d'étude'. In *Zeugma*. Vol. 6, *La Syrie romaine: Permanences et transferts culturels*, edited by Catherine Abadie-Reynal and Jean-Baptiste Yon, 97–121. Lyon: Maison de l'Orient et de la Méditerranée.

Vie d'Alexandre l'Acémète. 1911. *Vie d'Alexandre l'Acémète: Texte grec et traduction latine*, edited by Emile de Stoop. In *Patrologia Orientalis*. Vol. 6, 640–705. Paris: Diderot.

von Gerkan, Armin. 1935. 'Die Stadtmauer von Palmyra'. *Berytus* 2: 25–33.

Ward, John Hester. 1974. 'The Notitia dignitatum'. *Latomus* 33(2): 397–434.

Watson, Alaric. 1999. *Aurelian and the Third Century*. London: Routledge.

Will, Ernest. 1966. 'Le sac de Palmyre'. In *Mélanges d'archéologie et d'histoire offerts à André Piganiol*, edited by R. Chevallier, 1409–1416. EPHE, VIᵉ section. Paris: SEVPEN.

Will, Ernest. 1983. 'Développement urbain de Palmyre: Témoignages épigraphiques anciens et nouveaux'. *Syria* 60: 69–81.

Will, Ernest. 1992. *Les Palmyréens: La Venise des sables (Iᵉʳ s. avant – IIIᵉ s. après J.-C.)*. Paris: Colin.

Yon, Jean-Baptiste, ed. 2012. *Inscriptions grecques et latines de la Syrie*. Vol. 17.1, *Palmyre*. Bibliothèque archéologique et historique 195. Beirut: Institut français du Proche-Orient.

CHAPTER 10

PALMYRA AND THE THIRD-CENTURY CRISIS

UDO HARTMANN

THE third century was a period of profound change for Palmyra. The trade centre developed into an important political player within the Roman Empire. In the AD 260s and the early 270s, the leading family of Palmyra even took over the administration of the Roman Near East. But after a brief peak in political significance in 270–272 and two conquests by Emperor Aurelian (270–275) in 272 and 273, the city became a Syrian provincial town at the edge of empire without any political importance (Hartmann 2001; 2008; 2016; cf. also Will 1992, 167–197; Sommer 2005, 159–170, 220–224; 2008, 309–318; 2017, 154–179; Smith 2013, 175–181).

THE COLONY OF PALMYRA IN THE FIRST HALF OF THE THIRD CENTURY

Under the Antonines, the city of Palmyra was a flourishing centre of long-distance trade to Parthia and India. It was also a regional political player in Syria and, with that, responsible for the safety of the border region of the Palmyrene. The steppe from Palmyra to the Euphrates was therefore under the control of the city's militia. The rich urban elite concentrated on the organization and the protection of long-distance trade (see also Chapter 17, [Seland], this volume). The emperor Septimius Severus (193–211) and his son Caracalla (211–217) systematically supported the cities of Syria, one of the home regions of the new imperial family. Palmyra became one of the leading cities of the newly created province of Syria Phoenice. In 212, the Emperor Caracalla granted the city the status of a Roman *colonia* with *ius italicum* (*Dig.* 50.15.1.4–5; Millar 1990, 42; Sartre 1996, 394; Edwell 2008, 60). Nearly all citizens of Palmyra received Roman citizenship; this included the acquisition of the *nomen gentile* Iulius Aurelius, perhaps in reference to the Empress Julia Domna, Caracalla's mother (Schlumberger 1942/1943; Simelon 2013, 198–200). Only some aristocrats who had already received Roman citizenship under Septimius Severus kept their old *nomen gentile* of 'Septimius'.

The political institutions of the city were reorganized and restructured according to the model of a Roman colony (Millar 1990, 42–46; 1993, 143–144, 326–327; Sartre 1996, 394–395; Yon 2002, 38–40, 243–244; Smith 2013, 130–132; Hartmann 2016, 54–59). The two supreme annual magistrates were now called *duumviri*, while the *aediles* were the second annual pair of magistrates. In the inscriptions honouring them, these magistrates are called *strategoi* and *agoranomoi* ('controller of the market', with the Palmyrene translation, *rb šwq*; IGLS XVII.1, 53, 67, 97, 224). Beginning in 212, the Greek title *strategos*, until now the title of an officer of the Palmyrene militia (Young 2001, 157–166; Sommer 2005, 155–157), was exclusively used to denote the supreme civil annual magistrates of the colony. But even after 212, the city retained a special political and cultural position within the Roman province of Syria: Palmyra continued to maintain a militia to protect the caravans and the border region of the Parthian Empire against raiding nomads. Palmyra also preserved its unique culture; the Palmyrenes were able to use the Palmyrene language and script, even in official texts.

Since the first half of the third century, the Palmyrene aristocracy, composed of the clan chiefs and the heads of the city's rich merchant families, focused not only on the organization of long-distance trade and on their civic duties in Palmyra, but also on their opportunities as Roman citizens. The Palmyrene aristocrats emphasized three essential values in their political identity: their responsibilities as decurions (councillors) of the *colonia* Palmyra, their concern for the protection of the caravans, and their unconditional commitment to the Roman Empire and their loyalty to Roman imperial rule, which later, in the middle of the third century, also included their involvement in the Roman imperial service (Hartmann 2016, 53–65). These values of the aristocracy are evident in the honorary inscriptions at the *agora* (market) and on the Great Colonnade in Palmyra. These texts praise the aristocrats for the assumption of public duties and civic offices and for their contribution to the city's welfare. On the agora of Palmyra, the council and people of Palmyra dedicated three statues to Iulius Aurelius Malichus Malikō because he was generous in his former offices as *strategos* and *agoranomos* of the *colonia* and paid many expenses out of his own pocket; the god Yarḥibōl, the council, and the Roman governor are named as witnesses (IGLS XVII.1, 224; Millar 1990, 44; Yon 2002, 39–40, 55–56, 185, 243, 290; Smith 2013, 130). The council and the people emphasize Malichus's civic merits and his extensive public services, but, at the same time, they also represent the recognition of his merits by the Roman governor. This shared set of value can be found in the inscription of 242/243 honouring Iulius Aurelius Zenobius Zabdilah on a column in the Great Colonnade. The council and people of Palmyra honoured Zenobius for his administration as *duumvir* and *aedilis*. Then again, the council and the people also praised his commitment to the Romans: in 231/232, when Zenobius was *strategos*, he took good care of the Roman troops, accompanying the Emperor Severus Alexander (222–235) and the governor Rutilius Pudens Crispinus. Therefore, not only the god Yarḥibōl but also a representative of Rome was cited as witnesses: in this instance it was the praetorian prefect Iulius Priscus, the brother of the Emperor Philippus Arabus (244–249) (*IGLS* XVII.1, 53; Millar 1990, 43–44; 1993, 327; Smith 2013, 130).

Other *duumviri* of the colony were also recorded: in 224/225, Iulius Aurelius Seiba and Iulius Aurelius Titianus served as *duumviri* (*IGLS* XVII.1, 70; Sartre 1996, 394; Yon 2002, 9–10, 243, 292, 294), and later, Iulius Aurelius 'Ogā Seleucus held this office. He was honoured in October 254 for being *strategos* twice (*IGLS* XVII.1, 75; Millar 1990, 44; Yon 2002, 58, 61–62, 243, 249, 260, 291). In 262/263, the *strategos* Iulius Aurelius Nebuzabadus honoured the *procurator ducenarius* Septimius Vorodes with a statue (*IGLS* XVII.1, 65; Hartmann 2001, 204, n. 153; Yon 2002, 33, 244, 291, 294). Last, both Vorodes (*IGLS* XVII.1, 67), who was also *aedilis* of the *colonia*, and his colleague Iulius Aurelius Hermes served as *duumviri*, probably in 263/264 (*IGLS* XVII.1, 61; Sartre 1996, 395; Yon 2012, 73–75).

THE CRISIS OF PALMYRA AND THE RISE OF ODAENATHUS

In 224, the Sassanid Ardašīr I (224–240/242) defeated the Parthian king of kings Artabanus IV (213–224), near Hormizdagan. With the rise of the Sassanid dynasty in Persia, the political framework at the Roman frontier changed fundamentally. The rise also led to a crisis of the flourishing Palmyrene trade in southern Mesopotamia. Palmyra's unilateral focus on long-distance trade made it and its wealth extremely dependent on the political conditions in Mesopotamia. In the 220s, Ardašīr I occupied the Characene in southern Mesopotamia, and the free trade to the Persian Gulf was restricted by the Sassanians. The trading stations in the former Parthian vassal kingdom of Characene (Spasinou Charax and Forat) and in Vologesias, a Parthian emporium near Seleucia along the Tigris, were closed by the first two Sassanians. The existence of the emporium in Vologesias is attested until 247. After that, Palmyrene emporia were no longer mentioned in the caravan inscriptions of the third century. Following his victory over the Parthians, the new Sassanid king of kings, Ardašīr I, immediately initiated an aggressive policy against Rome and launched attacks on Roman Mesopotamia. His son Šābuhr I (239/240–272) continued this policy. In the 240s and early 250s, he also occupied the Palmyrene stations along the Euphrates, between Dura-Europus and the island of Anatha (Kettenhofen 1982, 50–51; Kennedy 1986). The Palmyrene network of military bases was destroyed. In 244, the Persian army under Šābuhr I defeated the Roman emperor, Gordian III (238–244) at Misiche, along the Euphrates. The Roman emperor died of an injury suffered during the battle. Therefore, Rome was no longer able to guarantee the security of Syria. At this point, a Persian attack on Palmyra became possible. The weakening of the Palmyrene military infrastructure in the steppe region also strengthened the position of the nomadic Arab tribes. Subsequently, the danger of raids by Arab nomads increased. Furthermore, the crisis in the Roman Empire led to a decline in sales of exotic luxury goods from India and China, which also caused a considerable decay in Palmyra's long-distance trade. The collapse of the trading network in Mesopotamia and the new, dangerous situation at the eastern Roman border plunged Palmyra into an economic and political crisis (Hartmann 2001, 76–85; Smith 2013, 175–177; but see Sommer 2005, 158–159).

A clear indication that the caravan trade over the Roman eastern border decreased dramatically is the decline of Palmyrene caravan inscriptions in the first half of the century. Only four caravan inscriptions have come down to us from between 212 and 273 (Gawlikowski 1983, 67–68; 1996, 143; Millar 1993, 331–332; Young 2001, 173–175; Daryaee 2022, 43): in April 247, the merchants and members of a caravan thanked Iulius Aurelius Zebidas Zebīdā for his support, probably in protecting their caravan. They moved down with Zebīdā to Vologesias (*IGLS* XVII.1, 89). Iulius Aurelius Nebumaeus is the last attested *synhodiarchos*, a caravan leader or leader of a community of merchants (*IGLS* XVII.1, 22). In 257/258 Palmyra honoured the *archemporos* (rb šyrt', 'chief merchant') Iulius Aurelius Šalāmallat because he brought back the caravan to Palmyra at his own expense (*IGLS* XVII.1, 74). The inscription describing Septimius Vorodes's career, probably dating to April 264, is the last testimony to the Palmyrene caravans and the *archemporoi* (*IGLS* XVII.1, 67). The aristocrat Vorodes brought back caravans at his own expense and was therefore honoured by the chief merchant.

During the difficult political and economic situation of the late 240s, the Palmyrenes raised Septimius Odaenathus to the office of city chief, with the irregular title, '*exarchos* of the Palmyrenes' in Greek, or 'head of Tadmōr' (rš' dy tdmwr) in Palmyrene (Hartmann 2001, 86–230; Sommer 2017, 154–168; Raja 2022, 108). This special office to manage the crisis and to restore stability in the border region is attested in three inscriptions. One is dedicated to the son of Odaenathus, Septimius Ḥairān, in October 251 (*IGLS* XVII.1, 58), and another to Odaenathus, in April 252 (*IGLS* XVII.1, 54); in both inscriptions Odaenathus and his son Ḥairān are called 'Roman senator' and *exarchos*. In the third, undated, inscription, 'Ogeilū, son of Maqqaī, calls Odaenathus only 'head of Tadmōr', so this inscription must have been erected a little earlier, perhaps in the late 240s (Cantineau 1931, 138, no. 17; cf. *HA trig. tyr.* 15.1).

In the second half of the 240s, Septimius Odaenathus and his son and heir Septimius Ḥairān received the title of *exarchos*. Without altering the constitution of the colony, the elite of Palmyra created a new, irregular position of power to manage the political and economic crisis. But with this political step, virtually a new dynasty of Palmyrene princes was established. Presumably, the military command of the Palmyrene militia was concentrated in the hands of the new *exarchos* and his heir (Hartmann 2001, 90–96; Sommer 2017, 156–158; but see Millar 1995, 417–419). Odaenathus increased its military capacity and established units of *cataphracti*, a very heavily armoured cavalry, following the Parthian model (Fest. 24; Zos. 1.50.3; Hartmann 2001, 98–100). Odaenathus was able to restore security with this new military power. Thus, he also became an important political factor in the Roman East. Around 250, the Roman emperor recognized this new position of Odaenathus as 'prince' of Palmyra, and appointed him (*IGLS* XVII.1, 54, 545) and his son Ḥairān (*IGLS* XVII.1, 58–60) to the senate: with that, the family of Odaenathus became the first Palmyrene members of the Roman senate (Hartmann 2001, 97–98; Hächler 2019, 581–588, no. 260; but see Gawlikowski 1985, 261; Strobel 1993, 248–249).

THE FAMILY OF ODAENATHUS

We do not know much about the ancestry of Odaenathus, but his family must have been part of the aristocracy of Palmyra since the second century, because his ancestors had already acquired Roman citizenship under Septimius Severus. Perhaps the *decurio* (city councillor) Odaenathus was a successful caravan leader and officer of the Palmyrene militia (Fest. 23; Zos. 1.39.1; Hartmann 2001, 86–90, 108–111). Odaenathus was the son of Ḥairān, the grandson of Wahballāt, and the great-grandson of Naṣōr (Cantineau 1931, 138, no. 17; IGLS XVII.1, 54, 545), but nothing has come down to us about these men. Born at the beginning of the third century, Odaenathus was married twice, first to an unnamed woman (*HA trig. tyr.* 16.1), then to Zenobia. His son from his first marriage was his designated heir, Septimius Ḥairān. In all likelihood, he is identical with Septimius Herodianus, known from an inscription and a *bulla* (IGLS XVII.1, 61; Seyrig 1937, 3). The author of the *Historia Augusta* calls this heir 'Herodes' (*HA trig. tyr.* 16.1, 16.3, 17.2). Ḥairān Herodianus, apparently an adult at about 250, received the title of *exarchos*, and, in 263, following the victory over the Persians, the title 'king of kings' (IGLS XVII.1, 61; Seyrig 1937, 3), together with his father (Hartmann 2001, 112–128). Odaenathus's second wife, Septimia Zenobia Bat-Zabbai (Equini Schneider 1993; Kotula 1997, 89–144; Hartmann 2001; 2021; Sartre and Sartre 2014; Sommer 2017, 168–179; Andrade 2018; more popular accounts in Stoneman 1992; Southern 2008; Winsbury 2010), was a daughter of Antiochus (CIS II, 3971; Milik 1972, 318; OGIS 650–651; CIL III, 6727). The oldest son from his second marriage was Lucius Iulius Aurelius Septimius Vaballathus Athenodorus, born around 258/260 (*HA Aurel.* 38.1; Pol. Silv. 521.49; cf. Zos. 1.59.1). The author of the *Historia Augusta* mentions two more sons of Zenobia, Herennianus and Timolaus, and incorrectly asserts that they were the heirs of Odaenathus. Since no other sources confirm the existence of these sons, the whole story may be a fiction. If they were historical persons, they did not take part in politics at the court of Palmyra (*HA Gall.* 13.2; *trig. tyr.* 14.4, 15.2, 17.2, 24.4, 27–28, 30.2; Hartmann 2001, 124–127).

ODAENATHUS AND THE IMPERIAL CRISIS IN AD 260

In 257/258, Odaenathus received the title *consularis*, as evidenced by some inscriptions from Palmyra (IGLS XVII.1, 55–56, 59–60, 143; Gross 2005, 94–97, no. 2). It is also confirmed by an undated inscription from Tyrus, the metropolis of the province of Syria Phoenice (Chéhab 1962, 19–20, plate VI, 1). The exact meaning of this title is unclear. Did Valerian (253–260) bestow on Odaenathus the honour of *ornamenta consularia* while he was in Syria at that time (e.g., Potter 1990, 389–390; Kotula 1997, 99; Watson 1999, 30; Young 2001, 234–235; Gawlikowski 2007, 301)? It is more probable that Odaenathus was *consul suffectus in absentia* and that Valerian appointed him as governor of Syria Phoenice in 257/258 (Ingholt 1976, 119; Gawlikowski 1985, 258; Hartmann 2001, 102–108). The governorship would also explain why Odaenathus could command Roman troops in Syria at the Euphrates after the capture of Valerian by Šābuhr in 260.

Valerian needed a strong military supporter in this region. In 259, he planned a great offensive against the Persians in northern Mesopotamia (Glas 2014, 163–167, 219–224). It was probably the task of the Palmyrene military leader to save the flank of this Roman offensive. But the Roman offensive ended in disaster. In June 260, the Roman and Persian armies met between Carrhae and Edessa. After the battle, Valerian and his staff were taken prisoner during the negotiations with Šābuhr. They were brought to and held captive in Persia, where the emperor died. His son Gallienus (260–268), co-ruler since 253 and responsible for the western part of the empire, was now emperor of the whole empire. But the invasions of the Germans and some usurpers along the Rhine and the Middle Danube forced Gallienus to stay in the west. Only with great difficulty could Gallienus and his generals reestablish control over the central regions of the empire in the years 260 and 261. After the Roman disaster in Mesopotamia, there was no Roman defence at the eastern frontier. In the summer of 260, Šābuhr crossed the Euphrates and invaded Syria, Cilicia, and Cappadocia (Glas 2014, 167–186, 319–341; Geiger 2013, 93–125).

Only Fulvius Macrianus, the commanding officer of the imperial war treasury at Samosata and in charge of the supplies for the troops, tried to organize resistance against the Persians (Hartmann 2001, 133–135; Glas 2014, 326–327). He had the support of the consular Odaenathus. He assembled an army of his Palmyrene militia and the remnants of Valerian's troops (Zos. 1.39.1; cf. Fest. 23; *HA Valer.* 4.2; *trig. tyr.* 15.2) and attacked the booty-laden army of Šābuhr, returning from Syria, on the banks of the Euphrates. His troops defeated Šābuhr and forced him to withdraw to Persia quickly (Sync. 466.24–25; Zon. 12.23 p. 595.18–21; Kettenhofen 1982, 122–126; Hartmann 2001, 138–140). For a few weeks, the equestrian officer Macrianus remained loyal to the Emperor Gallienus. But in the late summer of 260, the elderly and infirm officer seized power in the Roman East and declared his two sons, T. Fulvius Iunius Macrianus Iunior and T. Fulvius Iunius Quietus, Augusti (Hartmann 2001, 141–145; Geiger 2013, 120–125). For that he had to face civil war with Gallienus. While the two Macriani marched into the Balkans against Gallienus, Quietus and his *praefectus praetorio* Ballista remained in Syria to secure imperial power there. But Gallienus defeated the two Macriani in the summer of 261 in the Balkans, whereupon Gallienus commissioned Odaenathus to eliminate Quietus. The senator from Palmyra defeated the usurper Quietus at Emesa in the autumn of 261, and besieged him there. Quietus was probably lynched by the Emesan citizens, and Ballista was handed over to Odaenathus and executed (*Cont. Dio.* fr. 8, 1 = Petr. Patr. fr. 167; Zon. 12.24 p. 600.2–7; Sync. 466, 26–467, 1; Potter 1990, 53–54, 345–346; Geiger 2013, 124–125).

ODAENATHUS: THE RULER OF THE EAST

After these two military successes, Odaenathus was the most important officer in the Roman East. In 260/261 Gallienus appointed Odaenathus as a special representative of the emperor in the Roman East. He was now deputy to the emperor with an *imperium maius*, an extraordinary though temporary command over the Roman troops and the provincial administration in the region. He thus made the de facto most powerful general in the East his imperial deputy in order to prevent further usurpation in the East and to secure Rome's frontiers there. This appointment was probably made in two steps. Late in the summer of 260, following his victory over Šābuhr at the Euphrates, Gallienus presumably gave the successful commander and confidant Valerian the military position of *dux Romanorum*, to secure the Euphrates border. Gallienus also wanted to secure an ally against Macrianus. With this special command Odaenathus acquired command of the troops along the empire's eastern border (Sync. 466.25–26; Zon. 12.23 p. 595.21–22; cf. Zos. 1.39.1). Following the victory over Quietus in the autumn of 261, Gallienus elevated Odaenathus to *corrector totius Orientis* (attested only in Palmyrene: *mtqnn' dy mdnḥ' klh*) and thereby also entrusted him with civil power in the Roman East (*Inv.* III, 19; cf. Zon. 12.24 p. 600.7–9; *HA Gall.* 1.1, 3.3, 10.1; Clermont-Ganneau 1920, 386–401; Potter 1990, 391–394; 1996, 272–274; Hartmann 2001, 147–156; only an honorific title without political power according to Cantineau 1933, 217–220; Millar 1993, 170; Swain 1993). The power vacuum in the Roman East was now filled by Odaenathus. After 261, he began to extend his authority and his personal power in the East by providing security and prosperity to the region. Formally, he still governed in the name of Gallienus as *dux Romanorum* and *corrector totius Orientis*, as a military and civil official with an extraordinary command (Potter 1996; Hartmann 2001, 146–161; Sommer 2017, 161–163).

After the restoration of internal order in Syria and the reorganization of the Roman army, Odaenathus launched a large-scale offensive against Persia in 262. This campaign to avenge Valerian's capture was to restore the lost territories in northern Mesopotamia to Roman rule. Although there still were Roman troops in Edessa, the other parts of northern Mesopotamia around Nisibis and Carrhae were controlled by the Sassanians. Odaenathus crossed the Euphrates in the spring of 262, liberated Carrhae and conquered Nisibis, whose citizens had sympathized with the Persians after the occupation by Šābuhr in 252. The Severan province of Mesopotamia was once again under full Roman control. Odaenathus moved to the Euphrates and marched through Babylonia into the Persian heartland. He then reached the Tigris and the Persian residence at Ctesiphon, which he besieged but could not take. Apparently, there was no direct military confrontation with Šābuhr (Eutr. 9.10; Fest. 23; *HA Gall.* 10.1–8, 12.1; *trig. tyr.* 15.2–4; Zos. 1.39.1–2; Sync. 467.7–8; cf. *Orac. Sib.* 13.167–168, 171; Kettenhofen 1982, 125–126; Hartmann 2001, 162–185).

In the summer of 263, Odaenathus returned to Syria victorious. The security at the frontier and Roman authority in Mesopotamia were restored. Gallienus therefore celebrated a triumph in Rome in the second half of 263 (*HA Gall.* 10.5) and was awarded the title of *Persicus maximus* (*CIL* VIII, 22765). The victory of Odaenathus over the Persians was won under the emperor's auspices, although Gallienus never was in the East (Hartmann 2001, 175; Geiger 2013, 133; Sommer 2017, 165). As the actual vanquisher of the Persians, Odaenathus remained a loyal official of Emperor Gallienus.

But Odaenathus's victory was accompanied by an increase in his prestige as a military leader in the Roman East. His Palmyrene soldiers also demanded an increase in rank. Avoiding the usurpation of imperial titles, Odaenathus elevated himself and his son Septimius Herodianus to 'king of kings' at the Orontes near Antioch, following the Persian victory in the second half of the year 263. In a Palmyrene inscription dated March 263, Odaenathus is still referred to as *clarissimus consularis* (Hartmann and Luther 1999; but see Gawlikowski 2007, 301). But later in 263, he and his son bear the title of the defeated Persian king. The title is attested by an inscription honouring *rex regum* Herodianus on the tripylon of Palmyra, erected in 263/264 by the *duumvir* of the *colonia* Palmyra, Vorodes. A Palmyrene inscription for *rex* Odaenathus on a *krater*, probably from 266/267, and the posthumous inscription honouring *rex regum* Odaenathus in the Great Colonnade of Palmyra in 271 confirm this (*IGLS* XVII.1, 61; Schlumberger 1951, 60, no. 36; 151, no. 21; *Inv.* III, 19; cf. *IGLS* XVII.1, 120; *HA trig. tyr.* 15.2; Hartmann 2001, 176–185; but see Gawlikowski 2007, 305; Gnoli 2007, 81–94; against this title Mosig-Walburg 2023, 324–329). However, the title *imperator*, attributed to Odaenathus in the *Historia Augusta*, is not historical (*HA Gall.* 3.3, 13.1; *trig. tyr.* 15.5; Hartmann 2001, 184–185; historical according to Will 1992, 179; Strobel 1993, 248, n. 423; Winter and Dignas 2007, 160).

The new title of the dynasts symbolized first and foremost the victory over the Persian king of kings Šābuhr. Odaenathus thus upgraded his position without assuming the title of *augustus* and without risking civil war. But the charismatic general was able to establish a personal, dynastic power in the East in the mid-260s (Hartmann 2001, 180–184, 440–446). Under the good administration of Odaenathus, the Roman Near East was soon able to recover from the Persian invasions (Hartmann 2001, 186–200). The Syrian author of the thirteenth *Sibylline Oracle* celebrates him in the final passage of his poetry as a 'lion sent from the sun' and as the saviour of the East who would rule the Romans and defeat the Persians, expressing the sentiments of the local people (Orac. Sib. 13.164–171; Potter 1990, 141–142, 151–154, 328–347; Strobel 1993, 211–212, 247–248, 251–256; Hartmann 2001, 194–200; Sommer 2017, 163–164).

In the city of Palmyra, the constitution of the colony had now been adapted to the new 'royal' power structure (Hartmann 2001, 200–211; Yon 2002, 35, 70–71). In late 263 or early 264, the already-mentioned *decurio* Iulius Aurelius Septimius Vorodes, a Roman knight and the *duumvir* of the *colonia* in 263/264 (*IGLS* XVII.1, 61), who also served as *procurator ducenarius* (a Roman equestrian official in the imperial administration of the province) since 261/262 (*IGLS* XVII.1, 64–65, 67), became the *iuridicus* of the *metrocolonia* Palmyra, a judge and civil deputy to King Odaenathus in the city (*IGLS* XVII.1, 67). Finally, Vorodes was appointed as *argapet* of Palmyra in 264/265 (*IGLS* XVII.1, 66, 68–69; Ingholt 1936, 94, no. 4 = *CIS* II, 4105 ter), a royal 'city governor' with civil, fiscal, and military authority (Hartmann 2001, 203–211; 2008, 348, 355–356; Gnoli

2007, 95–113; Yon 2012, 76–86; Smith 2013, 79; 114–115, 117, 130–132). Thus, the Roman knight and procurator Vorodes served in the imperial administration of the Roman East and simultaneously organized the 'royal' administration of Palmyra on behalf of Odaenathus. The old institutions of the colony, such as the *duumviri* and the council, are now no longer attested in the inscriptions. Palmyra, upgraded to a *metrocolonia*, the most important city in the province (*IGLS* XVII.1, 67), thus stood under the command of the king's deputy with the Parthian title *argapet*.

Under Odaenathus, Palmyra became the centre of power in the Roman East. With Palmyra's increasing political significance in the empire in the late 250s and the early 260s, Palmyrene aristocrats tried to find new positions in the imperial administration. They sought to attain recognition and social prestige in the equestrian order and in the Roman senate. In the third century, several Roman knights and two senatorial families are attested. In addition to the dynasty of Odaenathus, we know of a second Roman senator from Palmyra: Septimius Ḥaddūdan, son of ʿOgeilū, the *symposiarchos* of priests of the temple of Bel, is mentioned in two inscriptions from March 272 and March 273, written only in the Palmyrene language. They list the 'guards' of the temple of Bel during the *symposiarchia* of Ḥaddūdan. The second inscription also mentions the support that the senator gave the army of the Emperor Aurelian during the first capture of Palmyra in August 272 (*Inv.* IX, 28; Gawlikowski 1973, 76–77, no. 11; Kowalski 1997, 41–42; Hartmann 2001, 91, 383–384; Kaizer 2002, 232–233, 237, 241; Smith 2013, 114; Raja 2022, 115).

Besides Odaenathus's confidant, the *procurator ducenarius* and *argapet* Vorodes, we know of five other Roman knights from Palmyra in the late 250s and early 260s. In April 259, the city council and the people of the city honoured the Roman knight and former *duumvir* Iulius Aurelius ʿOgā Seleucus with a statue (*IGLS* XVII.1, 76). Iulius Aurelius Hermes, *duumvir* in 263/264 and colleague of Vorodes, held the position of *procurator centenarius* in the imperial administration of the province of Syria Phoenice (*IGLS* XVII.1, 61). In the 260s, more aristocrats, for the most part probably military officers associated with Odaenathus, entered the Roman equestrian order: the Roman knights Iulius Aurelius Septimius Malchus Malkū, Iulius Aurelius Septimius Iades, son of Septimius Alexander, and Iulius Aurelius Salmes Šalmē are attested (*IGLS* XVII.1, 66, 68–69).

THE MURDER OF ODAENATHUS AND THE EMPIRE OF QUEEN ZENOBIA

In the spring of 267, Odaenathus set out on a second campaign against the Persian stronghold at Ctesiphon. He was probably planning to capture the city, which he had failed to accomplish 262/263. His troops once again advanced to the Tigris and Ctesiphon. A sudden invasion of the northern coast of Asia Minor by the Goths in the spring of 267 prevented the completion of this campaign. After receiving this news from Asia Minor, Odaenathus immediately broke off the Persian war and marched through Cappadocia to Heraclea Pontica in the summer or autumn of 267. By then the Germanic tribes had already left the region (Sync. 467.7–13; cf. *HA Gall.* 12.6–13.1; Zos. 1.39.2; Winter 1988, 126; Bleckmann 1992, 124; Hartmann 2001, 211–218).

According to the dates given in the Egyptian papyri relating the joint reign of Emperor Aurelian and King Vaballathus, the son and heir of King Odaenathus (the first year of Vaballathus's reign was 267/268), Odaenathus was killed in the winter of 267/268, probably at the end of 267 (Hartmann 2001, 213–216, 231–241). Zosimus (1.39.2) reports that this happened in Emesa at a birthday celebration. However, Syncellus's (467.10–14) version—according to which Odaenathus was murdered in Heraclea Pontica—is more probable. Similarly, the *Historia Augusta* (*Gall.* 12.6–13.1; *trig. tyr.* 15.5, 16.3, 17) establishes a connection between the Persian war, the Gothic invasion of Heraclea, and Odaenathus's murder in Asia Minor. Both authors probably used the contemporary chronicle of Dexippus. The reasons for the murder, as given by the available sources, are contradictory. According to the *Historia Augusta*, Odaenathus and his heir, 'Herodes', were victims of the king's *consobrinus* ('cousin' or 'nephew') Maeonius. Zonaras (12.24 p. 600.12–23) reports that the murder was committed by one of Odaenathus's nephews, whom the king had insulted during a hunt. According to the *Continuator Dionis* (fr. 7 = Petr. Patr. fr. 166), the gouty Roman official Rufinus was responsible for the murder, but the Emperor Gallienus praised him for this act. Finally, John of Antioch (fr. 152, 2) speaks of a plot by Gallienus. Odaenathus was probably assassinated in a plot organized by Rufinus on behalf of Gallienus, although Rufinus did not do the deed himself; he apparently took advantage of a quarrel in the Palmyrene dynasty. One of the king's nephews murdered Odaenathus and his heir Herodianus at a banquet in Heraclea Pontica; the nephew was then killed by the guards (Hartmann 2001, 218–230; but see Bleckmann 2007, 57–61). Whether or not this man's name was Maeonius remains open to question (Hartmann 2001, 222–223; a fictitious person, according to Barnes 1978, 69). This name is attested only in the *Historia Augusta*, a notoriously unreliable source, especially in the collection of the *vitae* of the *tyranni triginta*.

Why did Gallienus order the murder of his deputy in the Roman East? The background of the murder is disputed: Was this a plot by Gallienus (e.g., Equini Schneider 1993, 11; Strobel 1993, 252; Teixidor 2005, 198; Gnoli 2007, 50, n. 51; Andrade 2018, 143–149; Raja 2022, 111), a conspiracy by Zenobia (so Février 1931, 90), or an internal feud in the family of the dynasts of Palmyra (e.g., Bleckmann 1995, 93–96; 2007, 57–61; Potter 2004, 263)? Or are we to state that the problem cannot be resolved (e.g., Kaizer 2005; Sommer 2005, 162)? Gallienus probably feared that Odaenathus would rise as emperor after his second victory over the Persians or that he would demand further political power. A potential competitor was therefore eliminated. However, this attempt by Gallienus to eliminate the power of the Palmyrene dynasts in the East failed (Hartmann 2001, 218–230). After the murder of Odaenathus, the Palmyrene government did not collapse. To a great extent, the general's strong-willed widow, Septimia Zenobia, secured the rule for her still underage son, Vaballathus, and, as his father's heir, appointed him *rex regum, corrector totius orientis*, and probably also *dux Romanorum*. With the help of Odaenathus's loyal officials she was able to secure Palmyrene rule in Syria (*CIS* II,

3971; Fest. 24; Eutr. 9.13.2; *HA Gall.* 13.2; *trig. tyr.* 27.1, 30.2; *Aurelian.* 22.1, 38.1; Zos. 1.39.2; Sync. 467.13–14; Hartmann 2001, 242–271). The administrative sector in which Odaenathus officially commanded the Roman administrative and military forces on behalf of Gallienus became a realm of the Palmyrene dynasts Vaballathus and Zenobia within the structures of the Roman Empire. King Vaballathus and Queen Zenobia officially recognized the authority of the Roman emperor, but in fact acted independently.

Nathanael Andrade's Chapter 11 in this volume provides additional information about Zenobia's unusual rule. Between 268 and 272, Zenobia expanded her political power in the East. In 270, Arabia and Egypt were occupied, and Vaballathus was elevated to *vir clarissimus rex consul imperator dux Romanorum*. Officially, the rule of the new emperor, Aurelian, was still recognized. However, Aurelian did not accept the increasing political power of the Palmyrene emperor. Therefore, in early 272, he moved against the Palmyrenes' realm in the Roman East and forced Zenobia and Vaballathus to usurp imperial power. In late March or early April 272, Zenobia relinquished her previous policy and honoured her son with the title of the Roman emperor, establishing him as equal to Aurelian. Her son was now called 'Imperator Caesar Lucius Iulius Aurelius Septimius Vaballathus Athenodorus Persicus maximus Arabicus maximus Adiabenicus maximus pius felix invictus Augustus' (*ILS* 8924; for the coinage see Bland 2011). After being defeated by Aurelian in two battles near Antioch and Emesa, Zenobia fled to Palmyra but was captured on the Euphrates (Hartmann 2001, 242–394; Sommer 2017, 168–179). The city of Palmyra was handed over without a fight by a 'peace party' under the leadership of the previously mentioned Roman senator Septimius Ḥaddūdan in August 272. But Palmyra was treated mildly. Aurelian had its riches confiscated, but there was no major destruction (Zos. 1.54.2; 55–56.2; *HA Aurel.* 28.3; Sync. 470.5; Equini Schneider 1993, 85–86; Watson 1999, 76–77; Hartmann 2001, 375–386; 2008, 370–372). But now a garrison under the Roman officer Sandario secured the city (*HA Aurel.* 31.2; Hartmann 2001, 391).

In Emesa, Zenobia and her advisory staff were brought to trial. Zenobia and Vaballathus, however, were pardoned because they belonged to a senatorial family (*HA Aurel.* 30.1–3; Zos. 1.56.2–3). After securing the eastern border against the Sassanians, Aurelian left the East in the early autumn of 272 (*HA Aurel.* 30.4; Zos. 1.59; Hartmann 2001, 391–394). He presented Zenobia in his triumph in Rome together with the defeated Gallic usurper Tetricus in the late summer of 274 (Fest. 24; Eutr. 9.13.2; *HA tyr. trig.* 24.4, 30.3, 30.24–26; *Aurelian.* 30.2, 32.4, 33–34). The queen then received a villa in Concae, near Hadrian's Villa in Tivoli (*HA trig. tyr.* 30.27). According to Syncellus and Zonaras, she married a respected senator (Sync. 470.5–7; Zon. 12.27 p. 607.6–11; untrustworthy Zos. 1.59; Hartmann 2001, 411–424).

PALMYRA IN THE LATE THIRD CENTURY

Before leaving the Roman East, Aurelian presented the equestrian governor of Mesopotamia, Aurelius Marcellinus, with responsibility for the Eastern provinces and the protection of the eastern frontier (Zos. 1.60.1; Hartmann 2001, 371–73, 393). But the followers of the dynasts in Palmyra could not admit defeat. A group led by Septimius Apsaeus, the *prostates* (governor) of Palmyra, planned a new uprising of the Eastern provinces against Aurelian at the turn of the year 272/273 (Zos. 1.60.1; *IGLS* XVII.1, 77; Kotula 1997, 141–142; Hartmann 2001, 395–396; 2008, 372–373; Yon 2002, 143–144, 149–150, 284; Sommer 2005, 165). He initially tried to persuade Marcellinus to overthrow the emperor and accept the title of *augustus*. But Marcellinus was loyal to his successful Illyrian emperor. He stalled the rebels and informed Aurelian of the plans of the Palmyrenes. But Apsaeus sensed that Marcellinus would not support Palmyra's cause. To forestall the emperor's intervention, he ordered the commander of Palmyra, Sandario, and his soldiers to be assassinated. After the massacre, in the spring of 273, the Palmyrenes proclaimed Antiochus, probably the father of Zenobia, who remained in the city, *augustus*. The old man, whom the *Historia Augusta* calls 'Achilleus' and *parens Zenobiae* ('father of Zenobia'), was probably forced to usurp the title of *augustus* by Apsaeus (Zos. 1.60, 61.1; *HA Aurel.* 31.2; Pol. Silv. 521.49; Hartmann 2001, 117–124). The mastermind of the rebellion wanted to give the uprising dynastic legitimacy. The rebellion, however, remained regionally limited to the area around Palmyra. Without any military forces, the uprising was doomed from the outset. Aurelian took determined action against it. Immediately after receiving the message from Marcellinus, he marched east from the Balkans. From Antioch he moved on to Palmyra. In the early summer of 273, Aurelian was once again able to take the unfortified city without major problems (there was no city wall to besiege in the times of Zenobia, as the *History Augusta* assumes, cf. Hartmann 2001, 375–384; but see Intagliata 2017). The rebellion collapsed on the emperor's arrival. The backers of the uprising were punished, but Zenobia's elderly father, an emperor against his will, went unpunished (*HA Aurel.* 31; Zos. 1.60–61.1; Equini Schneider 1993, 85–86; Kotula 1997, 140–144; Watson 1999, 80–82; Hartmann 2001, 395–402; 2008, 372–374). In order to secure the East, Aurelian stationed the Legio I Illyricorum in Palmyra (*Not. Dig. or.* 32.15, 32.30; Hartmann 2001, 409–410).

The report of Aurelian's complete destruction of Palmyra, as found in the *Historia Augusta* and in Zosimus's account, is unhistorical. In 273, Palmyra was plundered and some buildings were heavily damaged in the fight. However, major destruction is not archaeologically detectable (*HA Aurel.* 31.3; Zos. 1.61.1; Kowalski 1997, 39–44; Hartmann 2001, 398–401; Raja 2022, 118). Moreover, one cannot speak of a sudden end of Palmyrene civilization following the pillage of 273. Palmyrene culture, writing, and language were not immediately suppressed by Aurelian (as suggested by Cantineau 1935, 7, 164). The most recent known Greek–Palmyrene bilingual text dates to 279/280. In this year, the *phyle* (tribe) of the Maththabolians honoured Malchus/Malkō, son of Mocimus/Moqīmō, with a statue because he rebuilt the roof of the great basilica of the god Ares/Arṣū with his own resources, together with those of his son, Mucianus (*IGLS* XVII.1, 81 = al-As'ad and Gawlikowski 1986/1987, 167–168, no. 8; cf. *IGLS* XVII.1, 80 = al-As'ad and Gawlikowski 1986/1987, 167, no. 7; Kaizer 2002, 122–123; Yon 2002, 70, 76–77, 252–253; 2012, 95–96). The text attests to the official use of the Palmyrene script and to the cult of the Palmyrene god Arṣū with its temple on the southern bank of the wadi and to one of the four tribes of the city of Palmyra. The temples of Baalshamin (*IGLS* XVII.1, 154; Kowalski 1997, 45; Kaizer 2002, 86) and Allat/Athene (Barański 1994, 11) were still used around AD 300. Palmyra also retained the status of a Roman *colonia*, even under Emperor Diocletian (284–305; *CIL* III, 6049; *CIS* II, 3971, note = *AÉ* 1921, 92; *AÉ* 1934, 262; *CIL* III, 14177/4, 1–2 = Bauzou 1989, vol. 2, 416, no. 113; *AÉ* 1993, 1606). However, we know almost nothing about the municipal organization after AD 273 (Kowalski 1997, 42–46; Hartmann 2001, 400–402, 425–426; 2016, 65–67). Thus, the abandonment of the specific culture of Palmyra in the last quarter of the third century was not the result of punitive imperial measures: it was the remainder of the upper class of Palmyra in the city after the pillage of 273 who gathered around the senator Ḥaddūdan and took the drastic step of testifying to their loyalty to Rome and the Illyrian emperors. They abandoned the Palmyrene language and script in official contexts and so relinquished their local culture. A rapid decline began in the years following Aurelian's devastation of the city, and it became an insignificant border town. The old trading centre could not be revitalized (Hartmann 2016, 65–67).

Under Diocletian, Palmyra once again experienced some recovery as a garrison town in the new Tetrarchic border fortification system along the Strata Diocletiana. Around 300, the governor of the province of Syria Phoenice, Sossianus Hierocles, built a camp for the Legio I Illyricorum in the eastern parts of the town and a bath in a house at the Great Colonnade (*IGLS* XVII.1, 100, 121; Millar 1993, 183; Barański 1994, 13; Kowalski 1997, 44–45; Delplace 2014, 225–226). With the construction of a new city wall under Diocletian, Palmyra was reduced to the core of the town surrounding the Great Colonnade, the agora, and the residential area north of the Great Colonnade that had been the centre of Palmyra since the second century (Barański 1994, 9–13; Intagliata 2018, 69–82, 98–100). The rest of the once-thriving city became deserted; the old Hellenistic parts of town, south of the Wadi, were abandoned.

The Historical Significance of Palmyra in the Third Century

Why did Palmyra become so politically significant in the third century? The peak of Palmyra's political importance, under the rule of Odaenathus and Zenobia in the 260s and early 270s, must be explained in the context of the crisis in the Roman Empire during the third century (Hartmann 2001, 427–466; for a different assessment Sommer 2005, 159–170, 220–224; 2008). The Palmyrene dynasts' particular form of rule in the Roman East was not an attempt to separate themselves from Rome and establish their own independent realm. Instead, their aim was to establish a regional rule by Roman senators from Palmyra who took the protection of their region into their own hands in a critical situation. The weakness of the central power in Rome and the many problems at the borders of the Rhine and the Danube forced Gallienus to appoint a representative of the emperor in the East, one who would fulfil his duties to protect the eastern frontiers, and to secure the imperial power of his dynasty in the East against possible usurpers. By elevating the consular and Palmyrene *exarchos* to *corrector totius Orientis* and *dux Romanorum* in 261, Gallienus gave the most powerful general in the East a temporary special command over the provinces and military forces. The experienced officer had proven himself as a loyal follower of the dynasty and had a strong reputation in the East. In the early 260s, the local dynast and senator from Syria distinguished himself by protecting his home region, acting as a representative of the interests of the Roman East. Over the next few years, a regional political power emerged in the East. Odaenathus successfully built his charismatic personal dynastic rule through his successful campaigns against the Persians and his skilled administration of the East. Odaenathus's new political position found expression in his adoption of the title *rex regum*. However, Odaenathus cannot be characterized as a client king established by Gallienus, as is often assumed by scholars (cf., inter alia, Février 1931, 84; Strobel 1993, 250–251; Kotula 1997, 98, 101, 114; Young 2001, 177). Even after this step, Odaenathus remained a Roman official. His political power arose, not from his position as *rex*, but from the *imperium* given to him by Gallienus.

With Vaballathus's assumption of governance after the murder of Odaenathus in 267/268, the character of Palmyrene power in the East changed. The mandate given by the emperor, with its temporal and regional limits, became a regional rule in the eastern part of the empire, legitimized by dynastic succession. Queen Zenobia, the real ruler in Syria, secured the position of the father for her son, Vaballathus. His title of *rex* secured a dynastic succession. At the same time, the Roman offices of the father supported this succession. With the expansion of this power, the conquest of Arabia and Egypt, and the adoption of the title *imperator* by Vaballathus in 270, the special character of this regional rule was openly expressed. The subruler Vaballathus understood himself as a regional leader under the supremacy of the emperor, protecting the eastern frontier on behalf of the emperor in the West.

The emergence of Palmyra's specific form of regional rule ('Teilreich') was necessary owing to the particular problems in the middle of the third century: the simultaneous threats at different borders requiring the presence of the emperor at several fronts simultaneously and the Roman soldiers' need for the leadership of a victorious *augustus*. Usurpations in various regions of the empire were the result of these problems and fundamentally destabilized imperial rule. The Palmyrene realm in the East was an attempt to resolve this problem by establishing local Roman rule led by a senatorial family. The regional ruler governed a limited part of the empire and assumed only certain aspects of imperial rule and without adopting the title of *augustus*. This form of decentralization of the Roman government was one way to resolve Rome's institutional and political crises of the third century. However, Zenobia ultimately failed in her policy of regional rule because she did not succeed in achieving recognition from Rome. Aurelian regarded the Palmyrene realm as a danger to the unity of the Roman Empire and as interference in his imperial authority. His two campaigns against Palmyra in 272 and 273 ended the brief interlude of the Palmyrene realm, and the short period of significance of this Syrian oasis in world history.

ABBREVIATIONS

AÉ   *Année épigraphique*. Paris: Presses universitaires de France, 1888–.

CIL   *Corpus inscriptionum Latinarum*. Berlin: Berlin-Brandenburgische Akademie der Wissenschaften, 1853–.

CIS   *Corpus inscriptionum Semiticarum*. Paris: Reipublicæ Typographeo, 1881–1962.

IGLS   *Inscriptions grecques et latines de la Syrie*. Paris: Geuthner, 1929–.

ILS   Dessau, Hermann, ed. 1892–1916. *Inscriptiones latinae selectae*. 3 vols. Berlin: Weidmann.

Inv.   Cantineau, Jean, Jean Starcky, Michał Gawlikowski, and Adnan Bounni, eds. 1930–1975. *Inventaire des inscriptions de Palmyre*. 12 vols. Beirut: Imprimerie catholique.

OGIS   Dittenberger, Wilhelm, ed. 1903–1905. *Orientis Graeci inscriptiones selectae*. 2 vols. Leipzig: Hirzel.

PAT   Hillers, Delbert and Eleonora Cussini, eds. *Palmyrene Aramaic Texts*. Baltimore: The Johns Hopkins University Press, 1996.

BIBLIOGRAPHY

Andrade, Nathanael. 2018. *Zenobia: Shooting Star of Palmyra*. Oxford: Oxford University Press.

al-As'ad, Khaled, and Michal Gawlikowski. 1986/1987. 'New Honorific Inscriptions in the Great Colonnade of Palmyra'. *Annales archéologiques arabes syriennes* 36–37: 164–171.

Baldini, Antonio. 1976. 'Problemi di storia palmirena: Nota sulla politica di Odenato'. *Corso di cultura sull'Arte Ravennate e Bizantina* 23: 21–45.

Barański, Marek. 1994. 'The Roman Army in Palmyra: A Case of Adaptation of a Pre-existing City'. In *The Roman and Byzantine Army in the East*, edited by Edward Dąbrowa, 9–17. Cracow: Jagiellonian University Press.

Barnes, Timothy D. 1978. *The Sources of the 'Historia Augusta'*. Brussels: Latomus.

Bauzou, Thomas. 1989. 'A finibus Syriae: Recherches sur les routes des frontières orientales de l'Empire Romain'. 3 vols. Unpublished doctoral thesis, Université de Paris I.

Bland, Roger. 2011. 'The Coinage of Vabalathus and Zenobia from Antioch and Alexandria'. *Numismatic Chronicle* 171: 133–186.

Bleckmann, Bruno. 1992. *Die Reichskrise des III: Jahrhunderts in der spätantiken und byzantinischen Geschichtsschreibung*. Munich: Tuduv.

Bleckmann, Bruno. 1995. 'Zu den Quellen der vita Gallieni duo'. In *Historiae Augustae Colloquium Maceratense 1992*, edited by Giorgio Bonamente and Gianfranco Paci, 75–105. Bari: Edipuglia.

Bleckmann, Bruno. 2007. 'Odainathos in der spätantiken Literatur'. In *Historiae Augustae Colloquium Bambergense 2005*, edited by Giorgio Bonamente and Hartwin Brandt, 51–1. Bari: Edipuglia.

Cantineau, Jean. 1931. 'Textes palmyréniens provenant de la fouille du Temple de Bêl'. *Syria* 12: 116–141.

Cantineau, Jean. 1933. 'Un *restitutor orientis* dans les inscriptions de Palmyre'. *Journal asiatique* 222: 217–233.

Cantineau, Jean. 1935. *Grammaire du palmyrénien épigraphique*. Cairo: Institut français d'archéologie orientale.

Chéhab, Maurice. 1962. 'Tyr à l'époque romaine'. *Mélanges de l'Université Saint-Joseph* 38: 13–40.

Clermont-Ganneau, Charles S. 1920. 'Odeinat et Vaballat, rois de Palmyre, et leur titre romain de *corrector*'. *Revue biblique* 29: 382–419.

Daryaee, Touraj. 2022. 'Palmyra and the Sasanians in the Third Century AD'. In *Palmyra and the East*, edited by Kenneth Lapatin and Rubina Raja, 39–44. Turnhout: Brepols.

Delplace, Christiane. 2014. 'Palmyre, de la ville – centre commercial international – à la ville – centre militaire et chrétien'. In *The Levant: Crossroads of Late Antiquity*, edited by Ellen Bradshaw Aitken and John M. Fossey, 225–253. Leiden: Brill.

Edwell, Peter M. 2008. *Between Rome and Persia*. London: Routledge.

Equini Schneider, Eugenia. 1993. *Septimia Zenobia Sebaste*. Rome: 'L'Erma' di Bretschneider.

Février, James Germain. 1931. *Essai sur l'histoire politique et économique de Palmyre*. Paris: Vrin.

Gawlikowski, Michał. 1973. *Le temple palmyrénien: Étude d'épigraphie et de topographie historique*. Palmyre 6. Warsaw: Państwowe Wydawnictwo Naukowe.

Gawlikowski, Michał. 1983. 'Palmyre et l'Euphrate'. *Syria* 60: 53–68.

Gawlikowski, Michał. 1985. 'Les princes de Palmyre'. *Syria* 62: 251–261.

Gawlikowski, Michał. 1996. 'Palmyra and Its Caravan Trade'. *Annales archéologiques arabes syriennes* 42: 139–145.

Gawlikowski, Michał. 2007. 'Odainat et Hérodien, rois des rois'. *Mélanges de l'Université Saint-Joseph* 60: 289–311.

Geiger, Michael. 2013. *Gallienus*. Frankfurt am Main: Lang.

Glas, Toni. 2014. *Valerian: Kaisertum und Reformansätze in der Krisenphase des Römischen Reiches*. Paderborn: Schöningh.

Gnoli, Tommaso. 2007. *The Interplay of Roman and Iranian Titles in the Roman East (1st–3rd Century A.D.)*. Vienna: Verlag der Österreichischen Akademie der Wissenschaften.

Gross, Andrew D. 2005. 'Three New Palmyrene Inscriptions'. In *A Journey to Palmyra: Collected Essays to Remember Delbert R. Hillers*, edited by Eleonora Cussini, 89–102. Leiden: Brill.

Hächler, Nikolas. 2019. *Kontinuität und Wandel des Senatorenstandes im Zeitalter der Soldatenkaiser*. Leiden: Brill.

Hartmann, Udo. 2001. *Das palmyrenische Teilreich*. Stuttgart: Steiner.

Hartmann, Udo. 2008. 'Das palmyrenische Teilreich'. In *Die Zeit der Soldatenkaiser*, edited by Klaus-Peter Johne, 343–378. Berlin: Akademie-Verlag.

Hartmann, Udo. 2016. 'What Was It Like to Be a Palmyrene in the Age of Crisis? Changing Palmyrene Identities in the Third Century AD'. In *The World of Palmyra*, edited by Andreas Kropp and Rubina Raja, 53–69. Copenhagen: Det Kongelige Danske Videnskabernes Selskab.

Hartmann, Udo. 2021. 'Zenobia of Palmyra: A Female Roman Ruler in Times of Crisis'. In *Powerful Women in the Ancient World: Perception and (Self)Presentation*, edited by Kerstin Droß-Krüpe and Sebastian Fink. 433–452. Münster: Zaphon.

Hartmann, Udo and Andreas Luther. 1999. 'Eine Weihung an den Gott Abgal'. *Welt des Orients* 30: 125–128.

Ingholt, Harald. 1936. 'Inscriptions and Sculptures from Palmyra I'. *Berytus* 3: 83–125.

Ingholt, Harald. 1976. 'Varia Tadmorea. II. The Odainat Family'. In *Palmyre: Bilan et perspectives; Colloque de Strasbourg (1973)*, 115–137. Strasbourg: Association pour l'étude de la civilisation romaine.

Intagliata, Emanuele E. 2017. 'Palmyra and Its Ramparts During the Tetrarchy'. In *New Cities in Late Antiquity*, edited by Efthymios Rizos, 71–83. Turnhout: Brepols.

Intagliata, Emanuele E. 2018. *Palmyra After Zenobia. 273–750: An Archaeological and Historical Reappraisal*. Oxford: Oxbow.

Kaizer, Ted. 2002. *The Religious Life of Palmyra*. Stuttgart: Steiner.

Kaizer, Ted. 2005. 'Odaenathus von Palmyra'. In *Politische Morde*, edited by Michael Sommer, 73–79. Darmstadt: Wissenschaftliche Buchgesellschaft.

Kaizer, Ted. 2007. '"Palmyre, cité grecque"? A Question of Coinage'. *Klio* 89: 39–60.

Kennedy, David L. 1986. 'Ana on the Euphrates in the Roman Period'. *Iraq* 48: 103–104.

Kettenhofen, Erich. 1982. *Die römisch-persischen Kriege des 3. Jahrhunderts n. Chr. nach der Inschrift Šāhpuhrs I. an der Ka'be-ye Zartošt (ŠKZ)*. TAVO-Beihefte B 55. Wiesbaden: Reichert.

Kotula, Tadeusz. 1997. *Aurélien et Zénobie: L'unité ou la division de l'Empire?* Wrocław: Uniwersytetu Wrocławskiego.

Kowalski, Sławomir P. 1997. 'Late Roman Palmyra in Literature and Epigraphy'. *Studia Palmyreńskie* 10: 39–62.

Milik, Jósef Tadeusz. 1972. *Dédicaces faites par des dieux (Palmyre, Hatra, Tyr)*. Recherches d'épigraphie Proche-Orientale 1. Paris: Geuthner.

Millar, Fergus. 1990. 'The Roman *Coloniae* of the Near East'. In *Roman Eastern Policy and Other Studies in Roman History*, edited by Heikki Solin and Mika Kajava, 7–58. Helsinki: Societas scientiarum Fennica.

Millar, Fergus. 1993. *The Roman Near East, 31 BC–AD 337*. Cambridge, MA: Harvard University Press.

Millar, Fergus. 1995. 'Latin in the Epigraphy of the Roman Near East'. In *Acta colloquii epigraphici latini*, edited by Heikki Solin, Olli Salomies, and Uta-Maria Liertz, 403–419. Helsinki: Societas scientiarum Fennica.

Mosig-Walburg, Karin. 2023. *Das frühe Sasanidenreich und Rom. Eine Forschungskritik*. Gutenberg: Computus.

Potter, David S. 1990. *Prophecy and History in the Crisis of the Roman Empire: A Historical Commentary on the Thirteenth Sibylline Oracle*. Oxford: Clarendon.

Potter, David. 1996. 'Palmyra and Rome. Odaenathus' Titulature and the Use of the *imperium maius*'. *Zeitschrift für Papyrologie und Epigraphik* 113: 271–285.

Potter, David S. 2004. *The Roman Empire at Bay, AD 180–395*. London: Routledge.

Raja, Rubina. 2022. *Pearl of the Desert: A History of Palmyra*. Oxford: Oxford University Press.

Sartre, Maurice. 1996. 'Palmyre, cité grecque'. *Annales archéologiques arabes syriennes* 42: 385–405.

Sartre[-Fauriat], Annie and Maurice Sartre. 2014. *Zénobie, de Palmyre à Rome*. Paris: Perrin.

Schlumberger, Daniel. 1942/1943. 'Les Gentilices romains des Palmyréniens'. *Bulletin d'études orientales* 9: 53–82.

Schlumberger, Daniel. 1951. *La Palmyrène du Nord-Ouest*. Paris: Geuthner.

Seyrig, Henri. 1937. 'Antiquités syriennes 19. Note sur Hérodien, prince de Palmyre'. *Syria* 18: 1–4.

Simelon, Paul. 2013. 'Aurelius dans les gentilices multiples à l'époque de Caracalla'. *Antiquité classique* 82: 195–215.

Smith II, Andrew M. 2013. *Roman Palmyra*. Oxford: Oxford University Press.

Sommer, Michael. 2005. *Roms orientalische Steppengrenze: Palmyra – Edessa – Dura-Europos – Hatra*. Stuttgart: Steiner.

Sommer, Michael. 2008. 'Der Löwe von Tadmor. Palmyra und der unwahrscheinliche Aufstieg des Septimius Odaenathus'. *Historische Zeitschrift* 287: 281–318.

Sommer, Michael. 2017. *Palmyra*. Darmstadt: von Zabern.

Southern, Pat. 2008. *Empress Zenobia: Palmyra's Rebel Queen*. London: Continuum.

Stoneman, Richard. 1992. *Palmyra and Its Empire: Zenobia's Revolt Against Rome*. Ann Arbor: University of Michigan Press.

Strobel, Karl. 1993. *Das Imperium Romanum im '3. Jahrhundert': Modell einer historischen Krise?* Stuttgart: Steiner.

Swain, Simon. 1993. 'Greek into Palmyrene. Odaenathus as "corrector totius Orientis"?' *Zeitschrift für Papyrologie und Epigraphik* 99: 157–164.

Teixidor, Javier. 2005. 'Palmyra in the Third Century'. In *A Journey to Palmyra: Collected Essays to Remember Delbert R. Hillers*, edited by Eleonora Cussini, 181–225. Leiden: Brill.

Watson, Alaric. 1999. *Aurelian and the Third Century*. London: Routledge.

Will, Ernest. 1992. *Les Palmyréniens: La Venise des sables*. Paris: Armand Colin.

Winsbury, Rex. 2010. *Zenobia of Palmyra: History, Myth and the Neo-Classical Imagination*. London: Duckworth.

Winter, Engelbert. 1988. *Die sāsānidisch-römischen Friedensverträge des 3. Jahrhunderts n. Chr.* Frankfurt am Main: Lang.

Winter, Engelbert and Beate Dignas. 2007. *Rome and Persia in Late Antiquity*. Cambridge: Cambridge University Press.

Yon, Jean-Baptiste. 2002. *Les notables de Palmyre*. Beirut: Institut français d'archéologie du Proche-Orient.

Yon, Jean-Baptiste, ed. 2012. *Inscriptions grecques et latines de la Syrie*. Vol. 17.1, *Palmyre*. Beirut: Institut français du Proche-Orient.

Young, Gary K. 2001. *Rome's Eastern Trade*. London: Routledge.

CHAPTER 11

QUEEN ZENOBIA

The Rise and Fall of Her Palmyra

NATHANAEL ANDRADE*

INTRODUCTION

> When Aurelian captured her and had her escorted into his presence, he addressed her with these words: 'Well, Zenobia? You dared to behave insolently towards Roman emperors [*imperatores*]?' She reportedly said: 'I acknowledge you, who conquers, to be an emperor [*imperator*]. I did not deem Gallienus, Aureolus, and the rest to be emperors [*principes*].' (*HA* Tyr. Trig. 30.23)

GIVEN such source testimonies, it is unsurprising that Zenobia captures our imagination today. Named Bathzabbai in Palmyrenean, she is the most famous Palmyrene on record and among the best-known women of antiquity. She has often been the subject of historical analyses (Sartre and Sartre 2014; Hartmann 2001; Equini Schneider 1993; Stoneman 1992; Hvidberg-Hansen 2002; Southern 2008; Teixidor 2005; Winsbury 2010; Weingarten 2018 and *Zenobia: Empress of the East* for an informative blog; Andrade 2018; Dirven 2021). Her stature as a virtuous woman, or a queen of the 'Orient', has been reiterated by medieval and modern European authors and artists (Sartre and Sartre 2014, 191–262; Sartre 2016; Sommer 2015). Legends of a Tadmorean queen named al-Zabba, based on her, circulated in medieval Arabic texts. For modern Arab writers, Zenobia has symbolized nationalist resistance to Western oppression (Woltering 2014; Weingarten 2018). Her reputation has also been exploited for darker purposes. The Assad government has leveraged it to legitimize its oppressive and brutal rule. Zenobia's portrait has appeared on its currency (Stoneman 1992, fig. 25d), and a chief official has portrayed her as an Arab nationalist (Tlass 1985; 1986; 2000; see Sartre and Sartre 2014,

* The material in this chapter condenses, summarizes, or rephrases material from Andrade 2018; I thank Oxford University Press for permission to use it.

253–255; 2016, 21–32, 219–221). When the Islamic State first occupied Palmyra in May of 2015 and initiated its atrocities and destruction there, the Assad government responded by parading a likeness of Zenobia in the cities that it controlled (Weingarten 2018, 144–145; on the civil war, see Chapter 37 [Sartre-Fauriat], this volume).

Because of her fame, any attempt to situate Zenobia in her historical and social context confronts a paradox. Although well known, little reliable source material documents her life. The extract above, from the *Historia Augusta*, depicts Zenobia as resisting an array of Roman emperors and usurpers. But it misleads. Zenobia never opposed the Emperor Gallienus or the usurper Aureolus. Claudius II ('Gothicus'), whom Zenobia resisted, is not mentioned.

With these challenges in mind, this chapter considers what it means to write a history of Zenobia. While outlining the sources' limitations, it describes how we may understand some of Zenobia's life experiences and political career. Since third-century Palmyra and the dynasty of Odainath are covered elsewhere (see Hartmann's contribution in Chapter 10), we will touch only on those aspects that help us to understand Zenobia better. Much is beyond our grasp, and people will inevitably debate how Zenobia should be depicted. Still, in light of the political agendas that have governed Zenobia's representations and the destruction of her Palmyra, it is important to base narratives about her on our knowledge of the Palmyrene context that she inhabited. In this chapter, we offer the basic outline of one such narrative.

ZENOBIA: THE SOURCES

Inscriptions are important sources of information on Zenobia's life and career, but only a few mention her. One valuable inscription (*PAT* 0317) states

[in Greek]:

> . . . for the safety
> of Septimia Zenobia,
> most illustrious queen [βασιλίσσης],
> mother of the king
> [μητρὸς τοῦ βασιλέως] . . .

[in Palmyrenean]:

> For the life and victory of Septimius
> Wahballath Athenodoros, illustrious king
> of kings [mlk mlk'] and epanorthotes
> of all the East ['pnrtt' dy mdnh' klh],
> son of Septimius Odainath, king of kings,
> and for the life of Septimia Bathzabbai,

illustrious queen [mlkt'], mother of the king of kings
['mh dy mlk mlk'], daughter of Antiochus
[bt 'ntywkws], mile 14.

Wahballath's titles date the inscription to 268–270. Zenobia had not yet claimed the titles of *imperator* or Augustus for her son (Hartmann 2001, 242; Southern 2008, 83–86). Wahballath was king of kings and *epanorthotes* of all the East. These titles were consistent with those of his father, Odainath. From the inscription, we learn that Zenobia's father was named Antiochus. Zenobia had Greek and Aramaic names (Zenobia and Bathzabbai). She also claimed to be queen and 'mother of the king of kings.' Thus the inscription conveys how Zenobia conceived of her legitimacy as ruler. As the guardian of Odainath's child, she exerted political authority on his behalf (Hartmann 2001, 259–277, 465; Southern 2008, 83–84, 92, 101; Andrade 2018, 165–166, 172; Dirven 2021, 261–263).

Literary texts communicate information about Zenobia, but their reliability is open to question. Zenobia figures prominently in the *Historia Augusta*. Now generally believed to be the composition of a single author ca. 395, it is notorious for its inaccuracies and invented material (Paschoud 2002; 2011 for material relevant to Zenobia). The historian Zosimus (ca. 500) also provides important testimony (Paschoud 2003, xxxvi–xlvi). The *Historia Augusta* and Zosimus shared some common source traditions, such as the works of Zenobia's contemporary, Dexippus (*BNJ* 100; Mecella 2013; Mallan and Davenport 2015). Even so, Zosimus's reliability is also inconsistent.

Zenobia is briefly mentioned by Byzantine historians and chroniclers, but many of these accounts are fragmentary. Notable are the *Continuator Dionis* (who may be Peter the Patrician), John of Antioch (seventh century), George Syncellus (ninth century), and Zonaras (twelfth century). These referenced various earlier traditions, especially Zosimus (Banchich 2015, 3–9; Potter 1990, 356–369, 395–397; Bleckmann 1992; Brecht 1999; Mariev 2008). Some fourth- and fifth-century Christian authors identify Zenobia as Jewish (Hartmann 2001, 319–321). But this is only because of her affiliation with Paul of Samosata, a Christian bishop of Antioch who denied the divinity of Jesus (Eus., *Hist. ecc.* 7.27 and 30; Riedmatten 1952, 135–158). Fragments of his correspondence with Zenobia survive (Declerck 1984, 134). Through such sources, we can comprehend certain aspects of Zenobia's reign.

Rabbinical Jewish texts impart at least one valuable reference to Zenobia (TJ *Ter.* 8: 10.46b in Guggenheimer 2000; Appelbaum 2011, 542). Legends about a Palmyrene queen named Tadi or Thadamor appear in later Manichaean texts. The figure from medieval Arabic literature named al-Zabba ('the hairy one'), apparently due to her long, braided pubic hair, also seems based on her (Gardner and Lieu 2004, 111–114; Weststeijn 2013; 2016; Hartmann 2001, 308–315, and 332–351; Woltering 2014, 38–40; Sommer 2015, 114–115). Although fascinating, such accounts shed little light on Zenobia herself. They indicate her fame long after she lived.

Between 270 and 272, Zenobia had coins minted at Antioch and Alexandria. Most celebrated Wahballath, but, in early 272, some issues featured profiles of Zenobia wearing a stephane crown (Bland 2011; Estiot 2004, 113–120, 222–223). On the Antiochene coins,

FIGURE 11.1 Antoninianus with likeness of Zenobia, Antioch, 272; British Museum 1974.1001.3.

Latin texts described her as S(eptimia) Zenobia Aug(usta) (Figure 11.1). Greek versions of these titles appeared on coins from Alexandria (Figures 11.2–11.3). Zenobia's portrait typically resembles that of the Empress Salonina, wife of Gallienus (Figures 11.1 and 11.2). But some Alexandrian coins featured a 'realistic' portrait of Zenobia with an aquiline nose and large ears (Figure 11.3) (Sartre and Sartre 2014, 75–76; Equini Schneider 1993, 95–96).

Zenobia has left no trace in the material record at Palmyra, including its statues and portraits (Balty 2005, 321–324, 337–338). Her name and royal title (*basilissa*) appear on some tesserae, but without her likeness (Equini Schneider 1993, 98, fig. 18, with 26–27; Hvidberg-Hansen 2002, 77, no. 21). Even so, we can still understand some of Zenobia's life experiences from Palmyra's material culture, including its funerary portraits (see Chapter 27 [Raja], this volume).

ZENOBIA'S FAMILY, CHILDHOOD, AND MARRIAGE

Reportedly, Zenobia's chastity was such that she slept with her husband only to attempt conception. After sleeping with him once, she waited to

FIGURE 11.2 Tetradrachm with likeness of Zenobia, Alexandria, 272; British Museum 1860.032.27.

FIGURE 11.3 Tetradrachm with likeness of Zenobia, Alexandria, 272; Bibliothèque nationale de France, Cabinet de Monnaies, Médailles, et Antiques, no. 3647.

> menstruate again and withheld herself in case she was pregnant. If not, she gave him the power to try for children again. (*HA* Tyr. Trig. 30.12)

Despite fascinating (and uncorroborated) statements such as this one, little is known about Zenobia's social and domestic world. However, recent inquiries into the lives of children and women in Palmyra (Chapters 28 and 29 [Heyn] and Chapter 31 [Bobou], this volume; Krag and Raja 2016; Heyn 2018) make it possible to surmise certain aspects of this world before her reign. The next paragraphs present a narrative of Zenobia's life before her rise to power. It constitutes a skeletal summary of my recent book, which explores what Palmyrene material culture can tell us about Zenobia's early years (Andrade 2018).

Since Wahballath was probably born in the late 250s (he was still in his minority in 268–272), we may infer that Zenobia was born around 240 (Stoneman 1992, 111–112; Equini Schneider 1993, 32). Like most Palmyrene women born after 212, she probably had the name Iulia Aurelia (Iulia Aurelia Bathzabbai) (on this possibility, Sartre and Sartre 2014, 79; Southern 2008, 4). Her natal household, and perhaps extended family, shared a courtyard house with an elaborately decorated interior (Chapter 22 [Zenoni], this volume). Its smells, colours, and culinary offerings permeated her youthful experiences. As a young girl, Zenobia interacted with her extended family and with domestic slaves, as well as with members of her clan and tribe. Her attire and hairstyle perhaps differed little from that of boys her age, with whom she interacted (see Chapter 28 [Heyn] and Chapter 31 [Bobou], this volume; Krag and Raja 2016, 143; Heyn 2018, 111–112). She wore earrings, learned to weave, and played childhood games. In the early 250s, Zenobia reached puberty. She had her hair, now longer, styled elegantly, and she wore more gendered clothing (see Chapter 28 [Heyn], this volume). She spoke Palmyrenean Aramaic as her native tongue and acquired fluency in Greek. Only later in life did she probably learn Latin, but not flawlessly (*HA* Tyr. Trig. 30.20–22; *BNJ* 626). Despite Arabian and Iranian traditions in Palmyra, Zenobia did not regard herself as an Arab, Parthian, or Persian. She was a Roman, even if she expressed it through Palmyra's distinctly local patterns.

In the late 250s or so, Zenobia and Odainath were married (Southern 2008, 4). Odainath was considerably older than Zenobia and had been married previously. His son, Hairan, also called Herodian, was fairly close to Zenobia's age (for Hairan and Herodian as the same person, Gawlikowski 1985; 2007; 2016). Throughout the 250s, the Roman imperial court recognized Odainath as a client king. But he only claimed the title of 'exarch' or 'leader' of Palmyra (*IGLS* XVI.1, 54 and 58, *PAT* 2753). At roughly the time of Zenobia's marriage, he governed Palmyra as a Roman *consularis* (*IGLS* XVI.1, 55–56, 143, with 59–60; Yon 2011, 61, 157; Rey-Coquais 2006, no. 32). In the 260s, Odainath claimed the title of 'king of kings' and authority as governor of all the East (*PAT* 0292; see Chapter 10 [Hartmann], this volume). Many courtiers now adopted his name of Septimius. Zenobia became Septimia (for this possibility, Sartre and Sartre 2014, 79; Potter 2014, 257).

Once married, Zenobia covered her hair (and perhaps her face) in public. She displayed the jewellery that Odainath had given her, but perhaps only domestically. As in her youth, she participated in religious processions; made offerings of burnt incense, wine, or oil; and prayed to her gods (see Chapter 28 [Heyn], this volume; Finlayson 2013). We do not know whether she or women in general served as priests or organized ritual banquets. She managed the textile production of her domestic slaves. She administered her property, including rural estates and perhaps burial plots (Cussini 2005). She began bearing children, and she survived the dangers of childbirth.

Wahballath is Zenobia's only undisputed child. The *Historia Augusta* repeatedly claims that she governed for two sons named Herennianus and Timolaus (*HA Gall.* 13.2, Tyr. Trig. 15.2, 24.4, 27–28, and 30.2; Stoneman 1992, 114–115; Sartre and Sartre 2014, 85–86; Southern 2008, 7–10), but refers to Wahballath only once (*HA Aurel.* 38.1–2). However, it alone mentions them, and they are probably the literary products of some sort of confusion over the identities of Odainath's actual sons (Sartre and Sartre 2014, 85 and 2016, 183; Bland 2011, 137, n. 10). Owing to misinterpreted inscriptions, scholars have sometimes erroneously surmised the existence of a son named Antiochus (on this issue, Sartre and Sartre 2014, 86–87, 275; Hartmann 2001, 119–120).

A tessera series displays images of figures reclining on dining couches while dressed as priests (*PAT* 2497 = *RTP* 736; Gawlikowski 2016, 132–133, fig. 6). Apparently dating to the 260s, their inscriptions identify Hairan, son of Odainath on one side, and Wahballath, son of Odainath on the other. No Palmyrene material mentions other sons in Odainath's household. Zosimus indicates that Aurelian removed only one son of Zenobia from Palmyra in 272 (Zos. 1.59.1; Sartre and Sartre 2014, 183). This was certainly Wahballath.

The Byzantine author Zonaras (12.27) claims that Zenobia had daughters, and Latin sources indicate that Zenobia's descendants lived near Rome well after Aurelian relocated her to Italy (*HA* Tyr. Trig. 27 and 30.27; Eutr. 9.13.2; Jer., *Chron.*, for year 274). Zenobia, reportedly married to a Roman senator (Syn. 721 (470); Zon. 12.27), may have had additional children (Sartre and Sartre 2014, 87). More probably, Wahballath and any daughters were born at Palmyra and lived with Zenobia in Italy after 272.

Such was Zenobia's life before her reign. In 267–268, her husband was murdered. For the next four years, Zenobia was the most powerful person in the Roman East. But she faced serious political challenges.

Zenobia's Widowhood and Rise to Power

Between August 267 and August 268, Odainath and Herodian Hairan were killed (Hartmann 2001, 230–241, esp. 238; Southern 2008, 76–78). Zenobia soon emerged as Palmyra's ruler. She governed on behalf of Wahballath, Odainath's surviving male heir.

Local Palmyrene customs apparently enabled support for Zenobia's claim to legitimate authority. At Palmyra, women could become guardians of underage children and their estates after their husbands' deaths if there were no surviving male heirs in their maturity (Cussini 2005, 35; Andrade 2018, 123–126). On this basis Zenobia now made formal decisions for Odainath's household, whether civic or domestic (Andrade 2018, 126 and 165–166; Dirven 2021, 261–263). Since Odainath's household governed the Roman East, Zenobia did too.

The *Historia Augusta* suggests that Zenobia was complicit in the deaths of Odainath and Herodian Hairan. Her motive was to transfer power to her offspring (*HA* Tyr. Trig. 17.2). But no other sources corroborate this. They mainly indicate that Odainath was murdered by a jealous relative in a local plot (*HA* Tyr. Trig. 17; Syn. 717 (467); Zon. 12.24). Another source tradition links a broader plot to the court of Gallienus, though its reliability is debated (*FHG* 4.195; Banchich 2015, 3–9, 120–122; Mecella 2013, 502–503). However, any conspiracy against Odainath's household put Wahballath in immense danger (Southern 2008, 81–83, 94). Zenobia was under harrowing pressure to seize power. This she did, even though the exact details evade us.

Since the surviving members of Odainath's household were children, Zenobia would have been the one who ensured that he was buried with proper funerary rites. Palmyra's material culture enables us to reconstruct some aspects of the funeral (for details, Andrade 2018, 152–161 and 2019). A surviving tomb inscription for Odainath suggests that he expected Zenobia to have him entombed (*IGLS* XVI.1, 545), presumably in a 'temple tomb' so popular in the third century (see Chapter 24 [Henning], this volume; Sartre and Sartre 2014, 127–128). After his body was prepared, which may have entailed a form of mummification involving layers of textiles (see Chapter 36, Schmidt-Colinet's contribution on textiles in this volume), Odainath may have been placed in a sarcophagus. Its lid would have borne a portrait of him reclining, surrounded by his household. A portrait of Zenobia would perhaps have adorned the sarcophagus or a nearby burial niche (see Chapter 27 [Raja], this volume, on funerary sculpture). Zenobia probably expected to be buried with Odainath. This did not happen. As she prepared Odainath's burial, Zenobia also had to worry about serious, imminent conflict. Her relationship with the Roman imperial court was tense. As far as many Palmyrenes were concerned, Odainath's heirs wielded legitimate authority, but according to the imperial court, they did not.

Zenobia's Reign and Civil War

For four years or so, Zenobia ruled much of the 'East' that her husband Odainath had governed. But even our knowledge of her reign is skeletal. The sources offer only slivers of information. Even so, we can draw certain inferences about Zenobia's governance.

After assuming power in 268, Zenobia initially claimed only the titles of 'king of kings' and *epanorthotes* of the East for her son, Wahballath (Southern 2008, 83–86; Hartmann 2001, 241–245 interprets slightly differently). These were essentially the titles that Odainath had held. There was no pretence that Wahballath had greater authority than Odainath. In fact, Zenobia apparently controlled less territory, only some Syrian and Mesopotamian provinces (Hartmann 2001, 259–277). Under Zenobia, the mint at Antioch produced coins with the emperor's portrait until 270 (Huvelin 1990).

Still, relations with the imperial court were tense. It did not recognize the transmission of Odainath's titles and powers to his heirs (Hartmann 2001, 244–245; Potter 2014, 262–263; Andrade 2018, 165–166, 172; Dirven 2021, 261–263). The *Historia Augusta* reports that Gallienus's praetorian prefect, Heraclianus, campaigned against the Persians but lost his army while confronting Zenobia (*HA* Gall. 13.4–6). The date implied by the narrative is 268, but since Heraclianus was involved in Gallienus's murder in Milan in the summer of 268, this seems impossible (Zos. 1.40.2; *HA* Gall. 14; Potter 2014, 259–260). One theory is that this expedition was cancelled when Aureolus tried to usurp the imperial throne in early 268 (Hartmann 2006). However, some surmise that this actually occurred in 269 (Potter 2014, 262). Anyhow, by 270 relations had so failed that Zenobia sent her armies into Arabia, Egypt, and then Asia Minor (Southern 2008, 90, 102).

Civil papyri from Egypt date Zenobia's campaign there (Hartmann 2001, 231–241; Southern 2008, 105–106, 114). They bear the name of Claudius II in the summer, but during the autumn they mention no emperors at all. By December they celebrate the joint reign of Wahballath (year 4) and Aurelian (year 1), since Claudius had died in September or thereabout (*P. Oxy.* 1544, 2906–2909, 2921; *SB* 11589, e.g.; Kreucher 1998, 267; Estiot 2004, 116–117). This suggests that Zenobia's protracted campaigns in Egypt absorbed the summer and autumn. Zosimus describes how the Palmyrenes invaded, suffered reversals against the prefect Probus, and ultimately prevailed (Zos. 1.44, with *HA* Claud. 11–12; Hartmann 2001, 281–294). Zenobia presumably invaded Arabia before invading Egypt, in early 270. Her conquests in Anatolia, otherwise very obscure, are best placed in 271 (Zos. 1.50.1; Hartmann 2001, 279–281, 294–296).

Zenobia's offensives marked a shift in the way she represented Wahballath's authority (Hartmann 2001, 245–254 for much of what follows). Milestones from Arabia and Syria Palestina celebrated him as *Vir Clarissimus, Rex, Consularis, Imperator*, and *Dux Romanorum* (Bauzou 1998, nos. 95–97; Isaac 1998, 70). On Antioch's coins, he was identified as *VCRIMDR: Vir Consularis* (or *Clarissimus*), *Rex, Imperator*, and *Dux Romanorum*. He appeared on their technical obverse with a laurel crown. On the reverse, Aurelian bore a radiate crown. At Alexandria, Wahballath appeared with the titles ὑπατικὸς αὐτοκράτωρ, στρατηγὸς Ῥωμαίων, abbreviated variously (Hartmann 2001, 250–254; Estiot 2004, 115–118; Bland 2011, including 141–142 for Antioch's coins). Wearing longer hair and a muscle cuirass, he resembled the Palmyrene divinities Iarhibol and Aglibol (Schwentzel 2011, 161–162). Images of Aurelian appeared on the obverses. The papyri and coins provide insight into how Zenobia was formulating her son's authority for her subjects and, presumably, the imperial court. While exercising autonomous discretion, Wahballath governed the East in harmony with the imperial court despite the military confrontations of 270. But his status was now much more elevated. While not Caesar or *Augustus*, he reigned as an *imperator*, notionally for life. Like Aurelian, he had regnal dates, and had arguably been ruling longer (Bland 2011,

142). Zenobia was now promoting Wahballath as being nearly the peer of the emperor, though not a co-emperor.

Intriguingly, Zenobia's titles changed little. She remained simply 'queen'. An inscription from 271 (August) made by Zenobia's senior commanders, who also may have been her relatives, indicates as much (*IGLS* XVI.1, 57; Sartre and Sartre 2014, 84):
[in Greek]:

> Septimia Zenobia, most illustrious pious queen [*basilissa*]. The Septimioi Zabdas, the chief general, and Zabbaios, who is general here, excellent, [honour] their lady. The year 582, the month Loos.

[in Palmyrenean]:

> This is the image of Septimia Bathzabbai, illustrious and just queen [*mlkt'*]. The Septimioi Zabda, chief of the great army, and Zabbai, chief of the army of Tadmor, excellent, raised it for their lady. In the month Ab, the year 582.

Zenobia's generals commissioned the inscription in tandem with another that post-humously celebrated Odainath as 'king of kings' and the governor of the East (*PAT* 292). Together, the inscriptions earmarked Odainath's household as exercising legitimate governance. They also linked Zenobia's authority to her role as its guardian, as her prior inscriptions had.

In early 272, as Aurelian invaded her territories, Zenobia initiated another shift in titles (Hartmann 2011, 255–258, 354–364; Southern 2008, 120–121; Andrade 2018, 195 discuss date and significance). She had Wahballath and herself proclaimed *Augusti*. Milestones in Arabia and Palestina reported:

> For *imperator* Caesar L. Iulius Aurelius Septimius Vaballathus Athenodorus, Persicus Maximus, Arabicus Maximus, Adiabenicus Maximus, pious, lucky, uncon-quered Augustus. (*ILS* 8924 – Bauzou 1998, nos. 98, with 99–101; Isaac 1998, 70)

An inscription near Byblos in Phoenicia stated:

> For . . . unconquered Augustus [*Sebastos*], and Septimia Zenobia Augusta [*Sebaste*], mother of [our] eternal [lord] *imperator* Vaballathus Athenodorus. (*IGR* III, 1065 = *CIG* 4503b = *OGIS* 647; Hartmann 2001, 355–356, 469)

Zenobia was now claiming that Odainath's dynasty's rule had parity with the impe-rial court.

We also notice a change in the coins of Antioch and Alexandria at this time. Aurelian no longer appeared. Instead, their obverses featured likenesses of Wahballath or, less fre-quently, Zenobia. Gods or divine personifications graced the reverses. The Alexandrian coins paired Zenobia with *Elpis* or *Homonoia*, the Antiochene ones associated her with

Iuno Regina (Figures 11.1–11.3) (Estiot 2004, 115–120; Bland 2011, 162–180). By and large, the imagery emulated that on the coins representing Gallienus or Claudius, but they identified Zenobia and Wahballath as *Augusti*. When Aurelian invaded her territory, Zenobia finally acknowledged a complete breach with the imperial court. Wahballath was now emperor.

Zenobia's Governance

Scarcely a trace remains of Zenobia's reign, with respect to surviving laws, decrees, and rescripts. We know precious little about how she ruled. But the Palestinian Talmud describes Zenobia as she governs (TJ *Ter.* 8: 10.46b in Guggenheimer 2000; Appelbaum 2011, 542). It states that two rabbis petitioned for her to release an imprisoned colleague. Zenobia responded by telling them to appeal to their creator to perform his usual wonders for them. But when a Saracen displayed a sword with which Odainath ('Bar Nezer') reportedly killed the brother of the detained rabbi, Zenobia let him go.

The passage dispels any doubt that Zenobia exercised real power. Her subjects petitioned her, and she exercised political authority. It also offers a brief glimpse of how some of Zenobia's subjects perceived her, for later generations to record. She could display a regal arrogance, but she gave petitions serious consideration.

The *Historia Augusta* offers the most detailed portrait of Zenobia's character. But it is inconsistent and largely uncorroborated. Her treatment in the 'Thirty Usurpers' is favourable; in Aurelian's biography, it is negative (Paschoud 2011, 182–184; Southern 2008, 10–12; Sommer 2015, 118–123; Jones 2015 for what follows). In the 'Thirty Usurpers', Zenobia is a brave and virtuous leader who protected the eastern frontier when Roman emperors had to direct their attention elsewhere. She is also chaste, a woman who only sleeps with her husband once per menstrual cycle, to beget children. She drinks moderately with her generals and foreign ambassadors. She hunts and endures harsh wilderness conditions (*HA* Tyr. Trig. 30.17–19, 15.8). Yet, in Aurelian's biography, she is a usurper who defied the Roman court (*HA* Aurel. 22–29, Claud. 4.4). Arrogant and intractable, she clings to power and aligns herself with eastern 'barbarians' to retain it. She betrays and informs on her supporters to save herself from Aurelian's wrath.

Given the *Historia Augusta*'s unreliability, we can only obliquely glimpse how Zenobia governed. The *Historia Augusta* states that Zenobia modelled herself on Cleopatra VII and on the largely mythical Semiramis and Dido. It also calls Zenobia 'Cleopatra' and claims that Zenobia wrote an epitome of Ptolemaic history (*HA* Tyr. Trig. 27.1, 30.2, and 30.22 and Probus, 9.4–5; *BNJ* 626). However, this is the only source to say all this explicitly, and, as it was written ca. 395, it may have been influenced by an earlier statement of the historian Ammianus (28.4.9; Teixidor 2005, 201). Even so, Zenobia may have been inspired by mythical or historical queens with roots in the Near East and Egypt, Cleopatra in particular.

Scholars have often surmised that Zenobia attracted intellectuals to her court. While this is an intriguing possibility, the evidence is underwhelming. Cassius Longinus's presence at Palmyra or nearby is fairly certain. He probably came from Emesa. After spending many years at Athens, he apparently returned to Syria (Porph., *VP* 19; Southern 2008, 95–97; Hartmann 2001, 302–304; Stoneman 1992, 129–131; Janiszewski et al. 2015, 219–222, no. 632). He wrote a speech in honour of Odainath (Lib., *Ep.* 1006, 1078), and, according to both Zosimus and the *Historia Augusta*, Aurelian had him killed in 272 because of his influence on Zenobia (Zos. 1.56.2–3; *HA Aurel.* 30.1–3; Mariev 2008, fr. 180).

More tenuously linked to Zenobia is Callinicus of Petra (for what follows, *BNJ* 281, T1a, with commentary). He reportedly wrote a history of Alexandria 'for Cleopatra'. Because the *Historia Augusta* describes her as emulating Cleopatra, Zenobia is often identified as the recipient. But caution is merited. Nothing indisputably places him, or his rival Genethlius of Petra (*BNJ* 281, T1b, with commentary), in Zenobia's realm.

Also tenuous is Zenobia's link to Nicostratus of Trapezos (*BNJ* 98, with commentary). He apparently wrote a history of Roman affairs from the reign of Philip the Arab to Valerian's Persian campaign and Odainath's governance of the East. Presumably, his work celebrated Odainath's reign. A certain Nicomachus allegedly translated an abrasive letter that Zenobia wrote to Aurelian into Greek (*HA Aurel.* 27.2–5). Some suggest that Nicomachus is Nicostratus or Nicomachus Flavianus, but we have no reliable information on this person or whether he existed (*PLRE* 1.630; Bleckmann and Gros 2016, 68–73; Barnes 1972, 165; Southern 2008, 97).

More secure is Zenobia's effort to tighten her grip on the Middle Euphrates and Upper Mesopotamia. According to Procopius (sixth century), Zenobia founded an eponymous city at Halabiyya, on the Euphrates' west bank (Procop., *Aed.* 2.8.8–15). Most of its remains and those of its sister site on the opposite bank (Zalabiyya, a corruption of Zenobia's name) date to the sixth century (Sartre and Sartre 2014, 93–94, 250). But Zenobia's city has left some third-century traces (Lauffrey 1983–1991; Blétry 2015, 469).

Zenobia is often associated with the renewal of the privileges of a Jewish community in Egypt. But the relevant inscription, in Latin and Greek, is not securely dated. It simply refers to a queen and a king, with 'queen' intriguingly preceding 'king'. Owing to the letter forms (that suggest a fairly late date), some have deemed the inscription to refer to Zenobia and Wahballath. But Cleopatra VII and one of her co-regents are also candidates (*CIL* III, 6583 = *ILS* 574 = *OGIS* 129 = Horbury and Noy 1992, no. 125, with commentary). The reconstruction of a colossal statue of Amenhotep III, famous for making a whistling sound, is also linked to Zenobia's occupation of Egypt. Greek and Roman travellers often visited the statue, which they identified as the mythical Ethiopian king Memnon, and inscribed graffiti on it (Bernand and Bernand 1960). However, more recent analyses of the graffiti indicate that the reconstruction happened before Zenobia's reign (Sartre and Sartre 2014, 109–110).

On the whole, even Zenobia's reign is poorly documented. We catch only glimpses of her as she governs. But the surviving sources suggest that Zenobia assumed and maintained power under immense pressure. She governed decisively and effectively, even if she would ultimately be defeated by Aurelian.

ZENOBIA'S FALL FROM POWER

In a fabricated exchange of letters, the *Historia Augusta* claims that Zenobia responded to Aurelian's request for surrender by claiming that she, like Cleopatra before her, would prefer to die a queen (*HA* Aurel. 27.2–5). The taunt is part of the *Life of Aurelian's* portrayal of Zenobia as a self-absorbed eastern despot. Nothing corroborates it. Even so, the basic details of Aurelian's campaigns against Zenobia are fairly certain.

In 272, the Emperor Aurelian initiated his campaigns into Zenobia's territory. He crossed Anatolia and reached Tyana before meeting serious resistance (Hartmann 2001, 354, and 364–368). Meanwhile, Zenobia had joined her main army at Antioch to confront him. Near the city, Aurelian won an overwhelming victory in May or June of 272, even if the different accounts are difficult to harmonize (Downey 1951 is widely accepted). He apparently lured Zenobia's heavily armoured cavalry (*clibanarii*) into making a prolonged charge and counterattacked when it was exhausted (Zos. 1.50.3–4, with Fest. 24; Hartmann 2001, 368–370; Southern 2008, 135–138). Zosimus records in unique detail how Zenobia responded at this moment of defeat. She and her general Zabdas found a local resident who resembled Aurelian. Parading him as a captive, they pretended that they had won a resounding victory. The ploy enabled Zenobia to flee to Emesa, where she assembled another army (Zos. 1.51.1–3; Southern 2008, 136–137).

After his victory, Aurelian entered Antioch and crushed a Palmyrene garrison that had remained at the suburb of Daphne (Zos. 1.52.1–2). He paused briefly, to offer clemency to anyone in north Syria and Mesopotamia who surrendered and to resolve the doctrinal disputes in which Paul of Samosata was heavily involved (Zos. 1.51.4–52.1; Eus., *Hist. ecc.* 7.30; Hartmann 2001, 321–323, 371, 388–90; Southern 2008, 138). He then marched south towards Emesa. In a mid-summer battle there, Aurelian's infantry repulsed a charge by Zenobia's cavalry and overwhelmed her army. Aurelian alleged that the god of Emesa, the divine sun, had appeared to him during the battle (Zos. 1.52.3–53.3; *HA* Aurel. 25.4–5; Hartmann 2001, 374–375; Southern 2008, 138–140).

At this juncture, Aurelian moved east to Palmyra and invested it. He apparently had some support from local nomads, including (it seems) the Tanukh (Hartmann 2001, 383; Graf 1989, 150–155). Zenobia escaped the city, but she was captured as she tried to board a boat on the Euphrates River (Zos. 1.55.1–3; *HA* Aurel. 28.2–4). As defeat became imminent, a faction at Palmyra, including a certain Ḥaddudan, arranged a surrender (Zos. 1.56.1; *PAT* 1358, 2812; Hartmann 2001, 383–384). It was August of 272.

After Zenobia was captured, Aurelian had her brought to Emesa for trial. There she allegedly informed on Longinus and other members of her senior staff. Both ancient and modern authors have considered this a disreputable moment in her career (Zos. 1.56.2–3; *HA* Aurel. 30.1–3; Mariev 2008, fr. 180). However, Zenobia had needs other than her own to consider. She was a mother, and Wahballath's fate, too, was in Aurelian's hands. Aurelian probably was inclined to believe that men at Zenobia's court had unduly influenced her. Zenobia's denunciations may even reflect a rumour circulated by Aurelian's court (Southern 2008, 146).

Zenobia was transported west. Aurelian certainly had her brought across Anatolia to the Bosporus. He entered Europe by January 273 (Potter 2014, 267). Meanwhile, Palmyra was not at rest. A rebellion broke out. A figure named Apsaios, who is attested in an inscription at Palmyra (*IGLS* XVI.1, 77), was responsible. He reportedly encouraged Marcellinus, Aurelian's senior governor in the East, to defect. When this failed, he dressed a certain Antiochus in regal attire and killed Aurelian's garrison in the city. However, the *Historia Augusta* calls this figure 'Achilles' and claims that he was related to Zenobia (Zosimus, 1.60.1–2; *HA* Aurel. 31.1–10). This testimony is dubious. Modern scholarship has sometimes theorized that Antiochus was Zenobia's father or her (non-existent) son by the name. But little supports these premises (Zos. 1.61.1–2; *HA* Aurel. 31.2; Hartmann 2001, 122–123, 395–398). The rebellion never took root outside Palmyra, and Aurelian returned to pillage it in 273. In Alexandria, a severe but short-lived rebellion associated with a figure named Firmus also occurred (*HA* Aurel. 32.1–3, Quadr. Tyr. 4, with Amm. Marc. 22.16.15; Hartmann 2001, 403–410; Potter 2014, 268).

Sources differ concerning Zenobia's fate. According to one tradition, Zenobia either starved herself to death or died of disease while crossing Anatolia. Her personal circle, save her son, died while crossing the Bosporus. Only Zosimus (1.59) and Zonaras (12.27), whose source is probably Zosimus, report Zenobia's death (Hartmann 2001, 414). According to a better-corroborated tradition, Aurelian took Zenobia to Italy. There, he had Zenobia displayed in a triumph at Rome, in jewels and gold chains so heavy that she could barely walk. She and her children were then settled at Tibur (modern Tivoli). Her descendants could be found in Rome or serving in imperial posts thereafter (*HA* Tyr. Trig. 27 and 30.24–27, Aurel. 34; Eutr. 9.13.2; Festus, *Brev.* 24; Jer., *Chron.*, for year 274; Syn. 721 (470); Zon. 12.27; Jordanes, *Rom.* 291; Lib., *Ep.* 1006, 1078; Hartmann 2001, 413–424; Sartre and Sartre 2014, 15–20, 184–185). Although defeated, Zenobia apparently survived the violence of the 260s and 270s. This achievement is often overlooked. Many political players, including the talented Aurelian, could not say the same.

At this point, Zenobia disappears from our view. We have no information on the later stages of her life or how she died. Even so, Zenobia continues to live through her images as one of the most famous people of the ancient world. Writers and artists from the Middle East and Europe ensured this. But thanks to her remarkable reign, Zenobia has seen to it too.

Bibliography

Andrade, Nathanael. 2018. *Zenobia: Shooting Star of Palmyra*. Oxford: Oxford University Press.
Andrade, Nathanael. 2019. 'Burying Odainath: Zenobia and Women in the Funerary Life of Palmyra'. In *Representations of Women and Children in Roman Period Palmyra*, edited by Signe Krag and Sara Ringsborg, 176–191. Copenhagen: Det Kongelige Danske Videnskabernes Selskab.

Appelbaum, Alan. 2011. 'The Rabbis and Palmyra: A Case Study on (Mis-)Reading Rabbinics for Historical Purposes'. *Jewish Quarterly Review* 101(4): 527–544.

Balty, Jean-Charles. 2005. 'La sculpture'. In *L'agora de Palmyre*, edited by Christiane Delplace and Jacqueline Dentzer-Feydy, 321–342. Bordeaux: Institut français du Proche-Orient.

Banchich, Thomas. 2015. *The Lost History of Peter the Patrician: An Account of Rome's Imperial Past from the Age of Justinian*. London: Routledge.

Barnes, Timothy. D. 1972. 'Some Persons in the *Historia Augusta*'. *Phoenix* 26(2): 140–182.

Bauzou, Thomas. 1998. 'La via nova en Arabie: le secteur nord, de Bostra à Philadelphie'. In *Fouilles de Khirbet es-Samra en Jordanie*. Vol. 1, *La voie romaine, le cimetière, les documents épigraphiques*, edited by Jean-Baptiste Humbert and Alain Desreumaux, 101–225. Turnhout: Brepols.

Bernand, André, and Étienne Bernand. 1960. *Les inscriptions grecques et latines du Colosse de Memnon*. Cairo: Imprimerie de l'Institut français d'archéologie orientale.

Bland, Roger. 2011. 'The Coinage of Vabalathus and Zenobia from Antioch and Alexandria'. *Numismatic Chronicle* 171: 133–186.

Bleckmann, Bruno. 1992. *Die Reichskrise des III. Jahrhunderts in spätantiken und byzantinischen Geschichtsschreibung: Untersuchungen zu den nachdionischen Quellen der Chronik des Johannes Zonaras*. Munich: Tuduv.

Bleckmann, Bruno, and Jonathan Gros. 2016. *Historiker der Reichskrise des 3. Jahrhunderts*. Vol. 1. Paderborn: Schöningh.

Blétry, Sylvie. 2015. *Zénobia-Halabiya, habitat urbain et nécropoles: Cinq années de recherches de la mission syro-française (2006–2010)*. Ferrol: Sociedade Luso-Galega de Estudos Mesopotámicos.

Brecht, Stephanie. 1999. *Die römische Reichskrise von ihrem Ausbruck bis zu ihrem Höhepunkt in der Darstellung byzantinischer Autoren*. Rahden: Leidorf.

Cussini, Eleonora. 2005. 'Beyond the Spindle: Investigating the Role of Palmyrene Women'. In *A Journey to Palmyra: Collected Essays to Remember Delbert Hillers*, edited by Eleonora Cussini, 26–43. Leiden: Brill.

Declerck, Jose H. 1984. 'Deux nouveaux fragments attribués à Paul de Samosate'. *Byzantion* 54: 116–140.

Dirven, Lucinda. 2021. 'Zenobia of Palmyra'. In *The Routledge Companion to Women and Monarchy in the Ancient Mediterranean*, edited by Elizabeth D. Carney and Sabine Müller, 256–267 Abingdon: Routledge.

Downey, Glanville. 1951. 'Aurelian's Victory over Zenobia at Immae, A.D. 272'. *Transactions and Proceedings of the American Philological Association* 81: 57–68.

Equini Schneider, Eugenia. 1993. *Septimia Zenobia Sebaste*. Rome: 'L'Erma' di Bretschneider.

Estiot, Sylviane. 2004. *Monnaies de l'Empire romain*. Vol. 12, *D'Aurélien à Florien (270–76 après J.-C)*. Paris: Bibliothèque nationale de France.

Finlayson, Cynthia. 2013. 'New Perspectives on the Ritual and Cultic Importance of Women at Palmyra and Dura Europos: Processions and Temples'. *Studia Palmyreńskie* 12: 61–85.

Gardner, Iain, and Samuel N. C. Lieu. 2004. *Manichaean Texts from the Roman Empire*. Cambridge: Cambridge University Press.

Gawlikowski, Michal. 1985. 'Les princes de Palmyre'. *Syria* 62: 251–261.

Gawlikowski, Michal. 2007. 'Odainat et Hérodien, rois des rois'. *Mélanges de l'Université Saint-Joseph* 60: 289–313.

Gawlikowski, Michal. 2016. 'The Portraits of the Palmyrene Royalty'. In *The World of Palmyra*, edited by Andreas Kropp and Rubina Raja, 126–134. Copenhagen: Det Kongelige Danske videnskabernes selskab.

Graf, David. 1989. 'Zenobia and the Arabs'. In *The Eastern Frontier of the Roman Empire*, vol. 1, edited by David H. French and Chris S. Lightfoot, 143–167. Oxford: British Archaeological Reports.

Guggenheimer, Heinrich. 2000. *The Jerusalem Talmud=Talmud Yerushalmi*. Berlin: de Gruyter.

Hartmann, Udo. 2001. *Das palmyrenische Teilreich*. Stuttgart: Steiner.

Hartmann, Udo. 2006. 'Der Mord an Kaiser Gallienus'. In *Deleto paene imperio Romano: Transformationsprozesse des Römischen Reiches im 3. Jahrhundert und ihre Rezeption in der Neuzeit*, edited by Klaus-Peter Johne, Thomas Gerhardt, and Udo Hartmann, 107–118. Berlin: Steiner.

Heyn, Maura. 2018. 'Embodied Identities in the Funerary Portraiture of Palmyra'. In *Palmyra: Mirage in the Desert*, edited by Joan Aruz, 110–120. New Haven, CT: Yale University Press.

Horbury, William, and David Noy. 1992. *Jewish Inscriptions of Graeco-Roman Egypt*. Cambridge: Cambridge University Press.

Huvelin, Hélène. 1990. 'L'atelier d'Antioche sous Claude II'. *Numismatica e antichità classiche* 19: 251–272.

Hvidberg-Hansen, Finn O. 2002. *Zenobia: Byen Palmyra og dens dronning*. Aarhus: SFINX.

Isaac, Benjamin. 1998. *The Near East Under Roman Rule*. Leiden: Brill.

Janiszewski, Paweł, Krystyna Stebnicka, and Elzbieta Szabat. 2015. *Prosopography of Greek Rhetors and Sophists of the Roman Empire*. Oxford: Oxford University Press.

Jones, Prudence. 2015. 'Rewriting Power: Zenobia, Aurelian, and the *Historia Augusta*'. *Classical World* 109(2): 221–233.

Krag, Signe, and Rubina Raja. 2016. 'Representations of Women and Children in Palmyrene Funerary *loculus* Reliefs, *loculus stelae*, and Wall Paintings'. *Zeitschrift für Orient-Archäologie* 9: 134–178.

Kreucher, Gerald. 1998. 'Die Regierungszeit Aurelians und die griechischen Papyri aus Ägypten'. *Archiv für Papyrusforschung* 44: 255–274.

Lauffray, Jean. 1983–1991. *Halabiyya-Zenobia: Place forte du limes oriental et la Haute-Mésopotamie au VIᵉ siècle*. Paris: Geuthner.

Mallan, Christopher, and Caillan Davenport. 2015. 'Dexippus and the Gothic Invasions: Interpreting the New Vienna Fragment (*Codex Vindobonensis Hist. gr. 73*, ff. 192v–193r)'. *Journal of Roman Studies* 105: 203–226.

Mariev, Sergei. 2008. *Ioannis Antiocheni Fragmenta quae supersunt omnia*. Berlin: de Gruyter.

Mecella, Laura. 2013. *Dexippo di Atene*. Tivoli: Tored.

Paschoud, François, ed. 2002. *Histoire Auguste*. Vol. 5.1: *Vies d'Aurélien et de Tacite*. Paris: Les belles lettres.

Paschoud, François, ed. 2003. *Histoire nouvelle: Zosime*. 2nd ed. Vol. 1. Paris: Les belles lettres.

Paschoud, François, ed. 2011. *Histoire Auguste*. Vol. 4.3, *Vies des trente tyrans et de Claude*. Paris: Les belles lettres.

Potter, David S. 1990. *Prophecy and History in the Crisis of the Roman Empire: A Historical Commentary on the Thirteenth Sibylline Oracle*. Oxford: Clarendon.

Potter, David S. 2014. *The Roman Empire at Bay, AD 180–395*. 2nd ed. Milton Park: Routledge.

Rey-Coquais, Jean-Paul. 2006. *Inscriptions grecques et latines de Tyr*. Beirut: BAAL.

Riedmatten, Henri de. 1952. *Les actes du procès de Paul de Samosate: Étude sur la Christologie du IIIᵉ au IVᵉ siècle*. Fribourg: Éditions St-Paul.

Sartre, Maurice. 2016. 'Zénobie dans l'imaginaire occidental'. In *The World of Palmyra*, edited by Andreas Kropp and Rubina Raja, 207–221. Copenhagen: Det Kongelige Danske videnskabernes selskab.

Sartre, Annie, and Maurice Sartre. 2014. *Zénobie: De Palmyre à Rome*. Paris: Perrin.

Sartre, Annie, and Maurice Sartre. 2016. *Palmyre: Vérités et legendes*. Paris: Perrin.

Schwentzel, Christian-Georges. 2011. 'La propaganda de Vaballath et Zénobie d'après le témoignage des monnaies et tessères'. *Rivista italiana di numismatica e scienze affini* 111: 157–172.

Sommer, Michael. 2015. 'Through the Looking Glass: Zenobia and "Orientalism"'. In *Reinventing "the Invention of Tradition": Indigenous Pasts and the Roman Present*, edited by Dietrich Boschung, Alexandra W. Busch, and Miguel J. Versluys, 113–125. Paderborn: Fink.

Southern, Pat. 2008. *Empress Zenobia: Palmyra's Rebel Queen*. London: Continuum.

Stoneman, Richard. 1992. *Palmyra and Its Empire: Zenobia's Revolt Against Rome*. Ann Arbor: University of Michigan Press.

Teixidor, Javier. 2005. 'Palmyra in the Third Century'. In *A Journey to Palmyra: Collected Essays to Remember Delbert Hillers*, edited by Elenora Cussini, 181–225. Leiden: Brill.

Tlass, Mustafa. 1985. *Zanūbiyā malikat Tadmur*. Damascus: Tlass.

Tlass, Mustafa. 1986. *Zénobie, reine de Palmyre*. Damascus: Tlass.

Tlass, Mustafa. 2000. *Zenobia: The Queen of Palmyra*. Damascus: Tlass.

Weingarten, Judith. 2018. 'Zenobia in History and Legend'. In *Palmyra: Mirage in the Desert*, edited by Joan Aruz, 130–147. New Haven, CT: Yale University Press.

Weingarten, Judith. Zenobia: Empress of the East. http://judithweingarten.blogspot.com/.

Weststeijn, Johan. 2013. 'Zenobia of Palmyra and the Book of Judith: Common Motifs in Greek, Jewish, and Arabic Historiography'. *Journal for the Study of the Pseudepigrapha* 22(4): 295–320.

Weststeijn, Johan. 2016. 'Wine, Women, and Revenge in Near Eastern Historiography: The Tales of Tomyris, Judith, Zenobia, and Jalila'. *Journal of Near Eastern Studies* 75(1): 91–107

Winsbury, Rex. 2010. *Zenobia of Palmyra: History, Myth, and the Neo-Classical Imagination*. London: Duckworth.

Woltering, Robbert A. F. L. 2014. 'Zenobia or al-Zabbā': The Modern Arab Literary Reception of the Palmyran Protagonist'. *Middle Eastern Literatures* 17(1): 25–42.

Yon, Jean-Baptiste. 2013. 'Palmyrene Epigraphy After PAT, 1996–2011'. *Studia Palmyreńskie* 12: 333–379.

CHAPTER 12

PALMYRA AND THE MILITARY

From the Roman Period to the Islamic Conquest

EMANUELE E. INTAGLIATA

INTRODUCTION

EXAMINING the military presence in Palmyra is an arduous task owing to the lacunose state of the evidence. Inscriptions provide the most informative set of data but cover mainly the period between the first and the third centuries. Written sources on the military are relatively few and reveal little. Archaeological evidence is also particularly problematic for little evidence of military quarters from the Roman period remain in the ground in Palmyra. Most of the relevant archaeological data date to after the late third century to the beginning of the fourth, when a monumental camp, the so-called Camp of Diocletian, was constructed within the urban perimeter defined by the late antique city walls.

This patchy and lacunose dataset has not prevented the scholarly community from investigating this topic. Secondary literature has focused mostly on Palmyra and the military in the Roman period. The most recent and comprehensive review of this is Yon's (2008, in French; English works have also been produced, e.g., Pollard 2000, 43; Edwell 2008, 50–62). Other contributions have focused on more specific questions. For example, Speidel (1972; 1984b) has shed light on the problem of the name of the Ala Vocontiorum; Young (2001, 163–166) has reviewed the evidence on the Palmyrene militia in his *Rome's Eastern Trade*; and Smith (2013, 165–172) has summarized the evidence of Palmyrene soldiers abroad (on this, also see the useful tables in Yon 2002, 265–274). Compared to this abundance of works, late antiquity has received little attention (especially, see Barański 1994; Kowalski 1998). This chapter, which fits into and benefits from this long history of studies, aims to provide a necessarily brief and incomplete overview of what is known about the military presence in Palmyra between the first and the early seventh centuries and Palmyrene soldiers.

THE GARRISON AT PALMYRA IN THE ROMAN PERIOD: A BRIEF HISTORY

Since the Roman period, the protection of Palmyra and its territory was entrusted to a garrison. One of the earliest epigraphic occurrences linked to the military at the site is dated to 27 BC, when a funerary stela was erected in honour of a certain Mabogaios, of the Cohors Damascenorum (*IGLS* XVII.1, 450; Gawlikowski 2010). The inscription does not necessarily prove that the *cohors* was quartered at Palmyra, although scholars now tend to believe that this was probably the case (Gawlikowski 2010, 50). More direct clues of a stable military presence at this site are attested only from the mid-second century. The name of the unit garrisoned in Palmyra in this period has given rise to much debate. The crux of the problem is an inscription on a column bracket reused in the sanctuary of Bēl and dedicated by the council and the people of Palmyra to Gaius Vibius Celer 'prefect of the *ala* that is here'. Frustratingly, the inscription does not name the *ala* (i.e., an auxiliary mounted unit), but two main candidates have been suggested: Ala I Thracum Herculana (Seyrig 1933, 153; Millar 1993, 108; Edwell 2008, 54) and Ala I Ulpia Singularium (Birley 1988, 157–158; Yon 2008, 130; Ala I Ulpia Dromedariorum Palmyrenorum has also been proposed: Spaul 1994, 105; Speidel [1984b, 167–169] locates the unit at Palmyra until 150; see summary of scholarly positions in *IGLS* XVII.1, 10).

However, it is reasonable to incline to the Ala I Ulpia Singularium. Gaius Vibius Celer is found in another inscription from Circeii (Italy) that provides details of his *cursus honorum* and identifies him as prefect of the Cohors I Montanorum, Cohors I Flaviae Hispanorum, and, more importantly in this discussion, Ala I Ulpia Singularium (*CIL* X, 6426; Birley 1988, 157–158). The garrisoning of this unit is also demonstrated at Palmyra by other fragmentary inscriptions and funerary stelae (*IGLS* XVII.1, 34?, 175?, 212, 486, and 487). The presence of the Roman army at that time demonstrates Palmyra's growing importance in the eyes of the Romans and the latter's need to maintain their position on the important trading route from the east to the Mediterranean coast via the plain of al-Daww and Emesa (modern-day Homs).

This unit does not seem to have remained in Palmyra for long. By about the mid-160s, the Ala I Thracum Herculana was in town, replacing the former Ala I Ulpia Singularium. Ala I Thracum Herculana served in Pannonia before being deployed in Syria in the mid-second century (*CIL* XVI, 106). In Palmyra, it was present as early as 167, when an inscription mentions the prefect of the *ala*, Julius Julianus (*IGLS* XVII.1, 11). Of the unit, we know of one Palmyrene soldier, Vibus Apollinarius, whose name accompanies a funerary relief now at the Louvre (*IGLS* XVII.1, 488; also see Brizanus in *IGLS* XVII.1, 172) and another *praefectus* besides Julius Julianus: Claudius Celsus (*IGLS* XVII.1, 204—on this unit, see Lesquier 1918, 78–79; Spaul 1994, 142–143; Yon 2008, 132–133).

Some twenty years after its deployment in Palmyra, the Ala I Thracum Herculana was moved to Coptos. It was replaced by the Ala Vocontiorum, which was present at Palmyra, either entirely or with a detachment, and which itself had been formerly stationed at Coptos. An inscription from Palmyra reports that a decurion of this unit was responsible for the construction of a training ground (*camp[um]*) in 183 (*IGLS* XVII.1, 171; on this unit, see Speidel 1972; Speidel 1984b; Spaul 1994, 238–239; Yon 2008, 133–134).

Besides the general necessity of guarding the city and the caravan trade, a number of other reasons may be suggested to explain the need to deploy the above-mentioned units in Palmyra. The presence of *alae* is unsurprising in the Palmyrene, as horses would have allowed for the mobility necessary to guard and patrol the vast Syrian steppe. One may also assume that these units were deployed in Syria because of their acquaintance with desert conditions. Yet it remains difficult to shed light on the reasons behind this complex pattern of military transfers from and to Palmyra, which saw three *alae* deployed over a span of a few decades.

The fate of the Ala Vocontiorum is unknown, but we know that, at a certain point, either at the end of the second century or the beginning of the third, this unit was replaced by the Cohors I Flavia Chalcidenorum Equitata Sagittariorum. The *cohors* included a cavalry element, infantrymen, and Palmyrene archers (Edwell 2008, 60). The earliest known inscription concerning this *cohors*, which was reused in the construction of the tower annexed to the *principia* (headquarters) of the Camp of Diocletian, is dated to 206–207, and is a dedication to Septimius Severus by the same unit (*IGLS* XVII.1, 118). The most recent, found in the new town, is dated to 247, and it suggests that the unit remained garrisoned in the city throughout the first half of the third century (*IGLS* XVII.1, 169; on this unit, see Spaul 2000, 430; Yon 2008, 134–135).

After this date, soldiers are attested in Palmyra in 271–272, when two Palmyrene generals dedicated two statues in honour of Zenobia and Odaenathus (*IGLS* XVII.1, 57; see discussion in Yon 2008, 134–135). Following the events of 272 and Zenobia's rebellion, a garrison of six hundred archers was left in the city. If one is to believe the *Historia Augusta Vita Aureliani*, this was slaughtered by rebellious Palmyrenes at the start of the second Palmyrene revolt in 273 (*HA Aurel.* 31.1–2). The *Historia Augusta* is undoubtedly an unreliable source; nonetheless, the installation of a garrison at Palmyra to keep the inhabitants at bay following the Zenobian collapse sounds like a reasonable step to take after the rebellion.

The military presence in Palmyra becomes archaeologically more visible in the late Roman period. At that time, Palmyra had lost its commercial role and had become an important outpost along a well-guarded military road, the Strata Diocletiana (on this *via militaris*, see Bauzou 1992; 1993). Between 293 and 303, while Sossianus Hierocles was governor of the province Phoenicia Libanensis, a camp was constructed in the westernmost section of the city (Figure 12.1). The compound's foundation inscription on the lintel of the main doorway of the *aedes* (Temple of the Standards) states that Sossianus himself was responsible for its construction (*IGLS* XVII.1, 121). The camp, known in modern literature by the name of the 'Camp of Diocletian' was by far the largest and most architecturally decorated compound of its kind constructed along the eastern *limes* in this period (see, among others, Kowalski 1998; Chapter 25 [Juchniewicz], this volume, for a summary description of the remains). The 'theatrical' setting of the fort may be explained by the necessity of impressing occasional visitors, such as representatives of

FIGURE 12.1 Entrance to the Camp of Diocletian.

Courtesy of the PAL.M.A.I.S. Syro-Italian archaeological team.

nomadic tribes unacquainted with monumentally scaled architecture (Intagliata 2015, 200; 2018, 81–82).

The *Notitia dignitatum* reports that Palmyra was the base of the prefect of the Legio I Illyricorum (*Not. Dig., Or.* 32.30), which is not attested elsewhere in the city. The presence of a legion—which in late antiquity may have numbered some one thousand men—rather than an auxiliary unit, is indicative of the growing importance of Palmyra as a stronghold along the eastern *limes*. The Legio I Illyricorum was either partially or entirely quartered in the Camp of Diocletian. The fort was separated from the civilian settlement via a row of shops, which functioned as a veritable physical barrier, like the mud brick wall dividing the military quarters from the settlement at Dura-Europos in earlier times (see Lenoir 2011, 49, with further bibliography). However, as at Dura-Europos, this would not have excluded the soldiers from being quartered in the city. The construction of a bathhouse in the city centre on top of a previously existing building by the same Sossianus Hierocles (*IGLS* XVII.1, 100), and the limited size of the Camp of Diocletian, support this conclusion (Fellmann 1976, 190).

No written sources attest to a military garrison in Palmyra in the century that follows, and the epigraphic record is almost silent in this regard (nonetheless, see *IGLS* XVII.1, 359). The fifth century is marked by relatively peaceful relations between Rome and Persia, and one cannot rule out the likelihood that the regular garrison in the city underwent a substantial reduction in strength at that time. Since one may assume that the military remained an important economic engine for the city in late antiquity, such a reduction must have had important repercussions for the civilian settlement (Intagliata 2015, 256–258; 2018, 101–102). As a matter of fact, when, at the time of Justinian, the decision was made to strengthen the garrison at Palmyra, the city underwent frenetic building activity that was unprecedented since the late third century.

According to Malalas (*Chr.* 17.2), Procopius (*Aed.* 2.9.10–12), and the later Theophanes (*Chr.* 1.174), early in Justinian's reign a *numerus* of soldiers was moved into the city together with the *dux* of Emesa and, probably, his large retinue. Malalas's text is rather confusing as it reports that the soldiers were transferred to Palmyra μετὰ τῶν λιμιτανέων, which may be translated as either 'with the *limitanei*' (frontier troops) or, more probably, 'among the *limitanei*', meaning that Palmyra had a garrison when the *numerus* and the *dux* were moved there. In any case, our sources do not reveal much about the fate of the Legio I Illyricorum, which might have been removed from the city by the fifth century.

What happened to the garrison after Justinian's reign is obscure, as both archaeological evidence and epigraphy are lacunose concerning this matter. It is probable that the soldiers had already been removed from their post before the brief Persian hiatus (613–628). Similarly, it is reasonable to assume that no regular troops were quartered in the city at the time of the Islamic takeover (634). In recounting the event, one of our sources, Ibn A'tham al-Kūfī (*Kitāb*, 1.140–142), reports that during the fight for the city, 'the Romans came out and approached Khālid b. al-Walīd like fierce lions' but makes no mention of soldiers.

Soldiers Not Belonging to the Garrison at Palmyra

In addition to the garrison, there is inscriptional evidence to suggest that Roman soldiers frequented Palmyra but that they were not necessarily quartered in the city when in service. A few were Palmyrene veterans who had decided to return to their native town (Yon 2008, 135), whereas there were more foreign soldiers. A number of these died in the city, in all likelihood while they were in town for specific missions, while others are known for their manifest, and certainly not disinterested, devotion to imperial authorities. For example, in 17–19, Minucius Rufus, *legatus* of the Legio X Fretensis, dedicated an inscription to Drusus, Tiberius, and Germanicus in the sanctuary of Bēl (*IGLS* XVII.1, 3).

In some cases, foreign soldiers were honoured with inscriptions and statues placed in the heart of the city by the council and people of Palmyra. Perhaps the most informative example of this is that of Celesticus, to whom were dedicated two inscriptions and statues in the agora in the late first century. The inscriptions, which are bilingual (Greek and Palmyrene) and are dedicated by one or more Palmyrenes, give the partial *cursus honorum* of Celesticus: the centurion served in the Legiones III Gallica, IV Scythica, VI Ferrata, was *curator* of the superior and inferior riverbanks (of the Euphrates), and *curator* of the Cohors I Sebastena (*IGLS* XVII.1, 207–208).

PALMYRENES IN THE ROMAN ARMY

Compared to the relative paucity of inscriptions and written sources attesting to a garrison in Palmyra before Verus's campaigns against the Parthians in the 160s, there is epigraphic evidence that demonstrates that Palmyrene soldiers had been swelling the ranks of the Roman army at least as early as the Trajanic period. It is reasonable to believe that the military skills of Palmyrene soldiers derive directly from a military tradition first developed to protect the caravan trade and that this 'caravan police' was later integrated into the Roman army (Young 2001, 162–163, see below). Their adaptability to arid conditions played a pivotal part in their recruitment not only at the desert's frontiers, such as northern Africa However, they were also employed in the newly created borderland of Dacia, from the time of Hadrian. In some cases, Palmyrenes constituted auxiliary troops of their own, whether *cohortes*, *alae*, or *numeri*, whose official names may betray their place of origin.

The earliest piece of evidence from Palmyra mentioning a Palmyrene unit is an inscription dated 156 (*IGLS* XVII.1, 202), dedicated to Tiberius Claudius Pi-, prefect of the Ala I Ulpia Dromedariorum Palmyrenorum (ἔπαρκον εἴλης πρῶτος [Οὐλπί]ας δρομαδαρίων Παλμυρη[νων]) by Marcus Ulpius Yarḥai. The *ala* is also attested in a number of earlier military diplomas from Syria and Arabia (*CIL* XVI, 106; Weiß and Speidel 2004, 254–255; on this unit, see Spaul 1994, 104–105; Weiß and Speidel 2004, 257–258; Yon 2008, 130–132; *IGLS* XVII.1, 202)—*diplomas* were official documents that certified the end of a soldier's military service). Although the inscription was found in Palmyra, there is no hard evidence to suggest that it was quartered there.

The rich corpus of inscriptions by Palmyrenes in Dacia confirms an earlier military involvement (for the evidence, see Yon 2002, 270–271; discussion in Bianchi 1987). Veterans and active soldiers of Numeri Palmyreni Sagittarii (Palmyrene archers) are known to have been present at Porolissum, Tibiscum, and Casei as early as the 120s, when four military *diplomata* afford evidence of the granting of Roman citizenship to soldiers after their discharge (*CIL* XVI, 68; *RMD* I, 17; *RMD* I, 27; *RMD* I, 28; see Smith 2013, 165–168; Southern 1989, 89–90). The enrolment of two of these soldiers might have occurred in or before 114, on the occasion of Trajan's preparation for the Parthian war, but their deployment to Dacia is dated to the reign of Hadrian (Mann in *RMD* II, 217–219). Hadrian's increasing use of Palmyrene troops, which may have been the hidden reason behind the economic privileges granted by the emperor to Palmyra (Seyrig 1941, 228, n. 5), might explain the transfer attested in an undated inscription (*ILS* 9173; see recently Le Bohec 2012, 90) of one Palmyrene Agrippa son of Themi from Cohors III Thracum Syriaca in Syria, to Cohors I Chalcidenorum, at al-Qanṭara in Numidia. A unit of Palmyrene archers was left under his *curam* (care—note that the inscription does not use the term *strategos*—στρατηγός). Al-Qanṭara has yielded an impressive number of inscriptions by Palmyrene soldiers, some of whom dedicated altars to their native gods (evidence in Yon 2002, 271–272; see Equini Schneider 1988; Southern 1989, 90–92; Smith 2013, 168–169).After Lucius Verus's campaigns, evidence of the conscription of Palmyrenes in the army in Syria increased considerably. The richest corpus comes from Dura-Europos, where Palmyrene soldiers are known to have been present soon after the (re-)conquest of the city in 165. A group of Palmyrene archers led by a *strategos* would prehave formed part of the garrison of the city; their existence is supported by two inscriptions dated 169 and 171 (*Dura Prelim. Report* VII–VIII, 845–846; James 2020, 244–245). However, this troop may well have been Palmyrene militia not in service in the Roman army at that time (Young 2001, 160). Not until the early third century, when the military quarters at Dura-Europos were considerably expanded (209–216), do we hear about the Cohors XX Palmyrenorum. This cohort was attested first in 208, and remained in the city until the Persian siege of 256. Their headquarters were in the temple of Azzanathkona, where the excavation of room W13 revealed an archive of eighty-four papyri, most of which pertain to the cohort. The unit was a *cohors* of approximately a thousand men led by a tribune, and included infantry and cavalry. Although only attested after 208, one of the two almost complete rosters from the temple of Azzanathkona suggests that it existed at least since 192. Yet the date of the formation of the cohort has been hotly debated by scholars, who have pushed it back to as early as 165 (*Dura Final Report* V.1, 22–46; on the cohort, see Spaul 2000, 434–436; James 2020, 245–247).

In the second and third centuries, Palmyrene units were also present in Numidia, as noted above, and in Egypt. For example, at Berenike, on the Red Sea, a statue and a bilingual inscription in Greek and Palmyrene dedicated to Yahribol testifies to the presence of one Aemilius Celer, 'prefect of Berenike and the Ala Heracliana' (ἐπάρχου Ὄρους Βερενείκης καί Εἴλης Ἡρακλιανῆς) and the chiliarch, Valerius Germanionos (Οὐαλερίου Γερμανίωνος χι(λιάρχου) εἴλης τῆς αὐτῆς—SEG XLIX, 2117). The inscription has been generally dated to between 180/185 and 212 A.D. . Similarly, Palmyrene archers are also attested at Coptos, where a 216 inscription refers to 'Hadriani Palmyreni Antoniniani Sagittari' (on this, see Speidel 1984a).

Other soldiers rose to prominence in units that did not bear the identifier *Palmyrenorum* in their official names; however, some of them took pride in stressing their identity in inscriptions using the adjective *Palmyrenus* after their personal names. An example of this is Publius Aelius Annius, who dedicated an altar in Rome to Fortuna. The associated inscription identifies him as an *eques singularis augusti* (i.e., a mounted praetorian guard) but also as a *Palmyrenus* (CIL VI, 3174). In Britain, a Palmyrene *vexillarius* is attested in a second-century inscription found at Corbridge (RIB 1171). The inscription is an incomplete funerary stela to a '. . . rathes Palmorenus', who died at the age of sixty-eight—probably the same 'Barathes Palmyrenus', husband of Regina, mentioned in another second-century inscription from South Shields (RIB 1065). However, in this case, the evidence is confusing. The term *vexillarius* is often translated as 'flag-bearer', but the advanced age of this individual suggests that he was not in service at the time of his death. Therefore, it has been postulated that Barathes may have been a 'flag-maker' or the *vexillarius* of a corporation (Birley 1953, 81–82).

The involvement of Palmyrene units in the Roman army in late antiquity is more obscure due to the lack of evidence in primary sources. The only written source to shed light on this is the late fourth-century *Notitia dignitatum* (7.34; 31.49), which attests to the existence of a Cuneus Equitum Secundorum Clibanarium Palmyrenorum and an Ala Octava Palmyrenorum. The document reports that both units were under the care of the *dux Thebaidis*. The Cuneus Equitum Secundorum Clibanarium Palmyrenorum was a *vexillatio comitatensis*—a cavalry unit—made up of an elite mounted unit of *clibanarii*, heavily armoured shock cavalry (on *clibanarii*, see Elton 1996, 106; on *vexillatio comitatensis*, see Southern and Dixon 1996, 30–31). The existence of Palmyrene *clibanarii* in late antiquity is confirmed by an inscription in the tombs of the prophets at Jerusalem mentioning one Anamos 'clibanarios teriius [or triarius?] of Palmyra', tentatively dated to the fourth or fifth century by Clermont-Ganneau (1899, 364–365). Although the inscription does not explicitly mention the Cuneus Equitum Secundorum Clibanarium Palmyrenorum, it is possible that the soldier belonged to that unit. The Ala Octava Palmyrenorum was probably the result of the transformation of the former Numerus Palmyrenorum stationed at Coptos (Speidel 1984a, 221).

SOME NOTES ON PALMYRENE MILITIA

Besides Palmyrene soldiers regularly serving in the Roman army, there is inscriptional evidence to suggest the existence of Palmyrene militia, the role of the latter being to protect the lucrative caravan trade to the east (on this, see Young 2001, 157–166). There are at least three known ways in which soldiers could have served in this militia. First, they could be recruited by the *synodiarch* or *archemporos* to provide caravans venturing east with military protection against the nomads. The most direct evidence of this are inscriptions mentioning prominent figures who 'provid[ed] safety for the merchants and caravans in every occasion' (*IGLS* XVII.1, 222; transl. Matthews 1984, 168; on this, also see Will 1957, 266). Second, some soldiers were actively combating the nomadic threat, and served under a '*strategos* of the peace' (στρατηγὸς ἐπὶ τῆς εἰρήνης). The command of these στρατηγοί was endorsed by the city itself, since, in the epigraphic record, these figures are honoured by the council and the people for raising commands against the nomads (Will 1957, 265–266; Young 2001, 161–162). There is further evidence concerning a third way of employing Palmyrene militia, which was to guard nodal trading posts in Persian territory. Perhaps the most informative case study is represented by the garrisons at ʿAna, Bijan, and Gambla on the Euphrates, which are attested in a number of inscriptions starting in 132, referring to detachments of horsemen and their commanders (*CIS* II, 3973; Cantineau 1933, 178–180; Dunant 1971, 65, n. 51; on these and other relevant inscriptions, see Isaac 1992, 150–151, n. 241; Matthews 1984, 168–169; Young 2001, 158–159). Here, the Palmyrene militia was deployed to protect the caravan route along the river. As already mentioned above, the continuous presence of Palmyrene soldiers at Dura suggests that at least some of these garrisons were later regularized and integrated into the Roman army (Young 2001, 162–163). However, like the Palmyrene army at the time of Zenobia, their composition and organization remain obscure.

CONCLUSION

What seems to emerge from the available data is that, at least since the second half of the second century, if not earlier, Palmyra was provided with a garrison of auxiliaries to the Roman army. Of this garrison, the names of four units from the Roman period are known: Ala I Ulpia Singularium (150–167), Ala I Thracum Herculana (167–183), Ala Vocontiorum (183 to the end of the second or beginning of the third century), and Cohors I Flavia Chalcidenorum (206/207 to 247). Little or nothing is known of the garrison at Palmyra in the turbulent second half of the third century, but, by the beginning of the fourth century, the city seems to have acquired a new unit, the Legio I Illyricorum, which was stationed in part or entirely in a newly constructed camp—the Camp of Diocletian. The military importance of Palmyra as a frontier post grew gradually, and, after a break in the fifth century, the city hosted the *dux* of Emesa, probably together with his retinue, a *numerus* of soldiers, and a group of *limitanei* (frontier troops).

Palmyra was not solely a garrisoned city, but also contributed actively to the Roman army with its own auxiliary units, at least in Dacia, northern Africa, and Syria. We know that Palmyrenes were much valued as soldiers in the Roman period, to the extent that one of them is known to have been a member of the emperor's personal escort in Rome. Two auxiliary units of recruits are also known from late antiquity, namely the Cuneus Equitum Secundorum Clibanarium Palmyrenorum and the Ala Octava Palmyrenorum, which are mentioned in the *Notitia dignitatum* as being under the command of the *dux Thebaidis*. In addition to the Roman army, the Palmyrenes are known to have formed a militia to protect the lucrative caravan trade to the east.

ABBREVIATIONS

CIL	*Corpus inscriptionum Latinarum.* Berlin: Berlin-Brandenburgische Akademie der Wissenschaften, 1853–.
CIS	*Corpus inscriptionum Semiticarum.* Paris: Reipublicæ Typographeo, 1881–1962.
Dura Final Report V.1	Welles, Bradford C., Robert O. Fink, and Frank J. Gilliam. 1959. *The Excavations at Dura-Europos: Conducted by Yale University and the French Academy of Inscriptions and Letters; Final Report.* Vol. 5, *Inscriptions, Parchment and Papyri.* Part 1, *The Parchments and Papyri.* New Haven, CT: Yale University Press.
Dura Prelim. Report VII/ VIII	Rostovtzeff, Michael I., Frank E. Brown, and Bradford C. Welles. 1939. *The Excavations at Dura-Europos Conducted by Yale University and the French Academy of Inscriptions and Letters: Preliminary Report of the Seventh and Eighth Seasons of Work, 1933–1934 and 1934–1935.* New Haven, CT: Yale University Press.
IGLS XVII.1	Yon, Jean-Baptiste, ed. 2012. *Inscriptions grecques et latines de la Syrie: Palmyre.* Beirut: Institut français du Proche-Orient.
ILS	Dessau, Hermann, ed. 1892–1916. *Inscriptiones latinae selectae.* 3 vols. Berlin: Weidmann.
Inv.	Cantineau, Jean, Jean Starcky, Michał Gawlikowski, and Adnan Bounni, eds. 1930–1975. *Inventaire des inscriptions de Palmyre.* 12 vols. Beirut: Imprimerie catholique.
RIB	Collingwood, Robin G. and Richard P. Wright, eds. 1965. *The Roman Inscriptions of Britain.* Vol. 1, *Inscriptions on Stone.* Oxford: Clarendon Press.
RMD	Roxan, Margaret M. and Paul A. Holder, eds. 1978–2006. *Roman Military Diplomas.* London, Institute of Classical Studies, School of Advanced Study, University of London.
SEG	*Supplementum epigraphicum Graecum.* Leiden: Brill, 1923–.

BIBLIOGRAPHY

Written Sources

Historia Augusta Vita Aureliani, edited and translated by François Paschoud. Paris: Les belles lettres, 1996.

Ibn A'tham al-Kūfī. *Kitāb al-futūḥ*, edited by Muhammad 'A. Khān and 'A. W. al-Bukhari. Hyderabad: Osmania Oriental Publications Bureau, 1968–1975.

John Malalas. *Chronographia*, edited by Ludwig A. Dindorf. Bonn: Weber, 1831; *The Chronicle of John Malalas: A Translation*, translated by Elizabeth Jeffreys, Michael Jeffreys, and Roger Scott. Melbourne: Australian Association for Byzantine Studies, 1986.

Notitia dignitatum, edited by Otto Seeck. Berlin: Weidmann, 1876.

Procopius. *De aedificiis*, edited and translated by Henry B. Dewing. London: William, 1961.

Theophanes. *Chronographia*, edited by Carolus de Boor. Leipzig: Teubner, 1884.

Secondary Literature

Barański, Marek. 1994. 'The Roman Army in Palmyra: A Case of Adaptation of a Pre-existing City'. In *The Roman and Byzantine Army in the East: Proceedings of a Colloquium Held at the Jagiellonian University, Kraków in September 1992*, edited by Edward Dabrowa, 9–17. Krakow: Uniwersytet Jagiellonski, Instytut Historii.

Bauzou, Thomas. 1992. 'Activité de la mission archéologique "Strata Diocletiana" en 1990 et 1992'. *Chronique archéologique en Syrie* 1: 136–140.

Bauzou, Thomas. 1993. 'Epigraphie et toponymie: Le cas de la palmyrène du sud-ouest'. *Syria* 70: 27–50.

Bianchi, Luca. 1987. 'I Palmireni in Dacia: Comunità e tradizioni religiose'. *Dialoghi di archeologia* 5: 87–95.

Birley, Eric. 1953. *Roman Britain and the Roman Army*. Kendal: Wilson.

Birley, Eric. 1988. 'The Equestrian Officers of the Roman Army'. In *The Roman Army: Papers, 1929–1986*, edited by Eric Birley, 133–153. Amsterdam: Gieben.

Cantineau, Jean. 1933. 'Tadmorea'. *Syria* 14: 169–202.

Clermont-Ganneau, Simon C. 1899. *Archaeological Researches in Palestine During the Years 1873–1874: With Numerous Illustrations from Drawings Made on the Spot by A. Lecomte du Noüy*. Vol. 1. London: Palestine Exploration Fund.

Dirven, Lucinda A. 1999. *The Palmyrenes of Dura-Europos: A Study of Religious Interaction in Roman Syria*. Leiden: Brill.

Dunant, Christiane. 1971. *Le sanctuaire de Baalshamin à Palmyre*. Vol. 3, *Les inscriptions*. Biblioteca Helvetica Romana, vol. 10, no. 3. Rome: Institut suisse de Rome.

Edwell, Peter. 2008. *Between Rome and Persia: The Middle Euphrates, Mesopotamia and Palmyra under Roman Control*. London: Routledge.

Elton, Hugh. 1996. *Warfare in Roman Europe, AD 350–425*. Oxford: Clarendon Press.

Equini Schneider, Eugenia. 1988. 'Palmireni in Africa: Calceus Herculis'. In *L'Africa Romana: Atti del V convegno di studio, Sassari, 11–13 December 1987*, edited by Attilio Mastino, 383–395. Sassari: Università di Sassari, Dipartimento di Storia.

Fellmann, Rudolf. 1976. 'Le "camp de Dioclétien" à Palmyre et l'architecture militaire du Bas empire'. In *Mélanges d'histoire ancienne et d'archéologie offerts à Paul Collart*, edited by

Pierre Ducrey, Claude Bérard, Christiane Dunant, and François Paschoud, 173–191. Cahiers d'archéologie romande 5. Lausanne: Bibliothèque historique Vaudoise.

Fellmann, Rudolf. 1995. 'L'inscription d'un "Optio Princeps" au temple de Ba'alshamin à Palmyre'. In *Actes du Colloque de Lyon 1994: La hiérarchie (Rangordnung) de l'armée Romaine sous le Haut-Empire*, edited by Yann Le Bohec, 239–240. Paris: de Boccard.

Gawlikowski, Michał. 2010. 'The Roman Army in Palmyra Under Tiberius'. *Studia Palmyreńskie* 11: 49–52.

Intagliata, Emanuele E. 2015. 'Palmyra/Tadmur in Late Antiquity and Early Islam. An Archaeological and Historical Reassessment'. Unpublished doctoral thesis, University of Edinburgh.

Intagliata, Emanuele E. 2018. *Palmyra after Zenobia (273–750): An Archaeological and Historical Reappraisal*. Oxford: Oxbow.

Isaac, Ben. 1992. *The Limits of Empire: The Roman Army in the East*. 2nd ed. Oxford: Clarendon Press.

James, Simon. 2020. *The Roman Military Base at Dura-Europos, Syria: An Archaeological Visualization*. Oxford: Oxford University Press.

Kowalski, Slawomir P. 1998. 'The Camp of the *Legio I Illyricorum* in Palmyra'. *Novaensia: Badania ekspedycji archeologicznej Uniwersytetu Warszawskiego w Novae; Studia i materialy* 10: 189–209.

Le Bohec, Yann. 2012. 'Décurions et centurions auxiliaires sous le principat en Afrique-Numidie'. *Acta classica* 55: 83–98.

Lenoir, Maurice. 2011. *Le camp Romaine: Proche-Orient et Afrique du nord*. Rome: École française de Rome.

Lesquier, Jean. 1918. *L'armée romaine d'Égypte d'Auguste à Dioclétien*. Cairo: Institut français d'archéologie orientale du Caire.

Matthews, John F. 1984. 'The Tax Law of Palmyra: Evidence for Economic History in a City of the Roman East'. *Journal of Roman Studies* 74: 157–180.

Millar, Fergus. 1993. *The Roman Near East, 31 BC–AD 337*. Cambridge, MA: Harvard University Press.

Pollard, Nigel. 2000. *Soldiers, Cities and Civilians in Roman Syria*. Ann Arbor: University of Michigan Press.

Schnädelbach, Klaus. 2010. *Topographia Palmyrena*. Vol. 1, *Topography*. Bonn: Habelt.

Seyrig, Henri A. 1933. 'Antiquités syriennes'. *Syria* 14: 152–168.

Seyrig, Henri A. 1941. 'Inscriptions grecques de l'agora de Palmyre'. *Syria* 22: 223–270.

Smith, Andrew M. 2013. *Roman Palmyra: Identity, Community, and State Formation*. Oxford: Oxford University Press.

Southern, Pat. 1989. 'The Numeri of the Roman Imperial Army'. *Britannia* 20: 81–140.

Southern, Pat, and Karen R. Dixon. 1996. *The Late Roman Army*. London: Batsford.

Spaul, John E. H. 1994. *Ala 2: The Auxiliary Cavalry Units of the Prediocletianic Imperial Roman Army*. Andover: Nectoreca Press.

Spaul, John E. H. 2000. *Cohors 2: The Evidence for and a Short History of the Auxiliary Infantry Units of the Imperial Roman Army*. Oxford: Archaeopress.

Speidel, Michael P. 1972. 'Numerus ou ala Vocontiorum a Palmyre'? *Syria* 49: 495–497.

Speidel, Michael P. 1984a. 'Palmyrenian Irregulars at Koptos'. *Bulletin of the American Society of Papyrologists* 21: 221–224.

Speidel, Michael P. 1984b. 'Numerus or Ala Vocontiorum at Palmyra'? In *Roman Army Studies*. Vol. 1, edited by Michael P. Speidel, 167–169. Amsterdam: Gieben.

Weiß, Peter, and Michael P. Speidel. 2004. 'Das erste Militärdiplom für Arabia'. *Zeitschrift für Papyrologie und Epigraphik* 150: 253–264.

Will, Ernest. 1957. 'Marchands et chefs de caravanes à Palmyre'. *Syria* 34: 262–277.

Yon, Jean-Baptiste. 2002. *Les notables de Palmyre*. Bibliothèque archéologique et historique 163. Beirut: Institut français d'archéologie du Proche-Orient.

Yon, Jean-Baptiste. 2008. 'Documents sur l'armée romaine à Palmyre'. *Electrum* 14: 129–147.

Young, Gary K. 2001. *Rome's Eastern Trade: International Commerce and Imperial Policy, 31 BC–AD 305*. London: Routledge.

PART THREE

PALMYRA AND LANGUAGE

CHAPTER 13

A BILINGUAL WORLD?

Language and Epigraphy in Palmyra

JEAN-BAPTISTE YON

INTRODUCTION: LANGUAGE IN PALMYRA

FOR most of the Roman period, Aramaic was one of the spoken languages of the population of Syria, used as a lingua franca, mostly alongside Greek, but with North Arabian, Latin, and other languages (Iranian, Armenian) spoken as well. Most of these languages were however rarely written, and the epigraphic evidence is strong only for Greek and North Arabian (Safaitic, various Thamudic scripts). Latin was rarer, as was Aramaic, except in some areas such as Nabatea, Osrhoene, and Palmyra. In this last city, almost uniquely in the public epigraphy of the cities of the empire, Palmyrene Aramaic was on an equal footing with Greek.

Palmyrene was a dialect of Aramaic (a member of the North-West Semitic group of the Semitic language family), combining Achaemenid Imperial Aramaic with some Eastern Aramaic traits (Gzella 2011). Although Greek, Latin, or Arabic loanwords were incorporated into Palmyrene, most of the vocabulary (for trade, law, or in the funerary sphere) is Aramaic. The language was written in an alphabet originally borrowed from the Phoenicians via official (Achaemenid) Aramaic, written from left to right. Like other Semitic alphabets, Palmyrene did not represent vowels. It was close to Syriac *estranghelo* in its more cursive form, frequently found in the graffiti found in the tombs and sometimes written vertically, but it also had a more 'monumental' script, used for official inscriptions. Its development from letters of rather irregular forms and varying dimensions to a script characterized by its letters with broken lines and rounded shapes can be seen as an influence from Greek epigraphy: the calibrated shape of each letter tended to fit into the same ideal rectangle (Cantineau 1935). For Greek, the script was usually of a rounded sort. Similar examples could be found all over the Roman East, but this particular script for Greek was consistently used and was remarkably regular. The stonecutters of the city were very well practised in both languages (Figure 13.1). Only in the early Byzantine period and chiefly for epitaphs did Greek script become much less elegant, evidencing the short supply of professional stonecutters. Obviously, the quality of the stone, a local whitish limestone, was a dominant factor for the visual aspect of the inscriptions during the Roman period. In the beginning a soft limestone was mostly used for carving and building, but in the first century AD this was replaced by a much

FIGURE 13.1 A bilingual Greek and Aramaic inscription dated AD 242/243 (*IGLS* XVII, 53).

harder variety. Other stones, such as marble, had to be imported and are very rare for inscriptions.

The balance between Greek and Aramaic inscriptions in the Palmyrene epigraphic corpus is clear. More than 2,500 Aramaic inscriptions compare to over five hundred Greek texts and about fifty in Latin. A great part of the Greek inscriptions are bilingual and include an Aramaic version. These statistics have also to be seen in the light of the literary evidence on the history of the city, which amounts to some lines of Pliny (*NH* 5.88) and Appian (*Bell. Civ.* 5.9) and several late antique narratives of the rise and downfall of Palmyra under Odainathus and Zenobia (mostly Zosimus). In other words, the documentary evidence for Palmyra would be next to nothing were it not for the information given by archaeology and epigraphy. This chapter describes the contribution of epigraphy to the history of the city, focusing on the public use of Aramaic alongside Greek, a singular feature in the cities of the Roman Empire (Millar 1993). This public bilingualism, almost unique and sometimes extending (with the addition of Latin) into trilingualism, has to be explained if we are to better understand the Palmyrene society of the first three centuries of the era.

An almost complete contemporaneity must be underlined between, on the one hand, epigraphy in Palmyra and, on the other, the period of the city's major buildings and its urban blossoming. The first dated inscription is a dedication by the priests of Bēl in the year 44 BC, not long before the construction of the temple of Bēl (*PAT* 1524). The absence of inscriptions does not mean that there were no buildings of importance before this period (such as a precursor of the temple of Bēl), but the monumentalization of Palmyra and the epigraphic habit seem closely intertwined. Similarly, after the downfall of Zenobia, the great period of Palmyra abruptly ceased. Edifices were still built, such as military camps, temples, or, later, churches, but never on the same scale as in the second and third centuries. Likewise, Greek inscriptions were still engraved until at least March AD 562 for the last dated example (*IGLS* XVII, 499), but much less than before, and, after the beginning of the fourth century, Latin is not seen. After the victory of Aurelian, Aramaic epigraphy came to a stop almost immediately. Only two or three Hebrew inscriptions (fourth century?) account for Semitic languages until the arrival of Arabic in the first centuries of the Hegira.

A SHORT HISTORICAL OVERVIEW: HISTORY OF RESEARCH

At the beginning of the epigraphy of Palmyra (in the sense of epigraphic science) stands the visit of the British cleric William Halifax in 1691. He made a copy of about twenty Greek and three Palmyrene Aramaic texts. The latter language was still unknown at the time, and the poor copies made by Halifax could not be used in a subsequent publication. The first reliable evidence came only with other British travellers, Robert

Wood and James Dawkins, in 1751. The book they published two years later (Wood and Dawkins 1753) presented the copies of eleven bilingual (Greek and Palmyrene Aramaic), fifteen Greek, and two Palmyrene inscriptions (Figure 13.2). It took only one year then for this dialect of Aramaic to be deciphered by the Abbot Barthélemy in France and by John Swinton in England, taking advantage of the drawings published by Wood and Dawkins and of their knowledge of other Semitic languages (Daniels 1988). Greek and Latin texts were used in the first corpus of inscriptions between the end of the century and the beginning of the next (*Corpus Inscriptionum Graecarum* was published in 1833 by A. Boeckhe), but the dangers and expenses of travelling to Palmyra until the last part of the nineteenth century resulted in only limited progress on this point. Only with the expedition of the French scholar and political figure William Henry Waddington in 1861 was it possible to increase the number of documents. Waddington's mission was organized following the advice of the Marquis Melchior de Vogüé, who had visited Palmyra in 1853 and had made copies of some documents. Waddington brought back copies and drawings of 144 new Aramaic texts, subsequently published by de Vogüé (Vogüé 1868), as well as numerous Greek and Latin inscriptions, marking the beginning of a more 'scientific' exploration of the city and its epigraphy (Waddington 1870). From the 1870s, the number of travellers began to increase, from simple tourists to scholars, some of whom were well versed in Semitic languages and biblical studies.

FIGURE 13.2 The Great Colonnade as seen in 1751. The consoles for the statues are easily distinguishable on the columns.

From Wood and Dawkins 1753, plate 35.

Notable among them are A. D. Mordtmann, Eduard Sachau, Otto Puchstein, and the Armenian Russian prince, Simon Abamalek Lazarew, who had the Tax Law brought back to St Petersburg some years after its initial discovery in 1881. In the same period, a flourishing traffic in antiquities from the oasis began, which explains why Palmyrene funerary busts are found in every major archaeological collection from Istanbul to Los Angeles—even in Cuba and Brazil—but mostly in Europe and the United States, in both public and private collections. At the same time, Semitic epigraphy was rapidly taking its due place alongside Latin or Greek. After the publication of textbooks with selections of inscriptions (Cooke 1903; Lidzbarski 1898) and numerous papers on specific aspects (script, language, vocabulary, syntax), the first attempt to document a complete corpus of Aramaic inscriptions from the site came with the dedicated volume of the *Corpus inscriptionum Semiticarum (CIS)* published in Paris between 1926 and 1949. The editor of the volume, Jean-Baptiste Chabot, drew heavily on the works of all his predecessors (among them Charles Clermont-Ganneau and Mark Lidzbarski); of the architect Émile Bertone, who had spent five months in Palmyra in 1895; and of the Dominican friars Antonin Jaussen and Raphaël Savignac, who made copies, squeezes, and photographs in their few months before the beginning of World War I. The corpus focused on Aramaic texts but in the case of bilingual inscriptions gave Greek and Latin texts. These were present as well in the selections of Greek and Latin inscriptions compiled at the beginning of the twentieth century (e.g., W. Dittenberger, *Orientis Graeci inscriptiones selectae*; R. Cagnat, *Inscriptiones Graecae ad res Romanas pertinentes*).

A second period began after World War I with the French Mandate over Syria. Excavations, mapping, and inventories were conducted under the supervision of Henri Seyrig (director of antiquities for Syria; Duyrat et al. 2016), with names such as Harald Ingholt and Jean Cantineau for Semitic epigraphy and Seyrig himself for Greek. Thanks to the more than seven hundred inscriptions then known by the *CIS* and to the new texts that were published at the time, a marked interest in the Aramaic dialect of Palmyra led to the publication of two grammars of the language, the first in French by Jean Cantineau (Cantineau 1935), the second in German by Franz Rosenthal (Rosenthal 1936). Jean Cantineau tried to supplement the *CIS* with his series of *Inventaire des inscriptions de Palmyre* (1930–1939, continued by Jean Starcky in 1949, then by Javier Teixidor and Adnan Bounni in 1965 and 1975) in order to keep abreast of the latest discoveries. Epigraphic publications then did not stop until the beginning of the 2010s, due to the continuous excavations and surveys that took place during the French Mandate, after World War II, and into Syria's independence. Syrian and foreign missions—among them most notably the Polish and Swiss teams—discovered and published inscriptions during their work. Jean Starcky, Michał Gawlikowski (Gawlikowski 1970; 1973; 1974), Józef Tadeusz Milik (Milik 1972), and Christiane Dunant (Dunant 1971) figure prominently among the epigraphists involved. *Palmyrene Aramaic Texts* by Delbert R. Hillers and Eleonora Cussini (for which the acronym *PAT* has become standard) was published in 1996 as a contribution to the Comprehensive Aramaic Lexicon Project. It gathered all known texts written in the Aramaic language of Palmyra, with a total number of ca. 2,830 items. This is now the standard reference for Palmyrene Semitic epigraphy, with its glossary, to be completed by some later contributions (al-As'ad et al., 2012; Yon 2013). The textbook published by E. Cussini (2022) offers a lucid assessment of the state of knowledge. In the near future, the Palmyrene Portrait Project will gather all known funerary portraits from the city, at the same time providing an important corpus of mostly Aramaic epitaphs (Raja 2018). The recent publication of the diaries of Harald Ingholt (Raja et al. 2021) and of his abundant archives (Bobou et al. 2022) is a first step. For Greek and Latin, the *IGLS* volume (*Inscriptions grecques et latines de la Syrie*, volume 17.1, *Palmyre*) came out in 2012, with all the texts in these languages—including Aramaic versions for bi- and trilinguals—discovered in the area of the city of Palmyra. The next volume (17/2, in preparation) will include the Tax Law and inscriptions from the hinterland of Palmyra (the Palmyrene region).

Latin: The Language of Empire

Even the most recent discoveries confirm the clear-cut division between languages for the genre of inscriptions. As elsewhere in the Roman East, Latin, which is rather rare, was used for texts connected mostly but not exclusively with the Roman army and with imperial administration. In Palmyrene epigraphy, Latin was used mostly for epitaphs of Roman soldiers and their families (*IGLS* XVII, 484–493) and for dedications to the emperors by soldiers or Roman officials (3, 118, 119, 121, 168, 169, 170, 297, 353). It covers a long period of Roman presence at Palmyra, from the beginning of the first century with a dedication by the legate of the tenth legion to Tiberius, Drusus, and Germanicus, to the fourth century, with the construction of a military camp by a governor on behalf of the first tetrarchy of Diocletian, Maximian, and their *caesares* Constantius and Galerius (between 293 and 303). Despite this restricted usage, Latin was occasionally used in official documents by the city of Palmyra at the time of its inception.

The Primacy of Aramaic

On the other side, during almost exactly the same time period, Aramaic was clearly the written language of the majority, above all of local people. The information given by personal names, overwhelmingly Semitic, confirms this (Stark 1971). This domain was marked to some extent by bilingualism: Palmyrenes of the upper class could have double names, with a Greek equivalent of their Aramaic name, as with 'Zabdilah' (in the Semitic version) who is in the other version 'Zenobios who is also called Zabdilas' (*IGLS* XVII, 53). The equivalence could be semantic (Iarhibolê, from Iarhibôl seen as a sun god, equated with Heliodôros), approximately phonetic (Queen Zenobia was Batzabbai, *PAT* 0293 = *IGLS* XVII, 57), or for no apparent reason, as when Oga is called Seleukos in Greek (*PAT* 0280–0281 = *IGLS* XVII, 75–76). Sometimes double names could be Semitic, as in the case of 'Elahbel who is called Marônâ', who appears curiously as 'Theodoros who is called Marônas' in the Greek version of the same text (*PAT* 0117 = *IGLS* XVII, 542). Greek names were also occasionally adopted by Palmyrenes without visible reference to a Semitic context, and a Heliodôros could be the son of one Raaios. It is manifest that Graeco-Roman onomastics were not predominant at Palmyra. Even when magistrates exercise the typical civic duties of Greek cities, they mainly have local names. When the Greek name is used, it is very often in parallel with the Aramaic name; more commonly, the Aramaic does not mention the Greek name but only the local version of the name. As always, it has to be underlined that the linguistic background of a name is not necessarily linked with the ethnic origin of an individual. Iranian names are well attested (Worod, Artaban), always as main names, but they apply to members of families in which all other names are Semitic or Greek. Fashion, or special relations with the Iranian world (for trade?) is an obvious explanation, but details remain uncertain (Yon 2000).

Aramaic was ubiquitous in two areas: for epitaphs and for dedications to deities. The epigraphic use of Aramaic corresponds to what has often been broadly defined as more private fields, as opposed to Greek, seen as the language of the public sphere. Inscriptions inside tombs—mostly epitaphs, but graffiti as well—were composed in Aramaic: they were to be read by members of the family or perhaps of an enlarged family circle (Figure 13.3). Obviously, the visitors to the tombs were local people, not foreigners, and they read their own language. In total, more than a thousand funerary inscriptions accompany the bust reliefs sculpted on plaques representing the dead. Those well-known reliefs, very identifiable, were engraved almost exclusively with Semitic texts. Exceptions, often bilingual, were restricted to a few families and a few random examples. The layout of these epitaphs is always very simple: the name of the deceased is followed by his father's and grandfather's names, sometimes with earlier generations, or the husband's name in the case of women. The epitaph usually ends with the word 'alas'. Dates or other details are very rare. Despite their succinct content, these epitaphs collectively inform us about family relations, genealogies. Combined with the depiction of deceased individuals and their family members, which constitute the largest group of portrait sculpture from the Roman Empire, the corpus originating inside the tombs yields an unmatched overview of Palmyrene society at the time of the Roman Empire. But it is a view from the inside. The message is different outside the tomb, where the foundation and concession inscriptions displayed on the tomb walls aimed at an audience of Palmyrenes and foreigners. This led to the use of Greek next to Aramaic, but proportions are worth underlining. On the more monumental tombs—the tower tombs and, later, temple tombs—Greek and Aramaic inscriptions often marked ownership, with lengthy genealogies going back to distant ancestors (great-grandfathers and beyond). The same genealogies also appear on less conspicuous monuments (i.e., underground tombs), but most of these are written only in Aramaic. Admittedly, there are exceptions, with Greek inscriptions for underground tombs and Aramaic-only inscriptions for monumental tombs, above all for earlier cases. Personal and family choices or social differentiation played a major role here.

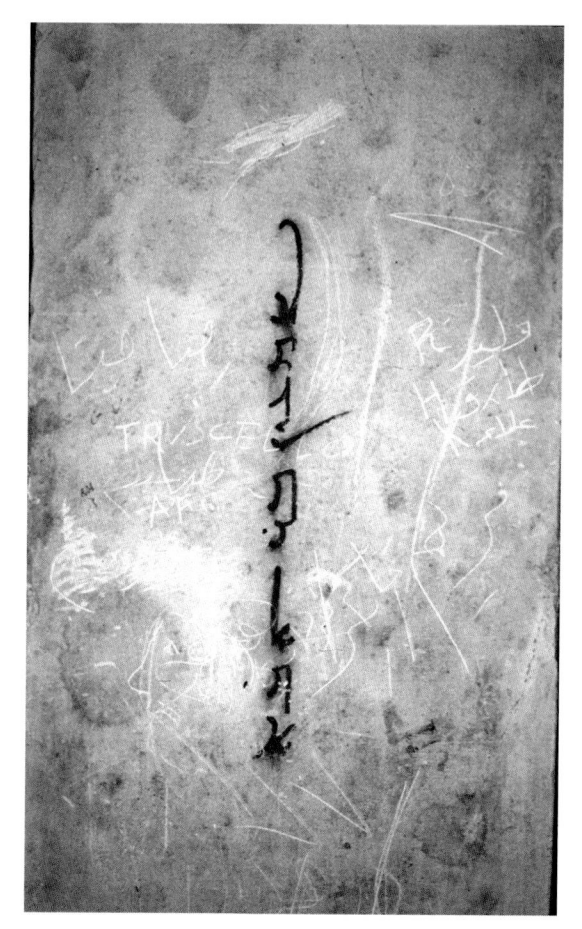

FIGURE 13.3 Vertical Aramaic graffito in the Three Brothers Tomb, with the name of Shimon son of Abba (*PAT* 0538).

© J.-B. Yon, Hisoma, CNRS.

Statistics are difficult because many texts have been found out of context, and inscribed stone slabs could belong to any type of tomb. In addition, the concession inscriptions reveal a different population partaking in the epigraphic habit. Many women and, indeed, freedmen were part of these transactions as they offered less privileged groups a way of participating in the elite's way of life, with both these categories using Aramaic as their mode of expression (Gawlikowski 1970; Yon 2002).

The same phenomena are clear for texts devoted to deities (Gawlikowski 1990; Kaizer 2002, on religious matters), a domain in which all categories of the population are represented, the elite as well as more modest individuals. From the small tesserae (terracotta tokens serving as entrance tickets to religious banquets; Ingholt et al. 1955) to the more impressive reliefs with figurations of Palmyrene or Greek divinities, Aramaic is the common language. For dedications to the so-called Anonymous God on stone altars, Greek is rare; where it exists, it often has an Aramaic counterpart. The altars, some of them rather small, and their inscriptions were offered as tokens of devotion to the gods by very different people—members of the affluent families, former slaves, and women (Dijkstra 1995; Yon 2002).

If, for traditional Semitic gods, the Greek counterpart sometimes used equivalents of the original names (Ares for Arsu, Hera for Herta, Poseidon for El Qonera), some gods consistently kept their Semitic names. This is particularly true for deities specific to Palmyra, such as Iarhibôl, Malakbel, or Aglibôl. Their characteristic personality could not be expressed in another language. Among Palmyrene expatriates, they were hugely popular: Iarhibôl and Malakbel are the most frequent deities in dedications made by soldiers and civilians of the diaspora in Dacia, Numidia, and Rome, their names always kept in Latin or Greek transcription, with inconsistent spellings. Even Bēl, the great god of Palmyra, sometimes kept his name (Greek Belos) alongside Zeus or in addition to him (Zeus Belos: *IGLS* XVII, 6). But Zeus never appears in Aramaic, and names of original Greek deities are rare in Aramaic. Nemesis (*nmsys*) is apparently the only case, but, as is clearly evidenced by Old Syriac (Edessean) epigraphy, there could have been transcriptions of Greek god names in some Aramaic dialects (Hera as *hr*). The scanty remains of cultic regulations ('sacred laws') discovered at Palmyra were written in the local language (e.g., *PAT* 0991 or 1981). Those texts are usually dated to the first century AD—admittedly, before the period of the full development of Greek in epigraphy. However, at the end of the period, the last dated Aramaic inscriptions (*PAT* 1358 and 2812: 272 and maybe 273), two lists of religious dignitaries and men responsible for religious duties in the sanctuary of Bēl, were written in Palmyrene Aramaic. At the same time, religious foundations, following a classical model widespread in Asia Minor and in Greece, are often expressed in Greek. Sometimes, with Palmyrene counterparts, there are also references to Palmyrene deities and practices ('the sedan chair of the god Bôrroaônos'), but, for the most part, gifts made 'for the everlasting well-being of the priests' or 'for the distribution of meat on that very day [16 August] to all guests' were in accordance with other examples from the Greek world (*IGLS* XVII, 308). Allusions to an imperial cult may be adduced to explain the use of Greek, but this was not always the case. It remains the case that, even allowing for a few exceptions as far as religion is concerned, this was mostly an Aramaic-speaking world. Conversely, when the Palmyrene population was engaging in self-representation on the scene of the Graeco-Roman world, Greek was the language used. It explains why there are few purely Aramaic honorific inscriptions dedicated to great individuals. Among the examples of Aramaic honorific inscriptions stand out those texts better understood in a purely family context, such as a dedication in the Transverse Colonnade to a grandfather by his grandson (*PAT* 0303), or with a clear religious content, as when in the same Transverse Colonnade a man is honoured by an unknown group (a tribe?) for his gift to the gods Shamash (the sun god), Allat, and Rahim (*PAT* 0301).

GREEK: A PUBLIC LANGUAGE?

Greek, conversely, appears alone or in bilinguals when it comes to relations with the army or with the Roman emperor and his subordinates, or in a civic context, with most of the dedications made by 'the council and the people' of Palmyra (*boule* and *demos*). There are exceptions when purely 'Palmyrene' topics dealing with religion are expressed only in Greek (*IGLS* XVII, 312) but not in the other direction: no exclusively Aramaic text deals with the emperor and imperial administration. Particularly striking in the same vein are the few dedications that involve the tribes of Palmyra: these are, to some extent, of an official nature, but deal mostly with religious matters, as is best exemplified by the so-called dedications made by the gods. At Palmyra, these inscriptions associate gods and a tribe as they honour a benefactor (or benefactress). As with other texts relating to the tribes (including the first dated inscription of Palmyra, 44 BC), Aramaic is the language of choice in the earlier period. Later, from the end of the first century, bilinguals become numerous, even for tribes and 'dedications made by the gods' (*PAT* 0312 = *IGLS* XVII, 124), until the almost complete disappearance of the latter. Tribes still appear in the epigraphy of the city, now in a definitely civic context, as 'the four tribes of the city' (*IGLS* XVII, 149), following a tradition firmly anchored in Greek civic procedure. Clearly, as the constitution of the city of Palmyra, with its *boule*, its *demos*, and its magistrates, apparently became more Greek, the language itself came to the forefront and even what was expressed in the local language could be expressed simultaneously in Greek (Sartre 1996). Other tribes coexisted with the civic tribes and expressed their dedications in Greek and Aramaic, such as those of the Matthabôlioi/Benê Mattabôl in the Great Colonnade and the Benê Zabdibôl in the Transverse Colonnade (Yon 2002). In an early phase of the process, an inscription is particularly enlightening on the importance of self-designation. In this text, discovered in the agora and dated to the last quarter of the first century, a Palmyrene called Zabdibôl records his identity as 'Zabdibôlos son of Ogèlos, the Palmyrene' in Greek, but as 'Zabdibôl son of 'Ogeîlû, who is from the [tribe of] Benê Ma'zîn' in Aramaic, thus making it clear that, according to the audience, he was concurrently a Palmyrene citizen and a member of a tribe (*IGLS* XVII, 241). For the foreigners, who were more likely to understand Greek, the more general reference was given; for fellow citizens, well versed in Aramaic, a more specific category was needed. In the same manner, inscriptions only in Greek generally concerned emperors, soldiers, governors, and administrators—that is, a category of population who did not have command of languages other than Latin and Greek. It was a matter of who was the addressee, not of who was producing the text.

A BILINGUAL SOCIETY

For this reason, the study of the use of bilinguals is of a paramount importance if we are to understand the specificities of the epigraphy of Palmyra. The use of the Seleucid era (beginning in 312 BC) for reckoning time clearly expresses a frame of reference organized around the Greek presence in the Near East, namely the Seleucid kingdom. The Seleucid era was still in use in the last Greek inscriptions of the sixth century and was kept as a dating system by the Syriac (Aramaic) world until modern times. However, it is clear that at Palmyra both public and private discourses of the first century BC were written in Aramaic. The first dated Greek inscriptions began only in the first years of the first century AD (with only one earlier example in 7 BC). Most of them belong to bilinguals, but with some surprising features: *IGLS* XVII, 318 = *PAT* 2779, for example, is a dedication to the god Elqonera, equated with Poseidon. So far, so good—but another look at the stone shows the lack of symmetry between the two versions: instead of the date with the complete name of the benefactor and of his tribe, the Greek has only 'to Poseidon the god'. In several cases of early bilingual inscriptions, it has often been surmised that the stones were engraved only in the second century (Cantineau 1933). Were they accurate copies of earlier inscriptions, or was the Greek version added only at a later stage? There is no evidence. Another interesting characteristic is the fact that the first funerary inscriptions that include Greek date to the mid-first century: some of them were not bilingual, but trilingual texts, with Latin in addition to Aramaic and Greek. This is a trait common to a small number of inscriptions of the first and second centuries: they offer examples of an official use of Latin by the city at its beginning, or by foreigners wishing to show their integration into local culture (Seigne and Yon 2005). That two of these early texts come from the civic authorities renders this phenomenon even more striking. Three others are funerary texts: of these, two belong to the tombs of freedmen, most likely tax collectors who, judging by their names, were foreign to Palmyra, but from the Greek-speaking world (*IGLS* XVII, 400 and 536). Apparently, Latin was a reference to their administrative function, Greek was their language of origin, and Palmyrene was a concession to the city in which they had been living. The last funerary text is even more instructive as it is the foundation of the tomb of Hairan son of Bonne (*IGLS* XVII, 535). The Greek and—mostly—the Aramaic versions are much more elaborate. The names of both the tribe of his father and that of his mother are specified only in Aramaic, but the Latin text is enhanced by its position on the stone and by the script, which is larger than the Greek and Aramaic. The same individual is honoured by the council and the people of Palmyra in AD 74 (*IGLS* XVII, 304): this last inscription marks the epigraphic appearance of the civic authorities of Palmyra as they remained until at least the third century. Hairan was undoubtedly one of the main promoters of the institutional changes taking place at that time. Attention should be drawn to the form, which uses in Latin the transcription of a Greek word to designate the civic council of Palmyra—'bule et civitas'. At Palmyra, the formula is entirely modelled on the Greek version. Another very fragmentary trilingual inscription substantiates this point of view with the same 'bule et civitas' (*IGLS* XVII, 72). One may wonder whether Latin was almost used as an official language of Palmyra, alongside Greek and Aramaic, at the time when the *polis* was being introduced. It seems very likely that practical reasons and the scarcity of Latin speakers in the area then put a stop to this. Indeed, the cities that had commercial relations with Palmyra were almost all Hellenophone. Palmyra nevertheless remains exceptional since it is one of the rare examples of an eastern city in which Latin was used officially. Paradoxically, as has been pointed out, from the moment Palmyra became a colony (probably under Caracalla), no official text using Latin is known.

One may also note that one of the earliest inscriptions in the agora is a bilingual in which Aramaic is complemented by Latin, not by Greek (*PAT* 0308 = *IGLS* XVII, 208; Figure 13.4). The individual honoured was a Roman centurion in charge of the banks of a river, presumably the Euphrates. This makes sense because he would have exercised responsibility over an area through which the caravan routes passed. In this context, Latin is not surprising, but it has to be underlined that this is the only example of a bilingual Latin and Aramaic inscription at Palmyra. The date (end of first century?) makes this console one of the earliest documents of the agora. During this period of the establishment of a civic constitution, a shift in the location of official honorific inscriptions occurred. What had previously been displayed in temples, mostly in the sanctuary of Bēl, was now set up in the agora, the location of civic activities. The position of inscriptions is inseparable from the institutional and urban history of the city. When later the Great Colonnade took shape and bore witness to a complete remodelling of the urban structure with the colonnade as its main axis, benefactors were honoured there, beginning in the second part of the second century. Still at the time of Odainathus and Zenobia, the greats of Palmyra received statues in what was now the civic centre.

FIGURE 13.4 A bilingual Latin–Aramaic inscription from the agora (*PAT* 0308 = *IGLS* XVII, 208).

© J.-B. Yon, Hisoma, CNRS.

Almost fifty years after the fall of the city, in 328, an inscription evidences a restoration of part of the portico thanks to the curator Flavius Diogenes (*IGLS* XVII, 101), another proof of the survival of institutions of some sort in this later period. The particular disposition of inscriptions and of statues on consoles attached to columns (see Figure 13.2) was another specificity of the Greek East, and particularly of Roman Syria (Apamea and Palmyra). Thus benefactors were put on the public stage in very dramatic scenery in which architecture and epigraphy were closely connected (Yon 2017).

Caravan inscriptions are iconic of the status of Palmyra as a caravan city: their locations are consistent with those of other official texts, with specificities. They also evidence the function of civic tribes and their sanctuaries: there, benefactors could be celebrated with statues offered by each tribe (*IGLS* XVII, 127, and 150). As always, bilingual texts are the norm, with only a few exceptions in a very early period. Some fragmentary texts could also have been bilingual. Clearly, caravans represented the city as a whole, with their texts directed at local citizens but at foreigners as well. This makes clear that the importance of Palmyra hinged on its relations with cities and populations beyond the empire; but still the only evidence is provided by the epigraphy, which supplies the names of foreign locations and of the people actually trading.

As with other inscriptions, there are striking features regarding onomastics. Most of the caravan leaders and notables had Semitic names, but Iarhai, who received at least ten statues in few years around AD 157, was a Roman citizen. Marcus Ulpius Iarhai son of Hairan is his full name, and he was one of the first citizens at a period when they were rare at Palmyra and in Syria generally. Even the famous Soados, recipient of more than sixteen statues between 140 and 150 and commended by several governors and by emperors themselves, was no Roman citizen. While benefactors and civic magistrates sometimes had Greek names, this is never the case with caravan leaders (Gawlikowski 1994).

Official Languages

If Aramaic was first, and if Greek prevailed alongside the local language, it is difficult to reconstruct how inscriptions were actually drafted. Which language was the first in the drafting of the decree that was a decision of the civic council? The same question is valid for the legal texts that were the basis for the foundation and concession inscriptions. In this case, Aramaic seems to have been the legal language, as could be evidenced by fragments of papyri found in tombs and by the fact that the specifications for concessions of parts of tombs are more precise in Aramaic while they very often do not appear in Greek (Gawlikowski 1970). The main characteristic of these very elliptical honorific inscriptions was the use of a very conventional vocabulary: the same words and expressions—'patriot', 'pious', 'as a testimony of honour'—are overused, and the actual content in terms of references to events, places, and actions is generally limited (Yon 2017). There was no difference between the languages in this regard, but rather a voluntary limitation on what was really important for Palmyrenes: genealogies and family links were preferred to civic positions. Texts reflect what seemed important to the notables of Palmyra: piety, patriotism, generosity. In addition, the texts carved on the stone are only short versions of more elaborate compositions kept in the archives. The Greek and the Aramaic are correct most of the time; syntax and vocabulary are rather simple. Thus it is an arduous task to establish which was the first language for a particular inscription: models—ready-made sets of expression—could have been the basis for most of the texts that were engraved: *teimes charin* 'as a proof of honour' corresponds to *lyqrh* 'in his honour'. It does not mean that the local scribe had no command of Greek, only that he could not disparage a benefactor by not using the same words as in the inscription situated close by. Words and concepts that were Greek in origin were adapted or translated. Thus *philopatris*, 'patriot', becomes *rḥym mdynth*, 'lover of his city', whereas *boule kai demos*, 'Council and People', is simply rendered as *bwl' wdms*. In another area, personal names could be translated, but most of the time Aramaic names were transcribed in Greek. In a way, each language kept its own tradition and its ways of expression, and it is appropriate to consider the different versions of a text as parallel (Yon 2002; Gzella 2005).

THE QUESTION OF THE EPIGRAPHIC HABIT

As shown by the few examples possibly anterior to the mid-first century BC, the epigraphic habit had a long standing at Palmyra. From the second part of the first century BC, first in Aramaic, then in Greek, it became a regular form of public and private expression. Other areas of the Near East witnessed a similar situation. In a way, the arrival of Rome around 64–63 BC with Pompey could be regarded as the starting date for the epigraphic habit in the region. At Palmyra, this habit did not die out until the fall of Zenobia in AD 272. The epigraphic flourish lasted a little more than three centuries. Not until the eighth century was the site virtually deserted but for the area of the temple of Bēl. But the fact that so many monuments were left standing made possible the preservation of inscriptions.

ABBREVIATIONS

IGLS XVII   Yon, Jean-Baptiste, ed. 2012. *Inscriptions grecques et latines de la Syrie.* Vol. 17.1, *Palmyre.* Bibliothèque archéologique et historique 195. Beirut: Institut français du Proche-Orient.

PAT   Hillers, Delbert R. and Eleonora Cussini, eds. 1996. *Palmyrene Aramaic Texts.* Baltimore: The Johns Hopkins University Press.

BIBLIOGRAPHY

al-Asʿad, Khaled, Michał Gawlikowski, and Jean-Baptiste Yon. 2012. ʿAramaic Inscriptions in the Palmyra Museumʾ. *Syria* 89: 163–183.

Bobou, Olympia, Amy C. Miranda, Rubina Raja, and Jean-Baptiste Yon. 2022. *The Ingholt Archive: The Palmyrene Material, Transcribed with Commentary and Bibliography*. Archive Archaeology 2. Turnhout: Brepols.

Cantineau, Jean. 1933. ʿTadmoreaʾ. *Syria* 14: 169–202.

Cantineau, Jean. 1935. *Grammaire du palmyrénien épigraphique*. Cairo: Institut français d'archéologie Orientale.

Cooke, George Albert. 1903. *A Text-Book of North-Semitic Inscriptions: Moabite, Hebrew, Phoenician, Aramaic, Nabataean, Palmyrene, Jewish*. Oxford: Clarendon Press.

Cussini, Eleonora. 2022. *Tadmorena. Documenti per lo studio della cultura e dell'aramaico di Palmira*. Testi del Vicino Oriente antico. Torino: Paideia Editrice.

Daniels, Peter T. 1988. "ʿShewing of Hard Sentences and Dissolving of Doubtsʾ": The First Deciphermentʾ. *Journal of the American Oriental Society* 108: 419–436.

Dijkstra, Klas. 1995. *Life and Loyalty: A Study in the Socio-Religious Culture of Syria and Mesopotamia in the Graeco-Roman Period Based on Epigraphical Evidence*. Religions in the Graeco-Roman World 128. Leiden: Brill.

Dunant, Christiane. 1971. *Le Sanctuaire de Baalshamin à Palmyre*. Vol. 3, *Les inscriptions*. Bibliotheca Helvetica Romana 10. Neuchâtel: Attinger.

Duyrat, Frédérique, Françoise Briquel Chatonnet, Jean-Marie Dentzer, and Olivier Picard, eds. 2016. *Henri Seyrig (1895–1973)*. Syria, Supplément 3. Beirut: Institut français du Proche-Orient.

Gawlikowski, Michał. 1970. *Monuments funéraires de Palmyre*. Warsaw: Państwowe Wydawnictwo Naukowe.

Gawlikowski, Michał. 1973. *Le temple palmyrénien: Étude d'épigraphie et de topographie historique*. Palmyre 6. Warsaw: Państwowe Wydawnictwo Naukowe.

Gawlikowski, Michał. 1974. *Recueil d'inscriptions palmyréniennes provenant de fouilles syriennes et polonaises récentes à Palmyre*. Paris: Imprimerie nationale.

Gawlikowski, Michał. 1990. ʿLes dieux de Palmyreʾ. In *Aufstieg und Niedergang der römischen Welt* Vol. 2, *Principat*, no. 18, *Religion*, 4, edited by Wolfgang Haase and Hildegard Temporini, 2605–2658. Berlin: de Gruyter.

Gawlikowski, Michał. 1994. ʿPalmyra as a Trading Centreʾ. *Iraq* 56: 27–33.

Gzella, Holger. 2005. ʿDie Palmyrener in der griechisch-römischen Welt: Kulturelle Begegnung im Spiegel des Sprachkontaktesʾ. *Klio* 87: 445–458.

Gzella, Holger. 2011. ʿLate Imperial Aramaicʾ. In *The Semitic Languages: An International Handbook*, edited by Stefan Weninger, 598–609. Berlin: de Gruyter.

Ingholt, Harald, Henri Seyrig, and Jean Starcky. 1955. *Recueil des tessères de Palmyre*. Bibliothèque archéologique et historique 58. Paris: Geuthner.

Kaizer, Ted. 2002. *The Religious Life of Palmyra: A Study of the Social Patterns of Worship in the Roman Period*. Oriens et Occidens 4. Stuttgart: Steiner.

Lidzbarski, Mark. 1898. *Handbuch der nordsemitischen Epigraphik nebst ausgewählten Inschriften*. Vol. 1, *Text*; vol. 2, *Tafeln*. Weimar: Emil Felber. Reprinted Norderstedt: Hansebooks, 2017.

Milik, Józef Tadeusz. 1972. *Recherches d'épigraphie proche-orientale*. Vol. 1, *Dédicaces faites par des dieux (Palmyre, Hatra, Tyr) et des thiases sémitiques à l'époque romaine*. Bibliothèque archéologique et historique 92. Paris: Geuthner.

Millar, Fergus. 1993. *The Roman Near East (31 BC–AD 337)*. Cambridge, MA: Harvard University Press.

Raja, Rubina. 2018. 'Compilation and Digitisation of the Palmyrene Corpus of Funerary Portraits'. *Antiquity* 92: 1–7.

Raja, Rubina, Julia Steding, and Jean-Baptiste Yon. 2021. *Excavating Palmyra: Harald Ingholt's Excavation Diaries: A Transcript, Translation, and Commentary*. Vol. 1, *Introduction and Ingholt's Diaries, 1–3*; vol. 2, *Ingholt's Diaries, 4–5*. Studies in Palmyrene Archaeology and History 4. Turnhout: Brepols.

Rosenthal, Franz. 1936. *Die Sprache der palmyrenischen Inschriften und ihre Stellung innerhalb des Aramäischen*. Mitteilungen der Vorderasiatisch–Ägyptischen Gesellschaft, vol. 41, no. 1. Leipzig: Hinrichs.

Sartre, Maurice. 1996. 'Palmyre, cité grecque'. *Annales archéologiques arabes syriennes* 42: 385–405 (Sartre 2016, 293–319).

Sartre, Maurice. 2016. *L'historien et ses territoires: Choix d'articles*. Scripta antiqua 70. Bordeaux: Ausonius.

Seigne, Jacques, and Jean-Baptiste Yon. 2005. 'Documents nouveaux de la grande colonnade de Palmyre'. In *Aux pays d'Allat: Mélanges offerts à Michal Gawlikowski*, edited by Piotr Bieliński and Franciszek M. Stępniowski, 243–261. Warsaw: Instytut Archeologii Uniwersytet Warszawski.

Stark, Jürgen Kurt. 1971. *Personal Names in Palmyrene Inscriptions*. Oxford: Clarendon Press.

Vogüé, Melchior de. 1868. *Syrie centrale: Inscriptions sémitiques publiées avec traduction et commentaire*. Paris: Baudry.

Waddington, William Henry, ed. 1870. *Inscriptions grecques et latines de la Syrie*. Paris: Firmin Didot.

Wood, Robert, and James Dawkins. 1753. *Les ruines de Palmyre: Autrement dite Tedmor au désert*. London: Millar.

Yon, Jean-Baptiste. 2000. 'Onomastique et influences culturelles: L'exemple de l'onomastique de Palmyre'. *Mediterraneo Antico* 3(1): 77–93.

Yon, Jean-Baptiste. 2002. *Les notables de Palmyre*. Bibliothèque archéologique et historique 163. Beirut: Français du Proche-Orient.

Yon, Jean-Baptiste. 2013. '1996–2011: L'épigraphie palmyrénienne depuis *PAT*'. In *Palmyra: Queen of the Desert; 50 Years of Polish Excavations in Palmyra*, 333–379. Studia Palmyreńskie 12. Warsaw: Uniwersytet Warszawski, Instytut Archeologii.

Yon, Jean-Baptiste. 2017. 'Le reflet des honneurs'. In *The Politics of Honour in the Greek Cities of the Roman Empire*, edited by Anna Heller and Onno Van Nijf, 496–526. Leiden: Brill.

CHAPTER 14

THE PALMYRENE TAX TARIFF

JOHN F. HEALEY

INTRODUCTION

THE Palmyrene Tax Tariff is one of the most important economic inscriptions of the Roman Empire. According to John F. Matthews (1984, 157) it is:

> one of the most important single items of evidence for the economic life of any part of the Roman empire, and, in the taxable services mentioned in the regulations, a vivid glimpse also of the social life of a great middle-eastern city.

Dated AD 137, it is a bilingual text consisting originally of 253 lines of Greek and 161 lines of Palmyrene Aramaic, set out in four panels. It was discovered in 1882 and subsequently transported to the Hermitage Museum in St Petersburg, where it is currently displayed (see Figure 14.1).

DISCOVERY OF THE TARIFF

The Tariff came to light as a result of the visit to Palmyra in March 1882 of the Russian industrialist and scholar Semyon S. Abamelek-Lazarev. He went to Palmyra as part of his grand tour of the Middle East. Shown some carved stone protruding from the sand, he quickly realized that the writing he could see was Greek and appeared to contain a title, part of a dating formula. It was evident that there was much more of the inscription buried under the sand, so he arranged for the excavation of the front of the stone, thereby revealing it in all its glory. There were seen to be four panels carved onto a massive block of limestone. It was still in its original position, standing vertically and photographed *in situ*, though no precise record was kept of where at the site of Palmyra it was found. Rather, in a story which was not untypical with respect to monumental

FIGURE 14.1 The Palmyrene Tariff in the State Hermitage Museum, St Petersburg.

© John Healey.

Near Eastern discoveries of the nineteenth century, focus quickly switched to the study of the text and the acquisition of the monument for display in Europe, in this case not London or Paris or Berlin, but St Petersburg.

On his return home, Abamelek-Lazarev quickly reported the discovery to the Russian Archaeological Society (May 1882), and specialist study of the text began on the basis of squeezes and drawings. At this point in the history of Imperial Russia, intellectuals envied the growing museum collections in the other European capitals, especially in Semitic epigraphic material. Thus the Archaeological Society began to discuss the possible acquisition of the Palmyrene Tariff for display (and study) in Russia. Although difficulties were encountered, these efforts culminated in the Ottoman Sultan Abdülhamid I presenting the Tariff as a gift to Tsar Nicholas II in 1900 (for details see Shifman 2014, 38–43).

The task of transporting the Tariff stone to Russia was formidable and involved cutting the stone base to save weight and then sawing the stone into four parts, corresponding to the four panels. After some further delays, the Tariff entered the Hermitage in 1904, the four pieces were reassembled, and the whole was put on display in the museum, where it still stands.

The question of the precise original location of the Tariff was definitively resolved by Michał Gawlikowski (2012), following Robert du Mesnil du Buisson's brief, earlier comments (1966, 176–177) and various clues. There were a number of such clues: (i) very early photographs of the stone (photographs preserved in the State Hermitage) gave some topographical indications in the form of other monuments which could be seen in the background; (ii) the text of the Tariff itself suggests that it was set up in front of a particular shrine or temple, that of the god Rab-Asīrē (I, 11 Greek; I, 23 Aramaic; panel and line numbers here cited according to Shifman 2014, with translations based on Healey 2009, no. 37). This temple is not among the various well-known Palmyrene temples subsequently excavated. However, (iii) two small fragments of the text of the Tariff *were* discovered in an area adjacent to the Palmyrene agora in 1940 and subsequently published by Jean Starcky (Starcky 1949 = *Inv.* X, no. 143; Delplace and Yon 2005, 162). Finally, (iv) elements of a small shrine were found in the same area, adjacent to the southern corner of the agora, including an epigraphic fragment which could be read as alluding to Rab-Asīrē.

This evidence was brought together by Gawlikowski, who also excavated outside the agora, in the area of the shrine and the adjacent wadi (Gawlikowski 2012; 2014). All the pieces of evidence agree, and the conclusion is now clear: the wadi had been paved during the Roman period and in fact formed a walkway. The Tariff was set up facing towards this walkway and towards the corner of the agora (with the Rab-Asīrē shrine between the two). In earlier times, the area south of the wadi was the main focus of the pre-Roman city: Roman-period replanning moved the focus to the north (to the colonnaded street, theatre, etc.).

Older maps and pictures often labelled the enclosed area to the east of the agora as 'the Tariff Court'. In fact, the Tariff stood outside that enclosed area, on the other side of the wadi/paved walkway, and its connection with that courtyard and the function of that courtyard remain uncertain.

HISTORY OF THE STUDY OF THE TARIFF

Detailed early studies of the text of the Tariff had already appeared on the basis of photographs and squeezes before it was transported to St Petersburg. De Vogüé (1883a; 1883b) provided the first full treatment, but we may also note Sachau 1883 (mainly Aramaic), Dessau 1884 (Greek), Schroeder 1884 (Greek and Aramaic, using squeezes made by Julius Euting), and Reckendorf 1888 (Aramaic). In English, Cooke's treatment (1903, no. 147, 313–340) made the Aramaic of the inscription widely known, while for the Greek, Dittenberger (1905, no. 629) became the standard text. In St Petersburg, the project of a definitive edition and translation was undertaken by the well-known Russian orientalist, Pavel K. Kokovtsov.

Kokovtsov's project did not, however, come to fruition. A probable reason is that the Tariff was included with full commentary in the Paris-based *Corpus Inscriptionum*

Semiticarum (*CIS*) where it has the siglum *CIS* II, 3913, published in 1926 (*CIS* II, iii, 33–73). This was accompanied by reproductions of squeezes in the possession of the editor, Jean-Baptiste Chabot, and a line drawing of the inscription originally made by Seymour de Ricci. It is likely that this edition was felt to offer the best possible treatment of the text, so that Kokovtsov's proposed edition had little to offer.

Russian interest in the Tariff revived in the 1970s. In 1980 Il'ia Sh. Shifman, one of the most prolific of the post World War II Russian orientalists, published a major monograph on the Tariff in Russian. Apart from providing a new edition, this dealt with virtually every detail of the text and included a lengthy analytical introduction as well as a translation and line-by-line commentary on philology and content. This new edition had little impact on Western scholarship: the Russian text was a formidable obstacle for most scholars, though a few began referring to Shifman's work (see, e.g., Javier Teixidor 1984, 57, n. 138; Glen Bowersock 1987). Belatedly, an English translation of his book was published (posthumously) in 2014. Shifman's book needs updating, but it is currently the only full work on the Tariff. (It may be noted that the text of the Tariff appears in Hillers and Cussini 1996, 57–63 as *PAT* 0259 and in Healey 2009, 164–205 as no. 37, with a full philological commentary on the Aramaic. The forthcoming second part of Jean-Baptiste Yon's *Palmyra* volume in the *IGLS* series will provide a new and definitive edition [for the first part see Yon 2012]).

Meanwhile, the Tariff has been studied many times for the light it throws on the Roman economy. Probably the most influential of these studies is that of Matthews (1984), though it focuses mostly on the Greek. Javier Teixidor's studies give equal attention to the Aramaic (1983; 1984). The Tariff has also often featured in studies related to economic issues (e.g., Heichelheim 1938, 250–254), though most of these have said little about the original Palmyrene context of the inscription. A bibliographical guide to the Tariff has been published recently (Perassi and Bona 2016).

Physical Arrangement and Outline of Content

The stone of the Tariff originally measured ca. 4.75 m wide and 1.5 m high (see Figure 14.2). As already noted, it is divided into four panels, their sequence running from left to right. Above the panels there is a dating formula pertaining to Roman authorities (restorations are not marked here, but see Shifman 2014).

> In the reign of the Emperor Caesar Traianus Hadrianus Augustus, son of the deified Traianus Parthicus, grandson of the deified Nerva, Chief High Priest, in the twenty-first year of his tribunician power, twice hailed *imperator*, three times consul, *pater patriae*, in the consulships of L. Aelius Caesar for the second time and Publius Coelius Balbinus.

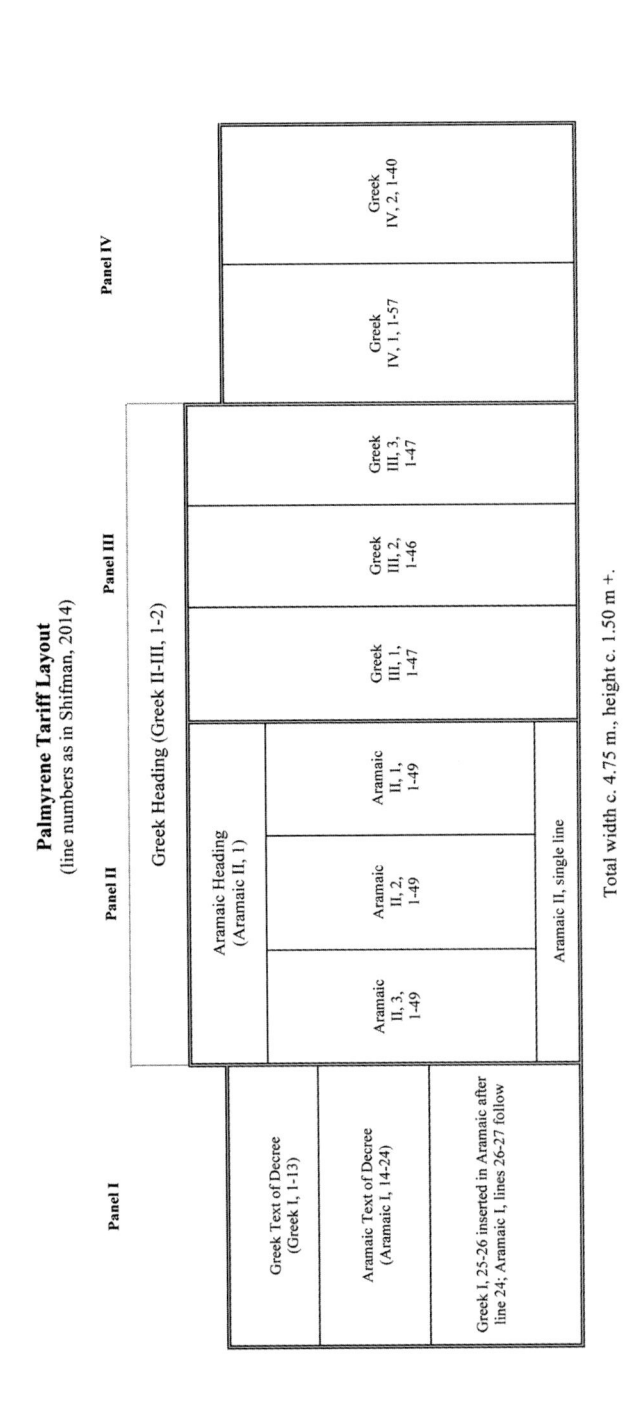

FIGURE 14.2 Palmyrene Tariff layout.

The details here establish the date as AD 137, which is subsequently confirmed by Panel I below, which is mainly devoted to the decree by the local authorities enacting the new tax tariff. It appears first in Greek and then, almost identically, in Aramaic.

The placing of the Greek first reflects the fact that Greek was, at least in public affairs, the more important language of the city, given the latter's position in the empire. There is, however, some evidence of Aramaisms in the Greek of the Tariff and it is not clear whether the older parts of the text (see below) had already been translated into Aramaic before the decisions of AD 137 were taken. It is obvious, however, that some of the Roman decisions on tax rules (below) were originally issued in Greek (Healey, forthcoming; Teixidor 1984, 58–59, 62, 69, 80 argued for a Latin original text, though the evidence is weak).

The decree which occupies most of Panel I gives us vital information on dating, on the municipal authorities of Palmyra, and on the motivation behind the issuing of the new tariff. To quote the Aramaic version,

> Decree of the Council. In the month of Nīsān on the 18th day, in the year 448, during the presidency [*proedria*] of Būna son of Būna son of Ḥayran and the secretaryship [*grammateia*] of Alexander son of Alexander son of Philopator, secretary [*grammateus*] of the Council and People, the archons being Malkū son of ʿAlī son of Muqīmu and Zabīda son of Nashsha, when the Council was assembled in accordance with law, it established what is written below:
>
> Since in former times many items subject to tax were not entered in the tax law and were charged according to custom with whatever (rate) was being written in the contracts of the tax collector and he was collecting according to the law and according to custom, and therefore many times there were disputes concerning these things between the merchants and tax collectors, it seemed good to the Council that the said archons and {to} the Ten [*dekaprōtoi*] {that they} should determine whatever was not entered in the law and it should be written in the new tax contract and there should be written for each thing its customary tax. And whatever has been established for the tax contract will be written down with the former law on the stela which is opposite the temple of Rab-asīrē. And it is made the responsibility of the archons who are (in office) at any time and the Ten [*dekaprōtoi*] and the Syndics that the tax collector should not be collecting from anyone anything more. (I, 14–24)

The date is fully elaborated in a format which would be expected for a public inscription enacting a municipal decree within the Roman Empire. The year 448 in the Seleucid dating current in the eastern part of the empire (and outside it) confirms the date of AD 137.

The motivation for passing a decree to revise the tax laws is made very clear:

1. Much (though not all) of the earlier tax regime had been based on custom rather than a written law, informed by clarifications issued in earlier times by various Roman authorities.
2. As a consequence, disputes had frequently arisen between the tax collectors and the taxpayers: with so much left unwritten, we can imagine that this would have been a

fertile source of tax evasion strategies, often resulting in the local authorities being called in to adjudicate.

The solution to these difficulties was to be a revised tax law, establishing a new basis for the work of tax collectors.

The decree goes on to state that the New Law, when approved by local officials (a noteworthy detail: What authority over the New Law did these officials have?), was to be publicly displayed alongside a copy of the less satisfactory, though not explicitly revoked Old Law, in a prominent place which we know was close to the agora, opposite the temple or shrine of Rab-Asīrē. It is not clear whether locating the Tariff opposite this shrine has something to do with the religious role of Rab-Asīrē: this deity is otherwise unknown in Palmyrene epigraphy though there are some uncertain traces elsewhere (e.g., in Mandaean literature). The divine name has no obvious etymology: 'Lord of the bound ones' (perhaps referring to the lions identified in the iconography of the shrine, or those bound in the underworld—the latter suggested by the Mandaean evidence), or even 'Lord of coins' (see Kaizer 2002, 152–153), which might have some connection with taxation.

Also rather unclear is the relationship between the various authorities mentioned in the text of the decree (and this is not made easier by the fact that, at this point, in lines 19 and 21, the Aramaic appears to contain some minor syntactical mistakes [marked with {} in the translation above]: Healey, forthcoming). The decree was issued by the *dēmos* and *boulē*, the leading authorities of the Palmyrene *polis*, but it also refers to the decisions of the *archons* and *dekaprōtoi*—both apparently treasury officials (Teixidor 1984, 61–64)—in detailed matters of the tax law, and to the agreement made with the contracted tax collector.

The two versions of the decree did not occupy the whole of the space available in Panel I, and the opportunity has been taken, probably as an afterthought, to insert below the Aramaic version of the decree a regulation concerning the equivalences between cart-loads, camel-loads, and donkey-loads. This too is bilingual.

> (Greek) For one wagon-load of any merchandise, the tax has been assessed at the rate of four camel-loads.
> (Aramaic) A wagon-load of any kind at all, the tax is collected for four camel-loads (I, 25–27).

Clearly, this regulation was important. The tax regulations which follow in Panels II–IV frequently distinguish between camel-loads (γόμος καμηλίκος/ṭʿwn gml) and donkey-loads (γόμος ὀνικός/ṭʿwn ḥmr). We can only speculate on whether this additional regulation on equivalences for cart- or wagon-loads was an afterthought, closing a fiscal loophole which could be exploited, but its location outside the main body of the tax document is certainly a little strange and suggests this. Panel II, containing the Aramaic text of the Tariff law, is tightly packed (concentrating into one panel the details which in Greek are spread over two panels, though there are some omissions from the

Aramaic). The empty space in Panel I may have been the only option when the need to add a rule about equivalences arose.

This supplementary regulation establishes that the weight ratio for taxation purposes between a cart and a camel was 4:1. Elsewhere in the Tariff, the tax on a camel-load of any particular item is double that of a donkey-load so the following ratio may be deduced—cart: camel: donkey = 8: 2: 1.

The Old and New Laws and Authorities Cited

Panel II contains the Aramaic text of the tax legislation, Panels III–IV the Greek text (which is badly damaged at some points and which contains some material not found in the Aramaic).

In the instructions contained in the council's decree, and in the way the details are set out, there is one very notable fundamental feature. Instead of composing a new, comprehensive tax document, the city council decided (or was instructed) to set out the New Law while at the same time not revoking the Old Law, but, on the contrary, quoting it in full. Both New and Old Laws are set out side by side. An additional complication is the fact that the law which is placed second in the text is in itself very short but appears to incorporate at great length a tax edict issued by Mucianus, governor of Syria in the 60s AD (which must have had a Greek original). Without the edict, this shorter law would be almost pointless (Aramaic II, 2, 13–23; missing from the Greek). It deals with only four items: dry goods (a catch-all term), purple wool, 'all kinds of goods' (even more of a catch-all term), and salt. More than half its space is devoted to salt. We thus have in effect,

Law A
Law B1 (a heading and ten lines of regulations) +
Law B2 (the edict of Mucianus)

This raises the question, long disputed, of which of the two legal documents incorporated into the inscription is the New Law and which the Old. It is widely accepted now that the New Law is presented first (A) and that it is followed by the Old Law (B), which consists mostly of a reiteration of the tax edict of Mucianus. It may be noted that this second legal document (here taken to be the Old Law) is introduced under a new heading which marks a clear break in the text.

The Tax Law of [= applicable in] Tadmūr and the water-springs and salt which are in the city and its territories according to the contracts which were drawn up before the governor Marinus. (Aramaic II, 2, 13–15; there is a lacuna in the Greek)

(Greek III, 3, 46: Λιμένος Π[αλμύρων καὶ πη]γῶν ὑδάτων Καίσαρος, remains problematic. It looks like a heading similar to the Aramaic heading at the top of column II, but, like the heading of the Old Law, it does not refer to Hadriana Palmyra. It has no exact parallel in the Aramaic and is probably a subheading giving authority for the rules that follow. It may be a misplaced parallel to the title of the Old Law of Aramaic II, 2, 13, otherwise missing from the Greek. The text and context are unclear.)

There are several reasons for thinking that what follows this heading is the Old Law. Perhaps most telling is the fact that this new heading does not use the city's relatively new title, Hadriana Palmyra, granted to it ca. AD 129. This makes it improbable that the material following this heading dates to AD 137. By contrast, the Aramaic heading above the three Aramaic columns of Panel II *does* use this title: 'The Tax Law of the *portus* of Hadriana Palmyra . . . '. Also, the phrase 'as is written above' (II, 2, 18) seems to refer to the earlier part of the inscription, containing, on the common view, the New Law. If so, the Old Law of Marinus may have been abbreviated using catch-all phrases which did not need specification.

In any case, the edict of Mucianus long predates the decree enacting the New Law: there is nothing new about it, and it would be odd for the municipality of Palmyra to proclaim it as new long after it had been promulgated. It does, however, make sense to include it in the definitive New Law since, as we shall see, many of its regulations remained in force.

A notable feature that supports the view that A is the New Law and explains the presentation of the regulations in this way is the frequent citation of authorities who had earlier made decisions about taxation which could not now be changed without special authority and, one assumes, Roman agreement. Almost all these citations of authority are found in the Old Law (B). This provides a strong reason for not simply ignoring the Old Law and, in association with it, the edict of Mucianus (from II, 2, 24 in Aramaic; IV, 1, 10 in Greek).

The cited authorities, in the order of their occurrence, are Kilix (a freedman of Caesar, probably to be dated to the early second century: Greek III, 2, 46; Aramaic II, 2, 12), Marinus (probably L. Julius Marinus Caecilius Simplex, an imperial legate in Syria in the early second century AD: Aramaic II, 2, 15 [not in Greek]), Mucianus (governor of Syria, AD 68–69: Greek IV, 1, 10; Aramaic II, 2, 24), Alkimos (C. Virius Alcimus, whose tomb cover was identified by Gawlikowski [1998: British Museum inv. WA 125036]) and an unnamed associate, Germanicus (active as imperial representative in Syria ca. AD 17–19: Greek IV, 1, 41–44; Aramaic II, 3, 4–5), and Cn. Domitius Corbulo (imperial legate to Syria ca. AD 60: Greek IV, 1, 55–57; Aramaic II, 3, 20–21, extending to ca. 41).

We can reconstruct the history of taxation at Palmyra on the basis of these citations. Already in the first century AD, Roman authorities were making decisions about municipal taxes in Palmyra. The first indication is provided by *Germanicus's* decision, communicated to a local official, Statilius, probably, ca. AD 17–19. The immediate issue of taxation involved is that of cattle brought in for slaughter, but it adds the interesting detail that tax of less than a *denarius* could be collected in local coin (κέρμα/῾rpn). This suggests direct Roman involvement early in the first century, if not before. Later in the century, ca. AD 60, we find decisions being made by *Corbulo* and communicated to Barbarus, another local official. Corbulo is partly quoted in the first person (Aramaic II, 3, 26, and 32), and his decision was to tax both laden and unladen camels at one *denarius*. A few years later, ca. AD 68–69, comes the edict of *Mucianus*, at least in part in response to disputes about tax (II, 2, 25). This is a much more elaborate set of decisions embodied in a first-person decree (Aramaic II, 2, 26; clearly reflected later in the Greek version: IV, 47ff.). It may be regarded as the precursor of the Old Law. He confirms the earlier decisions of Alkimos, another unnamed authority, Germanicus, and Corbulo.

The *Old* Law gives a new framework to the edict of Mucianus, and it was issued in the name of the imperial legate Marinus, probably early in the second century. He set the pattern of existing rules governing taxes prior to AD 137 and incorporated them into the tax-farming contract. Marinus is the first authority cited within the framework of the Old Law (II, 2, 15), but other material is attached to this Old Law, most importantly the edict of Mucianus. Finally, so far as our documentation is concerned, we have the *New* Law, revising a number of tax regulations and citing the more recent precedent created by Kilix, probably early in the second century. As part of this final revision in AD 137, the full Tax Tariff text was composed and promulgated in the newly named Hadriana Palmyra.

There are also some formal differences between the New and Old Laws. In the Old Law, which begins at II, 2, 13 in the Aramaic, the imposition of taxes is usually expressed from the point of view of the taxpayer: 'he will pay . . .' (*ypr'*). This verb, PR', is not used in the New Law, where the verb generally found is GB'/Y, with the tax collector as the subject or implied subject (when a passive is used): *ygb'*, 'he will collect . . .'. The Greek equivalent for the latter is normally πράξει, 'he will exact', though much of the Greek is damaged and the passive is used in some sections.

DETAILED TAXATION REGULATIONS

While it is not possible here to go through all the details, we can (i) list the goods and services specified as subject to tax and indicate, as far as is possible, the innovations of the New Law; (ii) note specific exemptions; and (iii) draw attention to one major difference between the Greek and the Aramaic—the omission from the Aramaic of a long section which appears in the Greek.

Items Subject to Taxation: New Law Versus Old Law

Goods and services covered by the tax laws are as follows (not all items are completely clear).

> *New Law*: Slaves, veteran slaves, dry goods, purple wool, perfumed oil, olive oil, fuel oil, fish, other animals (Shifman reconstructs a whole list: see Healey,

forthcoming), perfumed-oil sellers, prostitutes, craftsmen's shops, general shops, shoemakers, tailors, garment sellers, use of the two springs (the tax on which is high, eight hundred *denarii*, charged annually, according to the Greek version [Aramaic II, 2, 8; Greek III, 2, 41], and, according to Teixidor [1984, 75–76], the springs were used for agricultural irrigation), wheat, wine, straw, unladen camels (the precedent set by Kilix).

Old Law of Marinus combined with the edict of Mucianus: Slaves (called here 'persons'), veteran slaves, dry goods, purple wool, perfumed oil, prostitutes, tailors, hides, garment sellers, camels (laden or not: the decision of Corbulo), (fine) salt (mentioned by both the law of Marinus and Mucianus), butchers, foodstuffs, pine nuts, hides, vegetables, fruit, bronze images, sheep.

There is slight uncertainty whether the parts of the Old Law (to which the edict of Mucianus is attached) which are not mentioned in the New Law were still valid after AD 137. It seems likely that where general principles are concerned they *do* remain in force, for example, where the Old Law contains complex rules related to payment of tax (pledges), the exemption of certain goods (see below), and judgements issued by earlier Roman authorities (except where Kilix appears to contradict Corbulo: but see below). But some specific tax rates for items mentioned in both laws had their tax reduced under the New Law: dry goods and purple wool (II, 1, 7 v. II, 2, 16—three *denarii* instead of four for dry goods; II, 1, 10–11 v. II, 2, 17—8 *assarii* [i.e., half a *denarius* by the imperial standard] instead of four *denarii* for purple wool). In general, however, the Old Law appears to contain fewer specific details, and some of the repetitions may be seen as clarifications. For example, in the sections on slaves (II, 1, 1–5 and II, 2, 30–34), the specific taxes are repeated for clarity, and the Old Law used the term 'persons' rather than 'slaves'. Again, on perfumed oil (II, 1. 12–21 and II, 2, 48–II, 3, 2) there is a definite move towards clarification.

The New Law omits mention of salt (fine), butchers, foodstuffs, pine nuts, hides, vegetables, fruit, bronze images, sheep, all mentioned in the Old Law/Mucianus. We can assume that these omissions are not significant: the rules governing them must surely have remained in force after AD 137. On the other hand, the omissions from the Old Law by comparison with the New may point to areas of doubt which might have been disputed: olive oil, fuel oil, fish, other animals (Shifman's reconstruction), perfumed-oil sellers, craftsmen's shops, general shops, shoemakers, use of the two springs, wheat, wine, straw. There may be only a slight expansion of taxation here, but trades and goods seem to be explicitly mentioned which were not mentioned before. In the case of 'camels (unladen)', the older legislation was already clear: it may have been disputed in some way (see below).

Exemptions

There are a number of explicit exemptions from tax: wool from Italy II, 2, 44–47 (Mucianus), camel hides II, 3, 23 (Mucianus), and sheep from the locality of Palmyra, that is, from within its own territory (II, 3, 46–48). Also, and obviously in a different category, discarded animal carcasses are exempted (II, 3, 9). We can add that the ruling attributed to Kilix, to the effect that unladen camels entering the city are to be taxed at one *denarius*, does not *explicitly* contradict the ruling of Corbulo to the effect that all camels, laden and unladen, brought in *from outside the territory of Palmyra* should be taxed. The following of the precedent created by Kilix (a tax official after Corbulo's time?) may be intended to clarify that only unladen camels from *inside* the territories were to be taxed, whereas both laden *and* unladen camels from outside were to be taxed. This would amount to a tax exemption for local farmers who were bringing in goods on camels and taking unladen camels back to the territories.

There are other signs of special favour for local industries. Sheep brought in from outside the territory, even if only for shearing, would be taxed on entry, but sheep from within the territory were exempt. This general aspect of policy is summarized in II, 3, 13:

> Whoever exports to the villages or imports from the villages is not liable to tax (Mucianus). (See recently Meyer 2017, 38)

Omissions from the Aramaic

The omission from the Aramaic text of one whole section of the Old Law which appears in Greek III, 3, 26 to IV, 1, 5 (which is followed by a lacuna) is notable. The matters covered in this section are technical in the sense that they deal with complications in payments (the use of sureties in lieu of immediate payment, forfeiture of sureties, disputes to be resolved before the *juridicus/dikaiodotēs*). The omission of this material from the Aramaic version is hard to explain. There may not have been sufficient space, though it seems more likely that the technical regulations involved, concerning methods of payment of tax and the use of pledges in lieu of tax, may have been regarded as not in dispute or covered by other legislation.

IMPLICATIONS FOR THE PALMYRENE ECONOMY

Perhaps, in the Palmyrene context, the most important point to note from study of the Tariff is that it is only marginally relevant to the so-called caravan trade for which Palmyra is justly famous. It deals with customs taxes on goods traded locally rather than imperial taxes which were remitted to the central authorities (on this distinction, see Schürer 1973, 372–376). It is not concerned with exotic and expensive goods in transit to the Mediterranean or the role of Palmyra as a *portus*, where the *portoria* taxes were imposed on goods entering Roman territory on behalf of central Roman authorities (though this role is reflected in the description of the city as *lmn'* [Aramaic heading of Panel II] = Greek λιμήν [III, 3, 46]). Rather, it is a set of *municipal* tax regulations concerned with local trade in and out of the city and with services within the city, including access to the city's water supply and the activities of particular groups of tradesmen (and -women). Although it is a remarkable document from several points of view, such a tax-related inscription could have survived from any major city of the Roman world.

Particular local features which help us to understand the commercial and civic life of Palmyra, at least in the first half of the second century AD, include the important (if not always clear) distinction the Tariff makes between the city itself, the hinterland which was treated as part of its economic area, and the territories beyond. Pliny refers to the rich soil and fields of the city, as well as its springs (Plin., *NH* 5.88). That the Tariff distinguishes between goods brought in from outside the territories and those from the villages is clear (Greek IV, 1, 48–53; Aramaic II, 3, 10–18; Matthews 1984, 173). The Palmyra hinterland has long attracted research attention (e.g., Schlumberger 1951; Teixidor 1984, 71–75) and has recently been the subject of a detailed survey (Meyer 2017).

The same kind of principle applies to animals brought in for pasture and for shearing from outside the territories of Palmyra (II, 3, 46–48; IV, 2, 36–38). They are distinguished from those brought into the city from *within* the territories. The former are taxed, but not the latter. Thus, insofar as they are part of Palmyra's internal economy, they are exempt from tax. Both the Aramaic (II, 3, 46ff.) and the Greek (IV, 2, 36–38) texts are damaged, but the latter appears to impose a tax on sheep brought in for grazing (ἐπὶ νομήν), whereas the former exempts sheep brought in for shearing (*lmgz*). There is also reference at the very end of both texts (Aramaic II, the line under the three columns and Greek IV, 2, 39–40; see Matthews 1984, 173) to the possibility that the tax officials might brand the sheep, presumably to distinguish those liable for tax from those exempted. This implies some kind of official brand-mark, the use of which was restricted by law.

The key phrase in these distinctions is the application of tax regulations to 'Tadmūr and its territories'. The term translated as 'territories' (*thwmy'*) means, more literally, 'borders', but the reference is clearly to territories within the borders. In fact, the rural industries of rearing sheep and goats and the production of salt were integral to the city's success. They received preferential treatment under the tax law, though the details are often quite difficult to understand. The norm in the Tariff was that livestock brought into the city for sale were to be subject to taxation.

Salt production is known from various sites around Palmyra (Teixidor 1984, 78–82), and since salt was an essential item, special regulations applied to it. Again, these regulations are a little obscure, but salt was tightly controlled, and the edict of Mucianus seems to have added restrictions designed to prevent abuses and ensure that this staple product was available as necessary to Palmyra's citizens. Tax seems to have been paid both by the producers of salt and its purchasers (Aramaic II, 2, 19–23; II, 3, 31–37 and Greek III, 3, 23–27). Other products were clearly brought in from the hinterland: fruit, vegetables, nuts, straw, etc. and were essential for the functioning of the city.

Although, as indicated above, the Tariff is not directly concerned with long-distance trade, we may note the exemption applied to importation of wool from Italy destined for the local market: it was not taxed (II, 2, 44–47; IV, 1, 33–36). This rule appears to favour imports of Roman origin, presumably over regional products. This exemption must have been imposed by the Roman authorities, though no named official is cited.

Finally, we may note the details which are revealed incidentally in the text about Palmyra's monetary arrangements (a) in the first century AD and (b) in the second. It has been argued (Lönnqvist 2008) that one of the motives for Roman involvement in what was essentially a local document was connected with the imperial policy of introducing Roman currency and weights. This would explain the references in the Old Law (Germanicus to Statilius with regard to tax on butchers) to the specific form in which tax payments had to be made, in *denarii* or *assarii*, rather than in local coins (κέρμα), though the latter were allowed in the case of certain payments of less than a *denarius* (Aramaic II, 3, 6; Greek IV, 1, 43). This also explains the Tariff's concern with measures, especially of salt: II, 2, 19–21: '*modius* of sixteen *sextarii*' (not in the Greek); II, 3, 34 and III, 3, 25: 'for a *modius* an Italic *assarius*', both details being found in the Old Law. This argument about currency and measures seems to be most convincing in relation to the first-century regulations, still largely in force in the second, according to our view above. It is less easy to detect this idea in the New Law, which quotes taxes in *denarii* and *assarii* without mentioning any special regulations about methods of payment. The discussion does, however, demonstrate the potential of the Palmyrene Tariff to shed light on many aspects of the economic life of the Roman Near East.

ABBREVIATIONS

CIS   *Corpus Inscriptionum Semiticarum.* Paris: Reipublicæ Typographeo, 1881–1962.

IGLS   *Inscriptions grecques et latines de la Syrie.* Paris: Geuthner, 1929–.

PAT   Hillers, Delbert R. and Eleonora Cussini, eds. 1996. *Palmyrene Aramaic Texts.* Baltimore: Johns Hopkins University Press.

BIBLIOGRAPHY

Bowersock, Glen. 1987. 'Review of *Un port romain du désert: Palmyre et son commerce d'Auguste à Caracalla* by Javier Teixidor'. *Classical Philology* 82(2): 178–181.

Cooke, George A. 1903. *A Text-Book of North-Semitic Inscriptions.* Oxford: Clarendon Press.

Delplace, Christiane, and Jean-Baptiste Yon. 2005. 'Les inscriptions de l'agora'. In *L'agora de Palmyre,* edited by Christiane Delplace and Jacqueline Dentzer-Feydy, 151–254. Bibliothèque archéologique et historique 175. Beirut: Institut français du Proche-Orient.

Dessau, Hermann. 1884. 'Der Steuertarif von Palmyra'. *Hermes* 19: 486–533.

Dittenberger, Wilhelm, ed. 1905. *Orientis Graeci inscriptiones selectae.* Vol. 2. Leipzig: Hirzel.

du Mesnil du Buisson, Robert. 1966. 'Première campagne de fouilles à Palmyre'. *Comptes rendus des séances de l'Académie des inscriptions et belles-lettres* 110: 158–190.

Gawlikowski, Michał. 1998. 'Deux publicains et leur tombeau'. *Syria* 75: 145–151.

Gawlikowski, Michał. 2012. 'Le tarif de Palmyre et le temple de Rab'asirê'. *Comptes rendus des séances de l'Académie des inscriptions et belles-lettres* 156(2): 765–780.

Gawlikowski, Michał. 2014. 'Palmyra: Reexcavating the Site of the Tariff (Fieldwork in 2010 and 2011)'. *Polish Archaeology in the Mediterranean* 23(1): 415–430.

Healey, John F. 2009. *Aramaic Inscriptions and Documents of the Roman Period*. Textbook of Syrian Semitic Inscriptions 4. Oxford: Oxford University Press.

Healey, John F. Forthcoming. 'Language, Law and Religion: The Palmyrene Tariff in Its Roman Context'. In *Palmyra and the Mediterranean*, edited by Rubina Raja. Cambridge: Cambridge University Press.

Heichelheim, Fritz M. 1938. 'Roman Syria'. In *An Economic Survey of Ancient Rome*. Vol. 4, edited by Tenney Frank, 121–257. Baltimore: Johns Hopkins University Press.

Hillers, Delbert R., and Eleonora Cussini, eds. 1996. *Palmyrene Aramaic Texts*. Publications of the Comprehensive Aramaic Lexicon Project. Baltimore: Johns Hopkins University Press.

Kaizer, Ted. 2002. *The Religious Life of Palmyra: A Study of the Social Patterns of Worship in the Roman Period*. Oriens et Occidens 4. Stuttgart: Steiner.

Lönnqvist, Kenneth. 2008. 'The Tax Law of Palmyra and the Introduction of the Roman Monetary System to Syria: A Re-evaluation'. In *Jebel Bishri in Context: Introduction to the Archaeological Studies and the Neighbourhood of Jebel Bishri in Central Syria: Proceedings of a Nordic Research Training Seminar in Syria, May 2004*, edited by Minna Lönnqvist, 73–88. British Archaeological Reports, International Series 1817. Oxford: Archaeopress.

Matthews, John F. 1984. 'The Tax Law of Palmyra: Evidence for Economic History in a City of the Roman East'. *Journal of Roman Studies* 74: 157–180.

Meyer, Jørgen Christian. 2017. *Palmyrena: Palmyra and the Surrounding Territory from the Roman to the Early Islamic Period*. Oxford: Archaeopress.

Perassi, Claudia, and Alessandro Bona. 2016. 'La "tariffa" di Palmira. Un aggiornamento bibliografico ragionato'. *Rivista Italiana di Numismatica e Scienze Affini* 117: 73–115.

Reckendorf, Salomon [Hermann]. 1888. 'Der aramäische Theil des palmyrenischen Zoll- und Steuertarifs'. *Zeitschrift der Deutschen Morgenländischen Gesellschaft* 42: 370–415.

Sachau, Eduard. 1883. 'Über den palmyrenischen νόμος τελωνικός'. *Zeitschrift der Deutschen Morgenländischen Gesellschaft* 37(4): 562–571.

Schlumberger, Daniel. 1937. 'Réflexions sur la loi fiscale de Palmyre'. *Syria* 18: 271–297.

Schlumberger, Daniel. 1951. *La palmyrène du nord-ouest: Villages et lieux de culte de l'époque impériale; Recherches archéologiques sur la mise en valeur d'une région du désert par les Palmyréniens*. Bibliothèque archéologique et historique 49. Paris: Geuthner.

Schroeder, Paul. 1884. 'Neue Palmyrenische Inschriften'. *Sitzungsberichte der Königlich Preußischen Akademie der Wissenschaften zu Berlin* 1: 417–436.

Schürer, Emil. 1973. *The History of the Jewish People in the Age of Jesus Christ (175 B.C.–A.D. 135)*. Vol. 1, edited by Geza Vermes, Fergus Millar, and Matthew Black. Edinburgh: T. & T. Clark.

Shifman, Il'ia Sholeĭmovich. 2014. *The Palmyrene Tax Tariff*. Journal of Semitic Studies Supplement 33. Oxford: Oxford University Press. Russian original 1980.

Starcky, Jean. 1949. *Inventaire des incriptions de Palmyre*. Fasc. 10, *L'agora*. Damascus: Direction Générale des Antiquités de Syrie.

Teixidor, Javier. 1983. 'Le Tarif de Palmyre, I. Un commentaire de la version palmyrénienne'. *Aula Orientalis* 1: 235–252.

Teixidor, Javier. 1984. *Un port romain du désert: Palmyre et son commerce d'Auguste à Caracalla.* Semitica 34. Paris: Maisonneuve.

Vogüé, Melchior de. 1883a. 'Inscriptions palmyréniennes inédites'. *Journal asiatique* 8(1): 231–245.

Vogüé, Melchior de. 1883b. 'Inscriptions palmyréniennes inédites (suite)'. *Journal asiatique* 8(2): 149–183.

Yon, Jean-Baptiste, ed. 2012. *Inscriptions grecques et latines de la Syrie.* Vol. 17, fasc. 1, *Palmyre.* Bibliothèque archéologique et historique 195. Beirut: Institut français du Proche-Orient.

CHAPTER 15

ARAMAIC LEGAL LANGUAGE FROM PALMYRENE MONUMENTAL INSCRIPTIONS

ELEONORA CUSSINI

GATHERING PALMYRENE LEGAL LANGUAGE

The Palmyrene epigraphic corpus does not preserve legal contracts. Those documents were written on perishable writing materials, mostly on parchment and perhaps also on papyrus. In contrast to the scattered remains from nearby sites such as, for example, the AD 243 slave sale from Dura-Europos (Drijvers and Healey 1999, 232–134; Cussini 2010), Palmyrene contracts have not survived. However, elements of Palmyrene legal language are embedded in inscriptions in the funerary contexts. Additional lexical items with legal connotations may be gleaned from other Palmyrene epigraphs: the epitaphs on the relief-busts that sealed the burial niches and from other types of inscriptions (Cussini 2016). Therefore, although the contracts are now lost, monumental inscriptions may be used to investigate Palmyrene legal language, especially regarding the practice of selling and buying funerary properties and, to some extent, the inheritance of these same properties. The available sources record the alienation of parts of tombs. They are not complete copies of the original contracts, but citations, or brief excerpts: significant sections of the contracts were copied on architectural elements, door-lintels and jambs, or stone slabs, which were sometimes reused in later structures. The inscriptions were placed in visible positions and often rubricated: visibility was in fact an important aspect of these epigraphs, which recorded a legal change. In some cases sale inscriptions from a single tomb record subsequent sales of different pieces of property, up to twelve, in one case (e.g., Tomb of the Three Brothers, *PAT* 0523–*PAT* 0527: see below, 'Palmyrene Inscriptions Documenting Sale of Funerary Properties', nos. 5–6, 20–21, 59; of Maliku *PAT* 0044–*PAT* 0055: nos. 14–15, 18, 27–29, 57, 64, 73–75; Cussini 2016, 42) (see Figure 15.1).

FIGURE 15.1 Tomb of the Three Brothers, foundation and sale inscriptions

Photograph by E. Cussini.

Drawing on my previous research on the Aramaic language of sale and on the re-construction of Palmyrene legal language, I offer a synthesis of this subject in the broader framework of the Aramaic legal tradition. Leaving aside legal terminology defining capacities and functions of individuals who had a role in the raising of children discussed elsewhere, together with a detailed study of the obligation *PAT* 1624, AD 214 (Cussini 2016), the present analysis focuses on the formulation of the sale texts, including new evidence from inscriptions discovered or made available after the publication of *Palmyrene Aramaic Texts* (Hillers and Cussini 1996). The evidence has been entirely reconsidered: the structure of the sale clauses and the verbs expressing the legal change are examined alongside new occurrences (see below, Table 15.1). The new inscriptions confirm the understanding of the juridical act they relate— the sale of immovable (funerary) properties—and offer additional examples of formulas expressed by the verbs previously documented.

The sale texts under discussion are mainly written in the formal or monumental Palmyrene-script style, with some specimens in cursive script, and are usually carved next to the foundation inscriptions that record the construction of the tomb and the builder's dedication to his family and descendants. There are also about ten Greek–Palmyrene bilinguals, at least three inscriptions in Greek only, and some fragments (Gawlikowski and al-Asʿad 1997, no. 24, and no. 108; Cantineau 1933, no. 68). In a few cases, they record the sale of the whole tomb (e.g., see below, no. 49, AD 236). More

Table 15.1 Chronological distribution of verbs expressing sale

Year	b'd	zbn	'ḥbr	yhb	rḥq	'rḥq	šwtp	yhb wb'd	b'd wyhb	'ḥbr wyhb	yhb w'ḥbr	'ḥbr wrḥq	šwtp wrḥq
130		1					2, 3						
140							4						
150													
160					5								
170					6, 10, 11			7	8, 9				
180			12, 14, 17, 18							16			15
190			19	22	20, 21, 24						23		
200													
210					26, 27, 28, 29, 30, 33						31		
220			35		38, 39, 40, 41, 42	36						25, 37	34
230			51		45, 46, 47, 48, 50, 52, 54	43							
240					55, 56, 57, 58, 59, 61, 63, 64								
250					65								
260					67, 68, 69, 70, 71, 73, 74								
270					75								
n.d.	79	82	79, 81		77, 78								

frequently, of parts of it: rows of burial niches, entire walls with already-existing niches, or ones just outlined and to be carved out as needed. Other portions that were sold included rooms, called *exedrae*, or arched recesses, that provided space for sculpted sarcophagi and monumental reliefs of the dead, such as family banquet scenes. Together with the archaeological evidence, the texts show that each row of niches contained multiple burials (e.g., no. 59). The structure of underground tombs also made it possible to dig ground-burials. If necessary, the owners could enlarge their tombs by digging additional galleries and recesses for more burial spaces, as illustrated below (Gawlikowski 1970, 109). In building his tomb, Lishamshu son of Mokimu, offered his family and descendants that possibility: 'so that whoever wishes may dig for him inside' (*PAT* 1787, AD 123). The same was also granted to purchasers, as one reads in a AD 194 text from a hypogeum (no. 25) 'that they may dig and build burial chambers as they want', and, from another underground tomb: 'and if he wishes to make any holes [?] of his, he must build either a plastered wall, or one of bricks, then he may enlarge them, on the wall' (*PAT* 1624, AD 214). This last text, on a stone tablet found by Harald Ingholt in the tomb of Maliku, in the south-west necropolis, is a rather interesting inscription that was formerly analysed as a sale text. It records key sections of what turns out to be a unilateral obligation that prevented one party from damaging a neighbouring property and references its earlier purchase and the sale of other sections of that tomb (Ingholt 1962; Cussini 2016). Part of the original contract, the monumental inscription *PAT* 1624, was copied on a stone slab that was placed in the hallway beside the two neighbouring properties consisting of rows of burial niches. The obligation was stipulated to avoid future damage and safeguard the structure, and in light of its importance it was deemed necessary to make the core of the contract visible, monumentalized in the tomb.

The reason for the appearance of inscriptions recording the sale of burial spaces during the second part of the second century AD was first investigated by Gawlikowski in his 1970 study of the funerary texts and their context. He gathered fifty-two cession texts: five from tower tombs, five from funerary temples, and forty-two from fifteen hypogea. The wealth of cession texts from later funerary structures, the underground tombs, well explains the practice of selling funerary properties as a result of changes in Palmyra's socioeconomic situation (Gawlikowski 1970), which was due to two combined factors: the growth of a middle class affluent enough to provide burial places for their immediate family and descendants but without the means to build new monumental tombs, and the need for ready cash on the part of the tomb builders or, especially, their descendants. Moreover, I believe that instances of sales of entire structures implied the migration of family groups from Palmyra.

The corpus of Palmyrene inscriptions of sale now comprises over eighty specimens. Monolingual Palmyrene inscriptions still represent the majority, the number of Greek–Palmyrene bilinguals is almost unchanged, and there are some new fragments in Greek. A previously known damaged Greek inscription does not contain Aramaic elements that may be used to analyse Palmyrene legal language, but nonetheless it offers information about the presence of Jews at Palmyra and some insights into the interaction of different religious and social groups in the funerary context. Conceivably, it could also be an example of migration from Palmyra (Cussini, forthcoming). The inscription, on a framed stone slab from an unknown tomb, records the sale of the whole tomb (Cantineau 1933, no. 68; Gawlikowski 1970, Mfc 51; Cussini 1995; Yon 2012, no. 546). The seller bears a Jewish name and patronym, Samouelos, son of Samouelos. As the editor suggested, in the missing portion there was the foundation inscription in Greek (Cantineau 1930, 49). Perhaps there may also have been a Palmyrene section, which would make it another example of a bilingual sale inscription.

Before proceeding with the discussion, a brief description of the newly added texts is necessary. The first, on a stone slab of unknown provenance, records the sale of five niches by Julius Aurelius Samuel, son of Aurelius Shimḥay, to Yarḥay son of Barshaʿadu, in AD 215 (no. 30). The seller's name and patronym indicate he was probably Jewish. Three additional inscriptions come from the underground Tomb F, in the south-east necropolis, built in AD 128, as shown by the *in situ* foundation inscription on a stone tablet framed by a sculpted *tabula ansata* and decorated by a satyr's head (Sakai 1994, 133–138).

On the lintel there are two Palmyrene sale texts (Figure 15.2): the first, damaged, records the sale of a section by the owners, two cousins named Boropa and Bolyada, in AD 220 (no. 34). According to an AD 222 inscription (no. 36) on the upper portion of the lintel, above the previous text, the same two cousins and two others sold 'two of the three parts of the hypogeum' to another cousin (no. 36). In the main gallery, above a side recess with the relief of Hermes, 'freedman of Bolaḥa', is another partly preserved Palmyrene inscription (no. 80) (Figure 15.3).

It describes the specific area (the eastern side of the main gallery); mentions burial niches, a statue, and another relief; and contains the same word, *rbwʿt*, 'square, rectangular recess', found in the obligation from Maliku's tomb (*PAT* 1624, AD 214). The verb is lost, and it is unclear whether the inscription recorded a sale or another type of text.

FIGURE 15.2 Tomb F, sale inscriptions.

After Higuchi and Saito 2001, plate 5.

FIGURE 15.3 Inscription above the recess of Hermes, detail.

After Higuchi and Saito 2001, plate 8.

Possibly, Hermes bought that recess and the inscription above his relief related to it. A damaged bilingual text on a reused lintel from another unknown tomb records an AD 224 sale by Julius Aurelius Maqqay, son of Yarḥibola ʿAteʿaqab, to Julius Aurelius Shalma, son of Maliku (Yon 2012, no. 477) (no. 38). Finally, broken slabs bearing foundation and sale texts and used in antiquity as building material were excavated in the northern wall area (al-Asʿad et al. 2012, 164–165. Formerly, in the Palmyra Museum). A framed inscription on a tablet (inv. no. 2983/9507), broken into four parts with one section missing, recorded a sale, possibly a mid-second-century text (no. 81). Another fragmentary inscription on a stone tablet (inv. no. 1518/9318) probably records a sale. It is dated September AD 243, but the verb is lost (no. 62). Other stone tablet fragments with remains of framed inscriptions belonged to a foundation (inv. no. 1443/8601) and, possibly, to a sale text (inv. no. 1457/8672). Despite their poor condition, the northern wall findings are further examples of monumentalized legal language and deeds. New significant additions to the corpus are thirteen inscriptions copied by Ingholt in his excavation diaries but never published during his lifetime, which have been recently made available (Raja et al. 2021). They are Palmyrene monolingual texts, dated between August AD 131 (below, no. 3) and December AD 265 (no. 71).[1] They come from seven

---

[1] From Ingholt's diaries (IED = Raja et al. 2021) also fragmentary specimens, possibly cession texts: IED, 1800, 1–p. 80, May AD 189, tomb 'L'; IED 1800, 1–p. 90, date lost, tomb 'AG'; IED 1805, 4–p. 13, date lost. Moreover, an inscription framed by a *tabula ansata* from tomb 'P' or '112' records the division between three owners (Yon 2016, 123 = IED 1803, 2–p. 16–17) perhaps resulting from inheritance and/or sale.

different tombs: five from tomb 'O' or '24' (nos. 3, 10, 39, 45, 71), three from tomb 'AG' (nos. 33, 63, 68), two from tomb '25' (nos. 8, 9), and one each from tomb '106' (no. 69), tomb 'L' (no. 28), tomb 'P' or '112' (no. 13), and tomb 'U' or '33' (no. 83).[2] The sale is usually expressed by *rḥq*, 'to cede' (nos. 3, 10, 13, 39, 45, 63, 68, 69, 70), by *šwtp wrḥq*, 'to make a partnership and cede' (no. 33), and, in two inscriptions from the same tomb which record subsequent sale by the same woman, by *b'd wyhb* 'to cede and sell' (nos. 8 and 9), the last one a new version of the already known formula *yhb wb'd* 'to sell and cede' (see Table 15.I).

A fragmentary bilingual text (no. 53, AD 238) has been classified as a cession text, thanks to the verbal form εξεχώρησεν, also found in no. 58, AD 241. The verb εκχωρέω 'to withdraw, cede' is a calque of *rḥq*. The inscription mentions a woman, (Julia) Aurelia Shalmat, whose role is not entirely clear, and the seller, Julius Aurelius Ḥanaina. It has been suggested that the Greek portion contains a provision regarding 'permis[sion to alienate]' the property, or perhaps a prohibition, as in two fragmentary Greek texts (Yon 2012, 478; *PAT* 0571), and in a bilingual foundation (no. 79: 'and they shall not be [entitled to . . .] or to alienate it, or to take anyone in partnership, as I have written'). Moreover, a problematic inscription (no. 82, n.d.) warns against the sale of a surety (?) that guarantees the tomb (Gawlikowski 1970, 168: ' un autre texte peu clair qui avertit l'acheteur d'une dépendance du tombeau qu'il commet un péché'). The extant portion of both sections of no. 53, AD 238, does not allow a complete understanding of the provision. Perhaps, in contrast to what has been suggested, the 'permission' regarded the possibility of enlarging the tomb, as in other inscriptions. The woman's name, Shalmat, and her patronym (in Greek only: Αβδαρσας) suggest she may be 'Abda'astor's daughter, who, together with another woman, Ummadabu (no. 54, AD 239), sold the northern *exedra* in her father's tomb (Cussini 2016, 49). If the identification is correct, the stone tablet came from the same tomb and may have recorded provisions regarding another section of that tomb drawn from a contract issued in the same or the preceding year. However, it is difficult to reconstruct Shalmat's role. Perhaps she was mentioned here for reasons that concerned easements on her family tomb. However, it is also possible that the slab came from another tomb and mentioned another woman.

The most significant sale inscription, and certainly the starting point for an analysis of the language of sale at Palmyra, is the text on a door-lintel, copied by Cantineau at al-Bazuriya, 24 km south of Palmyra (no. 7, AD 171; Cantineau 1930, plate XXIII; Cussini 2010, 343; 2023, 46–48). Unfortunately, there are no photographs of the artefact *in situ*. It had been reused in a later structure, and, in Cantineau's photograph, the dilapidated building where it was found may be seen only in the distance. The inscription records the sale of one-third of an underground structure, as indicated by the term defining it,

---

[2] The inscriptions were transliterated by Ingholt in Hebrew letters and are only rarely accompanied by hand copies. The preliminary nature of the annotations in Ingholt's excavation diaries and the lack of photographs do not allow one to check some problematic readings (e.g., see below, no. 83). Two photographs only are available in Yon 2016, 123, figure 7 (=IED 1803, 2–p. 16–17), and 124, figure 9 (= no. 83 below).

m'rh 'hypogeum' (l. 5). Shalma, daughter of Boropa, owned half of it and acted 'on behalf' *bmqmwt* (l. 1) of her husband; she sold it to Maliku, son of Mokimu (l. 3). What makes this text unique, in addition to the specification of the active role of the woman, is the mention of the price paid by the purchaser: '120 silver denarii'. As in sale contracts, here one finds the payment receipt formula 'she acknowledges . . . that she received . . .' (l. 3), and the name of a witness. The sale clause, here expressed by *yhb wb'd* 'to sell and cede' (Table 15.1, no. 7), is followed by the description of the location of the property. In the final lines, the noun *šwtpw* occurs twice ('in partnership with Maliku . . . and in partnership with 'Ogailu, her husband', ll. 6–7). The noun *šwtpw* 'association' has a legal connotation, and the same root occurs as a verbal form *šwtp* in other inscriptions (Table 15.1, nos. 2, 3, 4, 15, 34). At al-Bazuriya, as in other cases, the 'association' or 'partnership' probably indicated a servitude and the right of way of the new owners to their property (Cussini 2015, 93–95). The poor state of the last lines does not allow for a full understanding of the provision.

The above-mentioned inscription offers the unique opportunity to hypothesize the structure and formulation of Palmyrene sale contracts. Although it is not a contract, this monumental inscription recorded more significant elements than the rest of the evidence. This may have been due to the site's distance from Palmyra and the city archives, where copies of the contracts held by the parties involved were presumably deposited, as illustrated by mentions of the archives, *bt 'rk'* in two instances (*PAT* 2760; *PAT* 2759). The purchaser may have believed it necessary to have a larger portion of the contract inscribed on the tomb to reiterate his title to access and use his portion. Also, as in the other sale texts, the inscription made his name visible since he was obviously not mentioned in the foundation text, which in this case has not survived. The tomb was probably built by Shalma's husband's family, possibly by his father or his grandfather. This would account for its division: one-third owned by 'Ogailu and Shalma, the rest presumably by other family members. The inscription contains the following key elements from the original contract: (a) date formula, (b) seller's name (and a specification of her capacity: 'in the place of' *bmqmwt*), (c) witness, (d) payment receipt and sale price, (e) sale formula, (f) property description and location, and (g) reference to partnership (indicating servitudes). The sequence does not necessarily reflect the order of the clauses in the contract now lost. There, the sale formula probably preceded the payment receipt, whereas the witness's name (and his signature) was at the bottom of the document.

Turning to the rest of the evidence, the monumental sale texts display key clauses from the original contracts, although not all are present in the extant inscriptions. What was copied on stone was the core of the original documents, specifically the operative section and the following elements:

1. Sale clause
2. Cession of rights
3. Property description and location
4. *Forever* formula

Occasionally, there are portions of the concluding section of the contract:

5. Restrictive covenant and conditions
6. Fines
7. Names of scribe and witnesses

Sale Clause

At Palmyra, the core of the contract, the sale clause, was monumentalized. The inscriptions record the date formula; the name(s) of the seller(s); the verb expressing the sale, constructed with the preposition 'to' (*l-*); and the name(s) of the purchaser(s). The clause is usually cast in the third person (objective style) and, in four cases, in the first person (subjective style) (nos. 3, AD 131; 15, AD 186; 26, AD 213; 42, AD 229). Once, an objective-style clause is followed by the seller's subjective-style declaration, specifying what part was sold (no. 17, AD 188: 'Lishamash . . . ceded in partnership, part of this hypogeum / to Bonne . . . / I have ceded to him as a partner . . . eight niches').

The sale clause, and the legal change that occurred, is expressed by six verbs (see Table 15.1.: *b'd*, 'alienate'; *zbn*, 'to sell'; *'ḥbr*, 'to make a partnership';[3] *yhb*, 'to give'; *rḥq*, 'to cede (literally, 'to distance oneself')' (and C form, *'rḥq*); and *šwtp*, 'to make a partnership' (a loanword from Akkadian *šutāpu*, 'partner, companion', CAD, Š, p. 397, also documented in later Aramaic sources, Sokoloff 1990, 543). There are also two-verb formulas, with different and alternate combinations of the same verbs: *yhb wb'd*, and *b'd wyhb* 'to sell and cede'; *ḥbr wyhb*, 'to take in partnership and cede' and *yhb w'ḥbr*, 'to sell and take in partnership'; *'ḥbr wrḥq*, 'to take in partnership and cede'; and *šwtp wrḥq*, 'to make a partnership and cede'. Apart from *zbn* (no. 1, AD 131) and *yhb* (no. 22, AD 192), which clearly indicate a sale, also found in combined forms *yhb wb'd* (no. 7, AD 171), *b'd wyhb* (nos. 8, AD 174; 9, AD 175), *ḥbr wyhb* (no. 16, AD 186), and *yhb w'ḥbr* (nos. 23, AD 193; 31, AD 215), the other verbs express the concept of *distancing* oneself from the property sold: in the first place *rḥq* (or *'rḥq*) and *b'd* (no. 79, n.d.), also found in the two-verb formula *yhb wb'd* or *b'd wyhb*.

The verb *rḥq* is the most frequently found, attested in the majority of inscriptions from AD 160 to 274 (see Table 15.1). It is also found in the two-verb formulas *'ḥbr wrḥq* (nos. 25, 37) and *šwtp wrḥq* (nos. 15, 34). It occurs in a 437 BC Aramaic house sale contract from Elephantine (Porten and Yardeni 1989, 64, B3.4). There, in the withdrawal formula, it expresses the relinquishment of rights to the property, whereas the sale clause has *zbn* 'to sell'. Although it is impossible to follow the line of transmission within the Aramaic legal tradition, *rḥq* became the most widespread Palmyrene expression of sale and, from AD 240 onward, the only one. One cannot say whether the sale was expressed by that verb in the Palmyrene contracts or whether they had a more articulated formulation,

---

[3] The D form, *ḥbr* in no. 16, AD 186, probable haplography, therefore another C form *'ḥbr*.

one comparable to other earlier or contemporary Aramaic contracts of sale. Perhaps the Palmyrene sale clause was followed by a withdrawal formula, as in Aramaic contracts, and this was the only part copied on stone. In terms of comparison, in the two AD 97/98 Nabataean sale deeds of immovables from Naḥal Ḥever, the withdrawal formula is expressed by another verb, *šbq*, 'to free' (Yadin et al. 2002, 201–244).

With regard to other verbs meaning 'making a partnership'—*'ḥbr* and *šwtp*—also found in two-verb formulas, I have argued that the concept of *partnership* could be explained in light of the specificity of the property conveyed. The section sold was in a hallway or in a room, beside another person's property, that of the original tomb owner or of another purchaser. Therefore, it was necessary to regulate access, and the contract may have included servitudes over the galleries or the recesses where the property was located. Therefore, the verbs expressing the idea of partnership specified that the buyers did not own the whole structure, but were *made partners* and granted the right to access their section (Cussini 2015).

Cession of Rights

Ten inscriptions recording the sale of parts of the tombs refer to cession of rights. They are all third-century specimens, from AD 236 to 267. Three are Greek and Palmyrene bilingual texts; they come from hypogea and a funerary temple, another from an unknown tomb. One inscription specifies that the sale includes 'ornaments and rights' (no. 58, AD 241). In another, the property is sold with its ornaments, with no reference to 'rights' (no. 40, AD 226). The inscriptions are on architectural elements and, in one case, on a reemployed stone tablet. Two come from the same tomb and feature the same parties: a woman named Amata bought two *exedrae* and, two years later, four niches (nos. 67, 263; 70, AD 265). There was no space left on the lintel, and the second inscription was written on the door-jamb. Also, from another tomb, two inscriptions: one records the sale of ten rows of niches and 'their rights' (no. 45, AD 234) by a woman named Bat'a. Some thirty years later she sold seven more niches and another portion 'and their rights' (no. 71, AD 265,). According to inscriptions from Maliku's tomb, a woman bought four niches in AD 267 (no. 73), and, a month later, she sold two (no. 74). Tomb decorations are mentioned also in foundation texts (IED 1804, 2–p. 31, AD 181; see below, no. 24, AD 193; *PAT* 0557, AD 212; *PAT* 1142, AD 232).

These are the sale texts mentioning 'cession of rights':

No. 45, February AD 234, Tomb 'O'. Seller: Bat'a daughter of 'Ogga (son of) 'Awedallat. Purchaser: Julia Aurelia She'ilata', daughter of Zubaida Diogenes. For the same seller also no. 71, AD 265.

No. 49, AD 236, bilingual, door-lintel. Tomb of Marona, funerary temple 150. Seller: Julius Aurelius Zubaida, son of 'Ashtor (son of) Zubaida. Purchaser: Julius Aurelius Theodoros, son of Agrippa, son of Marcellus.

No. 58, August AD 241, bilingual, stone tablet. Hypogeum of Yarḥay. Sellers: Julius Aurelius Ḥairan and Julius Aurelius Maloka, sons of Germana. Purchaser: Julius Aurelius Teopilos, son of Taimarṣu, (son of) Zubaida.

No. 62, September AD 243, stone tablet. Unknown tomb. Seller: Julius Aurelius Aelius. Purchaser: Julius Aurelius Adwan, son of Barʿate, son of Maʿan. Adwan was perhaps Baʿalay's grandfather, see below no. 74.

No. 67, June AD 263, bilingual, door-lintel. Hypogeum of Naṣrallat. Seller: Julius Aurelius Yadiʿbel, son of ʿAbdishamayya (son of) Malka. Purchaser: Julia Aurelia Amata, daughter of Bolḥazay, (son of) Mokimu.

No. 69, April AD 264. Tomb 106. Sellers: Julius Aurelius Ḥaruṣ, son of Ḥaruṣ and Shamshigeram, son of Shamshigeram. Purchaser: Julius Aurelius Male, son of Zabdibolno. 70, March AD 265, door-jamb. Hypogeum of Nasrallat. Seller: Julius Aurelius Yadiʿbel son of ʿAbishamayya (son of) Malka. Purchaser: Julia Aurelia Amata, daughter of Bolḥazay, (son of) Mokimu. Same parties of previous text, seller's patronym has different spelling: ʿAbdishamayya, Αβισαμαια (no. 67), and here ʿAbishamayya (no. 70).

No. 71, December AD 265, Tomb ʿO. Seller: Batʿa daughter of ʿOgga (son of) ʿAwed. Purchaser: Abgar son of Shalman (son of) Worod.

No. 73, February AD 267, inside doorway. Hypogeum of Maliku (founded in AD 121, *PAT* 1218). Seller: Dadion, son of Ḥabbay, son of Diogenes. Purchaser: Ummu, daughter of Bassa, (son of) Shaʿarona. From this tomb: twelve cessions on lintel and door-jamb (nos. 14–15, 18, 27–29, 57, 64, 73–75, AD 186–274), and an obligation (*PAT* 1624, AD 214).

No. 74, March AD 267, door-jamb. Hypogeum of Maliku. Seller: Ummu, daughter of Bassa (son of) Shaʿarona. Purchasers: Julius Aurelius Agathona, son of Bassa, (son of) Germana, and Julius Aurelius Baʿalay, son of ʿAbday, (son of) ʿAdwan. Ummu sold two of the four niches she bought in February (no. 73).

The sale clause is always expressed by *rḥq*, twice reconstructed and therefore not listed in Table 15.1 (no. 49, AD 236; no. 62, AD 243). Why the transfer of the property and rights was mentioned during the last forty years of attestation of Palmyrene sale texts and never before, and what these *rights* refer to, remain to be explained. It seems probable that these annexed rights had to do with servitudes, as in second-century AD Aramaic contracts concerning immovable property from Murabbaʿat and Naḥal Ḥever from Dead Sea caves, granting the easement of access 'to enter and exit as is proper' (Cussini 2015, 90 with previous bibliography) or other types of rights that cannot be reconstructed. For the sake of comparison, see for instance irrigation rights mentioned in contemporary Nabataean sale deeds from a Dead Sea cave: 'partnership and estate rights', *šwtpw wnḥlh* (Yadin et al. 2002, 201–244). As seen above, *šwtp* occurs in Palmyrene inscriptions (Table 15.1), and its attestation in Nabataean contracts points to a shared legal tradition.

Property Description and Location

The inscriptions describe the property conveyed: niches, rooms, and recesses. When the whole tomb is sold, there is no indication of its location in the necropolis or reference to neighbouring funerary buildings. This differs from extant Aramaic contracts of sale of immovables, in which neighbouring properties are always mapped. In Palmyrene inscriptions recording sales of tomb-sections, there is always a detailed description of the location of the property inside the tomb. Both description and location are significant parts of the original contract rather than reflecting what O'Connor termed 'tour-language' (O'Connor 1988). In Aramaic deeds of sale, the *clausula salvatoria*, or 'More or Less' clause, stated the exact extent of the property against future disputes concerning its precise dimensions, as in Naḥal Ḥever contracts, (the field) 'if less or more, it is the buyer's' and, in the Dura-Europos contract, about a slave, 'she is twenty-eight years old, more or less'. In the original Palmyrene contracts, one could posit a comparable clause whose introduction into the Aramaic language of sale derived from Neo-Babylonian models ('more or less', *iṣi u mâdu*). That clause is unattested in earlier Aramaic deeds, an indication of the complexity of the Aramaic legal tradition. Through Aramaic, it entered into Greek sale contracts (e.g., Dura-Europos, Welles et al. 1959, 139, no. 26, 'the land . . . however large it may be').

Palmyrene contracts probably contained easements regulating access to the portion sold, which granted the rights of the various buyers. As already seen, this is reflected by verbs indicating the notion of 'partnership'.

Forever Formula

The *forever* formula expressed the title to a property held by purchasers and their descendants. It is also present in foundation inscriptions, where it granted ownership to the builder's descendants, sometimes limited to male heirs only (*PAT* 0511, 114; *PAT* 0056, 142; *PAT* 0552, 184;[4] *PAT* 0024, AD 229, and in a sale inscription, see below, no. 6, AD 160). The evidence shows that female descendants inherited the tombs, or parts of them. To cite one example only, the seller mentioned in a foundation inscription (below, no. 24, AD 193) is the tomb builder's great-granddaughter (Figure 15.4). In addition to the inscriptions featuring women as sellers, who certainly had inherited the property they sold, at least four undated brief painted inscriptions from the tomb of the Three Brothers define Batmalku as 'heiress of house and tomb' (*PAT* 0528–*PAT* 0530; *PAT* 0540), and these texts labelled the sections of the tomb, originally her family's property, that remained hers (Cussini 2023). Moreover, in AD 241 (no. 59), the same woman sold four niches in the beautifully decorated *exedra* (Cussini 2016, 50–51).

---

[4] For an improved reading of this text, see Gawlikowski and al-As'ad 1997, no. 22.

FIGURE 15.4 Foundation inscription from al-Qaryatayn (no. 24, *PAT* 0555).

Former Palmyra Museum ©.

Restrictive Covenant and Conditions

Two inscriptions refer to a covenant between the parties involved: the obligation (*PAT* 1624, AD 214) 'And he shall not be entitled to extend the square in any way' and the above-mentioned bilingual foundation text (no. 79, n.d.). The *power* to modify a property, here denied, is expressed by the adjective *šlyṭ*, as in Aramaic contracts from Elephantine, Samaria, Naḥal Ḥever, and Dura-Europos (Cussini 1995, 247). Aramaic usage was probably modelled on late Babylonian forms of the cognate root *šalāṭu* (Muffs 1969, 153, 178). In Murabbaʿat and Naḥal Ḥever contracts we find the verb *ršy* with the same meaning (Cussini 1993, 103 with previous bibliography) and the same verb is also attested in monumental Nabatean inscriptions from Madāʾin Ṣāliḥ (Healey 1993, H3, H31, see below). A clause recording conditions that regulated the possibility of enlarging a tomb is found in three inscriptions from underground tombs: the obligation (*PAT* 1624, 'and if he wishes to make any holes [?] of his'), an earlier foundation (*PAT* 1787, AD 124, 'whoever wishes may dig'), and a sale text (no. 25, AD 194, 'they may dig and build burial chambers as they want').[5] The permission to modify the property should be viewed in the broader context of the Completion of Transaction clause, which defined the extent of the purchaser's control of the property. In the foundation text (*PAT* 1787), the right to dig is granted to the owner's cousins, in the other cases to the purchasers (no. 25, and *PAT* 1624). The permission is expressed by the verb *ṣby* 'to wish, desire', as in Aramaic contracts from Elephantine and Naḥal Ḥever (Cussini 1993, 98–99; 1995, 247). In the first-century AD Nabatean inscriptions from Madāʾin Ṣāliḥ, ancient Hegra (monumental tomb foundation inscriptions which contain portions of contracts now lost, comparable to some extent to the Palmyrene evidence), the conditions concerned the possibility of being buried upon production of a 'valid document' (Healey 1993, 189: H5, 7, 8, 20, 33, 34, 36, 37).

Fines

Two Palmyrene foundation texts mention a fine to be paid in case of the misuse of a tomb (in Aramaic contracts, fines are mentioned in the penalty clauses). The first in-scription is bilingual, and most of the extant portion is in Greek (*PAT* 0571, date lost), while the remaining Aramaic section only contains a brief fragment of the original text: 'This tomb, built . . .'. The Greek section forbids its sale and, in case of infringement, five thousand denarii must be paid to the treasury (Yon 2012, no. 531). The other in-scription (*PAT* 2760, date lost) limits the rights (probably to inheritance of the tomb) to male family members and specifies that a '1[000]' drachmas fine should be paid to the 'treasury' (*psqws*), if 'a corpse of a stranger, one who is not of my male descendants' is

---

[5] An inscription from Ingholt's excavation diaries specifies that all the burial niches were dug by one of the owners 'at his own expenses' *ḥpr gymḥyn klhyn mn kyš*, see below, no. 83.

buried there. Fines (combined with curses) occur in first-century Nabataean foundation inscriptions from Madāʾin Ṣāliḥ. In contrast to the Palmyrene evidence, they contain formulas forbidding the sale, pledge, lease, and other juridical acts concerning the
tombs (Healey 1993; 2013, 175–177).

Scribe and Witnesses

As with all examples of Palmyrene monumental inscriptions, the sale texts do not cite
their writers. An exception is the mention of the one who wrote the original contract,
in the al-Bazuriya inscription. The text records the declaration of a man that he wrote
on behalf of one party because he was illiterate. This, an odd statement in the monumental context, is a straightforward citation from the original contract. A comparable
declaration occurs in the Dura-Europos contract of sale, written by a professional
scribe: the seller's husband declares that he signed on her behalf because 'she does not
know writing' (Greenfield 1993). Mention of witnesses, another feature of the original
contracts, and another oddity in this type of monumental inscriptions, appears in two
inscriptions only. One is defined the 'expert witness' (no. 7), a loanword from γνώστης,
whose exact meaning at Palmyra escapes us. The names of two others, followed by šhd,
'witness', as commonly found in Aramaic contracts, are listed in the obligation (PAT
1624, AD 214).

   In comparison to contemporary or earlier Aramaic sale contracts, the Palmyrene
inscriptions preserve a limited portion of the operative section: almost exclusively only
part of the sale clause, usually cast in objective style. There are a few subjective-style
examples, possibly reflecting the original formulation of the contracts, in line with
Aramaic examples from Elephantine, Murabbaʿat, Naḥal Ḥever, and Dura Europos.
In those contracts the sale clause is cast in subjective style, it is always drawn up from
the seller's perspective, and it takes the form of a declaration pronounced by the seller
that he or she has sold the property. In contrast, the fourth-century Aramaic slave sale
contracts originally from Samaria, discovered in 1962 in a cave in the Wadi Daliyeh in
the Dead Sea region, are cast in objective style (Gropp 2001).

   Although the verbs attested in the Palmyrene formulas may have different primary
meanings and possibly originally conveyed different legal meanings, the sense of all
the expressions is the same—that is, *transfer of ownership* through sale. In one case,
at al-Bazuriya, the payment receipt clause was copied in stone, including mention
of the sale price (no. 7, AD 171). Although the Withdrawal formula is never attested,
verbs expressing the idea of *withdrawal* from the property sold state the legal change.
Verbs meaning *distancing oneself* from the property sold, indicating the relinquishment of rights, became the most widespread expression of sale in the monumentalized
summaries of the contracts, and *rḥq* is the most attested one in most of the specimens
(see Table 15.1). There are also examples of formulas expressing a restrictive covenant between the parties, conditions regarding the use of the property, and mentions of fines to
be paid in case of misuse of the property.

The lack of other clauses typical of the operative or concluding sections of sale contracts depends on the nature of Palmyrene sale inscriptions; not *contracts*, but selected portions of the original contract. In a few cases, there is a statement very close to the *clausula salvatoria*, intended to protect the seller from future disputes regarding the dimensions of the property. Witnesses are mentioned in the two inscriptions that contain longer portions of the original contracts for reasons that had to do with the distance from the city in one case or because of the seriousness of the situation involved in the other. Those who drafted the contracts, not mere scribes, but more complex professional figures, are never cited, with the only exception of the obligation from the tomb of Maliku (*PAT* 1624, AD 214).

Although only a selected section was copied, sometimes the original contract emerges quite vividly: this may be observed in the al-Bazuriya inscription (no. 7, AD 171) or in the obligation (*PAT* 1624) and, in other cases, in the subjective-style formulation of the sale formula. Two significant examples are in cursive script, written in vertical lines: one, a sale inscription carved on the door jamb of Maliku's tomb (no. 73, AD 267), the other painted on the stone door of 'Abd'astor's hypogeum, not a cession text, but an inscription warning against misuse of the funerary property (no. 82, n.d.).[6] The peculiar layout and the use of cursive indicate that the inscriptions were copied from contracts written on perishable material. The cursive vertical lines carved on the stone perhaps reproduced the contracts' original script and layout. That, in turn, was probably influenced by Old Syriac or earlier Seleucid Aramaic writing practices (Naveh 1976, 103). Cursive script and cursive influences may also be observed in the Nabataean monumental inscriptions from Hegra cited above (Healey 1993, 44, 54).

Thirty inscriptions feature women as tomb-owners, sellers, or buyers and span the period from 147 (no. 4) to AD 274 (no. 75) (Cussini 2005). Ten inscriptions from Ingholt's excavation diaries complete the picture and underline the active role of women with regard to sale and purchase of the funerary properties and their role of owners (e.g., no. 83). More than one-third of the extant cession texts feature women mostly as sellers and, to a lesser degree, as buyers. Women sell properties with men (nos. 4, AD 147; 14, AD 186; 15, AD 186; 25, AD 194; no. 66, AD 262), or sell or buy on their own. In one case, although the husband is mentioned, a woman alone sells a property (no. 7, AD 171). A similar situation may be noted in another case (no. 13): a portion is sold by a man in June AD 184, and later, in August, his mother sold another part of the same tomb (no. 13). The same woman and two other sellers are defined *brt ḥry* (nos. 13, AD 184; 54, AD 239; 60, AD 242), perhaps manumitted slaves, as indicated by the correspondence with *liberta* in a Latin-Palmyrene epitaph (*PAT* 0246, not dated).[7] In eight instances, the buyers are women. In AD 263, a woman bought two *exedrae* in a tomb and, two years later, four more niches (nos. 67; 70). We infer that women sold properties they had inherited, although that is never stated. A damaged bilingual inscription does not allow us to understand the role played by a woman: whether the tomb owner or the buyer, and she may be mentioned in connection to an obligation (although this is not preserved in the Palmyrene section,

---

[6] Also in cursive script, but apparently written in horizontal lines are no. 3, AD 131 and no. 68, AD 264.

[7] On this, Cussini 2004, with previous bibliography, and Levine 2005, 112–113.

and the Greek portion is quite fragmentary: '(to) Aurelia Salamathe, [. . .] Abdarsas, with permis[sion to alienate . . .] to said hypogeum as a [burial place . . .], no. 53, AD 238).

Late inscriptions show that the practice of selling funerary properties continued after the fall of Palmyra. One text from Maliku's tomb (no. 75) records the sale of five niches in AD 274, two years after the conquest, a year after the destruction of the city walls. According to that inscription, Tema, daughter of 'Abd'astor, sold part of her property to Abgar, son of Taime, who bought it for his children and grandchildren. This legal act bears witness to the continuity of the Palmyrene legal tradition after the great watershed date of AD 273. It also offers a glimpse into the lives of local residents and their permanence in Palmyra, as illustrated by Abgar's decision to provide his descendants with burial spaces in the monumental tomb built by Maliku for his family in AD 120, as we read in the foundation inscription (*PAT* 1218). Finally, one of the new cession texts from Ingholt's excavation diaries (no. 63, AD 248) contains an additional occurrence of a unique legal designation of the seller, a woman who is defined *mprnsny* of her own son.[8] The noun, from the root *prns* 'to provide' designates women who acted as legal guardians of their (underage) children, and, as the extant inscriptions point to, they managed and sold part of the funerary property on their behalf.

The legal language contained in the Palmyrene monumental inscriptions offers a glimpse into the formulation of the original contracts of sale, now entirely lost. Although one cannot reconstruct the complete structure of those contracts, the epigraphic records from Palmyra have preserved numerous examples of inscriptions recording the sale of portions of funerary properties, and their formulation may be studied in the framework of a shared Aramaic legal tradition and compared to contemporary and earlier Aramaic contracts of sale. As seen above, it is possible to pinpoint significant elements, sections, and key-clauses of the original contract. The legal change was expressed using different verbs and two-verb formulas, and their attestation and distribution varied in the course of time, as illustrated by Table 15.1. These elements allow for a reconstruction of the language of sale, and, together with provisions regarding inheritance and other scattered elements, they contribute to the study of Palmyrene legal language.

Palmyrene Inscriptions Documenting Sale of Funerary Properties

1. *PAT* 1843, October AD 131
2. *PAT* 1614, AD 131
3. IED, 1801, 11–p. 94, August AD 131[9]

---

[8] For a discussion of this term, Cussini 2016, 49, with reference to no. 54 (PAT 0095, AD 239).

[9] IED followed by page number and diary reference: texts from Ingholt's diaries, in Raja et al. 2021.

4. *PAT* 1815, April AD 147 (sellers: husband and wife)
5. *PAT* 0523, October AD 160
6. *PAT* 0524, November AD 160
7. *PAT* 1791, May AD 171 (seller: woman)
8. IED, 1801, 1- p. 96, April AD 174 (seller: woman)
9. IED, 1802, 1- p. 96, April AD 175 (seller: woman)[10]
10. IED, 1801, 5–p. 90, September AD 178
11. *PAT* 2761, October AD 178 (seller: woman)
12. *PAT* 0550, March AD 181
13. IED, 1803, 2–p. 16–17, June 184 (seller: man); August AD 184 (seller: woman)[11]
14. *PAT* 0044, July AD 186 (sellers: brother and sister)
15. *PAT* 0045, September AD 186 (sellers: brother and sister)
16. *PAT* 0072, May AD 186 (form *ḥbr*, unique occurrence, possibly a case of haplography, for it is preceded by *'m* 'the mother', in determined state, marked by *aleph*. This would explain *ḥbr* instead of the expected form *'ḥbr*)
17. *PAT* 0551, November AD 188
18. *PAT* 0046, June AD 188
19. *PAT* 1135, April AD 191
20. *PAT* 0525, May AD 191
21. *PAT* 0526, July AD 191
22. *PAT* 1790, July AD 192
23. *PAT* 0027, March AD 193
24. *PAT* 0555, July AD 193 (foundation mentioning earlier sale. Seller: woman)
25. *PAT* 0067, May AD 194 (sellers: husband and wife)
26. *PAT* 0047, January AD 213
27. *PAT* 0048, October AD 213
28. *PAT* 0050, AD 213
29. *PAT* 0049, August AD 214
30. Gawlikowski and al-As'ad 1997, no. 20, AD 215
31. *PAT* 0028, May AD 215
32. *PAT* 0118, February AD 215 (verb: lost)
33. IED, 1801, 1–p. 91, February AD 218 (seller: woman)
34. Sakai 1994, no. 8, November AD 220
35. *PAT* 1657, July AD 222
36. Sakai 1994, no. 7, October AD 222
37. *PAT* 0029, December AD 223
38. al-As'ad and Yon 2001, no. 1, October AD 224
39. IED, 1801, 1–p. 95, March AD 225 (seller: woman)

[10] Same woman as in no. 8.

[11] In June AD 184, a man sold two sides of an *exedra* to two brothers. Later on, in August, his mother sold the third side of that *exedra* to the father of the same brothers. Neither inscription records the verb indicating the sale, only the owners' names and their portions.

40. *PAT* 0560, November AD 226
41. *PAT* 0075, May AD 228
42. *PAT* 0562, January AD 229 (two sales from the same tomb, cf. no. 44)
43. *PAT* 1788, June (?) AD 232
44. *PAT* 0562, February AD 234 (purchaser: woman; verb lost)
45. IED, 1801, 5–p. 93, February AD 234 (seller: woman; purchaser: woman)[12]
46. *PAT* 0039, May AD 234
47. *PAT* 0040, February AD 235
48. *PAT* 0041, February AD 235 (same seller as previous text; different purchaser)
49. *PAT* 0565, AD 236 (verb lost)
50. *PAT* 0042, May AD 237
51. *PAT* 0567, August AD 237
52. *PAT* 0043, December AD 237 (purchaser: woman)
53. *PAT* 2820, AD 238 (bilingual, Greek verb only; purchaser (?): woman)
54. *PAT* 0095, April AD 239 (sellers: two women; purchaser: woman)
55. *PAT* 1945, May AD 240 (seller: woman)
56. *PAT* 2823, AD 240
57. *PAT* 0051, May AD 241
58. *PAT* 2786, August AD 241
59. *PAT* 0527, September AD 241 (seller: woman)
60. *PAT* 2725, March AD 242 (seller: woman; verb lost)
61. *PAT* 2729, July AD 243 (sellers: two women)
62. al-As'ad et al. 2012, no. 1, September AD 243 (verb lost)
63. IED, 1801, 1–p. 91–92, February AD 248 (seller: woman)
64. *PAT* 0052, August AD 249
65. *PAT* 0071, July AD 251
66. *PAT* 0568, September AD 262 (sellers: man and woman; verb lost)
67. *PAT* 0057, June AD 263 (purchaser: woman)
68. IED 1804, 2–p. 70, January AD 264 (seller: woman)[13]
69. IED, 1803, 2–p. 9, April AD 264
70. *PAT* 0058, March AD 265 (purchaser: same woman of no. 67)
71. IED, 1801, 1–p. 94–95, December AD 265 (seller: woman)[14]
72. *PAT* 1160, June AD 265 (verb lost)
73. *PAT* 0053, February AD 267
74. *PAT* 0054, March AD 267 (purchaser: woman)
75. *PAT* 0055, June AD 274 (seller: woman)
76. *PAT* 0073, n.d. (verb lost; almost a replica of no. 16)
77. *PAT* 1227, n.d.
78. *PAT* 1153, n.d. (second century, or later. Foundation: *PAT* 0514, AD 118)

[12] Seller is same woman as in no. 70.
[13] For the same text, see also Raja et al. 2021, 1689, 1801, 1- p. 92.
[14] Seller is same woman as in no. 45 above.

79. *PAT* 0570. n.d. (foundation text with provisions against sale and partnership)
80. Higuchi and Saito 2001, 22, n.d. (verb lost; cession text?)
81. al-As'ad et al. 2012, no. 2, n.d.
82. *PAT* 0097, n.d. (not a cession text, but contains verb *zbn* 'to sell')
83. IED, 1802, 1- p. 110, n.d. (cession text (?) problematic verb).[15]

BIBLIOGRAPHY

al-As'ad, Khaled, Michał Gawlikowski, and Jean-Baptiste Yon. 2012. 'Aramaic Inscriptions in the Palmyra Museum: New Acquisitions'. *Syria* 89: 163–184.

al-As'ad, Khaled, and Jean-Baptiste Yon. 2001. 'Textes et fragments grecs de Palmyre'. *Syria* 78: 153–162.

Benoit, Pierre, Jósef Tadeusz Milik, and Roland G. de Vaux. 1961. *Les Grottes de Murabba'at*. Discoveries in the Judaean Desert 2. Oxford: Clarendon Press.

Cantineau, Jean. 1930. 'Textes funéraires palmyréniens'. *Revue biblique* 39(4): 520–551.

Cantineau, Jean. 1933. *Inventaire des inscriptions de Palmyre*. Fasc. 8, *Le Dépot des Antiquités*. Beirut: Imprimerie catholique.

Cussini, Eleonora. 1993. 'The Aramaic Law of Sale and the Cuneiform Legal Tradition'. Unpublished doctoral dissertation, Johns Hopkins University, Baltimore (1993 Library of Congress, Washington DC, USA n. TX 3-631-179).

Cussini, Eleonora. 1995. 'Transfer of Property at Palmyra'. *ARAM* 7: 233–250.

Cussini, Eleonora. 2004. 'Regina, Martay and the Others: Stories of Palmyrene Women'. *Orientalia* 73: 235–244, tables XXIII–XXV.

Cussini, Eleonora. 2005. 'Beyond the Spindle: Investigating the Role of Palmyrene Women'. In *A Journey to Palmyra: Collected Essays to Remember Delbert R. Hillers*, edited by Eleonora Cussini, 26–43. Culture and History of the Ancient Near East 22. Leiden: Brill.

Cussini, Eleonora. 2010. 'Legal Formulary from Syriac Documents and Palmyrene Inscriptions: An Overview'. In *Trois millénaires de formulaires juridiques*, edited by Sophie Démare-Lafont and André Lemaire, 337–355. Geneva: Droz.

Cussini, Eleonora. 2015. 'Predial Servitudes and Easements in Aramaic Documents of Sale'. In *From Source to History: Studies on Ancient Near Eastern Worlds and Beyond*, edited by Salvatore Gaspa, Alessandro Greco, Daniele Morandi Bonacossi, Simonetta Ponchia, and Robert Rollinger, 87–98. Münster: Ugarit Verlag.

Cussini, Eleonora. 2016. 'Reconstructing Palmyrene Legal Language'. In *The World of Palmyra*, edited by Andreas Kropp and Rubina Raja, 42–52. Scientia Danica. Series H, Humanistica, 4, vol. 6. Palmyrene Studies 1. Copenhagen: Det Kongelige Danske Videnskabernes Selskab.

---

[15] On this inscription (probably not a cession, but recording the division of the property between a woman, Akamat, and her son Iadun, maybe after they had inherited it), Yon 2016, 124 reads *prš ydwn* 'Iadun separated' (his property from his mother's), on the basis of Ingholt's (uncertain) preliminary reading. Elsewhere in his diaries, Ingholt suggested to interpret it *wb. ydwn* 'has separated Iadun' (Yon in Raja et al. 2021, 1802). Both readings cannot be checked. From Ingholt's diaries see also a fragmentary cession text: IED 1800, 1- p. 80, May 189, verb and seller's name lost, Ingholt's tomb 'I', or 'the Head Tomb' (Raja et al. 2021, 1309).

Cussini, Eleonora. 2023. 'Circular Economy in Palmyra in Light of the Sale and Reuse of Funerary Spaces'. In *Exchange and Reuse in Roman Palmyra: Examining Economy and Circularity*, edited by Nathanel Andrade and Rubina Raja, 45–58. Studies in Palmyrene Archaeology and History, 8. Turnhout: Brepols.

Cussini, Eleonora. Forthcoming. 'Mobility and Identity of Palmyrene Jews'. In *Palmyra and the Mediterranean*, edited by Rubina Raja. Mediterranean Studies in Antiquity. Cambridge: Cambridge University Press.

Drijvers, H. J. W., and John F. Healey. 1999. *The Old Syriac Inscriptions of Edessa and Osrhoene: Texts, Translations and Commentary*. Handbuch der Orientalistik, section 1, Der Nahe und Mittlere Osten 42. Leiden: Brill.

Gawlikowski, Michał. 1970. *Monuments funéraires de Palmyre*. Warsaw: Państwowe Wydawnictwo Naukowe.

Gawlikowski, Michał, and Khaled al-As'ad. 1997. 'Inscriptions de Palmyre nouvelles et revisitées'. *Studia Palmyreńskie* 10: 23–38.

Greenfield, Jonas C. 1993. '"Because He/She Did Not Know Letters": Remarks on a First Millennium C.E. Legal Expression'. *Journal of the Ancient Near Eastern Society* 22: 39–44.

Gropp, Douglas M. 2001. *Wadi Daliyeh II: The Samaria Papyri from Wadi Daliyeh, and Qumran Cave 4. XXVIII; Miscellanea*, part 2. Discoveries in the Judaean Desert 28. Oxford: Clarendon Press.

Healey, John F. 1993. *The Nabatean Tomb Inscriptions of Mada'in Salih: Edited with Introduction, Translation and Commentary*. Oxford: Oxford University Press.

Healey, John F. 2013. 'Fines and Curses: Law and Religion Among the Nabataeans and Their Neighbours'. In *Law and Religion in the Eastern Mediterranean: From Antiquity to Early Islam*, edited by Anselm C. Hagedorn and Reinhard G. Kratz, 165–188. Oxford: Oxford University Press.

Higuchi, Takayasu, and Kiyohide Saito. 2001. *Tomb F: Tomb of BWLH and BWRP; Southeast Necropolis Palmyra, Syria*. Nara: International Foundation Research Center for Silk Roadology.

Hillers, Delbert R., and Eleonora Cussini. 1996. *Palmyrene Aramaic Texts*. Publications of the Comprehensive Aramaic Lexicon Project. Baltimore: Johns Hopkins University Press.

Ingholt, Harald. 1934. 'Palmyrene Sculptures in Beirut'. *Berytus* 1: 32–43.

Ingholt, Harald. 1962. 'Palmyrene Inscriptions from the Tomb of Malkū'. *Mélanges de l'Université Saint Joseph* 38: 99–119.

Levine, Baruch A. 2005. 'Lexicographical and Grammatical Notes on the Palmyrene Aramaic Texts'. In *A Journey to Palmyra: Collected Essays to Remember Delbert R. Hillers*, edited by Eleonora Cussini, 103–117. Culture and History of the Ancient Near East 22. Leiden: Brill.

Muffs, Yochanan. 2002. *Studies in the Aramaic Legal Papyri from Elephantine*. With Prolegomenon by Baruch Levine. Leiden: Brill. First edition: 1969.

Naveh, Joseph. 1976. 'Syriac Miscellanea'. *'Atiqot* 11: 102–104.

O'Connor, Michael. 1988. 'The Grammar of Finding Your Way in Palmyrene Aramaic and the Problem of Diction in Ancient West Semitic Inscriptions'. In *Fucus: A Semitic/Afrasian Gathering in Remembrance of Albert Ehrman*, edited by Yoël L. Arbeitman, 353–369. Current Issues in Linguistic Theory 58. Amsterdam: John Benjamins.

Porten, Bezalel, and Ada Yardeni. 1989. *Textbook of Aramaic Documents from Ancient Egypt Newly Copied: Edited and Translated into Hebrew and English*. Vol. 2, *Contracts*. Jerusalem: Hebrew University.

Raja Rubina, Jean-Baptiste Yon, and Julia Steding, eds. 2021. *Excavating Palmyra: Harald Ingholt's Excavation Diaries; A Transcript, Translation, and Commentary; Introduction and Ingholt's Diaries 1–3, Ingholt's Diaries 4–5.* Studies in Palmyrene Archaeology and History 4.1–2, Turnhout: Brepols.

Reiner, Erica, Robert D. Biggs and Martha T. Roth. 1992. *The Assyrian Dictionary of the Oriental Institute of the University of Chicago.* CAD, vol. 17, Š, Part III. Ann Arbor, MI: The Oriental Institute of the University of Chicago.

Sakai, Ryuichi. 1994. 'Eight Palmyrene Inscriptions Found in the Southeast Necropolis'. In *Tombs A and C: Southeast Necropolis; Palmyra Syria; Surveyed in 1990–92,* edited by Takayasu Higuchi and Takura Izumi, 127–138. Nara: Nara International Foundation Research Center for Silk Roadology.

Sokoloff, Michael. 1990. *A Dictionary of Jewish Palestinian Aramaic.* Tel Aviv: Bar Ilan University Press.

Welles, Charles B., Robert O. Fink, and James F. Gilliam. 1959. *The Excavations at Dura-Europos: Conducted by Yale University and the French Academy of Inscriptions and Letters; Final Report.* Vol. 5, *Inscriptions, Parchment and Papyri.* Part 1, *The Parchments and Papyri.* New Haven, CT: Yale University Press.

Yadin, Yigael, Jonas C. Greenfield, Ada Yardeni, and Baruch Levine. 2002. *The Documents from the Bar Kokhba Period in the Cave of Letters: Hebrew, Aramaic and Nabatean Documents,* with additional contributions by Hannah M. Cotton and Joseph Naveh. Judean Desert Studies 3. Jerusalem: Hebrew University of Jerusalem.

Yon, Jean-Baptiste. 2012. *Inscriptions grecques et latines de la Syrie.* Vol. 17, fasc. 1, *Palmyre.* Bibliothèque archéologique et historique 195. Beirut: Institut français du Proche-Orient.

Yon, Jean-Baptiste. 2013. 'Palmyrene Epigraphy After PAT, 1996–2011'. *Studia Palmyreńskie* 12: 333–379.

Yon, Jean-Baptiste. 2016. 'Inscriptions from the Necropolis of Palmyra in the Diaries of H. Ingholt'. In *The World of Palmyra,* edited by Andreas Kropp and Rubina Raja, 118–125. Scientia Danica. Series H, Humanistica, 4, vol. 6. Palmyrene Studies 1. Copenhagen: Det Kongelige Danske Videnskabernes Selskab.

PART FOUR

PALMYRA AND ITS CONTACTS

CHAPTER 16

THE PALMYRENE DIASPORA

KATIA SCHÖRLE

INTRODUCTION

BETWEEN the first and third centuries AD, Palmyra throve as an urban centre, due in part to the prosperity engendered by its long-distance commercial activities. Whether the Palmyrenes resided abroad and set up systems of trade based on diaspora communities that enabled them to thrive economically or as a broad community is a crucial question to examine. Of course, the answer is far more complex than this simple question could ever uncover: for one, the evidence we have represents only a minute fraction of the contacts, diaspora groups, and trade connections that existed, and, second, the Palmyrenes surely also relied on a network of traders, buyers, and agents of non-Palmyrene descent, of which there remains little archaeological or textual evidence to compare with the first group. As also pointed out by Smith, 'Since this is a matter of identity and our sources are not as explicit as we would like, the issue of what it meant to be a Palmyrene, or how the Palmyrenes perceived themselves and their community, is naturally elusive and debatable' (see Chapter 7 [Smith], this volume). But with this in mind, the aim of this chapter is to investigate the presence of Palmyrenes outside the realm of the city itself, since a number of Palmyrenes are known to have traded, resided, or worshiped both east and west of the city of Palmyra, as far as the Indian Ocean or Hadrian's Wall on Rome's northernmost frontier. This chapter will not discuss each and every known Palmyrene, and it certainly excludes the two stelae at Merv, Turkmenistan, initially thought to have belonged to Palmyrenes, but which were in fact part of a nineteenth-/twentieth-century collection (Cussini 1998).

It has been argued that Palmyra's success lay in the initial unification of its main tribes, but the same may be said about its economic prosperity, which relied on the successful establishment of strong social ties with merchants and groups outside of Palmyra and which served as the commercial backbone of the caravans or other Palmyrenes involved in the long-distance trade with the Roman or Parthian empires and other trading groups involved in the Indian Ocean. In Palmyra itself, even though over time the mention of the four main tribes became more of a convention (Dirven 1998, 82), their unification remained an institutional constant, with the dedications referring to them. Outside of Palmyra, Palmyrenes often preferred the city itself as their point of reference: such is the case of Barates of Palmyra in Roman Britain (*RIB* 1065) or the association of Palmyrene shipowners on the Red Sea.

IDENTIFYING DIASPORA COMMUNITIES: A CHALLENGE IN ITSELF

In its simplest meaning, a *diaspora* consists of the spread of people who wish to retain social or religious ties with their home location, regardless of their motivations, and whether or not the initial move is voluntary (Eckardt 2010, 7). But diasporas may be very different in nature and reasons. Palmyrenes are found far from their home city, and different communities will form different 'diasporas'. Dirven's article on the Palmyrene diaspora remains an essential article on Palmyrenes found in both the Roman West and Parthian East (Dirven 1998; but see also Smith 2013, ch. 6). Here I focus less on religion and include commercial and military ties while examining the role of Palmyrenes living outside their original city still wishing to retain a social or cultural bond with their home. Our overview of Palmyrene diaspora groups is necessarily biased because it is an overview of the available and surviving archaeological or literary evidence. We can discuss only those Palmyrenes whom we assume to have had a conscious link to their hometown and whose testimony has survived in the archaeological or textual record. The Palmyrenes who may be identified beyond Palmyra will be only those who have a distinctly Palmyrene personal name, use the Palmyrene script, or worship a Palmyrene deity. The shortcuts and underlying problematic assumptions of this type of reasoning should be obvious, but they are unavoidable if we wish to discuss the evidence that is available. Those who chose to assimilate or remain discrete within their new local surroundings for any reason—by using another name or worshipping or writing in local scripts without referring to their Palmyrene traditions—will disappear from the identifiable corpus even if they may still have been part of a diaspora group. Nevertheless, we must work on the assumption that the inscriptions and evidence that have survived are at least somewhat representative of the Palmyrene diaspora.

Another issue is the duration of stay. How long does one have to stay or reside in a place to be part of a diaspora? As pointed out by Dirven, the strength of the interaction between a diaspora group and the home city may be assessed only if we consider 'how many people from one place visited the other, whether or not they stayed, for how long and for what reasons' (Dirven 2013, 50). On the island of Socotra, known in ancient times as Dioscourides, a wooden tablet with a dedication dated AD 258 in Palmyrene Aramaic records the presence on the island of a Palmyrene named Abgar (Strauch 2012, esp. part 2). The well-preserved tablet was found in a two-thousand-metre-long cave that contained over two hundred graffiti in various Brahmi, Bactrian, Greek, Axumite, and south Arabian scripts, which have been dated to between the second century BC and the second century AD. A Greek graffito mentioning the uncommon name 'Aukar' may be the same Abgar, inscribing his name in Greek. But did he reside on the island, or even write his name during the trip during which he left his votive tablet? Did he belong to a 'multi-ethnic diaspora of traders' residing on the island? None of the evidence really suggests the duration of the stay, nor that the traders necessarily resided or worshipped in the cave at the same time. It is far more probable that Abgar dedicated in the cave during transit while on his maritime voyage in the Indian Ocean. Likewise, an inscription in a sanctuary outside the Hadramawt capital, Sabah, in the southern Arabian Peninsula, which mentions two Palmyrenes dedicating to the local god in company of the king of Hadramawt (Bron 1986), two Indians, and two Chaldeans, more probably represents an embassy to the Hadramawt kingdom than a diaspora community.

MERCANTILE DIASPORA

The most frequently occurring diaspora would have been triggered by Palmyra's mercantile activities and its associated trading network (see Chapter 17 [Seland], this volume). The Palmyrene presence is well known in the desert and along the Euphrates since Palmyrenes regularly and famously undertook caravan trips to the Euphrates. The earliest known inscription comes from Dura-Europos (Smith 2013, 64; *PAT* 1067) and records the construction in 33 BC of a shrine to Yarhibol and Bēl, which was jointly dedicated by Zabdibol of the tribe of Gadibol, and Malku, of the tribe of the Kmr. The inscription in Dura-Europos celebrating the dedication of the temple of Bēl perhaps suggests trade links to the Euphrates in the second half of the first century BC (*PAT* 1067 referring to the dedication of the temple in the necropolis; Edwell 2008, 36; Dirven 2013, 52). Consequently, it would appear that at some time between the end of the first century BC and the early first century AD, Palmyra gradually developed an urban centre with connections beyond its territories, in particular to the Euphrates. Peace in the Mediterranean, and with the Parthians in 20 BC, now ushered in an era of opportunities for the Palmyrenes, who could further develop their networks across the region. Various Palmyrenes resided in Dura-Europos over the course of the first three centuries AD, and, although the presence of Palmyrenes in Dura-Europos does not seem directly connected with the longer caravan trade with the Euphrates, the ties, perhaps of a commercial nature, between Palmyra and Dura were particularly strong and were eventually strengthened by the presence of Palmyrene soldiers in the city (see Chapter 20 [Dirven], this volume), which is further discussed below. Although much shorter routes to the Euphrates, such as the one via Dura-Europos, could have been taken, the longer desert route to Hit was most likely the preferred one (Gawlikowski 1988, 169; see Chapter 20 [Dirven], this volume). The desert route meant avoiding populated areas that could have reduced the speed of travel, but also the taxes and administrative delays at each of the cities along the Euphrates. It also meant avoiding the softer and wetter ground around the Euphrates to which camels are particularly unsuited and could constitute an additional risk for any caravan (Seland 2011, 403; for diseases in wetter climates, Adams 2007, 55).

The inscriptions from the agora and the colonnaded street of Palmyra highlight the importance of travel to the mouth of the Persian Gulf and to the maritime routes of the Indian Ocean. The earliest inscriptions on trade from Palmyra, dated to the first half of the first century AD, point to the fact that the city primarily traded with Babylon and Seleucia (Rostovtzeff 1932, 796–798). However, Vologesias and Spasinou Charax quickly superseded these cities as end destinations for the caravans (Young 2001, 126–129). These cities, however, were of interest to both the Palmyrenes and the Romans as early as AD 19, and they may be associated with a political embassy to the city of Spasinou Charax and to another ruler, the king of Elymaïs (PAT 1414; Gawlikowski 1994, 28; Healey 1996, 33; Smith 2013, Ch. 6, Palmyrenes in Foreign Services, and n. 68 for references). Later inscriptions also refer to citizens established at Vologesias and could imply that a resident merchant community of Palmyrenes participated in the logistics of trade in places of political significance in both the Parthian and Sassanid periods and also in important transhipment areas (Drexhage 1988, n. 17; on the Parthian connections, see Chapter 19 [Edwell], this volume).

Over time, it seems that the Palmyrenes developed their activities into the Persian Gulf and that their activities were followed by Palmyrene residents in these locations as well. On the island of Kharg, ca. 25 km off the coast of Iran and 44 km from the Gulf of Hormuz, several necropoleis and funerary reliefs displaying Palmyrene influence may suggest a community of Palmyrenes on the island (the evidence remains controversial, however, cf. Steve 2003). On the Persian Gulf, the presence of Palmyrenes determined the success of their commercial enterprises. The best-attested connections are to the Isle of Tylos (modern Bahrain) where a Palmyrene was satrap in AD 131 and also honoured at Palmyra (Young 2001, 144; Delplace and Dentzer-Feydy 2005, VI.04). Two other Palmyrenes are also known to have been archon (Ingholt 1932, 278–292; Gawlikowski 1994, 29. The satrap's power may also have extended over parts of Eastern Arabia). One of the tombs of the Janussan cemetery on Bahrain may also be that of a Palmyrene official (Healey 1996, 36). While residing there and assisting the king, these Palmyrenes would also have provided traders with important social connections and presumably promoted Palmyrene interests. By the second century AD, Palmyrenes relied on the island as a port of call for Palmyrene vessels on their way to India. Access to Bahrain would also have given them direct access to its pearl market: the island was already famed for its pearls by the time of Pliny (NH 6.148), and pearls may have been a major staple.

THE PALMYRENE COMMUNITY IN EGYPT

The past three decades of research in the Eastern Desert of Egypt and the harbours of the Red Sea have brought to light far more evidence about Palmyrenes serving in the military, doing business, or residing in Egypt. Similarly, continued research interests in the Indian Ocean trade has further confirmed that Palmyrene traders and shipowners, such as the Palmyrene trader or shipowner on Socotra Island, comprised one of the groups of many different origins present in the region. As argued by Seland, Indian Ocean goods coming in via the Persian Gulf and Palmyra reached the Mediterranean at the beginning of the sailing season, and this provided the longer Persian-Gulf–Palmyra–Rome route with a competitive economic advantage (Seland 2010). Nevertheless, it appears that Palmyrenes chose to invest in both the overland and maritime routes, which, as a community, enabled them to carve out a more significant portion of the luxuries market (Schörle 2017). However, as mentioned earlier with reference to the Hoq cave dedication and votive tablet on Socotra, it is not easy to disentangle temporary presence from long-term residence in the available evidence. Some of the Egyptian evidence allows us to infer the long-term presence of some members of the Palmyrene community in Egypt. An inscription from Koptos reveals that a Palmyrene by the name of Zabdallas built a propylaion with three porticoes there. The dedication specifies that it was given by 'the merchants from Hadriane Palmyra', but it also mentions the 'Palmyrene shipowners on the Red Sea', which probably implies the presence of a community residing in Egypt (*SEG* XXXIV, 1593 = *I.Portes* 103; Bingen 1984; Young 2001, 80–81). Palmyrene commercial interests may be further attested on the Nile and beyond Koptos: an inscription with Palmyrene writing on the left-hand side found at Denderah (i.e., on the Nile) displays the name of a Palmyrene, along with the mention of *sunemporoi* (i.e., fellow merchants) (*CIS* II, 3190). Denderah was a strategic location for fluvial commerce and transit on the Nile. Koptos and Denderah are only ca. 30 km (one day) apart on opposite shores, but if the winds failed, passing the Denderah bend would be very tricky. Although this does not entirely rule out temporary travel, it is possible that a presence at both cities enabled Palmyrenes to organize themselves and envisage land transport as an alternative to fluvial transport on this difficult section of the Nile and whilst on their way to their ultimate market place of interest, Alexandria.

The Palmyrenes' choice of residing, investing, and trading via the Egyptian routes was in all likelihood helped by the presence of Palmyrenes along the desert route to the Red Sea harbours. The majority of Palmyrene dedications were made by soldiers stationed in the various forts along the two routes between Koptos on the Nile and the harbours of the Red Sea. Although the forts of the Roman period were built and occupied from the Flavian period onwards, and Palmyrenes were recruited by the army from the Trajanic period onwards, we begin to find Palmyrenes in the Eastern Desert only from ca. AD 215/ 216 onwards (see also Brun 2018). They often served as mounted archers and also had other functions, such as the *vexillarius* of the *Hadriani Palmyreni sagittarii* mentioned in an inscription from Koptos (*I.Portes* 85). The inscription was acquired in Koptos, so its original provenance is unknown, although it is reasonable to suppose that it came from Koptos or one of the Eastern Desert forts). Palmyrenes were employed at the forts on both the Myos Hormos and Berenike routes: at Didymoi, a fort along the longer desert route to the harbour of Berenike on the Red Sea, four soldiers of Palmyrene origin made a bilingual dedication in the early third century AD (Cuvigny 2012, 48–49:

I.did.5). The *Notitia dignitatum* mentions the presence of the *Ala VIII Palmyrenorum* towards the end of the fourth century AD (*Or.* 31, 49) at Phoinikon, a fort close to the Nile along the Myos Hormos, and archers are also attested at Didymoi, Dion, and Xeron Pelagos. Extensive, long-term archaeological research in the Eastern Desert has enabled the French team to link specific dietary changes, potentially clothing preferences (textiles with arrow motifs) and changes in architectural layout changes to the arrival and presence of the Palmyrene community at these forts (Brun 2018, with references to M. Leguilloux and D. Cardon's work, n. 65 for Phoinikon). On the Red Sea, several Palmyrenes made offerings at Berenike. A shrine with the statue base of Hierobol was found there along with a Palmyrene dedication by the prefect and the second-in-command of the *Ala Thracum Herculiana*, a cavalry division stationed at Palmyra until ca. AD 185, at which point it was transferred to Koptos (*OGIS* 639). Several dedications are known from the Eastern Desert of Egypt, such as the one at the fort at Didymoi from the early third century AD (Cuvigny 2012, 48–49: *I.did.5*). Another inscription, dated to AD 215, records the dedication of a bronze statue, found *in situ*, of a woman or more probably a deity, by Marcus Aurelius Mokimos, a Palmyrene archer.

Although the majority of inscriptions in the Eastern Desert suggest Palmyrenes in active military service, which may not be accurately considered part of a diaspora (i.e., they did not retire there), the strong Palmyrene military presence cannot be separated from those who were residing in Egypt for mercantile reasons: the presence of Palmyrenes along the routes created a sense of security, familiarity, and especially trust, which enabled the Palmyrene Red Sea and Nile merchants and shipowners to successfully develop their activities.

THE MILITARY DIASPORA

Apart from the mercantile community, the army would have been the other main vector for dispersion and diasporas. As established in the previous paragraph, Palmyrenes were well represented in the army where they served in auxiliary units and from which they eventually retired as veterans. Palmyrenes retained a central role at Dura-Europos, where the military units appeared in the mid-second century AD. An exceptional mural painting on the north wall of the pronaos of the Temple of the Palmyrene gods at Dura represents the sacrifice of the Roman tribune Julius Terentius, a standard bearer, and the auxiliary *Cohors XX Palmyrenorum*, which was stationed there from AD 208 to 256, in the presence of the gods. In the painting, the fortunes (Tyche) of the cities of Palmyra and Dura are represented, conveying the strength of the relationship between the two cities. This motif is also found on reliefs depicting the Gad of Dura-Europos and the Gad or Tyche of Palmyra (Dura-Europos collection 1938.5313 and 5314; Andrade 2013, 225–227), which implies that the social ties between the two cities were not of a purely military nature and reinforces the idea that Palmyra and Dura were intimately connected.

The majority of references to Palmyrenes serving in the army come from the Balkans, particularly in Dacia, not only in the Dacian capital, Sarmizegetusa, where some of the soldiers also built a temple and served as priests (*IDR* 3.2.20 = *AÉ* 1927, 00056 = *AÉ* 1977, 00668 = *AÉ* 2004, 01212), but in various Dacian towns and forts, such as Arcobara (*AÉ* 2006, 01129), Potaissa (*CIL* III, 00907 = *CIL* III, 07693), and Apulum (*IDR* 3.5.2.559 = *AÉ* 1914, 00102). Their strong presence comes from the fact that several Palmyrene units were stationed there, such as the *Numerus Palmyrenorum sagittarorium* (Palmyrene archers) in the cities of Porolissum or Tibiscum (Dacia). During their stay, these soldiers—such as Aelius Zabdibol, *custos armorum* of the *Numerus Palmyrenorum* in Tibiscum—dedicated to Palmyrene gods (*IDR* 3.1.134). Some were eventually discharged and granted Roman citizenship after completing their military service, as known from military diplomas (*CIL* XVI, 68; *IDR* 1.5; *IDR* 1.8; *IDR* 1.9). Various contingents of Palmyrenes were also present in North Africa, along the margins of the desert frontier and along strategic mountainous passes, such as Calceus Herculis (El-Kantara, Algeria), where their skills as mounted archers were appreciated and where soldiers from the *Numerus Palmyrenorum* also settled as veterans, such as Maximus Zabdibol, whose wife set up a tombstone bearing his name (*CIL* VIII, 02505 = *CIL* VIII, 18005).

Not all veterans settling away from their homelands, nor all Palmyrenes, may be considered part of a diaspora. People chose identities, and those could be complex and multiple. For D. Noy, the term 'immigrant' serves as a heuristic tool to discuss an identity (Noy 2010). Barates, a *vexillarius* (flag-bearer) at Corbridge on Hadrian's Wall, is the only Palmyrene known from Roman Britain. Another bilingual inscription on a woman's grave found at Arbeia (South Shields), one of the forts protecting the seaport on the easternmost part of Hadrian's Wall, probably also refers to him since that woman calls herself 'wife of Barates, from Palmyra' (*RIB* 1065). Did Barates wish to maintain active social ties to his homeland, or did he simply wish to identify himself by his place of origin? In Barates's case, should we not argue that he chose to present himself as an immigrant rather than a member of a diaspora group? The question, I believe, remains open.

RELIGIOUS TIES

Religious devotion to Palmyrene gods is well attested in the examples already cited, but perhaps the single most important religious diaspora community of Palmyrenes in the Roman and late Roman Mediterranean known to us is that at Beth She'arim (ancient Besara), in Palestine. In the necropolis, the presence of several generations of Palmyrenes confirms the existence of ties between the city famous for its exceptional material evidence of Jewish religious life and cited in Talmudic texts and the Mishna as seat of the Sanhedrin rabbinical council (council of seventy-one rabbis). The necropolis contains at least thirty extensive catacombs, with substantial numbers of sarcophagi, epitaphs, and graffiti. Catacomb 20 alone had 130 sarcophagi, and an estimated two hundred persons are named in the epitaphs, of which ca. 20 percent are associated with localities outside Beth She'arim (Rajak 1998, 349 and 357). The study of the epitaphs revealed the presence of people from a wide range of places, including Babylon, Mesene, Palmyra, and south Arabia (Himyar). Of these people with external ties, the Palmyrenes were by far the largest community and in all likelihood settled in the city before the fall of Zenobia and Aurelian's punitive expedition in AD 272/273 (Rajak 1998, 358). Palmyrene burials and inscriptions were found in several catacombs, although Catacomb 1 seemed to have contained the largest number of persons identifiably Palmyrene: they are represented by thirty-three surviving inscriptions found in halls C, E, and G, although the number of extant inscriptions is far less than that of the estimated burial spaces, which further highlights the problem of estimating the size of the Palmyrene community at Beth She'arim.

The largest community of Palmyrenes in Italy whose bond was through their homeland ties and devotion was in the Roman capital itself (see Chapter 18 [Equini Schneider], this volume). In Rome, several inscriptions and dedications to the gods Arsu, Astarte, Iarhibol, Aglibol, and Bēl indicate a Palmyrene community residing and worshipping in the area of Trastevere, by the temple of Sol. Their presence, tantalizingly close to the harbours, quays, and warehouses (Horrea Galbana) of Rome poses the question of the presence of a probable mercantile diaspora without entirely confirming its active mercantile trading network (contra Terpstra 2013, 152–160; Schörle 2017; see also Chapter 18 [Equini Schneider], this volume). It does confirm the presence of a strong diaspora community maintaining their social ties with Palmyra, with some members well integrated into Roman society as pointed out by Equini Schneider, and it expresses the strong wish to also show cohesion as a social group, with some dedications in the same location. A grave stela on the Via Appia indicates other Palmyrene residents within or in the vicinity of the city (*CIS* II, 3905 = *CIL* VI, 19134) and extends the possibility that other Palmyrenes living in Rome belonged to it (see Chapter 18 [Equini Schneider], this volume, for an extensive overview).

CONCLUSION

Different forms of and reasons for diasporas can be identified from the corpus of Palmyrene inscriptions. These reasons, whether institutional (military, embassy, etc.), mercantile, or religious, are complex. Veterans in the army formed new settled communities such as at El Kantara in Algeria, merchants settled in Rome, others settled at Beth She'arim and formed a family dynasty of Palmyrene rabbis. In the best-case scenarios, we can identify groups and their motivations, but, in most cases, the evidence eludes us. Nor should we forget that identities may be multiple, and Palmyrenes form no exception to the rule: for instance, Heliodorus, one of the dedicants at Rome, dedicated under different names as Iulius Aurelius Heliodorus Hadrianus in the Greek inscription and as Iarhai, son of Haliphi, son of Lisams son of Soades, in Aramaic (*IGUR* 119; on multiple identities in the city, see Moatti 2014, 149–150).

Keeping these factors in mind, perhaps we should consider ourselves fortunate that the multiple identities, the mentions of places of birth, the identifiably Palmyrene names, and the often bilingual (or trilingual) dedications enable us to identify the diasporas of Palmyrenes venturing far outside of Palmyra during the Roman imperial era more easily than other individuals in the Roman world. That dietary changes, clothing tastes, or architectural adaptation to a newly arrived Palmyrene community can be detected or even suggested as in the Eastern Desert of Egypt, remains both exemplary and an inspiration for future research potential.

ABBREVIATIONS

AÉ	*Année épigraphique*. Paris: Presses universitaires de France, 1888–.
CIL	*Corpus Inscriptionum Latinarum*. Berlin: Berlin-Brandenburgische Akademie der Wissenschaften, 1853–.
IDR	Russo, Ioan I. et al., eds. 1975–. *Inscriptiile Daciei Romane: Inscriptiones Daciae Romanae*. Bucharest: Academiei Republicii Socialiste România.
IGUR	Moretti, Luigi, ed. 1968–1990. *Inscriptiones graecae urbis Romae*. 4 vols. Rome: Istituto italiano per la storia antica.
OGIS	Dittenberger, Wilhelm, ed. 1903–1905. *Orientis Graeci inscriptiones selectae*. 2 vols. Leipzig: Hirzel.
PAT	Hillers, Delbert and Eleonora Cussini, eds. 1996. *Palmyrene Aramaic Texts*. Baltimore: Johns Hopkins University Press.

BIBLIOGRAPHY

Adams, Colin. 2007. *Land Transport in Roman Egypt: A Study of Economics and Administration in a Roman Province*. Oxford: Oxford University Press.

Andrade, Nathanael. 2013. *Syrian Identity in the Greco-Roman World*. Cambridge: Cambridge University Press.

Bingen, Jean. 1984. 'Une dédicace de marchands Palmyréniens à Coptos'. *Chroniques d'Égypte* 59: 355–358.

Bron, François. 1986. 'Palmyréniens et Chaldéens en Arabie du Sud'. *Studi epigrafici e linguistici sul Vicino Oriente antico* 3: 95–98.

Brun, Jean-Pierre. 2018. 'Chronology of the Forts of the Routes to Myos Hormos and Berenike during the Graeco-Roman Period'. In *The Eastern Desert of Egypt during the Greco-Roman Period: Archaeological Reports*, edited by Jean-Pierre Brun et al. Paris: Collège de France. https://doi.org/10.4000/books.cdf.5239.

Cussini, Eleonora. 1998. 'Review of *Palmyra: Kulturbegegnung im Grenzbereich*, by Andreas Schmidt-Colinet'. *Journal of the American Oriental Society* 118(1): 142–143.

Cuvigny, Hélène, ed. 2012. *Didymoi: Une garnison romaine dans le désert Oriental d'Égypte*. Vol. 2, *Les textes*. Cairo: Institut français d'archéologie orientale du Caire.

Delplace, Christiane, and Jacqueline Dentzer-Feydy. 2005. *L'agora de Palmyre*. Beirut: Institut français du Proche-Orient.

Dirven, Lucinda. 1998. 'The Palmyrene Diaspora in East and West: A Syrian Community in the Diaspora in the Roman World'. In *Strangers and Sojourners: Religious Communities in the Diaspora*, edited by Gerrie ter Haar, 77–93. Leuven: Peeters.

Drexhage, Raphaela. 1988. *Untersuchungen zum römischen Osthandel*. Bonn: Habelt.

Eckardt, Hella, ed. 2010. 'Roman Diasporas: Archaeological Approaches to Mobility and Diversity in the Roman Empire'. *Journal of Roman Archaeology* 78: 246.

Edwell, Peter M. 2008. *Between Rome and Persia: The Middle Euphrates, Mesopotamia and Palmyra under Roman Control*. London: Routledge.

Evers, Kasper Grønlund. 2016. 'Cave of Revelations: Indian Ocean Trade in Light of the Socotra Graffiti'. *Journal of Indian Ocean Archaeology* 10–11: 19–37.

Gawlikowski, Michał. 1988. 'Le commerce de Palmyre sur terre et sur eau'. In *L'Arabie et ses mers bordières*. Vol. 1, *Itinéraires et voisinages*, edited by Jean-François Salles, 163–172. Lyon: GS Maison de l'Orient.

Gawlikowski, Michał. 1994. 'Palmyra as a Trading Centre'. *Iraq* 56: 27–33.

Healey, John F. 1996. 'Palmyra and the Arabian Gulf Trade'. *ARAM* 8: 33–37.

Ingholt, Harald. 1932. 'Deux inscriptions bilingues de Palmyre'. *Syria* 13: 278–292.

Moatti, Claudia. 2014. 'Mobility and Identity Between the Second and the Fourth Centuries: The Cosmopolitization of the Roman Empire'. In *The City in the Classical and Post-Classical World: Changing Contexts of Power and Identity*, edited by Claudia Rapp and Harold A. Drake, 130–152. Cambridge: Cambridge University Press.

Noy, David. 2010. 'Epigraphic Evidence for Immigrants at Rome and in Roman Britain'. In *Roman Diasporas: Archaeological Approaches to Mobility and Diversity in the Roman Empire*, edited by Hella Eckardt, 13–26. Journal of Roman Archaeology, Suppl. 78. Portsmouth, RI: Journal of Roman Archaeology.

Rajak, Tessa. 1998. 'The Rabbinic Dead and the Diaspora Dead at Beth She'arim'. In *The Talmud Yerushalmi and Graeco-Roman Culture*. Vol. 1, edited by Peter Schäfer, 349–366. Tübingen: Mohr-Siebeck.

Rostovtzeff, Michael I. 1932. *Caravan Cities: Petra, Jerash, Palmyra, Dura*. Oxford: Oxford University Press.

Schörle, Katia. 2017. 'Palmyrene Merchant Networks and Economic Integration in Competitive Markets'. In *Sinews of Empire: Roman Networks in the Near East and Beyond*, edited by Håkon Fiane Teigen and Eivind Heldaas Seland, 147–154. Oxford: Oxbow.

Seland, Eivind Heldaas. 2011. 'The Persian Gulf or the Red Sea? Two Axes in Ancient Indian Ocean Trade, Where to Go and Why'. *World Archaeology* 43(3): 398–409.

Smith, Andrew M. 2013. *Roman Palmyra: Identity, Community, and State Formation*. Oxford: Oxford University Press.

Steve, Marie-Joseph. 2003. *L'Île de Khārg: Une page de l'histoire du Golfe persique et du monachisme oriental*. Neuchâtel: Recherches et publications.

Strauch, Ingo, ed. 2012. *Foreign Sailors on Socotra. The Inscriptions and Drawings from the Cave Hoq*. Bremen: Hempen Verlag.

Terpstra, T. 2013. *Trading Communities in the Roman World: A Micro-economic and Institutional Perspective*. Leiden: Brill.

Young, Gary K. 2001. *Rome's Eastern Trade: International Commerce and Imperial Policy, 31 BC–AD 305*. London: Routledge.

CHAPTER 17

PALMYRENE TRADING NETWORKS

EIVIND HELDAAS SELAND

Geopolitical Context

NEXT to her spectacular archaeological record and the tragic story of her queen, Zenobia, Palmyra's role in the world trade of the Roman period looms large among the Syrian city's claims to fame. Yet there was nothing natural or predestined about the city's commercial success. Palmyra was never on the most convenient route between the Mediterranean and the Indian Ocean (Gawlikowski 1988; Young 2001, 137–138). This is perhaps best illustrated by the fact that although the oasis was settled continually since the Neolithic period, at no time other than in the first three centuries AD was the city a centre of more than regional importance.

Palmyra's window of opportunity seems to have opened when the Euphrates became the border between the Parthian/Arsacid Empire and the crumbling Seleucid kingdom in the mid-second century AD. After the loss of Mesopotamia in 141 BC, the weakened Seleucid state allowed or was forced to accept the formation of a number of small kingdoms and principalities in the Euphrates Valley and in Syria. Several of these, such as Nabataea, Iturea, Emesa, and Oshroene, had roots in Nomadic groups in the Arabian and Syrian Deserts (Yon 2002, 140–144; Myers 2010; Sartre 2005, 12–25, 32–34; Sommer 2018a, 65–66). This also seems to be a plausible context for Palmyrene state formation and early urbanization. Moreover, on the authority of the Roman geographer Strabo (*Geo.* 16.1.27), the existence of multiple polities along the traditional trade route in the Euphrates Valley, each levying tax on passing traders, seems to have made cooperation between merchants and nomads on the more difficult desert crossing a viable alternative (Gawlikowski 1996, 139; Millar 1998, 126–127).

The earliest actual reference to Palmyra's participation in long-distance trade points to the year 41 BC, when Appian (*Bell. Civ.* 5.1.9) reports that the city was sacked by Marcus Antonius (even if the results were disappointing) due to the wealth that the

Palmyrenes had amassed by conveying Indian goods to the Roman Empire by way of Persia. The reference is considered anachronistic by many commentators and related to Appian's own time (second century AD) rather than to the first century BC (Millar 1994, 321; Hekster and Fowler 2005; Sommer 2018a, 157). That said, it is consistent with the historical context outlined above (Seland 2016d, 27). Be that as it may, by the first century AD, Palmyrene merchants were active in Middle and southern Mesopotamia, where they were permanently settled in Parthian cities and took part in civic life (Gregoratti 2010).

Until the third quarter of the third century, caravans were organized between Palmyra, Mesopotamia, and the Persian Gulf. By the first half of the second century Palmyrenes were active in the Persian Gulf and western Indian Ocean, and, from the second half of the second century, there is evidence of Palmyrene shipowners, merchants, and caravans in Egypt (Gawlikowski 1994; Seland 2016d, 34–43). There was a Palmyrene expatriate community in the imperial capital of Rome that was probably also involved in trade (Palmer 1981, 372–381; Terpstra 2013, 152–160; Chapter 16 [Schörle], this volume), whereas most epigraphic evidence of Palmyrenes in the Western Empire (Yon 2002, 270–273), including the famous tombstone of Regina, wife of Barates from Palmyra, at South Shields (Collingwood and Wright 1965, 1171, commentary), most likely relate to army service. No references exist to Palmyrene commerce or merchants after the sack of the city in AD 272/273. Absence of evidence is not evidence, and it is possible that trade continued (al-As'ad and Gawlikowski 1986–1987, 168). However, our knowledge of the later organization of Roman trade with the east, which according to a Roman–Sassanian treaty of AD 299 was restricted to Nisibis in northern Mesopotamia, leaves no place for a reduced Palmyra (Petrus Patricius, *frag.* 14 = *FGH* IV, p. 189; Seland 2016d, 86).

EVIDENCE: LITERARY SOURCES, ICONOGRAPHY, EPIGRAPHY, ARCHAEOLOGY, AND ETHNOGRAPHY

The massive scholarly interest in Palmyrene long-distance trade is not due to an abundance of data but to the fact that the existing fragmentary record from Palmyra stands out from an even more dismal source situation from other parts of the Roman world. The entire record of literary sources for Palmyrene trade consists of the above-mentioned reference in Appian and a passage of dubious value in the *Historia Augusta* (*Firmus* 3.1–3). The famous inscription known as the Tax Law of Palmyra is primarily concerned with local trade (Matthews 1984; Teixidor 1983; Shifman and Healey 2014; Chapter 14 [Healey], this volume). The rich iconographic material from Palmyra contains only five possible depictions that may be related to trading activities (Seland 2017b; Meyer and Seland 2020; Raja and Seland 2020). Archaeological evidence of trade goods, with the notable and important exception of textiles from the Valley of Tombs (Schmidt-Colinet et al. 2000), may be only indirectly connected with the city (Parlasca 1992; Seland 2016d, 29–30).

The main evidence of Palmyrene trade is a corpus of approximately thirty inscriptions, all but one of them from Palmyra itself, each explicitly or apparently relating to the operation of caravans, and another approximately thirty inscriptions dedicated by Palmyrenes who were travelling outside their native city, probably in pursuit of trade (Map 17.1).

The numbers of inscriptions are approximate because the relation to trade is not certain in all instances. Several lists of the caravan inscriptions from Palmyra have been published (Drexhage 1988; Gawlikowski 1994; Yon 2002, 263–264, 272–273), and modern editions of all texts are available (Cantineu 1930–1949; Hillers and Cussini 1996; Yon 2012), as are translations of most (Cantineu 1930–1949, Fox et al. 2005; Yon 2012; Fox and Lieu n.d.).

The caravan inscriptions were dedicated by groups of merchants, caravan leaders, and Palmyrene civic institutions in gratitude for the benevolence extended to Palmyrene caravans and merchants by named individuals, in most cases members of the Palmyrene elite. Most inscriptions are bilingual (Greek–Aramaic) and were originally accompanied by statues (mentioned, but not preserved) and displayed in the agora of Palmyra, but there are also preserved inscriptions and references to inscriptions from other locations.

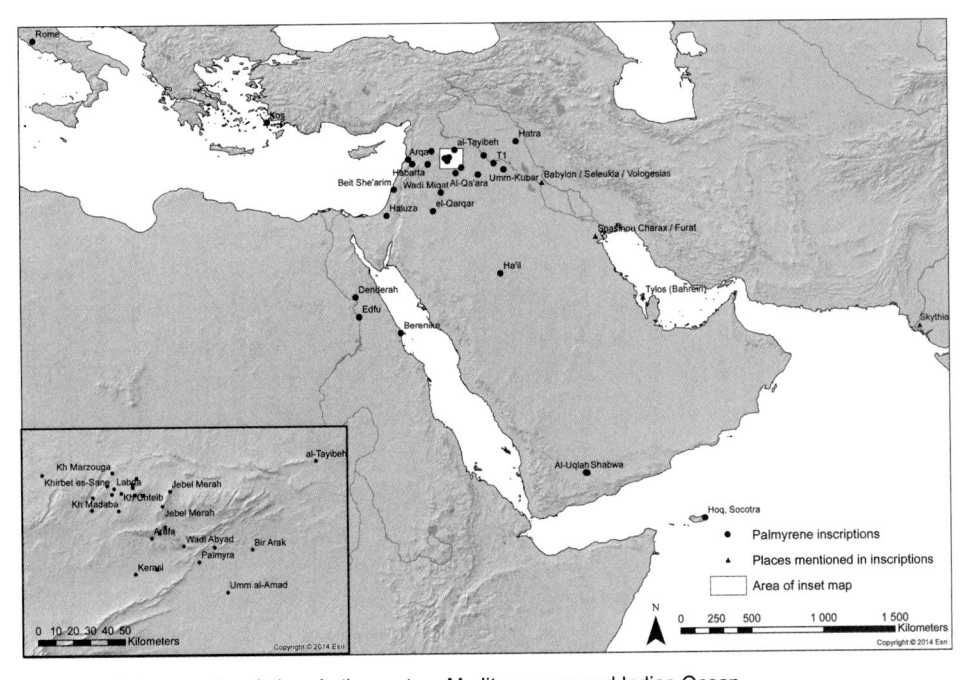

Palmyrene inscriptions in the eastern Mediterranean and Indian Ocean

MAP 17.1 Palmyrene inscriptions in the Mediterranean and Indian Ocean. Data compiled by Jørgen Christian Meyer and Eivind Heldaas Seland.

Basemap ©ESRI 2014.

The dates of many are preserved (between AD 19 and 257). Some are general with regard to the nature of the services offered. Others mention specific favours, such as military action against nomads (*PAT* 1378), payment of expenses (*PAT* 0294), or diplomatic aid (*PAT* 1414). The chronological distribution of the material has been utilized in discussions about the intensity of trade and to trace the impact of Roman–Parthian/Sassanian conflicts on trade (Teixidor 1984, 49–54; Will 1992, 63–66; Young 2001, 173–182; Sommer 2018b, 121–123). A challenge with this is that our record is likely fragmentary, that not all inscriptions are dated or contain preserved dates, and that inscriptions and statues seem to have been dedicated only when some kind of problem arose and was successfully resolved (Will 1992, 62; Young 2001, 147).

A final set of evidence for Palmyrene trade is comparative data. Roman period trade in the Red Sea and western Indian Ocean is well documented in literary and archaeological sources (Seland 2014a; 2017a; Cobb 2018). Likewise, fragmentary material from other parts of the Near East helps provide the context for Palmyrene inscriptions (Yon 2007), and ethnographic accounts of nomadism and trade in the Syrian Desert in other periods create parallels against which Palmyrene activities may be measured (Seland 2015). Geography, climate, and topography also constitute important parts of the jigsaw puzzle.

COMMODITIES

What did the Palmyrenes trade in? Actually, apart from certain textiles found in the funerary towers (Schmidt-Colinet et al. 2000), we cannot be certain, but there is good evidence of the general substance of trade between the Mediterranean and the Indian Ocean (Casson 1989). Chinese silk was traded both as cloth and as yarn. Indian cotton moved in a range of varieties and qualities (Seland 2016c). Indian and South-East Asian plant, animal, and mineral products were in demand for medicine, cosmetics, and as pigments (Casson 1989; Miller 1998). South Asia also supplied most gemstones in antiquity (Seland 2016b). From ports around the Gulf of Aden came frankincense, myrrh, and other commercially valuable resins (Groom 1981; Peacock et al. 2007). In return, glass, wine, gold, and silver from the Roman Empire were in demand in ports on the Indian Ocean rim (Casson 1989). On the evidence of the Palmyrene Tax Law, it also seems likely that there was a thriving traffic in slaves by way of Palmyra (Seland 2016d, 30–31).

CARAVANS

A *caravan* (Greek: *synodia*, Aramaic: *šyrh*) is a journey undertaken in company with others. Strength of numbers provided safety, comfort, and necessary expertise. We tend to consider a caravan to be an actual group of people, animals, and things moving from A to B, and although this was at the core of the undertaking, at the same time, a caravan was also a social organization consisting of agents pursuing a specific common goal (the journey) (Seland 2016d, 61–74).

The Palmyrene inscriptions mention either caravans or simply merchants (*emporoi/ tgr*) returning from Babylon, Vologesias, and Choumana in middle Mesopotamia, and from Spasinou Charax and Furat in southern Mesopotamia. In some cases, Palmyrene merchants from these places appear in the inscriptions without any mention of travel. One well-preserved and one very fragmentary inscription mention journeys to Skythia (at that time the Greek name for the Indus region), and some mention Palmyrenes in royal service or civic office in the kingdom of Mesene at the head of the Persian Gulf. This means that the inscriptions cover only one direction (homewards) and three segments (middle Mesopotamia, southern Mesopotamia, and the Persian Gulf) of a network that stretched at least from India to Rome. The rest has to be pieced together from the other kinds of evidence mentioned above.

In addition to occasional outsiders such as Romans, brigands, and regional client rulers, three groups of Palmyrene actors figure in the inscriptions. In most instances, the honorands are referred to by name and lineage, not by office or title, and must be considered members of the Palmyrene elite who probably drew on their pastoral resources and tribal and/or civic authority to finance, protect, equip, and staff the caravans (Will 1957; Young 2001, 135–142; Yon 2002, 100–106; 202–212; Andrade 2012; Sommer 2018a; 2018b, 195–199). The people who dedicated the inscriptions were mostly the merchants, acting as a collective. However, some inscriptions also mention named individuals with the office of *synodiarchês*—caravan leaders—and, in two late examples, *archemporoi*—head merchants. These seem to have been the people who actually managed the operation (Will 1957). Based on what we know about how magistrates were recruited in the Roman Near East and on the parallel Ottoman-period office of *caravanbashi*, these were probably senior and respected merchants who were also able to draw on lineage-based authority, but who were elected among the caravan members for the duration of a journey (Seland 2016d, 71–74).

DESERT–RIVER–SEA

Palmyra was a desert city, and the operation of caravans across the Syrian Desert was at the core and probably also the beginning of Palmyrene commercial activities. However, it has long been acknowledged that Palmyrene trade was not primarily a part of the Eurasian overland networks later to be known as the Silk Road, but instead a link between the maritime networks of the Indian Ocean and the Mediterranean (Seyrig 1936; Gawlikowski 1988; Healey 1996). Also, the Syrian Desert is skirted by one of the world's largest rivers, the Euphrates. An inscription from the colonnaded street of Palmyra reveals the existence of a guild of floating-skin makers (*askonautopoioi*)

(*IGLS* XVII.1, 59). This led to the realization that outbound Palmyrene caravans in all likelihood travelled partly by the rivercraft known in modern times as *kellek* (Seyrig 1963; Gawlikowski 1983; 1988; Rollinger and Ruffing 2013; Seland 2016d, 71–74; Meyer and Seland 2020). Last, inscriptions mentioning Palmyrene shipowners in the Persian Gulf (*PAT* 1403, 2763) and the existence of an association of Palmyrene shipowners (*naukleroi*) in Egypt (*I. Portes* 102) show that Palmyrenes were also actually sailing to destinations in the western Indian Ocean in pursuit of trade.

Caravans were major operations and were probably organized annually (Teixidor 1984, 16). Ancient seafaring in the Indian Ocean and the Mediterranean, as well as nomadic movement in the Syrian Desert and navigation on the Euphrates, were subject to strict seasonality. Smooth operation of Palmyrene caravan trade had to take all this into account. Drawing on ancient sources, ethnographic reports, and climate data allows us to reconstruct a tentative schedule of Palmyrene trade (Seland 2016d, 45–61): caravans would leave Palmyra in high summer, when camels were at their summer pastures in the northern Syrian Desert, providing access to animals and handlers. Transferring to rafts at the river port of Hit, they would reach ports in southern Mesopotamia in about a month. A maritime journey lasting approximately another month would take them to Indian ports, which, in any case, could not be approached before September due to the summer (SW) monsoon. Return from India with the north-east monsoon was feasible between October and March. At this time camels were at their winter pastures not far from the Persian Gulf, so pack animals were available. Another month-long overland journey would bring the caravan home to Palmyra; leaving ample time for practicalities and red tape, this probably happened in early spring.

The inscriptions are silent on what happened after the caravans reached Palmyra. Most commentators have assumed that the bulk of the goods imported from the East were destined for Mediterranean markets. From Palmyra goods would be transported eastwards, either the shortest way to Homs and from there through the Homs Gap to Aradus (Tartous) (Seyrig 1970, 89), or, in parallel to the situation in Egypt, to the provincial capital of Antioch for the collection of the special 25 percent tax levied on Indian Ocean imports (Young 2001, 148–149, 193; Seland 2008). Against this it has also been proposed that the main market for imports by way of Palmyra was Syria itself (Gawlikowski 2016), which, if correct, would render this problem less relevant.

Palmyrene maritime trade also took place by way of the Red Sea. It has been suggested that the extension of Palmyrene activities came as a response to the Roman–Sassanian wars of the mid-third century AD (Young 2001, 173–182). While this might have accelerated the process, important evidence from Egypt, including an inscription mentioning a clubhouse of Palmyrene Red Sea shipowners and merchants in Koptos, predate the Sassanian takeover (*I. Portes* 102; Bingen 1984). If trade across the Syrian Desert catered primarily for regional needs (Gawlikowski 2016), the Red Sea route would enable Palmyrenes to also tap into other Mediterranean markets. Alternatively, a rationale for trading by both the Red Sea and overland through Syria may be found in the different climate-imposed schedules along the two routes, which led to goods arriving by way of Syria and Palmyra being available at Mediterranean ports at different times of the year

(Seland 2011). In any case, the extension of Palmyrene activities to Egypt, the Red Sea, and into the western Indian Ocean, and the probable presence of Palmyrene merchants in Rome, reveals an ability and eagerness to engage in the wider commercial networks of the period (Schörle 2017; Cobb 2020).

Cooperation with Nomads, Protection of Routes

The caravan route to the Euphrates and the Persian Gulf would pass through territory with no permanent habitation and extremely limited access to water. However, the desert south of Palmyra was not uninhabited. The immediate hinterland of Palmyra, south of Wadi el-Miyeh, ca. 150 km south-east of Palmyra, enjoyed comparably ample access to water and was probably used by semi-nomadic groups that herded goats and sheep (Tucker 2009; Meyer and Seland 2016). Drawing on ethnographic parallels from the nineteenth and twentieth centuries and on Rowton's studies of sheep nomadism in late Bronze Age Mari, these groups would spend parts of the year in or near the city, and some members of the group would live there permanently while others followed the herds (Wirth 1969; Rowton 1973a, 1973b; Prag 1985). This is probably the rural population referred to as exempt from taxation in the tariff inscription (*PAT* 0259).

South of the present border between Syria and Iraq, water was extremely scarce outside the rainy season, with reliable wells being up to 150 km apart (Meyer and Seland 2016; Chapter 2 [Seland], this volume). The primary inhabitants of these regions would have been camel-pastoralists. These would also spend parts of the year in the northern or western Syrian Desert, for instance in the territory of Palmyra, but their stays in or near the city would be of shorter duration, and their annual cycle of transhumance considerably longer. Wells along this section of the route between Palmyra and Hit are associated with fortifications of uncertain date. Palmyrene inscriptions reveal that this region was also utilized by people from Palmyra, although whether for pasture, trade, military purposes, or even irrigated agriculture is not certain (Meyer and Seland 2016).

Two models have been used to describe Palmyrene involvement in the southern desert. The oldest and perhaps more widespread is that of the desert police, a corps of mounted Palmyrene soldiers patrolling the southern desert, maintaining guard posts, and keeping the caravans safe (e.g., Rostovtzeff 1932c, 807–808; Young 2001, 148; Yon 2002, 112–118). However, as has been pointed out, there is no positive evidence for the existence of such a force (Will 1992, 55; Sommer 2016), and the notion may have been inspired by the use of Arab camel cavalry forces under European command to police the desert in Syria and Transjordan during the mandate period (Sommer 2016, 13). The alternative is a mode of operation where protection for caravans was organized on an ad hoc basis (Seland 2016d, 69–70) and where territorial control in the deep desert was organized along tribal/traditional rather than civic/governmental lines (Sommer 2016). In either case, it is clear from the inscriptional record that protection and, at least occasionally, actual use of force were necessary.

THE PALMYRENE TRADING NETWORK

Trade in the ancient world depended on a social infrastructure that could overcome the otherwise prohibitive transaction costs imposed by structural restraints such as transport costs, cultural differences, predatory authorities, lack of legal and physical security, and scarcity of information (Bang 2008, 131–201). Arguably, the success of Palmyrene merchants stemmed from their ability to form strong social networks among themselves while remaining open to other groups.

The Palmyrene epigraphic record reveals not only that people from the city moved around, lived in, and traded in other parts of the world, but also outlines a Palmyrene diaspora that existed over generations, with a continued orientation towards their homeland. This is most evident in Mesopotamia, Egypt, and, in all likelihood, Rome, where we find communities identifying themselves as Palmyrenes and acting as collectives (Chapter 16 [Schörle], this volume). Also, further afield, Palmyrenes continued to identify as such through their script and reference to their gods and homeland (Seland 2016d, 77–84). The Palmyrene network was based on ethnicity in the sense that membership was decided by birth and that they maintained boundaries with respect to other groups, thus preserving a Palmyrene identity. Shared ties of language, religion, perceived ancestry, and civic and tribal institutions created social cohesion and facilitated trust within the network (Seland 2013). This proven 'business model' is well attested from better-documented cases, such as the medieval Jewish network known from the papers of the Cairo Geniza (Margariti 2007; Goitein and Friedman 2008) and the early modern Armenian trade network centred on New Julfa, in Iran (Aslanian 2011).

Strong social cohesion was only part of the key to Palmyrene success. For reasons unknown, Palmyrenes decided to maintain and highlight their own identity while also joining other social networks, such as the Roman army or the civic structure and royal bureaucracy of the Parthian client-kingdom of Mesene (Seland 2016a). In this way, they were able to combine internal trust with the ability to act as cross-cultural brokers that was necessary for success in premodern, long-distance trade (Curtin 1984). This also explains how the inhabitants of Palmyra were able to trade with the Parthian and Sassanian empires with little apparent friction, even in times when these were at war with Rome. Palmyra was a Roman city, no doubt, but the Palmyrenes living and working in the Parthian Empire were not Roman merchants abroad, following the sometimes invoked, but arguably anachronistic, model of early modern factories, *fondouks* or *comptoirs* (Rostovtzeff 1932a, 143–145; Teixidor 1984, 47–49; Gregoratti 2015). Rather, they belonged to Palmyrene local communities that had integrated with other local communities over generations.

THE CARAVAN CITY

The first discussion of Palmyrene caravan trade occurs in William Halifax's report of his visit to Palmyra in 1691. Relevant inscriptions known at that time were published by Waddington (1870), and Palmyra's reliance on caravan trade was already established by Theodor Mommsen (1904, 428–429). With the French Mandate, systematic excavations started, and going to Palmyra became less of an adventure. After visiting the city in 1928, the Russian-American scholar Mikhail Rostovtzeff published three extremely influential texts: a popular travelogue forever lending Palmyra the epithet of 'caravan city', a study of the caravan inscriptions establishing them as a kind of corpus, and a discussion of so-called caravan gods (Rostovtzeff 1932a, 1932b, 1932c). Rostovtzeff, following Mommsen's lead, saw the honorands of the caravan inscriptions as commercial magnates or even merchant-princes who were the real rulers of the city and who owed their fortunes and their positions to their trading activities (Rostovtzeff 1932c).

Several dedicated studies of Palmyrene trade have been made (Teixidor 1984; Drexhage 1988; Young 2001, 123–168; Grout 2016; Seland 2016d), and comprehensive reconstructions also exist as parts of more general works on Palmyrene society (Yon 2002; Andrade 2013; Sommer 2018a; 2018b). Questions of commodities, routes, and practicalities have been subject to numerous case studies. However, a main point of contention has been the role of the Palmyrene elite in the organization of trade, and vice versa, the role of trade in the civic life of the city.

It was Ernest Will who recognized the distinction between merchants, caravan leaders, and patrons described above. In his view, the caravan leaders were the technical experts who coordinated the rather complex operation of the caravan, which, apart from merchants and commodities, needed large numbers of animals, handlers, guides, and guards. The honorands of the inscriptions belonged to Palmyra's traditional elite. Will explicitly compares them with modern tribal leaders (sheikhs). With large pastoral holdings in the mountains north of Palmyra, tribal authority spanning from the city and deep into the desert, and good connections on both sides of the imperial borders, these notables not only supplied animals and manpower, but also used their influence and authority to assist the caravans in extraordinary situations, taking on the role of caravan protectors (Will 1957).

Will's model is a scholarly masterpiece. It introduces a consistent reading to the entire corpus of inscriptions, which integrates the civic world of the Hellenistic *polis* with the tribal universe of the Syrian steppe and the epigraphic sources with the ethnographic record. Moreover, although this has hardly been explicitly addressed in the scholarly debate and was most likely not on Will's agenda, it reconciled the evidence of large-scale trade and elite involvement in commercial activities with the substantivist/primitivist model of the ancient economy that was revived with Karl Polanyi's *Trade and Markets in Early Empires*, which appeared the same year (Polanyi et al. 1957) and gained traction with Moses Finley's *Ancient Economy* (1973): Palmyra's elite may well have profited from involvement in trade, but their status, self-perception, and wealth were based primarily on agricultural and pastoral holdings as well as on traditional/tribal authority. Palmyrene merchants were probably men of low status, as in other parts of the ancient world. This is perhaps most evident in Gary Young's interpretation of elite benevolence towards merchants as general acts of *euergetism*, in line with elite generosity in other cities of the Roman East, rather than as active involvement in trade (2001, 123–168).

Although the idea of a commercial aristocracy in Palmyra is alive (Drexhage 1988, 116–118; Gregoratti 2015), most subsequent scholarship has accepted Will's model, with some qualifications. It has become clear that the caravan leaders were not the mere technical subordinates he envisioned but that they could be men of considerable status and influence (Yon 1998). Commentators weigh the balance between tribal/traditional (Seland 2014b; Sommer 2018a; 2018b, 96–98, 199–201) and civic (Yon 2002; Andrade 2012; 2013; Seland 2016d) authority differently but acknowledge the importance of both. Recently Grout (2016) and Gregoratti (2020) have raised the issue of the role of temples and sanctuaries in the organization of Palmyrene trade, adding a new dimension to the debate.

Conclusion

As stated in the introduction, Palmyra was not predestined to become an important centre of trade. It was favourable geopolitical conditions and Palmyrene agency that created this success story. Save, perhaps, for the Red Sea/Indian Ocean trade of which Palmyrene merchants were also part and for which the archaeological evidence is more ample, Palmyrene trade is the best-documented case of long-distance commerce in Graeco-Roman antiquity. The combination of a unique epigraphic corpus that provides glimpses into the actual operation of long-distance caravan trade and the fragmentary and limited nature of this evidence renders any reconstruction of Palmyrene long-distance trade reliant on comparative evidence and theoretical assumptions, even if these more often remain implicit. This has stimulated vibrant scholarly debate, especially with regard to elite involvement, which has relevance far beyond the study of Palmyra.

Bibliography

al-As‘ad, Khaled, and Michał Gawlikowski. 1986–1987. 'New Honorific Inscriptions in the Great Colonnade of Palmyra'. *Annales archéologiques arabes syriennes* 36–37: 164–171.
Andrade, Nathanael J. 2012. 'Inscribing the Citizen: Soados and the Civic Context of Palmyra'. *MAARAV* 19(1–2): 65–90.
Andrade, Nathanael J. 2013. *Syrian Identity in the Greco-Roman World*. Cambridge: Cambridge University Press.
Aslanian, Sebouh David. 2011. *From the Indian Ocean to the Mediterranean: The Global Trade Networks of Armenian Merchants from New Julfa*. Berkeley: University of California Press.

Bang, Peter Fibiger. 2008. *The Roman Bazaar: A Comparative Study of Trade and Markets in a Tributary Empire*. Cambridge: Cambridge University Press.

Bingen, Jean. 1984. 'Une Dédicace de Marchands Palmyréniens à Coptos'. *Chronique D'Égypte* 59: 355–358.

Cantineau, Jean, Jean Starcky, and Michał Gawlikowski, eds. 1930–1949. *Inventaire des inscriptions de Palmyre*. 11 vols. Beirut: Imprimerie catholique.

Casson, Lionel. 1989. *The Periplus Maris Erythraei*. Princeton, NJ: Princeton University Press.

Cobb, Matthew Adam. 2018. *Rome and the Indian Ocean Trade from Augustus to the Early Third Century CE*. Leiden: Brill.

Cobb, Matthew Adam. 2020. 'Palmyrene Merchants and the Red Sea Trade'. In *Inter duo imperia: Palmyra between East and West*, edited by Michael Sommer, 65–83. Stuttgart: Steiner.

Collingwood, Robin G., and Richard P. Wright, eds. 1965. *The Roman Inscriptions of Britain*. Oxford: Clarendon Press.

Curtin, Philip D. 1984. *Cross Cultural Trade in World History*. Cambridge: Cambridge University Press.

Drexhage, Raphaela. 1988. *Untersuchungen zum Römischen Osthandel*. Bonn: Habelt.

Finley, Moses I. 1973. *The Ancient Economy*. Oakland, CA: University of California Press.

Fox, Greg, and Sam Lieu, eds. n.d. *Inscriptiones palmyrenae selectae ad commercium pertinentes. Select Palmyrene Inscriptions on Commerce*. http://www.mq.edu.au/__data/assets/pdf_file/0018/24525/106178.pdf. Accessed 24 February 2022.

Fox, Greg, Sam Lieu, and Norman Ricklefs. 2005. 'Select Palmyrene Inscriptions'. In *From Palmyra to Zayton: Epigraphy and Iconography*, edited by Ian Gardner, Samuel Lieu, and Ken Parry, 27–126. Turnhout: Brepols.

Gawlikowski, Michał. 1983. 'Palmyre et l'Euphrate'. *Syria* 60(1/2): 53–68.

Gawlikowski, Michał. 1988. 'Le commerce de Palmyre sur terre et sur eau'. In *L'Arabie et ses mers bordieres*. Vol. 1, *Itineraires et voisinages*, edited by Jean-François Salles, 163–172. Travaux de la Maison de l'Orient 16. Lyon: GS-Maison de l'Orient.

Gawlikowski, Michał. 1994. 'Palmyra as a Trading Centre'. *Iraq* 56: 27–33.

Gawlikowski, Michał. 1996. 'Palmyra and Its Caravan Trade'. *Les annales archeologiques Arabes Syriennes* 42: 139–144.

Gawlikowski, Michał. 2016. 'Trade Across Frontiers. Foreign Relations of a Caravan City'. In *Palmyrena: City, Hinterland, and Caravan Trade Between Occident and Orient*, edited by Jørgen Christian Meyer, Nils Anfinset, and Eivind Heldaas Seland, 19–28. Oxford: Archaeopress.

Goitein, Shelomo Dov and Mordechai Akiva Friedman. 2008. *India Traders of the Middle Ages: Documents from the Cairo Geniza ('India Book')*. Études sur le judaïsme médiéval. Leiden: Brill.

Gregoratti, Leonardo. 2010. 'The Palmyrenes and the Arsacid Policy'. In *Voprosy Epigrafiki: Sbornik statei (Problems of Epigraphy: Collected Articles): Vypusk 4; Russkii fond Sodeistviia obrazovaniiu i nauke, 4, 2010, 21–37*, edited by Aleksandr G. Avdeev, 21–37. Moscow: Russkij Fond Sodejstvija Obrazovaniju i Nauke.

Gregoratti, Leonardo. 2015. 'The Palmyrene Trade Lords and the Protection of the Caravans'. *ARAM* 27: 157–166.

Gregoratti, Leonardo. 2020. 'Temples and Traders in Palmyra'. In *Capital, Investment, and Innovation in the Roman World*, edited by Paul Erdkamp, Koenraad Verboven, and Arjan Zuiderhoek, 461–480. Oxford: Oxford University Press.

Groom, Nigel. 1981. *Frankincense and Myrrh: A Study of the Arabian Incense Trade*. London: Longman.

Grout, J. B. 2016. 'The Role of Palmyrene Temples in Long-Distance Trade in the Roman Near East'. Unpublished doctoral thesis, University of London.

Healey, John F. 1996. 'Palmyra and the Arabian Gulf Trade'. *ARAM* 8: 33–37.

Hekster, Olivier, and Richard Fowler. 2005. *Imaginary Kings: Royal Images in the Ancient Near East, Greece and Rome*. Stuttgart: Steiner.

Hillers, Delbert R., and Eleonora Cussini, eds. 1996. *Palmyrene Aramaic Texts*. Publications of the Comprehensive Aramaic Lexicon Project. Baltimore: Johns Hopkins University Press.

Margariti, Roxani Eleni. 2007. *Aden & the Indian Ocean Trade: 150 Years in the Life of a Medieval Arabian Port, Islamic Civilization and Muslim Networks*. Chapel Hill, NC: University of North Carolina Press.

Matthews, John F. 1984. 'The Tax Law of Palmyra: Evidence for Economic History in a City of the Roman East'. *Journal of Roman Studies* 74: 157–180.

Meyer, Jørgen Christian, and Eivind Heldaas Seland. 2016. 'Palmyra and the Trade Route to the Euphrates'. *ARAM* 28: 497–523.

Meyer, Jørgen Christian, and Eivind Heldaas Seland. 2020. 'A Raft, a Ship and a Lighthouse in the Desert Fluvial and Maritime Graffiti from Ancient Palmyra'. *Syria* 97: 305–314.

Meyer, Jørgen Christian, and Eivind Heldaas Seland, addendum Omar al-As'ad and Andreas Schmidt-Colinet. 2020. 'A Raft, a Ship and a Lighthouse in the Desert: Fluvial and Maritime Graffiti from Ancient Palmyra'. *Syria* 97: 305–314.

Millar, Fergus. 1994. *The Roman Near East, 31 BC–AD 337*. Cambridge, MA: Harvard University Press.

Millar, Fergus. 1998. 'Caravan Cities: The Roman Near East and Long Distance Trade by Land'. In *Modus operandi: Essays in Honor of Geoffrey Rickman*, edited by Michel Austin, Jill Harries, and Christopher Smith, 119–137. London: Institute of Classical Studies, School of Advanced Study, University of London.

Miller, James Innes. 1998. *The Spice Trade of the Roman Empire, 29 B.C.–A.D. 641*. Oxford: Oxford University Press. Original edition, 1969.

Mommsen, Theodor. 1904. *Römische Geschichte*. Vol. 5, *Die Provinzen von Caesar bis Diocletian*. Berlin: Weidmann. Original edition, 1885.

Myers, Elaine Anne. 2010. *The Ituraeans and the Roman Near East: Reassessing the Sources*. Society for New Testament Studies Monograph Series 147. Cambridge: Cambridge University Press.

Palmer, Robert E. A. 1981. 'The Topography and Social History of Rome's Trastevere (Southern Sector)'. *Proceedings of the American Philosophical Society* 125(5): 368–397. doi:10.2307/986199.

Parlasca, Klaus. 1992. 'Auswärtige Beziehungen Palmyras im Lichte archäologischer Funde'. *Damaszener Mitteilungen* 6: 257–265.

Peacock, David, David F. Williams, and Sarah James, eds. 2007. *Food for the Gods: New Light on the Ancient Incense Trade*. Oxford: Oxbow.

Polanyi, Karl, Conrad M. Arensberg, and Harry W. Pearson, eds. 1957. *Trade and Markets in Early Empires*. New York: Free Press.

Prag, Kay. 1985. 'Ancient and Modern Pastoral Migration in the Levant'. *Levant* 17: 81–88.

Raja, Rubina and Eivind Heldaas Seland. 2020. 'Horses and Camels in Palmyrene Art: Iconography, Contexts and Meanings'. *Zeitschrift Für Orient-Archäologie* 13: 300–344.

Rollinger, Robert, and Kai Ruffing. 2013. 'Schlauchflöße und Schwimmschläuche an Euphrat und Tigris in der römischen Kaiserzeit'. In *Calamus: Festschrift für Herbert Graßl zum 65.*

Geburtstag, edited by Rupert Breitwieser, Monika Frass, and Georg Nightingale, 403–418. Wiesbaden: Harrassowitz.

Rostovtzeff, Michael I. 1932a. *Caravan Cities: Petra, Jerash, Palmyra, Dura*. Oxford: Clarendon Press.

Rostovtzeff, Michael I. 1932b. 'The Caravan Gods of Palmyra'. *Journal of Roman Studies* 22(1): 107–116.

Rostovtzeff, Michael I. 1932c. 'Les inscriptions caravanières de Palmyre'. In *Mélanges Gustave Glotz*, edited by Gustave Glotz, 793–811. Paris: Les presses universitaires de France.

Rowton, Michael B. 1973a. 'Autonomy and Nomadism in Western Asia'. *Orientalia* 42(1): 247–258.

Rowton, Michael B. 1973b. 'Urban Autonomy in a Nomadic Environment'. *Journal of Near Eastern Studies*: 201–215.

Sartre, Maurice. 2005. *The Middle East Under Rome*. Cambridge, MA: Harvard University Press.

Schörle, Katia. 2017. 'Palmyrene Merchant Networks and Economic Integration in Competitive Markets. ' In *Sinews of Empire: Networks in the Roman Near East and Beyond*, edited by Håkon Fiane Teigen and Eivind Heldaas Seland, 147–154. Oxford: Oxbow.

Schmidt-Colinet, Andreas, Annemarie Stauffer, and Khaled al-As'ad, eds. 2000. *Die Textilien aus Palmyra: Neue und alte Funde*. Damaszener Forschungen 8. Mainz: von Zabern.

Seland, Eivind Heldaas. 2008. 'Trade Routes of Palmyra, with Special Notes on Western Routes in the Palmyrene Trade'. In *Jebel Bishri in Context*, edited by Minna Lönnqvist, 89–97. Oxford: Archaeopress.

Seland, Eivind Heldaas. 2011. 'The Persian Gulf or the Red Sea? Two Axes in Ancient Indian Ocean Trade, Where to Go and Why'. *World Archaeology* 43(3): 398–409. doi:10.1080/00438243.2011.605844.

Seland, Eivind Heldaas. 2013. 'Networks and Social Cohesion in Ancient Indian Ocean Trade: Geography, Ethnicity, Religion'. *Journal of Global History* 8(3): 373–390. doi:10.1017/S1740022813000338.

Seland, Eivind Heldaas. 2014a. 'Archaeology of Trade in the Western Indian Ocean, 300 BC–AD 700'. *Journal of Archaeological Research* 22(4): 367–406. doi:10.1007/s10814-014-9075-7.

Seland, Eivind Heldaas. 2014b. 'The Organisation of the Palmyrene Caravan Trade'. *Ancient West and East* 13: 197–211. doi:10.2143/AWE.13.0.3038738.

Seland, Eivind Heldaas. 2015. 'Camels, Camel Nomadism, and the Practicalities of Palmyrene Caravan Trade'. *ARAM* 27: 45–53.

Seland, Eivind Heldaas. 2016a. 'Ancient Trading Networks and New Institutional Economics: The Case of Palmyra'. In *Antike Wirtschaft und ihre kulturelle Prägung*, edited by Kerstin Droß-Krüpe, Sabine Föllinger, and Kai Ruffing, 223–234. Wiesbaden: Harrassowitz.

Seland, Eivind Heldaas. 2016b. 'Gemstones and Minerals in the Red Sea/Indian Ocean Trade of the First Millennium'. In *Gemstones in the First Millennium AD: Mines, Trade, Workshops and Symbolism*, edited by Susanne Greiff, Alexandra Hilgner, and Dieter Quast, 45–58. Mainz: Verlag des Römisch-Germanischen Zentralmuseums.

Seland, Eivind Heldaas. 2016c. 'Here, There and Everywhere: A Network Approach to Textile Trade in the Periplus Maris Erythraei'. In *Textiles, Trade and Theories: From the Ancient Near East to the Mediterranean*, edited by Kerstin Dross-Krüpe and Marie-Louise Nosch, 211–220. Münster: Ugarit-Verlag.

Seland, Eivind Heldaas. 2016d. *Ships of the Desert and Ships of the Sea: Palmyra in the World Trade of the First Three Centuries CE*. Wiesbaden: Harrassowitz.

Seland, Eivind Heldaas. 2017a. 'The Archaeological Record of Indian Ocean Engagements in the Red Sea'. In *Oxford Handbooks Online*. Oxford: Oxford University Press. doi:10.1093/oxfordhb/9780199935413.013.51.

Seland, Eivind Heldaas. 2017b. 'The Iconography of Caravan Trade in Palmyra and the Roman Near East'. In *Position and Profession in Palmyra*, edited by Anette H. Sørensen and Tracey Reeves, 106–114. Copenhagen: Det Kongelige Danske Videnskabernes Selskab.

Seyrig, Henri. 1936. 'Inscription relative au commerce maritime de Palmyre'. *Annuaire de l'Institut de philologie et d'histoire* 4: 397–402.

Seyrig, Henri. 1963. 'Les fils du roi Odainat'. *Annales archéologiques de Syrie* 13: 159–172.

Seyrig, Henri. 1970. 'Antiquités syriennes'. *Syria* 47(1/2): 77–116. doi:10.2307/4390577.

Shifman, Il'ia Sholemoivich and John F. Healey. 2014. *The Palmyrene Tax Tariff*. Oxford: Oxford University Press.

Sommer, Michael. 2016. 'The Venice of the Sands: Palmyrene Trade Revisited'. In *Palmyrena: City, Hinterland, and Caravan Trade between Occident and Orient*, edited by Jørgen Christian Meyer, Nils Anfinset, and Eivind Heldaas Seland, 11–17. Oxford: Archaeopress.

Sommer, Michael. 2018a. *Roms orientalische Steppengrenze: Palmyra, Edessa, Dura-Europos, Hatra; Eine Kulturgeschichte von Pompeius bis Diocletian*. Oriens et Occidens. Stuttgart: Steiner. Original edition 2005.

Sommer, Michael. 2018b. *Palmyra: A History*. New York: Routledge.

Teixidor, Javier. 1983. 'Le tarif de Palmyre I: Un commentaire de la version palmyrénienne'. *Aula Orientalis* 1: 235–252.

Teixidor, Javier. 1984. 'Un port romain du désert: Palmyre et son commerce d'Auguste à Caracalla'. *Semitica* 34: 1–127.

Terpstra, Taco T. 2013. *Trading Communities in the Roman World: A Micro-Economic and Institutional Perspective*. Leiden: Brill.

Tucker, David. 2009. 'Tracking Mobility in the Syrian Desert. Potential of Simple Features for Mapping Landscapes of Mobile Pastoralists'. *Computer Applications to Archaeology 2009: Online Proceedings Computer Applications to Archaeology 2009 Williamsburg, Virginia, USA. March 22–26, 2009.* http://archive.caaconference.org/2009/PapersProceedings.cfm.html.

Waddington, William Henry. 1870. *Inscriptions grecques et latines de la Syrie Recueillies et expliquées par W. H. Waddington*. Paris: Didot.

Will, Ernest. 1957. 'Marchands et chefs de caravanes à Palmyre'. *Syria* 34: 262–277.

Will, Ernest. 1992. *Les palmyréniens: La Venise des sables (Ier siècle avant – IIIème siècle aprè J.-C.)*. Paris: Armand Colin.

Wirth, Eugen. 1969. 'Das Problem der Nomaden im heutigen Orient'. *Geographische Rundschau* 21: 41–51.

Yon, Jean-Baptiste. 1998. 'Remarques sur une famille caravanière à Palmyre'. *Syria* 75: 153–160.

Yon, Jean-Baptiste. 2002. *Les notables de Palmyre*. Beirut: Institut français d'archéologie du Proche-Orient.

Yon, Jean-Baptiste. 2007. 'Les commerçants du Proche-Orient: Désignation et vocabulaire'. In *Vocabulaire et expression de l'économie dans le monde antique*, edited by Jean Andreau and Véronique Chanowski, 51–87. Bordeaux: Ausonius.

Yon, Jean-Baptiste, ed. 2012. *Inscriptions grecques et latines de la Syrie*. Vol. 1, *Palmyre*. Beirut: Institut français du Proche-Orient.

Young, Gary K. 2001. *Rome's Eastern Trade: International Commerce and Imperial Policy, 31 BC–AD 305*. London: Routledge.

CHAPTER 18

PALMYRENES IN ROME

EUGENIA EQUINI SCHNEIDER

PALMYRENE COMMUNITY IN ROME

THE existence of a Palmyrene community in Rome—particularly active during the second and third centuries AD, but present by the first century AD—is extensively attested by the epigraphic evidence and various well-known sculptural monuments. It is commonly accepted that religious worship, and probably part of the community's civic life, were concentrated in regio XIV Transtiberim, outside of today's Porta Portese and to the right of Via Portuense, in the area of Vigna Bonelli-Mangani: the archaeological evidence excavated on the eastern slopes of the Janiculum Hill during the nineteenth century came from here, as did many archaeological finds gathered since the fifteenth century, held by the collection of the Orti Mattei in Trastevere (Visconti 1860, 415–450; Lanciani 1901, 112). The excavations unearthed brick and *opus reticulatum* structures of uncertain and debated significance, seal-bricks from the Pontianus and Atilianus consulships (AD 135), reliefs and inscribed slabs, iconographic and epigraphic evidence of the presence of cults, and votive artefacts dedicated to the Palmyrene deities in this area of Rome.

Trastevere had a high concentration of slaves attached to its warehouses and to the merchants from the eastern part of the empire since the first century AD, when Ostia became an important centre for commercial traffic and the shipowners and the *negotiatores* brought their goods to the great port of Rome. Juvenal's well-known quotation (*Satyrae* 3.62–65), 'Iam pridem Syrus in Tiberim defluxit Orontes et linguam et mores' is strong evidence of the presence of Syrians in the capital, with their own institutions for preserving their language and customs.

The spread of Syrian cults in Rome is linked to the intensive commercial relations between Syria and Rome during the imperial period (most recently, Terpstra 2016, 39–48), and to the large influx of slaves destined for urban service and also engaged in activities connected to the port facilities.

ARCHAEOLOGICAL DOCUMENTATION

Two well-known dedicatory inscriptions found in Vigna Bonelli-Mangani, objects of intensive and ongoing study even today (Chausson 1995, 661–705; Fowlkes-Childs 2016, 195–196 with bibliography), attest to the existence of a temple in this area, one dedicated to the god Bēl and to Palmyrene divinities: a marble fragment with a bilingual Latin–Greek inscription (*CIL* VI, 50; *ILS* 4334; *IGUR* 117; *IG* XIV, 969; *IGR* I, 43), and the fragment of a relief in Luni marble—therefore produced in Rome—of which only the lower left side has been preserved, dedicated in Greek/Palmyrene by Palmyrenes residing in the city. Both are currently exhibited at the Capitoline Museums. The first fragment is an inscription dedicating a sacred building, and the Latin and Greek versions complement each other: of the Latin text it is possible to read the initial official formula, *pro salute imp* [——], the incomplete name of the first dedicator, 'C. Licinius N [—.]', and 'Palmyrenus', indicating the ethnicity of the second dedicator. The name of the latter, 'Heliodoros', and the reason for the dedication, the consecration of a naos to the god Bēl, appear in the Greek version. This same text appears in another bilingual Latin–Greek epigraph preserved by the British Museum, and it is reasonable to believe that the provenance of both is Vigna Bonelli-Mangani (*CIL* VI, 51; *IGUR* 118; *IG* XIV, 970; *IGR* I, 44). Although the inscription is very fragmented, there is no doubt about the identity of the dedicators or the reason for the dedication, which is addressed to the god Bēl in the Latin text and to Malakbel in the Greek one. The reference to the Roman emperor appears in the Latin inscriptions only, which precedes the Greek inscriptions in both instances (Adams 2003, 249).

Although in the two above-mentioned fragments only Heliodoros is clearly identified as a Palmyrene, in Hadrian's era, the *gentilicium* 'Licinius' is attested four times at Palmyra, in relation to a C. Licinius Flavianus Burrhi f(ilius), Sergia, Malichus, a prominent member of the priestly class, president of the *thiasos* of the god Bēl, and with the acquired right to Roman citizenship. In fact, Hadrian belonged to the Sergia tribe, in which the emperor registered the Palmyrenes who had been granted Roman citizenship during his visit to the city in AD 129. Therefore, we cannot exclude the possibility that the Licinius to whom we owe the consecration of the temple in Rome came from this same high-ranking Palmyrene family (Equini Schneider 1987, 71–72; 2001, 217–219). *Communis opinio* is that, in both inscriptions, the name 'Bēl' was followed by those of other Palmyrene gods or, more generally, by the expression 'et diis Palmyrae'.

It is interesting to note that the *gentilicium* 'Licinius' appears on an altar with a Greek dedication to Ares Patroos, found in Vigna Bonelli-Mangani, presently held by the Museo Nazionale Romano (*IG* XIV, 962; *IGR* I, 33; *IGUR* 122). In this inscription, Ares is to be identified with Arṣû, the god of the Palmyrene pantheon whose temple in Palmyra was one of the four sanctuaries dedicated to the *Dii Patrii*. The altar was dedicated to the well-being of Emperor Hadrian, by a Λούκιος Λικίνιος Ἑρμίας in the month of Xantico in the year 445 of the Seleucid era (April AD 134), a date that must be not long from that of the temple's construction (Fowlkes-Childs 2016, 200–201, with previous bibliography).

The Greek and Palmyrene inscription at the Capitoline Museums (inv. no. 105) is incised on the base of a slab with a fragmentary relief, on the lower part of which are traces of two male figures, one of which wears anaxyrides. The text of the inscription (*IGUR* 120; *IG* XIV, 972; *IGRR* I, 46; *CIS* II, 3, 3904) allows for the reconstruction of only part of the dedication to the *Dii Patrii*, Bēl and Yarhibol, and of the designation of the two dedicators, Maqqai and Soaʾdu, names that appear quite frequently in Palmyrene inscriptions. The integration of the name of the god Aglibol, one of the divine triad, proposed by the editors of the inscription, is plausible, if uncertain (Chausson 1995, 669; Adam 2003, 251; Fowlkes-Childs 2016, 197). This relief has been commonly dated to the end of second century or to the beginning of the third century AD and repeats the conventional stylistic and iconographic characteristics of votive sculptures of the motherland: several images of divinities represented as a group, in a rigidly frontal arrangement. Here, the dedicators' names have been only transliterated and are not translated into Greek.

The temple dedicated to the god Bēl and to the divinities of Palmyra was built in the regio XIV Transtiberim, on the site of the ancient Horti Caesaris, in the area outside the ancient walls, corresponding to the Vigna Bonelli-Mangani, south of the Naumachia Augusti, which extended towards the slopes of Monteverde and the Mons Janiculum (Papi 1996, 55–56; Ensoli 2003, 46–47; Manetta 2012, 538). The sacred building, associated with the brick structures amongst which the first dedicatory Latin and Greek inscription was found, was built towards the end of Hadrian's reign in an older sacred area, a religious centre whose existence is clearly attested by the many findings that have been brought to light and where several cults dedicated to Eastern divinities co-existed (Vincenti 2012, 554–557). This is also the provenance of a sculpted marble fragment initially attributed to the previously mentioned relief dedicated to Bēl and Yarhibol and which shows only a woman's head with a *calathos* and a veil (Capitoline Museums inv. no. 2970). The Greek inscription, engraved at the height of the head, identifies her as the goddess Astarte, the divinity that, assimilated to Allat, very frequently accompanies the triad of Bēl (Figure 18.1). The spread of the cult of this goddess in Rome is also testified by the finding of a marble bas-relief in the Villa dei Quintili, for which a second-century AD date has been proposed (Pisano 2008, 199–203).

In Palmyra, Astarte was worshipped in the temple of Bēl, where her cult image was kept in the southern *adyton*. The supreme god's association with other divinities of the Palmyrene pantheon, even without an evident cult relationship, is extensively attested by the reliefs in the temple at Palmyra and is very widespread in the city's votive inscriptions (Kaizer 2002, 70, 198–200; Dirven 1999, 173; Gawlikowski 2015, 249–252; Fowlkes-Childs 2016, 196). This religious traditionalism reveals the strong ties between the Roman Palmyrene community and the religious customs of the motherland.

Research and findings amply attest that, in the ancient area of the Horti Caesaris, a temple was built and dedicated to the goddess Syria-Atargatis—probably the first Syrian divinity introduced to the capital, as many documents from Nero's era confirm—and

FIGURE 18.1   Fragment of marble relief with the goddess Astarte.

© Rome Capitoline Museums Montemartini Powerstation depot MC2970/S.

for the construction of which a chronology going back to the Julio-Claudian period has been proposed (Ensoli 2003, 46–59; 2004, 193–194). It must have been an important place of worship, one closely related to the area's influx and concentration of slave labour originating from the East. Its ongoing attendance during the third century AD is attested by the Luni marble altar from the Orti Mattei—now on display in the Capitoline Museums (inv. no. 1936)—dedicated by a P. Acilius Felix to the goddess, who is presented sitting between two winged lions (Ensoli 2002, 138; Vincenti 2012, 553). The attribution of a marble relief of a male bust representing a priest of the goddess Syria-Atargatis to this temple is quite plausible, if still unconfirmed; it was purchased by the Municipality of Rome in the 1950s at the antiquarian market and is presently kept in the warehouse of the Centrale di Monte Martini Museum in Rome (inv. no. 2971; Manetta 2012, 534–537 with previous bibliography). A chronology dating to the mid-imperial period has been proposed for this relief, which appears to be closely related to Palmyrene sculpture of the same period in terms of iconography and style. However, the hypothesis that this is a Roman production seems warranted by the use of marble and by a few details of the workmanship on the face, such as the eyes, which have quite natural dimensions, and are not enlarged, and the creases that furrow the face, which suggest a vague attempt at portraiture rather than a strict, formal representation.

In the same regio XIV Transtiberim, there is ample evidence of the existence of a sun cult and of a series of associated votive structures: in particular, two Latin inscriptions found in the Vigna Bonelli-Mangani have been frequently reexamined by scholars (Chausson 1995, 664–666 with previous bibliography; Hijmans 2010, 416–418). The first (*CIL* VI, 31034), dated AD 102 owing to the names of the consuls, recalls the restorations or reconstructions effected by a 'C. Iulius Anicetus of a porti(cum—S)olis cum marboribus opere novo ampliato', work carried out with the authorization of the 'calatores pontificum et flaminum', a corporation with the authority to grant permits for votive constructions, sacrifices, and donations. The text of the second inscription (*CIL* VI, 52 = *ILS* 4335) is an invitation from the same person 'ex imperio Solis . . . ne quis velit parietes aut triclias inscribere aut scariphare'. Iulius Anicetus's name suggests that he was a priest of eastern origin who exercised his offices in the Transtiberim sanctuary.

The attribution of some structures and epigraphic documents to a sanctuary dedicated to Hadad-Jupiter Heliopolitanus between the end of the second century and the second half of the third century AD, which were brought to light during excavations carried out on the eastern slope of the Janiculum Hill in the area of Villa Sciarra, particularly beneath the 'Villino Würst', is somewhat problematic (De Romanis 2008, 149–169, also concerning more recent interventions in the area). The identification of the cult or cults followed in these structures is still under discussion (Filippi and Attilia 2008, 175–183; Papini and Cuccurullo 2015, 171–172). Investigations have led to the proposal of a new interpretation of the more recent phase of the complex, which is that this was a suburban villa with a private sanctuary dedicated to Osiris, dating to the fourth century AD (Goddard 2008, 165–174).

Among the findings collected and held by the Orti Mattei in Transtiberim were two other important votive monuments dedicated to the Palmyrene gods: of unknown provenance, they were attributed to Villa Bonelli-Mangani by Lanciani, a hypothesis that is now widely accepted (Palmer 1981, 372–381; Ensoli 2001, 123–128; Panciera 2006, 365). Both are presently held by the Capitoline Museums (inv. no. 2412 and inv. no. 1206).

Without doubt, the well-known marble altar dedicated 'to Sol Sanctissimus-Malachbel by a Tiberius Claudius Felix, his wife Claudia Helpis, his son Tiberius Claudius Alypus, Calbienses de cohorte tertia', constitutes highly valuable evidence. The altar is decorated on all four sides: on the front, above the Latin inscription, is a radiate bust of the sun god above an eagle with spread wings (Figure 18.2); on the left side is a sun divinity in oriental dress, in a quadriga drawn by four winged griffins, and, behind the chariot, a standing Victory is shown in the act of crowning the young god; in her left hand, she holds a palm branch (Figure 18.3). This scene has been compared to a similar one sculpted on an altar from the sanctuary of Baalshamin at Palmyra (Equini Schneider 1987, 78; Dirven 1999, 161–162), which strongly indicates the dedicators' ties to their home city. On the bottom half of the slab is the inscription in Palmyrene, with a dedication to Malakbel and to the Palmyrene gods; the names of only the first of the dedicators appears, and of 'the Palmyrenes', collectively. On the right side of the altar is the sculpted bust of the god Saturn, shown frontally, according to the most traditional iconography; on the back is a representation of a cypress tree with its top branches tied with a ribbon, and the bust of a child with a lamb on his shoulders emerges from the leaves.

FIGURE 18.2 *Sol Sanctissimus-Malachbel* marble altar: front.

© Rome Capitoline Museums MC 107-NCE2412.

The almost unanimously proposed chronology for this altar is the end of the first/
early second century AD, but the epigraphic texts and the figurative representations lead
to different and contrasting interpretations. The two inscriptions agree only in the name
of the first dedicator, Tiberius Claudius Felix, Roman citizen, a *libertus* or an imperial
official, whose remote Palmyrene origin is probable, if not explicitly stated. (Equini
Schneider 1987, 77; Chausson 1995, 675–677; Belayche 2007, 208; Adam 2003, 250–253;
Velestino 2017, 96–97; *contra* Houston 1990, 189–193; Dirven 1999, 179–180; Noy 2000,
242–245, who do not hold that Tiberius Claudius Felix was of Syrian origin). His privileged position among the members of the Palmyrene community in Rome, evident in
both the inscriptions, is probably related to his being granted Roman citizenship and
his social status. The term '*Calbienses*' in the Latin version seems to collectively identify the dedicators as staff attached to the Horrea Galbana, the warehouses located on

FIGURE 18.3 *Sol Sanctissimus-Malachbel* marble altar: left side.

© Rome Capitoline Museums MC 107-NCE2412.

the left bank of the Tiber, where the *cohortes* corresponded to the three courtyards that constituted the living quarters of the labourers, generally slaves belonging to the imperial family. Currently, most scholars agree with the interpretation proposed by Cumont (1928, 101–109), according to which the reliefs express a complete solar theology: the rising sun (the young god on the chariot), the midday sun (the god with the radiant halo and the eagle, the heavenly vault), the sun at night, symbolized by Saturn, according to a widespread astrological doctrine originating in Babylon; the final representation, the most discussed, refers to the *dies natalis Invicti*, 25 December. However, certain more recent interpretations of the significance of the altar's iconography propose that the altar is intended to separately commemorate—with two distinct and different dedications—the Roman cult of Sol and that dedicated to Malakbel and to the Palmyrene gods (Fowlkes-Childs 2016, 203–212). However, this hypothesis seems implausible: an inscription from the Hadrianic or post-Hadrianic era, engraved on a marble base fragment extracted from the Tiber's riverbed near the Aemilius Bridge (*CIL* VI, 31036 = *ILS* 4338, presently at the Museo Nazionale Romano), does indeed include a dedication in Latin only, to the one god *deo Soli invicto Malachibelo* on behalf of a (*P*) Aelius Longinus (centurio) frumentarius, who therefore had an official function specifically related to the imperial circle. This also confirms the link between persons of more or less distant Palmyrene origin (the Palmyrene family of *Publii Aelii* owed their right to citizenship to Hadrian: Equini Schneider 1987, 72), but residing in the capital and completely integrated into Roman society, yet with the religious culture of their motherland. The location in which the inscription was found suggests a possible provenance in the area of the sanctuary (Chausson 1995, 679; Ensoli 2003, 56; Hijmans 2010, 393–402; Fowlkes Child 2016, 206). The solar character and that of an agrarian deity are integral aspects of the nature of Malakbel, one of the most venerated divinities of the Palmyrene pantheon, also amongst the communities distant from the motherland, where he was the object of particular devotion and a constant diffusion of his cult (Dirven 1999, 170–180; Dirven 2011, 201–220). Therefore, the message conveyed by the Capitoline altar utilizes various codes that allowed the oriental worshippers to maintain their own religious traditions, making them comprehensible and adapting them, at least formally, to Roman traditions. However, 'the religion of Palmyrene expatriates cannot simply be explained as copying the religious world of the hometown, and different social and economic conditions are known to have had a strong effect on the choice of deities to whom dedications were made' (Kaizer 2002, 112).

The religion of Palmyrene soldiers seems to have been more influenced by their new setting: the Roman army actively promoted solidarity and a communal identity. In this connection, the Latin inscription of the 'eques sin(gularis) Aug(usti) P. Aelius Annius Palmyre(nus) d.d. Fortunae s' (*CIL* VI, 3174; Milik 1972, 229–321) is particularly significant. Acquired by Soane from the Roman collection of the neoclassical sculptor John Flaxman, the inscription is presently preserved in Sir John Soane's Museum in London (https://www.soane.org number: M1446; collection online). The epigraph, for which a date in the Flavian period has been proposed, is engraved on a fragmentary, sculpted Luni marble slab; the only part of the relief that is preserved shows the lower part of a female figure, dressed in long chiton and himation, presented frontally and seated on a throne, identified as Fortuna, probably Fortuna Redux—deducible from the attributes and from the monetary representations—to whom the votive inscription is dedicated (De Capraris 2005, 131–143). Beside the goddess's image stands a large, spoked wheel; her extended right hand grasps the tiller of a steering-paddle set on an orb on the ground.

As previously mentioned, the Orti Mattei collection also includes the votive aedicula in Pentelic marble (Figure 18.4) dedicated in Greek and Palmyrene to the gods Aglibol and Malakbel by Ioulios Aurelios Heliodoros son of Antiocos, Adrianos Palmirenos at his expense, for his health and that of his children, in the month of Sebat of the year 547 of the Seleucid era (i.e., in February AD 236). This is the latest monument of the Palmyrene community in Rome (*IGUR* 119; *IG* XIV, 971; *IGR* I, 45; *CIS* II, 3, 3962). The dedication also mentions the offering of a silver statuette, which probably decorated the top of the *naiskos*, as indicated by the presence of a hole with traces of a metal clasp. The local name of the dedicator, Iarhai, appears in the Palmyrene text, accompanied by his

FIGURE 18.4 Marble *aedicula* with the gods Aglibol and Malakbel.

© Rome Capitoline Museums MC1206/S.

complete genealogy. He must have been a wealthy citizen, probably a merchant or an important businessman residing in Rome, but clearly and deliberately attached to the religious pietas of his land of origin. Concerning this relief and its inscriptions, nothing significant may be added to what scholars have already said, also recently (Chausson 1995, 677–678; Ensoli 2001, 124; Fowlkes-Childs 2016, 201–203). The two divinities are shown in their traditional iconographic representation: Aglibol is outfitted in military dress, with cuirass, chlamys, and spear, with a radiate nimbus and the lunar crescent at his back; Malakbel instead wears Palmyrene civilian dress, trousers, a short tunic, and a slightly open overcoat. A cypress tree also appears in this relief, in front of which the two divinities shake hands in a brotherly gesture of alliance that supports the hypothesis that Aglibol and Malakbel should be referred to by the appellation of 'Holy Brothers', which appears in various Palmyrene texts (Equini Schneider 1987, 82; Gawlikowski 1990, 2605–2658; Dirven 1999, 175; Kaizer 2002, 124–141).

CONCLUSION

The archaeological documentation reveals a pronounced sense of traditionalism in the stylistic and iconographic elaboration and a strong influence stemming from the native city's models, often independent of the date of the relief's execution or the dedicators' social status. The presumably progressive adaptation of the Palmyrene community to a different social and cultural environment seems to have had a very limited influence on votive iconographic representation. Even in the execution of this material, a strong link to Palmyra's ancient tribal religious traditions and ancestral cults is palpable (Terpstra 2013, 152–160). In this regard, the epigraphic texts are particularly significant: the use of Palmyrene until the first half of the third century is symptomatic of the traditionalism within the community. However, Latin–Greek, Greek–Palmyrene, and Latin–Palmyrene bilingualism—and in other, albeit rare, cases, the use of Latin only is ascertainable—attest to a variety of situations and motivations within the group and perhaps also to various periods of residence and therefore of adaptation to the new linguistic reality (Adam 2003, 249–252; Belayche 2007, 243–260). Palmyrene was excluded from texts related to the founding of the temple to the god Bēl, which are instead written in Latin and Greek. The Latin version precedes the Greek in both these inscriptions, but Greek is present as one of the languages of Palmyra.

Palmyra was thoroughly absorbed into the Greek linguistic area. Greek, which was the language of the bureaucratic and administrative apparatus of the eastern provinces of the Roman Empire, must have been understood—and perhaps even spoken—within the Roman community and therefore was also employed here, given the same importance as Latin, to emphasize the official character of the two dedications. In private or semi-private inscriptions, the mother tongue was almost always present, although frequently in a subordinate or complementary role. The text, even if limited to the essentials, followed the typical Palmyrene epigraphic forms: the use of the family name and, generally, the lineage, and sometimes the Seleucid date, is evidence that the dedicators wished to preserve their identity. The writing is cursive and sometimes painstakingly precise, although in other cases the letters are uncertain—even if they are correct from the linguistic point of view—probably owing to the stonecutters' transcription skills.

Two funerary inscriptions testify to the fact that the use of Palmyrene in dedications was not linked to real linguistic necessity but to the desire to emphasize cultural links with the motherland. The first, from the Lapidarium Zeri collection in Mentana (Palmieri 1982, no. 55, 119–121), engraved on a marble slab, is dedicated to a 'Tiberio Claudio Onesimo ostiario imperatoris Caesaris . . . by his son Tiberius Claudius Onesimus, by his daughter Claudia Palmyris and by Iulia Feicula contubernalis suo', most likely a family of imperial *liberti* from the Julio-Claudian house. 'Onesimus' was a common cognomen among *liberti*; in contrast 'Palmyris' is very rare and not otherwise found in Rome. On the other hand, a 'Fresidia Palmyris' appears in a votive inscription from Preneste (*CIL* XIV, 2864; *ILS*, 3688). If the Palmyrene origins of the persons commemorated by this funerary inscription may be regarded as plausible, then the early use of Latin as the only language employed in this dedication should be noted. Another funerary inscription, engraved on a stela found on the Via Appia and dedicated to 'd. m. Habibi Annubathi f. Palmurenus' by his brother and heir (*CIL* VI, 19134; *CIS* I, 3, 3905), where, beside the Latin text, the Palmyrene version still appears, is generally attributed to the third century AD (Hillers and Cussini 1996, 55; Adams 2003, 253).

The available documentation attests to the fact that the progressive decline of the monumental temenos outside Porta Portese occurred after the conquest of Palmyra in AD 273, when emperor Aurelian confined the Transtiberim sanctuary to the exterior of the new city wall and promoted the construction of the great temple dedicated to Sol Invictus in regio VII, on the site that has been confirmed as corresponding to today's Piazza S. Silvestro, near the church of S. Silvestro in Capite. In this new temple, already dedicated by AD 274, the emperor placed the precious trophies that he had brought back from his sack of Palmyra (Zos. 1.61.5), while inside its porticoes was stocked the *vina fiscalia*, the wine that was distributed to the plebeians at a 'political' price (Muzzioli 2008, 50). This location was close to the site on the Tiber's shore where the wine was unloaded from the river barges.

BIBLIOGRAPHY

Adams, James Noel. 2003. *Bilingualism and the Latin Language*. Cambridge: Cambridge University Press.

Belayche, Nicole. 2007. 'Les immigrés orientaux à Rome et en Campanie: Fidélité aux *patria* et intégration sociale'. *Cahiers de la Villa Kérylos* 18(1): 243–260.

Chausson, François. 1995. 'Vel Iovi vel Soli: quatre études autour de la Vigna Barberini (191–354)'. *Mélanges de l'Ecole française de Rome, Antiquité* 107(2): 661–765.

Cumont, Franz. 1928. 'L'autel palmyrénien du Musée du Capitole'. *Syria* 9: 101–109.

De Capraris, Francesca. 2005. 'Fortuna Redux'. *Archeologia classica* 56: 131–143.

De Romanis, Federico. 2008. 'Cultores huius loci: Sulle coabitazioni divine del *lucus Furrinae*'. In *Culti orientali: Tra scavo e collezionismo*, edited by Beatrice Palma, 149–157. Rome: Artemide.

Dirven, Lucinda. 1999. *The Palmyrenes of Dura-Europos: A Study of Religious Interaction in Roman Syria*. Leiden: Brill.

Dirven, Lucinda. 2011. 'Strangers and Sojourners: The Religious Behavior of Palmyrenes and other Foreigners in Dura-Europos'. In *Dura-Europos: Crossroads of Antiquity*, edited by Lisa R. Brody and Gall L. Hoffman, 201–219. Chestnut Hill, MA: McMullen Museum of Art, Boston College.

Ensoli, Serena. 2001. 'Communautés et cultes syriens à Rome: Les sanctuaires de la regio XIV Transtiberim'. In *Moi, Zénobie, reine de Palmyre*, edited by Jacques Charles-Gaffiot, Henri Lavagne, and Jean-Marc Hofman, 123–128. Milan: Skira.

Ensoli, Serena. 2002. 'Comunità e culti siriani a Roma: i santuari della Regio XIV Transtiberim'. In *Zenobia: Il sogno di una regina d'Oriente*, edited by Palazzo Bricherasio (Turin, Italy), 137–143. Milan: Electa.

Ensoli, Serena. 2003. 'Il santuario della Dea Syria e i culti palmireni nell'area meridionale di Trastevere'. *Orizzonti rassegna di archeologia* 4: 45–59.

Ensoli, Serena. 2004. 'Deae Syriae Templum'. *Lexicon topographicum urbis Romae: Suburbium*. Vol. 2, *D-G*, edited by Eva Margareta Steinby, 191–196. Rome: Quasar.

Equini Schneider, Eugenia. 1987. 'Il santuario di Bēl e delle divinità di Palmira. Comunità e tradizioni religiose dei Palmireni a Roma'. *Dialoghi di archeologia* 1: 69–85.

Equini Schneider, Eugenia. 1996. 'Ritratti funerari palmireni del Museo Barracco'. *Studi miscellanei* 30: 293–300.

Equini Schneider, Eugenia. 2001. 'Beli Aedes'. *Lexicon topographicum urbis Romae, Suburbium*. Vol. 1, *A-C*, edited by Eva Margareta Steinby, 217–219. Rome: Quasar.

Filippi, Fedora, and Luigia Attilia. 2008. 'Tra Gianicolo e Tevere: le fonti documentarie sui culti orientali'. In *Culti orientali: Tra scavo e collezionismo*, edited by Beatrice Palma, 174–188. Rome: Artemide.

Fowlkes Childs, Blair. 2016. 'Palmyrenes in Transtiberim: Integration in Rome and Links to the Eastern Frontier'. In *Rome and the Worlds Beyond Its Frontiers*, edited by Daniëlle Slootjes and Michael Peachin, 193–212. Leiden: Brill.

Gawlikowski, Michał. 1990. 'Les dieux de Palmyre'. In *Aufstieg und Niedergang der Römischen Welt*. Vol. 2, *Principat*, no. 18, *Religion*, 4, edited by Wolfgang Haase, 2605–2658. Berlin: de Gruyter.

Gawlikowski, Michał. 2015. 'Bēl of Palmyra'. In *Religious Identities in the Levant from Alexander to Muhammed: Continuity and Changes*, edited by Michael Blömer, Achim Lichtenberger, and Rubina Raja, 247–254. Turnhout: Brepols.

Goddard, Christophe J. 2008. 'Nuove osservazioni sul Santuario cosiddetto "siriaco" al Gianicolo'. In *Culti orientali: Tra scavo e collezionismo*, edited by Beatrice Palma, 165–173. Rome: Artemide.

Hijmans, Steven. 2010. 'Temples and Priests of Sol in the City of Rome'. *Mouseion: Journal of the Classical Association of Canada* 54(3): 381–427.

Houston, George W. 1990. 'The Altar from Rome with Inscriptions to Sol and Malakbel'. *Syria* 67: 189–193.

Kaizer, Ted. 2002. *The Religious Life of Palmyra: A Study of the Social Patterns of Worship in the Roman Period*. Stuttgart: Steiner.

Lanciani, Rodolfo A. 1901. *Forma urbis Romae: Scala 1:2000*. Rome: Quasar. Reprinted 2007.

Manetta, Consuelo. 2012. '*Orientalia* da Villa Bonelli–Crescenzi–Mangani. Riesame e nuovi tentativi di contestualizzazione'. *Horti Hesperidum* 2(1): 533–543.

Milik, Józef Thadeusz. 1972. *Recherches d'épigraphie Proche-Orientale*. Vol. 1, *Dédicaces faites par des dieux (Palmyra, Hatra, Tyr) et des thiases sémitiques à l'époque romaine*. Paris: Geuthner.

Muzzioli, Maria Pia. 2008. 'I luoghi dei culti orientali a Roma: Problemi topografici generali e particolari'. In *Culti orientali: Tra scavo e collezionismo*, edited by Beatrice Palma, 49–56. Rome: Artemide.

Noy, David. 2000. *Foreigners at Rome: Citizens and Strangers*. London: Duckworth.

Palmer, Robert E. A. 1981. 'The Topography and Social History of Rome's Trastevere (Southern Sector)'. *Proceedings of the American Philosophical Society* 125: 368–397.

Palmieri, Raffaele. 1982. 'Un *apparitor* ed arti e mestieri'. In *Il Lapidario Zeri di Mentana*, edited by Guido Barbieri, 119–121. Studi pubblicati dall'Istituto Italiano per la storia antica, vol. 32, no. 1. Città di Castello: Arti Grafiche.

Panciera, Silvio. 2006. *Epigrafi, Epigrafia, Epigrafisti: Scritti vari e inediti (1956–2005) con note complementari e indici*. Rome: Quasar.

Papi, Emanuele. 1996. 'Horti Caesaris (Transtiberim)'. In *Lexicon topographicum urbis Romae*. Vol. 3, G-L, edited by Eva Margareta Steinby, 55–56. Rome: Quasar.

Papini, Massimiliano and Emanuele Cuccurullo. 2015. 'Una nuova divinità siriana dalle Terme di Elagabalo: Un Apollo di Hierapolis Bambyce a Roma?' *Scienze dell'Antichità: Storia, archeologia, antropologia* 21: 153–180.

Pisano, Giovanna. 2008. 'Note sull'Astarte della villa dei Quintili'. In *Cultu orientali: Tra scavo e collezionismo, Atti del Convegno Testimonianze di culti orientali tra scavo e collezionismo*, edited by Beatrice Palma Venetucci, 199–207. Roma: Artemide.

Terpstra, Taco T. 2013. *Trading Communities in the Roman World- A Micro-Economic and Institutional Perspective. Columbia Studies in the Classical Tradition*. Vol. 37. Leiden: Brill.

Terpstra, Taco T. 2016. 'The Palmyrene Temple in Rome and Palmyra's Trade with the West'. In *Palmyrena: City, Hinterland and Caravan Trade between Orient and Occident*, edited by Jorgen Christian Meyer, Eivind Heldaas Seland, and Nils Anfinset, 39–48. Oxford: Archaeopress.

Velestino, Daniela. 2017. 'Rome and Palmyra'. In *Portraits of Palmyra in Aquileia*, edited by Marta Novello and Cristiano Tiussi, 96–97. Rome: Gangemi.

Vincenti, Maria Cristina. 2012. 'Culti orientali: Contesti e rinvenimenti tra Roma e i Colli Albani'. In *L'Oriente nel collezionismo: Il collezionismo di antichità classiche e orientali nella formazione dei musei europei*, edited by Beatrice Palma Venetucci, 553–567. Rome: UniversItalia.

Visconti, Carlo L. 1860. 'Escavazioni della Vigna Bonelli, fuori della Porta Portese negli anni 1859 e 60'. *Annali dell'Istituto di corrispondenza archeologica*, 32: 415–450.

CHAPTER 19

PALMYRA AND THE PARTHIANS

PETER EDWELL

INTRODUCTION

THE political relationship between Palmyra and the Parthians from the first century BC to the early decades of the third century AD has received limited scholarly attention for a number of reasons. The surviving evidence relevant to the topic is very limited, and Palmyra's relationship with the Roman world has been the focus of a majority of the scholarship. While it is tempting to conclude that the increasingly close relationship between Rome and Palmyra from the first century AD automatically implies a more distant relationship between Palmyra and the Parthians, the reality might not be so clear-cut.

Despite evidence to indicate that Palmyra was either part of the Roman province of Syria or at least strongly within the Roman orbit of influence from the first century AD, there is evidence also to suggest that Palmyrene armed escorts of trading caravans were not only active on the Euphrates and in southern Mesopotamia, where Parthian power prevailed, but that some of them even held formal appointments within local power structures in the second century AD. This is especially evident in the Persian Gulf kingdom of Characene/Mesene but is also in evidence at the trading emporium of Vologesias, not far from the Parthian capital of Seleucia-Ctesiphon.

Characene/Mesene was admittedly a special case through much of the Parthian period, exercising a considerable degree of independence from Parthia. However, Palmyrene traders operating to and from Characene, and accompanied by armed escorts, passed through considerable sections of territory that were clearly under Parthian control. How was it possible for the movement, protection, and organization of trade in Parthian territory to be undertaken by armed allies of Rome who were even under the protection of Roman legionaries on occasion? The question may be informed by our ability to trace a change in the capacity of Palmyrene caravans and their leaders to operate in southern Mesopotamia in the second part of the second century AD following significant Roman territorial gains made at the expense of the Parthian Empire.

The political relationship only informs part of the story. Also of importance is the extent to which Parthian culture—including religion, sculptural styles, and Hellenism—influenced Palmyra from the first century BC to the third century AD. Cultural factors mark an important contrast with political ones at Palmyra, especially during the period in which Palmyra increasingly became a part of the Roman imperial system and was subsumed into the empire.

Geopolitical Developments

Developments and changes in imperial activity in Mesopotamia, Armenia, and Syria from the first century BC to the third century AD have important implications for how we might analyse the relationship between Palmyra and the Parthians. By the middle of the first century BC, in the immediate wake of Pompey's settlement of the regions to the west of the Euphrates and the Parthian defeat of Crassus, the long-term status of the upper Euphrates as a boundary between Roman and Parthian imperial interests in northern Mesopotamia and Syria was established. Despite Parthian attempts to threaten Roman imperial interests west of the Euphrates during the prolonged civil wars of the last decades of the Roman Republic and Roman attempts to prosecute military campaigns east of the Euphrates, the upper Euphrates came to represent a practical long-term boundary between the interests of the two imperial powers (Edwell 2013). This would remain the case until the second half of the second century AD.

Shorthand references in early Roman imperial texts to the Euphrates as a boundary between the Roman and Parthian empires were more relevant, however, to its upper reaches as it flowed north–south. As it flowed in a west–east direction beyond the bend at Barbalissos through territory adjacent to and increasingly dominated by Palmyra from the first century BC onwards, it is more difficult to define the Euphrates as a boundary between Roman and Parthian imperial interests. The city of Dura-Europos on the west bank of the Euphrates, for example, was clearly under Parthian control until ca. AD 163 but likely had a troop of Palmyrene archers stationed at it beforehand. Palmyra's relationship with Parthia up to this time was still relatively close despite the increasing dominance of Rome at the city, evident from the early Roman imperial period onwards. This is supported by other evidence, which will now be discussed.

A Destiny of Its Own?

The nature of Palmyra's political relationship with the Parthian and Roman empires and how this changed over time is the subject of ongoing debate. Much of the discussion revolves around the dating of Palmyra's incorporation into the Roman province of Syria and whether Parthian political influence at Palmyra was on the wane or snuffed out altogether as a consequence. A majority of scholars place Palmyra's inclusion in the Roman province of Syria by the early reign of Tiberius (AD 14–37), but there are other opinions suggesting that it dated from Pompey's original formation of the province ca. 63 BC (Bowersock 1973, 135–136; Pollard 2000, 16; Sartre 2005, 511 for the former claim. Colledge 1976, 16 for the latter). Others believe that Palmyra was part of the province of Syria by the reign of Vespasian (Seyrig 1932; Millar 1993, 34–35; cf. Sommer 2005, 152 who places it by the middle of the first century), while some analyse the relationship in less clearly defined ways. Matthews (1984, 161–162) sees Palmyra as within the Roman sphere of influence by the latter part of the first century AD, and Isaac (1992, 141–144) argues that Rome did not manage to exercise full sovereignty at Palmyra during the first century.

The primary reason for this lack of overall agreement is that the literary and epigraphic evidence do not always complement each other. The text typically seen as the earliest clear indication of where Palmyra's imperial loyalties initially lay is a reference by Appian (*Bell. Civ.* 5.9) to a raid on the city by Marcus Antonius.

> When Cleopatra had sailed homewards, Antony sent his horsemen to the *polis* of Palmyra, not far from the Euphrates, to plunder, accusing them of something insignificant, that they—being on the frontier between the Romans and the Parthians—showed tact to both sides (being merchants, they carry Indian and Arabian goods from the Persians and they dispose of them in the territory of the Romans), but in fact he had in his mind to enrich the horsemen. As the Palmyrenes learned about this beforehand and carried their essentials to the other side of the river and to the riverbank, preparing themselves with bows—with which they are by nature excellent—in case anyone would attack them, the horsemen, seizing the city empty, turned around, not having met anyone, not having taken anything.

Hekster and Kaizer (2004, 71) note the emphasis in modern scholarship on Palmyra's wealth and still 'nomadic' lifestyle ca. 41 BC, when the episode reported by Appian is meant to have taken place. That the Palmyrenes fled to the Euphrates and took up defensive positions might indicate their leanings towards the Parthians at this stage, although the passage makes no reference to the involvement of the Parthians in these events. Elsewhere, Kaizer (2002, 36) sees Antony's raid as an attempt to punish the Palmyrenes for their trading links with Parthia. Based on this passage, he argues that it is implausible to suggest that Palmyra was part of the province of Syria from the time of Pompey.

There are some overarching problems with this passage, which may not only be anachronistic but indicate defects in Appian's knowledge of Palmyra's geography. The suggestion that the city was close to the Euphrates is clearly incorrect, as Palmyra lies some 200 km from the river. Palmyra's reputation for bringing goods from India and Arabia may be more reflective of the time at which Appian was writing, ca. AD 120. On the other hand, the attack itself would suggest that Palmyra was not part of the Roman provincial system, which perhaps reflects the situation in 41 BC more than AD 120. Hekster and

Kaizer conclude that Appian is presenting the Palmyrenes as 'near-Parthian' in this passage and that this also reflects how Palmyra and the Palmyrenes were still perceived in the second century AD by Appian even though Palmyra and the surrounding territory were now within the Roman imperial system.

The only other literary reference indicative of Palmyra and its relationship with Parthia in antiquity is that of Pliny the Elder (*NH* 5.88), who claimed that Palmyra had a destiny of its own between the two empires of Rome and Parthia ('private sorte inter duo imperia summa Romanorum Parthorumque'). This contemporary observation of Pliny's, made ca. AD 70, has caused problems for those who date the inclusion of Palmyra within the Roman province of Syria, and hence the end of any political independence enjoyed by Palmyra, much earlier.

The most important evidence for those who see it this way is epigraphic. A number of inscriptions demonstrate that Roman influence at Palmyra was strong in the early decades of the first century AD. In the temple of Bēl, dedicatory statues were put up to members of the Roman imperial family, Tiberius, Drusus, and Germanicus ca. AD 18, while a fragmentary inscription in Palmyrene refers to Germanicus sending a Palmyrene envoy to the king of Mesene in the Persian Gulf at roughly the same time (*PAT* 2754). There are also references in the Hadrianic-era tariff inscription to Germanicus making earlier rulings on tariffs on certain items (Edwell 2008, 36–41). An inscription from Khirbet el-Bilaas, some 75 km north-west of Palmyra, is a boundary marker which refers to the 'fines regionis Palmyrenae constitutos a Cretico Silano'. Creticus Silanus was the Roman governor of Syria AD 11–17, finishing his term just before Germanicus arrived in the east.

Additional to this evidence is a Roman milestone discovered 27 km north-east of Palmyra, which dates to the fourth consulship of Vespasian (AD 75). The milestone is indicative of a Roman road, which would be strong evidence for Roman administrative and military control in and around Palmyra at the time Pliny was writing. How, then, do we explain Pliny's claim regarding Palmyra's status with reference to Rome and Parthia?

Some argue that Pliny's account was anachronistic, relying on a now lost and unnamed Augustan-era geographer who reported the situation prior to the reign of Tiberius (e.g., Bowersock 1973, 135–136). This is an unconvincing claim because Pliny tells us only a few lines earlier (*NH* 5.83) that his sources on the situation in Syria were Cn. Domitius Corbulo and Gaius Mucianus, successive governors of Syria only a few years before Pliny completed his work. What is likely for Pliny, and perhaps for the Roman nobility generally, is that conceptions of Palmyra were not unlike those of Appian fifty years later. The mystical stories of its splendour and exoticism made Palmyra distinctive in the Roman mind and perhaps in that sense Pliny believed it had a destiny of its own between the two imperial powers. The administrative, economic, and military reality on the ground painted a different picture, but the intricacies of these arrangements were not of great interest to Pliny when he made this brief reference to Palmyra.

Despite its closeness to Rome, Palmyra successfully continued to develop trading activities in territory that was either under direct Parthian suzerainty or at least within the Parthian Empire's orbit of control and influence. In the second century, in view of increased Palmyrene affiliation with the Roman military, the capacity of the Palmyrene merchants to prosper in the Parthian world was even more exceptional, especially given the Palmyrenes' characteristic tendency of providing armed escorts of the caravans into, through, and from Parthian territory.

PALMYRENE TRADE WITH THE CITIES OF SOUTHERN MESOPOTAMIA

The earliest evidence for mercantile links between Palmyra and the cities of southern Mesopotamia comes from the early Roman imperial period. Many Palmyrene inscriptions of the first and second centuries honour the leaders and escorts of the caravans to and from the city. The presence of armed Palmyrene agents guarding the caravans during a period in which political ties between Rome and Palmyra were strengthening is an indicator of the special position Palmyra continued to enjoy in relation to both empires. It is also informative of how Roman and Parthian imperialism operated in desert areas.

Early connections between Palmyra and Seleucia-Ctesiphon are indicated by a dedication of AD 19 in the temple of Bēl (*PAT* 0270). This inscription dedicated a statue of YDY'BL by the Palmyrene and Greek merchants of Seleucia, who gratefully acknowledged his beneficence to the cult of Bēl. Five years later merchants in the city of Babylon erected a statue, whose dedicatory inscription was also re-employed in the temple of Bēl, to MLKW, who had given generously to the Babylonian merchants out of his own funds and had helped in the building of the temple (*PAT* 1352). This phenomenon continued through the first century and expanded to the city of Spasinou Charax in Characene/ Mesene. (see Potts 1997, who believes that Mesene's level of autonomy from Parthia was similar to that of Palmyra from Rome).

In the early second century, an individual called 'Aqqayh was honoured with a statue in the temple of Bēl at Palmyra for his generosity in contributing to a temple in the Parthian city of Vologesias (*PAT* 0263 of AD 108). Vologesias, not far from Seleucia-Ctesiphon, was by then the most important trading emporium in southern Mesopotamia and one of the most significant in the whole of the Parthian Empire.

The protection of caravans as they made their way to and from Palmyra through destinations in the Parthian world was similarly honoured in the first century AD via statue dedications in prominent positions in the city of Palmyra. This became even more prominent in the second century. These dedications often gave thanks for the protection of caravans coming from Spasinou Charax in the Persian Gulf kingdom of Characene/ Mesene, but there are references to the protection of caravans originating in other cities in southern Mesopotamia.

This activity is somewhat extraordinary when considered in the context of Palmyra's developing military relationship with Rome. It is likely that a wing of Palmyrene cameleers (Ala I Ulpia Dromedarium Palmyrenorum) was attached to Trajan's army during the invasions of Parthia in 115/116, and there is some epigraphic evidence that indicates the honouring of Roman soldiers in prominent public locations at Palmyra from 115–135. *PAT* 1548 of 115 is a dedicatory inscription from the Grand Colonnade honouring a Roman centurion, Julius Maximus, and *PAT* 1397 of 135 from the agora also honours a Roman centurion of the same name. The latter, likely the same person, is of particular interest because the Palmyrene version of the inscription indicates that it was a dedication by a prominent Palmyrene caravan leader, Marcus Ulpius Abgar, in thanks to the centurion for his role in protecting a caravan originating in the Persian Gulf kingdom of Characene/Mesene. That a Roman centurion was able to lead an armed escort of a caravan through Parthian territory in the mid-130s before crossing the desert to Palmyra is an interesting example of what was still possible despite the heightened state of enmity between Rome and Parthia in the wake of the campaign of Trajan.

Further to this, at the time of Hadrian's visit to Palmyra in 131, the imperial loyalties of Palmyra were clearer than ever before. The subsequent codification in 137 of the setting of tariffs on locally traded items (*PAT* 0259) bore the authority of the emperor's name and clearly indicated the extent to which Roman imperial administrative authority extended to Palmyra at this time. As with Julius Maximus in 135, however, there is considerable epigraphic evidence to indicate that the armed escorts of the caravans to and from Characene/Mesene (in the Persian Gulf) and Vologesias (not far from Seleucia-Ctesiphon in Parthian-held southern Mesopotamia) continued unabated. If anything, the middle of the second century would witness the zenith of Palmyrene trade to and from the Gulf and southern Mesopotamia.

In 132, Soados received a dedication in the temple of Baalshamin in gratitude for his support for the merchants and caravans originating in Vologesias (*PAT* 0197). The inscription refers to him as a citizen of Vologesias and indicates that the Roman governor of Syria, Publicius Marcellus, honoured him in various ways for protecting a caravan originating in Vologesias. Soados had no fewer than four statues dedicated to him across different sanctuaries in Palmyra and was later honoured at the caravanserai of Gennaes, 22 km outside Palmyra for the many occasions on which he had supported merchants and caravans coming from Vologesias (145/146—*PAT* 1062). In the latter inscription, Soados was even honoured by Hadrian and Antoninus Pius for his deeds, and the *boule* and *demos* of Palmyra also funded statues of him at Spasinou Charax and Vologesias. The inscription concludes with the claim that Soados had also commissioned a temple to the Augusti in Vologesias.

Inscriptions indicating links with Spasinou Charax become even more numerous from ca. AD 130. One of the most interesting and informative of all Palmyrene inscriptions dating to AD 131 honours Iarhai (Iaraios) from Hadriana Palmyra, who was also satrap of Thilouanos (Tylos, modern Bahrain), appointed by Meherdates the king of Spasinou Charax (*PAT* 1374). Another individual, Iarhibol, was honoured in the agora in 138 for his dealings with the merchants of Spasinou Charax and also for his role in funding an embassy to Orodes, the king of Elymais, another vassal king of the Parthians

(*PAT* 1414). In this case, the *boule* of Palmyra was responsible for the dedication of the statue and, through the dedication, associated itself with the embassy to Orodes. For Iarhai and Iarhibol, clearly prominent Palmyrenes, the political nature of their activity in territories either directly under Parthian control or within the Parthian political orbit is important to consider when assessing the complex nature of Palmyra's relationship with Parthia and also, consequently, with Rome.

The links between Spasinou Charax, Vologesias, and Palmyra are given some context by another inscription from the agora, this time honouring an unnamed individual referred to as the archon of Forat (near Spasinou Charax: *PAT* 1412). Just as Vologesias was to Seleucia-Ctesiphon, Forat was the principal trading centre of Spasinou Charax. In September 140, this individual was honoured with a statue for assisting a caravan that had originated in Spasinou Charax and travelled to Palmyra via Vologesias. Forat is referred to by Pliny the Elder (*NH* 6.32.145) ca. AD 70 as a city subject to Characene/Mesene, which was frequented by traders from Petra. Pliny had access to information about Characene/Mesene from 'our traders' ('nostri negotiatores')—likely Palmyrenes or people who had dealt with them. The honouring of this individual at Palmyra while he held the title of archon of Forat is yet another indication of the political roles played by Palmyrenes in southern Mesopotamia. These political roles were likely tied closely to trade and indicate the extent to which trade and politics went hand in hand in the principalities of southern Mesopotamia, just as they did in Palmyra. In 142 an individual called Nesa was honoured in the temple of Bēl by a caravan leader and traders for assistance rendered in a journey from Forat to Palmyra, again via Vologesias (*PAT* 0262). The same Nesa was later honoured in the agora in 150 for his support of a caravan, this time travelling from Palmyra to Vologesias (*PAT* 1419).

A group of eight inscriptions from the 150s, five of which come from the agora at Palmyra (*PAT* 0274, 1411, 1399, 1409, *Inv.* X, 77—not in *PAT*), honour Marcus Ulpius Iarhai, perhaps the most famous of the caravan leaders of the second century. Five of these dedications refer to Iarhai's leadership and protection of the caravans to and from Spasinou Charax. Two inscriptions, one from 157 (*PAT* 1403) and another undated one (*PAT* 2763), refer to Iarhai being honoured by a range of people involved in the caravan trade, including merchants who had returned from Scythia (India) in ships belonging to Palmyrenes. As with the earlier honouring of individuals such as Soados, the inscriptions dedicating the statues of Iarhai convey a sense that his activities went beyond involvement in trade, extending perhaps to a formal level of authority and exercise of euergetism that allowed him to operate in a world that was under Parthian suzerainty and/or influence, and even perhaps beyond it, to India.

The extent to which Palmyra and Palmyrenes operated successfully between the Roman and Parthian worlds is indicated further by an inscription of 161, which again is from a statue dedication in the agora (*PAT* 1373). Here merchants and their leaders who had come from Spasinou Charax honoured Marcus Aemilianus Marcianus Asclepiades, who was a councillor from Antioch and responsible for the collection of the *Tetarte*, the 25 percent tariff levied on items coming into the empire. While it is of interest that a Roman tax collector was honoured with a statue in the agora at Palmyra alongside protectors of caravans coming from Spasinou Charax, Vologesias, and Forat, there is potentially further significance in this piece of epigraphic evidence.

PARTHIA'S WARS WITH ROME AND IMPLICATIONS FOR PALMYRA

From 161 there is a dramatic decline in surviving dedications to caravan protectors, especially from the agora at Palmyra, but also generally from across the city. Only one later inscription celebrated the actions of a protector of a caravan from Spasinou Charax, Thaimarsos, in 193 (*PAT* 0294), and this appeared in the Grand Colonnade. Another, also from the Grand Colonnade and dating to 211, also honoured Thaimarsos, this time for his support for a caravan that went from Palmyra to Vologesias (*PAT* 0295). There are a further three inscriptions dating to the post-161 period that refer to the protection of caravans without naming the cities or areas from which the protected caravans came. *PAT* 0309 (dating from either 88 or 188), *PAT* 1063, and *PAT* 1378 refer to individuals' protection or generosity towards caravans. Only one of these (*PAT* 0309) is from the agora, and there are issues with its precise dating due to the fragmentary nature of the last line of the inscription.

There are reasons for exercising a degree of caution in analysing this observation, including the possibility that the available space for honorific statues in the agora had filled up by the second half of the second century or that only the earlier inscriptions from the agora have survived. There is a possibility, however, that broader political events in the region had an impact on the ability of Palmyrenes to operate in territory under Parthian suzerainty and influence after the early 160s. The significant territorial changes that took place in northern Mesopotamia and eastern Syria in the wake of the wars between Rome and Parthia in the mid-160s and the territorial implications for Palmyra and for its role in the Syrian Desert and beyond may be an important part of the reason why the activity of Palmyrene caravan leaders in Characene and Vologesias declined rapidly after the early 160s.

Much like Trajan's war against Parthia fifty years before, the Romano-Parthian war of Lucius Verus and Vologases IV in the mid-160s resulted from problems in Armenia; but important territorial ramifications were felt further south in northern Mesopotamia and Syria. In 161, according to the Roman version of events, Vologases contravened an agreement between Rome and Parthia over Armenia, placing a member of his own family on the throne without the agreement of Rome (see Millar 1993, 111–114). Roman and Parthian armies soon engaged on the upper Euphrates, and the Roman province of Syria came under threat of invasion after the Parthians gained the initial advantage (Dio 71.2.1). An expanded Roman military response under Lucius Verus saw substantial gains made by the Romans in 163, and, by 165, Armenia was ruled by a Roman nominee. The Parthians had also been forced out of northern Mesopotamia, with the key city of

Nisibis now under Roman military control. The kingdom of Osrhoene, which occupied the western portion of northern Mesopotamia, became a dependent kingdom of Rome from this time (Edwell 2017).

In the wake of these territorial developments, the impact on Palmyra and its relationship with the cities and principalities within the Parthian sphere of influence was potentially significant. Roman power now extended along the middle Euphrates to the previously Parthian-held fortification of Dura-Europos and beyond. The Parthian capital of Seleucia-Ctesiphon was now more vulnerable, and the strongly Parthian-aligned desert kingdom of Hatra was closer to the Roman orbit of power. Connected to this was full Roman control of the Khabur River in the direction of Nisibis, which served as an important means of transport between eastern Syria and northern Mesopotamia.

As an ally of Rome, or as a part of the province of Syria and therefore the empire, Palmyra's close connection to the Syrian Desert and the various Euphrates River sites as far south as Hit and Anatha became potentially more of a threat to a Parthian Empire that was now under threat from an ascendant Roman Empire. The looser territorial arrangements in eastern Syria and the Parthian ascendancy in northern Mesopotamia up to the 160s had allowed the Palmyrenes to operate within Parthian territory with success at a commercial and even local political level. With the new territorial arrangements, however, the situation became more difficult, which is a possible explanation for the changing nature of the epigraphic evidence at Palmyra after 161.

Rome's wars with the Parthians in the 190s under Septimius Severus saw this factor develop further. During the Roman civil wars that preceded Severus's accession, a number of north Mesopotamian principalities, including Osrhoene, Adiabene, and likely Hatra, had sided with Pescennius Niger, the imperial rival Severus would eventually defeat (Dio 75.6.1ff.). By 195, Severus undertook a rearrangement of the territory of Osrhoene, with much of the kingdom converted into a Roman province. The city of Edessa was established as a client-kingdom, with Abgar VIII confirmed as king, and the province of Mesopotamia was likely established at this time.

In 197, Severus turned to confront the Parthians themselves (see Debevoise 1938, 255). The Parthians capitulated quickly; Seleucia and Babylon were both abandoned and Ctesiphon was captured easily. In early 199, the first unsuccessful siege of Hatra took place, while another unsuccessful siege of the city took place in the following year (Dio 75.10.1). In the wake of the military actions of the 190s, Severus reorganized the province of Syria, converting it into the two provinces of Syria Phoenice and Coele Syria. Along with the formation of the province of Mesopotamia and the reorganization of the kingdom of Osrhoene, this represents the most important and far-reaching territorial rearrangement in the Roman East since Pompey.

Provincia Mesopotamia was an expensive province to maintain and brought little by way of taxation to the Romans. Of greater concern was that it brought Rome closer to the Parthians and thus to foreign wars (Dio 75.3.2–3). All these developments were, of course, significant for Palmyra and its relationship with both the Parthians and the Romans. Palmyra was located within the newly formed province of Syria Phoenice and, at the beginning of the reign of Caracalla (AD 211/212), became a Roman colony with *ius italicum* (Ulpian, *De Censoribus*, 50.15.1.5). This made Palmyra one of the two most important cities in Syria Phoenice (the other being Emesa) and bound it as close to Rome as would seem possible. There is still some evidence to indicate Palmyrene trading activity into the Parthian world after this time, but it is even scarcer than between 161 and the 190s. The statue referred to earlier that was dedicated to Thaimarsos in 211 in the Grand Colonnade (*PAT* 0295) is the only extant example until that honouring Julius Aurelius Zebida, also in the Grand Colonnade, in 247 for his role in protecting a caravan bound for Vologesias (*PAT* 0279).

There is, of course, a complementary explanation for the distinct reduction in the number of inscriptions from the agora and/or the Grand Colonnade referring to the movement of trade between Vologesias and/or Spasinou Charax. After the 160s the Parthian Empire entered a prolonged period of internal division and civil war, brought on in part by the impact of the wars with Rome and the loss of territory in northern Mesopotamia and eastern Syria. The attendant reduction in demand, or more importantly supply, due to the breakdown of authority and the capacity to attract long-distance trade via Spasinou Charax and Vologesias was a possible symptom of the internal difficulties the Parthians faced. This may be another factor reflected in the marked reduction in epigraphic evidence related to the organization of long-distance trade at Palmyra after the 160s.

Not long after Caracalla came to power, Osrhoene, Armenia, and the Parthian Empire were all in a significant state of turmoil. In 213, Abgar IX of Edessa was removed and the city incorporated into the province of Osrhoene (Dio 77.12.1). Caracalla also removed the Armenian king, whose heirs became bitterly divided against each other, and Artabanus V and Vologases V were in open warfare in Parthia (Dio 77.1–2). Caracalla decided to deal with the turmoil in Armenia and at the same time took advantage of the divisions in Parthia. In early summer 216, the emperor crossed into Parthian territory and made his way to Arbela, forcing the Parthians to retreat. Artabanus V gathered a large army north of the upper Tigris in the spring of 217 aimed at challenging the Roman advances of the previous year (*HA Car.* 6.4). Soon after, Caracalla was murdered, and his successor, Macrinus, came to terms with Artabanus (Dio 78.1.4, 5.4; Herodian 4.13.3–8; *HA Car.* 6.6–7.2). Within a few short years, the Parthian dynasty would come to an end. Parthia's long period of decline, marked by civil war and division from the latter half of the second century, saw negative commercial ramifications for Palmyra.

Parthian Cultural Influences on Palmyra

The complicated geopolitical context in which Palmyra found itself from the first century BC to the early decades of the third century AD and the transformations in its status and imperial loyalties in relation to Parthia and Rome are, of course, only one part of the story. It is also important to analyse Parthian cultural influences on Palmyra during this period. In some ways, developments and changes in cultural expression at Palmyra can be linked with the changing imperial relationships between Palmyra and Parthia and between Palmyra and Rome; but, in other ways, the cultural elements tell a different story from the political and economic ones.

Henri Seyrig, one of the most influential scholars of Palmyra of the twentieth century, pointed to the consistent influence of Parthian religious and dress styles right up to what is often referred to (erroneously) as the last days of the city in the 270s (Seyrig 1950, 7). 'Their town', according to Seyrig, 'remained a stronghold of Graeco-Parthian civilization to the end'. In his opinion, there had been Roman influence, mostly architectural, but this was relatively superficial when compared to the ongoing importance of Parthian culture. For Seyrig, even the influences of Hellenism obvious at Palmyra were due more to Parthian influence than Roman influence.

Seyrig believed that, from its beginning as a city,

> Palmyra was entirely under the ascendancy of Lower Mesopotamia. Its policy looked towards the court of Ctesiphon. Its religion was strongly influenced by Babylonian religion. The costume of its wealthier classes copied that of Parthian noblemen or Greek merchants who were to be met in the Hellenistic colonies on the Tigris. Its artists learnt sculpture and architecture from the Graeco-Iranian workshops which developed that peculiar art which we begin to know as having been that of the Parthian Empire. Of Western influence we perceive nothing: even the Hellenism of Palmyra came from the East. (Seyrig 1950, 6)

Seyrig believed that the Palmyrenes looked to Seleucia more than any other city, including Antioch, for architectural, stylistic, and religious inspiration. Ultimately, he concluded, 'Most probably Palmyra is really a spiritual daughter of Seleucia-on-the-Tigris, and its earlier monuments reflect the civilization of that lost city'.

For Seyrig, it was also possible to observe the Roman impact on Palmyra from the first century AD onwards, but it was connected more to the outward appearance of the city than to the culture of its people. The Roman influence came primarily in the form of architectural influences on temples and also in the advent of the colonnaded streets, 'Yet in all probability these changes did not deeply affect their minds'. Ultimately, Parthian fashions and culture were with the people of Palmyra until the end.

Malcolm Colledge (1987, 26) saw greater Roman influence on Palmyrene sculptural styles after 150, but concluded that 'the basic art style remains the 'Parthian', and it still has a considerable complement of Iranian motifs, alongside the vast majority of Greek and Semitic'. Colledge believed that the Iranian influence was 'on the whole rather superficial', but finally conceded that 'the very fact that they were there at all is a striking testimony to the strength of Iranian elements in an area that was culturally fairly alien' (1987, 28).

Another important figure in the study of ancient Palmyra, Michal Gawlikowski, emphasizes the Babylonian influence on the religion of Palmyra, which he believes developed in the Neo-Babylonian or early Hellenistic period (Gawlikowski 2015, 247). Bel-Marduk, the chief god of the Babylonian pantheon, influenced the transformation of a local Palmyrene oasis god into Bēl. Nabu, the god of Borsippa who became known throughout Babylonia as the son of Bēl, became ensconced at Palmyra at about the same time. Other deities honoured in the Bēl temple complex of the Hellenistic period also had a likely Mesopotamian origin, according to Gawlikowski (2015, 248).

The Bēl temple and the complex surrounding it, however, were under construction through the first century AD and into the early second century, when Roman influence and administrative control became increasingly obvious. Rather than focusing on the long-accepted date of AD 32 for the completion of the temple, Gawlikowski points to an inscription of AD 19 (*PAT* 270) found in the temple that was erected by Palmyrene and Greek merchants from Seleucia as a terminus ante quem for the beginning of its construction. He suggests further that an inscription of AD 108 (*PAT* 263) from the temple indicates the end point of its construction. While the temple housed statues of the Roman imperial family ca. AD 18, this was more a nod to the reality of Roman imperial success in the broader region and to the increasingly undeniable fact that Palmyra's growing trading success was directly linked to a prosperous and expanding Roman Empire.

Some, including Seyrig, have seen the depiction of Bēl and a number of other gods in military cuirasses, including Yarhibol, Aglibol, Malakbel, and Arsu in the Bēl sanctuary and elsewhere, as possible evidence for increasing Roman military influence on Palmyra as the first century unfolded. Gawlikowski, however, points to sculptural depictions of some gods wearing cuirasses at Dura-Europos that date unquestionably to the middle of the first century AD as more likely Hellenistic than Roman in their origins.

An interesting development, however, which appears to signal at least some Roman influence on the military depiction of gods is the inclusion on sculpted reliefs of some Palmyrene gods such as Yarhibol and Aglibol in what is clearly Roman military attire (what Gawlikowski refers to as 'muscled breast-plate', 253). A relief of AD 121 depicting these two gods in Roman-style military attire alongside Bēl in the traditional Hellenistic cuirass is, perhaps, an interesting expression of the old and the new.

As for religion, Kaizer (2002, 261) concludes that while Palmyra took on the 'outward characteristics' of religious practice in many of the cities of the Roman Near East, 'direct Roman influence on Palmyrene religion was almost completely absent, but for the presence of the imperial cult'. Clear evidence for the Roman imperial cult at Palmyra dates to the latter half of the second century AD, but the dedication of Roman imperial statues in the temple of Bēl early in the reign of Tiberius is a possible indicator that it may have been present in some form quite early (Kaizer 2002, 148–51). It would seem, however, that Palmyra's own cults, mostly of Babylonian/Mesopotamian origins, always ruled the day in the religious life of the city.

CONCLUSION

To understand Palmyra's relationship with the Parthians, it is also necessary to understand Palmyra's relationship with the Roman Empire as it expanded further east from the middle of the first century BC to the early decades of the third century AD. In political and administrative terms, Palmyra was at the very least within the Roman orbit of influence by the early decades of the first century AD. As time passed, evidence mounts increasingly to show that Palmyra became enmeshed in the Roman provincial and imperial system. The visit of the living emperor Hadrian himself ca. AD 131 was perhaps the starkest indicator of where Palmyrene political and commercial loyalties lay by this time.

Roman military influence, marked by the presence and honouring of senior Roman military figures in the city, also grew from the time of Tiberius up until Palmyra received its first garrison of auxiliaries in the 160s. This was at approximately the same time when Roman military power had markedly increased throughout Syria and Mesopotamia due to the Parthian campaign of Lucius Verus. Palmyrene auxiliaries attached to the Roman army also made their first clear appearance after 160. Of these, the Cohors XX Palmyrenorum at Dura-Europos, likely formed ca. AD 170, is by far the best known. The extent to which Palmyra had been brought into the Roman provincial system and, therefore, the empire itself is marked ultimately by its grant of colonial status with *ius italicum* by the first decade of the third century AD.

While increasing Roman political, economic, and military power at Palmyra is undeniable from the early years of the first century AD, the capacity of Palmyrenes, even armed Palmyrene escorts of caravans, to operate in Parthian southern Mesopotamia is an interesting and potentially informative phenomenon. From the mid-first century up to the 160s, inscriptions from a number of locations at Palmyra, especially the agora, detail statue dedications to Palmyrenes who had protected and supported caravans both to and from Palmyra, especially the cities of Spasinou Charax and Vologesias. These were caravans protected by armed guards and led by individuals with something akin to military titles. It is possible that the eastern territorial gains of the Romans at the expense of the Parthians in the latter half of the second century, together with prolonged turmoil within the Parthian Empire during this time, had an impact on Palmyra's ability to participate in long-distance trade with the cities of southern Mesopotamia. A marked decrease in the relevant epigraphic evidence may be an indicator, but, as always, there is need for caution.

Culturally, it would appear, the world of southern Mesopotamia continued to dominate at Palmyra. Religion, dress, and sculptural styles continued to reflect an attachment to cultures older than the recently arrived Romans, whose architectural styles, at least, were attractive to aspirational Palmyrenes as their wealth from trade grew. Whatever the political and military realities, the Parthian world of southern Mesopotamia continued to dominate culturally at Palmyra.

Abbreviations

PAT   Hillers, Delbert R. and Eleonora Cussini, eds. 1996. *Palmyrene Aramaic Texts*. Baltimore: Johns Hopkins University Press.

Bibliography

Bowersock, Glen W. 1973. 'Syria Under Vespasian'. *Journal of Roman Studies* 63: 133–140.

Colledge, Malcolm A. R. 1976. *The Art of Palmyra*. Boulder, CO: Westview.

Colledge, Malcolm A. R. 1987. 'Parthian Cultural Elements at Palmyra'. *Mesopotamia* 22: 19–28.

Debevoise, Nielsen C. 1938. *A Political History of Parthia*. Chicago: University of Chicago Press.

Edwell, Peter M. 2008. *Between Rome and Persia: The Middle Euphrates, Mesopotamia and Palmyra under Roman Control*. London: Routledge.

Edwell, Peter M. 2013. 'The Euphrates as a Boundary Between Rome and Parthia in the Late Republic and Early Empire'. *Antichthon* 47: 191–206.

Edwell, Peter M. 2017. 'Osrhoene and Mesopotamia Between Rome and Arsacid Parthia'. In *Arsacids, Romans and Local Elites*, edited by Jason Schlude and Benjamin B. Rubin, 111–136. Oxford: Oxbow.

Gawlikowski, Michal. 2015. 'Bel of Palmyra'. In *Religious Identities in the Levant from Alexander to Muhammed: Continuity and Changes*, edited by Michael Blömer, Achim Lichtenberger, and Rubina Raja, 247–254. Turnhout: Brepols.

Hekster, Olivier, and Ted Kaizer. 2004. 'Mark Antony and the Raid on Palmyra: Reflections on Appian "Bella civilian" V.9'. *Latomus* 63: 70–80.

Isaac, Benjamin H. 1992. *The Limits of Empire: The Roman Imperial Army in the East*. Oxford: Oxford University Press.

Kaizer, Ted. 2002. *The Religious Life of Palmyra: A Study of the Social Patterns of Worship in the Roman Period*. Stuttgart: Steiner.

Matthews, John F. 1984. 'The Tax Law of Palmyra: Evidence for Economic History in a City of the Roman East'. *Journal of Roman Studies* 74: 157–180.

Millar, Fergus G. B. 1993. *The Roman Near East, 31 bc–ad 337*. Cambridge, MA: Harvard University Press.

Pollard, Nigel. 2000. *Soldiers, Cities and Civilians in Roman Syria*. Ann Arbor: University of Michigan Press.

Potts, Daniel T. 1997. 'The Roman Relationship with the Persicus Sinus from the Rise of Spasinou Charax (127 bc) to the Reign of Shapur II (ad 309–79)'. In *The Early Roman Empire in the East*, edited by Susan E. Alcock, 89–107. Oxford: Oxbow.

Sartre, Maurice. 2005. *The Middle East under Rome*. Cambridge, MA: Harvard University Press.

Seyrig, Henri. 1932. 'Antiquités Syriennes'. *Syria* 13: 266–277.

Seyrig, Henri. 1950. 'Palmyra and the East'. *Journal of Roman Studies* 40: 1–7.

Sommer, Michael. 2005. *Roms orientalische Steppengrenze: Palmyra, Dura-Europos, Hatra; Eine Kulturgeschichte von Pompeius bis Diocletian*. Stuttgart: Steiner.

CHAPTER 20

PALMYRA AND DURA-EUROPOS

Contact, Impact, and Differences

LUCINDA DIRVEN

INTRODUCTION

EVER since the accidental discovery of Dura-Europos in 1920, the contacts between this small fortified town on the left bank of the Euphrates and the thriving metropolis of Palmyra, located about 225 km to its west in the Syrian Desert, have been the object of research and speculation (Cumont 1926, introduction). Among the first finds from a temple situated in the north-west corner of the newly discovered ruins of Dura was a wall painting that depicts the tribune Julius Terentius and his men of the XX Palmyrene cohort sacrificing to three deities and two protective goddesses (Figure 20.1); the accompanying Greek *dipinti* identify the goddesses as the Tyche of Palmyra and the Tyche of Dura, respectively (Breasted 1924, 94–99). Not only did this find enable the excavators to identify the newly discovered town as Dura, but it suggested that the faiths of Palmyra and Dura had once been intimately connected. This impression was confirmed during subsequent excavations in the 1920s and 1930s by a wealth of finds that bear testimony to the relationship between the two cities (Dirven 1999, appendix; Smith II 2013, 150–160). The inscriptions and graffiti in Palmyrene (Mesnil du Buisson 1939) and Greek (Stuckenbruck 2016), the remains of at least six religious buildings and one private residence and of a substantial number of wall paintings and reliefs, as well as the frequent references to the Cohors XX Palmyrenorum in Roman military papyri dated to the third century (Welles et al. 1959), enable us to study the continuous history of Palmyrene visitors and immigrants in Dura from 33 BC until AD 256, when Dura was captured by the Sassanian army, after which it was quickly abandoned (James 1985). This period roughly coincides with the heyday of Palmyra, so richly documented by inscriptions and archaeological remains. As a result, the material remains that testify

FIGURE 20.1 Painting representing the sacrifice of the tribune Julius Terentius and his men of the Cohors XX Palmyrenorum to statues of three Palmyrene deities on pedestals, accompanied by the Tyche of Palmyra and Dura, respectively. Wall painting from the pronaos of the so-called Temple of the Palmyrene gods, ca. AD 240.

Courtesy YUAG.

to the presence of Palmyrenes in Dura can be compared and understood in the light of their city of origin. It is noteworthy that neither Dura-Europos nor its Palmyrene or Durene inhabitants are identifiable in records from Palmyra itself. Were it not for the finds from Dura, we would have been ignorant of the close relationship between the two cities.

Not only is the amount of Palmyrene material found in Dura-Europos abundant and spread over almost three centuries, it is also found in an exceedingly rich archaeological context (Hopkins 1979). As Ted Kaizer has recently pointed out once again, Dura-Europos is one of the best sources for the reconstruction of day-to-day life in a small provincial town in the eastern part of the Roman Empire in the first three centuries AD (Kaizer 2017a, 94).

Although Dura was founded at the beginning of the Hellenistic period, most finds date to the first three centuries AD, with the most spectacular finds dating to the last fifty years of the city's existence (Baird 2018). The best-known and most spectacular finds include a large quantity of inscriptions; an unusually rich record of domestic houses (Baird 2014); graffiti and *dipinti* in at least ten languages; documents relating to the local economy; at least twenty pagan sanctuaries (Welles 1969; Leriche 2016), plus the famous synagogue and house church (Kraeling 1956; 1967); an extraordinary number of wall paintings and sculptures (Perkins 1973; Dirven 2016); and an extraordinarily rich corpus of parchments and papyri (Welles et al. 1959), among which is one of the richest military archives found to date. The evidence relating to Palmyrenes can therefore be studied in its Durene context, and, from this, we may hope to ascertain whether, and if so, to what extent, the Palmyrenes influenced or were influenced by their new surroundings.

A Concise History of Dura-Europos

During the almost three centuries in which Palmyrenes are attested in Dura, the city was until its conquest by the Romans during the Parthian campaigns of Lucius Verus in AD 165 part of the Parthian Empire. These political allegiances had a profound influence on the city's economic and social functions and are therefore crucial for the interpretation of the Palmyrene material. During the period of Parthian domination, Dura functioned primarily as the centre of a rich agricultural and horticultural region along the Euphrates. Parthian documents among the parchments and papyri found at Dura testify to the city's interaction with this region (Millar 1998). From the first half of the first century onwards, a group of people from Anath, a village on the Euphrates about 50 km south of Dura, gathered in a small chapel in which they worshipped their god Aphlad. It is important to stress that Dura did not develop into a 'Parthian' town during this period and that no Parthian officials or soldiers resided in the city. Rather, the Parthian rulers made use of the existing Greek institutions. Dura's ruling class proudly propagated their (real or imagined) Greek origins, bore traditional Greek names, and used Greek in their inscriptions. This does not mean, of course, that Dura was still a profoundly Greek city during this period. Over the course of three centuries, indigenous traditions had a deep influence on the creation of a typically local, Durene culture. But the Greek language and real or imagined Greek traditions still played a prominent role in the creation of a local identity.

During the period of Roman domination, all this changed profoundly. During the last fifty years of its existence, especially, the city became primarily a frontier fortress, with a large Roman garrison stationed chiefly in the northern part of the city (Welles 1956; James 2019). We have good reasons to assume that the military became a dominant factor in Dura's social and economic life, with soldiers the main customers for local products (Rufing 2016, 198). The elite with Greek names disappears from our records, and their place is taken by people bearing predominantly Semitic names. Greek remains the primary language of inscriptions found in Roman Dura, but, in addition to Greek, Palmyrene, and Safaitic, we now also encounter Latin, Aramaic, Hebrew, and Middle Persian. This linguistic diversity reflects the great influx of new people with different cultural backgrounds who arrived at Dura in the wake of the Roman army.

THE SOURCES AND THEIR LIMITATIONS

Before turning to an in-depth discussion of the material, it is worth dwelling briefly on the limitations of the sources at our disposal. Apart from instances in which people explicitly identify themselves as originating from Palmyra, Palmyrenes can be identified on the basis of their use of the Palmyrene language and script, their 'typical' Palmyrene names, and/or their devotion to typical Palmyrene deities. Separately, none of these three categories provides firm proof of Palmyrene origin. In the first centuries AD, Palmyrene is attested in the region between Palmyra and the Euphrates, which shows that the language was not used only by inhabitants of the city. Many personal names attested in Palmyra are not exclusive to the oasis, and Palmyrene gods were also worshipped by people from the surrounding region, as clearly shown by the material found in the region to the north-west of the city (Schlumberger 1951). However, we frequently find many if not all of these characteristics in combination in finds from Dura. Consequently, it is highly plausible to identify these people as originating from Palmyra.

Problems of identification arise when one or several of these features are missing, but such instances are amazingly rare in the material from Dura-Europos. The most illustrative example is a relief dedicated to the god Baalshamin–Zeus Kyrios, in a Palmyrene–Greek inscription, by a certain Barateh, son of Leuqa, who is called Seleukos in Greek (Dirven 1999, 115–117) (Figure 20.2). Whereas the Palmyrene inscription, the iconography, and the name of the deity point to a Palmyrene context, the Greek and personal names are more at home in a Durene context. This example illustrates the difficulties in interpreting possible instances of interaction between people from Palmyra and Dura-Europos and shows that the nature of the material at our disposal leads to a focus on typical Palmyrene behaviour. Furthermore, Palmyrenes who assimilated to their new surroundings are bound to escape our notice since they can no longer be identified as Palmyrene. We should therefore be careful not to overestimate the cultural and religious conservatism of the Palmyrenes at Dura (Dirven 1999, 194).

Before turning to a more detailed discussion of the economic and political relationship between the two cities and the cultural and religious interaction between their inhabitants, it is useful to discuss the evidence in more detail. The oldest dated inscription from Dura-Europos is a Palmyrene dedication, dated to 33 BC, of a temple to the gods Bēl and Yarhibol by individuals identified as members of two Palmyrene tribes (Dirven 1999, 199–202). The fact that Dura's epigraphic record starts with a Palmyrene inscription is indicative of the close connection of the two cities from this time onwards. The temple is located on the plateau outside the city walls, and this prompted the excavators to label it the 'necropolis temple', despite the fact that it was unrelated to the cult of the dead. A Greek dedicatory inscription dated to AD 173 testifies to a remarkable continuity in the temple's cult after AD 165 (Dirven 1999, 203–207). Not only was the new temple also dedicated to Bēl, Palmyra's most important god, but this dedication was made by one of the descendants of the original founders, who served as its priest

FIGURE 20.2 Relief depicting Baalshamin-Zeus Kyrios, dated AD 31. The relief was made in Dura, in a style inspired by Palmyrene sculpture.

Courtesy YUAG.

and who was in turn succeeded by his son. In all likelihood, the temple remained in use until shortly before the fall of the city. We have no evidence that it was ever visited by others than Palmyrenes. The situation was similar in the so-called temple of the Gadde, an exclusively Palmyrene sanctuary located in the vicinity of the bazaar, Dura's commercial centre (Dirven 1999, 98–102). The temple was named after the protective deities of Tadmor and Dura that figure in two votive reliefs that were commissioned in Palmyra by a certain Hairan (Figure 20.3). The latter is represented as a priest wearing typical Palmyrene dress. The inscriptions are dated AD 159, but the history of the sanctuary undoubtedly begins much earlier. The two Gadde flanked a third relief on which the main deity was represented, who is probably to be identified as the Palmyrene god Malakbel (Dirven 1999, 248–253). Other finds from this temple also depict Palmyrene deities and were dedicated by Palmyrenes, but, in contrast to the main reliefs, these

FIGURE 20.3 Relief made in Palmyra depicting the Gad of Dura, dated AD 159.

Courtesy YUAG.

sculptures were produced in Dura. Like the sanctuary in the necropolis, this temple probably remained in use until the middle of the third century. In addition to these two exclusively Palmyrene temples, the relief dedicated to Baalshamin–Zeus Kyrios possibly testifies to a cult shared by Durenes and Palmyrenes.

The three older temples remained in use after Roman troops were stationed in Dura. In this period, the Palmyrene military probably joined the community of the temple of the Gadde. But although both the temple of the Gadde and the temple in the necropolis almost doubled in size, we have no reason to believe that their cult changed substantially during this period. To these long-known Palmyrene temples we may now add a room located in a building in block M5, where a small, locally produced relief was found; it was dedicated to the god Bēl in AD 173–174. The relief features a Palmyrene priest in front of a temple, carrying two standards topped by images of deities. The room possibly functioned as an *andron* for a Palmyrene community. Towards the end of its existence the room was used as a military depot (Leriche 1997, 897–904), but whether the earlier Palmyrene visitors were also military is impossible to determine. The *andron* from a domestic building in block M7 clearly served a Palmyrene clientele since the men who are depicted here ask to be remembered before Bēl, Yarhibol, Aglibol, and Arsu in a Palmyrene inscription dated to AD 194. The mural in a banquet hall, depicting the eunuch Otes and the councillor Iabsumos, son of Abdaates, with their acolyte and son, sacrificing before five Palmyrene deities standing on globes, probably dates to the third century AD. Again, the gods Bēl, Yarhibol, and Aglibol are represented, now with Arsu and Athena-Allat. The personal names of the men (written in Greek, strikingly) suggest that they were local inhabitants; it is telling that they worship Palmyrene deities in a temple that stands out for its strong Palmyrene military presence (Dirven 1999, 281–293).

Other finds from this period are more clearly related to Palmyrene militia or military personnel serving in the Roman army as members of the Cohors XX Palmyrenorum. In 168–169 and 170–171, two *strategoi* of the so-called Palmyrene archers dedicated a relief representing the god Mithras killing the bull (Dirven 1999, 260–272). These inscriptions are the first testimonies to a mithraeum that was probably founded by Palmyrene bowmen. It is not known whether, and, if so for how long, this was an exclusive Palmyrene community. The fact that the later relief bears a dedicatory inscription in Greek perhaps suggests that from early days the community comprised non-Palmyrenes. In any case, it is certain that by the beginning of the third century, this mithraic community consisted primarily of legionaries, among whom Palmyrenes were only a minority (Francis 1975). In addition, Palmyrenes serving in the Cohors XX Palmyrenorum (attested in Dura from the beginning of the third century) are known from a number of other cult sites which they shared with non-Palmyrene soldiers. An illustrative example is the above-mentioned Temple of the Palmyrene Gods, in which the mural representing the sacrifice of the tribune Julius Terentius and his men before three Palmyrene gods was found. Palmyrenes are also attested in the so-called temples of Azzanathkona and Zeus Megistos (Dirven 1999, 315–325). Thanks to the very rich military archive that was found at Dura, we are extraordinarily well informed about the organization and economic business of this auxiliary cohort. One very important source for our knowledge of ritual organization within the Roman army is the so-called *Feriale Duranum*, which presents us with a part of the daily ritual calendar of the Palmyrene unit (Fink 1971, no. 117). It is worth mentioning that this official document, which was probably used throughout the empire, does not mention the typical Palmyrene deities that figure prominently in the material evidence testifying to the religious practices of this unit.

ECONOMIC AND POLITICAL RELATIONS

From the beginning of the Common Era, Palmyra was subject to Rome, whereas Dura-Europos belonged to Parthian territory. Even if, following recent research, the situation along the eastern frontier is regarded as far more ambiguous than was formerly believed (Luther 2004; Sommer 2005, 58–65; Kaizer 2017a), there can be no doubt that until well into the second century the political loyalties of the two cities differed. The animosity between the two superpowers was obviously no reason to turn away Palmyrene immigrants from cities on Parthian soil. The evidence cited above clearly shows that, from the first century BC or even earlier, a Palmyrene community was permanently based in Dura-Europos. Palmyrene inscriptions show that the situation in Parthian Dura was by no means exceptional: merchants from Palmyra were also stationed in other cities in the Parthian Empire, such as Spasinou Charax, Babylon, and Seleucia on the Tigris (Seland 2016, 35–38). Eivind Heldaas Seland is probably right to argue that these people were viewed not so much as inhabitants of the Roman Empire as simply Palmyrenes.

The Palmyrenes stationed in Babylonia were primarily involved in the caravan trade, and it is no stretch of the imagination to suppose that the Palmyrene community at Dura was mostly involved in trading activities as well. Unfortunately, however, the sources are completely silent on the matter of the economic function of the Palmyrene community in Dura in the period preceding the Roman occupation. The location of a temple outside the city walls and the loyalty of the Palmyrene community towards the principal deities from their hometown suggest that this was a community that still maintained close contacts with their city of origin, a situation that accords well with mercantile activities on their part. The respect paid by the Palmyrenes in the temple of the Gadde to both their own protective deity and that of their new hometown also suggests that their fate depended on the good fortune of both cities, a situation well suited to a trading community engaged in business in both localities. So although evidence is missing, it is likely that until the Roman occupation of Dura-Europos the Palmyrene community mainly (but probably not exclusively) consisted of merchants (Smith II 2013, 150–160).

Even more enigmatic is the nature of the trading activities this community was involved in. Since Dura-Europos is located on the shortest route from Palmyra to the Euphrates, which Palmyrene merchants followed on their journey to southern Babylonia, Franz Cumont supposed that Dura was a station on the caravan route to the Gulf (Cumont 1926, esp. XXXVIII–XLI). He was followed by Michael Rostovtzeff (1932), who counted Dura among the so-called caravan cities of the Roman Near East. Specialists on Palmyra, however, pointed out long ago that this route must have been located further to the south, between Palmyra and Hit (Poidebard 1934). In a well-known article, Michael Gawlikowski pointed out that Palmyrene merchants used boats on the Euphrates to transport their goods southwards. Upstream, the river is only navigable as far as Hit, meaning that the caravans certainly chose this route on their way back to Palmyra (Gawlikowski 1988, 169). In an earlier publication, I suggested that Palmyrene merchants possibly embarked near Dura on their way down to the Gulf but were mainly involved in the trade of local produce between the two cities. Dura functioned as the commercial centre of an agricultural and horticultural region along the banks of the middle Euphrates, and it is probable that the growing metropolis used the Durene market to buy produce that was scarce in the surrounding territory (Dirven 1999, 38–40). Recent research by Jorgen Christopher Meyer and Eivind Heldaas Seland confirms that the caravans did indeed travel by way of Hit (Meyer and Seland 2016). These two researchers convincingly argue, furthermore, that this route was also used on the outbound journey. Between Dura and Hit the river has a meandering course and strong current, which is not attractive for riverine navigation. If this theory is correct, it follows that Dura never was a station for the Palmyrene caravan trade. In all probability, therefore, its Palmyrene community was primarily involved in trade involving local produce such as olive oil and wine (Kaizer 2017b, 48).

It is a vexed question whether Palmyrene troops were stationed in Parthian Dura. Palmyra possessed specialized police units that guarded the desert between the city and the Euphrates and contributed to the protection of the caravans and other trading expeditions. Assuming that Dura was a station on the route of the Palmyrene caravans, Rostovtzeff (1935b, 301) argued that Palmyrene police forces were stationed in the city. However, the first instances that testify to the presence of a group of Palmyrene archers in Dura originate from the mithraeum and date to AD 169 and 170–171 (i.e., after the Parthian campaign of Lucius Verus in AD 165). A third instance—a relief dedicated to Yarhibol by the archers belonging to the Bene Mita—is undated, but the style of the relief suggests a date in the second half of the second century (Downey 1977, 259). Hence Palmyrene troops are only attested in Dura after the city was at least nominally in Roman hands. It is true that before this date there is evidence testifying to the presence of Palmyrene (and Roman) troops in the desert area between Palmyra and the Euphrates, thus illustrating the porosity of this frontier area during the first two centuries of the Common Era. However, it does not necessarily follow that troops were also stationed in Dura at an early date. Inscriptions from Palmyra suggest their archers fell under the sphere of influence of the Roman army (Yon 2002, 114–116). I therefore find it hard to believe the Parthians would allow them to be stationed in a city under Parthian jurisdiction.

In a recent article, Ted Kaizer (2017a), building on a suggestion first made by Andreas Luther (2004), argues that the transition of Dura from Parthian to Roman control was far less clear than is generally assumed. The general opinion is that Dura fell into Roman hands in AD 165, after the Parthian campaign of Lucius Verus. During the first ten years of Roman occupation, however, no regular Roman troops are attested in the city (Baird 2014, 60; but now James 2019). The only attested military presence is the Palmyrene archers mentioned above, and it is therefore assumed that they indirectly controlled the town for Rome. In fact, this largely tallies with what was argued before, were it not for the suggestion that the Palmyrenes were acting largely on their own initiative and had stepped into a power vacuum in the middle Euphrates region. Kaizer suggests that the Palmyrenes acted from imperialistic motives to secure their local trading interests (Kaizer 2017a, 85). This hypothesis pushes the evidence a bit too far. Not only is there no evidence concerning this Palmyrene initiative, but the evidence we do have suggests that the archers were stationed in Dura in the wake of Rome's victory. Recent archaeological research into the mithraeum and the remainder of the Roman camp suggests that the Palmyrene militia were assimilated with Roman military culture and were soon joined by regular Roman troops (Dirven and McCarty, 2020, 177–178). This is confirmed by epigraphic evidence from Palmyra, which points to close connections between this Palmyrene militia and official Roman troops (Yon 2002, 114–115). It therefore is safest to assume that the Palmyrene archers were stationed in Dura on behalf of Rome. This does not, of course, preclude the possibility that they were also acting in their own interests.

Cultural Influences

During the first three centuries of the Common Era, Palmyra flourished. The city became an important artistic centre with a very particular local culture displaying strong Roman influences in certain categories, such as public buildings, architectural decoration, and the decoration of elite houses (Dirven, forthcoming). In view of the strong and consistent Palmyrene presence in Dura-Europos, it is to be expected that the oasis exerted a strong cultural influence on its much smaller neighbour. Although it can be shown that such an influence existed, it was in fact surprisingly small and was largely restricted to the first two centuries of the Common Era. It is important to stress that the outward appearance of both cities was very different during this period. As far as we can see, architecture in Dura was not influenced by Graeco-Roman traditions. Typical Roman features such as honorary statues and funerary portraits, both very prominent in Palmyra, are missing in Dura altogether (Downey 1988). Compared with Palmyra, Dura-Europos must have looked like a very provincial town indeed. Artistic influence between the two cities is restricted to sculptures and—to a lesser extent—paintings, the two artistic genres for which Dura is best known.

From the moment of their discovery, the figurative arts from Dura were frequently put on a par with the monuments of Palmyra. This is largely due to the publications of Michael Rostovtzeff, the head of the Dura mission from 1928, who laid great stress on the stylistic similarities between the figurative arts from the two cities (Rostovtzeff 1935a). According to Rostovtzeff, these stylistic similarities were due not to Palmyra exerting a cultural influence on Dura-Europos (in fact, Rostovtzeff tried to play down this influence), but to a communal source of inspiration: the arts of the Parthian court in Ctesiphon. Although this art has entirely been lost, Rostovtzeff argued that Parthian art could be reconstructed on the basis of the figurative arts found in cities on the edge of the Parthian Empire, such as Dura-Europos, Palmyra, Hatra, and Edessa. Nowadays, hardly anyone looks to the Parthian capital to explain the presumed artistic *koine* in these cities. Instead, it has become fashionable to stress the artistic independence of these so-called frontier cities. The characteristics of Parthian art as formulated by Rostovtzeff are, however, still considered an adequate description of the figurative arts from this region, and hence great stress is laid on reciprocal stylistic similarities. It is only recently that a number of scholars have argued for a greater variety in the artistic production of these Syro-Mesopotamian cities, which has in fact opened the door to a more profound study of mutual cultural influences (Hauser 2014; Dirven 2017).

The sculptures from Dura-Europos have been studied in detail by Susan B. Downey in her final report on the stone and plaster sculptures from the city (Downey 1977). Downey distinguishes five broad stylistic categories, which largely correspond to distinct cultural influences that made themselves felt in the city. The category that is most important in the present context is that of the sculptures that are stylistically related to Palmyra. This group consists of five works of Palmyrene limestone, produced

FIGURE 20.4 Relief depicting the Palmyrene god Yarhibol. Made in a local style in Dura, second half of the second century AD.

Courtesy YUAG.

by Palmyrene craftsmen in Palmyra and set up by Palmyrenes residing in Dura after the middle of the second century AD (Figure 20.3) (Downey 1977, 253–255), and about ten works of white limestone that were made locally and were clearly influenced by sculptures from Palmyra (Figure 20.2) (Downey 1977, 239–245). In contrast to the genuinely Palmyrene works, most local sculptures influenced by Palmyra are dated early, around the middle of the first century AD. They are characterized by a hieratic formalism and a neat, precise carving that differs significantly from the locally produced sculptures of a later date discussed below. Characteristic are the staring eyes, as well as the minute rendering of jewellery, weapons, and other details.

The high-end, early local sculptures are replaced by a large group of locally produced reliefs and heads of male figures, mostly carved from a poor-quality local gypsum. According to Downey, all the works belonging to this rather coarse group of sculptures can be dated to the middle of the second century or later and are characteristic of local artistic production in Roman Dura (Downey 1977, 259–264). The major characteristics of this group are flatness and linearity and a lack of naturalism (Figure 20.4). Stylistically, they are unrelated to contemporary sculptures from Palmyra. It is perhaps no coincidence that all genuinely Palmyrene sculptures found at Dura also date from this period. Due to the inferior quality of the local production, Palmyrenes looking for superior sculptures chose to import from their hometown. But not all Palmyrenes had the desire or the means to take this course. Quite a number of their sculptures were produced locally, in the coarse Durene style. Although the style of these sculptures deviates from contemporary Palmyrene sculptures, it is remarkable that the iconography, and frequently also the language, is in line with Palmyrene traditions.

As for the paintings, they are far more difficult to compare since few paintings from Palmyra have come down to us. By far the majority of the Durene paintings date from the last fifty years of the city's existence. Only a handful of paintings are dated earlier, to the first century AD (Dirven 2016, 79–83). As with the sculptures, we may note a remarkable stylistic difference between the early and later production. Since so few paintings have been preserved other than in Dura, it is difficult to establish their source of inspiration. However, the style of the earlier paintings is best compared to paintings from Palmyra, notably the paintings from the so-called Tomb of the Three Brothers (Dirven 2016, 85), an influence that accords well with Palmyrene influence on early Durene sculptures. Paintings found in a banquet room of a private residence in block M7 dated in 194 AD were made for Palmyrenes, probably by painters from Palmyra (Dirven 1999, 281–284). If this is correct, Palmyrene residents not only imported sculptures but also invited Palmyrene artists to work in Dura. The influence exerted by Palmyra on Dura's material culture is confirmed by the terracotta plaques and medallions found at Dura (Downey 2003). With the exception of Palmyra, terracotta artefacts of this kind are rare in Near Eastern sites in the Greek, Parthian, and Roman periods. These modest objects therefore illustrate the close connection between the two cities, notably in the period preceding the settlement of the Roman army.

RELIGIOUS INTERACTION

By far the majority of the Palmyrene material from Dura was found in a religious context. In their religious behaviour, the Palmyrenes demonstrated a remarkable loyalty to their local gods. Their religion did not, however, simply copy the religion in Palmyra but was instead determined by their social position as immigrants in a foreign city (Dirven 1999, throughout, esp. 190–195). Palmyrene immigrants can be subdivided into a group consisting primarily of merchants and a group of Palmyrenes who served in the Roman army. Whereas Bēl and his associates were most popular among the merchants, the soldiers showed a clear preference for the gods Yarhibol and Malakbel. This difference can be explained by the social position of the two groups. Palmyrene merchants constituted a small and close-knit community that gathered in sanctuaries predominantly visited by Palmyrenes: the temple outside the city in the necropolis and the so-called temple of the Gadde (Dirven 1999). Apart from the Gad of Dura, all the deities worshipped in these sanctuaries are distinctively Palmyrene. The most conspicuous feature of these gods is the municipal significance of their cult in Palmyra, which distinguishes them from the gods whose cult was typical of smaller social groups, such as clans and families. In all likelihood, these gods were chosen in Dura because their cult transcended the tribal organization within Palmyra, so that these gods provided the small immigrant community with a communal religious identity that connected them to their city of origin. This clearly illustrates the immigrants' desire to preserve a local religious identity in a foreign environment. This desire is underlined by the distinctively Palmyrene dress of the Palmyrene priests who served in these sanctuaries.

The relief dedicated to the Gad of Dura found in the temple of the Gadde clearly illustrates that the attachment of Palmyrene expatriates to their local gods did not preclude their participation in the religious life of their new residence (Figure 20.3). As inhabitants and merchants, they undoubtedly interacted with other groups in the city, and hence it is very likely that they participated in one or several of the numerous non-Palmyrene cult associations in the city. Since, however, their worship of local gods no longer identified them as Palmyrenes, this is impossible to establish with certainty. Conversely, it seems that the local community was scarcely influenced by the Palmyrene cults. A possible example of a shared cult of Palmyrene origin is provided by the sanctuary of Baalshamin–Zeus Kyrios. In the Roman period, we finally have evidence of non-Palmyrenes participating in the worship of Palmyrene gods in the so-called Temple of the Palmyrene Gods. Significantly, the chapel in which the relevant painting was found is located in a temple with a predominantly military clientele, primarily members of the Cohors XX Palmyrenorum.

Like Palmyrene merchants, Palmyrene soldiers associated with or serving in the Roman army conformed to the religion of their new environment. This was, first and foremost, the army itself, with its mixed social composition. The *Feriale Duranum* shows that Palmyrene soldiers adhered to the official religion within the Roman army, while archaeological remains show that they also participated in cults that were particularly popular among soldiers, such as those of Mithras and Jupiter Dolichenus. At the same time, they also revered typical Palmyrene deities. In comparison with the religion of non-military Palmyrenes, however, we note a remarkable shift towards the veneration of the gods Yarhibol and Malakbel, a preference best explained by the popularity of solar cults in the Roman army at this time (Dirven 1999, 157–189). It is noteworthy that such typical Palmyrene preferences are now found, in the main, in temples that were also used by other, non-Palmyrene soldiers. Unfortunately, we have no way of knowing whether these soldiers also participated in the cult of the Palmyrene gods.

CONCLUSION

In spite of the close and enduring ties between Palmyra and Dura-Europos, Palmyrene influence on Dura was minimal. Culturally speaking, this influence was strongest in the period before Dura became a Roman garrison town. At this time, Durene sculptors were clearly inspired by the artistic production in their prosperous neighbouring city. Palmyrene religion, however, was largely confined to the Palmyrene community and seems to have exerted little influence on its surroundings. Possibly Palmyrene immigrants interacted with the other inhabitants in local cult associations, but unfortunately this is very difficult to establish. The only possible instance testifying to such contact is the relief dedicated to Baalshamin–Zeus Kyrios (Figure 20.1). After the Roman conquest, Palmyra's cultural influence diminished drastically. This was not so much due to less contact (there had never, in fact, been more Palmyrenes in Dura), nor to the cultural production in Palmyra itself (which was now at its peak), as to a shift in the local economy, which came to be centred on the ever-increasing military population, which included many Palmyrenes. It is telling that now, for the first time, we encounter local Durenes paying homage to typical Palmyrene gods.

BIBLIOGRAPHY

Baird, Jennifer. 2014. *The Inner Lives of Ancient Houses: An Archaeology of Dura-Europos*. Oxford: Oxford University Press.

Baird, Jennifer. 2018. *Dura-Europos*. London: Bloomsbury Academic.

Breasted, James Henry. 1924. *The Oriental Forerunners of Byzantine Painting: Oriental Institute Publications*. Vol. 1. Chicago: University of Chicago Press.

Cumont, Franz. 1926. *Fouilles de Doura-Europos, 1922–3*. Paris: Geuthner.

Dirven, Lucinda. 1999. *The Palmyrenes of Dura-Europos: A Study of Religious Interaction in Roman Syria*. Leiden: Brill.

Dirven, Lucinda. 2016. 'The Problem with Parthian Art at Dura'. In *Religion, Society and Culture at Dura-Europos*, edited by Ted Kaizer, 68–88. Yale Classical Studies 38. Cambridge: Cambridge University Press.

Dirven, Lucinda. Forthcoming. 'Unity in Diversity? A Note on the Co-existence of Different Styles in Palmyrene Sculpture'. In *Life in Palmyra, Life for Palmyra*, edited by Dagmara Wielgosz and Marta Żuchowska. Warsaw: Uniwersytet Warszawski.

Dirven, Lucinda, and Matt McCarty. 2020. 'Rethinking the Dura-Europos Mithraeum. Diversification and Stabilization in a Mithraic Community'. In *The Archaeology of Mithraism: New Finds and Approaches to Mithras-Worship*, edited by Matthew McCarty and Mariana Egri, 165–181. Leuven: Peeters.

Downey, Susan B. 1977. *The Excavations at Dura-Europos Conducted by Yale University and the French Academy of Inscriptions and Letters: Final Report*. Vol. 3, *Sculpture, Figurines, and Painting*. Part 1, fasc. 2, *The Stone and Plaster Sculpture*. Los Angeles: Institute of Archaeology, University of California.

Downey, Susan B. 1988. *Mesopotamian Religious Architecture: Alexander Through the Parthians*. Princeton, NJ: Princeton University Press.

Downey, Susan B. 2003. *Terracotta Figurines and Plaques from Dura-Europos*. Ann Arbor: University of Michigan Press.

du Mesnil du Buisson, Robert. 1939. *Inventaire des inscriptions palmyréniennes de Doura-Europos (32 av. J. C. à 256 après J.C.)*. Paris: Geuthner.

Fink, Robert O. 1971. *Roman Military Records on Papyrus*. Cleveland: Case Western Reserve University Press for American Philological Association.

Francis, Eric D. 1975. 'Mithraic Graffiti from Dura-Europos'. In *Mithraic Studies: Proceedings of the First International Congress of Mithraic Studies*. Vol. 2, edited by John R. Hinnels, 424–445. Manchester: Manchester University Press.

Gawlikowski, Michael. 1988. 'Le commerce de Palmyre sur terre et sur eau'. In *L'Arabie et ses mers bordières*. Vol. 1, *Itinéraires et voisinages*, edited by Jean-François Salles, 163–172. Travaux de la Maison de l'Orient 16. Lyon: GS Maison de l'Orient.

Hauser, Stephan R. 2014. '"Parthian Art" or "Arts in the Arsacid Empire"'. In *'Parthische Kunst' Kunst im Partherreich: Akten des Internationalen Kolloquiums in Basel, 9. Oktober 2010*, edited by Bruno Jacobs, 127–178. Duisburg: Wellem Verlag.

James, Simon. 1985. 'Dura-Europos and the Chronology of Syria in the 250s AD'. *Chiron* 15: 111–124.

James, Simon. 2019. *The Roman Military Base at Dura-Europos, Syria: An Archaeological Visualization*. Oxford: Oxford University Press.

Kaizer, Ted. 2017a. 'Empire, Community, and Culture on the Middle Euphrates: Durenes, Palmyrenes, Villagers, and Soldiers'. *Bulletin of the Institute of Classical Studies* 60: 63–95.

Kaizer, Ted. 2017b. 'Trajectories of Hellenism at Tadmor-Palmyra and Dura-Europos'. In *Hellenism and the Local Communities of the Eastern Mediterranean, 400 BCE–250 CE*, edited by Boris Chrubasik and Daniel King, 29–51. Oxford: Oxford University Press.

Kraeling, Carl. 1956. *The Synagogue*. The Excavations at Dura-Europos, Final Report, vol. 8, part 1. New Haven, CT: Yale University Press.

Kraeling, Carl. 1967. *The Christian Building*. The Excavations at Dura-Europos, Final Report 8, part 2. New Haven, CT: Yale University Press.

Leriche, Pierre. 1997. 'Materiaux pour une reflexion renouvelée sur les sanctuaires de Doura-Europos'. *Topoi* 7(2): 889–913.

Leriche, Pierre. 2016. 'Recent Discoveries Concerning Religious Life in Europos-Dura'. In *Icon, Cult and Context: Sacred Spaces and Objects in the Classical World*, edited by Maura K. Heyn and Ann Irvine Steinshapir, 153–190. Los Angeles: UCLA Cotsen Institute of Archaeology Press.

Luther, Andreas. 2004. 'Doura-Europos zwischen Palmyra und den Parthern: Der politische Status der Region am Mittleren Euphrat am 2. Jh. n. Chr. und die Organisation des palmyrenischen Fernhandels'. In *Commerce and Monetary Systems in the Ancient World: Means of Transmission and Cultural Interaction*, edited by Robert Rollinger and Christoph Ulf, 327–351. Oriens et Occidens 6. Stuttgart: Steiner.

Meyer, Jorgen C., and Eivind H. Seland. 2016. 'Palmyra and the Trade Route to the Euphrates'. *ARAM* 28(1–2): 497–523.

Millar, Fergus. 1998. 'Dura-Europos Under Parthian Rule'. In *Das Partherreich und seine Zeugnisse: The Arsacid Empire; Sources and Documentation*, edited by Josef Wiesenhöfer, 473–493. Stuttgart: Steiner.

Perkins, Ann. 1973. *The Art of Dura Europos*. Oxford: Oxford University Press.

Poidebard, Antoine. 1934. *La trace de Rome dans le désert de Syrie*. Paris: Geuthner.

Rostovtzeff, Michael. 1932. *Caravan Cities: Petra, Jerash, Palmyra, Dura*. Oxford: Oxford University Press.

Rostovtzeff, Michael. 1935a. 'Dura and the Problem of Parthian Art'. *Yale Classical Studies* 5: 157–303.

Rostovtzeff, Michael. 1935b. 'Deux notes sur les trouvailles de la dernière campagne de fouilles a Doura-Europos'. *Comptes rendus des séances de l'Académie des inscriptions et belles-lettres* 79: 285–304.

Rostovtzeff, Michael. 1938. *Dura Europos and Its Art*. Oxford: Oxford University Press.

Rufing, Kai. 2016. 'Economic Life in Roman Dura-Europos'. In *Religion, Society and Culture at Dura-Europos*, edited by Ted Kaizer, 190–198. Yale Classical Studies 38. Cambridge: Cambridge University Press.

Schlumberger, Daniel. 1951. *La Palmyrène du Nord-Ouest*. Paris: Geuthner.

Seland, Eivind H. 2016. *Ships of the Desert and Ships of the Sea: Palmyra and the World Trade of the First Three Centuries CE*. Wiesbaden: Harrassowitz.

Smith II, Andrew M. 2013. *Roman Palmyra: Identity, Community and State Formation*. Oxford: Oxford University Press.

Sommer, Michael. 2005. *Roms orientalische Steppengrenze: Palmyra, Dura-Europos, Hatra; Eine Kulturgeschichte von Pompeius bis Diocletian*. Stuttgart: Steiner.

Stuckenbruck, Loren T. 2016. 'The Bilingual Palmyrene–Greek Inscriptions at Dura-Europos: A Comparison with the Bilinguals from Palmyra'. In *Religion, Society and Culture at Dura-Europos*, edited by Ted Kaizer, 177–189. Yale Classical Studies 38. Cambridge: Cambridge University Press.

Welles, C. Bradford. 1969. 'The Gods of Dura-Europos'. In *Beitrage zur alten Geschichte und deren Nachleben: Festschrift für Franz Altheim zum 6.10.1968*. Vol. 2, edited by Ruth Stiehl and Hans Erich Stier, 50–65. Berlin: de Gruyter.

Welles, C. Bradford, Robert O. Fink, and J. Frank Gilliam, eds. 1959. *The Excavations at Dura-Europos: Conducted by Yale University and the French Academy of Inscriptions and Letters; Final Report*. Vol. 5, *Inscriptions, Parchment and Papyri*. Part 1, *The Parchments and Papyri*. New Haven, CT: Yale University Press.

Yon, Jean-Baptiste. 2002. *Les notables de Palmyre*. Beirut: Institut français du Proche-Orient.

PART FIVE

PALMYRA AND ITS MONUMENTS

CHAPTER 21

URBAN LAYOUT AND PUBLIC SPACE

The Monuments of Palmyra in the Roman and Late Antique Periods

EMANUELE E. INTAGLIATA

Introduction: Urbanism and Public Space in Palmyra

IF it is beyond doubt that the origin of Palmyra goes back to at least the Bronze Age (see Figure 21.1; du Mesnil du Buisson 1966; al-Maqdissi 2000; Chapter 4 [Healey], this volume), it is from the Hellenistic period that archaeological evidence from this site become more frequent. Before the early Roman period (first century BC to first century), the settlement seems to have been mostly limited to the areas of the sanctuaries of Bēl and Baalshamin, and to the south of Wādī al-Qubūr (the so-called Hellenistic quarter) (Hammad 2010, 8–24; Schmidt-Colinet and al-Asʿad 2000; Chapter 5 [Schmidt-Colinet], this volume).

Later, and particularly from the early second century, Palmyra's urban area started expanding to the north. As it expanded, the urban layout had to face significant urbanistic challenges owing to the presence of previously existing compounds. Because of this, city blocks are not equal in size and streets do not always cross at right angles (Chapter 6 [Gawlikowski], this volume).

This expansion corresponded to a process of monumentalization of the public space that was common in many other cities in the Roman East and beyond. During this process, a theatre was constructed to the north of the agora, along the central stretch of the Great Colonnade, and an amphitheatre was probably erected further to the north, by the Dura Gate. The apparent 'incoherency' of the new city plan was partially mitigated by

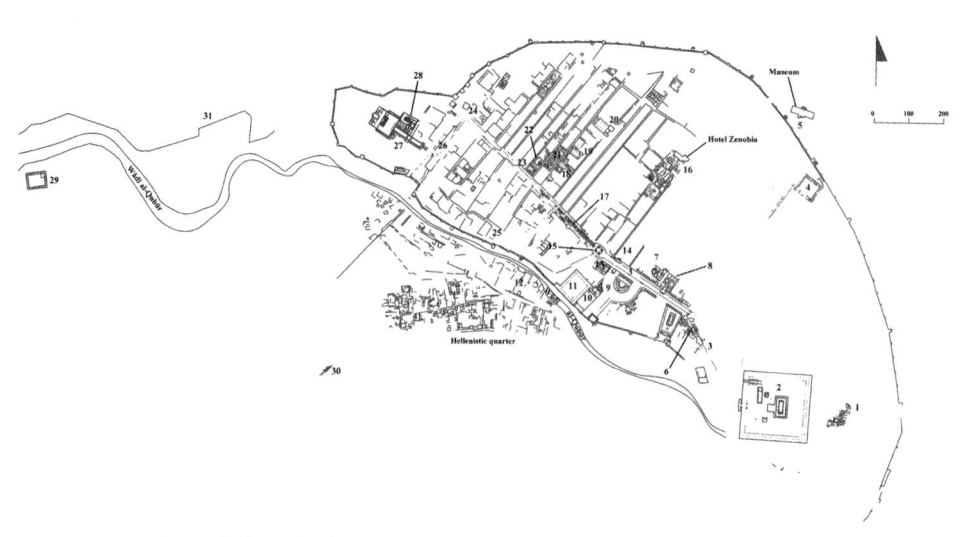

FIGURE 21.1 General plan of Palmyra: 1. Houses of Achilles and Cassiopea; 2. Sanctuary of Bēl, 3. Great Colonnade; 4. Suburban market; 5. Byzantine cemetery; 6. Buildings encroaching Section A of the Great Colonnade; 7. Church; 8. Baths of Diocletian; 9. Theatre; 10. Annexe of the agora; 11. Agora; 12. Sanctuary of Arṣū; 13. So-called *Caesareum* and congregational mosque; 14. Church; 15. Tetrapylon; 16. Sanctuary of Baalshamin; 17. Umayyad suq; 18. Church II; 19. Church III; 20. Church IV; 21. House F; 22. Church I; 23. Bellerophon Hall; 24. Church; 25. Peristyle building; 26. Transverse colonnade; 27. Camp of Diocletian; 28. Sanctuary of Allath; 29. Building [Q281]; 30. Efqa spring; 31. Western Aqueduct.

Redrawn after Schnädelbach 2010.

the construction of a number of wide colonnaded streets. These tied the urban framework together in a monumental way. They also had significant social, economic, and religious functions, as shown with the case of the Great Colonnade. In this chapter, we will provide a—necessarily brief and incomplete—overview of these monuments and how they transformed after the events of 272–273.

THE AGORA COMPLEX

The agora complex consists of three communicating components, namely an open-air courtyard of 84 × 71 m, the *curia*—or temple, and the annexe—or basilica. To the northeast, between the back wall of the annexe and the plaza of the theatre is the so-called senate, which does not communicate directly with the agora.

The open courtyard was surrounded by porticoes along its four sides, composed of columns with elaborate Corinthian capitals and brackets for supporting honorific statues. Whenever needed, light curtains were placed in the space between the columns to provide extra shade in the porticoes. The courtyard was accessible from all four sides through eleven openings, three of which were situated along its south-western wall, which opened onto the Wādī al-Qubūr and the Hellenistic quarter (Seyrig and Duru 2005, 23–38).

In the south-east of the courtyard was the *curia*. This was a rectangular, 12 × 14 m room protruding from the agora to the north-west. Originally opening onto the agora with two columns *in antis*, its access was later narrowed by blocking the *intercolumnia* with walls and constructing a gate. The internal arrangement of the *curia* also experienced two phases, the last consisting in the addition of benches against its walls (Delplace and Fournet 2005, 117–118).

Flanking the agora to the south-east is the annexe (or *basilica*), a rectangular (75 × 37 m) enclosure free from porticoes. The building could be accessed from the Wādī al-Qubūr through three large gates preceded by a vestibule. However, six more doors allowed access from the agora and the east. The high number of accesses suggests its public nature. (Delplace and Fournet 2005, 118–123).Squeezed between the theatre and the north wall of the annexe is a building that does not communicate directly with the latter, but opens onto a nearby western street and the theatre plaza. The building is traditionally known by the name of the 'senate'. It centred around a porticoed open courtyard whose main access was through the street via a narrow vestibule. Five small shops are situated along the street and three more by the portico of the theatre plaza. Opening onto the courtyard is a rectangular room (4.85 × 5.80 m) with a semicircular seating arrangement. During the excavations of the compound, five statues were brought to light, of which four were from the peristyled courtyard. The statues have been interpreted as representing Odaenathus and his family (Delplace and Fournet 2005, 123–124; Balty 2005).

The construction of the agora complex was already initiated by the last quarter of the first century, as evidenced by a number of honorific inscriptions on column brackets in the porticoes of the agora that bear dates ranging between 75/76 and 86 (*IGLS* XVII.1, 214, 225, 238, 241). However, its construction continued until approximately the first quarter of the second century. At a later point, the south-western wall of the agora was included into the city walls (on the city walls, see Chapter 25 [Juchniewicz], this volume; Juchniewicz et al. 2010; Juchniewicz 2013; Intagliata 2017; 2018, 83–96). It remains unclear who was responsible for the construction of the agora complex, but it is reasonable to assume that local benefactors might have been involved in funding this building project (Yon 2001; inscriptional evidence is silent in this regard).

In addition, the function of the *curia*, annexe, and senate remain uncertain. A long-standing theory considers the annexe to have been originally intended as a Roman basilica provided with four colonnades on its sides and a tribunal (Ward-Perkins et al. 1958, 180–182; Balty 1991, 52). Eventually, however, the tribunal was never constructed and the porticoes never completed. The incomplete annexe might have later been used as an open marketplace with temporary stalls (Delplace and Fournet 2005, 121–123).

The so-called *curia* has been interpreted as the senate and *tabularium* of the city. This hypothesis seems to be supported by the discovery, not far from the room and in the agora, of a thick layer of ash filled with terracotta stamps with inscriptions bearing the words 'Palmyra' and 'Adriana Palmyra' (Seyrig 1940, 242). These were interpreted as belonging to the archive situated within the *curia* (Delplace and Fournet 2005, 118; cf. Balty 1991, 52). As for the so-called senate, Delplace and Fournet (2005, 122–123) have advanced the hypothesis that the building may rest on the remains of a first- or second-century house, but that, in a later phase, the building was used as a meeting place for merchants.

PLACES OF ENTERTAINMENT: THE THEATRE AND AMPHITHEATRE

Evidence for places of entertainment at Palmyra in the Roman period come from the quarter to the north of the Wādī al-Qubūr. The theatre is situated along the central stretch of the Great Colonnade, between the so-called *Caesareum* and the sanctuary of Nabu. It was surrounded by a U-shaped colonnaded plaza that was accessible, *inter alia*, both from the Great Colonnade and a secondary colonnaded street leading to one of the main gates of the city walls, the Theatre Gate. These components, namely the theatre, the plaza, and the nearby portico of the Great Colonnade, were planned as part of the same building project. There is much disagreement in modern literature over the date of the construction of this building, with dates ranging from the mid-second to the mid-third centuries. However, it is clear that the theatre was never concluded, the dramatic events of 272–273 being likely responsible for this (Fourdrin 2009, 226–229).

Only the lower section of the *cavea* (*ima cavea*), the *orchestra*, and part of the stage (*scaena*) of this monument were completed. The *ima cavea* was divided by twelve staircases into eleven *cunei* (wedges) and twelve rows of seats. Had they been constructed, the *media* and *summa cavea*, that is, the middle and upper seating areas of the complex, would have occupied the greater part of the colonnaded plaza with a total diameter of 92 m (Sears 2006, 321). This suggests that the area surrounding the theatre was originally intended to accommodate the theatre and was not meant as an open square. The semicircular *orchestra* was divided from the *cavea* by a low wall and was paved with flagstones. The stage consisted of a low *frons pulpiti* decorated with alternated rectangular and semicircular niches and an elaborate *scaenae frons* of which only the first storey is left. This had five doors, the central one (the *valva regia*) being larger than the others. The *scaenae frons* consisted of columns on a continuous high pedestal with Corinthian capitals and supporting a horizontal architrave. The two columns flanking the *valva regia* are taller than the others and support a large triangular pediment. Rectangular niches with triangular pediments are situated above each door (Fourdrin 2009).

The existence of an amphitheatre in the north of the site has been suggested by Manar Hammad based on the analysis of a collection of aerial photographs taken in 1930 by the Forces Françaises du Levant (Hammad 2008). The photos show distinct traces of a sunken elliptical structure located close to the Dura Gate and suburban market and ca. 100 m long. The compound has never been excavated; therefore, its plan, architecture, and dating remain uncertain. Hammad has proposed a third-century dating, based on the historical development of the ancient site. He also noted the proximity of the structure to the Roman fort situated to the north of the Dura Gate, which finds *comparanda* elsewhere in the Roman Empire (for example, at Dura-Europos; James 2019, 124).

COLONNADED STREETS

Colonnaded streets represent an important addition to the second- and third-century Palmyrene townscape. The origin of this type of monument has been hotly debated, with theories ranging from it being a codified Roman urban marker that had evolved from the Greek model of the *stoa* to being a more localized Eastern phenomenon with little connection to the West. (The literature on this is vast: see, e.g., discussion in MacDonald 1986, 43–44; Bejor 1999; Ball 2016, 319; more recently, see Burns 2017 with extensive bibliography.) If their origin remains obscure, however, the principal functions of the colonnaded streets are not in doubt. Far from being solely necessary for circulation, with their rows of shops aligned along their sides, these monuments functioned as the commercial hub of cities in the Roman East. In some cases, as in Palmyra (Gawlikowski 1973, 80–86; Jakubiak 2013, 146–147), colonnaded streets may have also acted as monumental backdrops to religious processions. Certain also are their social and, at some sites, political functions. At Palmyra, for example, the Great Colonnade would have served not only as a meeting place, but also as a stage where the urban elite could display its political power in the form of honorific statues mounted on column brackets (Bejor 1999; Saliou 1996, 324).

The Transverse Colonnade might have been one of the earliest monuments of this kind initiated in Palmyra. The street is situated to the west of the city, by the later Camp of Diocletian, and stretched for 230 m from an oval plaza behind the Damascus Gate to the Funerary Temple 173d. There, it connected with the western section of the Great Colonnade. Its earliest inscription goes back to 110 (*CIS* 3984 = *Inv.* V, 9; Yon 2001, 156) but is problematic because it was not found *in situ* (see, Tabaczek 2002, 18, who proposes the mid-second century as a *terminus post quem* for the building of the street). Other inscriptional evidence and the style of the capitals suggest that the construction of this thoroughfare continued well into the second and third centuries (see Tabaczek 2002, 20–22: *IGLS* XVII.1, 113–117).

Yet the most iconic of these monuments undoubtedly remains the Great Colonnade. This majestic colonnaded street, approximately 1.1 km in length, runs from a square in front of Funerary Temple 173d to the *propylaea* of the sanctuary of Bēl and is one of the best-preserved examples of its kind from the Roman East. It consisted of a central carriageway flanked by two porticoes and rows of shops. The columns normally supported a horizontal architrave and were embellished with statues of prominent individuals on top of projecting brackets bearing honorific inscriptions (Tabaczek 2002, 22–41 for a full discussion and description of the monument).

The Great Colonnade is not to be intended as *decumanus* of the city since its course is not straight and the monument does not cross at a right angle with a *cardo* (Frézouls 1976, 192; Dentzer 2000, 159). Rather, it is better described as a collection of three sections built in different sizes and orientations. Within each section there is also much discontinuity. In examining the central stretch of the monument, Ostratz (1969) has concluded that its porticoes are the result of a collection of fourteen different sections, not always perfectly aligned. The width of the porticoes also varies, and this holds true for the whole carriageway (discussion in Saliou 1996, 320–321). This apparent architectural incoherency is due to the process of construction, which was financed by different families and tribes at different times (Saliou 1996).

There has been some disagreement over the construction sequence of the Great Colonnade, whose evolution is mostly understood thanks to inscriptional evidence (see Tabaczek 2002, 22–41 for a detailed description of the evolution of this monument and discussion of earlier literature; summary accounts in, *inter alia*, Barański 1995; Saliou 1996, 319–321; Yon 2002, 156). However, scholarship concurs in concluding that the western section, from the funerary temple to the *Tetrakionion*, was the first to be built, its earliest epigraphic evidence being dated to 158 (*IGLS* XVII.1, 73 = *Inv.* III, 26). After the events of 272–273, the construction of the eastern section of this stretch was still incomplete and building activity came to a halt, leaving it unfinished (al-As'ad and Stępniowski 1989, 206). The central section, from the *Tetrakionion* to the monumental arch, and the eastern section, from the monumental arch to the sanctuary of Bēl, were constructed at a later stage beginning in the second quarter of the third century (Tabaczek 2002, 31–41). The difference in orientation is apparent only when looking at the site plan; the *Tetrakionion* plaza and the wedge-shaped monumental arch were designed to deceive the eyes of passers-by and conceal this irregularity. This was needed in order to keep in place the cella of the sanctuary of Nabu, which is situated along the same trajectory as the eastern section of the Great Colonnade and whose northern enclosure portico had to be altered to make space for the new monument (Collart 1976, 85; Frézouls 1976, 197; more recently, see discussion in Yon 2002, 157).

Khans and *Marketplaces*

There is one group of buildings in Palmyra that has attracted much attention from archaeologists in the last couple of decades. Although their plans can vary, these compounds have in common a central open courtyard surrounded on all sides by small rectangular rooms. The intended function of these buildings has generated some debate in modern literature. During the excavation of one of these complexes in the Valley of the Tombs (Building Q281 in Schnädelbach's plan [2010]), the Polish team concluded that the building could be a military post dated to the second half of the third century (Gawlikowski 1993, 116–118). A thorough reanalysis of the diffusion of this type of monument in Syria and Arabia by Jean-Marie Dentzer (1994) has concluded that these could function as *khans* (i.e., inns for travellers). One of them, which was occupied from the mid-first century BC to the third century, has been excavated in the Hellenistic quarter and has yielded evidence for the existence of a rich trade network connecting the city to the East and West (Schmidt-Colinet, et al. 2013, 300, with further bibliography).

Recently, however, the excavation of one of these buildings team has led to the conclusion that some of these compounds could also be used for different purposes. The building in question, the so-called suburban market, is situated in the northern quarter of the city, close to the Dura Gate and by a colonnaded street that appears to be contemporary with it and dated to the Severan period. Its construction was, therefore, planned as part of the city's expansion to the north of the Great Colonnade. The plan of the building is rectangular (58 × 67 m) and consists of a central open courtyard surrounded by a row of rooms on all sides. As opposed to the building excavated in the Hellenistic quarter, the rooms of this compound are, in most cases, interconnected and open onto both the courtyard and the outside. The open character of the building does not appear to promote privacy, a common feature in *khans*. Rather, it betrays a more public function, which could fit well with a *macellum*—an open-air market (Delplace 2006–2007).

THE FATE OF PUBLIC MONUMENTS
AFTER ZENOBIA

After the defeat of Zenobia and the second Palmyrene revolt (272–273), the character of the city changed abruptly. From a caravan centre, Palmyra transformed into a stronghold along the Roman eastern frontier. Under Diocletian, a monumental camp hosting a legion was built at the westernmost edge of the site and its city walls were restored. The urban space also transformed dramatically. The construction of civic buildings, such as the theatre and the Great Colonnade, stopped and urban living became less monumental and more pragmatic. As was common in many sites in the Near East and beyond, private structures started encroaching into the public space, and abandoned buildings were transformed into open-air quarries. Encroachment also affected religious pagan buildings, which started being abandoned as a result of anti-pagan legislation and the diffusion of Christianity. The construction of new buildings often adopted reused building material and architecture—so-called *spolia* in modern literature (Intagliata 2018; Chapter 12 [Intagliata], this volume, with further references).

This transformation appears more clearly in the religious sphere. Excavations have revealed that the majority of the pagan sanctuaries were repurposed in this period, with the exception of the sanctuary of Allat in the Camp of Diocletian, which has yielded evidence of a violent destruction. The sanctuaries of Nabu and Baalshamin were abandoned and their precinct replaced by dwellings, workshops, and warehouses. The temple within the precinct of the sanctuary of Bēl was transformed into a church probably as early as the fifth century, its walls later being covered by Christian paintings (Chapter 12 [Intagliata], this volume, with further references).

Less is known about the fate of most of the public monuments after 273. No traces of late antique structures are left in the theatre, and the amphitheatre, as mentioned above, has never been excavated. Little is also known of the agora, which, at least in its annexe, experienced encroachment as workshops were constructed to its north-east half (Bounni and Saliby 1968, plate I).

The Great Colonnade remained the main thoroughfare of the city after 272–273. Flavius Diogenes, curator of the city in the early fourth century, was responsible for restoring an eight-column-long stretch of the street that had been ruined 'for a long time' and thought his effort worthy of record in an inscription (*IGLS* XVII.1, 101). The inscription is indicative of the necessity of maintaining the civic *decor* and *utilitas* (Bejor 1999, 7) and indicates the importance of the street in this period. The paving of the Great Colonnade seems also to have received constant upkeep throughout late antiquity, with numerous layers of gravel, one on top of another, being documented up to the seventh century (Żuchowska 2000, 187).

The thoroughfare continued to maintain a commercial function throughout late antiquity. Excavation of a shop in the southern portico of the western stretch of the street has revealed a complex stratigraphy dating back to the Roman period, including two sealed deposits, one dated to the Aurelianic reign and the other to the sixth/early seventh centuries (al-As‘ad and Stępniowski 1989, 211). In the early Islamic period, its commercial function continued. An open market or *suq* was constructed within the carriageway of the western section of the street. This consisted of a row of forty-seven shops flanked by two large lanes, large enough for pack animals to pass. The shops were constructed with reused architectural material and probably at different stages in the Umayyad period (al-As‘ad and Stępniowski 1989). The existence of four churches or chapels mentioned above as opening onto this street, as well as Greek graffiti made by devout passers-by, also points to a processional function for the Great Colonnade in this period (Intagliata 2018, 24). If this hypothesis is taken as valid, then the main functions of this monumental thoroughfare would seem not to have changed considerably since the Roman period.

The suburban market in the northern quarter also underwent major renovations after 300. The building was divided into two separate sections by blocking passageways. The western half was repurposed to accommodate private residential buildings and workshops, while the eastern part functioned as a cemetery. The small rooms that had been in use as shops in the Roman period had their entrances blocked and their space occupied by groups of five to seven burials. The excavations of these burials, which made use of wooden coffins, have not yielded grave goods but have, nonetheless, yielded rich textiles making use of golden threads (Delplace 2006–2007, 106–109).

Other Public Monuments of Late Antique Palmyra

Public buildings continued to be constructed and renovated after 273. On the central stretch of the Great Colonnade and opposite the theatre, a bathhouse was renovated under the care of the governor of Syria Sossianus Hierocles between 293 and 303. The inscription recording the event reports a total construction, although it is more likely to have been a renovation of an existing building (*IGLS* XVII.1, 100). The involvement of Sossianus Hierocles, who was also responsible for the construction of the Diocletianic fortress at the western edge of the city (Chapter 25 [Juchniewicz], this volume), suggests that the bathhouse might have been in use both by civilians and soldiers (Ostratz 1969, 114–115; more recently, Fournet 2009a; 2009b). The building was accessible through a monumental porticoed entrance with four reused monolithic columns of red granite of Aswan. Its floors were decorated in *opus sectile* and adopted reused marble material (Dodge 1988, 218–223; Wielgosz 2013, 320–321).

Perhaps the most common type of public building known in Palmyra after the third century is churches. At least eight churches are known to have been constructed in late antiquity, one of which certainly reused a previously existing pagan temple in the sanctuary of Bēl. Although churches in Palmyra are discussed in more detail in another chapter of this book (Chapter 12 [Intagliata], this volume), it remains important to stress here how these new buildings affected the public space. In the north-western quarter, access to Church III was embellished by a colonnaded *atrium* or monumental entrance which projected into the carriageway but without blocking its traffic (Gawlikowski 2002, 263–264). The ecclesiastical building next to Church II was similarly embellished, with a paved square entrance with four corner columns that, once again, projected into the street (Gawlikowski 2002, 261–264). The most disruptive change in the street layout occurred when Church IV was constructed, possibly in the sixth century. The ecclesiastical building, which counts as one of the largest of its kind in the whole of early Christian Syria, projects with its apse and *pastophoria* or flanking rooms into a nearby street, completely blocking its traffic (Schnädelbach 2010).

The impact of church construction on public space reflects the growing predominance of the clergy, and particularly the bishop, in decisions concerning urban development. In a way, then, urban planners in late antique Palmyra did not act dissimilarly from those in the Roman period when the course of the Great Colonnade had to be modified to accommodate the sanctuary of Nabu. It is important to stress, however, that although religion remained an important factor in determining urban planning in Roman Palmyra, it did not altogether prevent the construction of secular buildings by the civic administration. By contrast, in late antiquity, when the civic administration was mostly in the hands of bishops (Liebeschuetz 2001, 104–168), cities saw a gradual shrinkage in the number of secular buildings and, eventually, an explosion in church construction.

CONCLUSION

This chapter has briefly explored the use and monumentalization of public space in Palmyra between the Roman period and late antiquity. The urban expansion of Palmyra between the first and third centuries saw the construction of a number of public monuments, including places of entertainment and markets. The plan of the new city was architecturally tied together by colonnaded streets whose functions were numerous and not only commercial. The dramatic events that affected Palmyra in 272–273 brought about changes in urban living. The construction of some public buildings, such as the theatre and the Great Colonnade, was not brought to completion. There is no evidence to shed light on the fate of the theatre and amphitheatre after the fourth century. We know, however, that the Great Colonnade continued to be used as the main thoroughfare of the settlement and that the annexe of the agora complex was partially occupied by workshops. The suburban market also underwent major transformations, being reused as a residential quarter and a cemetery. In addition to the reconstruction of a bathhouse, the only public buildings worthy of note after 273 were churches. The construction of churches reflects the predominance of religious figures in civic administration who channelled public money into the construction of religious buildings.

ABBREVIATIONS

CIS	*Corpus inscriptionum Semiticarum*. Paris: Reipublicæ Typographeo, 1881–1962.
IGLS XVII.1	Yon, Jean-Baptiste, ed. *Inscriptions grecques et latines de la Syrie*. Vol. 17, fasc. 1, *Palmyre*. Bibliothèque archéologique et historique 195. Beirut: Presses de l'Institut français du Proche-Orient, 2012.
Inv.	Cantineau, Jean, ed. *Inventaire des inscriptions de Palmyre*. Vols. 1–9. Beirut: Imprimerie catholique, 1930–1936.
PAT	Hillers, Delbert and Eleonora Cussini, eds. *Palmyrene Aramaic Texts*. Baltimore: The Johns Hopkins University Press, 1996.

BIBLIOGRAPHY

al-As'ad, Khaled, and Franciszek Stępniowski. 1989. 'The Umayyad Suq in Palmyra'. *Damaszener Mitteilungen* 4: 205–223.

al-Maqdissi, Michel. 2000. 'Note sur les sondages réalisés par Robert du Mesnil du Buisson dans la cour du sanctuaire de Bēl à Palmyre'. *Syria* 77: 137–158.

Ball, Warwick. 2016. *Rome in the East: The Transformation of an Empire*. 2nd ed. New York: Routledge.

Balty, Jean-Charles. 1991. *Curia ordinis: Recherches d'architecture et d'urbanisme antiques sur les curies provinciales du monde romain*. Brussels: Académie Royale de Belgique.

Balty, Jean-Charles. 2005. 'La sculpture'. In *L'agora de Palmyre, sur la base des travaux de Henri Seyrig, Raymond Duru et Edmond Frézouls*, edited by Christiane Delplace and Jacqueline Dentzer-Feydy, 321–342. Beirut: Institut français du Proche-Orient.

Barański, Marek. 1995. 'The Great Colonnade of Palmyra Reconsidered'. *Aram* 7: 37–46.

Bejor, Giorgio. 1999. *Vie colonnate: Paesaggi urbani del mondo antico*. Rome: Giorgio Bretschneider.

Bounni, Adnan, and Nassib Saliby. 1968. 'Fouilles de l'annexe de l'agora à Palmyre. Rapport préliminaire'. *Les annales archéologiques Arabes Syriennes* 18: 93–102.

Burns, Ross. 2017. *Origins of the Colonnaded Streets in the Cities of the Roman East*. Oxford: Oxford University Press.

Collart, Paul. 1976. 'Á propos de l'autel du sanctuaire de Nébo'. In *Palmyre: Bilan et perspectives; Colloque de Strasbourg, 18–20 Octobre 1973, à la mémoire de Daniel Schlumberger et de Henri Seyrig*, edited by Edmond Frézouls, 85–95. Strasbourg: Centre de recherches sur le Proche-Orient et la Grèce.

Collart, Paul, and Jacques Vicari. 1969. *Le sanctuaire de Baalshamin à Palmyre: Topographie et architecture*. Rome: Institut suisse de Rome.

Delplace, Christiane. 2006–2007. 'La fouille du marché suburbain de Palmyre (2001–2005)'. *Les annales archéologiques Arabes Syriennes* 49–50: 91–111.

Delplace, Christiane, and Thibaud Fournet. 2005. 'Les complements sur le secteur'. In *L'agora de Palmyre, sur la base des travaux de Henri Seyrig, Raymond Duru et Edmond Frézouls*, edited by Christiane Delplace and Jacqueline Dentzer-Feydy, 117–125. Beirut: Institut français du Proche-Orient.

Dentzer, Jean-Marie. 1994. 'Khāns ou casernes à Palmyre? À propos de structures visibles sur des photographies aériennes anciennes'. *Syria* 71: 45–112.

Dentzer, Jean-Marie. 2000. 'Le développement urbain en Syrie á l'époque Hellénistique et Romaine: Modèles "occidentaux et orientaux"'. *Bulletin d'études orientales* 52: 159–163.

Dodge, Hazel. 1988. 'Palmyra and the Roman Marble Trade: Evidence from the Baths of Diocletian'. *Levant* 20: 215–230.

du Mesnil du Buisson, Robert. 1966. 'Première campagne de fouilles à Palmyre'. *Comptes rendus des séances de l'Académie des inscriptions et belles-lettres* 110: 158–187.

Fourdrin, Jean-Pascal. 2009. 'Le front de scène du théâtre de Palmyre'. In *Fronts de scène et lieux de culte dans le théâtre antique*, edited by Jean-Charles Moretti, 189–233. Lyon: Maison de l'Orient et de la Méditerranée Jean Pouilloux.

Fournet, Thibaud. 2009a. 'Les bains de Zénobie à Palmyre. Rapport préliminaire – août 2009'. http://balneorient.hypotheses.org/604.

Fournet, Thibaud. 2009b. 'Résumé de T. Fournet'. http://balneorient.hypotheses.org/1124.

Frézouls, Edmond. 1976. 'Questions d'urbanisme Palmyrénien'. In *Palmyre: Bilan et perspectives; Colloque de Strasbourg, 18–20 Octobre 1973, à la mémoire de Daniel Schlumberger et de Henri Seyrig*, edited by Edmond Frézouls, 191–207. Strasbourg: Centre de recherches sur le Proche-Orient et la Grèce.

Gawlikowski, Michał. 1973. *Le temple palmyrénien: Étude d'épigraphie et de topographie historique*. Palmyre 6. Warsaw: Państwowe Wydawnictwo Naukowe.

Gawlikowski, Michał. 1993. 'Palmyra 1992'. *Polish Archaeology in the Mediterranean* 4: 111–118.

Gawlikowski, Michał. 2002. 'Palmyra, Season 2001'. *Polish Archaeology in the Mediterranean* 13: 257–269.

Hammad, Manar. 2008. 'Un amphithéâtre à Tadmor-Palmyre?' *Syria* 85: 339–346.

Hammad, Manar. 2010. *Palmyre: Transformations urbaines; Développement d'une ville antique de la marge aride Syrienne.* Paris: Geuthner.

Intagliata, Emanuele E. 2017. 'Palmyra and Its Ramparts During the Tetrarchy'. In *New Cities in Late Antiquity: Documents and Archaeology*, edited by Efthymios Rizos, 71–83. Turnhout: Brepols.

Intagliata, Emanuele E. 2018. *Palmyra after Zenobia, AD 273–750: An Archaeological and Historical Reappraisal.* Oxford: Oxbow.

Jakubiak, Krzysztof. 2013. 'Via sacra or Sacral Space in Palmyra'. *Zeitschrift für Orient-Archäologie* 6: 144–155.

James, Simon. 2019. *The Roman Military Base at Dura-Europos, Syria: An Archaeological Visualisation.* Oxford: Oxford University Press.

Juchniewicz, Karol. 2013. 'Late Roman Fortifications in Palmyra'. *Studia Palmireńskie* 12: 193–202.

Juchniewicz, Karol, Khaled al-As'ad, and Khalil al-Hariri. 2010. 'The Defense Wall in Palmyra after Recent Syrian Excavations'. *Studia Palmyreńskie* 11: 55–73.

Liebeschuetz, John H. W. G. 2001. *The Decline and Fall of the Roman City.* Oxford: Oxford University Press.

MacDonald, William L. 1986. *The Architecture of the Roman Empire.* Vol. 2, *An Urban Appraisal.* New Haven, CT: Yale University Press.

Ostratz, Antoni. 1969. 'Note sur le plan de la partie médiane de la rue principale à Palmyre'. *Les annales archéologiques arabes syriennes* 19: 109–120.

Saliou, Catherine. 1996. 'Du portique à la rue à portiques: Les rues à colonnades de Palmyre dans le cadre de l'urbanisme Romain impérial, originalité et conformisme'. *Les annales archéologiques arabes syriennes* 42: 319–330.

Schmidt-Colinet, Andreas, and Khaled al-As'ad. 2000. 'Zur Urbanistik des hellenistischen Palmyra. Em Vorbericht'. *Damaszener Mitteilungen* 12: 61–93.

Schmidt-Colinet, Andreas, Khaled al-As'ad, and Waleed al-As'ad. 2013. 'Thirty Years of Syro-German/Austrian Archaeological Research at Palmyra'. *Studia Palmyreńskie* 12: 299–318.

Schnädelbach, Klaus. 2010. *Topographia Palmyrena.* Vol. 1, *Topography.* Bonn: Habelt.

Sears, Frank. 2006. *Roman Theatres: An Architectural Study.* Oxford: Oxford University Press.

Seyrig, Henri. 1940. 'Rapport sommaire sur les fouilles de l'agora de Palmyre'. *Comptes rendus des séances de l'Académie des inscriptions et belles-lettres* 84: 237–249.

Seyrig, Henri, and Raymond Duru. 2005. 'La fouille de l'agora'. In *L'agora de Palmyre, sur la base des travaux de Henri Seyrig, Raymond Duru et Edmond Frézouls*, edited by Christiane Delplace and Jacqueline Dentzer-Feydy, 23–38. Beirut: Institut français du Proche-Orient.

Tabaczek, Marianne. 2002. 'Zwischen Stoa und Suq. Die Säulenstraßen im Vorderen Orient in römischer Zeit unter besonderer Berücksichtigung von Palmyra'. Unpublished doctoral thesis, Universität zu Köln.

Ward-Perkins, John B., Michael H. Ballance, and Joyce M. Reynolds. 1958. 'The Caesareum at Cyrene and the Basilica at Cremna'. *Papers from the British School at Rome* 26: 137–194.

Wielgosz, Dagmara. 2013. 'Coepimus et lapide pingere: marble decoration from the 'Baths of Diocletian' at Palmyra'. *Studia Palmyreńskie* 12: 319–332.

Yon, Jean-Baptiste. 2001. 'Urbanism and Euergetism in Palmyra'. In *Recent Research in Late-Antique Urbanism*, edited by Luke Lavan, 173–181. Journal of Roman Archaeology Supplementary Series 42. Portsmouth, RI: Journal of Roman Archaeology.

Yon, Jean-Baptiste. 2002. *Les notables de Palmyre*. Beirut: Institut français d'archéologie du Proche-Orient.

Żuchowska, Marta. 2000. 'Quelques remarques sur la grande colonnade á Palmyre'. *Bulletin d'études orientales* 52: 187–193.

CHAPTER 22

DOMESTIC ARCHITECTURE IN PALMYRA

GIOIA ZENONI[*]

THE DISCOVERY OF PALMYRA'S HOUSES

THE study of domestic architecture in Palmyra has never flourished to the extent of that of the great monumental complexes; until recently it was a rather limited field of investigation.

However, records about structural evidence regarding Palmyrene houses has been collected in over a century of research and they have finally been located onto the new archaeological plan of the city included in the first volume of *Topographia Palmyrena* (Schnädelbach 2010), accompanied by detailed plans of all the houses that were published before its completion. In this plan each building has been given a new code number: this contribution refers to both the old and new designations (Figure 22.1).

The second volume of *Topographia Palmyrena* (Delplace 2023), dedicated to the urban centre, offers a description of the residential buildings identified in the various sectors of the city.

The earliest documentation of the few houses identified in Palmyra through surface investigations dates back to the Royal Museums of Berlin expedition led by Otto Puchstein in 1902, with drawings by Daniel Krencker (Wiegand 1932). It is to Albert Gabriel that we owe the positioning on the general plan of Palmyra of a dozen houses investigated by means of test pits. In the account of the archaeological campaign (Gabriel 1926), a rather meagre series of observations accompanies the photographs,

* I would like to express my deepest gratitude to Maria Teresa Grassi, for always encouraging my research and for offering her precious scientific supervision; to Christiane Delplace, who verified the references to the houses in the new general plan of Palmyra; to all the colleagues working on Palmyra who shared their studies and helped me in the preparation of this synthesis; and, last but not least, to all the friends and colleagues working in Palmyra and in Syria, for the sake of our heritage.

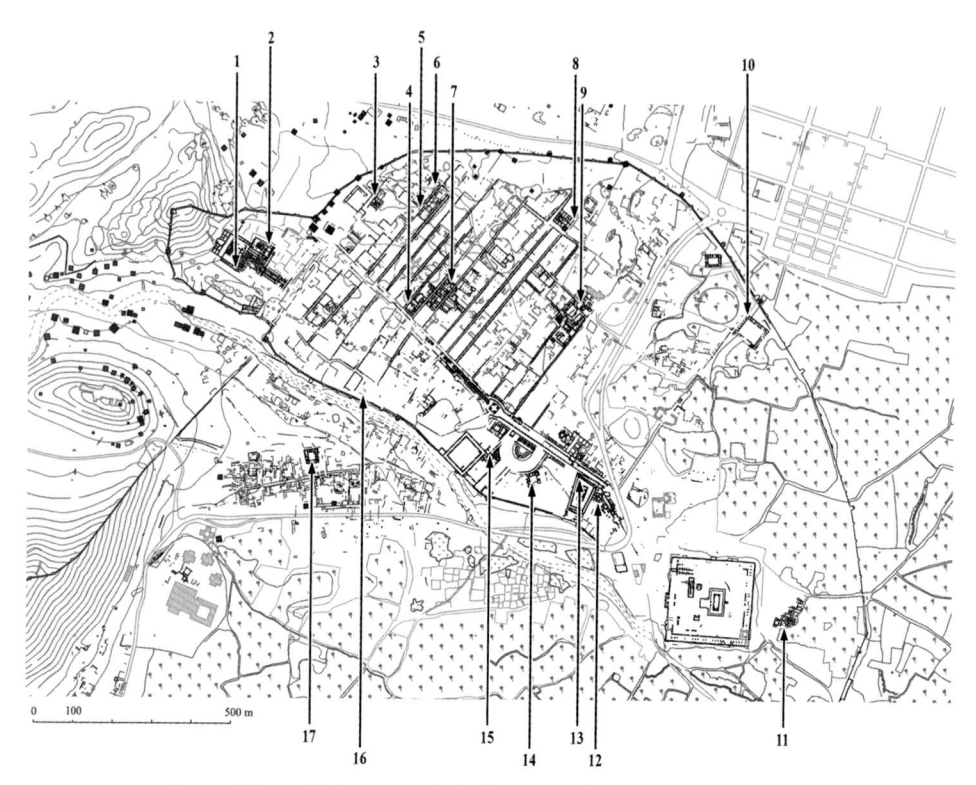

FIGURE 22.1 General plan of Palmyra with the location of the main houses.

1. D106 House under the Forum; 2. D700 "*Praetorium*"; 3. E205 House n. 38 of Gabriel's plan; 4. E807 Building in Insula E; 5. E404 House n. 39 of Gabriel's plan; 6. E405 House n. 40 of Gabriel's plan; 7. E902 House F; 8. F602 House n. 45 of Gabriel's plan; 9. G105 Houses in the *Grand Cour* of Baalshamin's sanctuary; 10. M103 Suburban Market; 11. L201-202 House of Achilles and Cassiopeia; 12. K901 Houses east of the Nabu's sanctuary; 13. K800 Nabu's sanctuary; 14. K702 House south-east of the Theatre; 15. K400 Annexe of the Agora; 16. H602 Peristyle Building; 17. N209 'Khan'.

After Schnädelbach 2010.

drawings, and schematic plans of four houses in the north-west sector of the city (38 = E205, 39/40 = E404/405, 45 = F602).

The evacuation of the modern village in and around the temple of Bēl made possible the first systematic excavation of a residential building in Palmyra, conducted by a French mission led by Henri Seyrig and Raymond Duru in 1940–1941. East of the sanctuary of Bēl, in an isolated position some distance from the town centre, were found the remains of a large, luxurious residence built in the Severan age and probably dismantled in conjunction with the rebuilding of the city wall during the Tetrarchy (L201–202).

The excavation records were lost except for the photographs, which are kept in the archive of Edmond Frézouls, author of the first study of the construction (Frézouls 1976), and some plans and reconstructive drawings made by Duru. These documents, together with the decoration fragments kept in the museum and the remains to be seen *in situ*, were studied and revised in the 2000s by a French team directed by Christiane Delplace, in collaboration with Jacqueline Dentzer-Feydy. Pending full publication, interesting observations and a new interpretation of the structures that compose the building have been put forward in an article recounting the work of the French mission up until field investigations were suspended in 2011 (Delplace 2013) and in a chapter on domestic buildings in an overview of Palmyra's archaeology (Delplace 2017).

The two mosaic floors depicting Achilles on Skyros and the Judgement of the Nereids, attributed at the time of discovery to two different buildings named respectively the 'House of Achilles' (L201) and 'House of Cassiopeia' (L202), are now attributed to a single extensive complex with more than one peristyle courtyard.

Inside this building, preferential routes mark the distinction between the public and private areas as well as the relative importance of different rooms. The main peristyle, accessed from the road through a monumental entrance (off-centre and *en chicane*), acts as a 'sorting area' for these routes, guaranteeing the privacy of family areas.

The most important room is situated opposite the entrance and service areas, opening directly onto the major portico of the large peristyle courtyard through a monumental entranceway. By its side there is a small peristyle with mosaic-floored porticoes, which leads to the south to private rooms including a small courtyard with a basin for collecting water. To the north—probably next to a *viridarium*—there is a further group of rooms dominated by a reception hall with a mosaic floor. Although the house plan's incompleteness obliges caution, one cannot but notice the zigzag diagonal path that joins together in scenographic fashion all the most prestigious areas of the house's various units. This impressive layout inspired the brilliant title of *petit palais* given to it by Frézouls (1976, 51). The presence of two staircases demonstrates the existence of an upper floor.

The building was dated on the basis of the wall construction technique called *opus palmyrenum* (large stone facing slabs joined by a slender mortar fill: Barański 1991), the style of the capitals, and the stuccoed and painted plaster decoration, composed of high-relief cornices ornamented with almost full-round plant motifs and human and animal figures on the upper wall, and other architectural finishings to painted decoration that imitates marble (Delplace 2019).

The remarkable floor mosaics seem to have been added subsequently (Stern 1977), during the third quarter of the third century according to a recent reinterpretation by Janine Balty (2014) who considers them among the best examples of post-Severan style and a production of the same workshop based at Antioch and active in Palmyra at the time of Zenobia, when the Neoplatonic philosophy was spread by Longinus.

With the birth of the Syrian Arab Republic in 1946, Palmyra opened its doors to research institutes of several nationalities to enable the systematic exploration of various monumental complexes, including through the establishment of joint missions.

A Swiss mission directed by Paul Collart between 1954 and 1956 identified three houses with courtyards in correspondence to the porticoes to the west (Building A), north (Building B), and east (Building C) of the Grande Cour of the temple of Baalshamin (G105), dating them to between the fourth and twelfth centuries (Collart and Vicari 1969). The chronology of these buildings, previously questioned by Jean-Charles Balty and Sławomir Kowalski, was delimited by Emanuele E. Intagliata (2017), who reexamined the copious archival documentation: they were erected after the

Grande Cour of the old pagan sanctuary—in use until the fourth century—had been abandoned, but before the end of the sixth century with regard to Building A (that underwent destruction), with their last phase of use corresponding to the early Islamic period. Their fairly complete plan gives a picture of how a house built starting from the Byzantine age might appear: large trapezoidal courtyards, cut by a wall or equipped with a reserved area, are flanked on two sides by one or two rows of rooms of varying shapes and dimensions.

The discovery of late antique and early Islamic-period houses continued with the start of investigations in the Camp of Diocletian, carried out from 1959 to 1964 by a Polish mission directed by Kazimierz Michałowski and presented in reports published almost yearly from 1960 to 1966 in the *Palmyre: Fouilles Polonaises* series (Michałowski 1966, with previous bibliography).

The most striking compound is the late fourth-/early fifth-century construction interpreted as the headquarters of the commander of the Legio I Illyricorum, the Praetorium (D700), since it dates to a period in Palmyra's history known more by way of epigraphic and literary attestations than from archaeological evidence (Kowalski 1994).

The asymmetrical plan of this building, only partly based on the preexisting structures—whose architectural components were largely reused—features two distinct functional centres grouped around two courtyards. On two adjoining sides of the main courtyard, which had porticoes on three sides, there was a linear series of reception rooms—including an alcove room—and private rooms. The service areas, on the other hand, overlooked a rear courtyard joined by a hallway: kitchen, storeroom, and stable. The bedrooms would have been on the first floor, reached by a staircase. The building techniques involve the use of three different types of stone, two types of grey mortar, and mud brick.

At the end of the sixth century or at the beginning of the seventh century the compound was comprehensively rebuilt, fulfilling only private residential functions in a completely different layout: only the ground floor survived, divided into smaller units and equipped with a well, water pipes, basins, storage, and cooking facilities.

Once their military function was lost, many other structures in Diocletian's Camp were reused from the end of the sixth century—when a violent earthquake occurred—and throughout the early Islamic epoch until the first half of the ninth century—as pointed out by Genequand (2008)—housing modest dwellings, shops, and workshops. These were built all along the Via Praetoria, occupying not just the porticoes, but also the road itself and the so-called Tetrapylon at the junction with the Via Principalis. They offer a great overview on functional installations, particularly those used for productive activities, such as stone or earthen benches, which often accompany *tannur* ovens built on flagstones or plaster floors or the sunken *pithoi*, mostly in solid prepared floors, inside rooms used for storage. Oil presses are also recorded encroaching into residential areas.

Houses seem, however, to have been present along the city's western border before the construction of the Camp of Diocletian: excavation between the extensive open area of the later military forum (D106) and the Grande Porte through which it was entered has brought to light the remains of a late first-century AD dwelling, built in turn over the remains of older buildings (Michałowski 1966). The uncovered pseudo-polygonal masonry refers to a courtyard flanked by rows of rooms on at least two sides (Krogulska 1984, fig. 22).

In the 1960s, the Syrian Service des Fouilles Archéologiques, directed by Adnan Bounni with the collaboration of Nassib Saliby, excavating the temple of Nabu, the theatre, and the areas around these also discovered that the city's monumental centre contained a number of houses.

The domestic buildings brought to light in the area between the wall of the sanctuary of Nabu (K901) and the Great Colonnade seem to predate the construction of the latter, sharing the preceding orientation with the first-century AD temple that they are either contemporary with or postdate (Saliby 1996).

The excavation of the dwellings built in the eastern and southern porticoes of the sanctuary of Nabu (K800) and in the area between the cella and the shops of the Great Colonnade led to the supposition of a generic late antique and early Islamic occupation (Bounni 2004), maybe starting already in the fourth century, as suggested by Gawlikowski (2009). The same generic chronology can be postulated for the dwelling unearthed by Bounni and Saliby (1968) in the northern part of the Annexe of the Agora (K400).

Facing onto the portico that borders the theatre area to the south-east, behind the shops, is a large dwelling (K702), equipped with at least two non-aligned peristyle courts leading respectively to public and private rooms and built adapting to the unusual curved shape imposed by the presence of the theatre, whose dating to the Severan epoch provides a firm chronological indication for the foundation of the house.

A plan and description of the rooms are given by Edmond Frézouls (1976) in an article in which he considers all the Roman houses in Palmyra of which he had documentation, including the 'maisons Gabriel' in the north-west quarter and the two units belonging to the House L201–202. This article was an important milestone in the history of research into Palmyra's domestic architecture, gaining attention and setting out the main issues that were subsequently debated by scholars.

Broadening Horizons on the Evolution of Domestic Architecture

In 1988, a new campaign by the Polish mission, directed by Michał Gawlikowski and focused on three blocks to the north of the western part of the Great Colonnade, constituted the first investigation of a largely residential quarter—which also contained no less than four churches and was thus known as the 'Christian Quarter'.

The systematic excavation, concluded in 1995, of a large house (E902) occupying the entire width of one block (indicated as Insula F on Gabriel's plan) marked a turning point in the study of domestic buildings: the house, built in the second half of the second century AD, was continuously inhabited until about AD 800 and bears witness to the changes in Palmyra's lifestyles over a period of more than six centuries.

The complex layout of this *demeure bourgeoise*, featuring two subunits with separate entrances, first-floor bedrooms, and terraces, also seems a very different scheme from that of the houses known until then, as observed by Gawlikowski (1997) in an article which was the first to question the interpretative models that Frézouls proposed. Descriptions of the house appeared in the annual excavation reports (published between 1990 and 1997 in *Polish Archaeology in the Mediterranean*); 2007 saw the appearance of an overview and a precise definition of the distinctive features of the 'Palmyrene House'—of which this became the representative example (Gawlikowski 2007).

The northern compound, with two small entrances and just one courtyard, has been interpreted as a private and service sector, while that to the south, with five entrances on two sides and interconnected L-shaped units arranged around five courtyards, as a reception suite accessible for guests. The two compounds were connected at a mezzanine level. According to Gawlikowski (1997), this division of space should be considered an anticipation of the subsequent oriental practice of splitting dwellings into a public 'male' sector and a more private 'female' sector. The general planning itself, agglomerative in style, would reflect Palmyra's particular social structure, one based on extended families (Gawlikowski 2007).

The dwelling's last phase of use in an Islamic urban context was discussed in a later article (Gawlikowski 2009), although the process by which it is subdivided into five independent units, each centred on a courtyard, is chronologically undefined. The long duration of decoration with painted stuccoes and cornices, which remained in view in numerous rooms in both portions of the building until it was abandoned, is noteworthy (Gawlikowski 2019b).

In the western block (Insula E), dating from the second half of the second century AD, a residential unit (E807) whose overall plan is unknown was located between the shops of the Great Colonnade's north portico—recently constructed—and Basilica I, which had a civil function (Żuchowska 2006; 2011). The large room with the exceptional mosaic floor representing Bēllerophon and dating to the latter half of the third century cannot be attributed to this house but is more likely to have been the 'banqueting hall' of one of Palmyra's religious confraternities (Gawlikowski and Żuchowska 2010). The area, which bears the signs of extensive destruction at the end of the third century (followed by reconstruction), was reorganized in the late fourth to early fifth centuries, following a second devastation. At this time all the rooms were united to form a single dwelling, entered from the Great Colonnade through a long vestibule that crossed it, with two doorways into the large hall—then without mosaic, but floored with a layer of dark grey mortar and divided lengthwise by a row of columns. North of the hall there was a service area with a latrine and two *tannur* ovens; the building had piped water and drains.

The close relationship between the construction of the western section of the Great Colonnade and the urban layout of the adjacent district—which has been understood since the first studies of the Polish mission and supported by the Insula E excavation—is reiterated in a study by Marta Żuchowska (2011), which examines the relationship between the houses and the urban layout in an attempt to identify the development over time of the residential areas.

Striking results in this field were obtained by the Syro-German/Austrian mission, directed by Khaled al-Asʿad, Waleed al-Asʿad, and Andreas Schmidt-Colinet, which, in 1997, began to explore the pre-Roman Palmyra settlement south of the wadi (Schmidt-Colinet et al. 2008). By means of geophysical prospections, the layout of the so-called Hellenistic City was mapped. Trial trenches allowed the area's earliest occupation to be dated to the third century BC and the establishment of the definitive layout to the late second century BC. The entire zone was abandoned in the late third century AD, perhaps as a result of Aurelian's sack in AD 273 and the construction of a new town wall north of the wadi.

In Trench II, a residential building (N209) was systematically excavated starting in 2006. The house was built in Augustan times on top of an earlier Hellenistic dwelling, rebuilt with the same plan after a fire in the mid-second century AD, and abandoned at the end of the third (Schmidt-Colinet and al-Asʿad 2013). Its plan features a simple series of rooms of different sizes around a rectangular courtyard, probably paved and equipped with a peristyle; the remains of a staircase suggest the existence of an upper-floor terrace. The house, built with wide massive standing wall bases in limestone blocks and with mud brick for the upper walls, was equipped with an external water supply and a latrine and perhaps also a well or cistern in the middle of the courtyard.

In its last phase, the building was strikingly decorated with stucco and painted plaster, maybe offering the best example of what can be considered the principal decoration of Palmyra's houses, as discussed in the 2013 international conference on *Stucs d'Orient*. The collected evidence points to the existence in Palmyra of a decorators' workshop that, from the last quarter of the second to the first third of the third century, developed a rather distinctive local style combining Hellenistic models with modified traditional oriental features.

Barbara Tober (2013; 2019) has drawn up a typology of stucco cornices of the west, north, and south-east wings of building N209 and has identified the decorative schemes formed by their use in combination with polychrome paintings that resemble stuccoes in two dimensions and with appliqués. She has proposed a reconstruction of the decoration system of each room which seems to reflect—with regard to quality and sumptuousness—the ranking of rooms in the house.

The quality of the data obtained from the systematic study of finds and decoration enabled the function of groups of rooms to be deduced in what is perhaps the best-documented Roman house in Palmyra. Proceeding anticlockwise from the stepped entrance that leads to the courtyard, there are areas used for religion and cult, cleaning and washing, entertainment, trade and economy, storage, food preparation, and banqueting. The plan of this sumptuous multipurpose building, residential and commercial at the same time, resembles both that of the Mesopotamian *Hofhaus* and the caravanserai of Parthian–Sassanian tradition.

Crucial to understanding the development of the town of Palmyra are the investigations launched in 2007 by the Syro-Italian mission directed by Waleed al-As'ad and Maria Teresa Grassi in the south-west quarter, located between the 'Hellenistic city' and the northern quarter: it is here that the early expansion of the city north of the wadi was thought to have taken place. The survey produced a detailed plan of all the *in situ* structural evidence, revealing the layout of the quarter and identifying some articulated building units featuring a rich architectural decoration that suggests that the probable residential function may have been combined with public use (Grassi 2012). The excavation of part of the courtyard and the northern and western wings of the Peristyle Building (H602) near the town wall—previously named *Grand péristyle* by Gabriel—adds further evidence for the evolution of domestic architecture from the Severan age to early Islamic times (Grassi and al-As'ad 2013). It also offered the opportunity to focus on building techniques in domestic architecture, including those using unfired clay (Grassi et al. 2012, 63–66; Zenoni 2012–2013), and on the stone types used in the residential buildings: pale brown arenaceous limestone, pale brown marly limestone, dark grey fossiliferous dolomite, and pinkish white nodular limestone (Bugini and Folli 2015).

High-quality architectural components such as the columns with Corinthian Asiatic capitals, monolithic shafts, and Attic bases carved from a single block (Rossi 2015); stuccos (Palmieri 2010; Grassi 2019); and marble slabs from throughout the Mediterranean used as wall and floor coverings, both in *opus sectile* and *opus interrasile* (Nava 2015) suggest that the oldest building, featuring a large reception room opening on the main portico of a three-sided peristyle, was quite luxurious, and probably residential.

In the last phase of use of this building (between the sixth and the eighth centuries), craft and/or commercial activities were perhaps also present in the new rooms obtained through the narrowing or closing of passages, the walling-up of peristyle column rows, the construction of internal partitions, and the modification of the internal circulation routes (Grassi 2018).

In the suburban market area (M103), dug by the Syro-French mission directed by Christiane Delplace between 2001 and 2005 in the north-east part of the city (Delplace 2013), shops and houses coexisted from the time of the Tetrarchy to the eighth century. In this quarter—developed in the Severan age, along a colonnaded road connecting the Great Colonnade to the Dura Gate in the late antique city wall— the presence of a number of houses with peristyles has been known since Gabriel's investigations.

In addition, several buildings identified outside the city boundary—known especially from 1930s aerial photography, but also from recent geophysical prospecting and excavations such as for Q281 (Byliński 1995)—are also worthy of mention. These are characterized by a rectangular enclosure bounded on each side by a row of rooms opening onto a large central courtyard. A study by Jean-Marie Dentzer (1994) discusses possible interpretations of these *enclos*—as caravanserais, barracks, or multipurpose buildings serving as residences, yet also with agricultural functions.

Perspectives of Interpretation and Further Investigation

The most recent field investigations in Palmyra, together with revision of previous documentation, have enlarged our knowledge on Palmyra's domestic architecture both topographically and chronologically thanks to a radical change in analytical approach showing that the more building-plan data can be integrated with the study of construction techniques, architectural components, decoration systems, domestic installations, and archaeological finds that functionally characterize the areas, the more understanding is gained. This is especially true for the residences of the Roman imperial age, whose classification according to type is still highly debated. There are two main lines of interpretation.

Starting from a classically based analysis of the few building plans then known, Frézouls (1976) maintains that the houses of Palmyra are strongly influenced by Hellenistic traditions. He distinguishes the large buildings of variable organization in the middle of the town (K702, L201, and L202), which he calls *petits palais*, from the *maisons cossues* that make up the northern quarter, whose plans Gabriel had drawn up with reference to Hellenistic models. Balty (1989)—who also considers the presence of *peristyle, prostas,* and *oikos* a proof of the Hellenistic origin of house layouts in Palmyra and Apamea—divides those residences that are symmetrical about central axes from those with radial plans and that have several courtyards which are the focus of sectors with different functions, suggesting that this second type has Eastern ancestry. Delplace (2017), who makes comparisons with Eastern and Western Roman models, identifies in Palmyra two main types of peristyle house on the basis of the internal pathways created by the arrangement of the courtyard and of the entrance (axial or *en chicane*).

Gawlikowski's approach (2007 and 2019a) is diametrically opposed to this. Appealing to the need to understand the plans of buildings in their sociocultural context, he sees Palmyra's houses as belonging to oriental tradition. An example of what this means is house E902, which in its internal organization into autonomous subunits respects the social organization of the Palmyrene clans and, in its use of courtyards, reflects the ancient Mesopotamian archetype also seen at Dura-Europos, while in its division between male and female sections it seems to anticipate an essential characteristic of Islamic houses. The key to the interpretation of residential premises is thus to be found in the way they are used—dictated by climatic factors, customs, beliefs, and particular functions—rather than by architectural style and decoration, which are mere expressions of aesthetic factors (and in fact largely reflect external influences).

Examination of how residences were used could also help to clarify the typological evolution through time of two architectural categories: reception and hospitality areas (*oecus, tablinum,* triclinium, alcove room, *iwan*) and courtyards with porticoes on one or more sides (which, according to Gawlikowski, were replaced by true peristyles only from the second half of the second century).

The particularities of the sociocultural and economic context of Palmyra—the 'caravan city' par excellence—are central also to Schmidt-Colinet's and al-As'ad (2013) interpretation of N209, a mixed residential-commercial building with similarities to the khans of Parthian–Sassanian tradition. This case points to an interesting field of investigation which deserves to be explored further: the identification of multipurpose buildings.

A number of other questions need to be answered. Do the *enclos* identified from aerial photographs also have a mixed residential-commercial function? Are there rural-type houses connected with agriculture in the area outside the walls? How was housing for the middle and lower class organized? Is it legitimate to think that some of what are considered 'urban palaces' might perhaps also have had administrative functions?

The location of residential areas within the town, and their layout and development over time, are urban themes that have fascinated many scholars and provoked intriguing suggestions, such as the hypothesis put forward by Dentzer (2000) that the settlement developed by way of the coalescence of originally independent nuclei. An overview of the various theories is given by Żuchowska (2011), who systematically analyses the evidence from all parts of the city—including those investigated recently, such as the south-west quarter—underlining the peculiar modes of adaptation of the 'multi-segmented' houses of the great Palmyrene families to the new urban grid established in imperial times, when the Great Colonnade was constructed. Thus the organization of the residential quarters gave rise to entirely original formulas that are not easily labelled, reflecting the singular combination of tradition and innovation that characterizes Palmyra's art and architecture.

The transformation of the inhabited area during late antiquity once more required an adaptation strategy since most of the houses resulted from the renovation of preexisting ones or from the installation in disused public compounds.

In his well-documented monograph on 'Palmyra after Zenobia', Intagliata (2018) reserves a whole chapter to post-Roman housing, systematically discussing the setting, layout, functional features, and chronology of the houses from the fourth to the eighth centuries.

Noting that, despite the trend toward opulence observed in many Syrian cities during Late Antiquity, the data available for Palmyra suggest the disappearance of monumentality in domestic architecture as early as the fourth century, Intagliata pinpoints the cause of this exception in a drastic shift in the composition of the Palmyrene society, possibly connected to the events of AD 272–273, that reasonably started the process of transformation from a 'caravan city' to a 'fortress city'. The replacement of the ancient aristocracy by middle-class merchants and artisans—a phenomenon that becomes apparent only under the Umayyads according to Gawlikoski (2009)—may therefore have started as soon as Palmyra gained a relevant role in the Tetrarchic frontier defensive system and may have caused the transition from a scenographic to a more utilitarian domestic architecture.

If we can easily draw up the main features of a generic 'post-Roman Palmyrene housing'—such as subdivision of large residential units into smaller ones, spread of internal partitions, convergence of apartments in a shared courtyard, transformation of the domus into multifunctional compounds, with productive installations, storage facilities, and shelters/mangers for animals in the core of the house—it is more difficult to reconstruct the precise timeline of the evolution of the houses up to their final stage of occupation.

As observed by Denis Genequand (2008) in his preliminary study on early Islamic Palmyra, the simplistic equation 'well built = Byzantine / poorly built = late Byzantine / badly built = Arab' has been for a long time the basic principle for determining relative chronology of building activities, thus impairing a synoptic study of late antique and early Islamic domestic architecture in Palmyra. Comparisons with the best-known models of houses in Apamea, Antioch, the villages of northern Syria, Resafe, Bosra, Jerash, and the civilian sectors of the Umayyad palaces in the Palmyrene therefore played a fundamental role in interpreting the elusive published records.

If the reconstruction of many buildings in all sectors of the city was due to an earthquake at the end of the sixth century—as is indicated by recent excavations and a review of old excavation records—then the absence of obvious rapid changes in domestic architecture between the Byzantine and Proto-Islamic epochs favours the idea of a gradual transition process 'from *polis* to *madina*'. The chronology of the final occupation of several houses, instead, has been made more precise in recent times based on the analysis of the published photographs of the pottery (Genequand 2008). This established that, after the boom of the Umayyad period, they have largely been abandoned in the first half of the ninth century, confirming the hypothesis based on historical sources.

In general, it can be noted that archaeologists' increasing attention to pre- and post-Roman Palmyra has made it possible both to reevaluate the buildings of the imperial age from a perspective less rigidly tied to the schemes proposed for urban houses in the eastern Mediterranean and also to find a common thread in the development of domestic architecture throughout the occupation of the city.

In a city like Palmyra, which maintained its social organization and cultural distinctions under the control of various political masters, the keys to interpretation of the architectural evidence are to be found precisely in those features of the inhabitants' lifestyles that show continuity over time. The openness of Palmyra's builders to new influences, often incorporated only at a superficial level and immediately modified to meet the needs of the local *modus vivendi*, is in fact one of the most striking features of Palmyra's domestic architecture.

Bibliography

Balty, Janine. 2014. *Les mosaïques des maisons de Palmyre*. Beirut: Institut français du Proche-Orient.

Balty, Jean-Charles. 1989. 'La maison urbaine en Syrie'. In *Archéologie et histoire de la Syrie*. Vol. 2, *La Syrie de l'époque achéménide à l'avènement de l'Islam*, edited by Jean-Marie Dentzer and Winfried Orthmann, 407–422. Saarbrücken: Druckerei und Verlag.

Barański, Marek. 1991. 'Opus Palmyrenum'. *Damaszener Mitteilungen* 5: 59–63.

Bounni, Adnan 2004. *Le sanctuaire de Nabu: Texte*. Beirut: Institut d'Archéologie du Proche-Orient.

Bounni, Adnan, and Nassib Saliby. 1968. 'Fouilles de l'annexe de l'agora à palmyre. Rapport préliminaire'. *Les annales archéologiques arabes syriennes* 81: 93–102.

Bugini, Roberto, and Luisa Folli. 2015. 'The Stone Architecture of Palmyra (Syria): From the Quarry to the Building'. In *ASMOSIA X: Proceedings of the Tenth International Conference of ASMOSIA, Association for the Study of Marble and Other Stones in Antiquity (Rome, 21–26 May 2012)*, edited by Patrizio Pensabene and Eleonora Gasparini, 683–688. Rome: 'l'Erma' di Bretschneider.

Byliński, Janusz. 1995. 'A III Century Open-Court Building in Palmyra: Excavation Report'. *Damaszener Mitteilungen* 8: 213–246.

Collart, Paul, and Jacques Vicari. 1969. *Le sanctuaire de Baalshamin à Palmyre: Topographie et architecture*. Rome: Institut suisse de Rome.

Delplace, Christiane. 2013. 'Les recherches de la mission française à Palmyre'. In *Fifty Years of Polish Excavations in Palmyra (1959–2009)*, edited by Michał Gawlikowski and Grzegorz Majcherek, 37–48. Studia Palmyreńskie 12. Warsaw: Wydawnictwa Uniwersytetu Warszawskiego.

Delplace, Christiane. 2017. *Palmyre: Histoire et archéologie d'une cité caravanière à la croisée des cultures*. Paris: CNRS.

Delplace, Christiane. 2019. 'Les influences orientales sur les stucs de la grande demeure à l'est du sanctuaire de Bêl à Palmyre'. In *Stucs d'orient: Traditions orientales et cultures hellénisées*, edited by Jacqueline Dentzer-Feydy Anne-Marie Guimier-Sorbets, and Christiane Delplace, 265–282. Syria, Supplément 5. Beirut: Institut français du Proche-Orient.

Delplace, Christiane. 2023. *Topographia Palmyrena. 2. Le centre urbain*. Paris: Académie des inscriptions et belles-lettres.

Dentzer, Jean-Marie. 1994. 'Khāns ou casernes à Palmyre? À propos de structures visibles sur des photographies aériennes anciennes'. *Syria* 61(1): 45–112.

Dentzer, Jean-Marie. 2000. 'Le développement urbain en Syrie à l'époque hellénistique et romaine: Modèles "occidentaux et orientaux"'. *Bulletin d'études orientales* 52: 159–163.

Frézouls, Edmond. 1976. 'À propos de l'architecture domestique à Palmyre'. *Ktema* 1: 29–52.

Gabriel, Albert. 1926. 'Recherches archéologiques à Palmyre'. *Syria* 7(1): 71–92.

Gawlikowski, Michał. 1997. 'L'habitat à Palmyre de l'antiquité au moyen-age'. In *Les maisons dans la Syrie antique du IIIe millénaire aux débuts de l'Islam: Pratique et représentations de l'espace domestique; Actes du colloque international, Damas, 27–30 juin 1992*, edited by Corinne Castel, Michel al-Maqdissi, and François Villeneuve, 161–166. Beirut: Institut français d'archéologie du Proche-Orient.

Gawlikowski, Michał. 2004. 'Palmyra: Season 2003'. *Polish Archaeology in the Mediterranean* 14: 313–324.

Gawlikowski, Michał. 2007. 'Beyond the Colonnades: The Domestic Architecture of Palmyra'. In *From Antioch to Alexandria: Recent Studies in Domestic Architecture*, edited by Katharina Galor and Tomasz Waliszewski, 79–93. Warsaw: Uniwersytet Warszawski, Instytut Archeologii.

Gawlikowski, Michał. 2009. 'Palmyra in Early Islamic Times'. In *Residences, Castles, Settlements: Transformation Processes from Late Antiquity to Early Islam in Bilad al-Sham; Proceedings of the International Conference Held at Damascus, 5–9 November 2006*, edited by Karin Bartl and Abd Al-Razzaq Moaz, 89–96. Rahden: Leidorf.

Gawlikowski, Michał. 2019a. 'Roman Housing in Palmyra'. In *Greco-Roman Cities at the Crossroads of Cultures*, edited by Grażyna Bąkowska-Czerner and Rafał Czerner, 103–108. Oxford: Archaeopress.

Gawlikowski, Michał. 2019b. 'La maison de la rue des Églises à Palmyre et son décor stuqué (Mission polonaise)'. In *Stucs d'orient: Traditions orientales et cultures hellénisées*, edited by Jacqueline Dentzer-Feydy Anne-Marie Guimier-Sorbets and Christiane Delplace, 231–242. Syria, Supplément 5. Beirut: Institut français du Proche-Orient.

Gawlikowski, Michał, and Marta Żuchowska. 2010. 'La mosaïque de Bēllérophon'. *Studia Palmyreńskie* 11: 9–42.

Genequand, D. 2008. 'An Early Islamic Mosque in Palmyra'. *Levant* 60: 3–15.

Grassi, Maria Teresa. 2012. 'Un nuovo scavo urbano della Statale di Milano: Il quartiere sud-ovest di Palmyra'. In *Interpretando l'antico: Scritti di archeologia offerti a Maria Bonghi Jovino*, edited by Cristina Chiaramonte Treré, Giovanna Bagnasco Gianni, and Federica Chiesa, 889–907. Quaderni di Acme (Annali della Facoltà di Studi Umanistici dell'Università degli Studi di Milano) 134. Milan: Cisalpino.

Grassi, Maria Teresa. 2018. 'Palmira islamica: I nuovi dati dal quartiere sud-ovest'. In *Nel ricordo di Gianfranco Fiaccadori: Atti della giornata di studi; Milano, 21 gennaio 2016*, edited by Vera von Falkenhausen, Federica Chiesa, and Fabio Eugenio Betti, 97–112. Quaderni di Artistonothos 6. Milan: Ledizioni.

Grassi, Maria Teresa. 2019. 'Mission conjointe italo-syrienne de Palmyre (quartier sud-ouest): Les nouvelles données du bâtiment à péristyle'. In *Stucs d'orient: Traditions orientales et cultures hellénisées*, edited by Jacqueline Dentzer-Feydy Anne-Marie Guimier-Sorbets and Christiane Delplace, 243–254. Syria, Supplément 5. Beirut: Institut français du Proche-Orient.

Grassi, Maria Teresa, and Waleed al-As'ad. 2013. 'PAL.M.A.I.S. Recherches et fouilles d'une nouvelle mission conjointe syro-italienne dans le quartier sud-ouest de Palmyre'. In *Fifty Years of Polish Excavations in Palmyra (1959–2009)*, edited by Michał Gawlikowski and Grzegorz Majcherek, 115–128. Studia Palmyreńskie 12. Warsaw: Wydawnictwa Uniwersytetu Warszawskiego.

Grassi, Maria Teresa, Gioia Zenoni, and Giorgio Rossi. 2012. 'Tecniche e materiali dell'architettura palmirena: Il caso dell'Edificio con Peristilio del quartiere Sud-Ovest (PAL.M.A.I.S. scavi 2008–2010)'. In *Novissima Studia: Dieci anni di antichistica milanese, atti dei seminari di dipartimento 2011*, edited by Maria Patrizia Bologna and Massimiliano Ornaghi, 53–82. Quaderni di Acme (Annali della Facoltà di Studi Umanistici dell'Università degli Studi di Milano) 129. Milan: Cisalpino.

Intagliata, Emanuele E. 2017. 'The Post-Roman Occupation of the Northern Courtyard of the Sanctuary of Baalshamin in Palmyra: A Reassessment of the Evidence Based on the Documents in the Fonds d'Archives Paul Collart, Université de Lausanne'. *Zeitschrift für Orient-Archäologie* 9: 180–199.

Intagliata, Emanuele E. 2018. *Palmyra after Zenobia AD 273–750: An Archaeological Reappraisal*. Oxford: Oxbow.

Kowalski, Sławomir P. 1994. 'The Praetorium of the Camp of Diocletian in Palmyra'. *Studia Palmyreńskie* 9: 39–70.

Krogulska, Maria. 1984. 'Le forum'. In *Palmyre*. Vol. 8, *Les principia de Dioclétien: 'Temple des Enseignes'*, edited by Michał Gawlikowski, 70–91. Warsaw: Panstwowe wydawnictwo naukowe.

Michałowski, Kazimierz. 1966. *Palmyre*. Vol. 5, *Fouilles Polonaises 1963 et 1964*. Warsaw: Panstwowe wydawnictwo naukowe.

Nava, Stefano. 2015. 'The Marble Decoration of the Peristyle Building in the SW Quarter of Palmyra (Pal.M.A.I.S. Mission)'. In *ASMOSIA X: Proceedings of the Tenth International Conference of ASMOSIA, Association for the Study of Marble and Other Stones in Antiquity (Rome, 21st–26th May 2012)*, edited by Patrizio Pensabene and Eleonora Gasparini, 241–252. Rome: 'l'Erma' di Bretschneider.

Palmieri, Lilia. 2010. 'Étude préliminaire sur les stucs trouvés dans le "bâtiment à péristyle" du quartier sud-ouest de Palmyre (Pal.M.A.I.S. – Fouilles 2008–2009)'. *Lanx* 6: 175–186.

Rossi, Giorgio. 2015. 'Architectural Elements of the Peristyle Building of the SW Quarter of Palmyra (Pal.M.A.I.S. Mission)'. In *ASMOSIA X: Proceedings of the Tenth International Conference of ASMOSIA, Association for the Study of Marble and Other Stones in Antiquity (Rome, 21st–26th May 2012)*, edited by Patrizio Pensabene and Eleonora Gasparini, 683–688. Rome: 'l'Erma' di Bretschneider.

Saliby, Nassib. 1996. 'Maisons palmyréniennes à l'est du temple de Nabū'. In *Palmyra and the Silk Road: International Colloquium; Palmyra 1992, Annales archéologiques arabes syriennes* 42: 289–290.

Schmidt-Colinet, Andreas, and Waleed al-As'ad, eds. 2013. *Palmyras Reichtum durch weltweiten Handel: Archäologische Untersuchungen im Bereich der hellenistischen Stadt.* Vienna: Verlag Holzhausen.

Schmidt-Colinet, Andreas, Khaled al-As'ad, and Waleed al-As'ad. 2008. 'Untersuchungen im Areal der "hellenistischen" Stadt von Palmyra. Zweiter Vorbericht'. *Zeitschrift für Orient-Archäologie* 1: 452–478.

Schnädelbach, Klaus. 2010. *Topographia Palmyrena. 1. Topography.* Documents d'archéologie syrienne 18. Bonn: Habelt.

Stern, Henri. 1977. *Les mosaïques des maisons d'Achille et de Cassiopée à Palmyre.* Paris: Geuthner.

Tober, Barbara. 2013. 'Stuck und Wandmalerei'. In *Palmyras Reichtum durch weltweiten Handel: Archäologische Untersuchungen im Bereich der hellenistischen Stadt.* Vol. 1, *Architektur und ihre Ausstattung*, edited by Andreas Schmidt-Colinet and Waleed al-As'ad, 170–253. Vienna: Verlag Holzhausen.

Tober, Barbara. 2019. 'The Hierarchical Use of Stucco Decoration and Wall Painting in a Representative Building in Palmyra'. In *Stucs d'orient: Traditions orientales et cultures hellénisées*, edited by Jacqueline Dentzer-Feydy Anne-Marie Guimier-Sorbets and Christiane Delplace, 255–264. Syria, Supplément 5. Beirut: Institut français du Proche-Orient.

Wiegand, Theodor, ed. 1932. *Palmyra: Ergebnisse der Expeditionen von 1902 und 1917.* Berlin: Archäologisches Institut des Deutschen Reiches/Abteilung Istanbul.

Zenoni, Gioia. 2012–2013. 'Tecniche edilizie dall'età romana all'età omayyade: I nuovi dati della missione archeologica italo-siriana a Palmira (Pal.M.A.I.S.)'. Unpublished thesis, University of Milan.

Żuchowska, Marta. 2006. 'Palmyra: Excavations 2002–2005: Insula E by the Great Colonnade'. *Polish Archaeology in the Mediterranean* 17: 439–450.

Żuchowska, Marta. 2011. 'Space Organisation and House Planning at Hellenistic and Roman Palmyra'. *Światowit* 9(50)/A: 141–153.

CHAPTER 23

RELIGIOUS ARCHITECTURE IN PALMYRA

The Temples and Sanctuaries

ROBYN L. LE BLANC

INTRODUCTION

IN AD 131, the council and assembly of Palmyra honoured Malè Agrippa, a two-time *grammateus* (a local magistrate), with a statue on a column of the temple of Baalshamin, a Semitic weather god. The dedicatory inscription in Greek and Palmyrene outlines Malè's euergistic activities on behalf of the community, which included funding large portions of a temple for the gods Baalshamin and Durahlun (*PAT* 0305). Malè's patronage of the sanctuary was consistent with expectations of prominent citizens, but it was also something of a family affair: in AD 67, his father, Yarhai, a member of the Bene Ma'ziyan tribe, had dedicated a portico with its columns and roof in the same sanctuary (*PAT* 0158).

The dedications of Malè and Yarhai provide a useful entry point for a discussion of the temples and sanctuaries of Palmyra from the first century BC to the third century AD. Several of these are still preserved today, including temples to Bēl-Hammon, Nabu, Allat, and Arsu. The temples of Bēl and Baalshamin unfortunately suffered major damage during the occupation of Palmyra by Da'esh in 2015–2017. Temples for other gods are known from inscriptions.

The earliest phases of many Palmyrene temples consisted of a simple *hamana* (a chapel; Drijvers 1988) or small temple, and an altar. This began to change in the first century AD as the sanctuaries and their temples were enlarged and monumentalized through the patronage of local elites. In this way, while only seventy years and a single generation separate the grants of Yarhai and Malè, the landscapes in which they were erected were fundamentally different.

In the first century AD, porticoes like the one paid for by Yarhai were progressively enclosing the archaic *hamana* of Allat, while new Graeco-Roman-style temples set on podiums and equipped with peristyles replaced earlier temples to Bēl and Nabu. By the time of Malè's second tenure as *grammateus* this flurry of construction was beginning to wind down, as indicated by the overall decline in inscriptions connected to building in sanctuaries after the mid-second century AD. The old *hamanas* of the first century BC had not entirely disappeared, but the trend was towards new Hellenistic architectural styles, a process that had only begun in Yarhai's time.

By the mid-second century AD, many Palmyrene sanctuaries followed a model consisting of a temple on a podium situated within a colonnaded precinct and approached through a monumental propylon. The cella door and propylon established a central axis. Staircases inside the cella led to the roof; sanctuary courts housed altars and buildings for dining. Architectural decoration typically appeared in the form of Corinthian capitals, Attic bases, and a rich variety of mouldings in the entablature and around windows and doors as well as stepped merlons above the cornices. Sculpted decoration included eagles and groups of deities, particularly used to decorate the lintels of the cult niches within the *adyta*.

The preserved temples famously combine local, Near Eastern, and Graeco-Roman architectural elements—a trend presaged, for example, by the bilingual inscription of Malè (also called 'Agrippa') and the rendering of Baalshamin as 'Zeus' in the Greek version of that inscription. Various architectural studies of the sanctuaries and temples have categorized these features by style, sorting temples into categories of Vitruvian sacred architecture (e.g., Segal 2013, 1–2, 8–32) and extracting typical Near Eastern elements, such as merlons (in use in Mesopotamia since at least the end of the third millennium: Bounni 1999, 508), the adoption of a Babylonian base measurement (Collart and Vicari 1969, 103), multiple *adyta*, and cult activity on the roof.

The benefactions by Yarhai and Malè in the same sanctuary demonstrate how temple complexes benefited from the patronage of several generations of the same family or clan. The exact nature (and antiquity) of this connection and whether particular complexes might be tribal sanctuaries is debated (Kaizer 2002, 43–51, with discussion and bibliography). However, the epigraphic evidence suggests that one or two tribes dominated each sanctuary. For example, Yarhai, Malè, and other members of the Bene Ma'ziyan were frequent patrons of the temple of Baalshamin, while the Bene Agrud were connected to Bēl-Hammon. Throughout, the local elite were patrons; no imperial benefactions can be associated with temples in Palmyra and few dedications are from non-Palmyrenes.

Malè's dedication to Baalshamin, Durahle, and a third deity (whose name is only partially preserved) reinforces an important tendency in Palmyrene religion to worship deities in association with one another. Multiple gods frequently received cult in spaces in the porticoes or in smaller chapels (such as the *hamana* to the god Shamash in the sanctuary of Allat in 30/31 BC; Gawlikowski 2006, 535) and, on occasion, within the main temple itself. Groupings, or triads, of deities were a characteristic of Palmyrene religion. The most famous of these is the association between Bēl, Aglibol, and Yarhibol (all of whom, arguably, were worshipped in the temple of Bēl). The exact nature of these associations is problematic, but ultimately it appears that the people of Palmyra were flexible in their identifications of and between deities, although certain deities (e.g., Bēl-Hammon and Manawat) appeared together more frequently than others (Kaizer 2016).

The sanctuaries also played a key role in the civic lives of the community as the setting for honours erected to important members of the community (such as Malè), as well as spaces for gatherings to reinforce social ties. Many of the sanctuaries had facilities for sacrifice and for communal dining (Will 1997; Kaizer 2002, 192–193, 220–229). Large numbers of tesserae, some decorated with images of priests, sacrifice, or deities, others inscribed with the names of Palmyrene tribes, suggest that banqueting delineated smaller groups within the community, acting as entrance tokens to events charged with both religious and social significance for the participants (Raja 2015a; Raja 2015b).

THE TEMPLES AND SANCTUARIES

An overview of the temples and sanctuaries will reinforce the trends sketched above while also demonstrating the multiplicity of ways in which the unique circumstances and building histories developed over the course of two centuries of construction. The goal is to provide non-specialist readers with an understanding of each complex and a sense of the major architectural features and trends within and across the temples and sanctuaries in the city of Palmyra. Readers interested in further details concerning the architecture are directed to the final reports of each sanctuary, most of which have been thoroughly published with a great many drawings and photographs. Likewise, references to comparative material outside Palmyra are intentionally minimal. More synthetic studies of the sacred spaces and cults of Palmyra can be found in the bibliography.

The Temple of Bēl

Bēl was a supreme cosmic deity with connections to Babylon (Drijvers 1976, 9–12; Seyrig et al. 1968–1975, 227–229), and his temple at Palmyra (Figure 23.1) was the largest and most important in the city, sometimes referred to in inscriptions as *lbt'lyn*, the 'temple of their gods' (i.e., the Palmyrene community as a whole) (*PAT* 1353; Kaizer 2002, 70–71). The sanctuary was the terminal point of the Great Colonnade, which functioned as a kind of monumental processional way during celebrations such as the Babylonian Akitu festival in April (Kaizer 2002, 200–211). The Corinthian temple, set on a high podium within a court bordered by porticoes, was a product of the first and second centuries AD. The court eventually included a dining hall and altar. Multiple gods were worshipped in the sanctuary, in particular Aglibol and Yarhibol (Drijvers 1976, 10–13; Gawlikowski 1990a, 2608–2624). Seyrig, Amy, and Will's publications (1968–1975) of

FIGURE 23.1 The temple of Bēl.

Photograph courtesy of Maura K. Heyn.

the temple, based on excavations beginning in the 1920s, are now supplemented by Pietrzykowksi's (1997a) generally accepted modifications to its chronology (published primarily in Polish but including a French summary; Gawlikowski 2015, 249; Kaizer 2002, 67–68).

The earliest temple to Bēl is dated to the mid-first century BC by architectural fragments found in a trench beneath the Roman-period sanctuary or reused in later constructions (Gawlikowski 1973, 54–66). Among these are inscriptions from 44 BC for a statue set up by the priests of Bēl (*PAT* 2766) and a dedication from 6 BC referring to a portico and spaces for sacrifice and dining (*PAT* 1524; Gawlikowski 1973, 60–63).

Inscriptions from 17 (*PAT* 0270) and AD 24 (*PAT* 1352) demonstrate that work on a new temple and porticoes was under way by the first quarter of the first century AD. The temple was officially dedicated (although incomplete) on 6 April AD 32 (*PAT* 1347), a date coinciding with the Akitu festival for Bēl. Construction on the cella extended into the early second century AD, as indicated by Aqqaih's gift of a gate and doors in AD 108 (*PAT* 0263; Pietrzykowski 1997a), while work on the porticoes and propylon continued up to the end of the second century AD (Filarska 1967, 103–115; Gawlikowski 1973, 67–68). These porticoes formed a sanctuary court more than twice as large as either of the sanctuaries of Allat and Nabu, and 30,000 m² larger in surface area than the sanctuary of Baalshamin. The exterior walls of the porticoes were decorated with Corinthian pilasters, the windows' edges with mouldings. Within, columns on Attic bases supported a decorated entablature, with double columns at the corners. Consoles for dedicatory inscriptions and statues were set up on the columns.

A monumental gateway (propylon) extended from the western portico, characterized by an octastyle Corinthian porch. The back wall of the propylon included three openings, divided by four small chambers opening east towards the sanctuary. Stairs in the two end chambers led to the roof, a common feature of Palmyrene temples, and probably related to open-air cult practice (Seyrig et al. 1975, 65–82).

The courtyard of the sanctuary was paved and contained several buildings between the propylon and the temple dating to the second century AD (Gawlikowski 1973, 68). Most notable is a ramp running beneath the western wall of the sanctuary and emerging into the north-west corner of the courtyard, presumably to facilitate processions of people and sacrificial animals towards the monumental altar in the courtyard beyond. Nearby were a rectangular building and an associated annex. A colonnade opened towards the altar beyond. A hoard of tesserae found in a nearby ditch confirms that this building was a banquet hall serving around one hundred attendees (Will 1997, 875–878). Across the court was a large basin; to the south, an enigmatic 'édifice à niches' (Gawlikowski 1973, 68).

Beyond this area and set on a high podium was the pseudodipteral temple. The main east–west axis in the sanctuary—followed also by the propylon—was created by the entrance to the cella on the long western end.

A stepped ramp led up from the court to the temple's stylobate, narrowing in width as it ascended (Seyrig et al. 1975, 11–12). The temple adopted a Corinthian order, a standard in the sacred architecture at Palmyra. Eight columns, fluted and set on Attic bases, were placed along the short ends of the temple, with fifteen in the long end on the east and twelve on the west to accommodate a span bridged by an arch over an entrance through the peristyle towards the cella (Seyrig et al. 1975, 17–18).

The Corinthian capitals were partially made of bronze. The entablature above was decorated with mouldings, some painted (Seyrig et al. 1975, 19–20, 94–95). A feature unique to the Bēl temple is the decorated beams spanning the gap between the peristyle and the cella. Carved in relief, these beams included images of animals, deities, processions, and sacrifice (Seyrig et al. 1975, 84–90, plates 42–45; Drijvers 1976, 10–12).

The exterior of the cella was decorated with engaged fluted Ionic columns on the north and south sides and four windows along each of the long sides (Seyrig et al. 1975, 27–40). Inside, the cella was divided into two *adyta* elevated above the level of the cella floor (and so necessitating stairs or a ramp to reach) and located against the short north and south walls.

The north *adyton* (Seyrig et al. 1975, 41–52) consisted of a large central niche decorated with Ionic pilasters on the sides and mouldings along the frame of the door and the lintel. On either side of the niche were smaller aedicular niches topped with blank pedestals. The central niche would have accommodated a cult statue; Gawlikowski (2015, 250) argues that there was only room for a statue of Bēl, while Seyrig, Amy, and Will (1975, plate 38) have reconstructed statues of Bēl, Aglibol, and Yarhibol within. Two doorways set on either side of the central niche led to subsidiary rooms. To the left was a staircase leading up to the roof, while to the right was a small room (Seyrig et al. 1968–1975, 47–48). The function of this smaller room is unknown, but Pietrzykowski (1997b) has argued that this may have been the original location of the couch of Bēl, illustrated on tesserae and perhaps housed in the later second *adyton*.

The most striking feature of this *adyton* was its domed ceiling, created from a carved monolith (Seyrig et al. 1968–1975, 45, 83–84). In the centre of the design were the busts of seven planets, carved in high relief and identifiable by their attributes, set in recessed frames and arranged around a central bust of Bēl or Zeus. Encircling this design were representations of the zodiac, with eagles with outspread wings creating four corners. Around this central schema were rows of framed rosettes and acanthus leaves. An eagle with spread wings was carved on the lintel, accompanied by a serpent, stars, and a cuirassed image of the sun god.

The south *adyton* (Seyrig et al. 1968–1975, 45, 53–64) was constructed at the opposite end of the cella and also consisted of a large central niche set between two rooms (Figure 23.2). The entrance to the niche was framed by two fluted Corinthian half-columns on each side; the lintel above was decorated with mouldings, rosettes, and floral decoration. A decorated dome can be found here as well, crowning the ceiling of the *adyton* and embellished with rosettes and geometric patterns around a large central rosette. The flanking rooms both contained staircases; a spiral staircase to the right and a squared staircase to the left.

FIGURE 23.2   The central niche of the south *adyton*, temple of Bēl.

Photograph courtesy of Maura K. Heyn.

The Temple of Nabu

The sanctuary of Nabu is located to the west of the Great Colonnade and south-west of the temple of Bēl. Publication of the Syrian and French excavations in the 1960s appeared in two comprehensive volumes (Bounni et al. 1992; Bounni 2004). Nabu, a god of Mesopotamian origin frequently associated with Apollo, dominates the dedications from the sanctuary (Bounni 2004, B14/63, B16/63, B20/64, B10/63), although Kaizer (2002, 91–94) notes that there is no specific mention of a temple to Nabu and that various other gods also receive dedications in the sanctuary (Bounni 2004, 47–48). Two families, the Elahbel and Bēlsuri, dominate the epigraphic evidence (Bounni 2004, 47–48). The form of the sanctuary was consistent in its outlines with the organization of the other large sanctuaries at Palmyra, comprising a porticoed court and a temple set on a central axis.

The Roman-period temple of Nabu is thought to have replaced an earlier sanctuary from the first century BC, represented by architectural fragments found in excavations (Bounni et al. 1992, 18). A new temple and the porticoes of the sanctuary were under construction by the first or second centuries AD (Bounni 2004, 14, 18, B14/63, B10/63; *PAT* 009; Bounni et al. 1992, figs. 8–19, 99).

This sanctuary was defined by a trapezoidal court surrounded by porticoes, with entrances through a propylon in the south and a door in the northern portico, decorated with scrolled vines and seven busts of deities over the exterior lintel (Bounni 2004, 5, 13–14). The original plan of the court had been more regular; it was transformed by changes to the north and south porticoes (Bounni 2004, 9–13). As part of the construction of the Great Colonnade, the street projected into the northern edge of the sanctuary (Bounni 2004, 11–13). The south portico was also modified at some time in the first century AD to angle more sharply to the north (Bounni 2004, 9, 18–19).The reason for the new course is unclear, but Bounni noted (2004, 5) that the result was an optical illusion which accentuated the size of the temple and created a sense of vastness. The new court was defined by a solid northern wall and by porticoes in the west. The columns were topped with Doric capitals and outfitted with consoles for dedicatory statues (Bounni 2004, 46–49).

The propylon was located in the southern end of the sanctuary, consisting of a hexastyle facade with Corinthian columns on Attic bases. Flanking the porch were small rooms that could be accessed from outside the sanctuary. The architrave above the columns and the doorway was decorated in a similar manner as found in the temple of Bēl, with a variety of mouldings. Two fluted pilasters flanked the doorway to the portico, which was originally equipped with a grille (Bounni 2004, 7).

Within the court was a square monument set on the same axis as the cella and propylon. Measuring 4.30 m on each side, the monument bore three columns at each corner, which supported a roof over a bas-relief of a series of deities (Bounni 2004, 13–14). The monument dates to perhaps the second century AD, but its function is unclear; both a *hamana* and a monumental altar have been suggested (Drijvers 1988, 175–176; Bounni 2004, 13; Dentzer 1990).

Elevated on a podium beyond was a 6 × 12 m peripteral Corinthian temple, oriented south. A staircase with a small inset altar led up to the peristyle, which appeared only in the second century AD, when it augmented the original colonnaded porch. The temple's entablature was decorated with ovals, dentils, rosettes, and lion-head gutter spouts. One preserved tympanum block was decorated with a fish and fragments of heads—including one wearing a nimbus, possibly Nabu—which had once been affixed to the capitals. Merlons were set along the edge of the roof, which was flat behind the triangular pediment (Bounni 2004, 16; Bounni et al. 1992, 85–86).

The cella enclosed a long approach to a flight of stairs up to an *adyton* with a niche at the north end (Bounni 2004, 17–18). As in the temple of Bēl, two rooms flanked the *adyton*; at least one contained stairs up to the roof (Bounni et al. 1992, plate LXXXVI).

Although the Nabu temple is more poorly preserved than that of Bēl, it appears to share many similar features: a central axis, Corinthian capitals and elaborate decorative features, and the worship of multiple deities within a complex. The excavators reconstructed both the temples of Bēl and Nabu with flat roofs equipped with short towers topped with merlons and with doors set into them, leading to the stairs flanking the *adyta* below, and thus facilitating rites on the roof.

The Temple of Allat

The temple of Allat was located in the north-west of the city, in the area of the Camp of Diocletian. Publication of excavations initiated in the 1970s is forthcoming, but Gawlikowski (1973, 101–104; 1977; 1983; 1990b; 2006; 2007; 2014) has published extensively on the ongoing work there. The goddess was depicted in Palmyrene art with lions or with the iconography of Athena, and is frequently associated with an Arabic origin (Gawlikowski 1990a, 2636–2643; Gawlikowski 1996). A dedicatory inscription from AD 115 set up by a member of the Bene Ma'ziyan identifies an ancestor, Mattanai, as the dedicant of the original cult image in the *hamana* of Allat, placing its earliest phase sometime in the first century BC (*PAT* 1929; Gawlikowski 1997). As was the case in each of the other sanctuaries, Allat was not worshipped alone; the Arabic gods Rahim and Shamash appear with Allat in inscriptions (*PAT* 0301; *PAT* 0297) and a *hamana* was dedicated to Shamash in Allat's sanctuary in 31/30 BC (Gawlikowski 2014, 81).

The original *hamana* was a simple windowless room entered from the east (Gawlikowski 1977, 271; Gawlikowski 1990b, 102; Gawlikowski 2014, 80–81). Merlons decorated the cornice, and a monolithic altar was set in front of the entrance. By the first century AD a niche decorated with eagles and vines was set into the west wall, probably to house the cult image donated by Mattani. Gawlikowski (2014, 81) suggests that the statue was composite and could be removed for use in ritual.

The typical outlines of a Palmyrene sanctuary began to take shape in the mid-first century AD, as indicated by dedicatory inscriptions from 54 (Gawlikowski 1977, 263) and AD 64 (*PAT* 0312; Kaizer 2002, 104). Porticoes enclosed a courtyard with the *hamana* set closer to the western edge. Inscriptions from the west and south porticoes show that construction in those areas was still ongoing in the mid-second century AD (Gawlikowski 1977, 271; Drijvers 1995b). Corinthian capitals were employed in the north and south, and Doric capitals in the west. The eastern portico is poorly understood in this period, but a dedicatory inscription from the entrance gate dates to the mid-second century AD (*PAT* 0331; Gawlikowski 1977, 256).

As in the other sanctuaries, the court included additional constructions. The foundations of two squared buildings were uncovered in the north-west corner and in front of the eastern entrance to the sanctuary. These structures were perhaps cultic spaces for other deities or monumental altars (Gawlikowski 2006, 534–535; Gawlikowski 2007, 520–521).

The temple itself underwent a substantial change in the second century AD, when the *hamana* was integrated into the cella of a Corinthian tetraprostyle temple. An inscription from the lintel dated to the mid-second century AD identifies a certain Taimarsu as the donor for the construction (*PAT* 1608; Gawlikowski 1977, 260–263). Set up on a podium, the new temple more than doubled the space of the old *hamana*, now measuring 18.40 × 9.20 m (Gawlikowski 1977, 258). The exterior walls of the cella and cornice were decorated with intricately carved mouldings and pilasters (Gawlikowski 1977, 259).

The cella was constructed around and at a slightly higher elevation than the *hamana* (Gawlikowski 2014, 80). Gawlikowski (1977, 258–260; 2007, 522) argues that the roof of the new temple was probably left open, as indicated by drainage channels and the lack of finish on a preserved fragment of the interior edge of the cella's pediment. A statue of Athena Parthenos made of Pentelic marble was also imported and set up somewhere in the temple in this period (Gawlikowski 1996).

The Roman sack in AD 272 resulted in widespread destruction in the sanctuary. Fragments from the temple and sanctuary were used in the construction of the Roman legionary camp, while additional pieces were found in pits and cisterns dated to the sack (Gawlikowski 2006, 236; 2007, 519). The temple was refurbished for its last century in use, now located within the boundaries of the camp. In place of the old temple, four columns now supported a canopy over a platform constructed over (and incorporating fragments of) the ruins of the shrine. The statue of Athena Parthenos was placed atop (Gawlikowski 1977, 264–271; 1996; 2014, 82). The eastern portico and its gate, dedicated in the mid-second century AD, were remodelled and brought in line with the Via Principalis (Gawlikowski 2006, 533; 1977, 256–258, 263–264), but lime kilns built in the fourth century AD demonstrate the relatively short-lived second life of the sanctuary (Gawlikowski 2006, 535–536).

The Temple of Baalshamin

If Bēl's sanctuary was the largest and most elaborate, that of Baalshamin was unique (Figure 23.3). Baalshamin, a Semitic weather and fertility deity (Drijvers 1976, 14–15; Gawlikowski 1990a, 2625–2627), was associated with a range of other deities in inscriptions and offerings within the sanctuary (particularly Durahle, e.g., Dunant 1971,

FIGURE 23.3 The temple of Baalshamin.

Photograph courtesy of Maura K. Heyn.

8–10; Kaizer 2002, 84–86). Located to the west of the temple of Allat, the sanctuary was composed of multiple colonnaded courtyards set up along a diagonal axis, similar in overall conception to the sanctuary of Baalshamin at Sia (Segal 2013, 206–213). In addition, the sanctuary had been constructed according to a Babylonian standard measurement of 28.75 cm, a feature also found in the sanctuary of Bēl (Collart and Vicari 1969, 102–107). Malè's temple was added only belatedly in the south of the sanctuary in the early second century AD; before this point, the focal point of cult seems to have occurred in a series of rooms further north. The association of the Bene Ma'ziyan with the sanctuary (Collart and Vicari 1969, 94–95; Dunant 1971, 10–11) was strengthened by the presence of tombs belonging to tribal members from the pre-Roman period located in and around the sanctuary; epigraphic evidence describes the opening and purification of several of these in the first century AD (*PAT* 0208; see commentary in Dunant 1971, 72–75). Excavations of the temple of Baalshamin, sadly destroyed in 2015, were published by Collart and Vicari (1969) and then supplemented by additional volumes (e.g., Dunant 1971).

The early sanctuary dates to the first quarter of the first century AD. It was from the beginning defined by an offset row of courts, measuring at its greatest extent 160 × 60 m (Collart and Vicari 1969, 25, 89–90, plate III). In this period the sanctuary was comprised of a solid exterior wall with an entrance in the south-west side and a large open court stretching out before a set of rooms fronting a large squared room bounded by two additional wall circuits (Collart and Vincari 1969, 47–53). These northern rooms probably functioned as a temple complex.

In AD 67, the sanctuary underwent a significant transformation with the erection of colonnaded courts. The main modification was the formalization of the central space between the northern temple complex and its southern extent through the construction of a large colonnaded court (Collart and Vicari 1969, 34–38, 54, 145–149, plate IV). Yarhai's dedication in AD 67 contributed to the southern extent, while dedications of columns by Zabdai and Malku in the north and east porticoes also date to the same year (PAT 0170; PAT 0329; Dunant 1971, 26–27, nos. 13–14). The year AD 67 also saw the dedication of a ritual dining hall in the south-east of the great court (PAT 0177; Dunant 1971, 33–34; Collart and Vicari 1969, 30).

A new period of construction, begun in AD 90, was the most consequential for the sanctuary as we know it today (Collart and Vicari 1969, 91–93, plate V). In the north, a Rhodian peristyle (in which one wing is higher than the others) was added within the central space of the old temple complex (Collart and Vicari 1969, 50). The southern extent of the sanctuary was not defined by a colonnade until AD 149, with the construction of a peristyle (PAT 0176; Dunant 1971, 31–32, no. 20). In addition, a central court (south of the great court) was constructed under the auspices of the same Malku who had previously given a column (Dunant 1971, 21–22; Collart and Vicari 1969, 145–149).

The Corinthian tetraprostyle temple built by Malè Agrippa was dedicated in AD 130/131 in the central court, with the entrance oriented to the south-east (Collart and Vicari 1969, 71–73, 111, plates IX–X). Consoles were affixed to the front of the columns; it was here that the dedicatory inscription of Malè was found (PAT 0305; Dunant 1971, 55–56, no. 44). Corinthian pilasters decorated the sides of the cella, and the sculpted cornices were crowned by merlons; one window framed by aedicular mouldings was also set into each long end (Collart and Vicari 1969, 108, 142, plates XIV–XV).

The 8-metre-long *adyton* inside the cella (Collart and Vicari 1969, 121) was built against the back wall and was more elaborate in design and conception than any of the other *adyta* excavated in the city. The *adyton* was dominated by a series of aedicular facades with heavy mouldings in various styles. Single and double columns and pilasters were set up on high pedestals and topped with Corinthian capitals (Gawlikowski and Pietrzykowski 1980, 426–430). Several of these columns were fluted, and niches were set into the eastern walls facing the entrance (Collart and Vicari 1979, plates XCV–XCVI). These smaller niches were decorated with shell designs, floral imagery, and griffins; Gawlikowski and Pietrzykowski (1980, 438–446) have suggested that some of these niches represent older material integrated into the new temple.

The passageway to the central niche was established by squared flanking rooms, and the aedicular superstructure formed a semicircular exedra over the large central niche. A relief was originally attached to the niche; although not preserved, it may have predated the construction of the temple (Gawlikowski and Pietrzykowski 1980, 446–447). In similar fashion, an earlier sculptural feature served as the lintel for the niche opening, depicting a central eagle with spread wings flanked by two smaller eagles on each side, a rosette, and bust of a deity with a nimbus (Collart and Vicari 1969, 129–132, plate XCVII). Above a series of mouldings was set a second carved lintel, decorated with the busts of seven (according to their attributes) planetary deities, flanked by two eagles (Gawlikowski and Pietrzykowski 1980, 426).

The Temple of Bēl-Hammon

The temple of Bēl-Hammon, dedicated in AD 89, was built into a bastion of the fortification walls south-west of the city near the Jebel Muntar (*PAT* 1561–1562). Explorations of the temple in the 1960s have been augmented by epigraphic evidence and tesserae which identify the Bene Agrud among the temple's primary patrons (du Mesnil du Buisson 1966, 165–176; Gawlikowski 1973, 12–14; Kaizer 2002, 114–115). Bēl-Hammon, an aspect of Bēl, received offerings in the city from at least the Hellenistic period, in conjunction with Manawat, a goddess related to good fortune who is also included in the dedicatory inscription for the temple (*PAT* 1523; *PAT* 1556; du Mesnil du Buisson 1966, 168–170; Kaizer 2002, 109–116).

The entrance and portions of the cella are preserved today, but the interior space was adapted into a mosque in the twelfth century. The temple is oriented to the south-east facing the city (Gawlikowski 1973, 12). The pronaos consisted of two columns flanking the entrance to the cella, of which only the Attic bases are preserved *in situ* (du Mesnil du Buisson 1966, 166–167; Gawlikowski 1973, 12). The dedicatory inscription, preserved on a lintel and console found nearby, describes the gifts of two members of the Bene Agrud, Moqimu, and Yarhibola. These included bronze doors and a marble portico in addition to porticoes and decorations for a temple of Manawat. Tesserae (*RTP* 99, *RTP* 214, *RTP* 22) inscribed with the name of the Bene Agrud appear to depict the temple as two towers of unequal height on a rock outcropping. Their roofs are flat; one is depicted with merlons. *RTP* 214 includes the detail of a window in the centre of the taller tower as well as an entrance in the smaller tower, flanked by two columns on Attic bases and crowned with merlons.

The Temple of Arsu

Emergency excavations in the 1980s uncovered the foundations of a temple and courtyard southwest of Palmyra's Agora (al-As'ad et al. 2005, 2–3). The building was identified as the temple of Arsu by an altar from AD 63 dedicated to the god and found there, as well as 125 tesserae depicting Arsu discovered in a jar in the sanctuary (al-As'ad and Teixidor 1985; al-As'ad et al. 2005). A series of small rooms in the sanctuary were likely associated with ritual dining. Arsu, a god of the desert and protector of caravans, was connected to the Bene Mattabol (Kaizer 2002, 116–119). His temple was identified as one of the main sanctuaries in two inscriptions of the early second century AD (*PAT* 0197; Drijvers 1995a, 34–36).

Others

Additional sanctuaries are known primarily from epigraphic sources. For example, inscriptions refer to the Sacred Garden of Aglibol and Malakbel as one of the city's main sanctuaries (*PAT* 0197; *PAT* 1944; Kaizer 2002, 124–143) and an inscription from AD 137 (Gawlikowski 1973, 24) situates a temple to the god Rabaseire across from the agora. Little is known about the sanctuary to Astarte or Atargatis aside from its existence (*PAT* 0197; Drijvers 1995a, 34–36; Kaizer 2002, 153–154). A Caesareum is mentioned in an inscription from AD 171, and Dirven (2011, 153–156) suggests that the imperial cult was an important nexus of activity. Finally, the 'Efqa spring served as the focal point for cult activity and is sometimes identified as a sanctuary for the solar god Yarhibol (du Mesnil du Buisson 1966, 161–162; Gawlikowski 1973, 25, 112–120; Kaizer 2002, 143–148). Stucco fragments uncovered in the 1970s near the spring included a pilaster depicting Aglibol, perhaps indicating the existence of a cult building there in the third century AD (Allag et al. 2010).

CONCLUSION

The sanctuaries of Palmyra share many commonalities—some drawn from the koine of the Hellenistic artistic world, others emerging from long-standing local or Near Eastern practices. A list of Hellenistic elements might include engagement with Hellenistic notions of proportions and space, so that nearly all Palmyrene temples fit neatly within Vitruvian architectural categories (Segal 2013, 2). Certainly the use of Corinthian columns and elaborate moulded decorations (to say nothing of the imported statue of Athena Parthenos) was part of a Graeco-Roman architectural style. Near Eastern elements include the use of merlons and Babylonian base measurements, as well as the organization of the sanctuary of Baalshamin and entrance to the temple of Bēl. The frequent reoccurrence of the eagle in the *adyta* and the specific phenomenon of local, familial, and/or tribal patrons evoke a certain sense of local priorities and expectations. However, the more compelling aspects of these sanctuaries are the stories they tell, in stone and stylobate and socle, of the ways in which peoples experienced the gods and used sanctuaries to forge and reforge ties within the community.

Much important work has been done on the cultural influences and threads brought together in the sanctuaries at Palmyra, but current emphasis on group and individual identities and on experiences within the temple complexes will forge new roads of inquiry and analysis. New categories of identity-based analysis (e.g., aspects of imperial identities or ideas about urban and rural sanctuaries) might be pursued. A key future direction—and a fruitful place for debate—is the use of digital tools and projects to map, render in 3-D (e.g., Silver et al. 2018), and catalogue the immense amount of architectural and artefactual material from the city and make it available more widely for study. New phenomenological approaches, aided by digital work, might study the role of lighting and viewing angles, access points, the role of polychromy, and sound and smell.

BIBLIOGRAPHY

al-As'ad, Khaled, Françoise Briquel-Chatonnet, and Jean-Baptiste Yon. 2005. 'The Sacred Banquets at Palmyra and the Function of the Tesserae: Reflections on the Tokens Found in the Arṣu Temple'. In *A Journey to Palmyra: Collected Essays to Remember Delbert R. Hillers*, edited by Eleonora Cussini, 1–10. Leiden: Brill.

al-As'ad, Khaled, and Javier Teixidor. 1985. 'Un culte arabe préislamique à Palmyre d'après une inscription inédite'. *Comptes rendus des séances de l'Académie des inscriptions et belles-lettres* 129(2): 286–293.

Allag, Claudine, Nicole Blanc, and Klaus Parlasca. 2010. 'Palmyre: Stucs trouvés près de la source Efqa (site de l'hôtel Méridien)'. *Syria* 87: 191–227.Bounni, Adnan. 1999. 'Couronnement des sanctuaires du proche-orient hellénistique et romain: Origine et développement du merlon'. *Topoi* 9(2): 507–525.

Bounni, Adnan. 2004. *Le sanctuaire de Nabu à Palmyre*. Beirut: Institut français d'archéologie du Proche-Orient.

Bounni, Adnan, Jacques Seigne, and Nassib Saliby. 1992. *Le sanctuaire de Nabu à Palmyre*. Beirut: Institut français d'archéologie du Proche-Orient.

Collart, Paul, and Jacques Vicari. 1969. *Le Sanctuaire de Baalshamin à Palmyre*. Vols. 1–2. Rome: Institut suisse de Rome.

Dentzer, Jean-Marie. 1990. 'Edicules d'epoque Hellenistico-Romaine et tradition des pierres cultuelles en Syrie et en Arabie'. In *Resurrecting the Past: A Joint Tribute to Adnān Bounnī*, edited by Paolo Matthiae, Maurits Nanning van Loon, and Harvey Weiss, 65–83. Leiden: Nederlands Historisch-Archaeologisch Instituut te Istanbul.

Dirven, Lucinda. 2011. 'The Imperial Cult in the Cities of the Decapolis, Caesarea Maritima, and Palmyra'. *ARAM* 23: 141–156.

Drijvers, H. J. W. 1976. *The Religion of Palmyra*. Leiden: Brill.

Drijvers, H. J. W. 1978. 'De matre inter leones sedente: Iconography and Character of the Arab Goddess Allât'. In *Hommages à Maarten J. Vermaseren*. Vol. 1, edited by T. A. Edridge and Margreet Boer, 331–351. Leiden: Brill.

Drijvers, H. J. W. 1988. 'Aramaic HMN and Hebrew HMN: Their Meaning and Root'. *Journal of Semitic Studies* 33(2): 165–180.

Drijvers, H. J. W. 1995a. 'Greek and Aramaic in Palmyrene Inscriptions'. In *Studia Aramaica: New Sources and New Approaches*, edited by Markham J. Geller, Jonas C. Greenfield, and Michael Weitzman, 31–42. Oxford: Oxford University Press.

Drijvers, H. J. W. 1995b. 'Inscriptions from Allat's Sanctuary'. *ARAM* 7: 109–119.

du Mesnil du Buisson, Robert. 1966. 'Première campagne de fouilles à Palmyre'. *Comptes rendus des séances de l'Académie des inscriptions et belles-lettres* 110: 158–190.

Dunant, Christiane. 1971. *Le sanctuaire de Baalshamin à Palmyre: Inscriptions*. Rome: Institut suisse de Rome.

Filarska, Barbara. 1967. *Studia nad dekoracjami architektonicznymi Palmyry*. Studia Palmyreńskie 2. Warsaw: Uniwersytetu Warszawskiego.

Gawlikowski, Michał. 1973. *Le temple palmyrénien: Étude d'épigraphie et de topographie historique*. Palmyre 6. Warsaw: Państwowe Wydawnictwo Naukowe.

Gawlikowski, Michał. 1977. 'Le temple d'Allât à Palmyre'. *Revue archéologique*: 2: 253–274.

Gawlikowski, Michał. 1983. 'Réflexions sur la chronologie du sanctuaire d'Allat à Palmyre'. *Damaszener Mitteilungen* 1: 59–67.

Gawlikowski, Michał. 1990a. 'Les dieux de Palmyre'. In *Aufstieg und Niedergang der römischen Welt*. Vol. 2, *Principat*, no. 18, *Religion*, 4, edited by Wolfgang Haase, 2605–2658. Berlin: de Gruyter.

Gawlikowski, Michał. 1990b. 'Le premier temple d'Allat'. In *Resurrecting the Past: A Joint Tribute to Adnān Bounnī*, edited by Paolo Matthiae, Maurits Nanning van Loon, and Harvey Weiss, 101–108. Leiden: Nederlands Historisch-Archaeologisch Instituut te Istanbul.

Gawlikowski, Michał. 1996. 'The Athena of Palmyra'. *Archeologia* 47: 21–32.

Gawlikowski, Michał. 1997. 'Du hamana au naos: Le temple palmyrénien hellénisé'. *Topoi* 7(2): 837–849.

Gawlikowski, Michał. 2006. 'Palmyra: Excavations in the Allat Sanctuary, 2005–2006'. *Polish Archaeology in the Mediterranean* 18: 531–541.

Gawlikowski, Michał. 2007. 'Palmyra: Preliminary Report on the Forty-Fifth Season of Excavations'. *Polish Archaeology in the Mediterranean* 19: 517–526.

Gawlikowski, Michał. 2008. 'The Statues of the Sanctuary of Allat in Palmyra'. In *The Sculptural Environment of the Roman Near East: Reflections on Culture, Ideology, and Power*, edited by Yaron Z. Eliav, Elise A. Friedland, and Sharon Herbert, 397–411. Leuven: Peeters.

Gawlikowski, Michał. 2014. 'Gods and Temples of Palmyra'. *Miscellanea anthropologica et sociologica* 15(3): 76–91.

Gawlikowski, Michał. 2015. 'Bēl of Palmyra'. In *Religious Identities in the Levant from Alexander to Muhammed: Continuity and Change*, edited by Michael Blömer, Achim Lichtenberger, and Rubina Raja, 247–254. Turnhout: Brepols.

Gawlikowski, Michał, and Michał Pietrzykowski. 1980. 'Les sculptures du temple de Baalshamin à Palmyre'. *Syria* 57(2–4): 421–452.

Ingholt, Harald, Henri Seyrig, and Jean Starcky. 1955. *Recueil des tessères de Palmyre*. Paris: Geuthner.

Kaizer, Ted. 2002. *The Religious Life of Palmyra: A Study of the Social Patterns of Worship in the Roman Period*. Stuttgart: Steiner.

Kaizer, Ted. 2016. 'Divine Constellations at Palmyra: Reconsidering the Palmyrene 'Pantheon''. In *The World of Palmyra*, edited by Andreas Kropp and Rubina Raja, 17–30. Copenhagen: Det Kongelige Danske Videnskabernes Selskab.

Pietrzykowski, Michał. 1997a. *Adyta świątyń palmyreńskich: Les adytons des temples palmyréniens*. Warsaw: Archet.

Pietrzykowski, Michał. 1997b. 'La couche du temple de Bēl'. *Études et travaux* 15: 324–325.

Raja, Rubina. 2015a. 'Cultic Dining and Religious Patterns in Palmyra: The Case of the Palmyrene Banqueting Tesserae'. In *Antike, Architektur, Geschichte: Festschrift für Inge Nielsen zum 65. Geburtstag*, edited by Stephan Faust, Martina Seifert, and Leon Ziemer, 181–199. Aachen: Shaker.

Raja, Rubina. 2015b. 'Staging 'Private' Religion in Roman 'Public' Palmyra: The Role of the Religious Dining Tickets (Banqueting Tesserae)'. In *Public and Private in Ancient Mediterranean Law and Religion*, edited by Clifford Ando and Jörg Rüpke, 165–186. Berlin: de Gruyter.

Segal, Arthur. 2013. *Temples and Sanctuaries in the Roman East: Religious Architecture in Syria, Iudaea/Palaestina and Provincia Arabia*. Oxford: Oxbow.

Seyrig, Henri, Robert Amy, and Ernest Will. 1968–1975. *Le temple de* Bēl *à Palmyre*. Vol. 1, *Texte et planches*; vol. 2, *Album*. Beirut: Institut français d'archéologie du Proche-Orient.

Silver, Minna, Gabriele Fangi, and Ahmet Denker. 2018. *Reviving Palmyra in Multiple Dimensions: Images, Ruins and Cultural Memory*. Dunbeath: Whittles.

Will, Ernest. 1997. 'Les salles de banquet de Palmyre et d'autres lieux'. *Topoi* 7(2): 873–887.

....

CHAPTER 24

BUILT FOR ETERNITY

The Funerary Monuments of Palmyra

....

AGNES HENNING

INTRODUCTION

IN the extended necropoleis of Palmyra, over four hundred monumental tombs have been documented in the past one hundred years (compare Schnädelbach 2010). This makes the oasis city one of the most important sites in the ancient world with regard to sepulchral architecture. The large number of tombs allows us to deduce that three particular tomb types are specific to Palmyra: the tall standing tower tombs, the less conspicuous (at least on the surface) hypogea, and the so-called temple tombs, with their magnificent facades (al-As'ad and Schmidt-Colinet 2005). Despite their different designs and their partially differing chronology, all three tombs are commonly referred to as 'houses of eternity' (*bt 'lm'*) in their preserved building inscriptions, which date to as early as the late first century BC (Will 1990, 438, n. 28; Hillers and Cussini 1996, 346). Irrespective of tomb type, in Palmyra this term was generally equated with funerary monuments, or a specific part of such (Henning 2013a, 85–86). It was primarily intended to emphasize the permanent commemoration and veneration of the deceased, which was expressed by the monumental architecture, the numerous burials within a single monument, the tombs' magnificent furnishings, and by the intentional representations of the Palmyrene families, which continue to fascinate us today.

STATE OF THE RESEARCH

The large number of funerary monuments in the Palmyrene necropoleis offer a great variety of information on not only their specific sepulchral contexts, but also on Palmyra's urban history in general. Although there are only a few remains left of some of the monuments, a sufficient number of tombs have retained their architecture, furnishings, and inscriptions sufficiently well that we can reconstruct a representative picture of Palmyrene funerary architecture. Above all, since Palmyra's earliest discovery, the tall standing tower tombs have fascinated travellers and explorers, most notably Louis-François Cassas, who visited Palmyra in the late eighteenth century (Schmidt-Colinet 1994; 1996, 361–368, 460–479, figs. 161–206; Henning 2016; Ketelsen 2016). In the early twentieth century, the first systematic survey of the necropoleis documented all then-known tombs and, as the approximately two hundred monuments were mapped and briefly catalogued, then published by Theodor Wiegand in 1932 (Watzinger and Wulzinger 1932, 44–76), this remains an essential basis for further research. A new and still unsurpassed overview was first presented by Michał Gawlikowski (1970), who not only analysed all three tomb types and designed a chronological framework, but also examined the funerary inscriptions and the overall structure of the necropoleis.

To date, the individual tomb types have received varying scholarly attention: Ernest Will (1949) developed the first chronology for the tower tombs. The Polish excavations of the following decades enriched the general picture and offered numerous important insights (Gawlikowski 1988; 1992; Witecka 1994). My detailed study (2013a; 2013b) documents all known tower tombs, extends the chronological development of their architecture and furnishings, and situates the tombs in the historical context of the oasis city. Anna Sadurska and Adnan Bounni (1994) compiled a catalogue of the sculptures of the then-known hypogea, which must be considered one of the first contextual studies of the tombs of Palmyra. However, the various hypogea are presented primarily in individual studies (see Sadurska and Bounni's compilation, 1994). In particular, the excavation reports of the Japanese archaeological team in Palmyra should be highlighted as they detected and revealed well-preserved subterranean structures in the southeastern necropolis by applying modern technology that revealed important findings such as skeletal remains. They were also able to establish the contextual relationship between burials and sculptures (Higuchi and Izumi 1994; Higuchi and Saito 2001; Saito 2005a). A comprehensive study of the chronological development of the architecture, construction history of the individual structures, construction techniques, and various furnishings of the hypogea is still missing. The same applies to the temple tombs, as Andreas Schmidt-Colinet's detailed study of temple tomb no. 36 (1992) remains the exception. Researching the temple tombs is fundamentally difficult and requires enormous logistic and documentary effort as most of the monuments have collapsed (see Saito 2016).

Numerous funerary inscriptions have been preserved, and these are a particularly valuable source, because—in combination with the archaeological evidence—they offer insights into various aspects of Palmyra's funerary culture, its family structure, and its urban community. These texts have been collected in various corpora and were constantly supplemented and extended (Chabot 1926; Cantineau 1930; 1931; 1932; Teixidor 1965; Hillers and Cussini 1996; Yon 2012).

The Necropoleis

Palmyra's necropoleis with their numerous funerary monuments extend outside the city's urban limits and at least partly follow the course of the most important trade routes entering the city (see general map of Palmyra in the opening pages of this volume). Today we also distinguish the western necropolis (Figure 24.1), which, owing to its natural setting in the landscape, is referred to as 'valley of the tombs', and stretches along the route to Emesa. The route towards the Euphrates runs through the extended northern necropolis. We also differentiate between the south-eastern necropolis, with its route towards Hit, and the south-western necropolis through which the route to Damascus runs. Apparently, there was also an eastern route that led directly to the Euphrates, as evidenced by isolated tombs discovered on a French cadastral map from 1930 (compare Dentzer and Saupin 1996); some of these tombs could still be surveyed quite recently (Schnädelbach 2010, Annex). In antiquity, there was probably no clear separation of the necropolis areas. In particular, the western and northern necropoleis were originally interconnected. However, the construction of Diocletian's Camp and the Diocletianic city wall caused a new urban shape, above all characterized by military needs. This created an architectural barrier. Numerous funerary monuments were sealed and

FIGURE 24.1 View from the city over the western necropolis with the tower tombs at Umm Belquis

Image © Agnes Henning.

incorporated into the fortification and thus lost their original function (Henning 2013a, 11; Gawlikowski 2021, 152). This clearly suggests that the Palmyrene tombs may once have encircled the city, although there was certainly a concentration on the surrounding hilltops and along roads.

As the tomb facades were oriented towards the roads, the pathways within the necropoleis may be reconstructed (Gawlikowski 1970, 147–166; Henning 2013a, 11). This is most clearly observable in the western necropolis, where the tombs' well-preserved facades, reliefs, and inscriptions are oriented towards a path that runs through the valley. However, the orientation of the tomb facades can also be applied to the other necropoleis, to detect pathways that once passed the tombs.

The beginning of Palmyra's necropoleis is difficult to determine. Isolated findings from the Hellenistic period do not indicate that a specific area of the settlement was reserved only for burials. Such findings include a hypogeum behind the temple of Baalshamin that, based on ceramic evidence, must have been built in the second century BC. This semi-subterranean tomb with a mud-brick superstructure is the earliest dated funerary monument in Palmyra (compare Fellmann 1970; Gawlikowski 2021, 152). Based on dendrochronological analyses, this individual burial of a man in the south-eastern necropolis (Tomb G) dates to between 380 and 160 BC (compare Saito 2005a, 34). It may be assumed that only since the first century BC were several above-ground funerary monuments erected in the form of tower tombs in the western necropolis (Henning 2013a, 117; 2013b, 160).

Since the first century AD, funerary monuments are also evidenced in the northern and south-western necropoleis. None of the necropoleis was preferred for one specific tomb type, and all include tower and temple tombs and hypogea. This suggests that, since the first century AD, the necropoleis were used simultaneously and did not develop successively. Whereas tower tombs were built mainly on gently inclined slopes or on small hilltops, the roadside was the preferred location for temple tombs. Hypogea required particular geological conditions because the soil had to be excavated for their construction.

BURIAL PRACTICES

Well into the third century AD, inhumation was the most common verifiable burial practice in all tomb types. Cremations are only exceptions. In some instances, mummification was also practised (Henning 2013a, 87–88). Individual burials of people not integrated into a large family tomb were set in simple pit-graves in the soil (Cantineau 1932, 4; de Jong 2017, 288), whereas in the monumental tombs of the wealthy Palmyrene clans, the deceased were laid in loculi. Tall, narrow shafts in the walls of the burial chambers, established by means of dividing slabs, created a system of shelves on which the deceased were laid. This system offered optimal use of space within the tomb. The openings were closed after the burial. This was achieved by a simple fill of rubble and mortar, or, from the mid-first century AD, by inserting limestone slabs featuring a relief portrait of the deceased (see Chapter 27 [Raja] this volume). In addition to the loculi, in the mid-first century AD, rather elaborate sarcophagus burials were introduced which required more space and often occupied prominent positions within the tombs. In the tower tombs, these sarcophagi were built of single stone slabs and mortar in specially designed chambers as monolithic stone cases did not fit through the tombs' narrow staircases (see Henning 2013a, 35; 2013b, 164). Monolithic sarcophagi were in evidence from the second century AD (see Colledge 1976, 77–78; Makowski 1985; Wielgosz 1997; also see Chapter 27 this volume).

A large number of funerary inscriptions have been preserved from the Palmyrene tombs. From the foundation texts, concession inscriptions, and individual epitaphs, it is clear that the large funerary monuments were built as family tombs in which several tribal branches were buried over several generations. Corresponding to the general development of the tombs, the number of burial places increased steadily, so that monuments erected in later times, in particular the temple tombs, contained more than four hundred burial places (Schmidt-Colinet 2005, 39). In addition to actual family members, slaves and freedmen probably also belonged to the extended family and were also buried in the large tombs (compare Yon 2002, 186, 199, 207–210).

The family tombs were not always full. Particularly in the hypogea, some sections were never completed and, instead, only prepared sufficiently to be expanded, if necessary (compare Michałowski 1963, 206; Higuchi and Saito 2001, 36–39). Since the second century AD, funerary inscriptions indicate that parts of the tombs were even conceded to other family branches or to outside individuals (Gawlikowski 1970, 204–16; Cussini 1995; Yon 2002, 223). However, in other tombs, burials were used successively several times (compare Fellmann 1970, 122; Higuchi and Izumi 1994, 108).

The Palmyrene tombs were not only burial places, but also intended to preserve the memory of the deceased. In addition to being 'houses of eternity', in some rare cases we also find the term 'nefesh', in reference to the various tomb types, which in the Semitic languages means 'breath', 'soul', or 'person'. Thus the tomb was a place where one imagined the soul of the deceased to reside (Gawlikowski 1970, 22–30; 1972, 10; Will 1990, 435; Mouton 1997; Triebel 2004; Henning 2013a, 86–87; Gawlikowski 2021, 155–156).

CHRONOLOGY

Palmyrene funerary monuments were provided with foundation texts that were carved on the lintels of the main entrances or on separate panels above them. Most of these are still incorporated within the original monuments, others were reused in the construction of other buildings. The necropoleis of Palmyra present the densest concentration of firmly dated, ancient funerary monuments in the ancient world.

The funerary inscriptions were in Aramaic or, from the second half of the first century AD, were bilingual, with an additional text version in Greek. Both texts are consistent in their statements and often also in their wording. Trilingual inscriptions with a text version in Latin are very rare (compare Yon 2012, 496). The building inscription gives the name of the tomb founder and, in many cases, also the date of construction of the respective tombs, according to the Seleucid calendar.

Around fifty Palmyrene tombs are currently firmly dated by building inscriptions, which allows us to follow a chronological sequence of the three tomb types (Figure 24.2) (see Gawlikowski 2005, 58–59). Accordingly, the tower tombs form the oldest epigraphically evidenced group of funerary monuments, dating from the late first century BC until the first half of the second century AD. From the second half of the first century AD, and thus simultaneously for a certain period, there are building inscriptions on underground tombs. The construction of temple tombs is documented only since the first half of the second century AD. The later tomb types, hypogea and temple tombs, continued to be built for burials until the mid-third century AD.

From the dense sequence of dated monuments from only a few years or decades, it is possible to reconstruct the development of the respective tomb types, as was already investigated for the tower tombs, but not for the other two tomb types so far (Will 1949; Gawlikowski 1970, 44–48; 2005; Henning 2013a; 2013b). This development is characterized mainly by an increasing regularity of the architectural design, the introduction of new techniques, and the increased use of elaborate furnishings. The emerging changes in the firmly dated monuments establish criteria that also allow us to classify those towers whose building inscriptions have been lost (compare Henning 2013a). However, this seemingly very linear development should not be considered too stringent. We have to assume that not all tombs fully followed the innovations of the time. For example, a family may have chosen deliberately a slightly older building and furnishings for the tower for the sake of tradition or owing to a lack of financial resources. In other tombs, new elements may have anticipated the general trend (compare Henning 2013a, 95).

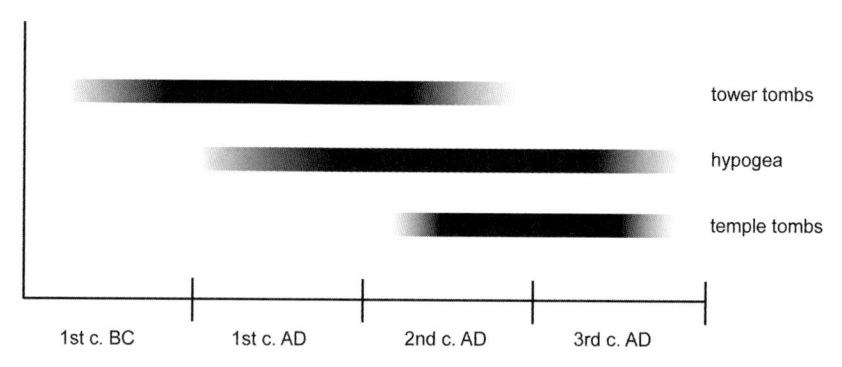

FIGURE 24.2 Schematic overview of the chronological development and overlapping construction of the funerary monuments

Image © Agnes Henning.

We must bear in mind that our archaeological knowledge remains fragmentary. Although the earliest funerary inscriptions of the Palmyrene hypogea date to the 80s of the first century AD, it may be assumed that this tomb type was introduced earlier, as suggested by the combined use of hypogea and tower tombs (Gawlikowski 1970, 60–71, 109–110; Henning 2013a, 37–38). The same applies to the tower tombs that are epigraphically dated to 9 BC (Chabot 1926, no. 4109; Cantineau 1930, no. 28) but seem to have appeared earlier in the western necropolis (Gawlikowski 1970, 54–60; Henning 2013a, 117–118).

From the last surviving foundation inscription in a tower tomb from AD 128 (Chabot 1926, no. 4164; Cantineau 1930, no. 19; Hillers and Cussini 1996, no. 0516), we know that this tomb type ceased to be built by approximately the mid-second century AD. Instead of the towers, temple-like funerary monuments were erected, the earliest evidence of which dates from AD 143 (Chabot 1926, 4167; Hillers and Cussini 1996, no. 0519; Yon 2012, no. 529). This suggests that the tower tombs were no longer considered fashionable and therefore completely abandoned. In some cases, this may be true, but there are inscriptions and reliefs that clearly imply that the towers were still used as burial places during the second and third centuries AD (Henning 2013a, 91–92).

A detailed chronological analysis reveals that there was indeed a sequence in the construction of the tomb types. Whereas the tower tombs belong to the oldest funerary monuments, the basic form of the so-called temple tombs did not develop until the late imperial era. The hypogea were apparently built simultaneously with the other tomb types. The reasons for choosing a particular tomb type may be determined in some instances. However, this first requires a detailed consideration of the individual tomb types.

Tower Tombs

Around 180 tower tombs are known today. Although the last well-preserved towers were demolished after the most recent destruction in 2015, many of them were originally more than 20 m tall, which must have made for an impressive landscape around the city in antiquity (Figure 24.1).

All Palmyrene tower tombs have a square ground plan, with sides between 5 and 13 m long, and stand on a pedestal (Figure 24.3). The upper part of the base leads into the tower shaft in several stages. To improve stability, the shaft tapers slightly upwards, and its upper section is stepped back at several points. The roof was probably flat. The external walls were left bare except for a few striking features. Only the door frame, the inscription panel, a relief niche, and a surrounding cornice were part of the repertoire of the facade design. The interiors of the Palmyrene tower tombs are characterized by several superimposed chambers—sometimes up to seven storeys tall—which were connected by staircases. The loculi shafts were built into the side walls of the tomb chambers. Since the second half of the first century AD, the chambers have been furnished

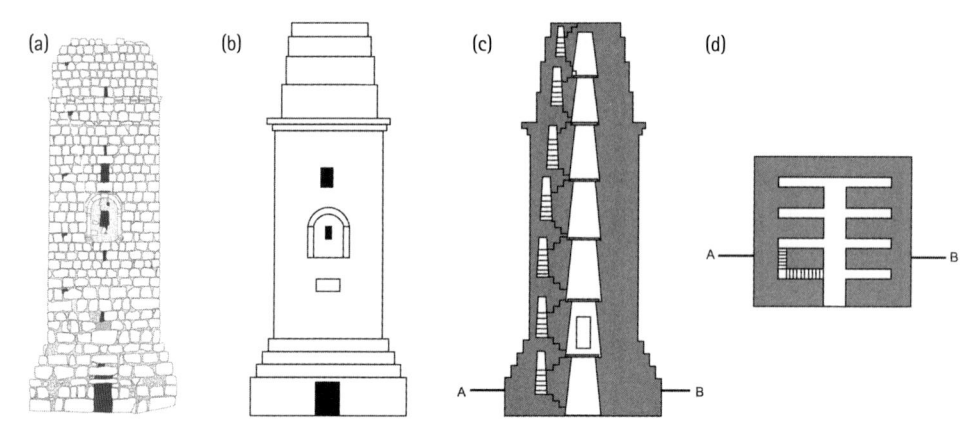

FIGURE 24.3 (a) Elevation of tower tomb no. 71; (b–d) Schematic view, section, and ground plan of a tower tomb

Image © Agnes Henning.

with architectural and sculptural decorations, in particular in the ground-floor chambers. Some of the tower tombs have associated hypogea accessible from the ground-floor chamber (Gawlikowski 1970, 60–71, 109–110; Henning 2013a, 37–38; Gawlikowski 2021, 162).

Some tower tombs in Palmyra, which, given their architecture and construction techniques, must have been erected before the earliest firmly dated monuments. Their external appearance corresponds to the later examples, although the facades were probably unadorned. The main difference is that their few burial spaces are situated in the bases of the towers and were only accessible from the outside. The interiors are characterized only by a rising staircase. The roofs are not preserved. The assumed construction period is set to the first century BC (Gawlikowski 1970, 54–60; Henning 2013a, 117–118; Gawlikowski 2021, 156).

Over the course of its development, the Palmyrene tower tomb developed from a tower-like marking with only a few burial spaces, to a monumental, multi-storey building with canonical decorative elements which could hold up to three hundred burial spaces (compare Henning 2013a, 14). The particular form of these tower tombs is exclusive to Palmyra. Other tower tomb types existed only in the Euphrates region (Henning 2013a, 101–113). Both groups are based on a similar concept. For example, in each case the base serves as the burial space, and the shaft is dominated by a staircase. The conceptual origin of the tower tombs apparently evolved out of the need to ascend a tall building that may have been related to a local ritual that took place on the roof. However, in Palmyra, the strict separation of burial place and staircase seems to have been abandoned quite early. An essential step in this development was putting the entire structure to use as a burial place by inserting chambers with loculi that were internally connected by the staircase. One reason for this may have been the need to include as many burial places as possible into one funerary monument. However, the original separation of burials in the base and the shaft's staircase was preserved in the Palmyrene monuments until the second century AD: although there was a separate entrance to the ground-floor chamber in the front, the staircase and the upper storeys could only be accessed by a back entrance (more in Henning 2013a, 117–118). This suggests that the Palmyrene tower tombs formerly followed a ritual-related architectural design that was subject to significant change corresponding to the Palmyrenes' specific demands of the funerary monuments.

HYPOGEA

In contrast to the tower and temple tombs, the hypogea are no longer recognizable by above-ground monuments, which explains why most of the now known monuments are missing from the 1932 inventory of Wiegand. Harald Ingholt also made a major contribution to the uncovering of the hypogea during the 1920s, and his documentation is still being evaluated today (Raja et al. 2021). Other underground burial chambers were either accidentally discovered when laying pipelines (Bounni 2005, 14) or identified through systematic geo-radar surveys (Higuchi and Izumi 1994; Higuchi and Saito 2001; Saito 2005a).

Even today, depressions in the landscape give evidence of apparently collapsed hypogea, indicating that at least one hundred fifty such monuments once existed (see Dentzer and Saupin 1996; Schnädelbach 2010). The fact that many hypogea collapsed or were covered by the desert sand preserved the furnishings of some chambers and protected them from looters.

Due to difficult static conditions of the soil, not only were the plains used for underground tombs but also the slopes of the western and north-western hills, creating burial caves (Gawlikowski 1970, 125–126; 2005, 53; Sadurska 1975; Schnädelbach 2010).

The oldest hypogeum of Palmyra is also the city's oldest known tomb. However, this is a semi-subterranean tomb with a mud-brick superstructure that, based on ceramic evidence, was constructed as early as the second century BC in the area behind the later temple of Baalshamin. The tomb features a long corridor from which the loculi shafts branch off, as is typical in Palmyra (Fellmann 1970). However, this early finding remains singular and is difficult to relate to the urban area.

The oldest building inscriptions from hypogea date two hundred years later than the tomb close to the temple of Baalshamin. The oldest, but decontextualized, dates to AD 81 (Cantineau 1931, no. 15), and the earliest firmly dated monument can be related to AD 87 (Hillers and Cussini 1996, no. 1784). However, underground tombs were also known in Palmyra in earlier periods owing to archaeological research. The latest epigraphically evidenced foundation of an underground tomb is AD 232 or 242 (Gawlikowski 1970, 201; 2005, 59; Hillers and Cussini 1996, no. 0569).

The hypogea were accessed by a stepped dromos. A stone door, which in many cases has been preserved, closed the chamber. The tomb facade consisted of only the elaborately crafted door frame with a lintel that usually bore the building inscription and possibly also a concession text. Inside, the complex extended over a central corridor approximately 10 to 20 m long and about 5 m wide. In most cases, two opposite arms branch off perpendicularly to the main corridor, so that often the ground plan resembles an inverted T (see Chapter 35 [Eristov et al.], this volume, Figure 35.1) (Gawlikowski 1970, 110–128; Sadurska and Bounni 1994; Schnädelbach 2010, 93–100). The central niche at the end of the main corridor, often adorned with reliefs depicting banqueting family members or *kline* sarcophagi arranged to resemble a triclinium, would have been the first thing to catch the attention of anyone entering the tomb (compare Amy and Seyrig 1936, 246; Sadurska and Bounni 1994, 174–177, figs. 248–253, plan 14). However, such scenes were also depicted on the side walls of the main corridor (Saito 2005a, 35, fig. 45), or in niches at the end of its two perpendicular side arms, as seen in the so-called Tomb of the Three Brothers (see Chapter 35 this volume). The shafts of the loculi were cut into the two long sides of the corridors. The side corridors of the hypogea were not always completely fitted with loculi, but only coarsely prepared in case they should be needed (Higuchi and Saito 2005a, plates 30, 32). This basic form of the Palmyrene hypogeum was established no later than the late first century AD and was frequently implemented with only slight modifications.

Owing to their good state of preservation, we have a vivid idea of the furnishings of the hypogea. In addition to the relief decoration, the walls were also adorned with rich architectural ornamentation (Amy and Seyrig 1936; Higuchi and Saito 2001). Other decorative elements were wall paintings and stucco applications (Ingholt 1932; 1935; Kraeling 1961; Sørensen 2016; Chapter 35 this volume). The paintings depict figural, mythological, and architectural themes.

The hypogea offer important insights into the Palmyrene funerary rituals as only here does one discover undisturbed findings in a larger context (Higuchi and Izumi 1994; Higuchi and Saito 2001). For example, it may be observed that the deceased were supplied with only a few grave goods, that there were small sacrificial hollows in the ground, and that lamps apparently played a role (see Saito 2005b). Also, it is not uncommon for the hypogea to be equipped with a well immediately to the right behind the entrance, which may also have had a ritual significance (see, e.g., Sadurska and Bounni 1994, plans 4, 7; Schnädelbach 2010, 93–100).

As the underground chambers were dependent on the prevailing geological conditions within the necropolis, it was not always possible to construct them in the immediate vicinity of roads. Therefore, further away from the routes through the necropoleis, immediate perception by travellers was not possible as it was for the other two tomb types. It may still have been important to visibly mark the site of a tomb for by-passers, as excavations may reveal. The exact appearance of these monuments, and whether they were truly visible from afar, remain unclear. Only at Tomb F in the south-eastern necropolis do the excavators believe that they can reconstruct a column-like structure in front of the entrance to the dromos (Higuchi and Saito 2001, 12). In other regions of Syria, above-ground markers of hypogea in various forms were quite common, mostly columns or stelae (de Jong 2017, 41–42, 65, 317), but this cannot simply be transposed to the Palmyrene situation.

TEMPLE TOMBS

The temple tombs form the smallest group of funerary monuments, comprising just over sixty. Today, the once large and magnificent structures are recognizable only as heaps of rubble. Apparently, they were less stable than the much taller tower tombs. These tombs, which are epigraphically dated between AD 143 and 253 (Gawlikowski 1970, 51; Hillers and Cussini 1996, no. 0519, 0569), are referred to as temple tombs because of their often temple-like exterior design. Above all, this impression is due to their facade: on top of a podium, a row of four or six columns with entablature characterized many temple tombs (Figure 24.4a). A pseudo-pediment then crowned the facade as the actual built

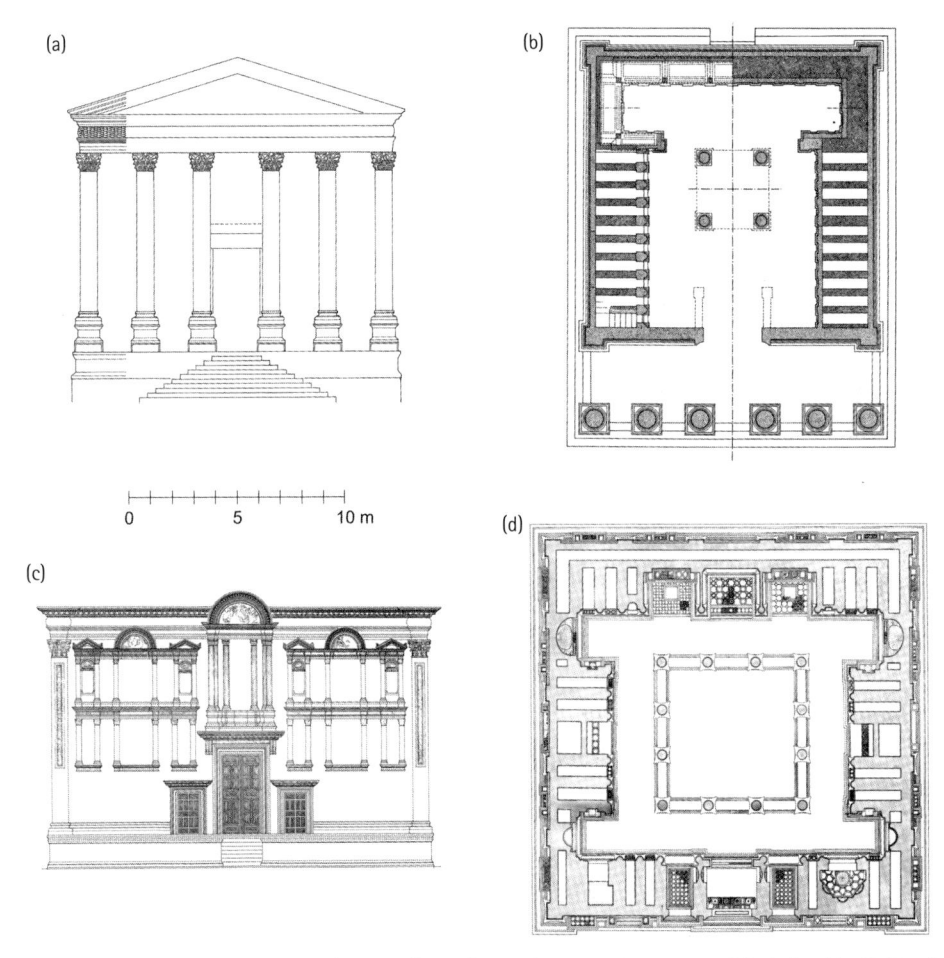

FIGURE 24.4 (a) Reconstructed view of temple tomb no. 86 (courtesy of A. Schmidt-Colinet). (b) Ground plan of temple tomb no. 86 (after Wiegand 1932, plates 39–41). (c–d) Reconstructed view and ground plan of temple tomb no. 36

Courtesy of A. Schmidt-Colinet.

roof extending behind the facade was flat (Schmidt-Colinet 1992, 23–24). Other facades also included pilasters (Schmidt-Colinet 1992, 42–52), half-column decorations (Saito 2016), or elaborate tabernacle architecture, as has been reconstructed for tomb no. 36 (Figure 24.4c) (Schmidt-Colinet 1992). The magnificent exterior design extended into the interior of the two- to three-storey-high funerary monuments. A characteristic feature was the peristyle courtyard, which is why the tombs are also referred to as 'house tombs' (concerning the definition, see Schmidt-Colinet 1992). The courtyard recurred on every floor, traversed as a halation the whole building, and greatly enhanced the overall architectural design of the tomb. Loculi shafts were grouped along the lateral sides (Figure 24.4b, d), as were symmetrically arranged niches in which sarcophagi could be displayed. In some tombs, the peristyle was uncovered, rendering it both a valuable source of light and a visual reference point (Schmidt-Colinet 1992, 47).

In contrast to the tower tombs, the facades of the temple tombs were highly varied (Figure 24.4a,c). The tomb owner was able to realize his own ideas about the design of his tomb to distinguish it from the other temple tombs. Therefore, the limited flexibility in influencing the facade decoration of the tower tombs may have been one factor that led to their abandonment. The apparent desire to represent oneself is also reflected in the positioning of the temple tombs directly beside roads so the rich ornamentation of the facades would impress passers-by.

The architectural design and decoration of the temple tombs testify to the increasing adaption of Hellenistic and Roman motifs by the Palmyrene artistic repertoire. For example, some Palmyrene reliefs may have been modelled after contemporary examples from Rome (Schmidt-Colinet 1992, 89–104), and the concept of temple-like tombs stems from funerary architecture widespread in the Roman Empire (compare von Hesberg 1992, 182–201). However, local funerary customs were maintained and integrated into the new tomb type through the use of loculi. But oriental architectural design elements were also incorporated, such as the flat roof behind the pseudo-pediment and the proportions of individual elements (Schmidt-Colinet 1992, 42–64), which render the overall design of the temple tombs specific to Palmyra.

Deviations and Unique Forms

Among the three basic Palmyrene tomb types described, certain characteristics were always evident so that almost every monument may be assigned to a specific group. This demonstrates how well-established the three tomb types were within Palmyrene society. However, the tower tomb from which a hypogeum could be accessed was a hybrid tomb type and appeared mainly in the first half of the first century BC, documented by three or four examples. From the ground-floor chamber of the tower a staircase led down to the hypogeum and another up to the floors with loculi. In such cases, two tomb types were combined, which may be related to the above-ground marking of the hypogeum (Gawlikowski 2005, 51).

There are individual tombs that deviate from the known patterns. From the exterior, some of these monuments appear to be one of the common above-ground tomb types, but the interiors are designed entirely differently. For example, tomb no. 03, situated in the western necropolis, shows architectural elements of both tower and temple tombs, possibly representing a transitional form between the two types (Parlasca 1989). Another monumental tomb in the northern necropolis does not fit to any of the familiar types and therefore must be referred to as a unique form. The date of the construction remains unclear, but it has been furnished with sculptures of the third century AD. The preserved ground plan suggests a round interior structure surrounded by a hexagonal exterior with the loculi placed side by side between these structures (compare Schnädelbach 2010, 40, no. P310; Gawlikowski 2016, 127). The superstructure can no longer be reconstructed. Nevertheless, it is clear that this funerary monument had an extraordinary architectural design and was built to be distinct from the prevailing norm. Thus, in individual cases there were deliberate deviations from the common tomb types that certainly aimed to meet the requirements of individual tomb owners and to enable the funerary monument to outshine the others.

SIMILARITIES AND DIFFERENCES IN PALMYRENE MONUMENTAL TOMBS

Despite the different and clearly identifiable tomb types, the Palmyrene tombs have certain common features that testify to shared aspirations for the three quite different architectural forms. This includes the monumentality of the individual tombs. Both the tower and the temple tombs, and the hypogea, were large complexes with numerous burial places which were intended from the outset as family tombs for several generations. There is no single monumental tomb that was intended for only a single individual or a very small group of people.

The monumentality of the tombs was accompanied by a strong desire to represent the tomb owner and his family, which caused a constant increase in decorative elaboration, beginning in the mid-first century BC. This was achieved by the use of predefined decorative patterns within the tombs, with little room for deviation. For the tower tombs, this mainly meant the design of the exterior facade, with its foundation text and a relief inserted into a niche depicting the banqueting tomb owner. The interior, particularly the ground floor, was richly adorned, with architectural decorations and additional reliefs of banquet scenes playing a central role (Henning 2013a; 2013b). The same applies to the hypogea, although here the representational patterns are found in the interior. Reliefs, ornaments, or wall decorations in the form of paintings or stucco were deliberately set in such a way that they immediately caught the eye of the observer when entering the tomb or its side corridors. This may be particularly observable at the so-called Tomb of the Three Brothers in the south-western necropolis (see Chapter 35 this volume).

The deliberate use of representational patterns was then advanced by the temple tombs. Although the tower tombs could no longer incorporate new representational patterns because of their traditional form, the facades of the temple tombs offered completely new design possibilities. The interior impressed with symmetrically arranged niches, pillars, sarcophagi, and reliefs (Figure 24.4).

The similarities described among the Palmyrene tombs suggest that the tomb types and their designs were socially accepted, and also—despite their monumentality—that their individual appearance was regulated to a certain degree. This led to the development of uniquely Palmyrene funerary monuments, which are unparalleled in the wider Syrian region (compare de Jong 2017, 58–59). Nevertheless, there were also differences, which are particularly expressed in the choice of a tomb type. This is most evident in the decision to create an above-ground or an underground tomb monument. Although the widespread use of hypogea is already in evidence in the Syrian region early on (de Jong 2017, 41), the tower tombs seem to have developed only during the late Hellenistic period, caused by ritual practices and the desire for the funerary monument to be highly visible (Henning 2013a, 117–118). The decision to build an above-ground or underground tomb was certainly not dependent on the financial resources of the tomb founder because both options were costly ventures. Instead, the various funeral beliefs of the various families may have played a role, although we have no way of knowing what these were.

The connection of tomb form and individual beliefs also concerned the transition from the tower tombs to the temple tombs during the second century AD, which was probably not as abrupt as the traditional foundation dates suggest (see above on the chronology). The tower form was strongly associated with traditional views that were firmly rooted in society and that were certainly only gradually replaced. However, they eventually lost their significance entirely with the new temple tombs becoming more fashionable.

The acceptance or rejection of particular construction techniques, decorative forms, motifs, or ritual practices may be detected by close inspection and reveal social changes in the urban fabric of Palmyra. For the tower tombs, a particular change in building techniques and the tombs' furnishing was observed between AD 50 and 80, which was accompanied by changes in Palmyrene society as the development of civic institutions is evidenced by inscriptions for that period (compare Henning 2013a, 121–123). Despite the readily available evidence, such aspects have not yet been investigated for the second and third centuries AD. Therefore, the continuities and discontinuities in the funerary monuments offer great interpretative potential for reconstructing the social history of Palmyra.

Bibliography

al-As'ad, Khaled, and Andreas Schmidt-Colinet. 2005. 'Kulturbegegnung im Grenzbereich'. In *Palmyra: Kulturbegegnung im Grenzbereich*, edited by Andreas Schmidt-Colinet, 36–62. Mainz am Rhein: von Zabern.

Amy, Robert, and Henri Seyrig. 1936. 'Recherches dans la nécropole de Palmyre'. *Syria* 17: 229–266.

Bounni, Adnan. 2005. 'Vierzig Jahre syrische Ausgrabungen in Palmyra'. In *Kulturbegegnung im Grenzbereich*, edited by Andreas Schmidt-Colinet, 13–21. Mainz am Rhein: von Zabern.

Cantineau, Jean, ed. 1930. *Inventaire des inscriptions de Palmyre*. Fasc. 4, *La vallée des tombeaux*. Beirut: Imprimerie catholique.

Cantineau, Jean, ed. 1931. *Inventaire des inscriptions de Palmyre*. Fasc. 7, *Les nécropoles nord-ouest et nord*. Beirut: Imprimerie catholique.

Cantineau, Jean, ed. 1932. *Inventaire des inscriptions de Palmyre*. Fasc. 8, *Le dépôt des antiquités*. Beirut: Imprimerie catholique.

Chabot, Jean-Baptiste. 1926. *Corpus inscriptionum Semiticarum*. Part 2, vol. 3. Paris: Typographeo Reipublicae.

Colledge, Malcolm A. R. 1976. *The Art of Palmyra*. London: Thames & Hudson.

Cussini, Eleonora. 1995. 'Transfer of Property at Palmyra'. *ARAM* 7: 233–250.

de Jong, Lidewijde. 2017. *The Archaeology of Death in Roman Syria: Burial, Commemoration, and Empire*. Cambridge: Cambridge University Press.

Dentzer, Jean-Marie, and René Saupin. 1996. 'L'espace urbain à Palmyre: Remarques sur des photographies aériennes anciennes'. In *Palmyra and the Silk Road: International Colloquium; Palmyra, 7–11 April 1992, Les annales archéologiques arabes syriennes* 42: 297–318. Damascus: Press of the Ministry of Culture.

Fellmann, Rudolf. 1970. *Die Grabanlage*. Le sanctuaire de Baalshamin à Palmyre 5. Rome: Institute suisse de Rome.

Gawlikowski, Michał. 1970. *Monuments funéraires de Palmyre*. Prace Zakładu Archeologii Śródziemnomorskiej Polskiej Akademii Nauk 9. Warsaw: Państwowe Wydawnictwo Naukowe.

Gawlikowski, Michał. 1972. 'La notion de tombeau en Syrie romaine'. *Berytus* 21: 5–15.

Gawlikowski, Michał. 1988. 'Palmyra'. *Polish Archaeology in the Mediterranean* 1: 37–44.

Gawlikowski, Michał. 1992. 'Palmyra'. *Polish Archaeology in the Mediterranean* 4: 111–118.

Gawlikowski, Michał. 2005. 'The City of the Dead'. In *A Journey to Palmyra: Collected Essays to Remember Delbert R. Hillers*, edited by Elenora Cussini, 44–73. Leiden: Brill.

Gawlikowski, Michał. 2016. 'The Portraits of the Palmyrene Royalty'. In *The World of Palmyra*, edited by Andreas Kropp and Rubina Raja, 126–134. Palmyrenske studier 1. Copenhagen: Det Kongelige Danske Videnskabernes Selskab.

Gawlikowski, Michał. 2021. *Tadmor – Palmyra: A Caravan City Between East and West*. Krakow: IRSA.

Henning, Agnes. 2013a. *Die Turmgräber von Palmyra: Eine lokale Bauform im kaiserzeitlichen Syrien als Ausdruck kultureller Identität*. Rahden: Leidorf.

Henning, Agnes. 2013b. 'The Tower Tombs of Palmyra: Chronology, Architecture and Decoration'. In *Fifty Years of Polish Excavations in Palmyra, 1959–2009: International Conference, Warsaw, 6–8 December 2010*, edited by Michał Gawlikowski and Grzegorz Majcherek, 159–176. Studia Palmyrenskie 12. Warsaw: Wydawnictwa Uniwersytetu Warszawskiego.

Henning, Agnes. 2016. 'Zwischen Realität und Phantasie: Louis-François Cassas und die Turmgräber von Palmyra'. In *Palmyra: Was bleibt? Louis-François Cassas und seine Reise in den Orient: Ausstellung im Graphischen Kabinett des Wallfraf-Richartz-Museums & Foundation Curbot, Cologne 2016*, edited by Thomas Ketelsen, 22–34. Der un/ gewisse Blick 20. Cologne: Asmuth.

Higuchi, Takayasu, and Takura Izumi, eds. 1994. *Tombs A and C in the Southeast Necropolis of Palmyra, Syria, Surveyed in 1990–92.* Nara: Research Center for Silk Roadology.

Higuchi, Takayasu and Kiyohide Saito, eds. 2001. *Tomb F: Tomb of BWLH an BWRP, Southeast Necropolis, Palmyra, Syria.* Nara: Research Center for Silk Roadology.

Hillers, Delbert R. and Eleonora Cussini, eds. 1996. *Palmyrene Aramaic Texts.* Publications of the Comprehensive Aramaic Lexicon Project. Baltimore: Johns Hopkins University Press.

Ingholt, Harald. 1932. 'Quleques fresques récemment découvertes à Palmyre'. *Acta archaeologica* 3: 1–20.

Ingholt, Harald. 1935. 'Five Dated Tombs from Palmyra'. *Berytus* 2: 57–120.

Ketelsen, Thomas. 2016. *Palmyra: Was bleibt? Louis-François Cassas und seine Reise in den Orient (Ausstellung im Graphischen Kabinett), Wallfraf-Richartz-Museums & Foundation Corboud, Cologne 2016.* Der un/ gewisse Blick 20. Cologne: Asmuth.

Kraeling, Carl Hermann. 1961–1962. 'Color Photographs of the Paintings in the Tomb of the Three Brothers at Palmyra'. *Annales archéologiques de Syrie* 11–12: 13–18.

Makowski, Krzystof C. 1985. 'La sculpture funéraire palmyrénienne et sa fonction dans l'architecture sépulcrale'. *Studia Palmyrenskie* 8: 69–117.

Michałowski, Kazimierz. 1963. 'Tombeau-Tour n° 19'. In *Palmyre: Fouilles Polonaises 1961,* edited by Kazimierz Michałowski, 197–231. Warsaw: Państwowe Wydawnictwo Naukowe.

Mouton, Michel. 1997. 'Les tours funéraires d'arabie, *nefesh* monumentales'. *Syria* 74: 81–98.

Parlasca, Klaus. 1989. 'Beobachtungen zur palmyrenischen Grabarchitektur'. *Damaszener Mitteilungen* 4: 181–190.

Raja, Rubina, Julia Steding, and Jean-Baptiste Yon, eds. 2021. *Excavating Palmyra: Harald Ingholt's Excavation Diaries: A Transcript, Translation, and Commentary. Studies in Palmyrene Archaeology and History 4.* Turnhout: Brepols.

Sadurska, Anna. 1975. 'Palmyre 1972: Tombeaux dans l'enceinte du camp de Dioclétien'. *Études et travaux* 8: 367–376.

Sadurska, Anna, and Adnan Bounni. 1994. *Les sculptures funéraires de Palmyre.* Rivista di Archeologia Supplementi 13. Rome: Giorgio Bretschneider.

Sadurska, Anna, and Krzystof C. Makowski. 1985. 'Les sculptures palmyréniennes provenant des fouilles polonaises en 1972 dans le tombeau turriforme (l'enceinte de Dioclétien)'. *Studia Palmyrenskie* 8: 35–41.

Saito, Kiyohide. 2005a. 'Die Arbeiten der japanischen Mission in der Südost-Nekropole'. In *Palmyra: Kulturbegegnung im Grenzbereich*, edited by Andreas Schmidt-Colinet, 32–35. Mainz am Rhein: von Zabern.

Saito, Kiyohide. 2005b. 'Palmyrene Burial Practices from Funerary Goods'. In *A Journey to Palmyra: Collected Essays to Remember Delbert R. Hillers*, edited by Elenora Cussini, 150–165. Leiden: Brill.

Saito, Kiyohide. 2016. 'Excavation of no. 129-b House Tomb at the North Necropolis in Palmyra'. In *Palmyrena: City, Hinterland and Caravan Trade Between Orient and Occident: Proceedings of the Conference Held in Athens, December 1–3, 2012*, edited by Jørgen C. Meyer, Eivind H. Seland, and Nils Anfinset, 115–129. Oxford: Archaeopress.

Schmidt-Colinet, Andreas. 1992. *Das Tempelgrab Nr. 36 in Palmyra: Studien zur palmyrenischen Grabarchitektur und ihrer Ausstattung.* Mainz am Rhein: von Zabern.

Schmidt-Colinet, Andreas. 1994. 'Cassas als Archäologe'. In *Louis-François Cassas: 1756–1827; Dessinateur–Voyageur; Im Banne der Sphinx, Ausstellungskatalog Tours und Köln, 1994–1995*, edited by Annie Gilet and Uwe Westfehling, 207–222. Mainz am Rhein: von Zabern.

Schmidt-Colinet, Andreas. 1996. 'Antike Denkmäler in Syrien: Die Stichvorlagen von Louis François Cassas (1756–1827) im Wallraf-Richartz-Museum in Köln'. *Kölner Jahrbuch* 29: 343–548.

Schmidt-Colinet, Andreas, ed. 2005. *Palmyra: Kulturbegegnung im Grenzbereich*. Mainz am Rhein: von Zabern.

Schnädelbach, Klaus. 2010. *Topographia Palmyrena*. Vol. 1, *Topography*. Documents d'Archéologie Syrienne 18. Bonn: Habelt.

Sørensen, Annette Høje. 2016. 'Palmyrene Tomb Paintings in Context'. In *The World of Palmyra*, edited by Andreas Kropp and Rubina Raja, 103–117. Palmyrenske Studier 1. Copenhagen: Det Kongelige Danske Videnskabernes Selskab.

Teixidor, Javier, ed. 1965. *Inventaire des inscriptions de Palmyre*. Vol. 11. Damascus: Direction général des antiquités et des musées de la république arabe Syrienne.

Triebel, Lothar. 2004. *Jenseitshoffnung in Wort und Stein: Nefesch und pyramidales Grabmal als Phänomene antiken jüdischen Bestattungswesens im Kontext der Nachbarkulturen*. Leiden: Brill.

von Hesberg, Henner. 1992. *Römische Grabbauten*. Darmstadt: Wissenschaftliche Buchgesellschaft.

Watzinger, Carl and Karl Wulzinger. 1932. 'Die Nekropolen'. In *Palmyra: Ergebnisse der Expedition von 1902 und 1917*, edited by Theodor Wiegand, 44–76. Berlin: Keller.

Wiegand, Theodor, ed. 1932. *Palmyra: Ergebnisse der Expedition von 1902 und 1917*. Berlin: Archäologisches Institut des Deutschen Reiches/Abteilung Istanbul.

Wielgosz, Dagmara. 1997. 'Funeralia Palmyrena'. *Studia Palmyrenskie* 10: 69–77.

Will, Ernest. 1949. 'Le tour funéraire de Palmyre'. *Syria* 26: 87–116.

Will, Ernest. 1990. 'La maison d'éternité et les conceptions funéraires des Palmyréniens'. In *Mélanges Pierre Lévêque*, edited by Marie-Madeleine Mactoux and Evelyne Geny, 433–440. Paris: Les belles lettres.

Witecka, Anna. 1994. 'Catalogue of Jewellery Found in the Tower-Tomb of Atenatan at Palmyra'. *Studia Palmyrenskie* 9: 71–91.

Yon, Jean-Baptiste. 2002. *Les notables de Palmyre*. Beirut: Institut français d'archéologie du Proche-Orient.

Yon, Jean-Baptiste, ed. 2012. *Palmyre: Inscriptions grecques et latines de la Syrie*. Vol. 17, fasc. 1, *Palmyre*. Bibliothèque archéologique et historique 195. Beirut: Institut français d'archéologie du Proche-Orient.

CHAPTER 25

THE FORTIFICATIONS AND MILITARY ARCHITECTURE OF PALMYRA

KAROL JUCHNIEWICZ

INTRODUCTION

IN the literature concerning Palmyra it is generally accepted that we are dealing with three major stages of fortification. The first stage is dated, with great caution, to the first/ second century AD. It is believed that the fortifications surrounding Palmyra served primarily as customs walls and as barriers which shielded the gardens from the sand blown from the desert. They did not constitute a closed circle because on the western side the city was sufficiently protected by steep, natural elevations. The walls were built only where they were needed for control—in the valleys and on flat terrain.

Only small sections of these walls were examined, among them a fragment stretching from the Damascus Gate to the Jebel Muntar summit, the so-called Damascus Gate in Wall K (not to be confused with the Damascus Gate at the end of the Transverse Colonnade), and a fragment of the embankment located north of the city. Excavations revealed the existence of a brick wall on a stone understructure reinforced with small towers. These fortifications were about 2.5 m wide. It is difficult to say unequivocally whether Palmyra's defensive wall was uniform. French research has shown that from the north the city was protected by a kind of embankment formed of compacted earth (Gabriel 1926, 75).

Dating is based on inscriptions. One of them—engraved on the altar and dating from AD 175—was found near the southern wall K, at the so-called Damascus Gate during the excavations conducted by Starcky. The second one, dating from AD 11, was found in the palm gardens in the south-east of the city. It mentions the wall at which customs duties are paid (Gawlikowski and al-As'ad 1993, 164–167). The third inscription, which was found in the temple of Bēl-Hamon at Jebel Muntar, gives us an idea when Wall N most likely ceased to function. Due to the lack of regular excavations, we are currently not able to determine the chronological interdependence of these fortifications. Their character also remains in the sphere of speculation.

The second stage in the city's military history is associated with the arrival of Aurelian's legions. After capturing the city, the emperor placed a small garrison in it, all of whom, according to *Historia Augusta*, were slain during a short-lived rebellion. Aurelian supposedly returned to the city to destroy it in revenge. Excavations proved, however, that it did not necessarily happen that way. However, a certain chronological hiatus occurs here. The next inscription about the fortifications comes from the period of the Tetrarchy and mentions the building of a camp (*castra*). There is no doubt that it refers to the so-called Camp of Diocletian. However, the question is whether the wall was erected at that time or whether it had been built earlier, during the reign of Aurelian. The latter certainly left a reinforced garrison there, most likely the Legio I Illyricorum, supposedly created specifically for the war with Zenobia. The legion's presence in Palmyra, however, is mentioned only by the *Notitia dignitatum*. Therefore, the question remains open whether Palmyra was completely devoid of walls from AD 273 to the period between AD 293 and 303, or whether at that time it was still protected by Zenobia's walls (most likely the walls which were partly exposed during the Polish excavations— see below), or whether the Diocletian-period walls had been built under Aurelian's rule by the garrison he had left. The description of these walls can be found in the latter part of this chapter.

The third, commonly accepted development stage is construction activity under the Emperor Justinian (527–565). The walls were reinforced at that time by the addition of huge U-shaped towers. Justinian ordered the renovation of aqueducts and public monuments, especially churches. It is also worth mentioning the fourth stage in the history of Palmyra, the Arab period. It is not known how the defensive walls functioned in this period. They were supposedly demolished in the middle of the ninth century during the revolt of the Christians in Homs. In the first half of the twelfth century, the temple of Bēl was rebuilt into a fort, thus protecting the Arab village inside.

Sections of the walls have been named with letters by von Gerkan, and his system is still widely used (von Gerkan 1935, fig. 1). Recently, a new system designating particular elements of the late antique fortifications has been proposed (Juchniewicz et al. 2010, 55).

Palmyra's Oldest Walls

Let us look at the first stage of development of the Palmyra fortifications. Our knowledge on this subject is actually based only on information obtained thanks to the Polish excavations conducted by M. Gawlikowski in 1971–1972 and on field observations (Gawlikowski 1974, 231–242).

The turning point for the study of the fortifications in Palmyra is 41 BC. Appian of Alexandria reports that Marcus Antonius sent a cavalry unit to plunder the city, but the Palmyrenes had learned of the plan so had transferred everything they needed to the other side of the Euphrates (Appian, 17.9.37–38).

Appian's passage concerning Palmyra is very problematic. On the one hand, he accurately describes the political situation of Palmyra as a city deriving profits from its location on the border between two superpowers. On the other hand, he shows some ignorance in terms of geography, locating Palmyra near the Euphrates, which is actually more than 200 km further to the east. Naturally, for a historian who had never been in such distant regions, such a mistake is of little significance, but the story that the city's inhabitants left it and took shelter on the other side of the Euphrates is at least puzzling. Travelling 200 km across the desert is a challenge even today. In those days, it had to be even more difficult, and numerous caravan inscriptions from Palmyra testify to the scale of such an undertaking.

If we take Appian's story seriously, we should conclude that Palmyra was not protected by any wall. However, the facts provided by the Roman historian are quite contradictory. On the one hand, he talks about lucrative trade; on the other, these merchants had no problem packing all their belongings and escaping in no time. It seems that Appian was describing the economic situation of Palmyra that corresponded to his time—namely to the middle of the second century AD—but that he placed the city in the time of Antonius (see also Chapter 19 [Edwell] this volume). This has extremely interesting implications for Palmyra's fortifications. The walls considered the oldest enclose the oasis from the south (Wall K) and from the north (Wall J). The section determined on von Gerkan's plan as N runs from the Damascus Gate (G8) to the top of Jebel Muntar. In the Valley of the Tombs there is a dividing wall, L. On von Gerkan's plan one more wall is visible—it runs along the ridge of the jebel, westwards from the summit of Muntar, and is marked as M. There is no proof, however, confirming its existence. The author of the plan must have mistaken the natural rock formation for the wall.

Archaeological research has shown that the wall on Jebel Muntar most likely ceased to function around AD 89, when the temple of Bēl-Hamon was consecrated at the top of the hill (Gawlikowski 1974, 236; du Mesnil 1966, 165–169). Unfortunately we do not know the exact location of the section that ran along the back of the Transverse Colonnade's shops. Perhaps its trace was preserved in the line of the Great Colonnade (Gawlikowski 1974, 236–237; 1975, 45).

Let us stop for a moment at Palmyra's western fortifications: Wall N, examined archaeologically by the Polish mission. Wall N is not homogeneous. It can be divided into two sections. The section at the foot of the hill was built of mud brick on a stone foundation. During the excavations, brick ramps placed along the inner front face and leading to the parapet were also exposed. Their discovery enabled the scientists to calculate that the wall was approximately 3.6 m high (up to the walking level), which, together with the battlements, gives a total height of approximately 5 m. No additional defensive devices, such as a dry moat, were found.

On the ridge leading to the peak of Jebel Muntar, the wall is built differently. No excavations were conducted there, but all the indications suggest that it was constructed of loosely arranged stones, not bonded with lime mortar. It was built directly on the bedrock. The wall was additionally fortified with towers. It is difficult to explain this change. Perhaps it was caused by technical or economic issues. The base of the wall had to be made more carefully because the rocky ridge had already been difficult to access, forming a natural glacis. There was no need to construct a brick wall on a stone foundation. The width and probably the height of the wall were retained, while the bricks were replaced with more accessible building material (Gawlikowski 1974, 235).

However, there is another serious difference regarding the architecture of these two sections. The section at the foot of Muntar has only ramps, while the section built on the slope was clearly fortified with towers. Moreover, there is no indication that the temple of Bēl-Hamon previously served as watchtower (Gawlikowski 1974, 234). It is possible, but all references to its military nature (e.g., the theory of R. du Mesnil du Buisson) fail to comply with the appearance of Wall K, which was built probably as a large fence rather than a defensive structure (du Mesnil 1966, 169). It seems that the temple did not have any other functions earlier.

Around the year AD 89, Wall N ceased to function and was most likely dismantled or remodelled. This is not necessarily the result of the watchtower having been transformed into the temple of Bēl-Hamon, but rather of significant urban changes, most notably the construction of the Transverse Colonnade built exactly along the line of the Wall N. It is worth noting that the stone part of the wall was never dismantled and is still clearly visible on the ridge leading to the top. Robert du Mesnil du Buisson proposed the theory that the wall was in fact a road leading to the temple of Bēl-Hamon (du Mesnil 1966; *contra* van Berchem 1970, 232). In the light of evident proofs of urban transformations in Palmyra in the first and second centuries AD, this theory is feasible, but it is not confirmed by archaeological research.

One of the hypotheses is that the control and defensive role of Wall N was taken over by another wall—still visible today in the Valley of the Tombs and marked on the von Gerkan plan as L (von Gerkan 1935, fig. 1; Crouch 1975, 34–35). However, this is pure speculation because this wall has never been examined archaeologically and its chronological attribution remains unknown. Its function is also unclear, apart from the fact that it divided the Valley of the Tombs.

In the absence of evidence proving that Wall N was replaced by another structure, we might venture a theory that, in the second century AD, Palmyra was partly an open city. Its fortifications at that time did not have a military character. Wall K, which probably functioned as late as AD 175, protected the city from the south. In terms of construction it was very similar to Wall N, being built from coarse stones with a core in the form of loosely bonded smaller stones. The base of the wall was constructed of quite large (about 1 m wide) coarse blocks of pink limestone. The section I explored, which runs from the summit of Jebel Muntar to the southern necropolis (further east, the wall is today imperceptible), was about 2.4 m wide. At the Damascus Gate the face of the wall is built of smaller, more tightly fitted stones. However, it still retains the same character.

The gate in Wall K constitutes a very interesting structure. A small shrine was found there bearing a date of AD 175. Judging from the photos, it stood outside the gate at its western corner, and, according to the inscription it was dedicated to the 'nameless god' (Starcky 1949, 395; Crouch 1975, fig. 24). It is not established when exactly the shrine was placed there, so the date AD 175 is only indicative and constitutes a terminus ante quem for the use of the wall and gate.

The passage was 4.7 m wide and led to an internal courtyard which was about 5.7 m wide. There are certain indications that this was not in fact a courtyard as there is no back wall with a second passage (as in the Theatre Gate). It is possible that two stone partitions perpendicular to the wall were parts of a gate, flanked by internal guard chambers or towers. If this is the case, these would be the only towers in Wall K. Its defensive capabilities are therefore even weaker than Wall N, which was fortified with towers.

Wall K disappears beneath today's gardens, and my attempts to find its traces proved futile. We do not know if and how the city was fortified from the east, but it must have been with a fence similar to Wall K or J surrounding the city from the north and today very poorly visible (in favourable light, its trace can be seen from the Arab castle).

Gabriel examined Wall J in the 1920s. According to his research, a ditch was dug along the northern face. Even in those years, Wall J was only a low, fuzzy hump. Gabriel did not find any traces of the stone structure, so naming the J structure a wall is at the very least an euphemism: it was simply an embankment constructed of compacted clay, sand, and lime with negligible defensive qualities. At present, it is impossible to see whether this structure climbs to the castle hill, as Gabriel observed (Gabriel 1926, 75–76).

The preceding short account demonstrates that Appian's record was not far from the truth. Palmyra's fortifications were built to protect the city from possible raids by nomads and marked the border of the oasis. They were not real protection against invading enemy armies.

The walls examined by the Polish mission were perfectly fitted to the tasks they were assigned. They facilitated the control of traffic and the collection of customs duties, and they protected against unexpected raids by nomads, although Palmyra was not particularly threatened by these, at least not in the second century BC. Nevertheless, they served a practical function as customs walls. This function is reflected in the modern tradition, according to which Wall K is still called by the inhabitants of Palmyra 'sur el-Ǧamarek', which can be translated as the 'customs wall'. The nature of these fortifications best reflects the position and role of Palmyra on the Syrian steppe during this period.

FORTIFICATIONS IN LATE ANTIQUITY: TRADITIONAL CHRONOLOGY

The attribution of the wall surrounding the current ruins still raises doubts among researchers. Some scholars have maintained until recently that the wall was built by Zenobia to protect the city against Aurelian. They argued that the use of a large number of *spolia* and the incorporation of graves into the wall proves their theory and that the choice of this type of construction was affected by haste (von Gerkan 1935, 28; Seyrig 1950, 240). It is now widely accepted that these fortifications were built during the reign of Diocletian. This hypothesis is confirmed, to a certain extent, by the Latin inscription from the Camp of Diocletian about the founding of the *castra* by Sossianus Hierocles between AD 293 and 303 (CIL III, 133 = 6661; Gawlikowski 1984, 10; Kowalski 1997, 44) and the record stating that Diocletian strengthened the entire eastern *limes* (Zos. 2.34.1, Ammianus Marcellinus 23.5.2). The next stage in the development of the fortifications was the period of Justinian's rule (Seyrig 1950, 239–242). The main change was adding U-shaped towers to the existing wall from the time of Diocletian.

The basic source on the basis of which we may claim that the camp was built during Diocletian's reign is the Latin inscription from the Principia (Kowalski 1997, 44). It is thus clear that this inscription was placed there after the introduction of the Tetrarchy in AD 293 and before Sossianus Hierocles (named in the inscription) became the governor of Bithynia in AD 303 (Jones et al. 1971). It is generally assumed that the camp was built at that time specifically for the legion, which was deployed there as part of Diocletian's programme of strengthening the borders. This is best rendered by the unsurpassed Zosimus (Zos. 2.34.1).

It was therefore assumed that the fortifications, which do not have a clear chronology but come from the second half of the third century AD, were built as part of Diocletian's activity. In the case of Palmyra, the situation seems extremely clear. The inscription from the Principia states clearly: 'during the reign of Diocletian and his companions, Sossianus Hierocles successfully built the *castra*'.

The chronology of buildings in the Camp of Diocletian in Palmyra is now accordingly defined as follows:

1. AD 293–303: Construction of the camp and the Principia, outlining the main streets, construction of the Porta Praetoria and *groma*, construction of defensive walls.
2. Second half of the fifth century: Construction of the C barracks.
3. Around AD 380: Destruction of the temple of Allat.
4. The turn of the fourth/fifth century: Construction of the Praetorium.
5. The sixth century: Destruction and reconstruction of the *horreum* and the Principia (Kowalski 1998, 206).

According to Kowalski, the rebuilding of the Principia took place in the sixth century after a great fire (perhaps caused by an earthquake). The archaeological sounding conducted near the western wall of the Principia provided ceramic material dated to the sixth century (Kowalski 1998, 201). It was found in the layer of ashes, which were interpreted as a trace of the above-mentioned fire.

New Approach: The Aurelian Wall

Although the chronology presented above is well established among scholars, perhaps one should consider the reasons for seeking the origins of the camp during the reign of Aurelian (Juchniewicz 2013, 194). The complex was set up on the ruins of the so-called western district, from which only the temple of Allat and some unidentified walls (unearthed during the excavations at the forum) are known (Krogulska 1984, fig. 22). It is probable that the western district was destroyed during the final siege of the city in 273. It was around the same time that the temple of Allat was devastated, although this was later rebuilt within the borders of the legion camp (Gawlikowski 1983, 62–63).

The hypothesis that the Roman legion was deployed in Palmyra already in Aurelian's time may be to some extent supported by the inscription found in the ruins of the Roman fort in the Azraq oasis (Christol and Lenoir 2001, 166).

The re-reading of this inscription by French researchers suggests that it originates from the time when Emperor Aurelian brought order to the eastern provinces after defeating Zenobia. The most important conclusion previously suggested by some earlier researchers is that the Legio I Illyricorum existed in the time of Aurelian (Parker 1933, 176). Judging from the record in the *Notitia dignitatum* that Palmyra was a base for this legion (Dodgeon and Lieu 1991, 341) and the inscription from the camp itself, dating back to its construction in Diocletian's time, one can presume that this legion had been present in Palmyra since AD 273. This would correspond to the events presented in the *Historia Augusta* and also to those described by Zosimus. The first source speaks clearly about the garrison of six hundred archers left in Palmyra just after Zenobia's defeat. Even if we take this story for granted, however, it is even more likely that after the final suppression of the rebellion by Zenobia's supporters, Aurelian left an even stronger garrison in the city (e.g., the Legio I Illyricorum, whose subunit is attested by the Azraq inscription). It is difficult to imagine that the legion would be deployed in such an open area. Most likely, the soldiers began to build their headquarters in the most convenient place, which could have been the destroyed western district, which had already been partially separated from the rest of the city by a wall, constituting the rear wall of shops in the west portico of the Transverse Colonnade. Another, though more speculative, argument is the fact that the Syrian steppe was undergoing significant change from the middle of the third century. We already know that Rome's new ally in the fight against Zenobia was the Tanukh tribal confederation. The question remains whether Aurelian would decide to leave the city unfortified in the face of completely new threats. Let us remember that the Tanukhs were newcomers who did not have any previous arrangements with Rome. Ancient sources, verified by archaeological research, indicate that Aurelian did not destroy Palmyra (al-As'ad and Gawlikowski 1986, 167–168; Gawlikowski 1970, 211). It is at least doubtful that the city remained unfortified for twenty years until the Camp of Diocletian was built.

Archaeological and epigraphic data, however rudimentary, seem to indicate that this was not the case.

The disappearance of the Aramaic inscriptions seems to indicate changes in the city's population structure. This may only be related to the influx of people for whom the Aramaic language was foreign, but this group had to be relatively large to make such an impact in such a short time. The most likely explanation is the presence of the Roman legion and the change in the city administration system.

It is regrettable that the direct archaeological findings supporting this hypothesis are quite scant. The chronological prerequisite that allows such dating is the bronze Aurelian coin found in the stylobate of the Via Principalis, undoubtedly coming from the times when the camp was founded, but this only gives us a terminus post quem (Kowalski 1994, 47).

The design of the forum, and more specifically its entrance, may also suggest the existence of an earlier phase of construction of the entire complex. The entrance to the forum was the so-called Great Gate, a monumental structure with three passages and a stone staircase leading to it (Michałowski 1963, 21–40; Krogulska 1984, 86). Excavations have shown that there were two phases of construction. In the first phase, a 3.5-m-wide staircase was built. The archaeologists, however, interpreted this as an unfinished construction which was replaced almost immediately by a new structure. Dating is not certain, but it has been suggested that this may be a remnant of constructions from the first century AD (Krogulska 1984, 83–84). However, after reexamining the excavation documentation it appears that such dating is not possible since at the base of these stairs lies a fragment of a column that was clearly reused during the construction of the stairs (Krogulska 1984, 85, fig. 26). This means that the first phase must be dated to the times when the use of *spolia* was common and therefore most likely after the year 273. Indeed, the construction of the new stairs took place soon after that, namely in the time of Diocletian. The conclusions seem obvious. The first stairs probably come from the times when Aurelian's soldiers were building their camp, while the monumental stairs from the second phase come from the times when Sossianus Hierocles was expanding the legionary base.

The object from this period may also be the Pretorian Gate, which was built at the expense of destroying some of the shops of the west portico of the Transverse Colonnade (Gawlikowski 1976, 275).

Other archaeological and architectural leads are the differences in the way individual camp structures were built, specifically the use of masonry. The basic difference, easily noticeable at first glance, is the type of stone used. The wall surrounding the city is built predominantly of a pink variety of local limestone. The most homogeneous in this respect is Section C, that is, the wall surrounding the Camp of Diocletian. It is certain that no matter how we date the fortifications, their construction started from the building of the Camp of Diocletian. Currently, the wall bears no traces of major modifications, so it can be assumed that this is an original construction which constitutes the earliest phase of late antique fortifications. This would mean that the Aurelian wall was reinforced only by monolithic quadrangular towers. In this respect, the Palmyrene walls would resemble the Aurelian Walls in Rome, which also had such towers—deprived of the internal chamber (at least to the level of the *corona muralis*) and almost quadrangle in plan (Richmond 1930, 76–77). As for the use of *spolia*, frequently quoted by supporters of the theory that the wall was built by Zenobia, their use in the construction has its analogy elsewhere. At the time, the use of such building material was very common in the west of the empire and can be attributed to the fact that the cities were getting smaller (Johnson 1973, 210; Lander 1984, 169). Another characteristic feature, also most noticeable in Rome, was the use of existing structures most likely to economize on the construction (Lander 1984, 168). In Palmyra, such a solution was also used as it perfectly suited the fortification trends of the era.

In conclusion, it is very likely that the wall of the Camp of Diocletian was built between 273 and 293 by the legion left in Palmyra by Aurelian, most likely the Legio I Illyricorum. The soldiers began building the fortifications of their own headquarters, and, when this work was completed, the construction of walls protecting the most important districts and city monuments began. Parts of the tombs from the northern necropolis and *spolia* from destroyed or dismantled structures (also mostly tombs) were used for this purpose. Inside the camp, streets were marked out and the basic plan outlined. At that time, the northern camp Gate G5 was probably not functioning and the Via Principalis had a dead end. Judging by the type of the construction, the eastern tower (Ts 36) was built at a later stage of the development of the camp.

DIOCLETIAN AND JUSTINIAN WALLS

In this respect, reconsideration of the inscription on the lintel found in the Principia and the activity of Sossianus Hierocles is overdue. The main contribution of Sossianus was probably the completion of the camp. In this case, archaeological data are extremely abundant. First, the interior of the camp was rearranged. Perhaps there were some changes in the structure of the legion itself, but this cannot be confirmed. It is certain, though, that it was Hierocles who built the military headquarters—the so-called Principia, consisting of the staff headquarters (the basilica) and the assembly square (the forum). The method of constructing the basilica, or, as it is sometimes called, the Temple of the Standards, is the starting point for further chronological consideration because, thanks to the inscription, this is the only well-dated building in the camp.

Let us take a closer look at the inscription. It relates to the activities of Sossianus Hierocles, *vir perfectissimus*, who served as provincial governor (Kowalski 1997, 44). It uses the phrase 'happily built' (*feliciter condiderunt*), which can mean 'happily completed construction'.

The entire complex consists of two main parts: a forum and a basilica. The forum was accessible from the east, via the stairs leading to the gate. Along the north and south walls there were single rows of rooms, in one of which, located in the south-eastern corner of the forum, there was a latrine. From the west, the square was enclosed by the wall of the basilica building. From the east, most likely there was a portico. In addition to the main gate, there was also a small gate located in the south-western corner (Krogulska 1984, 73–74).

Located at the foot of Jebel Husayniyet, the Temple of the Standards was built on a stone platform, levelling the slope of the area; its eastern wall was also a retaining wall. The building consisted of a large longitudinal hall (*scholae*), a centrally placed chapel in which the legion's standards were kept, and adjoining smaller halls and rooms. The platform also contained an aqueduct inside (Gawlikowski 1984, 10–13).

Principia were built of local limestone but in most cases a different variety than that used in the curtain of the defensive wall. This stone is harder, of beige/yellow hue. It erodes in a characteristic way—breaking and flaking off. The military headquarters were built of enormous blocks of this variety of stone, arranged in an easily identifiable manner, especially at the base of the western and eastern walls of the building.

The layout of the headers and stretchers is easily seen. The higher parts of the walls are no longer built with such care, and the rhythm of the stone blocks is difficult to determine.

The construction, which on grounds of its structural similarity dates back to the Tetrarchy, is a *horreum*—a mill and garrison granary. The building is located in the south-eastern corner of the camp and adjoins the defensive wall and the back wall of the western portico of the Oval Square, ending the Transverse Colonnade. In the *horreum*, two different types of masonry can be distinguished. One belongs to the defensive wall, whose inner face constitutes the *horreum*'s southern wall. This was built from blocks of pink limestone. The stones are processed only roughly and do not fit together perfectly, the contact surfaces bearing slight traces of processing. Large blocks lie at the base of the wall and were apparently reused. Originally they must have belonged to one of the tombs located nearby.

The second type of masonry, corresponding to that of the Principia, consists of blocks of light-yellow limestone, processed quite carefully from all sides. The stones cut in this way form thick slabs, which were joined in such a way that in one row of stones, two slabs parallel to the wall line and bonded by shorter sides are separated by a plate set perpendicularly, then next is a single slab set in parallel, then once again a perpendicular slab and two parallel slabs. This gives the following course: header-stretcher-header-stretcher-stretcher-header, and so on. It is telling that the walls built in this way have clearly been added to the outer walls of the camp—in other words, to the southern defensive wall and the back wall of shops in the portico of the Transverse Colonnade. They are not, however, constructionally bonded. This means that the *horreum* was built later than the fortifications. The use of another type of masonry and of stone also suggests a significant interval in time.

This might be another clue supporting the hypothesis that the camp and the surrounding wall were being built earlier than generally thought. Another change is the recognition that the U-shaped towers were modernized in Diocletian's times by Sossianus Hierocles. There are several important arguments supporting the theory that the towers are in fact two hundred years older than was assumed.

However, let us first look at the arguments for dating the fortifications back to the times of Justinian. The traditional dating of the U-shaped towers to the reign of this emperor resulted from the belief that the first late antique fortifications in Palmyra were built in the times of Diocletian. As these towers were clearly added to the wall, scholars began to search for a moment in history at which they could have been built. After Diocletian, another emperor whose building programme is well known to us is Justinian. His activity was widely described by Procopius, who dedicated a fragment of his work to Palmyra (Procopius, 2.11.10–12). And so the corresponding historical moment was found and certified by the ancient source, which also describes the remains visible in the field (Seyrig 1950, 239–241).

This hypothesis, however, is based on the assumption that, apart from the activity of the two emperors documented by the available sources, no other construction activity of this scale and character took place there. It is also worth noting that Procopius does not give any details and does not mention the towers. Meanwhile, the 'indescribable' fortifications can be described without much difficulty. Naturally, this is due to the fact that Procopius had never been to Palmyra and his information about it is second-hand. Most likely, he described what he considered probable, colouring the description for the needs of his otherwise useful work.

Seyrig's hypothesis was accepted by van Berchem and then by other researchers who continue to accept it today, most likely owing to the lack of other theories (van Berchem 1954, 257, n. 1). However, the arguments for dating the U-shaped towers back to the times of Diocletian are stronger.

Let us start with the comparative material from other sites. With the exception of the Dara Fortress, the vast majority of the sites I describe here which were equipped with U-shaped towers can be dated to the beginning of the fourth century. Dating of these towers is reliable because they usually form an integral part of the wall. An exception to this rule is the fortress in Udruh, where the U-shaped towers were added later, just as in Palmyra. In the case of Udruh, however, there is no doubt that these towers date from the Tetrarchy, while the wall to which they were added comes from the earlier period. The towers are well dated because of their twin resemblance to the fortifications of Lejjun, where the ceramic material leaves no doubt that these were built at the beginning of the fourth century.

We find a similar situation in Singara, where fortifications are also dated to the beginning of the fourth century. The similarities with Palmyra are even greater here than in Udruh and Lejjun. These two sites, however, from the very beginning were only legion camps, while Singara was a fortress city. Its U-shaped towers have a similar interior arrangement, namely the windows inclined inwards.

Another great comparison with Palmyra is the legion camp in Luxor, dated until recently to the beginning of the fourth century. Inscriptions found there, reinterpreted by Speidel and Pavkovic, prove that the camp could have been built as early as AD 293 (Speidel and Pavkovic 1989, 154). The common elements are U-shaped towers flanking the gates, with a quadrangular inner courtyard. This type of gate is also known in Singara.

Researchers agree that the U-shaped tower is characteristic of the Tetrarchy period and that it was in this period that it began to be widely used (Lander 1984, 218; Parker 1986, 72; Gregory 1996, 166). What is interesting is that most examples of sites from the Tetrarchy period equipped with U-shaped towers can be found in Moesia Inferior (Lander 1984, 218). This supports Kowalski's hypothesis that their origins should be sought there (Kowalski 1994, 207).

The reanalysis of the structure in Palmyra also supports my hypothesis that the U-shaped towers date from the times of Diocletian.

The starting point for us is the Principia building. The comparison of both constructions gives us results similar to those obtained in the case of the *horreum*. The U-shaped towers were built of the same material as the Principia. These are large slabs of light-yellow limestone, processed on each side. The masonry also shows great similarities. To a large extent, the course—header-stretcher, known also from the Principia—was applied here. But in the middle sections, wall fabric present in the *horreum* was applied: namely, one slab was positioned perpendicularly, then two in parallel, then once again, one perpendicular. The construction method applied in the case of buildings dated to the period AD 293–303 is therefore almost the same as in the case of the U-shaped towers.

The *horreum* and the Principia were therefore probably erected at the same time. The fortifications were equipped with new U-shaped towers that met the requirements of the reformed Roman army. They were in fact artillery platforms; however it is uncertain whether any kind of artillery was ever present in Palmyra. Some changes also occurred in the means of communication. Probably a new gate was built, the so-called northern camp gate (G5). This can be proved by the layout and construction of the quadrangular towers flanking it. The western tower is bonded to the wall and belongs to the original structure. The eastern tower, on the other hand, has clearly been added, built of light-yellow limestone and constructed similarly to the U-shaped towers.

In the light of the above considerations, it must be clearly stated that the late antique walls surrounding Palmyra bear no visible traces of Justinian's activity. That Procopius's description is usually misinterpreted does not mean that it is completely untrue.

According to John Malalas and Theophanes, to renovate the city, Justinian sent to Palmyra Patricius, the 'Komes of the East'. Only Procopius writes about the modernization of fortifications. Excavation carried out in the Camp of Diocletian points to the reconstruction phase of the Principia, which took place in the sixth century and resulted in changes to the arrangement of the interior and the addition of new rooms (Gawlikowski 1984, 43–45). This is also confirmed by the ceramic material discovered during the survey conducted behind the building (Kowalski 1998, 201). Perhaps these are the direct traces of Patricius's activity. However, there are no indications that any renovation work was carried out at that time on the defensive walls.

During the survey conducted by the Polish mission in Basilica III, the archaeologists excavated an apse which was supported from the outside by perpendicularly set stone blocks of light limestone, forming a kind of buttress (Gawlikowski 2003, 279–290). A hypothesis then arose that this was a construction similar to the perpendicular stone slabs used in the U-shaped towers, which would suggest similar dating of the building. I had the opportunity to reexamine both structures, and I can ascertain that they are completely different as far as their construction is concerned and that the similarity resulting from the transversal position is virtual. Blocks in the apse of Basilica III were outside the arc of the apse and were not built up. The perpendicularly arranged blocks in the U-shaped towers were designed to strengthen the structure of the wall from the inside and constituted a bonding element. The similarity is therefore only apparent.

BIBLIOGRAPHY

al-As'ad, Khaled, and Gawlikowski, Michał. 1986. 'New Honorific Inscriptions in the Great Colonnade of Palmyra'. *Annales archéologiques arabes syriennes* 36: 164–171.

Christol, Michel, and Maurice Lenoir. 2001. 'Qasr el-Azraq et la reconquête de l'orient par Aurélien'. *Syria* 78: 163–178.

Crouch, Dora P. 1975. 'The Ramparts of Palmyra'. *Studia Palmyreńskie* 6: 6–44.

Dodgeon, Michael H., and Samuel N. C. Lieu, eds. 1991. *The Roman Eastern Frontier and the Persian Wars (AD 226–362): A Documentary History*. London: Routledge.

du Mesnil du Buisson, Robert. 1966. 'Première campagne de fouilles à Palmyre'. *Comptes rendus des séances de l'Académie des inscriptions et belles-lettres*: 158–190.

Gabriel, Albert. 1926. 'Recherches archéologiques à Palmyre'. *Syria* 7: 71–92.

Gawlikowski, Michał. 1974. 'Les défenses de Palmyre'. *Syria* 51: 231–242.

Gawlikowski, Michał. 1975. 'Remarks on the Ramparts of Palmyra'. *Studia palmyreńskie* 6: 45–46.

Gawlikowski, Michał. 1976. 'Palmyre 1973'. In 'Chronique des fouilles'. *Études et travaux* 9: 273–281.

Gawlikowski, Michał. 1983. 'Réflections sur la chronologie du sanctuaire d'Allat à Palmyre'. *Damaszen Mitteilungen* 1: 59–67.

Gawlikowski, Michał, ed. 1984. *Palmyra*. Vol. 8, *Les principia de Dioclétien: Temple des enseignes*. Warsaw: Państwowe Wydawnictwo Naukowe.

Gawlikowski, Michał. 2003. 'Palmyra Season 2002'. *Polish Archaeology in the Mediterranean* 14: 279–290.

Gawlikowski, Michał, and Khalid al-As'ad. 1993. 'Le péage à Palmyre en 11 aprés J.-C'. *Semitica* 41–42: 163–172.

Gregory, Shelagh. 1996. *Roman Military Architecture on the Eastern Frontier, AD 200–600*. 3 vols. Amsterdam: Hakkert.

Johnson, Stephen. 1973. 'A Group of Late Roman City Walls in Gallia Belgica'. *Britannia* 4: 210–223.

Jones, A. H. M., John R. Martindale, and John Morris. 1971. *The Prosopography of the Later Roman Empire*. Vol. 1, *AD 260–395*. Cambridge: Cambridge University Press.

Juchniewicz, Karol. 2013. 'Late Roman Fortifications of Palmyra'. *Studia Palmyreńskie* 12: 193–202.

Juchniewicz, Karol, Khaled al-As'ad, and Khalil al-Hariri. 2010. 'The Defense Wall in Palmyra after Recent Syrian Excavations'. *Studia Palmyreńskie* 11: 55–73.

Kowalski, Sławomir P. 1994. 'The *Praetorium* of the Camp of Diocletian in Palmyra'. *Studia Palmyreńskie* 9: 39–70.

Kowalski, Sławomir P. 1997. 'Late Roman Palmyra in Literature and Epigraphy'. *Studia Palmyreńskie* 10: 39–62.

Kowalski, Sławomir P. 1998. 'The Camp of *Legio I Illyricorum* in Palmyra'. *Novensia* 10: 189–210.

Krogulska, Maria. 1984. 'Le forum'. In *Palmyra*. Vol. 8, *Les principia de Dioclétien: Temple des enseignes*, edited by Michał Gawlikowski, 70–91. Warsaw: Państwowe Wydawnictwo Naukowe.

Lander, James. 1984. *Roman Stone Fortifications: Variation and Change from the First Century A.D. to the Fourth*. British Archaeological Reports International Series 206. Oxford: British Archaeological Reports.

Michałowski, Kazimierz. 1963. *Palmyre*. Vol. 3, *Fouilles polonaises, 1961*. Warsaw: Państwowe Wydawnictwo Naukowe.

Parker, H. M. D. 1933. 'The Legions of Diocletian and Constantine'. *Journal of Roman Studies* 23: 175–189.

Parker, S. Thomas. 1986. *Romans and Saracens: A History of the Arabian Frontier*. Winona Lake: American Schools of Oriental Research.

Richmond, Ian A. 1930. *The City Wall of Imperial Rome*. Oxford: Clarendon Press.

Seyrig, Henri. 1950. 'Antiquités Syriennes'. *Syria* 27: 229–252.

Speidel, Michael P., and Michael F. Pavkovic. 1989. 'Legion II Flavia Constantia at Luxor'. *American Journal of Philology* 110: 151–154.

Starcky, Jean. 1949. 'Autour d'une dédicace palmyrénienne à Sadrafa et à Du'anat'. *Syria* 26: 43–85.

van Berchem, Denis. 1954. 'Recherche sur la chronologie des enceintes de Syrie et de Mesopotamie'. *Syria* 31: 254–270.

van Berchem, Denis. 1970. 'Le premiere rempart de Palmyre'. *Comptes rendus des séances de l'Académie des inscriptions et belles-lettres* 114(2): 231–237.

von Gerkan, Armin. 1935. 'Die Stadtmauer von Palmyra'. *Berytus* 2: 25–33.

PART SIX

PALMYRA AND ITS ART

CHAPTER 26

PUBLIC SCULPTURES FROM PALMYRA[*]

DAGMARA WIELGOSZ-RONDOLINO

INTRODUCTION: GENERAL OVERVIEW

LIKE many Graeco-Roman cities of the East, Palmyra expressed its own civic, communal, and political identity through inscriptions and sculptures set up in public. The statues were accompanied by honorific inscriptions, often bilingual, in Aramaic and Greek, and in a few cases also in Latin, and they provide evidence of the widespread nature of the free-standing public statuary in the city. In contrast to the written records, archaeological finds of honorific sculptures are exceptional. Executed in local limestone, bronze, and marble, they followed both local and Greek or Roman statuary types (see in general Colledge 1976, 88–93).

The statues were set up on inscribed bases or, in the majority of cases, on the inscribed column brackets that were the most emblematic and dominant feature of the Palmyrene architectural landscape owing to the fact that columns were one of the basic elements of all public buildings and spaces: temples, streets, and squares. Thus, column brackets became the most popular means of supporting a public statue and displaying an honorific inscription, although this was sometimes engraved directly into the column shaft. Each column was provided with one or two brackets on opposing faces of the column's shaft (Figure 26.1). The brackets for the public statues may also have been inserted directly into the wall of another architectural structure.

[*] The original manuscript of this chapter was submitted to the editor in 2018.

FIGURE 26.1 Great Colonnade in Palmyra.

Photograph by Dagmara Wielgosz-Rondolino.

EPIGRAPHIC EVIDENCE

The dated texts that refer to Palmyra's honorific statues stretch from October 44 BC (*PAT* 1524) to August of AD 271 (*IGLS* XVII.1, 57). They constituted a fundamental accompaniment to public statuary: the standardized formulas employed in the inscriptions— fewer than two hundred items are known to us—give us essential information about donors and honoured persons (Dijkstra 1995, 335–343, appendix G). The honorific inscription usually contains a patronymic followed by the paternal, multigeneration genealogy, and, especially in the first century AD, tribal affiliation. However, they occasionally mentioned the official position of the person represented (Yon 2002, 12). Thus, a special group of dedications refers to Palmyrene caravan leaders (συνοδιάρχης, e.g., *IGLS* XVII.1, 25; in later periods, ἀρχέμπορος, e.g., *IGLS* XVII.1, 74; see Yon 2002, 103– 104), of which, Sho'adu, son of Boliada' (in Greek, Soados son of Boliades), and Marcus Ulpius Iarḥai, son of Ḥairan, are well known from the epigraphical records, both having been active benefactors around the mid-second century AD. For their merits and deeds, they were recognized with several statues. Priests could be similarly recognized with public statues (e.g., *PAT* 0265), as could officers of local origin (e.g., *IGLS* XVII.1, 201) and private individuals—those whose public position was unknown and those with the most prominent roles in local society and policy, such as Septimius Odainathos (e.g., *IGLS* XVII.1, 56) or Septimius Worod (e.g., *IGLS* XVII.1, 64). Sometimes, one person was recognized with several statues simultaneously, which were precisely enumerated in the inscriptions (e.g., *IGLS* XVII.1, 127, 149, 150, 222, 307). Moreover, some honorific texts were dedicated to Roman administrative officials (e.g., publicans, *IGLS* XVII.1, 196–197) and military officers (e.g., *IGLS* XVII.1, 10, 11, 206, 208, 209) and to members of the imperial family (Yon 2002, 275; *IGLS* XVII.1, pp. 422–424).

Individuals might be honoured by several entities, in most cases by civic institutions and by groups of people: a city council (ἡ βουλή, e.g., *IGLS* XVII.1, 19, 113) on its own, the assembly of the people of Palmyra (Παλμυρηνῶν ὁ δῆμος, e.g., *IGLS* XVII.1, 16–17) on its own, or by both institutions at the same time (ἡ βουλὴ καὶ ὁ δῆμος, e.g., *IGLS* XVII.1, 20–22, 64, 67, 74, 76, 145, 159). They might be honoured also by the tribes, acting alone (e.g., *PAT* 0261, 0190, 0192, 0196; *IGLS* XVII.1, 79, 80–85, 114–116) or together with gods (e.g., *PAT* 0193–0194; *IGLS* XVII.1, 125; Gawlikowski 2017, nos. 30, 31, 34–35), on behalf of the civic authorities (by the decrees of *demos* and *bule*, e.g., *IGLS* XVII.1, 222), or even by the city of the Palmyrenes (Παλμυρηνῶν ἡ πόλις, e.g., *IGLS* XVII.1, 18). A conspicuous group of honorific inscriptions and statues was presented by members of caravans or merchants who originated mainly in Palmyra and resided in Palmyra or elsewhere (e.g., *IGLS* XVII.1, 16, 24, 240, 245). Last, there is a series of texts and statues dedicated by the priests (e.g., *PAT* 1524, 0191; *IGLS* XVII.1, 12, 123) and artisanal associations (e.g., *IGLS* XVII.1, 17, 56, 59, 143). Along with the collective donations, the epigraphic evidence also shows private individuals acting as dedicators, honouring their friends (i.e., patrons) (e.g., *IGLS* XVII.1, 29, 54, 63, 65–66, 68–69; Yon 2002, 145–148), members of their families, deceased or living (e.g., *PAT* 0268; *IGLS* XVII.1, 27–28, 128, 254–256, 258), and other individuals whose relation to the dedicators remains unknown (e.g., *PAT* 0198).

The texts specify not only by whom and for whom a statue was erected, but also commemorated the reason it was erected, an important factor in the act of honouring someone. Thus, the civic authorities, merchants or caravan members, and private individuals very often dedicated a statue to a particular individual in gratitude for his contribution to the success of a caravan (e.g., *IGLS* XVII.1, 74, 87, 127, 222, 227, concerning caravan inscriptions, Gawlikowski 1994, 27–33; 1996, 139–145; Yon 2002, 263–264).

Another kind of honorific inscription was related to the euergetic activity of local benefactors. It should be stressed that Palmyrene euergetism was mainly connected with religious contexts (Yon 2002, 150–155), with the texts often reporting that certain individuals had funded a particular part or feature of a sanctuary, for instance, portions of the porticoes, columns, or roof, a gilded bronze door, or the baths (e.g., *PAT* 0193, 0196; *IGLS* XVII.1, 18, 21, 312). Accordingly, these individuals must have offered large sums of money for building activities within the temple. In such circumstances, a collective often acted as the dedicator, that is, a tribe associated with a god or gods to whom the temple belonged, civic authorities, or associations of priests, alone or by order of gods (e.g., *PAT* 0193, 0275; Gawlikowski 2017, nos. 31, 35).

There is a special place within the Palmyrene honorific panorama for statues representing deceased family members. Most of these statues were erected by men: by a father for a son, by a son or sons for his/their father, by a brother for a brother, and so on (e.g., *IGLS* XVII.1, 179–180). On rare occasions, posthumous inscriptions and statues were set up by women. For example, a certain Ḥagge (in Greek, Iulia Aurelia Agge) commemorated her deceased father Taime and brother Ḥalafata in January of AD 214, or August of AD 216, according to the Greek version (*IGLS* XVII.1, 257). In a few cases, deceased females (a wife, sister, or daughter) were also commemorated. For instance, Tamma was commemorated in AD 168/169 by both parents with a statue erected in the sanctuary of Bēl (*IGLS* XVII.1, 30). Another Palmyrene woman, Hadirat, was commemorated by her father, Marcus Ulpius Elahbel, in the temple of Nabu (*IGLS* XVII.1, 181). On the other hand, five sculptures of members of a single family, including a posthumous one that a certain Shoraiku, son of Ḥairan, erected for his wife Marthi, were set up in the Transverse Colonnade by different entities almost simultaneously in March of AD 179 (*IGLS* XVII.1, 113–117). These posthumous inscriptions, displayed along with statues in a wider family context, were set up in the most frequented public spaces, such as the porticoes of temples, streets, and the agora, making them places of self-celebration and self-presentation for leading Palmyrene families. In such places of the city's collective memory, the living and the deceased coexisted.

It is worth noting that we know of inscriptions bearing dates from the first half of the first century that are engraved in an obviously second-century architectural context (*IGLS* XVII.1, 16–18, 24, 27, 214, 225, 238, 241)—both the circumstances of the incision and palaeography leave no doubt regarding this dating. This undoubtedly means that the inscriptions and statues commemorating important figures living in the first century were considered worth re-executing in a new context, on consoles, although it must be said that in none of these cases do we know how they were originally displayed (see also *PAT* 0191). This practice probably also existed in the third century, although on a smaller scale, when inscriptions from the second century were re-engraved (*IGLS* XVII.1, 25, 145). We also know of honorific sculptures being restored; for example, in March of AD 229 a certain Barʿateh restored the sculpture of his grandfather, Malku, which stood on the bracket of one of the columns in the Transverse Colonnade (*PAT* 0303).

The honorific inscriptions paired with the honorific statues illustrate a Palmyrene societal structure divided into tribes, clans, and families and very clearly mark the border between two worlds: the male and the female. Men were participants in the public and political life of the city, whereas women, with few exceptions, had little access to it and, in principle, did not play any role in civic identity. Women could, however, inherit and purchase funerary properties (Cussini 1995; Yon 2002, 166–175, 233–250; Cussini 2005; 2016).

In a society with such a sharp gender division, the beneficiaries of public honours, and eventually, those honoured with public sculptures, were (in most cases) men. Even though women are known to have sponsored the construction of individual parts of sanctuaries, such as the columns or sections of the porticoes (e.g., *PAT* 0167–0168), or to have contributed to the construction of the baths in the sanctuaries of local deities (*IGLS*

XVII.1, 312), their appearance in public/official epigraphy is uncommon, in contrast to that of other Hellenistic and Roman cities, especially those of Asia Minor. The very few (fewer than ten) female honorific sculptures, which are attested by inscriptions (the oldest is dated to March of 17 BC [*PAT* 0315; Yon 2002, 170, n. 32]), are mainly posthumous. Furthermore, in most cases, the female statues were displayed within a wider family or clan context as wives, sisters, or daughters, subordinate to the family, and not as independent individuals acting outside the family. For example, such is the case of Beththeis (*IGLS* XVII.1, 84), whose statue was probably erected during her life (in July of AD 208) and was set in the family context (al-Asʿad and Gawlikowski 1986–1987, 164–166, nos. 1–5), next to the statues of her husband, Shoʿadu son of Elahbel (dedicated in September of AD 201, *IGLS* XVII.1, 82), her son Malku (dedicated around AD 203, *IGLS* XVII.1, 83), and her husband's brother, Iarhai (dedicated in September of AD 197), and the case of Marthi, wife of Shoraiku, discussed above. A statue of Thomallachis, the last member of an important Palmyrene Firmon family seems to be somewhat unusual (Yon 2002, 152, 168–169). She was honoured in August of AD 182, during her life, for an act of euergetism, by her own tribe of Bene Komare (*IGLS* XVII.1, 312; Yon 2002, 152, 159). Even the most extraordinary case of Zenobia depended on familial links. Honoured as a queen, she had to demonstrate her ties to her family (legitimization of rule), to her deceased husband, honoured as king of kings (*PAT* 0292), beside a sculpture bearing her likeness (*IGLS* XVII.1, 57).

GENERAL ASPECT OF PALMYRENE PUBLIC STATUES

What did Palmyrene honorific statues look like? How did they evolve over the ages? The answer to these fundamental questions is limited by the fact that only a few of them have survived, although their manufacture must have been one of the most developed industries in Palmyra.

Commercial relations with the main *poleis* of the Graeco-Roman world must have favoured the influx of Hellenistic and Roman ideas, stimulating the demand for monuments and goods with a certain symbolic value for the wealthy classes of Palmyrene society. Of these, bronze and marble were considered markers of wealth.

Bronze Public Statues

We do not know the extent to which bronze was used as a material for honorific sculptures in Palmyra. However, one may assume that the majority, if not all the statues set up on hundreds of column brackets were made of bronze, as proved by the holes left by inserting the statues into their tops. The bronze sculptures may also have been displayed on other kinds of supports, such as bases or podia.

The oldest known bronze honorific statues came from the sanctuary of Bēl. They were cast between AD 17 and 19 by Minucius Rufus, the *legatus* of the Legio X Fretensis, who dedicated an imperial statuary group to Drusus, Tiberius, and Germanicus (*IGLS* XVII.1, 3). According to Ernest Will (1985, 268–269), the group originally stood on a base, but, following the new architectural setting of the sanctuary, especially of its court-yard, the bronze statues were probably inserted into the podium surrounding the sanctuary. This change took place around AD 70 or slightly later, and it was also the time when a dedicatory inscription in Latin was re-engraved.

Further testimony of an early first-century AD (February of AD 32) bronze public statue comes from the column bracket (which preserves the sockets for the statue insertion) at the sanctuary of Baalshamin that once exhibited the image of a certain Zabdilah, son of Bariki (*PAT* 0190), erected by Bene Ma'zin. Moreover, the first-century use of bronze statues is confirmed by the most spectacular bilingual Aramaic and Greek epigraphic source, known as the 'Tax Law of Palmyra'. This important text, dated to AD 137, preserves fragments of an earlier law (the so-called Old Law) that was probably promulgated at some point in the first century AD (Matthews 1984, 177–180) and that clearly mentions the import of bronze statues into the city (*CIS* II, 3913; II, 128–130 [Aramaic text]; *PAT* 0259: 128; Shifman 2014, panel II, col. III, lines 29–31). Unfortunately, the text says nothing about the character of these statues: Were they honorific or decorative? Nor does it say where they came from: Were they from the East or the West? Were they imported for local use or for further commerce, especially if they came from the western part of the Roman Empire? None of these questions has an answer. Henri Seyrig proposed the East as the place where the bronze statues were manufactured ('were cast in the Parthian cities of Lower Mesopotamia'), perhaps in Seleukeia-on-the-Tigris (1950, 4–5 *contra* Will 1992, 163), whereas Klaus Parlasca suggested the West (1985, 347). The very few fragments of bronze statues that survived in Palmyra, mainly from the agora, reproduce both Western and Eastern iconographic statue designs: fragments of draping, possibly parts of cuirassed statues; the front part of a plain, closed shoe (also considered to be a fragment of a thigh); a hand; and a fragment of a lingula-type Greek sandal of uncertain prove-nance (Balty 2005, 339–341, nos. 1–6, figs. 448–451).

Because of the importance of the statues putting as little weight as possible on the column shafts, cast bronze statues, which were hollow and lightweight, were better suited to column brackets than were stone sculptures. Eventually, they were also much more valuable and prestigious than the limestone statues. However, there is another reason for the widespread use of bronze in manufacturing public sculptures. The use of this material created the possibility of mass production and/or replicating an original using the lost-wax technique, a process that required the construction of a clay model from which the clay master moulds for producing a bronze statue in separate parts were created (concerning bronze casting, e.g., Mattusch 2006, 208–242). Thus, casting by the lost-wax technique gave the workshops the opportunity to create hundreds of identical bronze statues that might, if necessary, differ in gesture or iconographic detail. Reproducing numerous copies of the same model in various artistic media definitely conformed to the more general rules of Palmyrene art.

The serial production of bronze statues is also attested by epigraphic sources: the same person might be honoured by several bronze statues erected simultaneously in different places in the city. For example, an inscription from the temple of Allat, engraved in June of AD 144 in honour of the famous Sho'adu, son of Boliada' (Gawlikowski 2017, no. 36; see also *IGLS* XVII.1, 149), mentions four bronze statues erected in four sanctuaries belonging to the four tribes of Palmyra that constituted the city's civic body: the sanctuary of Allat, the Sacred Garden, the sanctuary of Arṣu, and the sanctuary of Atargatis.

The massive and widespread use of bronze public statues in Palmyra, proved, as I have argued above, by the holes for socketing left in the column brackets, and by the bilingual texts, more strongly supports the hypothesis of extensive local production than has been previously acknowledged.

Limestone Public Statues

Palmyra was very rich in one building and sculptural material—limestone—and exploited its various types and qualities. So far, ancient quarries have been identified in Jabal al-Tar, approximately 5 km north-west of the city (Figure 26.2), and the others 12–15 km north-east of Palmyra (Schmidt-Colinet 2017, 159–196; 2020; see also Chapter 36 [Schmidt-Colinet], this volume).

FIGURE 26.2 The quarries of Jabal al-Tar.

Photograph by Dagmara Wielgosz-Rondolino.

The oldest known examples of public statues, which are made of soft local limestone, come from Palmyrene sanctuaries, as do the honorary inscriptions dedicated with the representations of the city's outstanding citizens. They constitute the richest group of honorific monuments that have survived to our times from among thousands made mainly of bronze and melted down in later times. The most representative series were unearthed in the sanctuaries of Baalshamin and of Allat (Dunant and Stucky 2000, 95–105; Gawlikowski 2008, 397–411), both belonging to the tribe of the Bene Maʿzin (Dunant 1971, 10–11; Gawlikowski 2017, 152). Unfortunately, none of these oversized sculptures survived intact, and all the statues were discovered without heads, mainly in later constructions within the sanctuaries. They all look almost the same (Figure 26.3), replicating the same model and using an identical carving technique. The figures stand firmly in a frontal position and are usually dressed in a cloak and a chiton, visible on the chest and sometimes also emerging below the lower edge of the cloak. The cloak is wrapped tightly around the body; it is thrown over the left shoulder and falls down the back. Its other end is usually wound round the left wrist and falls down the left leg. The left arm, enveloped in drapery, is lowered; the hand may hold a bunch of laurel or olive leaves. The right arm is held in the arm-sling of the cloak. The feet bear closed shoes. The figure may also wear a ring (on the little finger). Men were represented in the most popular scheme for figures wearing civic costume in the Graeco-Roman Near East. However—in contrast to their classical counterparts—they wear closed shoes instead

FIGURE 26.3 Honorific sculptures from the temple of Allat on display at the Archaeological Museum of Palmyra before its demolition in 2015.

Photograph by Dagmara Wielgosz-Rondolino.

of sandals. In addition to chiton and cloak, some of the honorific statues also wear loose, full-length trousers in keeping with local tradition (e.g., Dunant and Stucky 2000, nos. 42–43, 50–51). Generally, draping of the garment is extremely simplified, with an unfinished or only outlined drapery design on the back of the statue. The bodies of the statues were carved separately from the portrait-heads and have sockets (the sockets differed in shape and dimensions) to hold the head and neck, which are provided with a large tenon for insertion. The earliest statues stood directly on the ground or perhaps on some kind of pedestal or base. They may have been displayed in the courtyards of the sanctuaries, perhaps in porticoes, and against the walls or columns since their backs were left unfinished. Of all these public statues, there is only one, fragmentarily preserved (found in the sanctuary of Allat) that bears an inscription identifying the person portrayed: 'Muqatil son of Moqimu Gura' (AMP inv. no. 100/75; Gawlikowski 2017, no. 28, see also inscription no. 27 from AD 68/69). In the course of the excavations of both sanctuaries, some portrait-heads made of soft limestone were also unearthed beside the bodies of the honorific statues (Dunant and Stucky 2000, nos. 103–105; Wielgosz-Rondolino 2016a, 171–176). They must have belonged to public statues as their dimensions fit well with the proportions of the sculpted bodies discovered. As brilliantly stated by Ernest Will, 'La vision de l'artiste oriental est en quelque sorte abstraite, l'idée l'emporte sur l'image; les choses, personnages ou objets, sont vues dans leur permanence, dans leur essence' (Will 1992, 157), so these portraits of meritorious Palmyrenes were rather symbolic images and did not reproduce the physiognomy of the individuals in question. The sculptor's attention focused on details and on the most important elements of the face, such as large eyes or mouths. Several of these portrait-heads find parallels in early first-century funerary sculpture and architectural elements, sharing the same sculptor's marks, technical handling, and style. This proves that, at the latest, from the first decades of the first century AD onwards, the same workshop and/or the same artist in Palmyra was involved in making various categories of sculptural objects (Wielgosz-Rondolino 2016a, 171–178). These sculptures very probably belonged to the earliest sculptural setting of the sanctuary of Allat (from the first century BC to the end of the first century AD), corresponding, in general, to the first phases of its construction (Allat I–Allat II, Gawlikowski 2017, 28–31). To more precisely determine a chronology for the founding and display of sculptures, the inscriptions may be helpful. However, they do not reflect the true state of affairs. For example, the oldest honorific inscription discovered so far, in the sanctuary of Allat, comes from AD 56/57 (Gawlikowski 2017, no. 26), but it is known that the early sanctuary of Allat was founded at least one hundred years earlier, around the middle of the first century BC (Gawlikowski 2017, 28–31). Therefore, we are dealing with finds that are entirely random, and we cannot rule out a priori the possibility of earlier honorific evidence.

Carving an honorific sculpture directly on the drum of a column shaft was a practice specific to Palmyra. This peculiar practice may be considered a transitional stage between honorific statues standing on bases or on the ground and those put on column brackets, which were to become the most widespread means of honouring individuals in Palmyra. All these traditions may have coexisted. The only dated honorific column with a human figure sculpted on the drum was erected in the sanctuary of Allat in February of AD 64 (Gawlikowski 2017, no. 31). The person honoured was a certain Shalamallat, son of Yarḥibol. Unfortunately, the whole figure has been hammered out. The same period is probably the source of two other male figures unearthed in the sanctuary of Baalshamin (Dunant and Stucky 2000, nos. 64–65; see also *PAT* 0158). Carved on the column drums of the large enclosure (probably in portico C4), they share an identical posture and similar draping with the free-standing honorific statues known from this sanctuary. Around the end of the first century AD or at the beginning of the second was possibly carved a relief representing Hagar and her sister, honoured by their brother Ma'nai (AMP inv. no. 454; *PAT* 1346; Yon 2002, 166, fig. 60). The relief is exceptional in terms of the visual evidence it provides of local women honoured in Palmyra (Figure 26.4). It shows two headless female figures standing stiffly in a rigidly frontal position and dressed in traditional Palmyrene garments: a chiton, a cloak, and a long veil covering the head. The iconography of the figures closely resembles that of the female funerary reliefs of the first or early second century AD. The images were carved on a column drum discovered in the garden south of the sanctuary of Bēl. The original setting of the column

FIGURE 26.4 Column drum with figures of Hagar and her sister. Palmyra, Archaeological Museum (old depot), inv. no. 454.

Photograph by Dagmara Wielgosz-Rondolino.

and the character of the dedication are uncertain (commemorative, posthumous?). However, one may imagine a sanctuary as its location (of Bēl or the Sacred Garden).

The honorific images of the meritorious individuals carved on the column drums disappear from the city's sculptural landscape not long after the first century AD.

Approaching the question of the public sculptures of the second and third centuries, we encounter considerable difficulties due to the almost complete lack of monuments. Some scholars considered a few heads from the second and third centuries to be parts of public sculptures, but in fact they formed parts of banquet slabs or funerary statues. Often found with no archaeological context, they were incorrectly considered to be public statues, sometimes because of their oversized dimensions, as, for example, two famous heads, one held by the Ny Carlsberg Glyptotek (inv. no. 1121) and the other by the Archaeological Museum of Istanbul (inv. no. D 111. 6), interpreted as public portraits of members of Odainathos's family (Ingholt 1976, 115–116, plate 3,1–2; Equini-Schneider 1992, 123–128; Ploug 1995, 230, *contra* Parlasca 1989, 206). But they have their counterparts in funerary art, in three identical male heads from the so-called Hexagonal Tomb in Palmyra; therefore, they were produced possibly in series for the private funerary contexts, and not the public sphere (Gawlikowski 2016, 126–127, fig. 1; Wielgosz-Rondolino 2016b, 75–76, fig. 14).

Another category of public sculpture widespread in the Graeco-Roman world was the statue representing a member of the local elite wearing either Greek civic garments or a Roman toga and seated on a chair. This popular statuary scheme, which is based on portraits of philosophers and poets of the third century BC, especially those of Menander and Poseidippos, was widely adopted by outstanding citizens for self-presentation, in both public and private/funerary spheres (Meyer 1989; Clairmont 1993). Its popularity increased from the second century BC onwards (the phenomenon of the intellectualization of citizens, Zanker 1997, 63, 211). In the Roman period, manifestations of Hellenic culture particularly attracted the upper classes of the provincial cities, which expressed their enthusiasm for Greek culture through statuary inspired by the Hellenistic iconography of the intellectual, for example (see e.g., Goette 1990, M1–M20). But, thus far, in Palmyra, seated male figures are very rare. Two male figures, carved in hard limestone, represented on chairs with animal legs and wearing tunics, cloaks, and plain shoes belong to this category. The first, that of "Ogeilu, son of Zabdibol", was discovered in the northern part of the so-called Senate (AMP inv. no. 4129; Tanabe 1986, no. 171). The second, preserved up to a height of 132 cm, was discovered south of the wall near the Damascus Gate (AMP inv. no. B 2229/7960; Tanabe 1986, no. 172). Both sculptures seem to belong to the third century AD. However, their honorific function remains uncertain.

Marble Public Statues

In contrast to other cities of the Graeco-Roman East, where marble sculptures usually disappeared into lime kilns, Palmyra preserved a relatively large number of marble public statues. This may be explained by the easy access to locally quarried pure limestone, an excellent material for high-quality lime production. In Palmyra, fifteen almost-complete or fragmentary public marble statues (Wielgosz 2010, 75–106; Wielgosz-Rondolino 2023, 537–554, nos. Palmy-22–36) survived, of which the oldest— skilfully carved in precious Dokimeian marble—come from the Hadrianic or early Antonine epoch, a time of economic prosperity for the city. Conversely, in later periods, the most common material used for marble sculptures was the relatively inexpensive Prokonnesian marble, which, over time, became the variety of choice across the entire Roman Empire. Unfortunately, the individuals honoured remain anonymous since no honorific inscriptions revealing their names have been discovered. The Palmyrene statues reproduced Graeco-Roman statuary types, excepting one male portrait-head carved in the oriental style. In the Graeco-Roman world, the custom of displaying sculptures in public is attested, not only in archaeological sources, but also in ancient written sources. For example, Pliny the Elder devoted a considerable part of book 34 of his *Naturalis historia* to this. The honorific sculptures were dedicated to meritorious people, including women (*NH* 34.17–32). Pliny provided not only names of honorands and benefactors, but also described statuary types, some of which were also used in Palmyra, such as men wearing togas, cuirassed statues, and equestrian statues. In Palmyra, of seven headless marble male statues, three depict individuals wearing a toga over the tunica (*statuae togatae*) and closed, strapped shoes (*calcei patricii* or *senatorii*); two are cuirassed statues (*statuae loricatae*); and two represent a man dressed in a chiton and himation—a typical civic garment of the Greek *poleis*. They may have been emperors or members of the imperial family, or magistrates or local benefactors. Of the female public effigies, five headless statues and two veiled heads have survived. The female figures are depicted conventionally—tightly wrapped in a himation over a chiton, the feet shod in traditional Greek sandals or closed shoes. The himation may be draped over the body in various ways, following the specific statuary conventions for depicting either married women or unmarried girls. In Palmyra, three iconographic schemes that were widely distributed throughout the Graeco-Roman cities of the Roman Empire were adopted for modest female presentation: Small and Large Herculaneum Women and *Pudicitia* (concerning these statuary types, e.g., Daehner 2008; Trimble 2011). Created throughout the Hellenistic period, in Roman times they became fashionable for the female portrait-statues set up in both public and private (funerary) contexts, especially in the second and third centuries AD. Through the appropriate gestures and postures (e.g., *Pudicitia* statue) they conveyed the conventional virtues of good and modest wives, mothers, or daughters, celebrated in both visual arts and literature.

Most of the fifteen honorific statues in Palmyra were discovered in public contexts. We may assume, however, with a fair degree of certainty that a significant number of these public statues were removed from their original settings and placed elsewhere (for this practice that continued well into the fourth and fifth centuries AD, see *CTh* XV.1, 14; XV.1, 19), which presumably occurred after AD 273, when the city went into an inexorable decline. The construction of new buildings or complexes produced the most favourable opportunities for the transfer of these sculptures, as may be seen in the case of what is known as the Baths of Diocletian, built by Sossianus Hierocles, governor of Phoenicia, probably between AD 293 and 303 (Wielgosz 2013, 319–332). Therefore, the chronological assessment of marble public statues from Palmyra is based mostly on stylistic and technical grounds.

Thus, three sculptures came from the so-called Baths of Diocletian (once kept in the Archaeological Museum of Palmyra [AMP] and today in the National Museum of Damascus [NMD]). Two of these are a cuirassed statue (AMP inv. no. B1806/6716) from the late Hadrianic or early Antonine period, probably representing an emperor, and a female statue (AMP inv. no. B2256/8117) executed sometime between the late second and early third centuries AD, and probably following the 'Kore' scheme. Both statues were carved in Dokimeian marble. The latest public sculpture from the Baths, and of all Palmyrene honorific sculptures in general, seems to be a *statua togata* (AMP inv. no. B2062/7390) in Prokonnesian marble. The possible dating of this statue covers a large time span, starting in the post-Severan period and ending in the mid-fourth century AD (for parallels e.g., Goette 1990, Bb 178, Bb 181, Cb 6, and Cb 21).

Five public statues—two male and three female—were unearthed in another public space, the so-called Senate of Palmyra. The male statues (NMD inv. no. C4024/8813, and C4025/8814)—the two *togati*—were made of marble from Prokonnesos; one of them (NMD inv. no. C4024/8813) was very probably represented pouring a libation over the altar situated next to his right leg and thus in the office of a magistrate (Figure 26.5). The date of the two *togati* was previously postulated as being around the

FIGURE 26.5 *Togatus* statue. Damascus, National Museum, inv. no. C 4024/8813.

Photograph by Dagmara Wielgosz-Rondolino.

beginning of the third century (Colledge 1976, 91–92). From the Severan period there are female statues of the Large Herculaneum Woman (NMD inv. no. C4021/8810) and *Pudicitia* (NMD inv. no. C4022/8811). Both were carved in Prokonnesian marble and were rendered in a simple schematic manner. The Small Herculaneum Woman (NMD inv. no. C4023/8812), the fifth sculpture from the Senate, displays completely different style, material, and carving technique. Executed in dolomitic marble from Thasos, it exhibits fairly good workmanship. For the five sculptures discussed above, Jean-Charles Balty postulated a common function as an official statuary group depicting Septimius Odainathos's and the Severan families (Balty 2005, 321–339, *contra* Wielgosz 2010, 80–81). Two other sculptures found not far from the Senate may have completed the presumed statuary group. The first, discovered south-west of the north-west entrance to the agora (NMD inv. no. C4020/8809, Ingholt 1936, 124–125), is a replica of the Herculaneum Woman from the Senate; both statues must, without any doubt, have been carved by the same artist. The stylistic elements advocate for the Antonine period as the date of their execution (for the middle Hadrianic period: Kruse 1975, 143), but the heads may have been rearranged in later periods. The second, discovered in 1940 in the agora and today known only from photographs from the Institut français du Proche-Orient (Ifpo), is the head of a mature, bearded man wearing an imposing headdress (a tiara?) only partially preserved. The head was comprehensively discussed by Jean-Charles Balty, who suggested that it might be a portrait of Odainathos, king of kings (Balty 2005, 333, n. 39–45, 50; Gawlikowski 2016, 126–134). A skilfully carved, female portrait-head of a veiled, mature woman (MND inv. no. C4026/8815) also comes from the agora in Palmyra. This beautiful piece of sculpture was made of Parian marble, most probably in the second quarter of the third century AD. Yet one public marble statue came from the sanctuary of Nabu (AMP inv. no. B39/64; Bounni et al. 2004, no. 36). The figure, probably executed late in the second century AD, wears typical Greek civic costume: a himation over a chiton, and sandals. The roughly carved cylindrical statue support in the form of a *modius*, the typical headgear characteristic of Palmyrene priests, is placed by the right foot and is adorned with a laurel wreath and a cabochon (Wielgosz 2010, 79–80). The base carries the Greek inscription ΗΒΟΚΑΤΩΝ (*IGLS* XVII.1, 176). This word is the genitive plural of ἠβοκᾶτος, a Greek equivalent of the Latin term *evocatus*, which denoted a soldier who, having served his time in the army and obtained a discharge (*missio*), was redrafted as a volunteer. Finally, a male public figure that depicted an individual in chiton and himation came from the sanctuary of Baalshamin (Dunant and Stucky 2000, 119, no. 154, pl. 32). Unfortunately, a reliable assessment of the statue is made problematic by the poor condition of the piece.

Regardless, the identity of the persons represented is purely speculative (Ingholt 1936, 124–125; Colledge 1976, 91). Although the male statues may represent residents of Palmyra, the ones of women pose a bigger problem. The female statuary types presented above were widely assumed to depict ladies of the local elite in the Graeco-Roman cities. Since public female statues were rather exceptional in Palmyra, it is possible that the marble statues may instead have represented women of the imperial family. The epigraphic evidence suggests honorific statues dedicated to the female members of at least two *domus Augustae* (*IGLS* XVII.1, 422–424). A significant number of dedications were connected to the Severan family. Among them, two, in Greek and Aramaic, refer to the imperial statuary groups. Both inscriptions were engraved on door lintels (*IGLS* XVII.1, 157; *IGLS* XVII.1, 191, also *IGLS* XVII.1, 192). Other dedications associated with the Severan family were issued by the members of the Cohors I Flavia Chalcidenorum equitata sagittariorum (*IGLS* XVII.1, 118–119, 168). Another honorific inscription, unfortunately preserved only partially, refers to Marcia Otacilia Severa (*IGLS* XVII.1, 170). The only sculpture that may possibly be associated with this empress is a portrait-head (MND inv. no. C4026/8815) previously interpreted as Iulia Cornelia Paula (wife of Elagabalus), based on numismatic parallels (e.g., Equini Schneider 1992, 141), although the portrait represents an elderly woman rather than a young one.

Last, one should also mention a life-size *capite velato* portrait, made of Thasian dolomitic marble (MND inv. no. C43). The head very probably belonged to a draped public statue from the Antonine period. However, the idealized and regular facial features do not suggest any association with any particular female member of the imperial family. It cannot be excluded that the woman portrayed belonged to one of the leading local families, although, as stressed above, female honorific statues are rather exceptional in Palmyra.

When approaching the marble sculptures displayed in cities of the Graeco-Roman Near East that lacked marble quarries, an essential question is whether they were imported or produced locally. Generally speaking, marble was imported to Palmyra both as a raw material and as finished or half-finished sculptures (Wielgosz 2010, 85–86). However, the answer should always take into account the historical period, the terms of the commission (public or private), the market conditions, and the financial means of the sponsor.

Conclusion

The evidence summarized in this chapter raises one fundamental question: What was the impact of public statues on Palmyrene sculpture? Well attested by inscriptions, official imperial statuary would certainly have been a good medium for transmitting Graeco-Roman models to the private sphere of Palmyrene art. In modern scholarship, the influence of the official statuary group of Drusus, Tiberius, and Germanicus on early Palmyrene funerary portraits has already been postulated (Sadurska 1988, 79–82). Moreover, on a number of funerary busts of male Palmyrenes one may observe the features of the official Roman portraiture of Hadrianic, Antonine, and later Severan times. Apparently, official Roman trends affected Palmyrene females less: among hundreds, only a few feature female hairstyles reminiscent of those in vogue in the major cities of the Roman Empire.

Additionally, adapted from the public statues displayed in Palmyra, the models were probably replicated in a funerary context, both as free-standing sculpture and on sarcophagi (Tanabe 1986, 440–443, 452–453; Schmidt-Colinet et al. 1992, 140, R1–R2, plate 56a–f; Sadurska and Bounni 1994, nos. 186–187, 235; Wielgosz 2004, 942, 947, fig. 12f; Wielgosz-Rondolino 2016b, 78–80, figs. 17a, 18–20), and in architecture (Wielgosz-Rondolino 2016a, 171–174; Tanabe 1986, no. 474). They represented male figures in himation and chiton, in togas, or finally in local garments and female figures in chiton and himation, sometimes following Ceres and *Pudicitia* statuary types. On the basis of hundreds of figural and architectural sculptures we may suggest that, in a single workshop, funereal, religious, and honorific sculptures and architectural details were produced side by side and thus replicated the same figurative and/or symbolic models in various artistic media. This seems to me to have been one of the fundamental features of Palmyrene art.

Abbreviations

CIS	Chabot, Jean-Baptiste, ed. 1926–1947. *Corpus inscriptionum semiticarum*. Part 2, vol. 3, *Inscriptiones palmyrenae*. Paris: Typographeo Reipublicae.
IGLS XVII.1	Yon, Jean-Baptiste, ed. 2012. *Inscriptions grecques et latines de la Syrie: Palmyre*. Bibliothèque archéologique et historique 195. Beirut: Institut français du Proche-Orient.
PAT	Hillers, Delbert E. and Eleonora Cussini, eds. 1996. *Palmyrene Aramaic Texts*. Baltimore: Johns Hopkins University Press.

Bibliography

al-Asʿad, Khaled, and Michał Gawlikowski. 1986–1987. 'New Honorific Inscriptions in the Great Colonnade of Palmyra'. *Annales archéologiques arabes syriennes* 36–37: 164–171.

Balty, Jean-Charles. 2005. 'La sculpture'. In *L'agora de Palmyre*, edited by Christiane Delplace and Jacqueline Dentzer-Feydy, 321–341. Mémoires 14. Bordeaux: Ausonius.

Bounni, Adnan, Jacques Seigne, and Nassib Saliby. 2004. *Le Sanctuaire de Nabū à Palmyre*. Institut français du Proche-Orient. Bibliothèque archéologique et historique 131. Beirut: Geuthner.

Clairmont, Christoph W. 1993. *Classical Attic Tombstones*. Kilchberg: Akanthus.

Colledge, Malcolm A. R. 1976. *The Art of Palmyra*. London: Thames & Hudson.

Cussini, Eleonora. 1995. 'Transfer of Property at Palmyra'. *ARAM* 7: 233–250.

Cussini, Eleonora. 2005. 'Beyond the Spindle: Investigating the Role of Palmyrene Women'. In *A Journey to Palmyra: Collected Essays to Remember Delbert R. Hiller*, edited by Eleonora Cussini, 26–43. Culture and History of the Ancient Near East 22. Leiden: Brill.

Cussini, Eleonora. 2016. 'Reconstructing Palmyrene Legal Language'. In *The World of Palmyra*, edited by Andreas Kropp and Rubina Raja, 42–52. Scientia Danica. Series H, Humanistica, 4, vol. 6. Palmyrene Studies 1. Copenhagen: Det Kongelige Danske Videnskabernes Selskab.

Daehner, Jens, ed. 2008. *The Herculaneum Women: History, Context, Identities*. Los Angeles: J. Paul Getty Museum.

Dijkstra, Klaas. 1995. *Life and Loyalty: A Study in the Socio-Religious Culture of Syria and Mesopotamia in the Graeco-Roman Period Based on Epigraphical Evidence*. Religions in the Graeco-Roman World 128. Leiden: Brill.

Dunant, Christiane. 1971. *Le Sanctuaire de Baalshamîn à Palmyre*. Vol. 3, *Les inscriptions*. Bibliotheca Helvetica Romana, vol. 10, no. 3. Rome: Institute suisse de Rome.

Dunant, Christiane, and Rolf Andreas Stucky. 2000. *Le Sanctuaire de Baalshamîn à Palmyre*. Vol. 4, *Sculptures*. Bibliotheca Helvetica Romana, vol. 10, no. 4. Rome: Institute suisse de Rome.

Equini-Schneider, Eugenia. 1992. 'Scultura e ritrattistica onoraria a Palmira. Qualche ipotesi'. *Archeologia classica* 44: 111–145.

Gawlikowski, Michał. 1994. 'Palmyra as a Trading Centre'. *Iraq* 56: 27–33.

Gawlikowski, Michał. 1996. 'Palmyra and Its Caravan Trade'. *Annales archéologiques arabes syriennes* 42: 139–145.

Gawlikowski, Michał. 2008. 'The Statues of the Sanctuary of Allat in Palmyra'. In *The Sculptural Environment of the Roman Near East: Reflections on Culture, Ideology, and Power*, edited by Yaron Z. Eliav, Elise A. Friedland, and Sharon Herbert, 397–411. Interdisciplinary Studies in Ancient Culture and Religion 9. Leuven: Peeters.

Gawlikowski, Michał. 2016. 'The Portraits of the Palmyrene Royalty'. In *The World of Palmyra*, edited by Andreas Kropp and Rubina Raja, 126–134. Scientia Danica. Series H, Humanistica, 4, vol. 6. Palmyrene Studies 1. Copenhagen: Det Kongelige Danske Videnskabernes Selskab.

Gawlikowski, Michał. 2017. *Le sanctuaire d'Allat à Palmyre*. PAM Monograph Series 8. Warsaw: Uniwersytet Warszawski.

Goette, Hans Rupprecht. 1990. *Studien zu römischen Togadarstellungen*. Beiträge zur Erschliessung hellenistischer und kaiserzeitlicher Skulptur und Architektur 10. Mainz am Rhein: von Zabern.

Ingholt, Harald. 1936. 'Inscriptions and Sculptures from Palmyra I'. *Berytus* 3: 83–128.

Ingholt, Harald. 1976. 'Varia Tadmorea'. In *Palmyre: Bilan et perspectives; Colloque de Strasbourg 18–20 octobre 1973*, edited by Edmond Frézouls, 101–137. Strasbourg: Association pour l'étude de la civilisation romaine.

Kruse, Hans J. 1975. 'Römische weibliche Gewandstatuen des zweiten Jahrhunderts n. Chr'. Unpublished doctoral thesis, the University of Göttingen.

Matthews, John F. 1984. 'The Tax Law of Palmyra: Evidence for Economic History in a City of the Roman East'. *Journal of Roman Studies* 74: 157–180.

Mattusch, Carol C. 2006. 'Archaic and Classical Bronzes'. In *Greek Sculpture: Function, Materials, and Techniques in the Archaic and Classical Periods*, edited by Olga Palagia, 208–242. Cambridge: Cambridge University Press.

Meyer, Marion. 1989. 'Alte Männer auf attischen Grabstelen'. *Mitteilungen des Deutschen Archäologischen Instituts: Athenische Abteilung* 104: 49–82.

Parlasca, Klaus. 1985. 'Das Verhältnis der palmyrenischen Grabplastik zur römischen Portätkunst'. *Mitteilungen des Deutschen Archäologischen Instituts: Römische Abteilung* 29: 343–356.

Parlasca, Klaus. 1989. 'Palmyrenische Bildnisse aus dem Umkreis Zenobias'. In *Festschrift Robert Werner zu seinem 65. Geburtstag dargebracht von Freunden, Kollegen und Schülern*, edited by Werner Dahlheim, Wolfgang Schuller, and Jürgen von Ungern-Sternberg, 205–209. Xenia 22. Konstanz: Universitätsverlag Konstanz.

Ploug, Gunhild. 1995. *Catalogue of the Palmyrene Sculptures: Ny Carlsberg Glyptotek*. Copenhagen: Ny Carlsberg Glyptotek.

Sadurska, Anna. 1988. 'Le portrait officiel romain et la diffusion du portrait funéraire dans les provinces orientale'. In *Ritratto Ufficiale e Ritratto Privato: Atti della II Conferenza internationale sul Ritratto Romano, Roma 26–30, settembre 1984*, edited by Nicola Bonacasa and Giovanni Rizza, 75–86. Rome: Consiglio nazionale ricerche.

Sadurska, Anna, and Adnan Bounni. 1994. *Les sculptures funéraires de Palmyre*. Rivista di archeologia. Supplementi 13. Rome: Giorgio Bretschneider.

Schmidt-Colinet, Andreas, Khaled al-Asʿad, and Carla Müting-Zimmer. 1992. *Das Tempelgrab Nr. 36 in Palmyra. Studien zur palmyrenischen Grabarchitektur und ihrer Ausstattung*. Damaszener Forschungen 4. Mainz am Rhein: Philipp von Zabern.

Schmidt-Colinet, Andreas. 2017. 'Die antiken Steinbrüche von Palmyra. Ein Vorbericht'. *Mitteilungen der Deutschen Orient-Gesellschaft zu Berlin* 149: 159–196.

Schmidt-Colinet, Andreas. 2020. 'A Method to Date Stones, Just Stones: The Quarries of Palmyra'. In *Methods and Models in Ancient History: Essays in Honor of Jørgen Christian Meyer*, edited by Ingvar B. Mæhle, Per Bjarne Ravnå, and Eivind Heldaas Seland, 53–64. Athens: The Norwegian Institute at Athens.

Seyrig, Henri. 1950. 'Palmyra and the East'. *Journal of Roman Studies* 40: 1–7.

Shifman, Ilia S. 2014. *The Palmyrene Tax Tariff*. Journal of Semitic Studies Supplement 33. Oxford: Oxford University Press (English translation by Svetlana Khobnya *of Пальмирский пошлинный тариф*, Moscow 1980, edited by John F. Healey).

Tanabe, Katsumi. 1986. *Sculpture of Palmyra*. Vol. 1. Memoirs of the Ancient Orient Museum 1. Tokyo: Ancient Orient Museum.

Trimble, Jennifer. 2011. *Women and Visual Replication in Roman Imperial Art and Culture*. Cambridge: Cambridge University Press.

Wielgosz, Dagmara. 2004. 'Osservazioni sul sarcofago palmireno'. In *Studi di archeologia in onore di Gustavo Traversari*, edited by Manuela Fano Santi, 929–962. Roma: Giorgio Bretschneider.

Wielgosz, Dagmara. 2010. 'La sculpture en marbre à Palmyre'. *Studia Palmyreńskie* 11: 75–106.

Wielgosz, Dagmara. 2013. '*Coepimus et lapide pingere*: Marble Decoration from the So-Called Baths of Diocletian in Palmyra'. In *Fifty Years of Polish Excavations in Palmyra 1959–2009, International Conference, Warsaw, 6–8 December 2010*, edited by Michał Gawlikowski and Grzegorz Majcherek, 319–332. *Studia Palmyreńskie* 12. Warsaw: Wydawnictwa Uniwersytetu Warszawskiego.

Wielgosz-Rondolino, Dagmara. 2016a. 'Palmyrene Portraits from the Temple of Allat. New Evidence on Artists and Workshops'. In *The World of Palmyra*, edited by Andreas Kropp and Rubina Raja, 166–179. Scientia Danica. Series H, Humanistica, 4, vol. 6. Palmyrene Studies 1. Copenhagen: Det Kongelige Danske Videnskabernes Selskab.

Wielgosz-Rondolino, Dagmara. 2016b. 'Orient et Occident unis par enchantement dans la pierre sculptée. La sculpture figurative de Palmyre'. In *La Syrie et le désastre archéologique du Proche-Orient: "Palmyre cité martyre"*, edited by Michel al-Maqdissi and Eva Ishaq, 65–82. Beirut: Beiteddine Art Festival.

Wielgosz-Rondolino, Dagmara. 2023. 'Palmyra/Tadmor/Hadriana Palmyra'. In *Sculptures from Roman Syria II. The Greek, Roman and Byzantine Marble Statuary*, edited by Mustafa Koçak and Detlev Kreikenbom, 502–562. Berlin: De Gruyter.

Will, Ernest. 1985. 'Pline l'Ancien et Palmyre. Un problème d'histoire littéraire?' *Syria* 62: 263–269.

Will, Ernest. 1992. *Les Palmyréniens: La Venise des sables, Ier siècle avant – IIIème siècle après J.C.* Paris: Armand Colin.

Yon, Jean-Baptiste. 2002. *Les notables de Palmyre*. Institut français du Proche-Orient. Bibliothèque archéologique et historique 163. Beirut: Institut français d'archéologie du Proche-Orient.

Zanker, Paul. 1997. *La maschera di Socrate: L'immagine dell' intellettuale nell'arte antica*. Torino: Einaudi.

CHAPTER 27

THE PALMYRENE FUNERARY SCULPTURE

RUBINA RAJA

PALMYRENE FUNERARY SCULPTURE AND RESEARCH HISTORY

PALMYRENE funerary sculpture has long been recognized as constituting a significant group of material culture giving insight into the funerary representational habits in both Palmyra and, by extension, the rest of classical world (Ingholt 1928; Colledge 1976; Bobou, Jensen et al. 2021; Raja 2019a). Due to its location at an oasis in the Syrian Desert and functioning as a trade route node which flourished in the first three centuries AD, Palmyra's society was in constant touch with numerous parts of the ancient world (see Chapters 16 [Schörle], 17 [Seland], 19 [Edwell], and 20 [Dirven], this volume). This integration into a wider cultural framework is heavily reflected in the art of the Roman-period city, while, on the other hand, strong local trends and traditions also clearly persisted.

Already in the second half of the nineteenth century the funerary sculpture began to find its way into European private collections and museums and a bit later into American collections and museums (Raja 2018, 2019c; Sartre-Fauriat 2019). Since the sculpture was relatively easy to transport or parts of it could easily be detached from their larger setting, it was the one group of material culture from the site which was already dispersed early and widely, and, due to the fact that so much had survived throughout the millennia, there was a lot which could be distributed by European collectors and their agents as well as occasional visitors. The portraits fascinated due to their distinct style, so far from the mainstream styles found within Graeco-Roman portraiture but still recognizable, and, after their discovery, they were soon used as comparanda to Greek and Roman-period portraiture, however, usually to underline the character of their provincial style and settings and usually not taking into consideration the entire span of Palmyrene society's cultural and social setting (Kropp and Raja 2014; Raja 2017b; Nielsen 2019; Raja 2019a). Since these portraits were rediscovered, they have been the topic of intense scholarly debates and publications. However, often these discourses have taken place on the basis of a fairly small number of portraits stemming from a corpus which everyone knew was in fact much larger, but one that no one had the opportunity or patience to collect (Parlasca 1982, 1985, 1995, 1998). One exception to this pattern was the Danish archaeologist Harald Ingholt, who, in his 1928 monograph, published 528 Palmyrene funerary portraits and thereafter kept up a personal archive to which he kept adding at least until the 1970s, at which point it amounted to more than a thousand objects (Ingholt 1928; Bobou et al. 2023).

The Corpus of the Funerary Portraits

Since 2012, the Palmyra Portrait Project (https://projects.au.dk/palmyraportrait/) has compiled a database that now holds 3,704 portraits, 329 tomb buildings, and 769 individual burials based on material in collections and publications (Raja et al. 2021; Romanowska et al. 2021; Raja 2021b). With such an immense amount of material new steps have recently been taken towards reintegrating this abundant material into its archaeological and historical contexts and re-evaluating its significance to our understanding of historical developments (Raja 2022a). However, despite the fact that the number of preserved portraits might seem staggering, we of course must not forget that, divided across roughly three hundred years, it only amounts to about twelve to fifteen per year left to us.

Each type of funerary sculptural object was entered into the database and thereafter divided up into a number of portraits. In the graves, objects could be either sarcophagi, banqueting reliefs, loculus reliefs, or wall paintings depicting deceased Palmyrenes, sometimes in the company of their family members, as well as a few partly preserved examples of free-standing sculpture. The sculptures have all been examined and assigned a stylistic dating, which is based on the development of carving techniques and stylistic features, and the collection also contains absolutely dated pieces, of which there are 156 objects (Raja 2021e). The 156 portraits which give us a date by inscription constitute an important, though small group since, despite being few and far between, they indicate what stylistic features, such as clothes, hairstyles, and attributes, were popular in the years in which they were produced (Krag and Raja 2016, 2017, 2018; Raja 2017a, 2017f, 2018; Krag 2018). Another 661 portraits are dated with a relatively high certainty because they stem from grave complexes that were in use for specific decades (Bobou and Raja 2023; forthcoming). The rest of the portraits are dated based on comparison with these 817 portraits (Bobou, Jensen et al. 2021; Colledge 1976; Raja et al. 2021; Raja 2021e).

A new study modelling the production intensity of the portraits held together with the development of the funerary structures shows intricate processes which, in numerous cases, relate to societal factors and known historical events (Bobou, Raja et al. 2021; Raja et al. 2021; Romanowska et al. 2021). Such developmental studies can be used

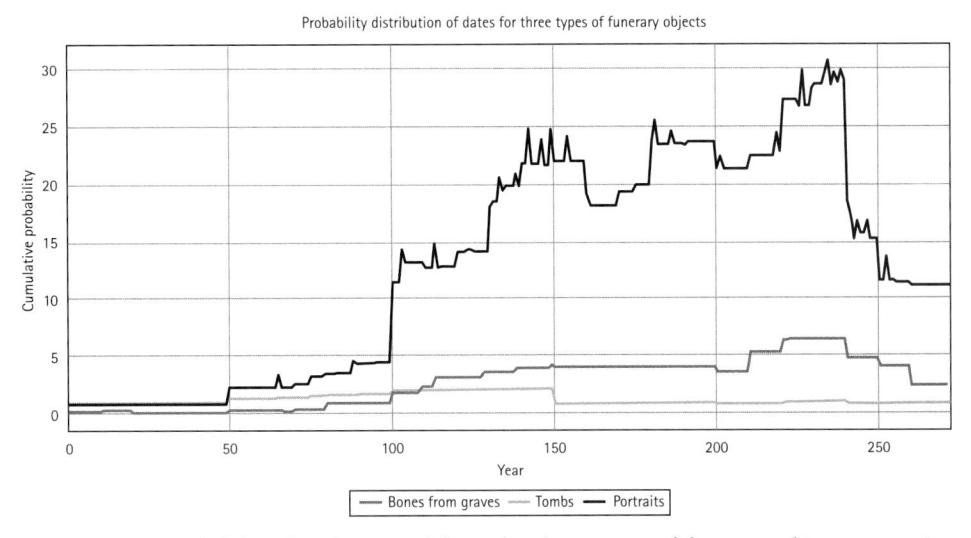

Probability distribution of dates for three types of funerary objects

FIGURE 27.1 Probability distribution of dates for three types of funerary objects: portraits, tombs, bones from graves.

© Raja et al. 2021, fig. 7.

to trace general trends in flows and fluctuations in the production of portraits. They may also in some cases give insight into overall patterns of death rates within the elite and upper middle classes for whom the sculpture was produced. But what they first and foremost show are general developments in terms of economic and societal trends, thus underlining that the archaeology of a site is the history of it to the same degree as written sources are. The modelling showed that production rose dramatically in the first and early second centuries AD, to reach a plateau in the middle of the second century AD. A dramatic drop beginning approximately AD 160 was detected, which continued until AD 175. A further plateau can be seen between AD 175 and 220 and another peak between AD 220 and 240. Last, a dramatic drop in the period AD 240–272 (Figure 27.1) is clear from the data (Raja et al. 2021; Romanowska et al. 2021).

It is noteworthy that both portrait and the burial curves follow this pattern, whereas the tomb data agree only until the mid-second century, after which the tomb numbers and capacity drop dramatically. When investigating the last pattern in more detail the study showed that the society was most likely saturated with burial capacity by the middle of the second century AD. The cession texts from the graves support this observation (Gawlikowski 1970; Cussini 1993, 1995, 2010; Henning 2013a, 2013b, 2019a).

TYPES OF FUNERARY SCULPTURE

The funerary portrait habit in Palmyra seems to have been introduced around the beginning of the first century AD. It drew on earlier Hellenistic sculptural traditions in the region, which were revived in numerous places in the Near East with the growing intensity of Roman rule, which created a more stable environment in the wake of many decades of political and military instability (Blömer and Raja 2019; Raja 2019a, 2019d). The production of the funerary sculpture cannot be traced further than to the time of the last sack of the city in AD 273 (Ingholt 1928; Bobou, Raja et al. 2021). The funerary sculptures therefore provide a terminus post quem and a terminus ante quem, which is an entirely unique situation when considering the amount of sculpture left for us to study and this despite the fact, as mentioned above, that, divided over three hundred years, the material is not overwhelming although still much better than that from other places.

There are several types of Palmyrene funerary sculpture (Ingholt 1928; Colledge 1976; Raja 2015). Palmyrene funerary reliefs, commonly referred to as *Palmyrene portraits*, are depictions of the deceased on locally carved limestone slabs; these were located in front of the burial shelves, the *loculi*. These were predominantly representations which showed the individual down to about the navel level and more rarely in full figure, and they could depict one or multiple individuals. The stelai usually show full-figure representations. In the later second century AD, limestone sarcophagi were introduced, on the lids of which family dining scenes (banquets) were depicted and on the boxes further portraits could be carved, usually in bust format (Bobou and Raja forthcoming).

The most common type is the *loculus relief*, which was a rectangular limestone slab upon which one or more portraits were carved in high relief (Figure 27.2). Of these 1,409 are known: 1,114 are loculus reliefs with single portrait busts on them, and 162 carry multiple representations. Within the group of multiple representations there are 137 double loculus reliefs, twenty-one triple, three quadruple, and one loculus relief showing five individuals. Another group is the *stele motif*, also a rectangular limestone slab on which full-figure, usually under life-size, representations of individuals were carved in high relief (Figure 27.3). Banqueting reliefs that showed dining scenes from the lifetime of the deceased person (Figure 27.4) and which are not to be confused with the burial banquet constitute a third type (Audley-Miller 2016; Krag and Raja 2016, 2017; Raja 2019d; Raja et al. 2021). All these types of reliefs were used to cover burial niches in Palmyrene tower tombs and underground graves, as well as in temple or house tombs (Gawlikowski 1970; Sadurska and Bounni 1994; Henning 2013a, 2013b; Raja 2019d, 2022a, 57–86).

The earliest funerary portrait representations, as far as we know, appear on stelai as full-figure representations (Seyrig 1936). However, with the introduction of funerary buildings, of which the tower tombs were the earliest, this habit shifted and the loculus reliefs were introduced, of which the earliest inscribed example dates to AD 65/66 (Raja 2019c, 66–67, cat. no. 1). Most of the stelai and banqueting reliefs are not *in situ* and are today located in collections outside of Syria. A total of 157 stelai and ninety-nine banqueting reliefs are currently in the Palmyra Portrait Project's database. The stelai chronologically span all three centuries of production, with the majority dating to the first and second centuries AD. Most banqueting reliefs are dated to the second and third centuries AD. Sometimes elaborate versions of banqueting reliefs were also set up on the facade of tower tombs as founder reliefs or in prominent niches in the graves (Henning 2013a, 2013b). These reliefs

FIGURE 27.2 Loculus relief with a male and a female. Copenhagen, Ny Carlsberg Glyptotek, I.N. 1028.

© Courtesy of Ny Carlsberg Glyptotek, photograph by Anders Sune Berg.

underlined the importance of the owner of the tomb and his high societal standing but were not associated directly with any burial (Henning 2019a, 2019b). Rather, these simply underlined that the tomb was founded and paid for by a *pater familias* who then was depicted on its exterior, which could also have happened during his lifetime. In particular, the tower tombs, which were so visible in the landscape of Palmyra, would have been status markers for rich families (see Chapter 24 [Henning], this volume).

In the later second century AD, locally produced limestone sarcophagi, large burial boxes often with elaborate relief lids, were introduced in Palmyra (Figure 27.5). More than six hundred of these still exist, most of them in fragmented shapes (Bobou and Raja 2023; Schmidt-Colinet 2007; Schmidt-Colinet and As'ad 2007). These were set up in underground graves and temple or house tombs (Bobou and Raja 2023). The sarcophagi could carry lavish banqueting scenes on their lids, with many individuals shown together, and several portraits were depicted on the boxes (Krag and Raja 2017; Schmidt-Colinet 2007). The sarcophagi commemorated entire families by depicting banquet scenes and could hold numerous burials.

FIGURE 27.3   Stele with a standing boy. Copenhagen, Ny Carlsberg Glyptotek, I.N. 1147.

© Courtesy of Ny Carlsberg Glyptotek, photograph by Palmyra Portrait Project.

CHRONOLOGY AND STYLE

The funerary portraits were produced in local limestone quarries around the city (see Chapter 36 [Schmidt-Colinet], this volume). They were produced over approximately three hundred years, from about the beginning of the Common Era until the sack of the

FIGURE 27.4 Banquet relief depicting a family of four. New York, Metropolitan Museum of Art, inv. no. 02.29.1.

© Metropolitan Museum of Art, Purchase, 1902.

city in AD 273 by Roman troops during the reign of the Emperor Aurelian. The vast majority of the known portraits are today ex situ (Raja 2021e). The earliest dated sculptural object from Palmyra is a votive relief on which an inscription gives the date AD 21/22 (Palmyra Museum, Palmyra, Syria; Gawlikowski 2017, 245–246, cat. no. 15). The earliest dated foundation relief comes from a tower tomb and dates to AD 40 (tower tomb no. 44, Tower of Kithot, Palmyra, Syria). The earliest dated loculus relief dates to AD 66 (Ny Carlsberg Glyptotek, Copenhagen, Denmark, IN 2816; Raja 2019c, 66–67, cat. no. 1).

Despite the fact that most are today ex situ, the more than 3,700 portraits make up a statistically solid group datable, on the one hand, by fixed points given by objects carrying inscriptions (Raja 2021e, table 1) and, on the other hand, by stylistic dating (Raja 2021e, tables 2–4). There are 101 objects with reference to individuals whose year of death is specified through the accompanying inscriptions (Raja 2021e, table 1). The remaining portraits are dated on stylistic grounds (Raja 2021e, tables 2–4; Ingholt 1928; Colledge 1976). The stylistic dating of these portraits has been done through a number of criteria pertaining to the development of dress styles, jewellery styles and combinations, distribution and types of attributes, hairstyles, etc. (Krag 2018; Steding 2022; Raja 2015, 2017b, 2019a). Furthermore, a number of attributes and sets of features also appear to cluster in

FIGURE 27.5 Sarcophagus box and lid. The box shows four busts of priest and the bust of a woman. The lid depicts a reclining man, a reclining woman, and a seated woman at the foot-end.

© Rubina Raja and Palmyra Portrait Project.

certain chronological periods (Heyn and Raja 2021; 2023), as do certain types of iconographic motifs, such as the so-called former priests, the Faustina hairstyle, certain types of brooches, or bilingual inscriptions (Krag and Raja 2016, 2017, 2018; Raja 2017b, 2017d, 2018; Cussini 2019; Raja and Yon forthcoming). These attributes, which often also are related to specific techniques for carving eyes, hairstyles, beards, textiles, jewellery, and other attributes, allow for a closer relative dating of the portraits with a point of departure in the large corpus and make it possible to place them within specific groups (Raja 2021e; Raja and Steding 2021; Steding 2022).

THE INDIVIDUALS REPRESENTED IN THE FUNERARY SCULPTURE

Palmyrene men, women, and children were represented in the funerary sculpture (Heyn 2012; Krag and Raja 2016, 2017; Ringsborg 2017; Krag 2018; Heyn 2019; Heyn and Raja 2019; Krag 2019; Krag and Raja 2019a; 2019b). In a few cases, foreigners were depicted as well. Usually these were in one way or another connected to the Roman military and could be either men who had moved to Palmyra with the army and who held high positions or women who had married a man with military connections (Raja and Yon forthcoming). The portraits divide as follows: 1,643 male portraits, 481 portraits of priests, 1,205 of women, and 216 of children. Furthermore, 151 portraits are fragmented to a state at which it is not possible to make out the gender of the original representation. The gender division stayed fairly consistent over time, with an approximate 70:30 male–female ratio. Children were also represented, but most often together with deceased parents (Krag and Raja 2018, 2019a; 2019b). The representations of Palmyrene priests have been split out into their own group since they make up such a large group of male representations. Their consistent iconography underlines the conservative status symbol that it was to hold a priesthood in Palmyra, a status which, much more than an actual office, was an elite societal position, with priesthoods being passed on and extended within families, from fathers to sons and potentially also from grandfathers to grandsons or uncles to nephews (Stucky 1973; Raja 2016, 2017c, 2017e, 2017f, 2017g, 2017h, 2019b, 2021a, 2021c, 2021d). The structure of Palmyrene priesthood pertained to Palmyra's societal structure, which was tribal-based (Kaizer 2002).

While it is perhaps not surprising that fewer females are represented in the funerary sculpture than males, it is still a crucial observation that they constitute just above 30 percent of the body of material. Elite women in Palmyra were continuously represented in the funerary sphere, just like their male counterparts, and not only as wives and mothers, but also in individual constellations on the single loculus reliefs. Although their representations were, like the male representations, always embedded in family settings (whether we can disentangle them today or not), the fact is that women were not just attributes to male representations.

The male representations, including dress codes and hairstyles, continuously kept to a more conservative style than the female portraiture (Heyn 2008; Raja 2017d, 2017g, 2021a, 2022b; Heyn and Raja 2019). However, for example, hairstyles do show Roman imperial and Parthian influences, and, through these broader trends circulating in the Roman and Parthian Empires and beyond can be traced (Albertson 2016; Krag 2018; Krag and Raja 2018). Children were represented in their own right in a number of cases (42 examples) (Krag and Raja 2016, 2017, 2019). However, most often children were depicted together with one deceased parent, which underlined the importance of showing societal status through reproduction and the continuation of the family beyond parental generations (169 examples). In terms of language used in the funerary contexts, the Palmyrene Aramaic script was used almost exclusively, despite the fact that Palmyra displays more bilingual inscriptions than any other city in the Roman Near East in its public sphere (Yon 2002). Out of a total 1,189 funerary inscriptions, only twelve are in Greek and five in Latin (Raja and Yon forthcoming). Palmyrene Aramaic consistently stayed the dominating language in the funerary sphere throughout the three centuries that the funerary sculptural tradition was in place and underlines the focus on the elite's strong local traditions. The Greek and Latin inscriptions in the funerary sphere appeared almost exclusively in the later second century AD, hinting at the fact that this was a time of renewed influence from the Roman world; these inscriptions often were connected to people who had moved to Palmyra from outside the city in connection with the mobility of the Roman army.

While Palmyrene funerary sculpture usually stands out as colourless to us today, we do have some examples which still carry colour traces, thus giving some insight into the fact that these white limestone figures were at least partly polychrome in Antiquity and painted in bright colours, with inlays of glass paste and potentially even semi-precious stones used to imitate jewellery stones (Blume 2021; Brøns et al. 2022). Eyes also could be inlaid in black stone or glass paste.

CONTEXTUALIZATION OF THE FUNERARY SCULPTURE INTO THE WIDER REALM OF PALMYRENE ARCHAEOLOGY AND HISTORY

In Palmyra, several hundred tomb buildings existed (see Chapter 24 [Henning], this volume). The three main types were tower tombs, underground tombs (hypogea), and the somewhat smaller but still monumental house or temple tombs. These were re-served for the elite and were usually founded by and paid for by a *pater familias*. They were maintained by following generations, and sometimes the foundations are dated by inscriptions, thus giving further fixed points to our chronology (see above). Legal texts inscribed on some of the graves inform us that parts of graves could be sold off to other families (Cussini 2010). Written evidence also tells us that older burials could to be taken out of the tombs and that new ones could be installed in their place, which would have made the tombs dynamic spaces. Other groups of inhabitants would have been buried in more insignificant graves, such as single-shaft graves without any sort of lavish embellishments. The funerary monuments give insight into Palmyrene burial traditions and rituals; the Palmyrenes practised inhumation (de Jong 2017, 111; Higuchi and Saito 2001; Saito 2005a, 2005b). Bodies were wrapped in textiles, perfumed and oiled, and placed on burial shelves in niches and sarcophagi. Cremations seem to have been exceedingly rare, and only two examples are known (Amy and Seyrig 1936, esp. 256; Al-Hariri 2013, esp. 151). Another practice rarely found in Palmyra is that of mummifi-cation, which is only known in two cases (de Jong 2017, 111 with further bibliography). So, it was as covering plates for these inhumations that the representations should be seen or, in the case of the banqueting reliefs and sarcophagi scenes, as commemorative monuments showing the deceased person with family members in scenes set in life be-fore death. The funerary sculpture and portraits from Palmyra display a strong conti-nuity in local cultural and societal traditions, underlining the Palmyrene identity, which was based on strong family ties with a *pater familias* heading the wider family groups. The Palmyrene funerary sculpture and portraits were entirely adapted to the local burial custom, namely to be used as commemorative monuments in the monumental grave buildings, although they also draw on artistic influences both from East and West, the Parthian and Roman cultural realms (Raja 2017b). The basic portrait style and the scheme of depicting the longer than bust-sized representations of individuals and the full figures on the later sarcophagi lids stayed fairly consistent across all three centuries of production.

The persistence of the portrait habit in Palmyra across approximately three hundred years allows us to study the fluctuations in their production, and recently it has been shown that they can be studied as expressions of economic and societal developments (Bobou, Raja et al. 2021; Raja et al. 2021; Romanowska et al. 2021). This has moved the importance of these objects from being exclusively of archaeological and art historical value to being studied as proxies for historical events and processes that might have implications for other studies of archaeological material in the future. The important overall conclusion drawn from the modelling of these funerary sculptural material, graves, and burial evidence is that the fast rise in the production of sculpture reflects an upswing in the economy, which would have been a result of political and military stability in the region in the wake of the Roman take-over of the region after the invasion of Pompey the Great in the 60s BC. In general, such a stabilizing period is observed throughout the region, where urban development began to flourish, in particular from the later first century AD onwards. It is also in this period that we can trace a rapid growth of Palmyrene society, along with all the parameters that would follow with such growth, such as labour specialization, societal expansion, and stronger hierarchies. Palmyra flourished in the middle of the second century AD, and this is traceable in sculptural production as well. However, crises such as the pandemic around AD 160—the Antonine Plague—can also be traced in portrait production. Production dropped dramatically from AD 160 until approximately AD 175, but recovered fairly quickly, and, by about AD 175, production reached a new high level which lasted for more than a generation and then increased again in the early third century, a time during which we know that Palmyra was politically, militarily, and trade-wise a strong player in the Roman East. Around AD 240, there was a significant drop in production of the portraits, indicating a drop in resources dedicated to the funerary sphere. Most likely the Parthian invasion of Dura-Europos in AD 239, a border town east of Palmyra, and a second invasion in AD 240 of Hatra further east, would have been significant for Palmyra and might have meant that the city had to mobilize its army and increase its size, which all would have been financed and led by the city's male elite. After this, the production of funerary sculpture never recovered, and, as stated above, after the second sack of the city by the Roman army in AD 273, no funerary portraits can be traced. This does not mean that the city did not live on, but its splendid funerary sculptural tradition seems to have died out and numerous loculus reliefs have been found in secondary use in the post-sack monuments, such as the military camp, which also incorporated tower tombs into its walls for example. The funerary portrait habit was one closely connected to the Palmyrene upper classes, and, with the dissolution of this layer, which made up the core of Palmyrene society, it disappeared entirely.

ACKNOWLEDGEMENTS

The author acknowledges the funding received by the Danish National Research Foundation's Centre for Urban Network Evolutions (grant no. 119) as well as the funding received from the Carlsberg Foundation for the various Palmyra projects based at Aarhus University, first and foremost the Palmyra Portrait Project. Furthermore, I thank the ALIPH Foundation as well as the Augustinus Foundation for funding for further Palmyra-related projects.

BIBLIOGRAPHY

Albertson, Fred. 2016. 'Typology, Attribution, and Identity in Palmyran Funerary Portraiture'. In *The World of Palmyra*, edited by Andreas Kropp and Rubina Raja, 150–165. Copenhagen: Royal Danish Academy of Sciences and Letters.

Al-Hariri, Khalil. 2013. 'The Tomb of 'Aqraban'. *Studia Palmyrenskie* 12: 149–157.

Amy, Robert, and Henri Seyrig. 1936. 'Recherches dans la nécropole de Palmyre'. *Syria: Archéologie, art et histoire* 17: 229–266.

Audley-Miller, Lucy. 2016. 'The Banquet in Palmyrene Funerary Contexts'. In *Dining and Death: Interdisciplinary Perspectives on the "Funerary Banquet" in Ancient Art, Burial and Belief*, edited by Catherine M. Draycott and Maria Stamatopoulou, 553–590. Leuven: Peeters.

Blömer, Michael, and Rubina Raja. 2019. 'Shifting the Paradigms: Towards a New Agenda in the Study of the Funerary Portraiture of Greater Roman Syria'. In *Funerary Portraiture in Greater Roman Syria*, edited by Michael Blömer and Rubina Raja, 5–26. Turnhout: Brepols.

Blume, Clarissa. 2021. 'The Polychromy of Palmyrene Portraits: Workmen and Colouration'. In *Production Economy in Greater Roman Syria: Trade Networks and Production Processes*, edited by Julia Steding and Rubina Raja, 33–48. Turnhout: Brepols.

Bobou, Olympia, and Rubina Raja. 2023. *Palmyrene Sarcophagi*. Studies in Palmyrene Archaeology and History 10. Turnhout: Brepols.

Bobou, Olympia, and Rubina Raja. Forthcoming. *Palmyrene Funerary Portraits in Context: The In-Situ Situations from the Palmyrene Graves*. Turnhout: Brepols.

Bobou, Olympia, Jesper V. Jensen, Nathalia B. Kristensen, Rubina Raja, and Rikke Randeris Thomsen. 2021. *Studies on Palmyrene Sculpture: A Translation of Harald Ingholt's Studier over Palmyrensk Skulptur, Edited and with Commentary*. Studies in Palmyrene Archaeology and History 1. Turnhout: Brepols.

Bobou, Olympia, Rubina Raja, and Iza Romanowska. 2021. 'Historical Trajectories of Palmyra's Elites Through the Lens of Archaeological Data'. *Journal of Urban Archaeology* 4: 153–166.

Bobou, Olympia, Amy C. Miranda, Rubina Raja, and Jean-Baptiste Yon. 2023. *The Ingholt Archive: The Palmyrene Material, Transcribed with Commentary and Bibliography*. Archive Archaeology. 4 vols. Turnhout: Brepols.

Brøns, Cecilie, Jens Stenger, Jørn Bredal-Jørgensen, Fabiana Di Gianvincenzo, and Luise Ø. Brandt. 2022. 'Palmyrene Polychromy: Investigations of Funerary Portraits from Palmyra in the Collections of the Ny Carlsberg Glyptotek, Copenhagen'. *Heritage* 5: 1199–1239. https://doi.org/10.3390/heritage5020063.

Colledge, M. A. R. 1976. *The Art of Palmyra*. London: Thames & Hudson.

Cussini, Eleonora. 1993. 'The Aramaic Law of Sale and the Cuneiform Legal Tradition'. Unpublished doctoral thesis, Johns Hopkins University.

Cussini, Eleonora. 1995. 'Transfer of Property at Palmyra, in Palmyra and the Aramaeans'. *ARAM Periodical* 7: 233–250.

Cussini, Eleonora. 2010. 'Legal Formulary from Syriac Documents and Palmyrene Inscriptions: An Overview'. In *Trois millénaires de formulaires juridiques*, edited by Sophie Démare-Lafont and André Lemaire, 337–355. Geneva: Droz.

Cussini, Eleonora. 2019. 'Daughters and Wives: Defining Women in Palmyrene Inscriptions'. In *Women, Children, and the Family in Palmyra*, edited by Signe Krag and Rubina Raja, 67–81. Copenhagen: Det Kongelige Danske Videnskabernes Selskab.

de Jong, Lidewijde. 2017. *The Archaeology of Death in Roman Syria: Burial, Commemoration, and Empire.* Cambridge: Cambridge University Press.

Gawlikowski, Michał. 1970. *Monuments funéraires de Palmyre.* Warsaw: Panstwowe Wydawnictwo Naukowe, Éditions scientifiques de Pologne.

Gawlikowski, Michał. 2017. *Le sanctuaire d'Allat à Palmyre.* Warsaw: Polish Centre of Mediterranean Archaeology, University of Warsaw.

Henning, Agnes. 2013a. 'The Tower Tombs of Palmyra: Chronology, Architecture and Decoration'. *Studia Palmyrenskie* 12: 159–176.

Henning, Agnes. 2013b. *Die Turmgräber von Palmyra: Eine lokale Bauform im kaiserzeitlichen Syrien als Ausdruck kultureller Identität.* Rahden: Leidorf.

Henning, Agnes. 2019a. 'Houses of Eternity: The Funerary Monuments of Palmyra'. In *The Road to Palmyra*, edited by Anne Marie Nielsen and Rubina Raja, 155–172. Copenhagen: Ny Carlsberg Glyptotek.

Henning, Agnes. 2019b. 'The Representation of Matrimony in the Tower Tombs of Palmyra'. In *Women, Children and the Family in Palmyra*, edited by Signe Krag and Rubina Raja, 19–37. Copenhagen: Royal Danish Academy of Sciences and Letters.

Heyn, Maura K. 2008. 'Sacerdotal Activities and Parthian Dress in Roman Palmyra'. In *Reading a Dynamic Canvas: Adornment in the Ancient Mediterranean World*, edited by Cynthia S. Colburn and Maura K. Heyn, 170–193. Newcastle: Cambridge Scholars.

Heyn, Maura K. 2012. 'Female Portraiture in Palmyra'. In *A Companion to Women in the Ancient World*, edited by Sharon L. James and Sheila Dillon, 439–441. Chichester: Wiley-Blackwell.

Heyn, Maura K. 2019. 'Valuable Impressions of Women in Palmyra'. In *The Road to Palmyra*, edited by Anne Marie Nielsen and Rubina Raja, 175–192. Copenhagen: Ny Carlsberg Glyptotek.

Heyn, Maura K., and Rubina Raja. 2019. 'Male Dress Habits in Roman Period Palmyra'. In *Fashioned Selves: Dress and Identity in Antiquity*, edited by Megan Cifarelli, 41–54. Oxford: Oxbow.

Heyn, Maura K., and Rubina Raja, eds. 2021. *Individualizing the Dead: Attributes in Palmyrene Funerary Sculpture.* Studies in Palmyrene Archaeology and History 3. Turnhout: Brepols.

Heyn, Maura K., and Rubina Raja. 2023. *Odds and Ends: Attributes in Palmyrene Funerary Art.* Turnhout: Brepols.

Higuchi, Takayasu, and Kiyohide Saito. 2001. *Tomb F. Tomb of BWLH and BWRP: Southeast Necropolis Palmyra, Syria.* Nara: Publication of Research Center for Silk Roadology.

Ingholt, Harold. 1928. *Studier over Palmyrensk Skulptur.* Copenhagen: Reitzel.

Kaizer, Ted. 2002. *The Religious Life of Palmyra: A Study of the Social Patterns of Worship in the Roman Period.* Stuttgart: Steiner.

Krag, Signe. 2018. *Funerary Representations of Palmyrene Women: From the First Century BC to the Third Century AD*. Turnhout: Brepols.

Krag, Signe. 2019. 'Palmyrene Funerary Buildings and Family Burial Patterns'. In *Women, Children and the Family in Palmyra*, edited by Signe Krag and Rubina Raja, 38–66. Copenhagen: Royal Danish Academy of Sciences and Letters.

Krag, Signe, and Rubina Raja. 2016. 'Representations of Women and Children in Palmyrene Funerary Loculus Reliefs, Loculus Stelae and Wall Paintings'. *Zeitschrift für Orient-Archäologie* 9: 134–178.

Krag, Signe, and Rubina Raja. 2017. 'Representations of Women and Children in Palmyrene Banqueting Reliefs and Sarcophagus Scenes'. *Zeitschrift für Orient-Archäologie* 10: 196–227.

Krag, Signe, and Rubina Raja. 2018. 'Unveiling Female Hairstyles: Markers of Age, Social Roles, and Status in Funerary Sculpture from Palmyra'. *Zeitschrift für Orient-Archäologie* 11: 242–277.

Krag, Signe, and Rubina Raja. 2019a. 'Families in Palmyra: The Evidence from the First Three Centuries CE'. In *Women, Children and the Family in Palmyra*, edited by Signe Krag and Rubina Raja, 7–18. Copenhagen: Royal Academy of Sciences and Letters.

Krag, Signe, and Rubina Raja, eds. 2019b. *Women, Children and the Family in Palmyra*. Palmyrene Studies. Copenhagen: Royal Danish Academy of Sciences and Letters.

Kropp, Andreas, and Rubina Raja. 2014. 'The Palmyra Portrait Project'. *Syria: Archéologie, art et histoire* 91: 393–408.

Nielsen, Anne Marie. 2019. 'Palmyra in the Glyptotek'. In *The Road to Palmyra*, edited by Anne Marie Nielsen and Rubina Raja, 23–40. Copenhagen: Ny Carlsberg Glyptotek.

Parlasca, Klaus. 1982. *Syrische Grabreliefs hellenistischer und römischer Zeit: Fundgruppen und Probleme*. Mainz am Rhein: von Zabern.

Parlasca, Klaus. 1985. 'Das Verhältnis der palmyrenischen Grabplastik zur römischen Porträtkunst'. *Mitteilungen des Deutschen Archäologischen Instituts, Römische Abteilung* 92: 343–356.

Parlasca, Klaus. 1995. 'Some Problems of Palmyrene Plastic Art'. *ARAM Periodical* 7: 59–71.

Parlasca, Klaus. 1998. 'Palmyrenische Sarkophage mit Totenmahlreliefs: Forschungsstand und ikonographische Probleme'. In *Akten des Symposiums '125 Jahre Sarkophag-Corpus', MarBurg, 4.-7. Oktober 1995*, edited by G. Koch, 311–317. Mainz am Rhein: von Zabern.

Raja, Rubina. 2015. 'Palmyrene Funerary Portraits in Context: Portrait Habit Between Local Traditions and Imperial Trends'. In *Traditions: Transmission of Culture in the Ancient World*, edited by Jane Fejfer, Mette Moltesen, and Annette Rathje, 329–361. Copenhagen: Museum Tusculanum Press.

Raja, Rubina. 2016. 'Representations of Priests in Palmyra. Methodological Considerations on the Meaning of the Representation of Priesthood in Roman Period Palmyra'. *Religion in the Roman Empire* 2(1): 125–146.

Raja, Rubina. 2017a. 'Between Fashion Phenomena and Status Symbols. Contextualising the Dress of the So-Called "Former Priests" of Palmyra'. In *Textiles and Cult in the Mediterranean Area in the 1st Millennium BC*, edited by Cecilie Brøns and Marie-Louise Nosch, 209–229. Oxford: Oxbow.

Raja, Rubina. 2017b. 'Going Individual: Roman Period Portraiture in Classical Archaeology'. In *The Diversity of Classical Archaeology*, edited by Achim Lichtenberger and Rubina Raja, 271–286. Turnhout: Brepols.

Raja, Rubina. 2017c. 'Networking Beyond Death: Priests and Their Family Networks in Palmyra Explored Through the Funerary Sculpture'. In *Sinews of Empire: Networks in the*

Roman Near East and Beyond, edited by Eivind Heldaas Seland and Håkon Fiane Teigen, 121–136. Oxford: Oxbow.

Raja, Rubina. 2017d. 'Powerful Images of the Deceased: Palmyrene Funerary Portrait Culture Between Local, Greek and Roman Representations'. In *Bilder der Macht: Das griechische Porträt und seine Verwendung in der antiken Welt*, edited by Dietrich Boschung and Franåois Queryel, 319–348. Paderborn: Fink.

Raja, Rubina. 2017e. 'Priesthood in Palmyra: Public Office or Social Status?' In *Palmyra: Pearl of the Desert*, edited by Rubina Raja, 77–85. Aarhus: Sun-Tryk.

Raja, Rubina. 2017f. 'Representations of the So-Called "Former Priests" in Palmyrene Funerary Art. A Methodological Contribution and Commentary'. *Topoi* 21: 51–81.

Raja, Rubina. 2017g. 'To Be or Not to Be Depicted as a Priest in Palmyra: A Matter of Representational Spheres and Societal Values'. In *Positions and Professions in Palmyra*, edited by Tracey Long and Annette H. Sørensen, 115–130. Copenhagen: Royal Academy of Sciences and Letters.

Raja, Rubina. 2017h. 'You Can Leave Your Hat on. Priestly Representations from Palmyra: Between Visual Genre, Religious Importance and Social Status'. In *Beyond Priesthood: Religious Entrepreneurs and Innovators in the Imperial Era*, edited by Richard L. Gordon, Georgia Petridou, and Jörg Rüpke, 417–442. Berlin: de Gruyter.

Raja, Rubina. 2018. 'Palmyrene Funerary Portraits: Collection Histories and Current Research'. In *Palmyra: Mirage in the Desert*, edited by Joan Aruz, 100–109. New York: Metropolitan Museum.

Raja, Rubina. 2019a. 'Funerary Portraiture in Palmyra: Portrait Habit at a Crossroads or a Signifier of Local Identity?' In *Funerary Portraiture in Greater Roman Syria*, edited by Michael Blömer and Rubina Raja, 95–110. Turnhout: Brepols.

Raja, Rubina. 2019b. 'It Stays in the Family. Palmyrene Priestly Representations and Their Constellations'. In *Women, Children and the Family in Palmyra*, edited by Signe Krag and Rubina Raja, 95–156. Copenhagen: Royal Academy of Sciences and Letters.

Raja, Rubina. 2019c. *The Palmyra Collection*. Copenhagen: Ny Carlsberg Glyptotek.

Raja, Rubina. 2019d. 'Portrait Habit in Palmyra'. In *The Road to Palmyra*, edited by Anne Marie Nielsen and Rubina Raja, 137–154. Copenhagen: Ny Carlsberg Glyptotek.

Raja, Rubina. 2019e. 'Stacking Aesthetics in the Syrian Desert: Displaying Palmyrene Sculpture in the Public and Funerary Sphere'. In *Visual Histories of the Classical World: Essays in Honour of R. R. R. Smith*, edited by Catherine M. Draycott, Rubina Raja, Katherine Welch, and William T. Wootton, 281–298. Turnhout: Brepols.

Raja, Rubina. 2021a. 'Adornment and Jewellery as a Status Symbol in Priestly Representations in Roman Palmyra: The Palmyrene Priests and Their Brooches'. In *Individualizing the Dead: Attributes in Palmyrene Funerary Sculpture*, edited by Maura K. Heyn and Rubina Raja, 75–117. Turnhout: Brepols.

Raja, Rubina. 2021b. Funerary Data from Palmyra, Syria Collated by the Palmyra Portrait Project (Version 1.0.0). Zenodo. Available from: http://doi.org/10.5281/zenodo.4669962.

Raja, Rubina. 2021c. 'Managing the Middle Ground: Priests in Palmyra and Their Iconographies'. In *The Middle East as Middle Ground? Cultural Interaction in the Ancient Middle East Revisited*, edited by Julia Hoffman-Salz, 129–146. Vienna: Holzhausen.

Raja, Rubina. 2021d. 'Negotiating Social and Cultural Interaction Through Priesthoods: The Iconography of Priesthood in Palmyra'. In *The Middle East as Middle Ground? Cultural Interaction in the Ancient Middle East Revisited*, edited by Julia Hoffman-Salz, 129–146. Vienna: Holzhausen.

Raja, Rubina. 2021e. Palmyra Portrait Typology and Chronology (Version 1.0.0). Zenodo. Available from: http://doi.org/10.5281/zenodo.4736592.

Raja, Rubina. 2022a. *Pearl of the Desert: A History of Palmyra*. Oxford: Oxford University Press.

Raja, Rubina. 2022b. 'The Way You Wear Your Hat: Palmyrene Priests Between Local Traditions and Cross-Regional Trends'. In *Imperium sine fine? Der romisch-parthische Grenzraum als Konflikt- und Kontaktzone*, edited by Udo Hartmann, Frank Schleicher, and Timo Stickler, 81–118. Stuttgart: Kohlhammer.

Raja, Rubina, Olympia Bobou, and Iza Romanowska. 2021. 'Three Hundred Years of Palmyrene History. Unlocking Archaeological Data for Studying Past Societal Transformations'. *PloS one* 16(11): e0256081. https://doi.org/10.1371/journal.pone.0256081.

Raja, Rubina, and Julia Steding. 2021. *Production Economy in Greater Roman Syria: Trade Networks and Production Processes*. Turnhout: Brepols.

Raja, Rubina, Olympia Bobou, and Jean-Baptiste Yon. Forthcoming. *Palmyrene Funerary Sculpture*. Turnhout: Brepols.

Raja, Rubina, and Jean-Baptiste Yon. Forthcoming. 'Palmyrene Funerary Sculptural Representations with Greek, Latin and Bilingual Inscriptions'. *Zeitschrift für Orientarchäologie*.

Ringsborg, S. 2017. 'Children's Portraits from Palmyra'. In *Palmyra: Pearl of the Desert*, edited by Rubina Raja, 66–75. Aarhus: SUN-Tryk, Aarhus University.

Romanowska, Iza, Olympia Bobou, and Rubina Raja. 2021. 'Reconstructing the Social, Economic and Demographic Trends of Palmyra's Elite from Funerary Data'. *Journal of Archaeological Science* 133: 105432. https://doi.org/10.1016/j.jas.2021.105432.

Sadurska, Anna, and Adnan Bounni. 1994. *Les sculptures funéraires de Palmyre*. Rome: Giorgio Bretschneider.

Saito, Kiyohide. 2005a. 'Palmyrene Burial Practices from Funerary Goods'. In *A Journey to Palmyra: Collected Essays to Remember Delbert R. Hillers*, edited by Eleonora Cussini, 150–165. Leiden: Brill.

Saito, Kiyohide, ed. 2005b. *The Study of Funerary Practices and Social Background in Palmyra*. Nara: Archaeological Institute of Kashihara.

Sartre-Fauriat, Annie. 2019. 'The Discovery and Reception of Palmyra'. In *The Road to Palmyra*, edited by Anne Marie Nielsen and Rubina Raja, 65–76. Copenhagen: Ny Carlsberg Glyptotek.

Schmidt-Colinet, Andreas. 2007. 'Nochmal zur Ikonographie zweier palmyrenischer sarkophage'. In *Lokale Identität im Römischen Nahen Osten: Kontexte und Perspektiven; Erträge der Tagung 'Lokale Identität im Römischen Nahen Osten', Münster, 19–21. April 2007*, edited by Michael Blömer, Margherita Facella, and Engelbert Winter, 223–234. Stuttgart: Steiner.

Schmidt-Colinet, Andreas, and Khaled As'ad. 2007. 'Zwei Neufunde palmyrenischer Sarkophage'. In *Akten des Symposium des Sarkophag-Corpus, Marburg 2001*, edited by Guntram Koch, 271–278. Sarkophag-Studien 3. Mainz am Rhein: von Zabern.

Seyrig, Henri 1936. 'Note sur les plus anciennes sculptures palmyréniennes'. *Berytus* 3: 137–140.

Steding, Julia. 2022. *Carvers and Customers in Roman Palmyra*. Turnhout: Brepols.

Stucky, R. A. 1973. 'Prêtres syriens I: Palmyre'. *Syria* 50(1–2): 163–180.

Yon, Jean-Baptiste. 2002. *Les notables de Palmyre*. Beirut: Institut français du Proche Orient.

....

CHAPTER 28

PALMYRENE WOMEN

Breaking the Glass Ceiling or Window Dressing?

....

MAURA K. HEYN

INTRODUCTION

....

WRITING about the life of women in Palmyra is a tricky task. On the one hand, there is an abundance of evidence in the form of funerary portraits[1] and both funerary and civic inscriptions. On the other hand, much of this evidence must be taken with a grain of salt, produced to be displayed in tombs or in public venues where the priority may not have been to commemorate the individual woman for her sake as much as to advertise paradigms of comportment and to draw attention to what the woman contributed to the family, by her presence, her appearance, and her associations (Hodder 1982; Hope 2001; Fisher and Loren 2003, 227; Joyce 2005, 146–147; Dillon 2006, 62; Davies 2008). For this reason, it is problematic to trace changes in the ways that women are represented in the funerary sphere, where a minority go from displaying items associated with the domestic sphere to wearing copious amounts of jewellery, to find an explanation for the startling success of Zenobia, the third-century queen of the Palmyrene Empire.[2] This is not to assert that the role of women did not change in the first three centuries AD, but that the evidence indicates that, for most Palmyrene women, life remained centred on the domestic sphere (Yon 2002, 165–166).

THE FUNERARY SPHERE

....

Funerary representations of women from the tombs outside the city are numerous and rich in detail. The earliest depictions are found on stelae that were used to mark

---

[1] As of 2018, there were 884 female portrait reliefs in the Palmyra Portrait Project database, which represent 42 percent of the funerary sculpture (Krag 2018, 68).

[2] For recent scholarship on Zenobia, see Weingarten 2018; Andrade 2018; 2019.

graves in the first half of the first century AD (Colledge 1976, 64). These small-scale figures in low relief represent men and women frontally and full-length on individual stelae. The figures are stiff in their frontality and reveal little other than the wish to commemorate and a glimpse into styles of dress. Both men and women wear tunic and cloak, and women add a veil and jewellery. A more nuanced view of the status of women in this early period may be provided by the banquet reliefs that were introduced to the exteriors of the monumental tombs that became popular during this time. The relief on the tower tomb of Kithôt, dated to AD 40 (Will 1951, 70), depicts the founder of the tomb reclining on his left elbow on a thick mattress in the foreground, with his wife and two sons standing behind him. The priestly hats worn by both sons and the ladle and vessels held in their hands, connect them to the father in an allusion to a ritual banquet (Colledge 1976, 64). The mother is included in the scene, but her dress and attributes do not connect her to the activities of the men; her role in the scene is unclear, unless it is to complete the family group (Henning 2019). The importance of this banquet scene for the prestige of the family is indicated by its placement with the inscription on the side of the tomb facing the main route in and out of the city (Gawlikowski 1970, 147–148; Yon 1999, 388). Judging from the remains of niches, similar scenes were duplicated on the exterior of other tower tombs in the vicinity (Will 1949, 99; 1951, 84).

Inside the Palmyrene tombs, representations of women appear in a variety of forms from the mid-first century AD onwards. The small-scale, full-length figures persist, now carved in low relief on rectangular slabs that sealed the burial niches (loculi) in the tomb (Colledge 1976, 66–67). The banquet scene also moved inside the tomb early in the second century AD and became a popular means of depicting the larger family group (Ingholt 1970/1971; Seyrig 1971; Colledge 1976, 73–79; Makowski 1985). Women in these scenes would appear either seated at the end of the couch or in the family group that surrounded the reclining figure. Occasionally, women and men were also depicted in the painted decoration on the walls and ceiling (Colledge 1976, 83–87; Sørensen 2016). However, the most popular form of portraiture was the (just under) life-size depiction of the deceased from the waist up, which adorned the rectangular limestone slabs that sealed the loculi (Figures 28.1–28.4). Although maintaining the frontality and basic dress choices of the earlier representations, this new style of portraiture in the second half of the first century AD allowed for greater animation via the hand gestures, cloak and veil arrangements, attributes, headgear, and jewellery (Krag 2019b).[3]

Most of the women depicted in the portrait busts wear a long- or short-sleeved tunic over which a cloak and veil are draped (Figure 28.1). The cloak is usually attached at the left shoulder with a brooch (Figures 28.2–28.4), and a turban is worn on

---

[3] The earliest dated loculus portrait is that of 'the wife of Bar'atê', dated to AD 65/66. Ny Carlsberg Glyptotek, inv. no. 2816 (Ploug 1995, 35–36; Hvidberg-Hansen 1998, 25–26).

FIGURE 28.1 Funerary relief of a woman. Limestone, ca. AD 125–150.

Yale University Art Gallery. Gift of Mr. and Mrs. J. Edgar Munroe, 1954.30.1 (www.artgallery.yale.edu).

the head, underneath the veil (Figures 28.1–28.4). Despite these being the customary garments in most representations of women in the loculus reliefs, the female portraits exhibit tremendous variety and individuality (Raja 2015; Krag and Raja 2016, 158; Raja 2017; Krag and Raja 2019). Difference was commonly created by the attributes held in the left hand, the adornment of the headband that was worn across the forehead (Finlayson 1998; 2002–2003; Krag 2017b, 47–48; 2018, 106–109), the gesture of the hands and position of the arms (Heyn 2010; Krag 2018, 38–41, 75–78), and the endless possibilities created by the different types and combinations of jewellery: earrings, bracelets, rings, necklaces, brooches, and hair ornaments (Mackay 1949; Krag 2017b; 2018, 95–110).

FIGURE 28.2 Funerary relief of a woman and two children. Limestone, ca. AD 150.

Harvard Art Museums/Arthur M. Sackler Museum. Gift of Alden Sampson, Richard Norton,
and Edward W. Forbes, 1908.3.

Photograph by Imaging Department © President and Fellows of Harvard College.

Female Attributes

Objects held or displayed in a funerary portrait that have symbolic significance for the deceased are not unusual in Hellenistic or Roman funerary portraiture,[4] but in Palmyra their significance is not always straightforward. The most common female attributes are

[4] For example, see Zanker 1993.

FIGURE 28.3 Funerary relief of a woman. Limestone, ca. AD 150–200.

The Metropolitan Museum of Art, New York, 02.29.5 (www.metmuseum.org).

the tools used for weaving thread from raw wool, the spindle and distaff (Figures 28.1 and 28.2). A small group of women also have a P-shaped or L-shaped key suspended from their brooch or held in one hand (Figure 28.3) (Krag 2017b, 46). There are various opinions as to the function of this key, whether it unlocks the house, the tomb, the jewellery box, or the gates to the afterlife (Gawlikowski 1966, 414; Colledge 1976, 70; Drijvers 1982, 720; Parlasca 1988, 216–220; Ploug 1995, 91; Balty 1996, 438–439; Sadurska 1996, 286; Finlayson 2008, 115; Sokołowski 2014, 393; Krag 2017b, 46). If its significance is related to that of the spindle and distaff, the key may well unlock the door to the house, but the key to the jewellery box is just as likely, given the display of jewellery and the occasional depictions of jewellery boxes (Colledge 1976, 155). Additional unusual attributes include a circular object with seven knobs that appears in three portraits and has been identified as a wreath, key-ring, rattle, tambourine (Colledge 1976, 156, n. 608), or a calendar (Sadurska 1983, 152–156), and a round object that may be a pinecone, with connotations of immortality (Colledge 1976, 155). Finally, many women (and some men) simply hold a loop of their veil or cloak in their left hand (Colledge 1976, 155).

The child who is held on the left arm of thirty-three women should probably also be considered an attribute, in the sense that the child communicates something about the woman's identity as a mother (Krag and Raja 2016, 146–147; Krag 2018, 83–85)

FIGURE 28.4 Funerary relief of a woman. Limestone, ca. AD 200–273.

The University of Pennsylvania Museum of Archaeology and Anthropology, B8904 (image courtesy of Penn Museum and Dorling Kindersley, Image #250891).

(Figure 28.2). Four of the women who hold children bare their breasts in a simulation of breastfeeding (Krag and Raja 2016, 147; Krag 2018, 84–85, cat. nos. 410, 411, 423, 431). Children are also depicted full-length, as small-scale adults, behind one or both shoulders of the bust-length figures in the loculus reliefs (Figure 28.2), though the relationship is not always that of a parent and child: sisters may appear together, or a man with his nephews.[5] Despite this variety of possible relationships between

[5] E.g., funerary portrait of a man with his two nephews, in the Seattle Art Museum, inv. No. 42.11.

the child and adult, women are pictured with children far more commonly (seventy-two loculus portraits) than are men (twenty-six loculus portraits) (Krag and Raja 2016, 137).

GESTURES

The strong bond between the child and adult in these portraits is often reinforced by gesture, with the smaller-scale child reaching out to touch the adult (Heyn 2010, 639, appendix 4; Krag 2018, 76–78) (Figure 28.2).[6] Another gesture that is primarily associated with a mother and her children is the so-called mourning gesture. Approximately five double portraits depict a woman with an unusual appearance who puts her arm around her full-size companion (Heyn 2010, 637, appendix 2; Krag 2017a, 237; 2018, 90–92, 130). With the exception of a relief that depicts a sister and brother, the inscriptions indicate that most of these women are pictured with their children, possibly adult children (Krag and Raja 2016, 152; Krag 2017a, 237). Apart from the arm position, these portraits attract attention because the mourning woman wears her dishevelled hair unbound and bares her chest, where ritual gashes are displayed. The combination of the altered appearance and the hand gesture makes it likely that these women are highlighting the mourning process. Furthermore, these double images, similar to the depictions of breast-feeding women, draw attention to a gender-specific role that the women had in the domestic sphere.[7]

The raising of the right or left arm to grasp the veil at the level of the shoulder or chin is another gesture specifically associated with women, but its connection to the domestic sphere is more tenuous. Most of the male portraits in Palmyra display the 'arm-sling' pose, which is created by wearing the cloak in such a way that it catches the right arm in a sling as it passes from the right shoulder to the left. Alternatively, most female portraits produced after the mid-second century raise the right or left arm to grasp the veil or touch the body at the level of the shoulder or chin (Heyn 2010, 636) (Figures 28.2–28.4). Both gestures, the right hand extended over the sling of the cloak and the hand raised to the level of the shoulder, are similar to gestures seen in the Hellenistic Greek world and in Roman republican funerary reliefs (Brilliant 1963; Kleiner 1977, 159–163; Davies 2017, 27). The Roman version of the female posture has been linked with *pudicitia* (Kleiner 1992, 40; Aldrete 1999, 65, n. 48; George 2005, 44–45), but it is not clear whether the Palmyrene versions were also associated with modesty.[8] Davies (2017, 39) suggests that

---

[6] For this phenomenon of illustrating family bonds more generally through gesture, see again Heyn 2010, 639, and Sadurska 1995. Also see Boatwright (2005) for a similar argument for the significance of gesture on Pannonian stelae.

[7] For similar gender-specific mourning rituals in Rome, see Corbeill 2004, 72.

[8] Davies (2017, 25–31) argues for a less limiting interpretation of the *pudicitia* gesture in Rome and Palmyra.

the raised arm should be more generally associated with appropriate behaviour for an elite Palmyrene woman, in the same way that the men's arm-sling pose associated them with good citizenship.[9]

A final gesture that is made almost exclusively by women in Palmyrene portraiture, and one that may provide information regarding activities outside the tomb, is the 'palm-out' gesture (Colledge 1976, 138, n. 493; Parlasca 1980, 150–152, n. 17–21; Sadurska and Bounni 1994, 32, cat. no. 31; Ploug 1995, 38; Heyn 2010, 636–637, appendix 1). There are twenty-six examples of the gesture in portraits known from Palmyra (Krag 2018, 39–40), and only one represents a man (Lagrange 1902, 94–97; Ingholt 1928, *PS* 183; Parlasca 1980, 151, fig. 51.1). More generally, the gesture has apotropaic connotations (Cumont 1926, 72; Corbeill 2004, 23) and may be used to communicate prayer or supplication, but its connection with women in Palmyra and its appearance in particular contexts in the city and elsewhere suggest its association with a particular kind of ritual behaviour. Full-length figures of men, women, and children appear on votive altars from the second and third centuries with the hands raised and held palm outward.[10] These figures are engaged in prayer (Ingholt 1936, 92; Colledge 1976, 138) that is often associated with the god known as 'He whose name is blessed forever'. The identity of this god is significant because epigraphic evidence reveals that women dedicated votive altars to him in thanks or in honour of family members in the second and third centuries AD (Cussini 2005, 29–30; Krag 2018, 120–123; Klaver 2019), and his cult is argued to be more personal and private in nature (Gawlikowski 1990, 2632). This type of cult activity fits the overall impression of the role of women in Palmyra, for whom the family was the primary concern, and in the tomb the gesture may have the same significance. One of the few contemporary examples from the region, which depicts a mortal woman making the palm-out gesture with her right hand, appears in a wall painting in the naos of the Temple of the Palmyrene Gods at Dura-Europos (Cumont 1926, 41–52, plates XXXII–XXXVI), where she is shown worshipping in the company of her family (Yon 2016, 101).

WOMEN'S SUBORDINATE POSITION

In the funerary portraiture, the clear association of women with the domestic sphere does not coincide with a reduced presence in the tombs. The bust-length loculus reliefs originating in the tombs surrounding Palmyra represent men and women in almost equal numbers. As of December 2015, there were 517 bust-length reliefs of women versus 670 similar reliefs of men recorded in the database of the Palmyra Portrait Project

[9] For the significance of the gesture in Rome, see Kleiner 1992, 40; Aldrete 1999, 65, n. 48). A similar gesture is made by women, also in a funerary context (mosaics) in Edessa (see Leroy 1957, 306–342), which may suggest that it was a regional cliché.

[10] E.g., on a votive relief to 'He whose name is blessed forever' in the Ny Carlsberg Glyptotek; I.N. 1081 (Hvidberg-Hansen 1998, 35).

(Krag and Raja 2016, 137).[11] Thus women are depicted in approximately 44 percent of the loculus reliefs. Also, the rare reliefs that were still *in situ* in some of these Palmyrene tombs reveal that the portraits of men and women were intermingled in the same spaces of the tomb.[12] However, as with the banquet scenes on the fronts of the tombs, there are indications of the subordinate position of women. The inscriptions in Palmyrene Aramaic, situated above one or both shoulders of the deceased, identify both men and women by name, but usually the additional genealogical information identifies male ancestors. Also, when the funerary epitaph identifies the person who commissioned the portrait, it is usually a male relative (Cussini 2005, 27).[13] Finally, turning to the iconographic evidence, women are represented in group portraits more often than men, implying the importance of family connections in their portraits (Krag 2018, 69). Occasionally, when a man and woman are depicted next to each other in a double portrait, the position of the male portrait will overlap the female portrait, thereby demonstrating his superior social position (Sadurska 1995, 585; Davies 2017, 31).[14]

In his 1928 study of the Palmyrene portraits, Ingholt placed the funerary portraits into three chronological groupings according to their stylistic similarities to the small number of dated portraits.[15] The portraits in the first group, from AD 50 to AD 150, are simple: the women wear a tunic, cloak, and veil with a diadem across the forehead and a turban on the head underneath the veil, but are otherwise fairly unadorned. Their jewellery is usually limited to earrings and a trapezoidal brooch, holding the cloak on the left shoulder. The spindle and distaff are the most common attributes for this first group (Figure 28.1), and most of the women who display the palm-out gesture with their right hand are in this group. In the second group of portraits, from AD 150 to 200, the women are portrayed with much more jewellery (necklaces, bracelets, rings, and so on), and there is more variety in the shape of the brooch. The women also adopt a new pose, using the right hand to hold back the veil (Figures 28.2 and 28.3). In the final group, which begins in AD 200 and lasts until the destruction of the city in AD 273, some of the female portraits become increasingly ornate, with lavish displays of jewellery. The pose of the arms changes as well, with the left arm now raised to catch the veil, or to touch the cheek (Figure 28.4) (Ingholt 1954; Colledge 1976, 255–261).

Ingholt's groupings allow for an analysis of the changes in the ways in which women were portrayed from the mid-first century AD to the third quarter of the third century

[11] http://projects.au.dk/palmyraportrait/ (Kropp and Raja 2014).

[12] E.g., the hypogeum of Bôlhâ, son of Nebôsûrî (Sadurska and Bounni 1994, 70); the hypogeum of Iarhai, son of Barikhi (Amy and Seyrig 1936, 233–234); the hypogeum of Šalamallat, son of Maliku (Sadurska and Bounni 1994, 149–151); and the hypogeum of the family of Artaban, son of 'Ogga (Sadurska and Bounni 1994, 25).

[13] There are exceptions, as when a woman is identified as having commissioned the portrait: *PAT* 0840, by a foster-mother; *PAT* 0877, by a wife; *PAT* 0901, by a daughter, and *PAT* 0915, by a sister (Cussini 2005, 27).

[14] E.g., the position of the male in a double portrait of brother and sister from the Tomb of the Sassans, AD 180–220; MP 1967/7059 (Sadurska 1995, 585).

[15] There are thirty-five portraits with an 'absolute date' (Krag 2018, 11).

AD. They reveal that most of the female attributes, with the exception of the child held on the left arm (Krag and Raja 2016, 147; Krag 2018, 83–85), fell out of use by the end of the second century. Women also no longer made the palm-out gesture, and instead they held first their right arm, and later their left, in a raised position to grasp the veil or touch the chin, with their other arm occasionally extended across the body to grasp the veil (Figure 28.4). Also, these groups clearly indicate that, as the common female attributes disappeared from female iconography, women wore increasing amounts of jewellery.

The shift in the items displayed in Palmyrene women's portraits, from spindle and distaff to jewels, has been argued to indicate the increasing emancipation of Palmyrene women in the second and third centuries AD (Sadurska 1996). This interpretation is problematic because it assumes that the female attributes were real, rather than symbolic, and that their disappearance from the female portraiture indicates an actual change in duties (Heyn 2012). Certainly, as symbols, attributes such as the spindle and distaff could be considered references to the ideal housewife (Sadurska 1983, 154; Sadurska 1995, 585; Sadurska 1996, 286; Balty 1996, 438),[16] but whether they were employed by these elite women to weave cloth is impossible to know (Cussini 2004, 236, n. 7).[17] The significance of the jewellery must also be considered. The jewellery found in the Japanese excavations of Tomb F (Higuchi and Saito 2001) attests to the existence of such adornment and increases the likelihood that the jewellery displayed in the portraiture was realistic, as asserted by Mackay (1949, 162). In terms of significance for the women's identity, the jewellery may have demonstrated their families' wealth or their association with the caravans bringing exotic goods from the east and cultivating trade connections with the west (Heyn 2016, 201–203). However, as pointed out by Krag (2017b, 37–38), the jewellery worn by the women depicted on the stelae from the earliest period of funerary portraiture weakens the argument that greater amounts of jewellery are associated with increasing wealth and suggests that at least part of the explanation for its popularity should be sought elsewhere. She concludes that jewellery was used in female portraits to communicate wealth and social status (Krag 2017b, 39), but that its surge in popularity in the later periods was also due to increased competition in the funerary context, with its myriad possibilities for display (Krag 2017b, 41).

Perhaps even more curious than the transition from spindle and distaff to jewellery is the degree to which portraiture of women changes compared to that of men (Heyn 2016, 200; Heyn 2017, 212), and this may be related to the function of the female portrait in the tomb. Male iconography remains stable throughout the two and a half centuries of production, whereas female iconography changes in very noticeable ways, such as most female attributes displayed in the left hand being replaced by the loop of the veil

---

[16] Finlayson (2008, 115) asserts that the spindle and distaff 'associate women with the powerful goddesses of resurrection and cosmic renewal venerated in Greater Syria, including the Great Goddess of Syria discussed in Lucian's *de Dea Syria*'.

[17] Cf. Krag 2017b, 236; Zouhdi 2001, 211; 1983, 316. Also see Sokołowski (2014, 393) who argues that attributes such as the stylus, open poliptych, or keys with engraved inscriptions were evidence of the literacy of the woman depicted.

and the increasing amounts of jewellery. Also, female gestures, such as the palm-out gesture, with its connotations of worship, fall from use and are replaced by the raising of the hand to grasp the veil in a display of 'appropriate behaviour'. This demonstrable change in female gestures and attributes seems to move away from providing evidence of active contributions to the community. Instead, the purpose is to draw attention to the strength of the family by depicting the woman wearing copious amounts of jewellery or emphasizing her connection to her children (Krag 2018, 82–93; Krag 2019a). The importance of the woman to the family is indicated by the number of female loculus portraits that include children (Figure 28.2) and the increasing popularity of the child held in the mother's left arm when all other attributes fall from use (Krag and Raja 2016, 141, 149; Krag 2018, 83–85), revealing the importance of the female identity as mothers (Sadurska 1995, 585; Krag and Raja 2016, 137–139). In addition to portraits that link mothers with their children, individual female portraits also enhance the picture of the family by their presence.

A similar phenomenon may be demonstrated in the mural decoration of the tomb of Hairan, where the full-size portrait of the son or grandson of the founder was painted on the side wall of an exedra of the tomb in AD 149–150 (Sørensen 2016, 107). The frontality of the portrait and the draping of the man's cloak in the arm-sling arrangement are similar to the bust-length loculus portraits (Colledge 1976, 84). Painted on the opposite wall of the exedra, facing the portrait of the male, is a full-length portrait of a woman in a green tunic and brown cloak. She wears black shoes and has two keys suspended from her brooch (Colledge 1976, 84). In addition to the placement of their portraits, facing each other, the arm positions of the two figures suggest parity:[18] despite the different draping of her cloak, the woman holds her arms across her torso in a similar pose to that of Hairan. Nevertheless, the subordinate position of the woman is indicated by the absence of an identifying inscription: Hairan is identified by means of an inscription painted over his head, giving his name and the date of the painting; the woman, presumably his wife, has no identifying inscription (Sørensen 2016, 107). It is perhaps her presence rather than her identity which is most important.

BANQUET SCENES

The banquet scenes that became a popular means of portraying the family in the second and third centuries AD provide additional evidence of the subordinate position of women in Palmyrene society and their inclusion for the purpose of advertising the strength of the family. As explained previously, the banquet scene first made its appearance in the funerary sphere on the facades of Palmyrene tower tombs, where it was used to advertise the prestige of the family to passers-by. When it moved inside the tomb

---

[18] For more on the idea of similar arm positions indicating equal status, see Davies 2016, 31.

in the second century AD, it was carved on large rectangular slabs or sarcophagus lids that sealed banks of loculi in highly visible areas of the tomb. The basic characteristics of these large-scale scenes remained fairly consistent, with a male or males depicted reclining on the left side on the banqueting couch while holding a drinking vessel in the left hand. The reclining figure's wife or mother would be included on a chair at the end of the couch, and his other family members: children, siblings, grandchildren, nieces, or nephews would stand behind him or be depicted in bust form between the legs of the *kline* below (Colledge 1976, 73–79; Krag and Raja 2018).

The significance of the banquet scene in Palmyrene tombs, whether it portrays a funerary banquet, a meal in the afterlife, a ritual banquet, a family banquet, or is just a convenient excuse to depict the entire family together, has been much debated (Ingholt 1970/1971; Seyrig 1971; Colledge 1976, 73–79; Makowski 1985; Sadurska 1995, 587; Cussini 2016; Audley-Miller 2016; Krag 2018, 52–53). It is also possible that the reclining figure on its own may be an indication of prestige (Dentzer 1971). His frequent choice of Parthian dress, and his position and larger scale, certainly set him apart. Women, on the other hand, are often depicted at a smaller scale at the foot of the couch. Their subordinate position is further emphasized by the simplicity of their clothing, in contrast to the embroidered Parthian dress and priestly headgear frequently worn by the reclining male figure (Krag 2017a, 236). Despite the fact that there are a handful of banquet scenes in which women recline,[19] perhaps as a result of the prestige associated with this position, the overall message of the banquet scene in the Palmyrene tombs is of the superior position of the reclining male: 'These scenes display a clear distinction between dominant male and subordinate female postures: men recline, and women sit, often performing a veiling gesture. Their seated position signals their subordinate position in relation to the male, and their veiling gesture suggests their fidelity to him' (Davies 2017, 33).

Epigraphic Evidence

Cussini (2004; 2005, 38; 2019) has argued that the image of a 'demure' Palmyrene woman who is restricted to the house is a biased impression created by focusing too heavily on the iconographic evidence from the tombs. Epigraphic evidence does attest to women's more active presence in the funerary and civic spheres. Within the funerary sphere, several foundation texts explicitly mention female names among those for whom a tomb was built, and cession texts that survive on certain tombs reveal that women could buy and sell portions of the tombs and commission reliefs inside the tomb (Cussini 2005, 27–28, 30–39, table 1). Also, inscriptions on the columns of the porticoed streets of the city and on the votive altars from its sanctuaries provide evidence of women making and

---

[19] There are thirteen reliefs (miniature banquets and sarcophagus lids) of reclining women (Krag 2018, 64–66).

receiving dedications (Yon 2002, 166–167; Cussini 2005, 28–30). Additional involvement in ritual activities in the city early on is also attested by fragmentary reliefs that show women observing religious processions (Seyrig 1934, 159–165, plate XIX; Colledge 1976, fig. 20; Tanabe 1986, plates 42–44, plate 156; Sadurska 1996, 286), and occasionally assisting with the ritual itself (Morehart 1956/1957, 55–56, figs. 1 and 2; Colledge 1976, 40, fig. 20, plate 26; Finlayson 2013, 64–65, figs. 1 and 2; Krag 2017a, 232–233, fig. 20.3).[20] However, this evidence of greater agency in the non-domestic sphere is not abundant[21] and should not be overestimated when considering the role of women in Palmyrene society. Indeed, Yon (2002, 167) has argued that the inscriptions accompanying honorific statues of women placed in sanctuaries and on the colonnaded streets of the city make it likely that these statues appeared when it was advantageous to emphasize the strength of the family.

Conclusion

The Palmyrene reliefs present a potentially fruitful body of evidence for understanding the role of women in antiquity because of their large number of female portraits, but conclusions must be approached with caution because of the nature of the evidence and the paucity of comparative material from elsewhere in the city. At one end of the spectrum, we have images of women holding spindles and distaffs and, at the other, is Zenobia leading an empire. Despite the century or more that separates one set of images from the other, linear progression towards greater female independence and agency in the city should not be assumed because of changing female attributes depicted in tomb reliefs.[22] This is not to suggest that the roles of women remained stagnant in the intervening one hundred years, but that the lived experience of most Palmyrene women was somewhere between those of the idealized funerary portraits and the unusual queen. Although the epigraphic evidence does nuance the 'demure' impression given by the funerary portraits, these examples represent exceptions to an overall trend of a female identity that is strongly connected to the family and the domestic sphere.

Bibliography

Aldrete, Gregory S. 1999. *Gestures and Acclamations in Ancient Rome*. Baltimore: Johns Hopkins University Press.

[20] For a fuller and more nuanced discussion of the civic and religious activities of Palmyrene women, see Krag 2018, 111–128.

[21] 'Only six texts out of hundreds of surviving honorific inscriptions are dedicated to women' (Cussini 2004, 239, n. 24).

[22] Cf. Zouhdi 2001, 111.

Amy, Robert, and Henri Seyrig. 1936. 'Recherches dans la nécropole de Palmyre'. *Syria* 17: 229–266.

Andrade, Nathanael J. 2018. *Zenobia: Shooting Star of Palmyra*. Women in Antiquity. Oxford: Oxford University Press.

Andrade, Nathanael J. 2019. 'Burying Odainath: Zenobia and Women in the Funerary Life of Palmyra'. In *Women, Children, and the Family in Palmyra*, edited by Signe Krag and Rubina Raja, 168–183. Palmyrene Studies 3. Copenhagen: Det Kongelige Danske Videnskabernes Selskab.

Audley-Miller, Lucy. 2016. 'The Banquet in Palmyrene Funerary Contexts'. In *Dining and Death: Interdisciplinary Perspectives on the 'Funerary Banquet' in Ancient Art, Burial and Belief*, edited by Catherine M. Draycott and Maria Stamatopoulou, 553–590. Leuven: Peeters.

Balty, Jean-Charles. 1996. 'Palmyre entre Orient et Occident: Acculturation et résistances'. *Annales archéologiques arabes syriennes* 42: 437–441.

Boatwright, Mary T. 2005. 'Children and Parents on the Tombstones of Pannonia'. In *The Roman Family in the Empire: Rome, Italy and Beyond*, edited by Michele George, 287–318. Oxford: Oxford University Press.

Brilliant, Richard. 1963. *Gesture and Rank in Roman Art*. New Haven, CT: Memoirs of the Connecticut Academy of Arts and Sciences.

Charles-Gaffiot, Jacques, Jean-Marc Hofman, and Henri Lavagne, eds. 2001. *Moi, Zénobie, reine de Palmyre*. Paris: Seuil.

Colledge, Malcolm A. R. 1976. *The Art of Palmyra*. London: Thames & Hudson.

Corbeill, Anthony. 2004. *Nature Embodied: Gesture in Ancient Rome*. Princeton, NJ: Princeton University Press.

Cumont, Franz. 1926. *Fouilles de Doura-Europos*. Paris: Geuthner.

Cussini, Eleonora. 2004. 'Regina, Martay and the Others. Stories of Palmyrene Women'. *Orientalia* 73: 235–244.

Cussini, Eleonora. 2005. 'Beyond the Spindle: Investigating the Role of Palmyrene Women'. In *A Journey to Palmyra: Collected Essays to Remember Delbert R. Hillers*, edited by Eleonora Cussini, 26–43. Leiden: Brill.

Cussini, Eleonora. 2016. 'Family Banqueting at Palmyra: Reassessing the Evidence'. In *Libiamo ne' lieti calici: Ancient Near Eastern Studies Presented to Lucio Milano on the Occasion of his 65th Birthday by Pupils, Colleagues and Friends*, edited by Paola Corò, Elena Devecchi, Nicla De Zorzi, and Massimo Maiocchi, 139–159. Münster: Ugarit Verlag.

Cussini, Eleonora. 2019. 'Daughters and Wives: Defining Women in Palmyrene Inscriptions'. In *Women, Children, and the Family in Palmyra*, edited by Signe Krag and Rubina Raja, 67–81. Palmyrene Studies 3. Copenhagen: Det Kongelige Danske Videnskabernes Selskab.

Davies, Glenys. 2008. 'Portrait Statues as Models for Gender Roles in Roman Society'. In *Role Models in the Roman World: Identity and Assimilation*, edited by Sinclair Bell and Inge Lyse Hansen, 207–220. Ann Arbor: University of Michigan Press.

Davies, Glenys. 2017. 'The Body Language of Palmyra and Rome'. In *Positions and Professions in Palmyra*, edited by Tracey Long and Annette Højen Sørensen, 20–35. Palmyrene Studies 2. Copenhagen: Det Kongelige Danske Videnskabernes Selskab.

Dentzer, Jean-Marie. 1971. 'L'iconographie iranienne du souverain couché et le motif du banquet'. *Annales archéologiques arabes syriennes* 21: 39–50.

Dentzer-Feydy, Jacqueline and Javier Teixidor, eds. 1993. *Les antiquités de Palmyre au Musée du Louvre*. Paris: Réunion des musées nationaux.

Dillon, Sheila. 2006. *Ancient Greek Portrait Sculpture: Contexts, Subjects, and Styles.* Cambridge: Cambridge University Press.

Drijvers, H. J. W. 1982. 'After Life and Funerary Symbolism in Palmyrene Religion'. In *La soteriologia dei culti orientali nell'Impero Romano*, edited by Ugo Bianchi and Maarten J. Vermaseren, 709–733. Études préliminaires aux religions orientales dans l'Empire romain 92. Leiden: Brill.

Finlayson, Cynthia. 1998. 'Veil, Turban and Headpiece: Funerary Portraits and Female Status at Palmyra'. Unpublished doctoral thesis, University of Iowa.

Finlayson, Cynthia. 2002–2003. 'Veil, Turban, and Headpiece: Funerary Portraits and Female Status at Palmyra'. *Annales archéologiques arabes syriennes* 45/46: 221–235.

Finlayson, Cynthia. 2008. 'Mut'a Marriage in the Roman Near East: The Evidence from Palmyra, Syria'. In *The World of Women in the Ancient and Classical Near East*, edited by Beth Alpert Nakhai, 99–138. Newcastle: Cambridge Scholars.

Finlayson, Cynthia. 2013. 'New Perspectives on the Ritual and Cultic Importance of Women at Palmyra and Dura-Europos: Processions and Temples'. *Studia Palmyreńskie* 12: 61–85.

Fisher, Genevieve and Diana DiPaolo Loren. 2003. 'Embodying Identity in Archaeology: Introduction'. *Cambridge Archaeological Journal* 13(2): 225–230.

Gawlikowski, Michal. 1966. 'Remarques sur l'usage de la fibule à Palmyre'. In *Mélanges offerts à Kazimierz Michałowski*, edited by Maria Ludwika Bernhard, 411–419. Warsaw: Państwowe Wydawnictwo Naukowe.

Gawlikowski, Michał. 1970. *Monuments funéraires de Palmyre.* Warsaw: Państwowe Wydawnictwo Naukowe.

Gawlikowski, Michał. 1990. 'Les dieux de Palmyre'. *Aufstieg und Niedergang der römischen Welt.* Vol. 2, *Principat*, no. 18, *Religion, 4*, edited by Wolfgang Haase, 2605–2658. Berlin: de Gruyter.

George, Michele. 2005. 'Family Imagery and Family Values in Roman Italy'. In *The Roman Family in the Empire: Rome, Italy, and Beyond*, edited by Michele George, 37–66. Oxford: Oxford University Press.

Henning, Agnes. 2019. 'The Representation of Matrimony in the Tower Tombs of Palmyra'. In *Women, Children, and the Family in Palmyra*, edited by Signe Krag and Rubina Raja, 19–37. Palmyrene Studies 3. Copenhagen: Det Kongelige Danske Videnskabernes Selskab.

Heyn, Maura K. 2008. 'Sacerdotal Activities and Parthian Dress in Roman Palmyra'. In *Reading a Dynamic Canvas: Adornment in the Ancient Mediterranean World*, edited by Cynthia S. Colburn and Maura K. Heyn, 170–193. Newcastle: Cambridge Scholars.

Heyn, Maura K. 2010. 'Gesture and Identity in the Funerary Art of Palmyra'. *American Journal of Archaeology* 114: 631–661.

Heyn, Maura K. 2012. 'Female Portraiture in Palmyra'. In *A Companion to Women in the Ancient World*, edited by Sharon James and Sheila Dillon, 439–441. Malden, MA: Wiley Blackwell.

Heyn, Maura K. 2016. 'Status and Stasis: Looking at Women in the Palmyrene Tomb'. In *The World of Palmyra*, edited by Rubina Raja and Andreas Kropp, 197–209. Copenhagen: Det Kongelige Danske Videnskabernes Selskab.

Heyn, Maura K. 2017. 'Western Men, Eastern Women? Dress and Cultural Identity in Roman Palmyra'. In *What Shall I Say of Clothes? Theoretical and Methodological Approaches to the Study of Dress in Antiquity: Selected Papers in Ancient Art and Architecture*, edited by Megan Cifarelli and Laura Gawlinski, 203–219. Boston: Archaeological Institute of America.

Higuchi, Takayasu, and Kiyohide Saito, eds. 2001. *Tomb F: Tomb of BWLH and BWRP; Southeast Necropolis, Palmyra, Syria.* Nara: Research Center for Silk Roadology.

Hillers, Delbert R. and Eleonora Cussini, eds. 1996. *Palmyrene Aramaic Texts*. Baltimore: Johns Hopkins University Press.

Hodder, Ian. 1982. *Symbols in Action*. Cambridge: Cambridge University Press.

Hope, Valerie M. 2001. *Constructing Identity: The Roman Funerary Monuments of Aquileia, Mainz and Nimes*. Oxford: Archaeopress.

Hvidberg-Hansen, Finn O. 1998. *The Palmyrene Inscriptions: Ny Carlsberg Glyptotek*. Copenhagen: Ny Carlsberg Glyptotek.

Ingholt, Harald. 1928. *Studier over Palmyrensk Skulptur*. Copenhagen: Reitzel.

Ingholt, Harald. 1932. 'Quelques fresques récemment découvertes à Palmyre'. *Acta archaeologica* 3: 1–20.

Ingholt, Harald. 1936. 'Inscriptions and Sculptures from Palmyra I'. *Berytus* 3: 83–128.

Ingholt, Harald. 1954. *Palmyrene and Gandharan Sculpture: An Exhibition Illustrating the Cultural Interrelations Between the Parthian Empire and Its Neighbors West and East, Palmyra and Gandhara*. New Haven, CT: Yale University Art Gallery.

Ingholt, Harald. 1970/1971. 'The Sarcophagus of Beʾelai and Other Sculptures from the Tomb of Malkû, Palmyra'. *Mélanges de l'Université Saint-Joseph* 45: 173–200.

Joyce, Rosemary A. 2005. 'Archaeology of the Body'. *Annual Review of Anthropology* 34: 139–158.

Kaizer, Ted. 2002. *The Religious Life of Palmyra: A Study of the Social Patterns of Worship in the Roman Period*. Stuttgart: Steiner.

Klaver, Sanne. 2019. 'The Participation of Palmyrene Women in the Religious Life of the City'. In *Women, Children, and the Family in Palmyra*, edited by Signe Krag and Rubina Raja, 157–167. Palmyrene Studies 3. Copenhagen: Det Kongelige Danske Videnskabernes Selskab.

Kleiner, Diana E. E. 1977. *Roman Group Portraiture: The Funerary Reliefs of the Late Republic and Early Empire*. New York: Garland.

Kleiner, Diana E. E. 1992. *Roman Sculpture*. New Haven, CT: Yale University Press.

Krag, Signe. 2016. 'Females in Group Portraits in Palmyra'. In *The World of Palmyra*, edited by Andreas Kropp and Rubina Raja, 180–193. Palmyrene Studies 1. Copenhagen: Det Kongelige Danske Videnskabernes Selskab.

Krag, Signe. 2017a. 'Women in Palmyrene Religion and Religious Practices'. In *Textiles and Cult in the Ancient Mediterranean*, edited by Cecilie Brøns and Marie-Louise Nosch, 230–240. Oxford: Oxbow.

Krag, Signe. 2017b. 'Changing Identities, Changing Positions: Jewellery in Palmyrene Female Portraits'. In *Positions and Professions in Palmyra*, edited by Tracey Long and Annette Højen Sørensen, 36–51. Palmyrene Studies 2. Copenhagen: Det Kongelige Danske Videnskabernes Selskab.

Krag, Signe. 2018. *Funerary Representations of Palmyrene Women: From the First Century BC to the Third Century AD*. Studies in Classical Archaeology 3. Turnhout: Brepols.

Krag, Signe. 2019a. 'Palmyrene Funerary Buildings and Family Burial Patterns'. In *Women, Children and the Family in Palmyra*, edited by Signe Krag and Rubina Raja, 38–66. Palmyrene Studies 3. Copenhagen: Det Kongelige Danske Videnskabernes Selskab.

Krag, Signe. 2019b. 'Palmyrene Funerary Female Portraits: Portrait Tradition and Change'. In *Funerary Portraiture in Greater Roman Syria*, edited by Michael Blömer and Rubina Raja, 111–132. Studies in Classical Archaeology 6, Turnhout: Brepols.

Krag, Signe, and Rubina Raja. 2016. 'Representations of Women and Children in Palmyrene Funerary *loculus* Reliefs, *loculus stelae* and Wall Paintings'. *Zeitschrift für Orient-Archäologie* 9: 134–178.

Krag, Signe, and Rubina Raja. 2018. 'Representations of Women and Children in Palmyrene Banqueting Reliefs and Sarcophagus Scenes'. *Zeitschrift für Orient-Archäologie* 10: 196–227.

Krag, Signe, and Rubina Raja. 2019. 'Unveiling Female Hairstyles: Markers of Age, Social Roles, and Status in Funerary Sculpture from Palmyra'. Zeitschrift für Orient-Archäologie 11: 243–277.

Kropp, Andreas, and Rubina Raja. 2014. 'The Palmyra Portrait Project'. *Syria* 91: 393–405.

Lagrange, Marie-Joseph. 1902. 'Notes d'épigraphie sémitique'. *Revue biblique* 11: 94–99.

Leroy, Jules. 1957. 'Mosaïques funéraires d'Édesse'. *Syria* 34: 306–342.

Mackay, Dorothy. 1949. 'The Jewellery of Palmyra and Its Significance'. *Iraq* 11: 160–187.

Makowski, Krzystof C. 1985. 'La sculpture funéraire palmyrénienne et sa fonction dans l'architecture sépulcrale'. *Studia Palmyrenskie: Études palmyréniennes* 8: 69–117.

Morehart, Mary. 1956/1957. 'Early Sculpture at Palmyra'. *Berytus* 12: 52–83.

Parlasca, Klaus. 1980. 'Ein frühes Grabrelief aus Palmyra'. *Eikones* 12: 149–152.

Parlasca, Klaus. 1988. 'Ikonographische Probleme palmrenischer Grabreliefs'. *Damaszener Mitteilungen* 3: 215–221.

Ploug, Gunhild. 1995. *Catalogue of the Palmyrene Sculptures, Ny Carlsberg Glyptotek*. Copenhagen: Ny Carlsberg Glyptotek.

Raja, Rubina. 2015. 'Palmyrene Funerary Portraits in Context: Portrait Habit between Local Traditions and Imperial Trends'. In *Traditions: Transmission of Culture in the Ancient World*, edited by Jane Fejfer, Mette Moltesen, and Annette Rathje, 329–361. Acta Hyperborea 14. Copenhagen: Collegium Hyperboreum and Museum Tusculanum Press.

Raja, Rubina. 2017. 'Powerful Images of the Deceased: Palmyrene Funerary Portrait Culture between Local, Greek and Roman Representations'. In *Bilder der Macht: Das griechische Porträt und seine Verwendung in der antiken Welt*, edited by Dietrich Boschung and Francois Queyrel, 319–348. Morphomata 34. Paderborn: Fink.

Sadurska, Anna. 1983. 'Le modèle de la semaine dans l'imagerie palmyrénienne'. *Études et travaux* 12: 151–156.

Sadurska, Anna. 1995. 'La famille et son image dans l'art de Palmyre'. *Arculiana*: 583–589.

Sadurska, Anna. 1996. 'L'art et la société: Recherches iconologiques sur la sculpture funéraire de Palmyre'. *Annales archéologiques arabes syriennes* 42: 285–288.

Sadurska, Anna, and Adnan Bounni, eds. 1994. *Les sculptures funéraires de Palmyre*. Rome: Giorgio Bretschneider.

Seyrig, Henri. 1934. 'Antiquités syriennes 17. Bas-reliefs monumentaux du temple de Bel à Palmyre'. *Syria* 15: 155–186.

Seyrig, Henri. 1939. 'Antiquités syriennes'. *Syria* 20: 189–194.

Seyrig, Henri. 1971. 'Le repas des morts et le 'banquet funèbre' à Palmyre'. *Annales archéologiques arabes syriennes* 21: 67–70.

Sokołowski, Łukasz. 2014. 'Portraying the Literacy of Palmyra: The Evidence of Funerary Sculpture and Its Interpretation'. *Études et travaux* 27: 376–403.

Sørensen, Annette Højen. 2016. 'Palmyrene Tomb Paintings in Context'. In *The World of Palmyra*, edited by Andreas Kropp and Rubina Raja, 103–117. Palmyrene Studies 1. Copenhagen: Det Kongelige Danske Videnskabernes Selskab.

Tanabe, Katsumi, ed. 1986. *Sculptures of Palmyra*. Tokyo: The Ancient Orient Museum.

Weingarten, Judith. 2018. 'Zenobia in History and Legend'. In *Palmyra: Mirage in the Desert*, edited by Joan Aruz, 130–145. New York: The Metropolitan Museum of Art.

Will, Ernst. 1949. 'La tour funéraire de Palmyre'. *Syria* 26: 87–116.

Will, Ernst. 1951. 'Le Relief de la tour de Kithôt et le banquet funéraire à Palmyre'. *Syria* 28: 70–100.

Yon, Jean-Baptiste. 1999. 'La présence des notables dans l'espace périurbain à Palmyre'. In *Construction, reproduction, et représentation des Patriciats urbains de l'Antiquité au XXe siècle*, edited by Claude Petitfrère, 387–400. Tours: Presses Universitaires François-Rabelais.

Yon, Jean-Baptiste. 2001. 'Zénobie et son milieu social'. In *Moi, Zénobie, reine de Palmyre*, edited by Jacques Charles-Gaffiot, Henri Lavagne, and Jean-Marc Hofman, 43–47. Paris: Skira.

Yon, Jean-Baptiste. 2002. *Les notables de Palmyre*. Beirut: Presses de l'Institut français du Proche-Orient.

Yon, Jean-Baptiste. 2016. 'Women and the Religious Life of Dura-Europos'. In *Religion, Society and Culture at Dura-Europos*, edited by Ted Kaizer, 99–113. Cambridge: Cambridge University Press.

Zanker, Paul. 1993. 'The Hellenistic Grave Stelai from Smyrna: Identity and Self-Image in the Polis'. In *Images and Ideologies: Self-Definition in the Hellenistic World*, edited by Anthony Bulloch, Erich S. Gruen, Anthony A. Long, and Andrew Stewart, 212–230. Berkeley: University of California Press.

Zouhdi, Bachir. 1983. 'La femme dans l'art de Palmyre'. *Damaszener Mitteilungen* 1: 315–316.

Zouhdi, Bachir. 2001. 'Le rôle de la femme dans la société de Palmyre'. In *Moi, Zénobie, reine de Palmyre*, edited by Jacques Charles-Gaffiot, Henri Lavagne, and Jean-Marc Hofman, 111. Paris: Skira.

....

CHAPTER 29

REPRESENTATIONS OF MEN IN PALMYRA

....

MAURA K. HEYN

INTRODUCTION

....

DURING its heyday, in the first through third centuries AD, the city of Palmyra bristled with representations of men. Statues of men sat on consoles that were attached to the columns of the long colonnaded streets, the public spaces, and the sanctuary enclosures of the city; busts and full-length figures in relief occasionally adorned its monuments; and images of men participating in religious rituals dotted its sanctuaries. With rare exceptions, these public images have not survived the passage of time, but the inscriptions that frequently accompany the statues identify the showcased men as religious benefactors, associates of the caravans, and civic officials (Colledge 1976, 89–90; Yon 2002). Although most of the municipal images have not survived, we do have an abundance of funerary portraits. These torso-length relief portraits of men, women, and occasionally children, carved on rectangular limestone slabs that were used to seal the burial compartments in the tombs, present the elite of Palmyra in the way that they wanted to be recorded for posterity. This chapter analyses the significance of these funerary representations of the male public persona to gain insight into those aspects of their identity that were emphasized. Recent scholarship has challenged the 'generic' label that is often ascribed to these portraits, citing particularities of dress, adornment, attribute, and feature that allow for an assertion of identity (Stauffer 2012; Albertson 2016; Raja 2015; 2017b). There is also considerable debate concerning the degree to which this self-representation has anything to do with the Romans during the period of Roman hegemony in the eastern Mediterranean (Colledge 1976; Parlasca 1985; Balty 1996; Heyn 2010; Kropp and Raja 2014; Raja 2015; 2017b). The question of identity is not easily answered, and it seems likely that some of the same ambiguity existed in the past. The message of the portraiture was rarely univocal or static, and the ancient Palmyrenes drew on this shifting kaleidoscope to advertise their multifaceted identities with portraiture that was simultaneously generic and specific, individual, familial and communal, Greek, Roman, Parthian, and Palmyrene.

SETTING THE STANDARD

The earliest individual representations of men in the funerary sphere appear on stelae that served as free-standing grave markers. Dating to the first half of the first century AD, these stelae depict small-scale, low relief, full-length frontal figures of men and women, often with a curtain included in the background (Colledge 1976, 64). All the men on these stelae wear a similar costume: a chiton with a himation draped over the shoulders and wrapped around the right arm in an 'arm-sling' arrangement. In the mid-first century, these grave markers were moved indoors, and their shape was modified slightly so they could serve as seals for the loculi (burial niches) in the tombs (College 1976, 64). The torso-length, almost life-size, relief portrait developed alongside these full-length figures and became the preferred way to portray the deceased on the slabs that sealed the individual niches, from the mid-first century to the late third century AD (Colledge 1976, 68; Tanabe 1986; Dentzer-Feydy and Teixidor 1993; Sadurska and Bounni 1994; Ploug 1995) (Figure 29.1).

These individual relief portraits, of which well over a thousand examples survive, represent by far the most numerous representations of men and women from Palmyra in the first three centuries AD (Kropp and Raja 2014; Raja 2015; 2017b, 329; 2019d). Men and women appear in almost equal numbers (Heyn 2016, 194–195; Raja 2017b, 330) and are depicted frontally, from the waist up, a presentation whose basic features varied little throughout the period in which they were produced (Colledge 1976, 68). The chiton and himation remain the most popular garments for the men, and the himation is typically presented in the familiar arm-sling arrangement (Heyn and Raja 2019). Most of the men extend the right hand over the fold of the cloak, and the left holds the attribute, if one is present, usually a book-roll, but occasionally a leaf. A ring or two often appear on the little finger of the left hand (Colledge 1976, 247–254). The preferred hairstyle is short and abundant, with the *coma in gradus formata* hairstyle being a popular choice in the first two centuries (Ploug 1995, 46). Harald Ingholt's (1928) stylistic grouping of the portraits according to the dated examples does indicate some changes over time; for example, the beard becomes a common feature in the second century, certain hairstyles come and go, and the folds of the cloak are configured differently (Colledge 1976, 68). However, for the most part, were it not for the inscriptions identifying the deceased in Palmyrene Aramaic above one or both shoulders, many of the representations of these men would be indistinguishable.

The frontal position and general arrangement of garments seen in the relief portraits in Palmyrene tombs is echoed by the relief busts of men (alongside those of women) that adorned other areas of the tomb, perhaps as decoration, and occasional painted images of men in these tombs (Colledge 1976, 84). An exceptionally well-preserved example of such a painting from the second century AD adorns the left wall of an exedra in the hypogeum of Ḥairan in the south-west necropolis, accompanied by the image of a woman painted on the right wall (Ingholt 1932; Sørensen 2016, 107–108). The full-length figure

FIGURE 29.1 Palmyrene funerary portrait. Limestone. Second century AD. 20.51 × 17.01 in. (52.1 × 43.21 cm).

The Metropolitan Museum of Art, 02.29.2.

of the man, identified as Ḥairan, son of Taimarsû, shows him from the front. He wears the chiton and himation, similar to the garment worn in the relief portraits, with the right arm held in the folds of the cloak extending across his chest. His tunic is adorned with a black stripe, and he wears two rings on his left hand. Images such as this one of Ḥairan, with his orientation, pose, and dress, strengthen the impression created by the torso-length limestone reliefs that there was a standardized way of depicting elite men in Palmyra (Colledge 1976, 86).

GENERIC VERSUS INDIVIDUATED REPRESENTATIONS

The tendency of Palmyrene men's funerary portraits to lack clear individuality is, perhaps, to be expected since the funerary representations were not intended to be realistic depictions of the actual features of the deceased (Parlasca 1985, 387; Long 2016). As several early inscriptions indicate, the relief bust began as a *nefesh*, a tomb-marker or metaphorical dwelling place for the soul that took the form of a figural relief (Colledge 1976, 62) and later developed into a representation that approximated the appearance of the deceased but was not meant to be a true portrait. This assertion is corroborated by nearly identical reliefs that depict two different people (Colledge 1976, 62; Parlasca 1985, 350–351; Albertson 2016, 152) and by two reliefs of the same person that do not look alike (Colledge 1976, 62, n. 185; Ploug 1995, 39–42). The relief busts were clearly produced in workshops that worked from a limited number of models (Colledge 1976, 68). Some choice existed in terms of adornment and attributes, and research indicates that the depiction of clothing was accurate (Stauffer 2012, 94), but, in general, options would have been limited (Albertson 2016, 151).

The similarity of the faces in the Palmyrene tomb portraits, the narrow range of poses, and the alikeness of the costumes from one portrait to the next seem to contradict Chabot, who asserted (1922, 114) that a simple glance would show that the artists wanted to create real portraits and that they offer true images of the deceased. And yet, Chabot is not wrong: the impression of a standard manner of representing men in Palmyra, as demonstrated by most of sculpted reliefs and painted images, holds true only under cursory observation. Closer inspection reveals clear particularities that distinguish the individual portraits and make them unique (Albertson 2016, 162; Long 2016, 143–144; 2017, 69; Raja 2017b, 329–330). The inscription, highlighted with red (and thus clearly a critical feature), identified the deceased by name and genealogy (College 1976, 68). Additional differentiation among male portraits was created by changing the types of garments, their arrangement, and the decoration of the tunic and cloak (Stauffer 2012; 2012, 90); choosing different attributes; the presence of a wreath on the head; different gestures (Heyn 2010); depicting a dorsalium behind the figure (Raja 2019c); or including additional family members on the loculus slab. These additional family members may be children (although not necessarily sons or daughters), shown full-length at a smaller scale in the background (Pierson 1984; Heyn 2010, appendix 4), or a mother, wife, cousin, brother, or sister, among others, shown adjacent to the man in the loculus relief (Colledge 1976; Heyn 2010, appendix 3; Krag 2016).

Two groups of men in the Palmyrene portraits stand out more prominently because of their distinguishing dress and attributes. The first group, identified by their attributes as men who had some affiliation with the caravans (Will 1957; Colledge 1976, 68; Raja 2020), often wear the cloak thrown back across the shoulders, rather than in the arm-sling arrangement (Colledge 1976, 147) (Figure 29.2). Also, instead of the usual short-sleeved tunic, a man in this group may wear a long-sleeved tunic (Dentzer-Feydy and Teixidor 1993, 71). These same men eschew the usual attributes of the book-roll or leaf, opting instead for the sword and whip held in one or both hands (Albertson 2000). In terms of gesture, rather than extending the hands, some of these men extend the index and middle fingers of each hand so they touch (Heyn 2010, 643, appendix 6). The second group that stands out are the men who wear a tall, cylindrical hat and who are identified as priests (Rumscheid 2000; Raja 2017a; 2018). In addition to their special hats, which

FIGURE 29.2 Funerary portrait of Zabda, son of 'Oggâ, from Palmyra. Palmyra, Palmyra Museum, inv. no. 2027/7225.

Photograph by author.

are often adorned with a wreath and a miniature bust, these men appear to have shaved heads, since no hair is visible. Also, they often wear a smaller cloak with embroidered edges, attached at the right shoulder with a brooch (Colledge 1976, 68; Taha 1982, 119–121; Raja 2021). Some of them hold ritual vessels: a jug and a bowl filled with incense (Stucky 1973, 175).

Banquet Scenes

Palmyrene men associated with the caravans or with priestly activities in the city are conspicuous in the corpus of torso-length reliefs because of variations of dress and attribute. A third group of men attracted attention in the Palmyrene tombs because they eschewed the frontal half-length portrait altogether and opted instead for the banquet motif. This type of scene appears early in the first century AD on the front of some tombs and then moves inside the tombs by the second century (Colledge 1976, 239). Inside the tomb, the banquet motif was featured on a large scale on flat rectangular stelae or sarcophagus lids that sat on rectangular slabs or sarcophagi that were carved to look like couches (Colledge 1976, 73–75) or on a smaller scale on rectangular slabs that sealed individual burial niches (Colledge 1976, 78; Makowski 1985, 69–71). The main figure is usually male, and reclines on his left side on a cushion, with his left leg tucked under his bent right leg, and a bowl or cup in his left hand. His family is depicted around him on a smaller scale, with his wife seated at his feet and his children behind him. More members of the family are depicted by the busts between the legs of the couch. Finally, in terms of costume, most of the men who recline in the banquet reliefs wear what is called 'Parthian' dress (but is perhaps more accurately called 'Mesopotamian' [Butcher 2003, 329]). It consists of a round-necked, long-sleeved tunic that is belted at the waist and decorated with bands of embroidery. Loose trousers, also adorned with stripes of embroidery, are worn beneath the tunic. A short cloak may be pinned on the right shoulder, as in the funerary reliefs of priests, or a longer cloak may be draped over the tunic and trousers. Soft, embroidered boots are worn on the feet (Seyrig 1937; Taha 1982; Curtis 2017; Long 2017).

Images of men reclining in the banqueting pose also appear on the tesserae, the small tokens that granted access to banquets in the city's sanctuaries (Seyrig 1940). The similarity of the reclining pose to that seen in the tombs prompted some scholars to identify the tesserae as tickets to funerary banquets (du Mesnil du Buisson 1962, 504), but their find-spots associate them with religious activities (Seyrig 1940, 52; Raja 2016; 2019e; 2019f). The repetition of the reclining-figure motif in the tomb may be associated with its connection to the prominent activities in the city (Heyn 2008) or its high-status connotations in the region (Dentzer 1971). The banqueting motif may also have been a convenient way of drawing attention to the family (Ingholt 1970/1971, 182–183), though not everyone in the scene holds banqueting items (Seyrig 1951, 67–70).

The clear popularity of Parthian dress in the banquet scenes in tombs is notable (Taha 1982; Curtis 2017, 59–62; Long 2017, 73, 77–81). Its association with the lucrative caravan trade may have made it both a status and a cultural symbol at Palmyra (Curtis 2017, 65; Long 2017, 79–81), but it is also true that priests often wear it. The significance of the choice is difficult to ascertain, but patterns in the selection of the costume with regard to the position of the wearer and his attributes suggest that it was not a haphazard occurrence (Heyn 2008). Whatever the motivations of the wearer, the choice of the Parthian costume corroborates what is already suspected about Palmyra: dress was a way in which the inhabitants of Palmyra expressed identity. Even their gods had particular styles of dress.

REPRESENTATIONS OF GODS

In the sanctuaries of Palmyra there are numerous representations of gods who are clearly identifiable because of their individuated dress (and attributes). Both Bēl and Baalshamin are usually represented with a *calathos* on their heads. Also, Bēl, Aglibol, and Yarhibol are always depicted in military dress. Bēl is further distinguished by a type of 'scaled' cuirass, as well as the baggy trousers he wears under this cuirass (Bounni 1966,

313–320). In contrast, Baalshamin often wears a tunic and cloak which are in the Graeco-Roman style, and he may be identified by his attributes, the thunderbolt and sheaves of grain (Colledge 1976, 25–26; Gawlikowski 1990, 2627). Aglibol and Yarhibol, the moon and sun gods, are usually depicted with the radiate nimbus, and Aglibol has a crescent on his nimbus.

Further evidence of costume as an identifying characteristic of Palmyrene gods is seen in the depiction of the gods worshipped by those living in outlying areas. These gods, known as *genneas*, are most often seen in *ex-voto* reliefs from rural sanctuaries in the area around Palmyra (Bounni 1966, 319). The costume worn by the *genneas* is generally assumed to be the most similar to the local costume: a long tunic belted below the waist with a piece of rolled material (Taha 1982, 118, 121–122). The iconography of Malakbel, the sacred brother of Aglibol, is also distinctive. Aglibol was a moon god, and Malakbel was a sun god. When Aglibol and Malakbel are featured side by side, Aglibol is depicted in military costume, and Malakbel wears local costume (Seyrig 1938). In this case, as with the other gods, the function of the god in the particular context may govern costume choice. These images of male deities give some indication of the power of costume, or at least offer insight into the ways in which dress was used as an identifying feature in the civic sphere.

Representations of Men in the Public Sphere

Turning to the statues of Palmyrene men who are represented in the public sphere, the evidence is not well preserved, and the paucity of surviving examples makes any definitive statements problematic (Colledge 1976, 89; Raja 2017b, 325–327). As stated in the introduction, statues of men and, much less frequently, women (Yon 2002, 166), featured prominently on the brackets that were attached to the columns of the colonnaded streets, public spaces, and religious sanctuaries (Figure 29.3). Most of this multitude of free-standing civic statues, many of which were bronze, have not survived, but we do have a few stone examples, both in fragments and in their entirety, from several sanctuaries in the city (Colledge 1976, 89–90; Gawlikowski 2008; Wielgosz-Rondolino 2016). Six statues from the temple of Baalshamin, dating to the late first and early second century, are life-size, standing portraits of men who wear the chiton and himation and feature the arm-sling pose (Colledge 1976, 90). Additional evidence, dating to the mid-second century, includes two more frontal, standing portraits of men, wearing the chiton and himation, and a third man who is seated and wears trousers beneath his cloak (Colledge 1976, 91). Finally, from the third century, there is evidence of the increasing popularity of honorific statues of men in togas. Two life-size limestone statues depict men in the Roman toga (Colledge 1976, 91), as do three

FIGURE 29.3 Grand Colonnade in Palmyra.

Photograph by author.

more in marble: two from the senate building and one from the Baths of Diocletian (Wielgosz 2010, 81).

The above-mentioned honorific statues of men, especially those from the third century, diverge stylistically from the funerary examples. This divergence in representational styles is due to their civic context (Butcher 2003, 328; Raja 2017b, 326–327), though it is likely that the public statues in limestone were produced in the same workshops as the funerary examples (Wielgosz-Rondolino 2016, 178). The statues of men in chiton and himation do provide some justification for concluding that the arm-sling motif was a well-known way of portraying mortal men in the civic sphere. The arm-sling pose shows up again in the sanctuary of Bēl, where men are portrayed in a variety of costumes in several of the reliefs that adorn the temple's peristyle beams (Seyrig 1934). In one of these scenes, eight men are discernible, and two of the pairs of men stand at either side of two *thymiateria*, presumably making an offering of incense (Seyrig 1934, plate 18). All the men wear the priestly hat. It is difficult to distinguish the costumes clearly, but one of the sacrificing pairs wears matching attire: long tunics belted at the waist. Two other men stand in the middle of the scene and are not directly beside either *thymiaterion*. These men may represent bystanders, and their attire is worth noting: both wear the chiton and himation and hold their right arms in the arm-sling pose. In a second relief, the men are grouped in pairs, with six pairs flanking six *thymiateria* (Seyrig 1934, plate 23). Though this relief is also in bad shape, the costumes of two of these groups may be discerned. Interestingly, the two men in each pair that flanks a *thymiaterion* wear matching costumes. The two men farthest to the right in the relief wear loose trousers and cloaks. The costumes of the next pair consist of long tunics belted at the waist and cloaks that hang down the back to the knees. The remaining four groups are too fragmentary to draw any conclusions about their attire.

STANDARDIZATION AND COMMUNITY IDENTITY

Although the various representations of men in Palmyra are not identical, with men opting for the toga much more often in the public arena, the chiton and himation, paired with the arm-sling pose, are the most frequent choice overall. Even in the tombs, where individuation is established in a variety of ways, the arm-sling motif still appears in the vast majority of male portraits (Heyn 2010, 114). The prominent aberrations from this standard, the priests, represent only 20 percent of men's portraits (Raja 2017a, 116), and far fewer men are securely linked to the caravan trade. It is worth considering the possibility that this consistency in male iconography is deliberate. In other words, the assertion that these funerary representations were powerful symbols of individual identity (Butcher 2003, 327–328; Raja 2015, 333) does not rule out the possibility that their standardization was also deliberate (Long 2016, 141–143). Distinguishing details, such as dress, attribute, and gesture drew attention to the deceased as individuals, and the decision to be represented in a chiton and himation, with the right arm held across the chest in the sling, indicated their inclusion in the group (Albertson 2016, 163).

The idea that a generic style of representation could emphasize the importance of the community and the individual's place in that community is described by Koortbojian (2009) in his analysis of the popularity of togate statues in Rome. He argues that the nearly identical appearance of toga-clad bodies, which were depicted on public monuments in Rome throughout the imperial period, demonstrates the power of the toga as an expression of civic ideology. The faces of the men, and their attributes, drew attention to them as individuals, and their togate bodies demonstrated their inclusion in the community (Koortbojian 2009, 72–73). Referring to the Villa Doria Pamphilj togatus, Koortbojian (75) says: 'What is truly distinctive about all such Roman statues is that both the head and body always served to articulate now the particularity, now the generality, of any given portrait'. A similar duality may have existed in Palmyra with respect to the popular arm-sling pose characteristic of representations of the city's upper-class men. The visual similarity may be due to a variety of factors, such as the portraits not being intended to be likenesses of the individuals or their being purchased ready-made from workshops, but some consideration should be given to the idea that the standardization or 'sameness' was deliberate because it contributed to a sense of elite identity in the Palmyrene community (Raja 2017a, 129).

In addition to strengthening the sense of community, the standardization of portraiture also drew attention to family groups, which were extremely important in Palmyra (Sadurska 1995). Although the portraits mostly depicted individuals, they were not meant to be seen in isolation: they were placed beside, and above, and below dozens, and even hundreds, of other portraits of the same family tomb (Raja 2017b, 333–334). Again and again, attention was drawn to the family: by the tomb itself (Yon 1999), the double portraits (Heyn 2010, 637–638; Krag 2016, 180–181; Raja 2017b, 332), the banquet scenes (Sadurska and Bounni, 70–73), the inscriptions (Yon 2002), and the similar styles of representation in the individual portraits. Even non-standard choices of representation, such as unusual attributes or dress styles, drew attention to the family if these choices were echoed in other portraits in the tomb (Albertson 2012, 157; 2016, 156; Raja 2017a, 129). The portraits of priests could also draw attention to the family if they were representative of hereditary positions associated with that particular family (Raja 2017b, 335).

Cultural Identity

It is difficult to assess the extent to which these frontal representations of Palmyrene men—particularly the bust-length funerary portraits—were popular because they were connected to a Roman cultural identity in some way. Palmyra is located in a region that was renowned for being a complex cultural web of Hellenistic, Roman, Parthian, and local practices (Colledge 1976, 235; Butcher 2003; Andrade 2013; Raja 2019a). There is no pre-Roman tradition of funerary portraiture in Palmyra (Raja 2015, 335), but there are prototypes in the region (Raja 2017b, 322). Also, the emphasis on a frontal presentation and the large eyes that are seen in the torso-length portraits may have been adopted from the Parthians to the east (Ingholt 1954, 5).

The timing of the production of these portraits—the first three centuries AD—and the similarity of their style to freedmen reliefs in Rome (Kleiner 1977; 1992) suggests that the Romans were the source of inspiration (Colledge 1976, 138, 239; Zanker 1992). The

Romans were certainly the dominant political force in the region (Sartre 2005; Edwell 2008), which would have resulted in some negotiation of social and political positions in Palmyra that may have been expressed in the material culture produced in the city and in its tombs (Schmidt-Colinet 1997; Albertson 2016, 150; Magnani and Mior 2016). The Palmyrene men are wearing the Greek-style chiton and himation rather than the toga, but this preference does not preclude the Romans as a reference or audience. The Romans were responsible for the dissemination of new 'Greek' or 'Hellenistic' styles of material culture in the provinces (Butcher 2003, 270–275). So, for example, the chiton and himation, rather than the toga, are typical of public statuary of the Roman elite in the East (Smith 1998, 65; Fejfer 2008, 196–197; Borg 2012, 318). Also, though it is true that the arm-sling pose, so popular for freedmen reliefs in Rome in the first century BC, would have been 'old-fashioned' by the first millennium in Palmyra (Davies 2017, 23–24), it is a male pose that was popular throughout the eastern provinces of the empire in the first few centuries AD (Colledge 1976, 138; Boatwright 2005; Davies 2017, 24), including other regions of Syria (Parlasca 1982; Skupinska-Løvset 1985; 1999). The regional popularity of this style of representation may indeed suggest that the inhabitants of Palmyra were participating in a phenomenon that characterized the regional elite. Thus the new style of portraiture was a vessel for advertising an identity that was not cultural, per se, but (or additionally) a regional, communal, or even individual expression of status (Woolf 1998; Audley-Miller 2012; Stauffer 2012, 95–97).

Conclusion

Although drawing attention to the individual portrait in the tomb by varying the depictions of hand gesture, hairstyles, attributes, and clothing was not uncommon in Palmyra, the frontal portrait in chiton and himation, featuring the arm-sling pose, was the standard for representations of men in the city. This repetition of a recognizable representational style was deliberate: it created and strengthened a sense of commonality in the tomb as well as in the community (and perhaps even in the region). The inhabitants of Palmyra adapted a style of regional relief portraiture to suit their own needs and to advertise their own priorities (Colledge 1976, 239; Raja 2017b, 325, 343). The message behind this unique style of representation may have been individual, familial, communal, regional, or imperial. These interchangeable connotations would have allowed for any of these meanings at different times or for different audiences. Despite a style of representation that, in its general outlines, linked the inhabitants of Palmyra to a wider world and served to indicate status, the funerary portraits in Palmyra also allowed for the communication of an identity that was distinctly Palmyrene (Albertson 2016, 15; Raja 2015, 333).

BIBLIOGRAPHY

Albertson, Fred C. 2000. 'A Palmyrene Funerary Bust of a Roman Cavalryman'. *Damaszener Mitteilungen* 12: 141–153.

Albertson, Fred C. 2012. 'Two Unpublished Palmyrene Funerary Reliefs in North American Museums'. *Syria* 89: 151–162.

Albertson, Fred C. 2016. 'Typology, Attribution, and Identity in Palmyran Funerary Portraiture'. In *The World of Palmyra*, edited by Andreas Kropp and Rubina Raja, 150–165. Palmyrene Studies 1. Copenhagen: Det Kongelige Danske Videnskabernes Selskab.

Andrade, Nathanael. 2013. *Syrian Identity in the Greco-Roman World*. Cambridge: Cambridge University Press.

Audley-Miller, Lucy. 2012. 'Dressed to Impress: The Tomb Sculpture of Ghirza in Tripolitania'. In *Dressing the Dead in Classical Antiquity*, edited by Maureen Carroll and John Peter Wild, 99–114. Stroud: Amberley.

Balty, Jean Charles. 1996. 'Palmyre entre Orient et Occident: Acculturation et résistances'. *Palmyra and the Silk Road: International Colloquium; Palmyra, 7–11 April 1992, Les annales archéologiques arabes syriennes* 42: 437–441.

Boatwright, Mary T. 2005. 'Children and Parents on the Tombstones of Pannonia'. In *The Roman Family in the Empire: Rome, Italy and Beyond*, edited by Michele George, 287–318. Oxford: Oxford University Press.

Borg, Barbara. 2012. 'Recent Approaches to the Study of Roman Portraits'. *Perspective* 2: 315–320.

Bounni, Adnan. 1966. 'Nouveaux bas-reliefs religieux de la Palmyrène'. In *Mélanges offerts à Kazimierz Michalowski*, edited by Maria Ludwika Bernhard, 313–320. Warsaw: Państwowe Wydawnictwo Naukowe.

Butcher, Kevin. 2003. *Roman Syria and the Near East*. Los Angeles: The J. Paul Getty Museum, Getty Publications.

Chabot, Jean-Baptiste. 1922. *Choix d'inscriptions de Palmyre*. Paris: Imprimerie nationale.

Charles-Gaffiot, Jacques, Jean-Marc Hofman, and Henri Lavagne, eds. 2001. *Moi, Zénobie, reine de Palmyre*. Paris: Seuil.

Colledge, Malcolm A. R. 1976. *The Art of Palmyra*. London: Thames & Hudson.

Curtis, Vesta Sarkhosh. 2017. 'The Parthian Haute-Couture at Palmyra'. In *Positions and Professions in Palmyra*, edited by Tracey Long and Annette Højen Sørensen, 52–67. Palmyrene Studies 2. Copenhagen: Det Kongelige Danske Videnskabernes Selskab.

Davies, Glenys. 2017. 'The Body Language of Palmyra and Rome'. In *Positions and Professions in Palmyra*, edited by Tracey Long and Annette Højen Sørensen, 20–35. Palmyrene Studies 2. Copenhagen: Det Kongelige Danske Videnskabernes Selskab.

Dentzer-Feydy, Jacqueline, and Javier Teixidor, eds. 1993. *Les antiquités de Palmyre au Musée du Louvre*. Paris: Seuil.

Dentzer, Jean-Marie. 1971. 'L'Iconographie iranienne du souverain couché et le motif du banquet'. *Annales archéologiques arabes syriennes* 21: 39–50.

Edwell, Peter M. 2008. *Between Rome and Persia: The Middle Euphrates, Mesopotamia and Palmyra under Roman Control*. London: Routledge.

Fejfer, Jane. 2008. *Roman Portraits in Context*. Berlin: De Gruyter.

Gawlikowski, Michal. 1970. *Monuments funéraires de Palmyre*. Warsaw: Państwowe Wydawnictwo Naukowe.

Gawlikowski, Michal. 1990. 'Les dieux de Palmyre'. In *Aufstieg und Niedergang der römischen Welt*. Vol. 2, *Principat*, no. 18, *Religion*, 4, edited by Wolfgang Haase, 2605–2658. Berlin: de Gruyter.

Gawlikowski, Michal. 2008. 'The Statues of the Sanctuary of Allat in Palmyra'. In *The Sculptural Environment of the Roman Near East: Reflections on Culture, Ideology, and Power*, edited by Yaron Z. Eliav, Elise A. Friedland, and Sharon Herbert, 397–411. Leuven: Peeters.

Heyn, Maura K. 2008. 'Sacerdotal Activities and Parthian Dress in Roman Palmyra'. In *Reading a Dynamic Canvas: Adornment in the Ancient Mediterranean World*, edited by Cynthia S. Colburn and Maura K. Heyn, 170–193. Newcastle: Cambridge Scholars.

Heyn, Maura K. 2010. 'Gesture and Identity in the Funerary Art of Palmyra'. *American Journal of Archaeology* 114: 631–661.

Heyn, Maura K., and Rubina Raja. 2019. 'Male Dress Habits in Roman Period Palmyra'. In *Fashioned Selves: Dress and Identity in Antiquity*, edited by Megan Cifarelli, 41–53. Oxford: Oxbow.

Ingholt, Harald. 1928. *Studier over Palmyrensk Skulptur*. Copenhagen: Reitzel.

Ingholt, Harald. 1932. 'Quelques fresques récemment decouvertes à Palmyre'. *Acta archaeologica* 3: 1–20.

Ingholt, Harald. 1954. *Palmyrene and Gandharan Sculpture: An Exhibition Illustrating the Cultural Interrelations between the Parthian Empire and Its Neighbors West and East, Palmyra and Gandhara*. New Haven, CT: Yale University Art Gallery.

Ingholt, Harald. 1966. 'Some Sculptures from the Tomb of Malkû at Palmyra'. In *Mélanges offerts à Kazimierz Michalowski*, edited by Maria Ludwika Bernhard, 457–476. Warsaw: Pánstwowe Wydawnictwo Naukowe.

Ingholt, Harald. 1970/1971. 'The Sarcophagus of Be'elai and Other Sculptures from the Tomb of Malkû, Palmyra'. *Mélanges de l'Université Saint-Joseph* 45: 173–200.

Kleiner, Diana E. E. 1977. *Roman Group Portraiture: The Funerary Reliefs of the Late Republic and Early Empire*. New York: Garland.

Kleiner, Diana E. E. 1992. *Roman Sculpture*. New Haven, CT: Yale University Press.

Koortbojian, Michael. 2009. 'The Double Identity of Roman Portrait Statues: Costumes and Their Symbolism at Rome'. In *Roman Dress and the Fabrics of Roman Culture*, edited by Jonathan Edmondson and Alison Keith, 71–93. Toronto: University of Toronto Press.

Krag, Signe. 2016. 'Females in Group Portraits in Palmyra'. In *The World of Palmyra*, edited by Andreas Kropp and Rubina Raja, 180–193. Palmyrene Studies 1. Copenhagen: Det Kongelige Danske Videnskabernes Selskab.

Kropp, Andreas J. M., and Rubina Raja. 2014. 'The Palmyra Portrait Project'. *Syria* 91: 393–408

Long, Tracey. 2016. 'Facing the Evidence: How to Approach the Portraits'. In *The World of Palmyra*, edited by Andreas Kropp and Rubina Raja, 135–149. Palmyrene Studies 1. Copenhagen: Det Kongelige Danske Videnskabernes Selskab.

Long, Tracey. 2017. 'The Use of Parthian Costume in Funerary Portraiture in Palmyra'. In *Positions and Professions in Palmyra*, edited by Tracey Long and Annette Højen Sørensen, 68–83. Palmyrene Studies 2. Copenhagen: Det Kongelige Danske Videnskabernes Selskab.

Magnani, Stefano, and Paola Mior. 2016. 'Palmyrene Elites: Aspects of Self-Representation and Integration in Hadrian's Age'. In *Official Power and Local Elites in the Roman Provinces*, edited by Rada Varga and Viorica Rusu-Bolindet, 95–113. London: Routledge.

Makowski, Krzysztof C. 1985. 'Recherches sur le banquet miniaturisé dans l'art funéraire de Palmyre'. *Studia Palmyrenskie: Études palmyréniennes* 8: 119–130.

du Mesnil du Buisson, Robert. 1962. *Les tessères et les monnaies de Palmyre*. Paris: de Boccard.

Parlasca, Klaus. 1980. 'Ein frühes Grabrelief aus Palmyra'. *Eikones* 12: 149–152.

Parlasca, Klaus. 1982. *Syrische Grabreliefs hellenistischer und römischer Zeit: Fundgruppen und Problem.* Mainz am Rhein: von Zabern.

Parlasca, Klaus. 1985. 'Das Verhältnis der palmyrenischen Grabplastik zur römischen Porträtkunst'. *Mitteilungen des Deutschen Archäologischen Instituts Römische Abteilung* 92: 343–356.

Parlasca, Klaus. 1987. 'Aspekte der palmyrenischen Skulpturen'. In *Palmyra: Geschichte, Kunst und Kultur der Oasenstadt*, edited by Erwin M. Ruprechtsberger, 276–282. Linz: Gutenberg.

Parlasca, Klaus. 1988. 'Ikonographische Probleme palmrenischer Grabreliefs'. *Damaszener Mitteilungen* 3: 215–221.

Parlasca, Klaus. 1989. 'La sculpture grecque et la sculpture d'époque romaine impériale en Syrie'. In *Archéologie et histoire de la Syrie*. Vol. 2, edited by Jean-Marie Dentzer and Winfried Orthmann, 537–556. Saarbrücken: Saarbrücken Druckerei und Verlag.

Parlasca, Klaus. 1990. 'Palmyrensiche Skulpturen in Museen an der amerikanischen Weskuste'. *Roman Funerary Monuments in the J. Paul Getty Museum.* Vol. 1, 133–144. Malibu: J. Paul Getty Museum.

Parlasca, Klaus. 2005. 'Zu palmyrenischen Inschriften auf Reliefs'. In *A Journey to Palmyra: Collected Essays to Remember Delbert R. Hillers*, edited by Eleonora Cussini, 137–149. Leiden: Brill.

Pierson, Francis. 1984. 'Recherches sur les costumes des enfants dans l'iconographie palmyrénienne'. *Revue des archéologues et historiens d'art de Louvain* 17: 95–108.

Ploug, Gunhild. 1995. *Catalogue of the Palmyrene Sculptures, Ny Carlsberg Glyptotek.* Copenhagen: Ny Carlsberg Glyptotek.

Raja, Rubina. 2015. 'Palmyrene Funerary Portraits in Context: Portrait Habit between Local Traditions and Imperial Trends'. In *Traditions: Transmission of Culture in the Ancient World*, edited by Jane Fejfer, Mette Moltesen, and Annette Rathje, 329–361. Acta Hyperborea 14. Copenhagen: Collegium Hyperboreum and Museum Tusculanum Press.

Raja, Rubina. 2016. 'In and out of Contexts: Explaining Religious Complexity Through the Banqueting Tesserae from Palmyra'. In *The Significance of Objects: Considerations on Agency and Context*, edited by Rubina Raja and Lara Weiss, 340–371. Heidelberg: Mohr Siebeck.

Raja, Rubina. 2017a. 'To Be or Not to Be Depicted as a Priest in Palmyra: A Matter of Representational Spheres and Societal Values'. In *Positions and Professions in Palmyra*, edited by Tracey Long and Annette Højen Sørensen, 115–130. Palmyrene Studies 2. Copenhagen: Det Kongelige Danske Videnskabernes Selskab.

Raja, Rubina. 2017b. 'Powerful Images of the Deceased: Palmyrene Funerary Portrait Culture between Local, Greek and Roman Representations'. In *Bilder der Macht: Das griechische Porträt und seine Verwendung in der antiken Welt*, edited by Dietrich Boschung and Francois Queyrel, 319–348. Morphomata 34. Paderborn: Fink.

Raja, Rubina. 2018. 'The Matter of the Palmyrene "Modius". Remarks on the History of Research into the Terminology of the Palmyrene Priestly Hat'. *Religion in the Roman Empire* 2(4): 237–259.

Raja, Rubina. 2019a. 'Funerary Portraiture in Palmyra: Portrait Habit at a Cross-Road or a Signifier of Local Identity?' In *Funerary Portraiture in Greater Roman Syria*, edited by Michael Blömer and Rubina Raja, 95–110. Studies in Classical Archaeology 6. Turnhout: Brepols.

Raja, Rubina. 2019b. 'It Stays in the Family: Palmyrene Priestly Representations and Their Constellations'. In: *Women, Children and the Family in Palmyra*, edited by Signe Krag and Rubina Raja, 95–156. Palmyrene Studies 3. Copenhagen: Royal Danish Academy of Sciences and Letters.

Raja, Rubina. 2019c. 'Reconsidering the Dorsalium or "Curtain of Death" in Palmyrene Funerary Sculpture: Significance and Interpretations in Light of the Palmyra Portrait Project Corpus'. In *Revisiting the Religious Life of Palmyra*, edited by Rubina Raja, 67–151. Contextualizing the Sacred 9. Turnhout: Brepols.

Raja, Rubina. 2019d. 'Portrait Habit in Palmyra'. In *The Road to Palmyra*, edited by Anne Marie Nielsen and Rubina Raja, 137–154. Copenhagen: Ny Carlsberg Glyptotek.

Raja, Rubina. 2019e. 'Religious Banquets in Palmyra and the Palmyrene Banqueting Tesserae'. In *The Road to Palmyra*, edited by Anne Marie Nielsen and Rubina Raja, 221–234. Copenhagen: Ny Carlsberg Glyptotek.

Raja, Rubina. 2019f. 'Dining with the Gods and the Others: The Banqueting Tickets from Palmyra as Expressions of Religious Individualisation'. In *Religious Individualisation: Historical Dimensions and Comparative Perspectives*. Vol. 1, edited by Martin Fuchs, Antje Linkenbach, Martin Mulsow, Bernd-Christian Otto, Rahul Bjørn Parson, and Jörg Rüpke, 243–255. Berlin and Boston: De Gruyter.

Raja, Rubina. 2020. 'Men of the Desert or Men of the World? Revisiting the Iconography of Palmyrene Men and Their Camels'. In *Methods and Models in Ancient History Made in Honor of Jørgen Christian Meyer*, edited by Ingvar B. Mæhle, Per Bjarne Ravnå, and Eivind Heldaas Seland, 129–150, Papers and Monographs from the Norwegian Institute at Athens 9. Athens: The Norwegian Institute at Athens.

Raja Rubina. 2021. 'Adornment and Jewellery as a Status Symbol in Priestly Representations in Roman Palmyra: The Palmyrene Priests and Their Brooches'. In *Individualizing the Dead: Attributes in Palmyrene Funerary Sculpture*, edited by Maura Heyn and Rubina Raja, 75–117. Studies in Palmyrene Archaeology and History 3. Turnhout: Brepols.

Rumscheid, Jutta. 2000. *Kranz und Krone: Zu Insignien, Siegespreisen und Ehrenzeichen der römischen Kaiserzeit.* Istanbuler Forschungen 43. Tubingen: Wasmuth.

Sadurska, Anna. 1995. 'La famille et son image dans l'art de Palmyre'. *Arculiana*: 583–589.

Sadurska, Anna. 1996. 'L'art et la société: Recherches iconologiques sur la sculpture funéraire de Palmyre'. *Palmyra and the Silk Road: International Colloquium; Palmyra, 7–11 April 1992, Les annales archéologiques arabes syriennes* 42: 285–288.

Sadurska, Anna, and Adnan Bounni, eds. 1994. *Les sculptures funéraires de Palmyre*. Rivista di Archeologia Supplementi 13. Rome: Giorgio Bretschneider.

Sartre, Maurice. 2005. *The Middle East under Rome*. Translated by Catherine Porter and Elizabeth Rawlings. Cambridge, MA: The Belknap Press of Harvard University Press.

Schmidt-Colinet, Andreas. 1997. 'Aspects of 'Romanization': The Tomb Architecture at Palmyra and Its Decoration'. In *The Early Roman Empire in the East*, edited by Susan E. Alcock, 157–177. Oxford: Oxbow.

Schmidt-Colinet, Andreas. 2004. 'Palmyrenische Grabkunst als Ausdruck lokaler Identität(en): Fallbeispeile'. In *Lokale Identitaten in Randgebieten des römischen Reiches: Akten des Internationalen Symposiums in Wiener Neustadt, 24–26 April 2003*, edited by Andreas Schmidt-Colinet, 189–198. Vienna: Phoibos.

Seyrig, Henri. 1934. 'Antiquités syriennes 17: Bas-reliefs monumentaux du temple de Bel à Palmyre'. *Syria* 15: 154–186.

Seyrig, Henri. 1937. 'Armes et costumes iraniens de Palmyre'. *Syria* 18: 4–31.

Seyrig, Henri. 1938. 'Iconographie de Malakbel'. *Antiquités Syriennes* 2: 95–107.

Seyrig, Henri. 1940. 'Les tessères palmyréniennes et le banquet ritual'. In *Mémorial Lagrange*, edited by Hugues Vincent, 51–58. Paris: Gabalda.

Seyrig, Henri. 1951. 'Le repas des morts et le 'banquet funèbre' à Palmyre'. *Annales archéologiques arabes syriennes* 2: 32–41.

Skupinska-Løvset, Ilona. 1985. 'Funerary Portraiture of Seleukeia-on-the-Euphrates'. *Acta archaeologica* 56: 101–129.

Skupinska-Løvset, Ilona. 1999. *Portraiture in Roman Syria: A Study in Social and Regional Differentiation within the Art of Portraiture*. Łódz: Wydawnictwo Uniwersytetu Łódzkiego.

Smith, Roland R. R. 1998. 'Cultural Choice and Political Identity in Honorific Portrait Statues in the Greek East in the Second Century AD'. *Journal of Roman Studies* 88: 56–93.

Sørensen, Annette Højen. 2016. 'Palmyrene Tomb Paintings in Context'. In *The World of Palmyra*, edited by Andreas Kropp and Rubina Raja, 103–117. Palmyrene Studies 1. Copenhagen: Det Kongelige Danske Videnskabernes Selskab.

Stauffer, Annemarie. 2012. 'Dressing the Dead in Palmyra in the Second and Third Centuries AD'. In *Dressing the Dead in Classical Antiquity*, edited by Maureen Carroll and John Peter Wild, 89–98. Stroud: Amberley.

Stucky, Rolf A. 1973. 'Prêtres syriens I. Palmyre'. *Syria* 50: 163–180.

Taha, Ahmed. 1982. 'Men's Costume in Palmyra'. *Annales archéologiques arabes syriennes* 32: 117–132.

Tanabe, Katsumi, ed. 1986. *Sculptures of Palmyra*. Tokyo: Ancient Orient Museum.

Tanner, Jeremy. 2000. 'Portraits, Power, and Patronage in the Late Roman Republic'. *The Journal of Roman Studies* 90: 18–50.

Wielgosz, Dagmara. 2010. 'La sculpture en marbre à Palmyre'. *Studia Palmyreńskie* 11: 75–106.

Wielgosz-Rondolino, Dagmara. 2016. 'Palmyrene Portraits from the Temple of Allat: New Evidence on Artists and Workshops'. In *The World of Palmyra*, edited by Andreas Kropp and Rubina Raja, 166–179. Palmyrene Studies 1. Copenhagen: Det Kongelige Danske Videnskabernes Selskab.

Will, Ernest. 1957. 'Marchands et chefs de caravanes à Palmyre'. *Syria* 34: 262–277.

Woolf, Greg. 1998. *Becoming Roman: The Origins of Provincial Civilization in Gaul*. Cambridge: Cambridge University Press.

Yon, Jean-Baptiste. 1999. 'La présence des notables dans l'espace périurbain à Palmyre'. In *Construction, reproduction et représentation des patriciats urbains de l'Antiquité au XXᵉ siècle*, edited by Claude Petitfrère, 387–400. Tours: Université Francois Rabelais.

Yon, Jean-Baptiste. 2002. *Les notables de Palmyre*. Beirut: Institut français d'archéologie du Proche-Orient.

Zanker, Paul. 1992. 'Bürgerliche Selbstdarstellung am Grab in römischen Kaiserreich'. In *Die römische Stadt im 2. Jahrhundert n. Chr.: Der Funktionswandel des öffentlichen Raumes*, edited by Hans Joachim Schalles, Henner von Hesberg, and Paul Zanker, 339–359. Cologne: Rheinland-Verlag.

CHAPTER 30

RELIGIOUS LIFE AND PRIESTLY REPRESENTATIONS IN PALMYRA

RUBINA RAJA

The Religious Life of Palmyra and the Place of Priesthood

The religious life of Palmyra has been a focus of research over the past decades. Ted Kaizer's book remains one of the most recent prominent contributions to the field, giving a comprehensive overview of what we know about the structure of the religious life of the city during the Roman period, as seen from an ancient historical perspective (Kaizer 2002). Recently a new volume revisiting Palmyrene religious life from a broad perspective has contributed to the debates by presenting a set of articles on various aspects of religious practice and opening up new avenues of research as well as revisiting work already done on the city's religion and cults (Raja 2019d with further references). There are numerous contributions on various aspects of the city's religious life, and entire monographs have been written, including very recently, on several special niches of Palmyrene religion. These works answer important questions about the local society's way of viewing religious life (e.g., Kubiak-Schneider 2021). While Palmyra's local religious life has received much attention in terms of the written and epigraphic evidence, other aspects of the local religious life remain understudied, such as the continuity and changes in the city's religious life as traceable through its portrait habit (Raja 2015; 2019a; 2019c).

From the evidence available to us, it is clear that the structure of religious life in the city differed from that of many other places in the Roman world (Raja 2019d; 2019e; Kaizer 2002, 163–260, also see Chapter 23 [Le Blanc], this volume). For one, there is no evidence of women having held priesthoods, for example (Klaver 2019). Furthermore, their participation in the city's public religious life seems to have been limited to dedications of votives of various kinds and sacrifices. From fragments of reliefs we can deduce that when women participated as spectators at religious processions they were entirely veiled (Alley 2012; Krag 2018, 115–122). This, of course, does not mean that they would not have been active in the religious rituals taking place in domestic settings in Palmyra and even in public, as some votive altars with representations of women seem to indicate (Krag 2018, 120–121). However, we know little to nothing about these settings in Palmyra since no archaeological or written evidence survives. Because archaeological work mostly has focused on the large public and religious monuments and complexes in the city, the domestic sphere remains underexplored (see Chapter 22 [Zenoni], this volume). The social structure of Palmyrene society and its religious life was based on the tribal system, the tight-knit extended family system in which men would head their own family and most likely also several branches of it (Kaizer 2002, 234–241). This can be traced through in the funerary sphere, where *pater familias* would found monumental grave complexes to house themselves, their families, and their extended families, who would then fill these spaces over the centuries and in which different parts of the family could also buy spaces or spaces could even be sold off to people from outside the family (Henning 2013).

The sanctuaries of Palmyra have yielded significant insights into the importance of religion to the life of the city (Raja 2022a, 38–48 with further references). Palmyrenes worshipped a string of deities, male as well as female. Palmyra's main sanctuary was that of Bēl, which had an enclosure (temenos) measuring approximately 205 × 205 m (673 × 673 ft) with a monumental temple situated almost centrally in the courtyard. The temple, modelled on Graeco-Roman temple plans, had its main entrance along one of the long sides of the building (Seyrig et al. 1975), which made it quite different from other Roman temples of that period. Other known sanctuaries from Palmyra include those of Baalshamin, 'Allât, and Nabû, while several others are attested in the written records but have not yet been archeologically verified (Collart and Vicari 1969; Collart et al. 1969; Bounni 1981; Bounni et al. 1992a; 1992b; 2004; Gawlikowski 2017). Much has been written about the religious life of Palmyra, but, despite the fact that many deity names and physical sanctuaries are known, actual religious beliefs and practices are only partly known to us (Kaizer 2002; 2019a; 2019b; 2019c). These were structured around rituals and sacrifices, which often involved distribution of food and drink as well as ritual dining in groups. Our main sources of information, apart from often fragmented inscriptions, about the structure of religious life comprise the religious architecture, representations of religious processions, representations of Palmyrene deities and priests, and the so-called banqueting tesserae (tiny clay tokens with impressions on them), as well as the sanctuaries themselves (see Chapter 33 [Raja], this volume, on the tesserae). As in so many other places in the Near East, it is clear that religious life involved communal ritual dining; this is testified by both the banqueting tesserae and by the banqueting halls found in some of the sanctuaries (Chapter 33, this volume). At these feasts, the gods would have been honoured, and food, paid for by the banquet's sponsors, would have been served. Although these banquets were religious events, they were equally important as social events at which people would mingle and the donor would be celebrated as a good citizen and a devout follower of the gods.

While all the evidence summarized above has already been studied in much detail, two groups of material concerning the religious life of the city have not been examined in extensive detail: the so-called banqueting tesserae from the site (see Chapter 33 this volume) and the funerary portraits representing Palmyrene priests (Raja 2016; 2017a; 2017d; 2017e; 2017f; 2017g; 2018b; 2021a; 2021b; 2022b). Studies of Palmyrene priests have been conducted by Rolf Stucky, who gave an overview of the basic iconography connected with them (Stucky 1973). Klaus Parlasca has also addressed priestly representations (Parlasca 1976; 1987; 1988; 1998). Furthermore, Maura Heyn also has published on the priestly representations, emphasizing in particular the Parthian influence in their dress habit (Heyn 2008; also see Heyn and Raja 2019 on male dress habits in Palmyra in general).

Over recent years it has become clear that representations of priesthoods should therefore be understood as both social and religious status markers rather than necessarily just as representations of men in actual public positions (Raja 2017d; 2017f; 2019b). This explains why the representations of priests make up a large and distinct segment within the funerary corpus as a whole and why they were consistently produced over almost three hundred years. We do not know much about the structure of priesthoods in Palmyra from written sources. The known evidence was most recently collected and published as a monograph by Ted Kaizer (Kaizer 2002). An edited volume by Raja (2019d) was intended as a supplement to this 2002 publication, and the contributions treated various topics in a state-of-the-art manner.

Portraits, representations of individuals, were one of the prime media through which identities, senses of belonging, and cultural values were communicated in the Roman world and beyond. The Palmyrene portraits, mostly from funerary contexts, make up an excellent group of evidence through which Palmyrene society's attitude—both locally and beyond—can be examined (see Chapter 27 [Raja], this volume, on the funerary sculpture). This contribution takes its point of departure in the several hundred representations of Palmyrene priests, representations which stem from the first three centuries AD and which depict Palmyrene men dressed as priests in their funerary portraits (for overviews of the funerary portraiture, the chronology, and stylistic developments see Bobou et al. 2021; Raja et al. 2021; Romanowska et al. 2021). Since 2012, the Palmyra Portrait Project has been collecting all known funerary sculpture from the city, and today the corpus amounts to approximately four thousand locally produced limestone portraits, making this assemblage of material the largest group of Roman-period portraits stemming from one place in the ancient world (Raja 2017b; 2022a). Palmyra is unique in the ancient world, outside Rome, in possessing such a strong and continuous tradition of producing funerary portraits using the local limestone, a tradition that remained in place for almost three hundred years, from around the turn of the Common Era until the sack of Palmyra by the Romans in AD 273. The abundant visual material testifies to the ways in which the Palmyrene upper classes had themselves represented in the funerary sphere and today gives us a unique possibility for tracking stylistic developments, fashion phenomena, and Palmyrene society's general values as reflected in the portraits styles and their use of a wide range of attributes and inscriptions (Raja 2018b; Heyn and Raja 2021a; 2021b).

PRIESTS IN PALMYRA

Representations of Palmyrene priests make up a significant group within the corpus of funerary sculpture (Raja 2017g; 2019a; 2019d). Apart from the funerary sphere, priestly representations are also found in the public and religious spheres, although not in as large numbers. Priestly representations make up 13 percent of the entire funerary sculptural corpus and approximately 20 percent of all male representations in the funerary corpus. In total, there are 338 representations of Palmyrene priests in the sculptural corpus. These were produced consistently across almost three hundred years and seem to have been spread more or less evenly across the time span of production. In the iconography of the so-called banqueting tesserae, priestly representations are very common (see Chapter 33 [Raja], this volume, on tesserae).

Priestly representations are found in all categories of the visual sculptural art of Palmyra. They are depicted in religious settings, such as in architecture, as part of reliefs, or as architectural decorative elements (see, e.g., a ceiling coffer from the Temple of Bēl, first published with image by Drijvers 1976, 22, plate 78). They are also depicted on altars and in procession reliefs (see, e.g., a beam from the Temple of Bēl, first published in Seyrig 1934, 152, 165, plates 18–19), as well as in freestanding sculpture (see an example from a private collection in Beirut, published in Stucky 1973, 166–167, fig. 3). In the funerary sphere, they are depicted on founders' reliefs on graves (see, e.g., Tower Tomb of Kithot, first published by Will 1949, 94–95, fig. 8), on the lavish sarcophagi lids and boxes, and on banqueting reliefs, as well as in the loculus reliefs (see, e.g., a priest from the Palmyra Museum, first published in Bounni and Saliby 1957, 43, cat. no. 1, plate 1.1).

In most of the objects displaying priests, they are shown together with other priests or with family members. Often on sarcophagi several priestly representations are found on the same lid (Figure 30.1) or in the combination between lid and box. In the religious reliefs showing processions or sacrifices, numerous priests are also shown together. In the loculus reliefs, however, priests are usually shown on their own (Figure 30.2); only in five cases are they shown with another family member. However, by far the majority of loculus reliefs are single representations and should be seen within the wider framework of the family graves, where numerous loculus reliefs would have been displayed together (Chapter 27 this volume, on funerary sculpture).

The priestly sculptural representations can be assumed to have been more expensive to produce than the often fairly plain male representations since the priestly representations included a set of details not used in other male sculptural representations (Raja and Steding 2021a; 2021b; Steding 2022). This would have located these portraits at the higher end of the production economy spectrum of funerary sculpture. The

FIGURE 30.1 Sarcophagus lid with two reclining priests, a standing priest, a standing male, and a seated woman.

© Rubina Raja and Palmyra Portrait Project, Ingholt Archive at Ny Carlsberg Glyptotek, PS 890.

attributes and features included in the priestly representations included the distinct Palmyrene priestly hat, which was often decorated with wreaths or a central medallion that sometimes depicted a male person, either youngish without any attributes or a priestly bust (Figures 30.1 and 30.2). The priestly attire was usually an under tunic often showing at the neck with a decorated neckline, a cloak worn on top of the tunic, and sometimes a belt was also tied around the waist. Very often Palmyrene priests held a bowl and pitcher in their hands (Figure 30.3), objects used in connection with making sacrifices and therefore symbols closely connected to their duties as priests.

Brooches were another attribute which often went with priestly representations. These would hold together the cloak directly in front of the right shoulder. Brooches are very common in Palmyrene funerary art, but priests wear them more often than do other men. Brooches also occur in the funerary portraits of Palmyrene women. Almost half of the female representations are shown with brooches (Krag 2016; Krag and Raja, 2016; 2017; Krag 2018). Krag (2018) correctly emphasized that brooches also seem to have been a gender-distinctive symbol. And she also noted that young women with uncovered hairstyles are never depicted wearing brooches (Krag 2018; see also Krag and Raja 2018). It seems that, in the case of the women, brooches were used as an expression of coming of age and therefore status within the family as well. When held up against the fact that priests, who belonged to the uppermost elite of Palmyra, also wore brooches, these pieces of jewellery also seem to indicate a high status, underlining the importance and wealth of the family to which the individual, male or female, belonged. Krag distinguishes seven main groups of brooches in the female representations (Krag 2018, 103–104), but the variety is not that wide in the iconography of Palmyrene priests. As in the case of male dress in general, there seems to have been a greater degree of

FIGURE 30.2 Loculus relief depicting a priest wearing a Palmyrene priestly hat. Copenhagen, Ny Carlsberg Glyptotek, I.N. 1033.

© Courtesy of Ny Carlsberg Glyptotek, photograph by Anders Sune Berg.

conservatism in the choice of attributes in the male sculptural representations than in the female representations.

Often, however, the brooches in all types of representations are large, emphasizing that this attribute was connected closely to social status since they originally would have been made of metal (Raja 2023; 2021a).

To sum up, Palmyrene priests were distinguished first and foremost through priestly hats, but a number of other traits, such as brooches, high-quality garments, and the pitcher and bowl attributes, would also serve to emphasize the priestly status of these more than three hundred representations. Thus, a wide set of attributes went hand in hand with the representations of priests. Not all attributes were always included in the visual representations, but the priestly hat and attire made up

FIGURE 30.3 Loculus relief depicting a priest holding a pitcher and a bowl. Damascus, National Museum of Damascus.

© Rubina Raja and Palmyra Portrait Project, Ingholt Archive at Ny Carlsberg Glyptotek, PS 1283.

the basic elements needed to differentiate priests from other male representations. Sometimes the priestly hat was shown on a pedestal beside a male representation (Figure 30.4).

In earlier scholarship, it was suggested that this meant that the man was a former priest. However, new studies of these about twenty representations have shown that this was instead a fashion phenomenon, one that would allow the men to be shown with both elaborate hairstyles and beards (Raja 2017a; 2017e; 2017g; 2018b). These representations, which all date to around the same period, are certainly reflections of fashion phenomena influenced by the impact that images of bearded emperors with curly, bushy hairstyles had on the local portrait style. This underlines that Palmyrene men most likely did

FIGURE 30.4 Loculus relief depicting a priest with a Palmyrene priestly hat on the side. Copenhagen, Ny Carlsberg Glyptotek, I.N. 1043.

© Courtesy of Ny Carlsberg Glyptotek, photograph by Anders Sune Berg.

not act as priests all the time, but only at certain points in time, as when having to undertake sacrifices and partake in religious rituals and activities since they are usually shown clean-shaven and without hair (as far as we can tell from the amount of head exposed on representations that wear hats). This observation also questions the nature of priesthood in Palmyra. If one did not act as a priest the entire time, what was one then? It is very likely that priesthoods in Palmyra were held by the utmost elite and that priesthoods were extended from father to son and from uncle to nephew and so should be seen within a broader Semitic religious framework and not within a Roman religious framework (Raja 2021b).

The representations of Palmyrene priests are usually not accompanied by inscriptions identifying them as priests. The image would have been enough. But, in general, the funerary inscriptions place emphasis on family genealogies (Brughmans et al. 2021 with further references; Sadurska and Bounni 1994). Only very rarely are professions mentioned in the more than a thousand funerary inscriptions that accompany many of the portraits (Cussini 2017; Long and Sørensen 2017; Raja 2017f). The only funerary representation mentioning a priestly office is one in which the male individual is not even depicted in priestly clothes (Loculus relief from the Hypogeum of Artaban; Hillers and Cussini 1996, PAT 2644; Tanabe 1986, cat. 235, fig. 235). While this at first sight might seem odd, it is not: in this case, it was necessary to write it in the inscription since the portrait representation did not make the man's status clear. In this one case, we can assume that the person had chosen not to be depicted in the attire of a priest but still wanted for some reason to include this title, most likely since it would emphasize his social status.

While first overview studies have been made of the Palmyrene priestly hat as a central attribute for the identification of Palmyrene priests, only recently has an attempt been made to develop a typology of these hats and discuss the cross-cultural milieu within which they were set (Raja 2022b; 2016; 2017g; 2017f; 2017c; 2017d; 2017a; 2017e; 2018a; 2018b). First, the terminology connected to these hats is misleading. The term 'modius' simply slipped into the literature in the early twentieth century without any firm reasons. The priestly hat does not look like a modius (a measure for corn, like those sometimes carried by deities) (Raja 2018b). We have no written evidence that tells us what these hats were called in Antiquity. These priestly hats could range from being plain to highly decorated. The hat was, in the first instance, a status symbol and an entirely embedded part of the priestly attire; in the second instance, it was an attribute that could be scaled in terms of details included or left out during the portrait's production process and so became an expression of the value of the overall portrait. The representations of the hats do tell us that the priestly hats could be decorated in different ways, but what exactly the different types in fact meant, apart from being expressions of different trends, fashions, and choices, is more complex. Did a plain hat mean that a priest was of a lower rank? Do the wreaths often seen tied around the hats carry a particular honorific or religious meaning? What do the busts of young men and priests inserted centrally on numerous hats signify? How do we get closer to understanding the dynamics of the production economy and the reality of how the priestly hats would have looked? These are all questions which relate to art historical and archaeological methods of interpretation, and we cannot answer them all with much certainty. However, it does not seem likely that the level of elaborateness of the hat and its decoration had anything to do with the potential rank or importance of the priesthood. It is much more likely that the elaborateness had something to do with the amount of resources that the commissioner had been willing to put into the production of the representation. And, of course, these representations should also always be seen within the wider framework of the entire object and the grave setting. The wreaths often tied around the hats might indicate civic and religious honours, as are known from other categories of sculptural representations from across the Roman world (Rumscheid 2000). The busts represent a fairly enigmatic category. The young male bust shown without attributes, in a plain cloak and with curly hair, does not give many clues to interpret his identity. The other type of busts set in priestly hats are clearly representations of Palmyrene priests, which might underline the hereditary nature of the priesthoods. If that is so, then the youngish male bust might be explained as being an ancestor, mythical or real—potentially rather mythical since it is the same type of bust shown across all priestly hats. One is tempted to suggest that this might have been the mythical founder of Palmyra, but there is no evidence which supports this conclusion.

To be represented as a priest in one's funerary portrait, or to be represented in priestly attire together with a deceased family member, certainly served to underscore the high status which one had held or still held in life. Therefore, these representations can also be seen as firmly underlining the importance of the family as such—a tradition that went hand in hand with the family-based (tribal structure) society of Palmyra (Kaizer 2002; Gawlikowski 2003).

Conclusion: Religion and Priests in Palmyra—A Matter of Societal Structure

While a comprehensive study of the entire corpus of the priestly representations is under way (Raja, forthcoming), this chapter has given an overview of the priestly representations and their significance for our understanding of the religious life of Palmyra. Through a study of the representations of Palmyrene priests, plentiful evidence from the funerary sphere, and material from the public and religious spheres, we come a bit closer to understanding Palmyra's dynamic religious realm and the ways in which it might have differed from other places in the Roman world. There is no doubt that Palmyrene society displayed a very strong local identity, one that scaffolded the family as its basic unit. This structure is well attested in the material evidence, family graves, and inscriptions which accompany all portraits from the funerary sphere. The priestly representations and the constellations in which they are shown underline this. Furthermore, their distinct and recognizable iconography, despite variations in the details, also emphasizes the conservatism that was inherent to male representations in Palmyra across the first three centuries AD.

Acknowledgements

The author acknowledges the funding received by the Danish National Research Foundation for Centre for Urban Network Evolutions (grant no. 119) as well as the funding received from the Carlsberg Foundation for the various Palmyra projects based at Aarhus University, first and foremost the Palmyra Portrait Project. Furthermore, I thank the ALIPH Foundation as well as the Augustinus Foundation for funding for further Palmyra-related projects.

BIBLIOGRAPHY

Alley, Kelly D. 2012. 'The Paradigm Shift in India's River Policies: From Sacred to Transferable Waters'. In *Water, Cultural Diversity, and Global Environmental Change: Emerging Trends, Sustainable Futures?*, edited by Barbara R. Johnston, Lisa Hiwasaki, Irene J. Klaver, A. Ramos-Castillo, and Veronica Strang, 31–48. Paris: UNESCO.

Bobou, Olympia, Rubina Raja, and Iza Romanowska. 2021. 'Historical Trajectories of Palmyra's Elites through the Lens of Archaeological Data'. *Journal of Urban Archaeology* 4: 153–166.

Bounni, Adnan. 1981. 'Les représentations d'Apollon en Palmyrene et dans le milieu syrien'. In *Mythologie gréco-romaine, mythologies périphériques: Études d'iconographie*, edited by Lilly Kahil and Christian Augé, 107–112. Paris: Editions du C.N.R.S.

Bounni, Adnan, and Nessib Saliby. 1957. 'The Tomb of Shalamallat'. *Annales archéologiques arabes syriennes* 7: 25–52.

Bounni, Adnan, Jacques Seigne, and Nessib Saliby. 1992a. *Le sanctuaire de Nabū à Palmyre (planches)*. Paris: Geuthner.

Bounni, Adnan, Jacques Seigne, and Nessib Saliby. 1992b. *Le sanctuaire de Nabū à Palmyre*. Vol. 2. Paris: Geuthner.

Bounni, Adnan, Jacques Seigne, and Nessib Saliby. 2004. *Le sanctuaire de Nabū à Palmyre (texte)*. Beirut: Institut français du Proche-Orient.

Brughmans, Tom, Olympia Bobou, Nathalia B. Kristensen, Rikke R. Thomsen, Jesper V. Jensen, Eivind H. Seland, and Rubina Raja. 2021. 'A Kinship Network Analysis of Palmyrene Genealogies'. *Journal of Historical Network Research* 6(1): 41–84. doi: 10.25517/jhnr.v6i1.65.

Collart, Paul, and Jacques Vicari. 1969. *Le Sanctuaire de Baalshamîn à Palmyre*. Vols. 1–2, *Topographie et architecture*. Basel: Institut suisse de Rome.

Collart, Paul, Jacques Vicari, Christiane Dunant, Rudolf Fellmann, and Institut suisse de Rome. 1969. *Le sanctuaire de Baalshamin á Palmyre: Topographie et architecture*. Rome: Institut suisse de Rome.

Cussini, Eleonora. 2017. 'The Pious Butcher and the Physicians: Palmyrene Professions in Context'. In *Positions and Professions in Palmyra*, edited by Tracey Long and Annette H. Sørensen, 84–96. Copenhagen: Royal Danish Academy of Sciences and Letters.

Drijvers, H. J. W. 1976. *The Religion of Palmyra*. Leiden: Brill.

Gawlikowski, Michał. 2003. 'Palmyra: From a Tribal Federation to a City'. In *Kulturkonflikte im Vorderen Orient an der Wende vom Hellenismus zur römischen Kaiserzeit*, edited by Klaus S. Freyberger, Agnes Henning, and Henner von Hesberg, 7–10. Rahden: Leidorf.

Gawlikowski, Michał. 2017. *Le sanctuaire d'Allat à Palmyre*. Warsaw: University of Warsaw: Polish Centre of Mediterranean Archaeology.

Henning, Agnes. 2013. *Die Turmgräber von Palmyra: Eine lokale Bauform im kaiserzeitlichen Syrien als Ausdruck kultureller Identität*. Rahden: Leidorf.

Heyn, Maura K. 2008. 'Sacerdotal Activities and Parthian Dress in Roman Palmyra'. In *Reading a Dynamic Canvas: Adornment in the Ancient Mediterranean World*, edited by Cynthia S. Colburn and Maura K. Heyn, 170–193. Newcastle: Cambridge Scholars.

Heyn, Maura K., and Rubina Raja. 2019. 'Male Dress Habits in Roman Period Palmyra'. In *Fashioned Selves: Dress and Identity in Antiquity*, edited by Megan Cifarelli, 41–54. Oxford: Oxbow.

Heyn, Maura K., and Rubina Raja. 2021a. 'Attributes in Palmyrene Funerary Sculpture: Functions and Meanings'. In *Individualizing the Dead: Attributes in Palmyrene Funerary Sculpture*, edited by Maura K. Heyn and Rubina Raja, 1–11. Turnhout: Brepols.

Heyn, Maura K., and Rubina Raja, eds. 2021b. *Individualizing the Dead: Attributes in Palmyrene Funerary Sculpture*. Studies in Palmyrene Archaeology and History 3. Turnhout: Brepols.

Hillers, Delbert R, and Eleonora Cussini. 1996. *Palmyrene Aramaic Texts*. Baltimore: John Hopkins University Press.

Kaizer, Ted. 2002. *The Religious Life of Palmyra: A Study of the Social Patterns of Worship in the Roman Period*. Stuttgart: Steiner.

Kaizer, Ted. 2019a. 'Family Connections and Religious Life at Palmyra'. In *Women, Children, and the Family in Palmyra*, edited by Signe Krag and Rubina Raja, 82–94. Copenhagen: Royal Danish Academy of Sciences and Letters.

Kaizer, Ted. 2019b. 'Gods, Temples, and Cults. Religious Life in Palmyra'. In *The Road to Palmyra*, edited by Anne Marie Nielsen and Rubina Raja, 207–220. Copenhagen: Ny Carlsberg Glyptotek.

Kaizer, Ted. 2019c. 'Patterns of Worship at Palmyra: Reflections on Methods and Approaches'. In *Revisiting the Religious Life of Palmyra*, edited by Rubina Raja, 7–24. Turnhout: Brepols.

Klaver, Sanne. 2019. 'The Participation of Palmyrene Women in the Religious Life of the City'. *Women, Children, and the Family in Palmyra*, edited by Signe Krag and Rubina Raja, 157–167. Copenhagen: Royal Danish Academy of Sciences and Letters.

Krag, Signe. 2016. 'Females in Group Portraits in Palmyra'. In *The World of Palmyra*, edited by Andreas Kropp and Rubina Raja, 180–193. Copenhagen: Royal Danish Academy of Sciences and Letters.

Krag, Signe. 2018. *Funerary Representations of Palmyrene Women: From the First Century BC to the Third Century AD*. Turnhout: Brepols.

Krag, Signe, and Rubina Raja. 2016. 'Representations of Women and Children in Palmyrene Funerary Loculus Reliefs, Loculus Stelae and Wall Paintings'. *Zeitschrift für Orient-Archäologie* 9: 134–178.

Krag, Signe, and Rubina Raja. 2017. 'Representations of Women and Children in Palmyrene Banqueting Reliefs and Sarcophagus Scenes'. *Zeitschrift für Orient-Archäologie* 10: 196–227.

Krag, Signe, and Rubina Raja. 2018. 'Unveiling Female Hairstyles: Markers of Age, Social Roles, and Status in Funerary Sculpture from Palmyra'. *Zeitschrift für Orient-Archäologie* 11: 242–277.

Kubiak-Schneider, Aleksandra. 2021. *Dédicaces sans théonyme de Palmyra: Béni (soit) son nom pour l'éternité*. Leiden: Brill.

Long, Tracey, and Annette Højen Sørensen, eds. 2017. *Positions and Professions in Palmyra*. Palmyrene Studies. Copenhagen: Royal Danish Academy of Sciences and Letters.

Parlasca, Klaus. 1976. 'Probleme Palmyrenischer Grabreliefs: Chronologie und Interpretation'. In *Palmyre: Bilan et perspectives: Colloque de Strasbourg 18–20 Octobre 1973*, edited by Edmond Frézouls, 33–44. Strasbourg: Association pour l'étude de la civilisation romaine.

Parlasca, Klaus. 1987. 'Aspekte der palmyrenischen Skulpturen'. In *Palmyra: Geschichte, Kunst und Kultur der Oasenstadt*, edited by Erwin M. Ruprechtsberger, 276–282. Linz: Gutenberg.

Parlasca, Klaus. 1988. 'Ikonographische Probleme palmyrenischer Grabreliefs'. *Damaszener Mitteilungen* 3: 215–221.

Parlasca, Klaus. 1998. 'Palmyrenische Sarkophage mit Totenmahlreliefs - Forschungsstand und ikonographische Probleme'. In *Akten des Symposiums '125 Jahre Sarkophag-Corpus'*, *MarBurg, 4–7. Oktober 1995*, edited by Guntram Koch, 311–317. Mainz am Rhein: von Zabern.

Raja, Rubina. 2015. 'Palmyrene Funerary Portraits in Context: Portrait Habit between Local Traditions and Imperial Trends'. In *Traditions: Transmission of Culture in the Ancient World*, edited by Jane Fejfer, Mette Moltesen, and Annette Rathje, 329–361. Copenhagen: Museum Tusculanum Press.

Raja, Rubina. 2016. 'Representations of Priests in Palmyra. Methodological Considerations on the Meaning of the Representation of Priesthood in Roman Period Palmyra'. *Religion in the Roman Empire* 2(1): 125–146.

Raja, Rubina. 2017a. 'Between Fashion Phenomena and Status Symbols. Contextualising the Dress of the So-Called "Former Priests" of Palmyra'. In *Textiles and Cult in the Mediterranean Area in the 1st Millennium BC*, edited by Cecilie Brøns and Marie-Louise Nosch, 209–229. Oxford: Oxbow.

Raja, Rubina. 2017b. 'Going Individual: Roman Period Portraiture in Classical Archaeology'. In *The Diversity of Classical Archaeology*, edited by Achim Lichtenberger and Rubina Raja, 271–286. Turnhout: Brepols.

Raja, Rubina. 2017c. 'Networking Beyond Death: Priests and Their Family Networks in Palmyra Explored Through the Funerary Sculpture'. In *Sinews of Empire: Networks in the Roman Near East and Beyond*, edited by Eivind Heldaas Seland and Håkon Fiane Teigen, 121–136. Oxford: Oxbow.

Raja, Rubina. 2017d. 'Priesthood in Palmyra: Public Office or Social Status?' In *Palmyra: Pearl of the Desert*, edited by Rubina Raja, 77–85. Aarhus: Sun-Tryk.

Raja, Rubina. 2017e. 'Representations of the So-Called "Former Priests" in Palmyrene Funerary Art. A Methodological Contribution and Commentary'. *Topoi* 21: 51–81.

Raja, Rubina. 2017f. 'To Be or not to Be Depicted as a Priest in Palmyra: A Matter of Representational Spheres and Societal Values'. In *Positions and Professions in Palmyra*, edited by Tracey Long and Annette Højen Sørensen, 115–130. Copenhagen: Royal Academy of Sciences and Letters.

Raja, Rubina. 2017g. 'You Can Leave Your Hat on: Priestly Representations from Palmyra – Between Visual Genre, Religious Importance and Social Status'. In *Beyond Priesthood: Religious Entrepreneurs and Innovators in the Imperial Era*, edited by Richard L. Gordon, Georgia Petridou, and Jörg Rüpke, 417–442. Berlin: de Gruyter.

Raja, Rubina. 2018a. 'Individualising Palmyrene Priesthood Through Priestly Attributes'. Paper presented at the Attributes in Palmyrene Art and Sculpture conference, Aarhus, 19 June 2018.

Raja, Rubina. 2018b. 'The Matter of the Palmyrene "Modius": Remarks on the History of Research of the Terminology of the Palmyrene Priestly Hat'. *Religion in the Roman Empire* 4(2): 237–259.

Raja, Rubina. 2019a. 'Funerary Portraiture in Palmyra: Portrait Habit at a Crossroads or a Signifier of Local Identity?' In *Funerary Portraiture in Greater Roman Syria*, edited by Michael Blömer and Rubina Raja, 95–110. Turnhout: Brepols.

Raja, Rubina. 2019b. 'It Stays in the Family. Palmyrene Priestly Representations and Their Constellations'. In *Women, Children and the Family in Palmyra*, edited by Signe Krag and Rubina Raja, 95–156. Copenhagen: Royal Academy of Sciences and Letters.

Raja, Rubina. 2019c. 'Portrait Habit in Palmyra'. In *The Road to Palmyra*, edited by Anne Marie Nielsen and Rubina Raja, 137–154. Copenhagen: Ny Carlsberg Glyptotek.

Raja, Rubina, ed. 2019d. *Revisiting the Religious Life of Palmyra*. Contextualizing the Sacred 9. Turnhout: Brepols.

Raja, Rubina. 2019e. 'Revisiting the Religious Life of Palmyra: Or Why It Still Matters to Focus on Ancient Religious Life Within the Context of a Single Site'. In *Revisiting the Religious Life of Palmyra*, edited by Rubina Raja. Turnhout: Brepols: 1–6.

Raja, Rubina. 2021a. 'Adornment and Jewellery as a Status Symbol in Priestly Representations in Roman Palmyra: The Palmyrene Priests and Their Brooches'. In *Individualizing the Dead: Attributes in Palmyrene Funerary Sculpture*, edited by Maura K. Heyn and Rubina Raja, 75–117. Turnhout: Brepols.

Raja, Rubina. 2021b. 'Managing the Middle Ground: Priests in Palmyra and Their Iconographies'. In *The Middle East as Middle Ground? Cultural Interaction in the Ancient Middle East Revisited*, edited by Julia Hoffman-Salz, 129–146. Vienna: Holzhausen.

Raja, Rubina. 2022a. *Pearl of the Desert: A History of Palmyra*. Oxford: Oxford University Press.

Raja, Rubina. 2022b. 'The Way You Wear Your Hat. Palmyrene Priests Between Local Traditions and Cross-Regional Trends'. In *Imperium sine fine? Der romisch-parthische Grenzraum als Konflikt- und Kontaktzone*, edited by Udo Hartmann, Frank Schleicher, and Timo Stickler, 81–118. Stuttgart: Kohlhammer.

Raja, Rubina. 2023. 'Luxury Jewellery in Palmyrene Funerary Art. Necklaces with Portrait Busts Carried by Women Represented the Funerary Sculpture'. In *Odds and Ends: Attributes in Palmyrene Funerary Art*, edited by Maura Heyn and Rubina Raja, 85–113. Turnhout: Brepols.

Raja, Rubina. Forthcoming. *The Palmyrene Priests. Visual Representations and Sources*. Turnhout: Brepols.

Raja, Rubina, Olympia Bobou, and Iza Romanowska. 2021. 'Three Hundred Years of Palmyrene History. Unlocking Archaeological Data for Studying Past Societal Transformations'. *PloS one* 16(11): e0256081. https://doi.org/10.1371/journal.pone.0256081.

Raja, Rubina, and Julia Steding. 2021a. *Production Economy in Greater Roman Syria: Trade Networks and Production Processes*. Turnhout: Brepols.

Raja, Rubina, and Julia Steding. 2021b. 'Production Economy in Roman Syria: New Views on Old Stones'. In *Production Economy in Roman Syria*, edited by Rubina Raja and Julia Steding, 1–8. Turnhout: Brepols.

Romanowska, Iza, Olympia Bobou, and Rubina Raja. 2021. 'Reconstructing the Social, Economic and Demographic Trends of Palmyra's Elite from Funerary Data'. *Journal of Archaeological Science* 133: 105432. https://doi.org/10.1016/j.jas.2021.105432.

Rumscheid, Jutta. 2000. *Kranz und Krone: Zu Insignien, Siegespreisen und Ehrenzeichen der römischen Kaiserzeit*. Tübingen: Wasmuth.

Sadurska, Anna, and Adnan Bounni. 1994. *Les sculptures funéraires de Palmyre*. Rome: Giorgio Bretschneider.

Seyrig, Henri. 1934. 'Antiquités syriennes'. *Syria* 15(2): 155–186.

Seyrig, Henri, Robert Amy, and Ernest Will. 1975. *Le temple de Bel á Palmyre: Texte et planches*. Paris: Geuthner.

Steding, Julia. 2022. *Carvers and Customers in Roman Palmyra: The Production Economy of Limestone Loculus Reliefs*. Brepols: Turnhout

Stucky, R. A. 1973. 'Prêtres syriens I: Palmyre'. *Syria* 50(1–2): 163–180.

Tanabe, Katsumi. 1986. *Sclptures of Palmyra, I*. Tokyo: Ancient Orient Museum.

Will, Ernest. 1949. 'La tour funéraire de Palmyre'. *Syria* 26(1–2): 87–116.

CHAPTER 31

CHILDREN IN PALMYRA

OLYMPIA BOBOU[*]

THE presence of children in the ancient world is an elusive one in our sources: it has been estimated that persons younger than fifteen comprised 33 percent of the population of imperial Rome (Laes 2011, 27–28). In our written sources, though, children do not appear as often: even though there are several references to children, childhood, and their behaviour in literature, these appear when the text necessitates them and, naturally, reveal adult ideas and attitudes. For example, a reference to how Alcibiades played is used not to discuss play itself, but rather an aspect of Alcibiades's character that revealed itself from childhood (Plut., *Alc.* 2.2–3.2; on the use of childhood stories in the *Life of Alcibiades*, see Verdegem 2010, 121–130). In fact, there are only three works of Roman authors dealing explicitly with the period of childhood (Laes 2011, 6–7). In the material culture record, children appear on their own in around nine hundred funerary monuments from the western part of the Roman Empire (Mander 2012). The monuments often give the date of death, thus revealing how children were portrayed frequently as older than they were (Grossmann 2013, 52; Carroll 2018, 248).

We do not have any written sources about Palmyra from the Palmyrenes themselves, and the Roman authors who wrote about the city were more interested in military or political history. Adult expectations and the life experiences of Palmyrene children have to be gleaned from the material culture record: inscriptions from the public sphere, religious dedications, and funerary monuments. Thus the information we get is limited, scattered, and often repetitive, yet it allows us a glimpse into Palmyrene children's lives.

[*] This work was supported by the Danish National Research Foundation under the grant DNRF119—Centre of Excellence for Urban Network Evolutions (UrbNet), and the Carlsberg Foundation, Palmyra Portrait Project, grant held by Professor Rubina Raja. For more information on the project see: http://projects.au.dk/palmyraportrait/.

CHILDREN AND SOURCES

What Is a Child? Terms and Definition

Without literary sources from Palmyra itself, we have to rely on other evidence for the definition of a child. As Harald Ingholt had already observed, there is no distinction between 'son' and 'child' in Palmyrene Aramaic. Only when the word for 'child' is accompanied by the adjective 'male' can we be certain that it refers to 'son' (Ingholt 1935, 61; see also Hillers and Cussini 1996, s.v. *br*, 349). If the object carries two inscriptions, one in Greek or Latin, and one in Palmyrene Aramaic, then it is possible to differentiate between 'son' and 'child', as, for example, in an altar dedicated for the sake of the health of the dedicant, his children (τέκνα in the Greek text), and his brothers (Yon 2013, 141–142, cat. no. 130 with previous bibliography).

In Palmyrene funerary or public inscriptions, however, the words 'son', 'daughter', or 'child' can refer to anyone descended—or adopted—by a particular individual: it is not indicative of the age of the person. Even in the only example of a verse inscription from Palmyra (the so-called *Steinepigramm*), we cannot be certain that the 'child recently mourned' is a child in our modern understanding of the term (Yon 2013, 190, cat. no. 194 with previous bibliography). A hint to when a person stopped being a minor (i.e., a 'child' in our understanding of the term) can be provided by literary sources about Zenobia. In *Historia Augusta*, Zenobia is said to have exercised power in the name of her young sons Hereniannus and Timolaus (*HA* 30.27–28: 'duos parvulos'). *Parvulus*, meaning 'small' is used in reference to young children in Latin literature, those still dependent on their mother (e.g., in Ovid's Aeneid, 4.328). (http://penelope.uchicago.edu/Thayer/E/Roman/Texts/Historia_Augusta/Tyranni_XXX*.html#note96). This is the only instance where Hereniannus and Timolaus are recorded.

Wahballath: A Child in the Spotlight

Zenobia's son Wahballath is perhaps the only child in Palmyra who appears in more than a single source. He is mentioned in Roman texts, and we also have inscriptions as well as coins honouring him. This does not mean that we have any information about his childhood. Numismatic and epigraphic evidence from outside Palmyra shows that Wahballath was honoured together with Zenobia, as well as represented together with her in coins. In several of the inscriptions, Wahballath is mentioned first, and, in the coin series minted at Alexandria and Antioch after March 272, his portrait appears on the privileged obverse side of the coin, replacing the image of the emperor. The careful placement of Wahballath's name first, as well as his individual portraits on coins, show

Zenobia's intention to present herself as a mother acting in the name of her son and that her power nominally stemmed from his—even though she effectively exercised it in her own right (Chapter 11 [Andrade] this volume; Chapter 34 [Kristensen] this volume). The divergence between the *Historia Augusta* and the Palmyrene coins and inscriptions reveals more than the difference between sources created by opposing forces, namely the Palmyrenes and the Romans. It reveals how children could be used for manipulating public opinion, especially when they were still too young to be able to function as political entities separate from their parents.

Epigraphic evidence shows that the oldest son of Odainat, Septimius Hairan or Herodian, who ruled together with Odainat between 251/252 and 267/268, had received statues placed on consoles of the columns of the Grand Colonnade (Yon 2012, 69–73, cat. nos. 58–60) and one equestrian monument (Yon 2012, 73–75, cat. no. 61). In the inscriptions, the emphasis is on Septimius Hairan and his own titles: he is called λαμπρότατος, λαμπρότατος συνκλητικός (the Greek translation of *clarissimus senator*, a member of the senate) and βασιλεὺς βασιλέων (king of kings), both titles he shared with his father. Even though his descent from Odainat is mentioned and the inscriptions make clear that they have titles in common, Septimius Hairan, who is an adult, is shown as patron and a powerful political figure in his own right (Yon 2012, 69–75, cat. nos. 58–62).

In contrast to this prominent display, the only surviving representations of Wahballat, Odainat's younger son, who ruled together with Zenobia between 267/268 and 273, are on coins and tesserae. These representations, though, portray him as a young man carrying insignia of royal and military power (diadem, radiate crown, cuirass, *paludamentum*) and so they are in line with other representations of rulers, offering little to our understanding of children's iconography (Gawlikowski 2016; Chapter 34 this volume).

CONTEXTS

Mentioned earlier were the statues for Septimius Hairan set up in prominent public locations in Palmyra. These are the only known statues of a child set up in public in Palmyra—if he can be called a child. The religious sphere has yielded more evidence for statues: there are a few inscriptions from the sanctuary of Nabû recording dedications by parents in memory of a son, grandson, or daughter on the occasion of their death (Yon 2012, 179–180, cat. no. 179: for a son; Yon 2012, 180–181, cat. no. 180: for a grandson; Yon 2012, 181–182, cat. no. 181: for a daughter). These were inscribed on wall consoles, and the last one carries an explicit reference to the statue of the daughter. They date from the second century AD, but we cannot know how these children of prominent families were represented in the sanctuary. The houses of Palmyra, and so the private sphere, have not been explored to a great degree (Gabriel 1926; Schmidt-Colinet and al-As'ad 2013). A few of the houses of the elite were decorated with mosaics inspired by the art of Greek and Hellenized East (Balty 2014; Gawlikowski 2015, 293), but so far no images of children have been found within the houses either in paintings or statues. The funerary sphere is the area where we can find almost all of the representations of children.

Spaces for or used by children have also not been located either in the houses or the public/religious areas of Palmyra. It is true that then, as now, children could be found in every location of a town, but, without being aware during excavations of how children might use space, it is extremely difficult to find traces of their existence in the material record (see Baxter 2008). Another difficulty in locating spaces for children in the ancient world is that they did not have designated spaces, as in other historical periods: for example, there were no nurseries, and lessons could take place in various locations within a town, for example, the forum, or the dining area of a house (see Bloomer 2013). In Palmyra, the lack of literary sources adds another difficulty in finding areas where children would have been active. This leaves us with only one context where children can be located: the funerary sphere.

The necropoleis of Palmyra are located to the north, west, and south of the city. The south-east necropolis had already been devastated in antiquity, but evidence from the other locations shows that the Palmyrene elite preferred the west of the city as the prime location for their tombs. It is also possible to trace the trends in use of monumental tombs: tower tombs were the earliest built structures, followed by underground tombs and house tombs (Higuchi and Saito 2001, 3–4). Despite the numerous tombs, though, there is little evidence about Palmyrene burial practices because several of the tombs had been looted or excavated in earlier periods, when human remains ranked low in importance. Our best evidence for the burials of children comes from the excavations of hypogea: the tombs of the families of Zabdâ (Michałowski 1960, 171–177) and tomb N (Michałowski 1962, 261–269) in the west necropolis, excavated by the Polish Archaeological Mission of Sassans and Mattaî (Saliby and Parlasca 1992) and Taai (Abdul-Hak 1952); in the south-east necropolis, excavated by the Syrian Directorate of Antiquities; and Tombs A, C, and F at the south-east necropolis excavated by the Nara Archaeological Mission to Palmyra (Higuchi and Izumi 1994; Higuchi and Saito 2001).

The excavations revealed that, in five of these tombs (hypogea of Zabdâ, Sassans and Mattaî, tomb N, C, and F), neonates and very young infants were interred in grave pits dug into the floor of the tombs, while older children were buried together with either male or female adults in loculus burials. There is no evidence for burial pits in the hypogea of Taai and A. In the tombs of Sassans and Mattaî, of Taai and A, children could be buried on their own, or together with another adult in loculus burials or sarcophagi. The artefacts found together with the child and infant burials included beads, indicating necklaces, as well as bronze bells and amulets (Michałowski 1962, 265; Higuchi and Izumi 1994, 53; Higuchi and Saito 2001, 99).

ICONOGRAPHY AND INSCRIPTIONS

Funerary

General Observations: Age Groups, Family Groups, Inscriptions, Clothes

Thanks to the corpus of Palmyrene portraits compiled by the Palmyra Portrait Project, we know that there are approximately four thousand portraits, predominantly from the funerary sphere (Heyn and Raja 2021, 1; Raja 2022, 72). Of these, 1,654 portraits depict men and 1,025 depict women, and most were represented alone in loculus relief slabs (Raja 2022, 72). The earliest representations appear on stelae (also the earliest types of representations used in Palmyra: see Colledge 1976, 63, 66–67; Krag and Raja 2016, 155), while the majority of these are on loculus reliefs followed by portraits on sarcophagi (mostly reliefs depicting sarcophagi rather than free-standing sarcophagi) and banqueting reliefs (Krag and Raja 2016, 136). Children appear on almost 7 percent of all funerary representations (Ringsborg 2016, 67; Krag and Raja 2019, 12).

It is not easy to identify age groups in Palmyrene sculpture, but it is possible to distinguish three groups: (a) very young children (infants), (b) young children (from toddlers to pre-adolescents), and (c) adolescents. Very young children are always depicted in the arm of an adult female figure, identified as their mother because of the posture (Heyn 2010, 638). Young children are usually depicted with one parent or, less frequently, an older relative, such as an uncle or other sibling. In some sarcophagi and sarcophagi reliefs, however, children can be depicted together with both parents. Only on rare occasions do young children appear unaccompanied by an adult, and these images only occur on stelae. The least common group, and the one most difficult to identify, is that of adolescents. They can appear either with one parent or other relative or together with a sibling.

There are only forty-eight instances where a child or children are shown unaccompanied by adults, and they all occur on stelae, most of which were meant to cover loculus burials (see Colledge 1976, 63, 66–67 for the development of stelai in Palmyra). However, with only 146 stelae recorded in the Palmyra Portrait Project corpus database, the percentage of representations of children amounts to 70 percent, making this the category with the most images of children. Out of thirty-nine stelae depicting a single child, only nine show girls, while, of the nine stelae showing two children together, two show girls, two show a boy and a girl, and the other five have two boys. This means that boys were more often depicted (thirty-five boys, or 72 percent, compared to thirteen girls, or 28 percent).

The stelae with children also often carry inscriptions. Out of thirty-nine stelae with single children thirty-one are inscribed, while, of the nine stelae with portraits of two children, seven are inscribed. Of the fifteen stelae showing children with adults, six are inscribed. This means that stelae with children represent 44 percent of all the recorded inscribed stelae of the corpus with individual portraits, while inscribed stelae with children and adults represent 16 percent of all the stelae with multiple portraits carrying inscriptions (Figure 31.1).

The presence of an inscription provides us with information about the person's genealogy. A typical inscription gives us the name of the child, the name of his or her father, sometimes the name of the paternal grandfather, and the interjection 'alas'. The emphasis is clearly on patrilineal descent (Ringsborg 2016, 73). Only in the two examples where the children are portrayed with their mother do we have mention of their maternal grandfather: one stela at the Robert Mouawad Private Museum in Beirut (inv. no. 0166: Krag and Raja 2016, 156–157, 171, cat. no. 77, fig. 32, with previous bibliography), and one stela at the Palmyra Museum (inv. no. A 130: Krag 2018, 234, no. 260).

FIGURE 31.1 Stela with mother and two children, AD 130–150. Palmyra, Palmyra Museum, inv. no. A 130.

Copyright Palmyra Portrait Project, Ingholt Archives at the Ny Carlsberg Glyptotek.

Inscriptions also emphasize the significance of a monument. When we consider the high percentage of inscribed stelae with depictions of children, it becomes apparent that commemoration of children alone was a deliberate choice that was emphasized further by the use of the inscription.

One distinctive feature of Palmyrene art is that all but one of the children are dressed, regardless of their age, and this separates their imagery from contemporary images of children in the Roman Empire (see, e.g., Carroll 2011, figs. 2, 8, for images of infants in Roman funerary monuments from the second century AD, roughly contemporary with the Palmyrene stelae). In the stela from the Palmyra Museum inv. no. A 130, a female is depicted holding a standing child by the left arm and with a child on her left arm and cradled against her chest. The child on her arm is shown on a smaller scale than the other child, indicating that it is younger in age, while the motif of being held close to the mother's breast also emphasizes young age and dependency on the mother, thus making it likely that the child depicted is particularly young, possibly even an infant. Both children are dressed in long-sleeved tunics that reach to their ankles. Each child also wears a necklace composed of round beads and holds an object visible in outline: the older child holds it in the right hand and the younger child in the left hand. The objects could be birds or bunches of grapes.

The undecorated tunic, either with long sleeves or sleeves that reach to the elbows, is the most common garment for boys and girls on the stelae (Ringsborg 2016, 68). An overfold indicates the presence of a belt, although on some rare occasions the belt is shown (e.g., at a stela at the British Museum, inv. no. BM 125048: http://www.britis hmuseum.org/research/collection_online/collection_object_details.aspx?objectId= 282173&partId=1&searchText=palmyra&page=2). Almost always, the tunic falls to the ankles of the girls, covering them, while in the case of boys it ends a little above the ankles or even at the middle of the lower legs (as, e.g., a stela depicting Ogg[â], son of Hûrâ, son of Bôlhâ, son of Nebôšûrî from the hypogeum of Bôlhâ: Sadurska and Bounni 1994, 73–74, cat. no. 95, fig. 15. There are two known examples, however, where a girl is depicted wearing a tunic that reaches to the middle of her lower legs: one stela at the National Museum of Damascus (inv. no. 13: Ingholt Archive, PS 522) and one in Palmyra Museum (inv. no. 1986/7078: Sadurska and Bounni 1994, 68–69, cat. no. 94, fig. 17). See Figure 31.2.

A less common option is a 'Parthian-style' costume for boys composed of trousers and long-sleeved tunic. In one case, the child is depicted wearing over-trousers as well, a type of chaps, probably made of leather. In iconography of adults, this type of costume is associated with wealth, luxury from the east, and banquet scenes, however its exact meaning in depictions of children is not clear (see Ringsborn 2016; Curtis 2017).

Boys and girls are shown with short hair, although there are a few rare examples where girls are also depicted wearing a veil (e.g., Istanbul, Archaeological Museum, inv. no. 3727/O.M.179: Ingholt 1928, 142, PS 451; see also Krag and Raja 2018, esp. 251). Children of both sexes are also depicted wearing jewellery, although of the twenty-nine cases where it is possible to differentiate the gender of the child, only two boys are shown with jewellery: one in a stela confiscated by the Turkish police and one a stela

FIGURE 31.2 Stela with girl, AD 150–200. Damascus, National Museum of Damascus, inv. no. 13.
Copyright Palmyra Portrait Project, Ingholt Archives at the Ny Carlsberg Glyptotek.

depicting a boy called Moqimu, sold in the Beirut art market (Teixidor 1966, 178–179, no. 6, plate II, 6). They both wear different types of jewellery: Moqimu wears a necklace and bracelets, while the other boy wears a necklace, a bracelet, and possibly a head ornament. The centrepiece of his necklace is a small bell. Girls wear earrings and necklaces, but no brooches (Ringsborn 2016). As they are not shown wearing a himation, it seems that the brooch was not necessary. Finally, children are shown holding small birds and bunches of grapes, attributes that are also common in images of children from the Graeco-Roman world (Krag and Raja 2016, 143; see also Cohen 2007, 15–20; Carroll 2018; Green 2023).

The depictions on stelae offer us the typical representations of young children; these are repeated in the reliefs where children are shown with adult figures and which form the most common way of representing children. There are more than 1,100 loculus reliefs from Palmyrene tombs, out of which only ninety-eight depict adults with children: seventy-two women and twenty-six men are depicted with children. This means that less than 10 percent of the total representations are showing the deceased in the role of a parent, a fact that highlights that parenthood was just one aspect of a person's social identity and one that was prioritized in the funerary depictions only by a minority of Palmyrenes (Krag and Raja 2016, 139).

There are very few reliefs showing siblings together. There are only four loculus reliefs, of which one shows three children of different age groups together, a young child together with two older (adolescent?) siblings (National Museum of Damascus, inv. no. C28: Tanabe 1986, 40, 404, fig. 373); one shows an adult, bearded male next to his beardless brother (Palmyra Museum, inv. no. B 1948/7040: Sadurska and Bounni 1994, 50, cat. no. 56, fig. 99); one shows two beardless brothers (however, they are depicted with age markers so perhaps the textual evidence that they are the sons of Nora reflects their lineage and not their youth: Palmyra Museum, inv. no. B 2683/9084: al-As'ad 1993, 297, no. 237); and one shows two adolescents (National Museum of Damascus, inv. no. 15020: Raja 2017b, 339–340, fig. 10). This last one is of great importance as it is one of the very few Palmyrene reliefs that record the age of death of the depicted persons: one of the brothers died at nineteen and the other at sixteen years of age. Both are depicted dressed as adults, in a tunic and himation, and with wreaths on their heads. This relief highlights the discrepancy between social and physical adulthood and serves as a reminder that the visual material record can be deceptive when trying to locate children and young people in the past.

There are eight stelae altogether showing two children, twelve stelae with women and one or more children, and two stelae with men and children (Krag and Raja 2016, 155). When the children are depicted together with a sibling, they are both shown as young but their different heights suggest a slight age difference between them. They can be shown either wearing similar clothes (as, e.g., in a stela at the Istanbul Archaeological Museum, inv. no. 3729: Ingholt 1928, 154, PS 527, no. 3, where both children wear a tunic and hold a bunch of grapes) or in different garments. For example, in a stela once in the possession of the antique dealer Marcopoli at Aleppo, where two sisters are depicted, both girls have long hair and wear a necklace and a bracelet each, but each wears a different costume: the tallest of the two is wearing a tunic that reaches above the ankles and himation, while the shorter is wearing an ankle-length tunic (Pierson 1984, 91, fig. 4). In this case, the clothes accentuate the age difference as much as the height. When the children are shown together with an adult, however, there is a clear differentiation between the depiction of younger children, shown seated or beside an adult figure or in an adult female's arm, in ancillary and attribute roles, and that of older children, who are depicted at almost the same scale as the adult figures (Krag and Raja 2016, 155–158).

Representation of Infants and Very Young Children on Loculus Reliefs

In twenty-eight loculus reliefs we find depictions of very young children: they are shown either held by or seated on the left arm of a female figure, who must be their mother (Krag and Raja 2016, 149). Most of the children face the viewer; however, in several reliefs, they turn towards the woman, often reaching for her clothes, jewels, hand, or breast, gestures indicating connection and intimacy between the figures (Krag and Raja 2016, 147). It is these criteria (mode of being held and gesture) that characterize these children as infants, as their physiognomy and clothes do not differ from those of older children. They, too, are shown with short hair, jewels, wearing tunics or 'Parthian-style' costume, and holding grapes or birds. Only on two occasions are the children shown fully or partly naked, a feature emphasizing their youth and vulnerability (fully naked: Istanbul Archaeological Museum, inv. no. 3814/O.M. 316: Krag and Raja 2016, 146–147, cat. no. 48, fig. 14, with previous bibliography; partly naked, lower body covered with mother's veil: Beirut, Robert Mouawad Private Museum, inv. no. 1339: Forge 2004, 96, cat. no. 35).

One more relief (Palmyra Museum, inv. no. B 2692/9094: Charles-Gaffiot et al. 2001, 345, cat. no. 153) shows a young child dressed in a tunic sitting cross-legged over the mother's right shoulder, while in a stela another child, also dressed in a tunic, is seated cross-legged on the ground to the right of his mother (currently in an unknown location: Teixidor 1966, 178–179, cat. no. 7, plate II, 7). The seated posture emphasizes the children's youth and suggests an identification as infants.

In all the other reliefs, visually the children have an ancillary role. In all of the reliefs depicting them with men, and in thirty of the reliefs where they are represented with women, children are depicted next to the adult, either as standing full-figures or in bust-shaped portraits (Krag and Raja 2016, 139). When the reliefs are inscribed, then the portraits of the children are usually accompanied by inscriptions, indicating that they were not considered a mere attribute of the adult (as has been suggested was the case with depictions of infants in ancient Greek reliefs; see Beaumont 2012, 98), however, the focus of the depiction is on the adult figure, always portrayed in a bust-shaped portrait that occupies two-thirds of the relief field. The discrepancy in size between adult and child figures is especially striking when the portrait bust is chosen for the depiction of the child.

The inscriptions relating to images of children in loculus reliefs do not necessarily imply the premature death of the child, as the formula 'alas' could accompany the recording of names and genealogies of people who were still alive at the construction of the funerary monument (Krag and Raja 2016, 145, n. 62). The image of a still-living child together with that of a deceased parent could serve as a reminder of the family's continuity, as well as accentuate the grief felt at the loss of the adult.

The inscriptions also reveal how children could form part of both paternal and maternal lineage. Descent from the father's side was the one prioritized in the ancient world, and Palmyra was no exception, yet, in 34 percent of the reliefs showing a mother together with her child or children, only her genealogy is recorded and not that of the father (Krag and Raja 2016, 143, cat. nos. 1–3, 1–11, 18, 21, 30). In the other reliefs commemorating a deceased mother, the child is associated with his or her father epigraphically, either in the inscription accompanying the child's portrait or by having the father mentioned as the woman's husband in the text accompanying her portrait (Krag and Raja 2016, 143). This divergence reveals that, in some cases at least, the bond between mother and child was the one that was accentuated both visually and epigraphically, implying that the high status of some women in Palmyra was independent of that of their husbands (Krag and Raja 2016, 144).

The depiction of young children in these reliefs does not differ from that of children on stelae: boys and girls are again depicted wearing a tunic and jewellery, as well as holding fruit, especially bunches of grapes, but also bunches of dates, and birds (Krag and Raja 2016, 143). There are very few examples where the children are depicted wearing a tunic and a himation: a girl in a loculus relief at Gaziantep Museum (inv. no. 211; Parlasca 2005, 144, fig. 4) and a boy in a relief at Palmyra Museum (inv. no. B 1961/7053; Sadurska and Bounni 1994, 56–57, cat. no. 69, fig. 56). The children in both reliefs have distinct costumes and, in the case of the girl, jewellery, that separate them from common images of children. The girl wears an ornate headdress that is more often seen in depictions of young women (see Krag and Raja 2019), while the boy is dressed in the manner of adult men (compare, e.g., with a loculus relief at the Ny Carlsberg Glyptotek, inv. no. IN 1049, Ploug 1995, 45–48, no. 5; stela with two males, Ny Carlsberg Glyptotek, inv. no. IN 1024, Ploug 1995, 255–256, no. 126). It is significant that in the Palmyra Museum relief there is a second child who is shown wearing just a tunic. This implies that costume could be used to differentiate between children of different ages, perhaps suggesting that these were on the cusp of or in adolescence.

Representation of Adolescents on Stelae and Loculus Reliefs

The third group is that of adolescents. They are difficult to identify in the funerary visual material culture because they and young adults share the same iconography. Mothers and daughters are depicted in similar clothes and jewellery, while young males are depicted in the same way as older men (i.e., in tunic and himation) (Krag and Raja 2016, 151). Without epigraphic evidence on the age of the child it is impossible to decipher the age of a young person depicted next to an older relative. The iconography emphasizes the generational gap only in some cases: a young male person is depicted consistently as beardless and without any wrinkles, but, in the case of a relief at the Palmyra Museum (inv. no. 1949/7041: Sadurska and Bounni 1994, 50–51, cat. no. 57, fig. 53), the father is also depicted as beardless and without noticeable age markers such as forehead furrows or nasolabial lines. What identifies him as the father is the accompanying inscription, and what separates him from his son is his depiction in a much larger scale. In another example, both father and son are depicted as priests, a role that we know was limited to adults (Krag and Raja 2016, 152; Raja 2017a). We know, however, that adulthood was a fluid concept in the ancient world. In the Roman world, it is documented that adulthood was acquired in several stages, from donning the *toga virilis* to becoming head of one's own household (*pater familias*) (Laes and Strubbe 2014, 37–40). This means that even if an individual was considered socially an adult and was able to hold a priesthood, his actual age might have been closer to an older adolescent's or a young adult's in our modern world.

The reliefs where we have these group depictions are also very few. We know of one loculus relief where we have the depiction of an uncle together with his nephew (Portland Art Museum, inv. no. 54.2: Heyn 2010, app. 3, cat. no. 24a–24b, fig. 3, with previous bibliography), and there are four reliefs where we have the depiction of a father together with his son (Krag and Raja 2016, 150–151). In fourteen loculus reliefs, we have mothers depicted with older children, some of whom might have been adolescents (Krag and Raja 2016, 149–154). Also, a few are loculus reliefs where mothers are shown bare-breasted and mourning children who have reached social adulthood (Krag and Raja 2016, 151–152).

Representations of Children on Sarcophagi

The other large category of Palmyrene funerary monuments is that of sarcophagi. This is also the last category of funerary commemoration to be introduced in Palmyra, and was in use from the second century AD onwards. A typical sarcophagus carried the representation of a banqueting scene on the lid (whether carved in the round or in the form of a covering slab) and a series of busts on the box (Krag and Raja 2017, 198–199; see also Bobou and Raja forthcoming). Out of 205 sarcophagi that have been recorded as surviving in a good condition (before the recent vicissitudes of Palmyra, that is), forty-one include depictions of children (Krag and Raja 2017, 204). The evidence shows that there was a clear preference for depicting adult male sons on the sarcophagi compared to depictions in other types of commemoration, while more emphasis is placed on the relationship between fathers and sons rather than mothers and children (Krag and Raja 2017, 207–208, 213), and so it is worth discussing them separately from the depictions of children on other funerary monuments.

There are no infants in the banqueting scenes that have survived well; however, there is one fragment from a sarcophagus depicting a child in 'Parthian-style' dress and seated cross-legged (Ny Carlsberg Glyptotek, inv. no. IN 1082: Raja 2019, 248–249, no. 75), a posture that in loculus reliefs is associated with very young children. If this is indeed a portrayal of an infant, it suggests that their depiction was extremely rare and reflected a personal choice.

On the sarcophagus lids only eight figures can be securely identified as young children through the use of costume and attributes: seven boys and one girl dressed in tunics and holding grapes, while two more figures, young children dressed in tunics and in smaller scale are depicted on sarcophagus boxes. The figures on the sarcophagus lids are arranged paratactically, with a reclining male figure on one end, a seated female figure on the other, and a series of standing figures between them and partly behind the reclining male (Figure 31.3) Children occupy these middle positions, and it significant that they are often seen touching the arm or knee of the male figure (Krag and Raja 2017, 210).

FIGURE 31.3 Fragment of sarcophagus lid with seated child, AD 135–150. Copenhagen, Ny Carlsberg Glyptotek, inv. no. IN 1082.

Copyright Palmyra Portrait Project, Ingholt Archives at the Ny Carlsberg Glyptotek.

Religious

Piety, hope, and gratitude were all common emotions associated with religious experience in the ancient world (see Chaniotis 2013; Chaniotis and Ducrey 2014; Kazantzidis and Spatharas 2018), but they were expressed differently from region to region. In Palmyra, altars decorated with bas-reliefs were one of the most common ways of expressing these emotions (Seyrig 1933, 263–266; Dunant and Stucky 2000, 38; see also Kubiak-Schneider 2021), together with reliefs. These were usually placed on niches on sanctuary walls and had a decorative frame, or they were incorporated in the structural components of the sanctuary as, for example, on ceilings or beams connecting the cella with the peristyle (Drijvers 1976, 8).

There are thirty-seven objects where worshippers can be identified either as cult agents (priests) together with a deity or as supplicants: sixteen altars and twenty-one architectural or other types of reliefs. These supplicants, though, are almost always depicted as adult figures: in all these reliefs, only one altar has the representation of a young child dressed in a tunic next to a female figure. Both have their hands raised (Ny

Carlsberg Glyptotek, inv. no. IN 1080: Raja 2019, 352–353, cat. no. 136; see Vuolanto 2019 for children in the religious sphere of Palmyra).

Conclusion

The preceding survey of the existing material culture relating to the presence of children in Palmyra and how they were depicted shows the paucity of evidence for their early lives, surroundings, social context, and roles. Even so, the representations reveal that children were valued both in their own right (as can be evidenced from their numerous single-portrait depictions in stelae reliefs) and as family members. In loculus reliefs depicting deceased parents, the presence of a still-living child ensured the continuity of the family line, while the depiction of infants cradled by their mothers highlighted the vulnerability of the children as well as the importance of motherhood as an aspect of female social identity in Palmyra. The few loculus reliefs depicting mothers mourning their adult children, as well as the presence of mostly adult sons in sarcophagus reliefs, show that affective bonds between parents and children persisted past the age of childhood (Krag and Raja 2016; 2017). In the public and religious sphere, votive columns show that children could be displayed on their own, with the inscriptions declaring them members of particular families but important in their own right. Votive altars and reliefs reveal that the health of children was a constant concern for Palmyrenes, one that was valued above all else (Vuolanto 2019).

The iconographic evidence reveals that childhood was considered a separate period in a person's life. Sweet things (dates and grapes) and pets (small birds) were suitable for children. Bunches of grapes and birds also appear in depictions of children outside Palmyra, but the presence of dates hints that these attributes were not represented only because of their conventionality or knowledge of fashions outside Palmyra but also because children did have them as part of their meals—either often or as cherished treats. The grounding of the imagery of children in Palmyrene reality is also revealed by the fact that all children are shown dressed; in the Graeco-Roman world, dress serves as a gender-dividing motif, with boys appearing from naked to dressed and girls appearing dressed always. Furthermore, it is possible to identify bead necklaces and bracelets, bell pendants, and possibly amulets among the jewels worn by the children in their depictions, objects that have been found also in child burials.

The burial of infants in grave pits near the tombs of adults (as in the tomb of Zabdâ, and tombs C and F), as well as of children and infants together with older members of their family (as in Tomb F) reveals the importance of children within a family context, their incorporation into the family even after death, and the continuous emotional ties between family members. The presence of bead necklaces, amulets, and bronze bells in infant and child burials reveals the grounding of iconographic conventions in reality as well as the parental desire to beautify and protect their children.

Researh on Palmyrene children may be in its beginning, compared to that on children from other areas of the ancient world, but even so the evidence can shed some light on their lives and deaths.

ACKNOWLEDGEMENTS

The author acknowledges the funding received by the Danish National Research Foundation for Centre for Urban Network Evolutions (grant no. 119) as well as the funding received from the Carlsberg Foundation for the various Palmyra projects based at Aarhus University, first and foremost the Palmyra Portrait Project. Furthermore, I thank the ALIPH Foundation as well as the Augustinus Foundation for funding for further Palmyra-related projects.

BIBLIOGRAPHY

Abdul-Hak, Selim. 1952. 'L'hypogée de Taai à Palmyre'. *Les Annales Archéologiques Arabes Syriennes*, 2: 193–251.

al-As'ad, Khaled. 1993. 'Bas-relief funéraire de deux frères'. In *Syrie: Memoire et Civilisation*, edited by L'Institut du Monde Arabe, 297. Paris: Flammarion.

Balty, Janine. 2014. *Inventaire des mosaïques antiques de Syrie*. Vol. 2, *Les mosaïques des maisons de Palmyre*. Beirut: Presses de l'Institut français du Proche-Orient.

Baxter, Jane Eva. 2008. *The Archaeology of Childhood: Children, Gender, and Material Culture*. Lanham: Rowman Altamira.

Beaumont, Lesley A. 2012. *Childhood in Ancient Athens*. Abingdon: Routledge.

Bloomer, Martin W. 2013. 'The Ancient Child in School'. In *The Oxford Handbook of Childhood and Education in the Classical World*, edited by Judith Evans Grubbs, Tim Parkin, and Roslynne Bell, 446–461. Oxford: Oxford University Press.

Bobou, Olympia and Rubina Raja. forthcoming. *Palmyrene Sarcophagi*. Studies in Palmyrene History and Archaeology 10. Turnhout: Brepols.

Carroll, Maureen. 2011. 'Infant Death and Burial in Roman Italy'. *Journal of Roman Archaeology* 24: 99–120.

Carroll, Maureen. 2018. *Infancy and Earliest Childhood in the Roman World: 'A Fragment of Time'*. Oxford: Oxford University Press.

Chaniotis, Angelos, ed. 2013. *Unveiling Emotions: Sources and Methods for the Study of Emotions in the Greek World*. Heidelberger Althistorische Beiträge und epigraphische Studien 52. Stuttgart: Steiner.

Chaniotis, Angelos, and Pierre Ducrey, eds. 2014. *Unveiling Emotions*. Vol. 2, *Emotions in Greece and Rome: Texts, Images, Material Culture*. Heidelberger Althistorische Beiträge und epigraphische Studien 55. Stuttgart: Steiner.

Charles-Gaffiot, Jacques, Henri Lavagne, and Jean-Marc Hofman. 2001. *Moi, Zénobie, reine de Palmyre*. Paris: Centre Culturel du Pantheon.

Cohen, Ada. 2007. 'Introduction: Childhood Between Past and Present'. In *Constructions of Childhood in Ancient Greece and Italy*, edited by Ada Cohen and Jeremy B. Rutter, 1–22. Hesperia, suppl. 41. Princeton: American School of Classical Studies at Athens.

Colledge, Malcolm A. R. 1976. *The Art of Palmyra*. London: Thames & Hudson.

Curtis, Vesta Sarkhosh. 2017. 'The Parthian haute-couture at Palmyra'. In *Positions and Professions in Palmyra*, edited by Tracey Long and Annette Højen Sørensen, 52–67. Palmyrene Studies 2. Scientia Danica. Series Humanistica 4, vol. 9. Copenhagen: Det Kongelige Danske Videnskabernes Selskab.

Drijvers, H. J. W. 1976. *The Religion of Palmyra*. Iconography of Religions: Section 15, Mesopotamia and the Near East. Leiden: Brill.

Dunant, Christiane, and Rolf A. Stucky. 2000. *Le Sanctuaire de Baalshamin a Palmyre*. Vol. 4, *Sculptures*. Rome: Institut suisse de Rome.

Forge, Oliver. 2004. 'Antiquities'. In *The Future of the Past: The Robert Mouawad Private Museum*, 76–111. Beirut: The Robert Mouawad Private Museum.

Gabriel, Albert. 1926. 'Recherches archéologiques à Palmyre'. *Syria* 6: 71–92.

Gawlikowska, Krystyna. 2015. 'The Glass Industry in Palmyra'. *Syria* 92: 291–298.

Gawlikowski, Michal. 2016. 'The Portraits of the Palmyrene Royalty'. In *The World of Palmyra*, edited by Andreas Kropp and Rubina Raja, 126–134. Palmyrene Studies 1. Scientia Danica. Series Humanistica 4, vol. 6. Copenhagen: Det Kongelige Danske Videnskabernes Selskab.

Green, Ashleigh. 2023. *Birds in Roman Life and Myth*. London: Routledge.

Grossmann, Janet Burnett. 2013. *Funerary Sculpture*. The Athenian Agora 35. Princeton, NJ: American School of Classical Studies at Athens.

Heyn, Maura. 2010. 'Gesture and Identity in the Funerary Art of Palmyra'. *American Journal of Archaeology* 114(4): 631–661.

Heyn, Maura, and Rubina Raja. 2021. 'Attributes in Palmyrene Funerary Sculpture: Functions and Meanings'. In *Individualizing the Dead: Attributes in Palmyrene Funerary Sculpture*, edited by Maura Heyn and Rubina Raja, 1–12. Studies in Palmyrene History and Archaeology 3. Turnhout: Brepols.

Higuchi, Takayasu, and Takura Izumi. 1994. *Tombs A and C: Southeast Necropolis; Palmyra Syria; Surveyed in 1990–92*. Nara: Research Center for Silk Roadology.

Higuchi, Takayasu, and Kiyohide Saito. 2001. *Tomb F: Tomb of BWLH and BWRP; Southeast Necropolis; Palmyra Syria*. Nara: Research Center for Silk Roadology.

Hillers, Delbert R., and Eleonora Cussini, eds. 1996. *Palmyrene Aramaic Texts*. Baltimore: Johns Hopkins University Press.

Ingholt, Harald. 1928. *Studier over Palmyrensk Skulptur*. Copenhagen: Reitzel.

Ingholt, Harald. 1935. 'Five Dated Tombs from Palmyra'. *Berytus: Archaeological Studies* 2: 57–120.

Kazantzidis, George, and Dimos Spatharas, eds. 2018. *Hope in Ancient Literature, History, and Art*. Ancient Emotions 1. Trends in Classics, Supplementary Volumes 63. Berlin: de Gruyter.

Krag, Signe. 2018. *Funerary Representations of Palmyrene Women: From the First Century BC to the Third Century AD*. Studies in Classical Archaeology 3. Turnhout: Brepols.

Krag, Signe, and Rubina Raja. 2016. 'Representations of Women and Children in Palmyrene Funerary *loculus* Reliefs, *loculus stelae* and Wall Paintings'. *Zeitschrift für Orient-Archäologie* 9: 134–178.

Krag, Signe, and Rubina Raja. 2017. 'Representations of Women and Children in Palmyrene Banqueting Reliefs and Sarcophagi'. *Zeitschrift für Orient-Archäologie* 10: 196–227.

Krag, Signe, and Rubina Raja. 2018. 'Unveiling Female Hairstyles: Markers of Age, Social Roles, and Status in Funerary Sculpture from Palmyra'. *Zeitschrift für Orient-Archäologie* 11, 243–277.

Krag, Signe, and Rubina Raja. 2019. 'Families in Palmyra: The Evidence from the First Three Centuries CE'. In *Women, Children and the Family in Palmyra*, edited by Signe Krag and

Rubina Raja, 7–18. Palmyrene Studies 3. Scientia Danica. Series Humanistica 4, 10. Copenhagen: Det Kongelige Danske Videnskabernes Selskab.

Kubiak-Schneider, Aleksandra. 2021. *Des dédicaces sans théonyme de Palmyre*. Leiden: Brill.

Laes, Christian. 2011. *Children in the Roman Empire: Outsiders Within*. Cambridge: Cambridge University Press.

Laes, Christian, and Johan Strubbe. 2014. *Youth in the Roman Empire*. Cambridge: Cambridge University Press.

Mander, Jason. 2012. *Portraits of Children on Roman Funerary Monuments*. Cambridge: Cambridge University Press.

Michałowski, Kazimierz. 1960. *Palmyre 1. Fouilles Polonaises 1959*. Warsaw: Państwowe Wydawnictwo Naukowe.

Michałowski, Kazimierz. 1962. *Palmyre 2. Fouilles Polonaises 1960*. Warsaw: Państwowe Wydawnictwo Naukowe.

Parlasca, Klaus. 2005. 'Zu palmyrenischen Inschriften auf Reliefs'. In *A Journey to Palmyra: Collected Essays to Remember Delbert R. Hillers*, edited by Eleonora Cussini, 137–149. Leiden: Brill.

Pierson, Francis. 1984. 'Recherches sur les costumes des enfants dans l'iconographie palmyrénienne'. *Revue des archéologues et historiens d'art de Louvain* 17: 85–111.

Ploug, Gunhild. 1995. *Catalogue of Palmyrene Sculptures: Ny Carlsberg Glyptotek*. Copenhagen: Ny Carlsberg Glyptotek.

Raja, Rubina. 2017a. 'Networking Beyond Death: Priests and Their Family Networks in Palmyra Explored Through the Funerary Sculpture'. In *Sinews of Empire: Networks in the Roman Near East and Beyond*, edited by Håkon Fiane Teigen and Eivind Heldaas Seland, 121–136. Oxford: Oxbow.

Raja, Rubina. 2017b. 'Powerful Images of the Deceased: Palmyrene Funerary Portrait Culture between Local, Greek and Roman Representations'. In *Bilder der Macht: Das griechische Porträt und seine Verwendung in der antiken Welt*, edited by Dietrich Boschung and François Queyrel, 314–348. Morphomata 34. Paderborn: Fink.

Raja, Rubina. 2019. *Catalogue: The Palmyra Collection; Ny Carlsberg Glyptotek*.Copenhagen: Ny Carlsberg Glyptotek.

Raja, Rubina. 2022. *Pearl of the Desert: A History of Palmyra*. New York: Oxford University Press.

Ringsborg, Sara. 2016. 'Children's Portraits from Palmyra'. In *Palmyra, Pearl of the Desert*, edited by Rubina Raja, 67–76. Aarhus: SUN-Tryk, Aarhus Universitet.

Sadurska, Anna. 1977. *Palmyre 7. Le tombeau de famille de 'Alainê*. Warsaw: Państwowe Wydawnictwo Naukowe.

Sadurska, Anna, and Adnan Bounni. 1994. *Les sculptures funéraires de Palmyre*. Rome: Giorgio Bretschneider.

Saliby, Nasib, and Klaus Parlasca. 1992. 'L'hypogée de Sassan fils de Malê à Palmyre'. *Damaszener Mitteilungen* 6: 267–292

Schmidt-Colinet, Andreas, and Waleed al-As'ad, eds. 2013. *Palmyras Reichtum durch weltweiten Handel: Archäologische Untersuchungen im Bereich der hellenistischen Stadt*. Vienna: Verlag Holzhausen.

Seyrig, Henri. 1933. 'Antiquités syriennes'. *Syria* 14(3): 253–282.

Tanabe, Katsumi. 1986. *Sculptures of Palmyra*. Tokyo: Ancient Orient Museum.

Teixidor, Javier. 1966. 'Monuments Palmyrénies divers'. *Mélanges de l'Université Saint-Joseph* 42(2): 177–179.

Verdegem, Simon. 2010. *Plutarch's Life of Alcibiades: Story, Text and Moralism*. Leuven: Leuven University Press.

Vuolanto, Ville. 2019. 'Children and Religious Participation in Roman Palmyra'. In *Women, Children and the Family in Palmyra*, edited by Signe Krag and Rubina Raja, 201–213. Palmyrene Studies 3. Scientia Danica. Series Humanistica 4, 10. Copenhagen: Det Kongelige Danske Videnskabernes Selskab.

Yon, Jean-Baptiste, ed. 2012. *Inscriptions grecques et latines de la Syrie*. Vol. 17.1, *Palmyre*. Beirut: Presses de l'Institut français du Proche-Orient.

Yon, Jean-Baptiste. 2013. 'Palmyrene Epigraphy after PAT, 1996–2011'. *Studia Palmyreńskie* 12: 333–379.

Online Resources

British Museum: http://www.britishmuseum.org/research/collection_online/collection_obj ect_details.aspx?objectId=282173&partId=1&searchText=palmyra&page=2.

Historia Augusta: http://penelope.uchicago.edu/Thayer/E/Roman/Texts/Historia_Augusta/ Tyranni_XXX*.html#note96.

CHAPTER 32

THE PRODUCTION ECONOMY OF FUNERARY PORTRAITURE

JULIA STEDING[*]

INTRODUCTION

THE production economy of portraiture in the ancient Mediterranean world is rarely studied within classical archaeology. Palmyrene funerary portraiture—the largest corpus of portraiture in antiquity outside Rome, including more than 3,700 portraits (Chapter 27 [Raja] this volume, on funerary sculpture; Raja 2017, 9)—is a resource on which we can draw to shed light on a number of questions relating to the production economy of funerary portraiture in ancient Palmyra, and particularly to the techniques of limestone carving in ancient Syria.

This chapter presents an overview of the potential of detailed studies of tool traces in these portraits when set within the context of various questions regarding the organization of Palmyrene carving workshops. One loculus relief from Palmyra will be discussed in a case study to explain the various kinds of tool traces detectable and propose ways of reaching further conclusions on the use of tools over the whole span of portrait production and how this might provide new insight into the workshops and the organization of production processes. Sadly, no carving workshop has ever been found in Palmyra, but comparisons with sites such as Aphrodisias in Asia Minor, as well as epigraphic and iconographic sources, may shed some light on the structure of the Palmyrene workplaces. The chapter also briefly addresses questions associated with the use of graves as a carving location: in this light, two partly carved objects found inside a grave will be discussed.

[*] This research is part of the Palmyra Portrait Project (http://projects.au.dk/palmyraportrait) that was funded by the Carlsberg Foundation from 2012 to 2020 and headed by Professor Rubina Raja at Aarhus University.

Classical archaeology has tended to focus on sculptures and portraits as pieces of art of the elite and from an exclusively Graeco-Roman perspective (Lichtenberger and Raja 2017b, 1–2; Blömer and Raja 2019b, 5). If production processes have been explored at all, the main area of focus has been the traces, attempting to reconstruct the tools and carving steps used. Carl Blümel was one of the first scholars to study methods of stone carving in his book *Griechische Bildhauerarbeit* (1927), translated into English as *Greek Sculptors at Work* in 1955. Blümel presented many interesting observations on the work of carvers, using various examples from different cities and quarries. He explained the carving process as layered, meaning that the carver worked all sides of a statue to the same stage before he took his carving to the next step. This made it possible to keep the whole object in view during the whole carving process (Blümel 1969, 11–12). The next most important publication on sculptural techniques, building upon Blümel's work, was by Sheila Adam (1966). Adam focused on techniques of Greek marble sculpture from the archaic to the classical periods. After surveying the most common carving tools, she discusses free-standing statues as well as grave reliefs. Another important publication on marble carving was Herz and Waelkens's edited collection, *Classical Marble: Geochemistry, Technology, Trade*, which discusses different types of marble and the various steps involved in choosing, quarrying, and using stone in ancient Greece and Rome (Herz and Waelkens 1988). A symposium on marble at the J. Paul Getty Museum resulted in a collection of papers covering the art historical approach as well as scientific developments in marble research (True and Podany 1990). In 1993, Peter Rockwell shifted the focus from the archaeological material to the actual craft of carving, describing the different tools, processes, and methods from a carver's point of view and generating important insight into the theoretical understanding of the carving process. More recently, Amanda Claridge discussed marble carving techniques, workshops, and artisans (Claridge 2015). A few years earlier, Olga Palagia explored the process of carving Greek sculptures rather than concentrating on the various kinds of tools and traces (Palagia 2006).

The publications just mentioned all focus on marble, which is understandable in view of the very large body of extant marble sculptures and reliefs and the popularity of marble in antiquity. Also, limestone and other materials have been less well studied within classical archaeology because of the focus on the elite, which used marble (Lichtenberger and Raja 2017b, 1), and the close connection between classical archaeology and art history in the past (Millett 2008, 30–36; Snodgrass 2008, 13–20).

However, interest is growing in other materials besides marble and their importance for understanding ancient societies (Dillon 2017, 223; on new approaches within classical archaeology in general, see Lichtenberger and Raja 2017; on funerary portraiture in Greater Roman Syria, see Blömer and Raja 2019a). The project 'The Art of Making', which ran from 2011 to 2013 and was based at King's College London, supervised by Will Wootton, centred on the topic of stone carving and published a large online database with a wide range of photos showing tool traces on a range of materials used for different purposes (http://www.artofmaking.ac.uk). This database also includes information on the carving of limestone and other less commonly used stones. Even though the available archaeological sources are small in number, the website offers a very useful overview of the available tools and their use, as well as of the carving process itself.

Although many works include small sections on the production of the sarcophagi or sculptures they discuss (for Roman sarcophagi, see, e.g., Huskinson 2006, 79–86; for Roman portraits, see, e.g., Fejfer 2008, 162–190; Kleiner 1992, 15–16; Lahusen 2010, 59–71, 189–204; for Palestine portraits, see Skupinska-Løvset 1983, 272–273; for Greater Roman Syria, see Raja and Steding 2021; on literary sources, see, e.g., Skupinska-Løvset 1999, 31–34), a comprehensive study of the carving of limestone has not been undertaken until recently (Steding 2022; see also Russell and Wootton 2021). As this chapter demonstrates, detailed study of the surface of the Palmyrene funerary portraits can glean information on both the tools and the carving processes used and thus provide insight into the broader lines of production.

Carving Stone

The Material

The first information needed to reconstruct the production process involves determining the type of stone used for particular sculptures or reliefs. This information allows us to draw conclusions about the resources used to create portraits. If the stone was carved locally, for instance, how did the quarry, the carver, and the customer collaborate with one another? If the stone was imported, what kind of transport was used? The provenance of stone has attracted increasing attention in recent years and adds important information about the choices made in different regions and periods (Dillon 2017, 223; Russell 2013, 1–3, 12–18; for recent results on marble provenancing, see the proceedings of the annual Association for the Study of Marble and Other Stones [ASMOSIA] conferences; for an overview on materials and techniques of art, see Lapatin 2015; for an overview of different types of stone, see Rockwell 1993). Once the type of stone and (if possible) its origin have been determined, the first assumptions about its choice can be made, shedding light on the question of whether the product was carved locally or abroad, whether the customer spent money on importing material, and whether certain types of stone were preferred in certain contexts. Based on these findings, further examinations of the carving concerned can be carried out.

Tools and Traces

The most notable research on limestone carving has been undertaken by Jean-Claude Bessac and Thomas F. C. Blagg. Bessac gave a comprehensive overview on handheld tools, percussion tools, and abrasion tools in connection with limestone, including drawings of the traces left on the stone surface (Bessac 1986). Further, he published on the limestone carving in Petra (Bessac 2007) and Roman Gaul (Bessac 1988; 1992). Blagg focused on the tools and techniques of stonemasons in relation to architecture in Roman Britain (Blagg 1976). Even though these publications deal mainly with the carving of architectural elements, they are important overviews of limestone carving in those regions and can help with the understanding of production processes of portraiture.

Stone carving has a long tradition and even though cultures have differed in their preferences for materials and tools, the general process of stone carving has remained the same until today (for a general introduction to the tools, see Bessac 1986, 14–24, 108–148, 231–270; Blagg 1976, 159–165, 170–171; Rockwell 1993, 31–54; Wootton et al. 2013a, 2–9; for the general process of carving, see Rockwell 1993, 69–88, 107–126; Wootton et al. 2013b). A standard set of tools was adapted to suit particular circumstances, such as the hardness of the material in question or the demands made by a specific carved shape (Rockwell 1993, 22). In many cases, tool traces are hard to detect on the finished objects because the desired finish included smoothing the surface and erasing visible tool traces. However, close examination makes it possible to reconstruct the various steps in the carving process and the tools used.

In general, after the material was quarried, the carver would start with a handheld pick, which roughed out an appropriately sized block, for instance, for a loculus relief. The tool marks of a pick can still be seen on the reverse, the sides, and the top of many objects, but never appear on the front, where finer tools were used to shape the actual figures and the background. This was done by a point chisel that roughed out the forms. This process was continued by a tooth chisel (also called a claw chisel) when required. Both these tools are percussion tools, used with a hammer that hits the upper end of the tool and drives the cutting edge into the stone. Portraits were shaped with these tools to quite some extent, only leaving the fine shaping to a finer tool. In most cases, the second-to-last step was the flattening of the background with a small-toothed tooth chisel or a flat chisel, followed by the fine shaping of the portrait with a flat chisel (a finer tool with a straight cutting edge, also used with a hammer), which erased most of the traces of the previous tools and added detail to the figures. Held vertical to the surface of the stone, the blade created a straight, flat surface; held more horizontal to the surface, the sharp rim created a groove, for instance to incise the eyebrows or the outline of the lips. The use of a drill was optional and was used either to outline figures by determining the final depth of a portrait by setting multiple holes in a line and carving the stone away up to this outline, or to add details (e.g., the pupils of the eyes or the nostrils). It was also used to elaborate certain shapes by giving them greater depth and more defined forms and to create undercuts. The final step in carving a portrait was to smooth and polish the stone, using a rasp or some form of abrasive. This was not done in all cases: the degree of smoothing depended on the type of stone in question.

To sum up, the process of carving follows a simple rule: as the process progresses, the tools used (and the marks left) become finer and finer. Rough marks from the early steps are probably to be found only on less visible surfaces (Bessac 1988, 41; Steding 2022, 77, 139) because elsewhere their traces have been removed by finer tools later in the process.

Limestone Portraits from Palmyra

The Palmyrene carvers used the locally available limestone for their architecture (see, e.g., Henning 2013, 27–39, 41; Schmidt-Colinet 2017, 161) as well as for their portraits and other art forms (Colledge 1976, 109, 117; Steding 2022). The stone was extracted in the nearby quarries, situated 12–23 km north of the city. Blocks of about 60 cm height or more were broken out of the rock. The presence of roughly carved sarcophagi, pillars, and altars in the quarries themselves indicates that these were carved roughly on site (on the quarries, see Schmidt-Colinet 2017, 168–181; Abdul Massih 2021; Bessac 2021; Chapter 5 [Schmidt-Colinet] this volume; other quarries are also mapped in Schnädelbach 2010). No loculus reliefs or any other kind of loculus slab have been found in the quarries, so these were probably either cut to size and brought to the city without further carving activity or simply cut to size in their final location (Steding 2022, 39–40). By contrast, sarcophagi were precarved in the quarries, then brought to the city after all redundant stone had been removed to reduce the weight of the object to be transported (Schmidt-Colinet 2017, 181). This was common practice and shows that the transportation of objects was taken into consideration when production was planned (Blagg 1976, 155; Russell 2013, 260–271). In Palmyra, the short distance between the quarries and the necropoleis can therefore be seen as a conscious decision to keep the costs and labour involved in the construction and interior of funerary monuments as low as possible.

The most important research on the techniques applied to the making of Palmyrene art was undertaken by Malcolm A. R. Colledge. His book, *The Art of Palmyra*, contains a broad overview of the portraiture of Palmyra, including a chapter on the materials and techniques that were most common (1976, 107–121). According to Colledge, the colour of the limestone that was used varied between white or grey, shading into yellow or pink (Colledge 1976, 109). The stone used from the first century AD onwards can be characterized as hard limestone, and this type was used for the tombs as well as the portraits (Henning 2013, 41; Schmidt-Colinet 1990, 88; Bessac 2021, 52).

Colledge has listed the various tools used at Palmyra: the pick-hammer, the punch, the point, the claw chisel, the flat chisel, the curved chisel, the drill, and the rasp (Colledge 1976, 110–114, fig. 56. See also Russell and Wootton 2021; Steding 2022, chapters 3 and 4). The traces of all these tools can be found on the objects themselves, aligned with the carving techniques discussed above.

Colledge's observations reveal not only which tools were used, but also their purposes. For instance, let us take a quick look at the flat chisel, the tool used most frequently. The traces of this tool can be found on all parts of a portrait, including the background, face, and clothing. The blade can vary in size and can serve multiple functions, including carving finer forms, adding details, or smoothing the surface after using the tooth chisel or point. Depending on the desired outcome, the flat chisel was held more or less horizontal to the stone, creating different kinds of traces on it (Colledge 1976, 112; Rockwell 1993, 42–43).

Colledge was also able to detect some changes in the use of the tools, showing one of the most significant outcomes of the study of tool traces. When tool traces are carefully examined and recorded, it is possible to work out whether and when carvers changed their process, which can in turn constitute evidence of economic changes (Steding 2002, especially chapter 4). This enables researchers to frame investigations on the use of tools and the process of carving within a broader framework of questions focusing on the economy behind individual portraits and connecting traces and tools to processes that can in turn supply information on the workshops and the way they were organized. With a view to explaining further details about what these traces could look like, the following section discusses a loculus relief from Palmyra to illustrate which traces can be observed on portraiture in the funerary context.

A Case Study: Tool Traces on a Loculus Relief from Palmyra

To illustrate the potential of close examination of the surface of portraits, I have selected a loculus relief, now in the Ny Carlsberg Glyptotek in Copenhagen (inv. no. IN 1155; Raja 2019, 72–73, no. 4). The relief is made from grey limestone and depicts a female within a wreath. The inscription dates the object to AD 125 (Figure 32.1).

The plaque is quite thin and rectangular in shape, with all its sides carved straight. In general, this plaque can be described as evenly carved when seen frontally. The sides are less carefully carved, and the traces of a point that was used to shape a square block of the desired size at the beginning of the carving process are still visible. After this, the bust was carved on the front surface of the block. This first stage of a portrait could also have been created by a point, but those traces have been erased. What is still visible are traces of a tooth chisel. These can be found on the bust, below her right breast, in a spot that was not clearly visible to the viewer. Still, these traces prove that a tooth chisel was used to rough out the bust. At the same time, the background was deepened to carve out the bust. Again, a point could have been used to deepen this space, but a tooth chisel certainly was used to create a flat surface behind the woman and the wreath. The marks are visible all over the plaque. They are characteristic small grooves that are parallel to each other. The carver used the tool in a vertical direction, working his way from the top of the plaque to the bottom, so the grooves run vertically across the plaque. Only around the upper part of the wreath did the direction change. Here, the grooves of the chisel follow the curve of the wreath. On the lower part of the plaque, below the bust, the tooth chisel was used in a similar way, following the curve of the wreath again and creating a pattern that runs diagonally across the stone.

While the tooth chisel is obviously visible on the background, nearly all traces have vanished on the bust itself. As mentioned above, traces have survived only on those parts barely visible to the viewer. In the next step, a flat chisel was used to shape the finer form of the bust and the wreath. The straight blade creates a smoother surface than the ridged blade of a tooth chisel or the uneven marks of a point. Depending on the angle

FIGURE 32.1 Loculus relief depicting a female.

Courtesy of the Ny Carlsberg Glyptotek, Copenhagen, IN1155, © Palmyra Portrait Project.

at which it is held, the flat chisel can flatten larger surfaces or be used to carve detail. The latter can be seen on the various parts of the object. The single leaves of the wreath as well as the three acorns on each side are defined by lines indicating their structure. Furthermore, both the tunic and veil are carved with individual folds, creating a livelier appearance. The same holds true for the face and hair. Single strands are evident, and the lips, nose, eyes, and eyebrows are indicated by incised lines. All of these details were rendered with a flat chisel, using the edge of the tool to cut lines into the stone. The work with the flat chisel has erased traces of the tooth chisel. The more angular flakes left by the flat chisel are visible on the wreath and on the clothes. Even though both look smooth, the individual forms are still quite angular rather than rounded. This is not the case with the woman's face, where a rasp was used to erase the marks still left by a flat chisel on the stone. Only on the face, then, do the incised lines survive as obvious marks of the flat chisel indicating details of eyes, nose, and mouth. Other than that, the surface of the face has been smoothed as much as possible.

A few observations can be made after studying all the traces in detail. First, it is possible to identify which tools were used. Second, we can reconstruct the sequence of carving. In this case, the carver started by roughing out the block using a point chisel, after which the bust and wreath were roughly shaped with a tooth chisel. During this same stage, the background was deepened. When the carver needed to refine the forms, he switched to a flat chisel for the bust and wreath, carving the final appearance. For the background, he decided to stick to the tooth chisel rather than reworking the surface with a flat chisel to get rid of the obvious marks. The flat chisel was used only to incise the frame running along the edge and the inscription. After the portrait and wreath were completely carved, another decision was made: while the woman's wreath and clothes were not smoothed any further, the carver used a rasp on the face. Here the forms are more rounded, and all traces of earlier tools have vanished. This complete sequence of carving reveals how the portrait was made and what decisions the carver made during the process. It also highlights which parts of the object were treated with greater care to accentuate them, namely the face.

Artisans and Workshops

The Archaeological Evidence

Of course, as stated above, the study of tools and traces cannot stand on its own and needs to be connected to broader queries. One of these concerns the workshops that were used. How many workshops existed, and how were they organized? To answer this, we need a definition of an ancient carving workshop. Such a definition could not cover all ancient cities, but needs to be adjusted to suit the circumstances in question. Depending on the size of the economy and the demand for portraiture, the way in which workshops were organized could vary. The carving workshop excavated in Aphrodisias gives an impression of how archaeological traces and structures can add to our knowledge of workshops. There, the two rooms of a modified *stoa* to the north of the bouleuterion have been excavated together with a yard that was used as a working and storage space for sculptures. Marble sculptures at different stages of carving and datable to the different architectural phases of the workshop can be dated to AD 200–400

(Rockwell 1991, 127–129; Smith 2008, 29, 111; van Voorhis 2012, 39–41). Twenty-eight pieces with carved feet or hands seem to have functioned as pieces for apprentices. Even though the findspots do not help with the contextualizing process, the pieces show that workshops were used as a place to train new artists (van Voorhis 1998, 176–183; van Voorhis 2008, 120–135). Furthermore, the variety of carved objects attests to the wide range of activities taking place within this one physical workspace: small figurines have been found as well as full-size portrait statues, and some objects can be seen as products of recycling. This shows not only that one workshop provided various different kinds of product, but also that objects may have been used again for other purposes or by other customers (Smith 2008, 111–118).

Iconographic and Epigraphic Sources

Because the archaeological sources give so little information, we need to look at both the available iconographic representations of workshop scenes and at inscriptions indicating the profession of the deceased. Only a few of these are known, but they can supply some information about the working process within a workshop. A sarcophagus from Ephesus, now in the Archaeological Museum in Istanbul (inv. no. 775; Smith 2008, 108–110), depicts various scenes in a workshop. On the left a seated figure, wearing a worker's short tunic, is drawing on a tabula, which can possibly be interpreted as the design process (Smith 2008, 109). To his right sits a master sculptor, wearing a knee-length tunic, chiselling the hand of a standing statue. Next to him, a slave, wearing a loin cloth, leans over a bench trough, polishing a lion-headed table leg using abrasives and water from the basin below. The last person is a master carver (possibly the same figure who is sculpting the standing figure), wearing a knee-length tunic. He chisels the shoulder drapery of a bust, and a slave stands behind him, with freshly sharpened tools (Russell 2013, 345; Smith 2008, 109). This shows that several persons could be involved in the carving process, a theory that is supported by a loculus slab from Rome, now in the Palazzo Ducale in Urbino (Neg. D-DAI-Rom 75.1102), showing another workshop scene. The carver Eutropos is sitting on a chair, directing a strap drill along a *strigilis* sarcophagus. He is assisted by another person who is operating the cord of the drill (Russell 2013, 291). This shows clearly that some tools, such as this special drill, needed to be operated by two people. Furthermore, multiple reliefs show tools or mention the profession of the deceased (for an overview of representations and inscriptions of stoneworkers, see Zimmer 1982, 35–37, 153–160).

A sarcophagus from Aphrodisias mentions various professions: an *agalmatoglyphos* and a *pimentarios*, terms that can be translated as 'sculptor' and 'paint supplier' (Smith 2008, 105). Another sarcophagus carries an inscription that was added when the object was reused. Together with the name Stratonikos, a profession is mentioned. *Epistēmē Graphikē*, referring to the knowledge of painting (Smith 2008, 107), indicates that different aspects of portrait production may have been covered by different specialists. Due to the relatively good preservation of colour on some of the Palmyrene loculus reliefs, we need to consider painters as part of the production process of funerary portraits. For instance, in the collection of loculus reliefs in the Ny Carlsberg Glyptotek in Copenhagen (Raja 2019), red pigments appear in the inscription, particularly in the background. On twenty-two of sixty-five loculus reliefs, this colour is used to highlight the inscription (personal observation). This procedure probably did not require a specialist, but could have been carried out by anyone working in the workshop. However, looking at the so-called 'Beauty of Palmyra' (Ny Carlsberg Glyptotek, Copenhagen, inv. no. IN 2795; Raja 2019, 198–201, no. 57), it becomes clear that different colours have been added to the surface. Red, yellow, black, and golden pigments have been found on the female portrait, covering parts of her skin, jewellery, and headdress (Hedegaard and Brøns 2019; Blume 2021). This shows that a specialist was used to add elaborate painting to the limestone portrait and that he must have worked either at the workshop or at least in collaboration with it, providing the material and knowledge required to add colour to the carved stone (see also Blume 2021; Steding 2022, 131–133). Other questions relating to workshops are harder to answer: for example, the use of master carvers and adjutants, the presence of various specialists, and the division of labour.

The next section gives a brief overview of the potential of research on the workshops of Palmyra and discusses how these questions should be addressed in future research.

Workshops in Palmyra

Without any archaeological evidence from new excavations pointing to the existence of workshops—the accumulated presence of tools, stored or carved objects, or accumulated waste—the only available evidence is the portraits themselves. Furthermore, neither epigraphic nor iconographic evidence from Palmyra can directly answer questions about the workshops in the city. Nonetheless, various approaches may help us to find some answers.

One of the aims of studying workshops is to trace different artists by studying the techniques used by the carvers. In her research on portraits from the temple of Allat, D. Wielgosz-Rondolino has compared funerary portraits with honorific statues and architectural decoration. Based on her study of the carving techniques used, she concludes that some of these portraits were carved in the same workshop, while others were carved by a different sculptor (Wielgosz-Rondolino 2016, 178). The study of a broader range of funerary reliefs and their carving may make it possible to identify the work of sculptors with particular areas of specialization working at different workshops (for an example see Steding 2022, 115– 118).

Another approach is to reconstruct how many portraits were produced over a particular period. Palmyra offers a unique closed context in which tight chronology allows us to actually elaborate on the increase or decrease of production (Raja et al. 2021). This permits us to think about the number both of workshops and of the carvers who were involved in the supply of funerary portraiture to the city (Steding 2022, 124–125). Thanks to Harald Ingholt's chronology of the loculus reliefs based on dated reliefs and stylistic analyses (Ingholt 1928) and the *in situ* contexts, the portraits can be dated with relative certainty, showing an increase in production over time.

The question remains how the production of the portraits was organized: Did customers buy portraits off the shelf, or did they order customized portraits? A comparative study of eight hundred loculus reliefs has shown how diverse they are, leading to the conclusion that the customers' influence on the final depiction was significant (Steding 2022, chapter 5). The loculus reliefs were thus, most likely, commissioned, and the workshops had to adjust to customers' requests and changing styles and the works were not pre-produced.

Even if we do not know exactly how much of the evidence is missing, certain questions relating to the scale of the production also need to be asked. How great was the total production, and how many workshops were sustained by the demand for portraiture? As we seek answers to these questions, it is necessary to calculate the carving times. We also need to remember that some workshops may have been involved in the construction of urban buildings in addition to portrait production. A comparison of tools and tool marks on architectural carvings and portraiture will help us to determine whether these pieces were produced in the same way—and therefore possibly by the same individuals. The opposite assumption would be that the two areas of business were divided, with carvers specializing in either one area or the other.

The last question to be addressed is where the carving took place. Once again, in the absence of archaeological evidence indicating the exact location of a workshop, the carved objects themselves must serve as our source of information. The *in situ* context of a banqueting scene discussed below is the first attempt to determine whether graves were used as a workspace.

Partly Carved Objects from an *in situ* Context

As the excavated workshop from Aphrodisias demonstrates, we can assume that in some cities portraits were carved in a specific location at which a variety of carving tasks were performed. Still, the connection between the tombs, their architects, and their owners must have been close, and it is not likely that these objects were produced with no knowledge of where they were going to be placed in the grave and what they would depict when finished. A study of the remaining *in situ* contexts (e.g., Higuchi 1994) shows that there must have been collaboration between tomb architects and carvers of funerary portraiture, as well as between carvers and customers. A loculus relief or banquet relief had to fit into the aperture of a loculus opening (Steding 2022, chapter 2), as did the larger sarcophagi constellations. With regard to the less movable banqueting scenes and sarcophagus lids in particular, an interesting phenomenon can be studied. Partly carved individuals and faces in the Roman period have been discussed in the past, and the most common are blank portraits on sarcophagi (see, e.g., Birk 2009; 2013; Russell 2013; Turnbow 2011). In Palmyra, the partly carved faces appear only on banqueting scenes that were used either as sarcophagus lids or as reliefs placed on the wall (Steding 2021). Colledge refers to partly carved objects as a source of information about tools used early in the carving process (Colledge 1976, 116), but a more in-depth study of these objects can provide greater insight into the way carving was organized.

As an example, let us look at a banqueting scene, found inside the hypogeum of Yarhai (Ingholt 1938, 99–100, plate XXXVI,I; Ingholt Archives, PS 997. Also discussed in Steding 2021, 19–20). The banqueting relief shows two reclining males and a seated female on the foot of the *kline*. In between them, two standing figures are laid out. Upon closer examination, all figures except the central male are only roughly outlined: the bodies as well as the faces stay undefined. Again, while parts of the relief were finished right up to the last detail, other parts were neglected, maybe to be completed later.

The fact that these banqueting reliefs were found inside a hypogeum suggests that they were put to use already and that the carver may have planned to come back to the grave to add the missing family members. This, of course, does not mean that there was no working space outside the tombs or that there were no workshops around the tombs or in the city; but it does indicate that carvers sometimes needed to be flexible and finish their work inside a tomb in response to the customer's wishes—for instance, that the portraits of additional family members should be added after their death (Figure 32.2).

FIGURE 32.2 Partly carved banqueting scene from the hypogeum of Yarhai.
Ingholt Archive, PS977, Courtesy of the Ny Carlsberg Glyptotek, Copenhagen, © Palmyra Portrait Project.

Conclusion

A broad range of questions arise when we consider the production economy of Palmyrene portraiture, covering all steps from the quarrying of stone through to the placement in a grave. The issues involved include the choice of material as well as that of the form of representation and stylistic preferences. Consequently, one of the main points of focus in the study of the production economy of portraits is the interplay between carver, customer, and traditional influences on the depiction of the deceased in particular periods and regions.

An essential first step is the detailed study of the stone surface to reveal the process of carving and the tools that were used. Setting this information within a chronological framework enables us to detect changes over time in the use of tools, and this in turn can supply evidence of changes in the process of carving that can be attributed to changes in the economy. When demand increases, there are two possibilities: open more workshops or speed up the process. Such a change in the economy could be seen either in increased numbers of individual sculptors or in changes to the carving process. Tool traces reveal even more about the emergence of new tools and how these might have resulted in new techniques for the carving of particular shapes.

The detection of tool traces can also help to identify different artists or—at least—distinct traditions of carving that can be connected to specific workshops. Naturally, such traces are hard to distinguish, and a standardized carving process will lead to similar outcomes, but while stone carving may be localized and highly standardized (Rockwell 1993, 1–7), it is also true that it is at the same time unique to each carver (Wootton et al. 2013b).

Our understanding of the sculpture workshops of antiquity cannot be fully established until further archaeological evidence of a workspace is unearthed. However, the portraits themselves can at least provide some evidence when studied carefully. The addition of costly colour suggests the work of a painting specialist in collaboration with the carver. Furthermore, partly carved objects that have been found *in situ* lead towards the assumption that parts of the carving could also have been undertaken inside the tombs, even though workshops must have existed, as the example of Aphrodisias shows. This may have been for practical as well as financial reasons—both of which are part of the discussion concerning the production of portraits.

As this chapter has shown, many unanswered questions remain over portrait production in Palmyra. But it is also clear that the resource of Palmyrene portraiture gives us the opportunity to change this picture and that the rich evidence of funerary portraiture and its context has much to contribute to the study of the production economy. Detailed studies will allow us to reconstruct the tools and carving process used, and the large corpus provides enough evidence to create a good picture of the way limestone was carved in Palmyra and how the production of the funerary sculpture was organized.

ACKNOWLEDGEMENTS

The author acknowledges the funding received by the Danish National Research Foundation for Centre for Urban Network Evolutions (grant no. 119) as well as the funding received from the Carlsberg Foundation for the various Palmyra projects based at Aarhus University, first and foremost the Palmyra Portrait Project (CF15-0493). Furthermore, the author thanks the ALIPH Foundation as well as the Augustinus Foundation for funding for further Palmyra-related projects.

BIBLIOGRAPHY

Abdul Massih, Jeanine. 2021. 'Quarrying in the Roman Near East: Palmyra and Baalbek – A Comparative Study'. In *Production Economy in Greater Roman Syria: Trade Networks and Production Processes*, edited by Rubina Raja and Julia Steding, 71–86. Turnhout: Brepols.

Adam, Sheila. 1966. *The Technique of Greek Sculpture in the Archaic and Classical Periods.* London: Thames & Hudson.

Bessac, Jean-Claude. 2021. 'Le calcaires de Palmyre face aux autres roches de décoration architecturale et de sculpture'. In *Production Economy in Greater Roman Syria: Trade Networks and Production Processes*, edited by Rubina Raja and Julia Steding, 49–70. Turnhout: Brepols.

Blume-Jung, Clarissa. 2021. 'The Polychrome of Palmyrene Portraits: Workmen and Colouration'. In *Production Economy in Greater Roman Syria: Trade Networks and Production Processes*, edited by Rubina Raja and Julia Steding, 33–48. Turnhout: Brepols.

Bessac, Jean-Claude. 1986. *L'outillage traditionnel du tailleur de pierre: De l'antiquité à nos jours.* Montpellier: CNRS.

Bessac, Jean-Claude. 1988. 'Problems of Identification and Interpretation of Tool Marks on Ancient Marbles and Decorative Stones'. In *Classical Marble: Geochemistry, Technology, Trade*, edited by Norman Herz and Marc Waelkens, 41–53. Dordrecht: Springer.

Bessac, Jean-Claude. 1992. 'Pierres et techniques utilisées pour les sculptures et inscriptions tardo-hellénistiques de "Villa Roma" à Nîmes''. *Documents d'archéologie méridionale* 15: 103–111.

Bessac, Jean-Claude. 2007. *Le travail de la pierre à Pétra: Technique et économie de la taille rupestre.* Paris: Éditions Recherche sur les civilisations.

Blagg, Thomas F. C. 1976. 'Tools and Techniques of the Roman Stonemason in Britain'. *Britannia* 7: 152–172.

Blömer, Michael, and Rubina Raja, eds. 2019a. *Funerary Portraiture in Greater Roman Syria.* Turnhout: Brepols.

Blömer, Michael, and Rubina Raja. 2019b. 'Shifting the Paradigms: Towards a New Agenda in the Study of the Funerary Portraiture of Greater Roman Syria'. In *Funerary Portraiture in Greater Roman Syria*, edited by Michael Blömer and Rubina Raja, 5–26. Turnhout: Brepols.

Blümel, Carl. 1927. *Griechische Bildhauer an der Arbeit.* Berlin: de Gruyter.

Blümel, Carl. 1969. *Greek Sculptors at Work.* London: Phaidon.

Birk, Stine. 2009. 'Reading Roman Sarcophagi: Aspects of Identity, Commemoration and Production'. Unpublished doctoral thesis, Aarhus University.

Birk, Stine. 2013. *Depicting the Dead: Self-Representation and Commemoration of Roman Sarcophagi with Portraits*. Aarhus: Universitetsforlag.

Claridge, Amanda. 2015. 'Marble Carving Techniques, Workshops, and Artisans'. In *The Oxford Handbook of Roman Sculpture*, edited by Elise E. Friedland, Melanie Grunow Sobocinski, and Elaine K. Gazda, 107–122. Oxford: Oxford University Press.

Colledge, Malcolm A. R. 1976. *The Art of Palmyra*. London: Thames & Hudson.

Dillon, Sheila. 2017. 'Approaches to the Study of Greek Sculpture'. In *The Diversity of Classical Archaeology*, edited by Achim Lichtenberger and Rubina Raja, 223–234. Turnhout: Belgium.

Fejfer, Jane. 2008. *Roman Portraits in Context*. Berlin: de Gruyter.

Hedegaard, Signe B., and Cecilie Brøns. 2019. 'New Research from Ny Carlsberg Glyptotek: Pigments in Ancient Palmyra'. In *The Road to Palmyra*, edited by Anne Marie Nielsen and Rubina Raja, 251–274. Copenhagen: Ny Carlsberg Glyptotek.

Henning, Agnes. 2013. *Die Turmgräber von Palmyra: Eine lokale Bauform im kaiserzeitlichen Syrien als Ausdruck kultureller Identität*. Orient-Archäologie 29. Rahden: Leidorf.

Herz, Norman, and Marc Waelkens. 1988. *Classical Marble: Geochemistry, Technology, Trade*. Dordrecht: Kluwer.

Higuchi, Takayasu. 1994. *Tombs A and C in the Southeast Necropolis in Palmyra Syria: Surveyed in 1990–92*. Nara: Research Centre for Silk Roadology.

Huskinson, Janet. 2006. *Roman Children's Sarcophagi: Their Decoration and Its Social Significance*. Oxford: Clarendon Press.

Ingholt, Harald. 1928. *Studier over palmyrenske skulptur*. Copenhagen: Reitzel.

Ingholt, Harald. 1938. 'Inscriptions and Sculptures from Palmyra'. *Berytus* 5: 93–140.

Kleiner, Diana E. E. 1992. *Roman Sculpture*. New Haven, CT: Yale University Press.

Lahusen, Götz. 2010. *Römische Bildnisse: Auftraggeber – Funktionen – Standorte*. Mainz: von Zabern.

Lapatin, Kenneth. 2015. 'The Materials and Techniques of Greek and Roman Art'. In *The Oxford Handbook of Greek and Roman Art and Architecture*, edited by Clemente Marconi, 203–240. Oxford: Oxford University Press.

Lichtenberger, Achim, and Rubina Raja, eds. 2017a. *The Diversity of Classical Archaeology*. Turnhout: Belgium.

Lichtenberger, Achim, and Rubina Raja. 2017b. 'Introduction: The Diversity of Classical Archaeology'. In *The Diversity of Classical Archaeology*, edited by Achim Lichtenberger and Rubina Raja, 1–7. Turnhout: Brepols.

Millett, Martin. 2008. 'What Is Classical Archaeology? (b) Roman Archaeology'. In *Classical Archaeology*, edited by Susan E. Alcock and Robin Osborne, 30–50. Oxford: Blackwell.

Palagia, Olga. 2006. 'Marble Carving Techniques'. In *Greek Sculpture: Function, Materials, and Techniques in the Archaic and Classical Periods*, edited by Olga Palagia, 243–279. Cambridge: Cambridge University Press.

Raja, Rubina. 2017. *Palmyra: Pearl of the Desert*. Aarhus: SUN-Tryk, Aarhus Universitet.

Raja, Rubina. 2019. *The Palmyra Collection: Ny Carlsberg Glyptotek*. Copenhagen: Ny Carlsberg Glyptotek.

Raja, Rubina, and Julia Steding, eds. 2021. *Production Economy in Greater Roman Syria: Trade Networks and Production Processes*. Turnhout: Brepols.

Raja, Rubina et al. 2021. 'Three Hundred Years of Palmyrene History. Unlocking Archaeological Data for Studying Past Societal Transformations'. *PLoS ONE* 16(11).

Rockwell, Peter. 1991. 'Aphrodisias: Unfinished Sculpture Associated with the Sculptor's Studio'. In *Aphrodisias Papers*. Vol. 2, *The Theatre: A Sculptor's Workshop, Philosophers, and*

Coin-Types, edited by Roland R. R. Smith and Kenan T. Erim, 127–143. Ann Arbor, MI: University of Michigan.

Rockwell, Peter. 1993. *The Art of Stoneworking: A Reference Guide*. Cambridge: Cambridge University Press.

Russell, Ben. 2013. *The Economics of the Roman Stone Trade*. Oxford: Oxford University Press.

Russell, Ben, and Will Wootton. 2021. 'Carving the Palmyrene Portrait Reliefs: Observations on the Collection in the Ny Carlsberg Glyptotek'. In *Production Economy in Greater Roman Syria: Trade Networks and Production Processes*, edited by Rubina Raja and Julia Steding, 9–16. Turnhout: Brepols.

Schmidt-Colinet, Andreas. 1990. 'Considérations sur les carrières de Palmyre'. In *Pierre éternelle du Nil au Rhin: Carrières et prefabrication*, edited by Marc Waelkens, 88–92. Brussels: Crédit Communal.

Schmidt-Colinet, Andreas. 2017. 'Die antiken Steinbrüche von Palmyra: Ein Vorbericht'. *Mitteilungen der Deutschen Orient-Gesellschaft zu Berlin* 149: 159–196.

Schnädelbach, Klaus. 2010. *Topographia Palmyrena*, Vol. 1, *Topography*. Bonn: Habelt.

Skupinska-Løvset, Ilona. 1983. *Funerary Portraiture of Roman Palestine: An Analysis of the Production in its Culture-historical Context*. Gothenberg: Paul Åströms förlag.

Skupinksa-Løvset, Ilona. 1999. *Portraiture in Roman Syria: A Study in Social and Regional Differentiation within the Art of Portraiture*. Łódz: Wydawnictwo Uniwersytetu Łódzkiego.

Smith, Roland R. R. 2008. 'Sculptors' Workshops: Inscriptions, Images, and Archaeology'. In *Roman Portraits from Aphrodisias: Exhibition and Catalogue*, edited by Roland R. R. Smith and Julie L. Lenaghan, 103–119. Istanbul: Yapı Kredı Bank Publications for Yapı Kredı Vedat Nedim Tör Museum.

Snodgrass, Anthony. 2008. 'What Is Classical Archaeology? (a) Greek Archaeology'. In *Classical Archaeology*, edited by Susan E. Alcock and Robin Osborne, 13–29. Oxford: Blackwell.

Steding, Julia. 2018. 'Producing Funerary Portraits: An Urban Tradition in the Syrian Desert'. In *Urban Network Evolutions: Towards a High-Definition Archaeology*, edited by Rubina Raja and Søren M. Sindbæk, 87–92. Aarhus: UrbNet/Aarhus Universitet.

Steding, Julia. 2021. 'Partly-Finished Objects from the Palmyrene Funerary Context'. In *Production Economy in Greater Roman Syria Trade Networks and Production Processes*, edited by Rubina Raja and Julia Steding, 17–32. Turnhout: Brepols.

Steding, Julia. 2022. *Carvers and Customers: The Production Economy of Limestone Loculus Reliefs from Roman Palmyra*. Turnhout: Brepols.

Steding, Julia. 2023. 'Recarving of Palmyrene Funerary Portraits'. In *Exchange and Reuse: Economy and Circularity at Roman Palmyra*, edited by Nate Andrade and Rubina Raja, 59–74. Turnhout: Brepols.

Turnbow, Heather N. 2011. *Sarcophagi and Funerary Display in Roman Aphrodisias*. New York: ProQuest.

True, Marion, and Jerry Podany, eds. 1990. *Marble: Art Historical and Scientific Perspectives on Ancient Sculpture*. Malibu, CA: J. Paul Getty Museum.

van Voorhis, Julie. 1998. 'Apprentices' Pieces and the Training of Sculptors at Aphrodisias'. *Journal of Roman Archaeology* 11: 175–192.

van Voorhis, Julie. 2012. 'The Working and Reworking of Marble Sculpture at the Sculptor's Workshop at Aphrodisias'. In *Ateliers and Artisans in Roman Art and Archaeology*, edited by Birte Poulsen and Troels Myrup Kristensen, 38–45. Journal of Roman Archaeology, Supplementary Series 92. Portsmouth, RI: Journal of Roman Archaeology.

Wielgosz-Rondolino, Dagmara. 2016. 'Palmyrene Portraits from the Temple of Allat: New Evidence on Artists and Workshops'. In *The World of Palmyra*, edited by Andreas Kropp and Rubina Raja, 166–179. Copenhagen: Det Kongelige Danske Videnskabernes Selskab.

Wootton, Will, Ben Russell, and Peter Rockwell. 2013a. 'Stoneworking Tools and Toolmarks (Version 1.0)'. In *The Art of Making in Antiquity: Stoneworking in the Roman World*. http://www.artofmaking.ac.uk/content/essays/2-stoneworking-tools-and-toolmarks-w-wootton-b-russell-p-rockwell/.

Wootton, Will, Ben Russell, and Peter Rockwell. 2013b. 'Stoneworking Techniques and Processes (Version 1.0)'. In *The Art of Making in Antiquity: Stoneworking in the Roman World*. http://www.artofmaking.ac.uk/media/uploads/uploads/stoneworking_techniques_and_processes-wootton_russell_rockwell-v1.0.pdf.

Zimmer, Gerhard. 1982. *Römische Berufsdarstellungen*. Berlin: Mann.

Other Sources

The Art of Making. http://www.artofmaking.ac.uk.

CHAPTER 33

THE BANQUETING TESSERAE FROM PALMYRA

Tokens for Religious Events

RUBINA RAJA

THE PALMYRENE BANQUETING TESSERAE

THE small tokens from Palmyra, also usually called 'banqueting tesserae' in the literature, constitute a fascinating group of material from the famous oasis city in the Syrian Desert. They make up our richest source to the city's religious life, and their varied iconographies give insight into the cults, deities, and priesthoods or groups of priests who organized religious events, including the banquets, which took place in the various sanctuaries at various points in time. The tesserae received their modern name due to their shape, taken from the Latin word *tessera*: many of them are small rectangular or square objects, resembling the facets of a dice. This terminology was first introduced for such objects by F. Ficoroni in 1740 (Ficoroni 1740; with reference from Rostovtzeff 1897, 463; and Crisà et al. 2019, 1–3). However, we do not know what they were in fact called in antiquity. No written sources tell us about them. Judging from their iconography, they all stem from the Roman period; however, their chronology remains fairly broad and is based on a few that are dated by year and span between AD 89 and AD 188 (Colledge 1976, 54). However, through a thorough study of the inscriptions combined with a new study of the prosopography, which is ongoing, surely more information will soon be available to us on this topic (Kubiak-Schneider et al., forthcoming).

Already in the late nineteenth century, publications on the tesserae began to appear (Simonsen 1889a; 1889b; Spoer 1905; de Vogüé 1868), and these continued during the Mandate period, when Palmyra was under French control, and culminated in the two major publications by Ingholt, Seyrig, and Starcky in 1955 and the two-volume work by Comte du Mésnil du Buisson, who in 1944 published his volume of plates and in 1962 brought out an accompanying text volume (du Mesnil du Buisson 1944; Ingholt et al.

1955; du Mesnil du Buisson 1962). The early publications on the tesserae were mostly concerned with the small inscriptions that are found on many of them. Almost all of these, with only very few exceptions, were imprinted in the local Palmyrene Aramaic dialect. It was only with the publications in 1955 and 1944/1962 that focus shifted to also include the rich iconography of these fascinating small objects. While many of the interpretations in Mesnil du Buisson are not to be trusted, they provide plenty of fun to read and the plate volume is of a wonderful quality for its time, reproducing both tesserae and Palmyrene coins in large scale, which allows for appreciation of the detailed iconography. However, Ingholt, Seyrig, and Starcky's publication provides the first attempt at a systematic overview of the known types of the tesserae, of which there then were more than 1,100 types. In the foreword to this publication Henri Seyrig makes a statement worth reiterating here since it gives background to the problem we have with placing these tesserae in their original contexts. He states that it was only during the clearance of the sanctuary of Bēl from 1929 onwards, under the direction of M. Robert Amy, that it became possible to obtain a large amount of the tesserae from the locals (Ingholt et al. 1955, unpaginated preface by Henri Seyrig). This sums up the situation very well: for the vast majority of the tesserae we have no original archaeological context, but if we read his statement correctly, then these tesserae might in fact have been found during the clearing of the sanctuary area by local workers who would have been employed by the French to dismantle their own houses while being displaced to new housing in the village built by the French military for the local community (see for this period Baird et al., 2023). Only one series of tesserae have been found *in situ* (see below). Colledge in his monograph on the art of Palmyra made several very useful observations and gave short summaries of these, although often without references to the examples he mentions (Colledge 1976, in particular 54–56). In recent years, there has been a renewal of focused studies on the tesserae, and various aspects of their production, iconography, and usage have been treated in recent publications (see, e.g., the contributions in Raja 2022c; 2015a; 2015b; 2016, Kaizer and Raja 2019; Raja 2019a; 2022b). Today numerous further types have been established, and these are currently under publication as a collected update to the publication from 1955 (Kubiak-Schneider et al., forthcoming; Raja 2022b).

It has often been asked how we can be sure that these tokens were used as entrance tickets to events since not all of them carry iconography which can be connected directly to banqueting. There are in fact two ways in which we can view the use of the tesserae. Both connect to religious rituals and sacrifices made in the city. Some of the tesserae carry inscriptions explicitly telling us about banquets and bear the phrase 'come'—a few even give dates for these events (Ingholt et al. 1955, no. 737). A few tesserae hold measures of food or drink to be distributed (Ingholt et al. 1955, nos. 160, 707, 709), many display images of vessels for food and drink (Ingholt et al. 1955, nos. 97, 307, 552). Many of them show reclining Palmyrene priests at banquets, distinguishable by their hats, those round hats with a flat top so particular to the Palmyrene religious sphere (see Chapter 30 [Raja], this volume, on priests). And some tesserae even carry scenes where food and drink are being served (Ingholt et al. 1955, nos. 10, 12). These iconographic elements, together with the explicitly religious iconography showing deities and religious symbols, point firmly to the conclusion that these tokens were either used as entrance tickets to religious banquets, paid for by individual priests or by priestly groups, or that they were used as tokens to prove that one was entitled to receive parts of foodstuff or drink in connection with religious sacrifices. Most likely the tokens were used for both sorts of events, which in any case were related to ritual sacrifices involving ritual dining (Ingholt et al. 1955, IV, followed by Colledge 1976, 54 without reference to Ingholt et al. 1955; Gnoli 2016; Raja 2020; Kaizer 2008; 2002, 220–233).

Within the framework of religion in the ancient world the Palmyrene tesserae constitute a unique group of material. While tokens as such in the wide understanding of small objects for some sort of exchange, sometimes also within religious settings, are known from other contexts across the Mediterranean, they are by no means that plentiful at any other site, and no other evidence comes even close to the phenomenon in Palmyra (e.g. Crisà et al. 2019). And when compared with the evidence from other sites, the Palmyrene tesserae in fact cannot be usefully put into this framework of tokens as such. On the one hand, they differ in the materials that they are made of and they clearly do not seem to have been for exchange outside Palmyra, only for exchange within small communities and groups in Palmyra. The Palmyrene tesserae, a term then used for lack of a better word, must be viewed as a strictly local phenomenon as tickets made for particular events for a specific group of individuals.

Religious Ritual Dining in Palmyra

Dining under the gaze of the gods was common in antiquity. The tesserae even quite literally reflect this situation on the types which carry reclining priests at banquets, above which busts of deities are shown. Banqueting halls, small or large, and triclinia were inherent features of many sanctuaries in the ancient world, and ritual dining—in its widest sense dining under the auspices of the god/gods—was an integrated part of religious life (Nielsen 2014; Martens 2015; as well as Nielsen 2015 with further literature, also see Chapter 23 [Le Blanc], this volume on religious architecture). At the sacrifices which would often go with these banquets, animals and other foodstuff could be sacrificed to the gods and the human beings would be offered the parts that were left, which fortunately were the good parts of the meat, for example. So it is no surprise that we also find banqueting halls in the sanctuaries of Palmyra (for a summary see Raja 2015a; Kaizer 2002, 229–234).

Four banqueting halls are found in Palmyra: one in the courtyard of the sanctuary of Bēl and one in the sanctuary of Baalshamin and two banqueting halls outside temple complexes. The banqueting hall in the sanctuary of Baalshamin, immediately north of the cella of temple of Baalshamin, is known through an inscription (Kaizer 2002, 229–234). However, the largest banqueting hall in Palmyra was located in the courtyard in the sanctuary of Bēl (Seyrig et al. 1975). It is also in this banqueting hall that the vast majority of the tesserae were found in the underground drainage system (Seyrig et al. 1975). The complex measured 33.5 × 10.75 m, totalling 360.1 m^2 (Nielsen 2015, 51), excluding the kitchen annexe to the north. It would have been able to hold more than a hundred dining individuals at one time. Of the two further banqueting rooms, not much is known. Several other banqueting halls are known through inscriptions from the site (Kaizer 2002, 220–229). Banquets could of course also have been held under the open sky; nothing speaks against this, and, in these cases, even more people could have been accommodated for such events. The sanctuary enclosures in Palmyra varied in size, but that of the sanctuary of Bēl, which was by far the largest measured more than 200 × 200 m (Raja 2022a, 42–44). The sides of the temenos walls were lined with columns, which would have provided shade for the spectators on days when religious rituals and sacrifices took place. We have to imagine that the tesserae gave access to certain groups for certain of these events hosted by religious groups or by individual members of such groups, as the inscriptions and representations of priests on the tesserae indicate.

The Production and Usage of the Tesserae

The tesserae, which measured between a few centimetres up to about 5 centimetres in diameter, were usually made of terracotta, but examples made of metal (bronze, iron, lead) as well as glass have also been found (Ingholt et al. 1955, V). Not many of those are known though. Ingholt et al. list one of bronze, one of iron, nine of lead, and three made of glass. By far the most common material was the local terracotta. The tesserae were certainly all produced locally, as their iconography and inscriptions also testify, and they bear witness to a high level of craftsmanship available for this task in Palmyra, which was related to the area of glyptic, carving gems, and making fine small moulds. In this way, despite all the research done on them, the tesserae still remain an understudied source when it comes to understanding labour specialization in Roman Palmyra (Raja 2022b). Many of them were square or rectangular in shape, but more than ninety other distinguishable shapes exist, making the tesserae very diverse even in their basic shape (Raja 2022b, table 2.1, 14–17).

The clay tesserae were produced in moulds, in series. The clay would have been pressed into the moulds, which must have consisted of two parts, one for each side, and the images came out in high relief. The wet clay was placed between the moulds and the exact thickness of the tesserae depended on how hard the moulds were pressed together. Usually, tesserae from the same series have more or less the same thickness, indicating that the pressing of the moulds was done with consistency. Each tessera was pressed into the series' mould, then taken out to dry, whereafter they would have been fired before they were ready to be used. This entire process—the choice of the iconography and potentially the inscription to go on the tesserae, the making of the mould, the making of each single tessera—together emphasize that making an entire series of tesserae was something which required the involvement of various people, from the customer (usually the male person or group of male persons hosting a religious banquet), to the mould maker, to the potentially different individual in charge of making every single tessera, pointing to the fact that this process was one of some importance. Considering that only about 1,300 types, including those currently under publication, are known, and speculating that these might even have been produced over the course of more than a hundred years, we are in fact not left with many series having been produced per year. Even if they fall within a shorter time span, such as a hundred or even fifty or twenty years, then these banquets would not have been events that occurred often. This underlines that either the tesserae as tokens to gain entrance to religious banquets were a short-lived fashion phenomenon, potentially replaced by some other entrance system, or that these kinds of banquets were not continued for the entire duration of Palmyra's religious life, or that they only took place quite infrequently, or that several different entrance check possibilities were in place at the same time, some of which are simply not known to us anymore.

At least 410 of the types recorded in Ingholt, Seyrig, and Starcky carry signet seal impressions (Raja 2022b, table 2.2, 18–26; forthcoming). We must assume that these signet seals belonged to individuals and would have been their personal marking on the token. That each and every tessera in a series would have received such a signet seal imprint is of course significant and forces us to think about production processes. Would the person who had commissioned the series be imprinting each and every one himself? Or would he perhaps have entrusted this to a servant or secretary? Or even to the producer of the tesserae? In any case, the signet seal imprint would have closely connected the series to a particular person, either as a single person or as spokesperson for a group.

As for potential original colouring, the tesserae do not give us much information. One example might carry a bit of red colour, but overall they do not seem to have been painted.

We do not know in exactly what numbers each series was produced, but since several examples are attested for numerous types, we can therefore with certainty conclude that they were made in series. Only one *in situ* find of a most likely complete set of tesserae was discovered, buried in the sanctuary of Arsu in Palmyra (al-As'ad et al. 2005, with further references) and containing 125 tesserae belonging to the same series. These were excavated in 1980, and found in a complete pot under a floor level within the temenos of the Arsu sanctuary (al-As'ad et al. 2005). It is impossible to tell whether these tesserae had already been in use and distributed as entrance tickets to a banquet and then collected when the invitees came to the event or whether they had not yet been distributed. The authors of the *in situ* find conclude that the tesserae most likely would have been used as entrance tickets already and had been collected upon entrance to the banquet and thereafter deposited under floor level (al-As'ad et al. 2005, 6). This seems plausible, of course, but one might ask why more such finds have not been made if it was the standard for collected tesserae series to be deposited within the sanctuaries where they had been used as tickets to gain entrance. One of the answers of course lies in the fact that the clearance of the sanctuary of Bēl, which began in 1929, might have destroyed any *in situ* contents (see above). But further tesserae are found strewn across the site, as publications from later years have shown, as well as across the sanctuaries and also in the drainage system connected to the banqueting hall in the sanctuary of Bēl, the city's main sanctuary (Ingholt et al. 1955, 3–5). So, in conclusion, we do not know whether the tesserae were always collected upon entry or upon people receiving their share of food or drink, and it seems plausible that there were different modes in place for collecting them (or not) upon entry to the event at which they served as tickets.

THE ICONOGRAPHY

While the tesserae were quite small objects, they could be extremely elaborate when it came to the images imprinted on them (Ingholt et al. 1955; Colledge 1976, 54–56). It is, as shown above, certain that they were produced in series and that no two series were alike. Each series, despite the fact that many carry, for example, priestly busts or reclining priests, was unique and held details which would set them apart from other series. The iconography could range from very basic patterns, such as a simple signet seal imprint on one side and nothing on the other (although rarely were they so basic) to tesserae with elaborate banqueting scenes on one side and scenes with a multitude of religious symbols and inscriptions on both sides. Overall, the iconography was extremely varied and creative but always connected to the religious sphere of Palmyra. Depictions of Palmyrene priests were very common (Figure 33.1).

These could be shown either in bust shape or in full figure standing, with both motifs shown frontally. Priests could also be reclining on a banqueting couch (kline) either alone or together with another priest. The priests can be identified by their distinctive Palmyrene priestly hats (Chapter 30 [Raja], this volume, on priests). Often they are shown together with inscriptions in Palmyrene Aramaic (Figure 33.2) giving their names or the name of the religious group to which they belonged.

In the scenes where they are found reclining, they are often surrounded by floral garlands or other decorative motifs or together with busts of deities or imprints of signet seals over their heads. The priests were the commissioners of the tesserae series and would have been the ones who paid for the religious banquets. We do not know much about how exactly these events were organized (see above), but they seem to have been events that also offered the opportunity for social/religious mixing and in which men from across various religious affiliations potentially came together to celebrate a variety of deities at various points in time (Raja 2016; 2019a; 2020). We of course cannot be sure that women did not take part in some of these banquets, but we do not have any hard evidence for this.

Other very common motifs were deities (Figure 33.3). These range from deities whose names we cannot assert from the iconography itself to deities named in inscriptions or recognizable through their attributes. Both local Palmyrene gods and goddesses appear,

FIGURE 33.1 Banqueting tessera with a reclining priest. Copenhagen, Ny Carlsberg Glyptotek, I.N. 2771.

© Courtesy of Ny Carlsberg Glyptotek, photograph by Anders Sune Berg.

as do Graeco-Roman and eastern deities. It is really on these tiny objects that we get a glimpse of the variety of patterns of worship in place in Palmyra. This, combined with the fact that many tesserae depicting gods other than the city's main gods were found in the drainage system under the banqueting hall in the sanctuary of Bēl, points to the conclusion that such sanctuaries might have been in use for celebrations of rituals dedicated to gods other than the god to which the sanctuary was dedicated, which in turn informs us about the multifunctionality of such sacred spaces. Apart from these iconographic motifs, numerous other symbols and scenes are found on the tesserae (Figure 33.4), ranging from astral symbols, to signs underlining the sacrality and importance of the highest god of the city (Kaizer and Raja 2019), floral designs, architectural elements, and animals personifying gods or carrying gods or simply shown on their own, such as camels or horses (Raja and Seland 2020).

The signet seals (Figure 33.5) also represent a group of images which can be studied in more detail to great effect in relation to artistic influences present in Roman Palmyra (Raja 2022b). From a first overview study it is clear that most of these motifs can be connected directly to the Graeco-Roman cultural spheres. Numerous deities in

FIGURE 33.2 Banqueting tessera with an inscription. Copenhagen, Ny Carlsberg Glyptotek, I.N. 3190.

© Courtesy of Ny Carlsberg Glyptotek, photograph by Anders Sune Berg.

Graeco-Roman style, such as Tyche, Athena, and Nike, are found on the tesserae (Raja, forthcoming). So are busts shown in profile of male individuals. While these cannot be identified as Roman emperors or mythical figures, they must have carried some specific meaning to the owner of the signet seal. Most of these are also shown in Graeco-Roman style. However, a range of signet seals also show motifs in local style, and some show Parthian-inspired or Parthian-imported motifs. These signet seals would most likely have belonged to the commissioner of the specific tesserae series. It is interesting to note that in the funerary sculpture (see Chapter 27 [Raja], this volume, on the funerary sculpture) the men depicted in all types of funerary sculpture often carry signet seal rings on one of their fingers. Obviously, these rings were an integrated part of the way in which the Palmyrene men shaped their public and therefore also religious identities.

It is difficult, if not impossible and quite frankly also unnecessary to try to come up with a systematic typology of the iconography of the tesserae. A typological development or strict pattern simply does not exist. Certain elements were common, such as priestly representations, images of deities, inscriptions, religious symbolism, and all were connected to the religious sphere, whereas the signet seals for obvious reasons

FIGURE 33.3 Banqueting tessera with a bust of the sun god Shamash/Malakbêl. Copenhagen, Ny Carlsberg Glyptotek, I.N. 3248.

© Courtesy of Ny Carlsberg Glyptotek, photograph by Anders Sune Berg.

would not necessarily be connected to the religious realm but rather reflect on the personal identity of the owner of the ring. Overall the design of the various series must be understood as reflections of personal or group choices made by the commissioners of these tokens. It is first and foremost their specific wishes that are expressed on the tesserae, wishes which did, however, take place within a certain religious framework, where combinations could be drawn from a wide repertoire and where it seems that the most important things to underline were the donorship, the religious euergetism displayed through the donation of the banquet, and the specific religious affiliation (the deity or deities, which are not always clear to us), as well as a personal touch that was often underlined through the use of the signet seal. The tesserae are, together with the large corpus of the funerary sculpture, our richest source for understanding Palmyrene art and undoubtedly our largest group of evidence pertaining directly to the religious life of Palmyra. As such, they deserve in-depth study and disentanglement to push the borders of their meaning within the conceptual framework of Palmyrene religion, which was structured so very differently from Roman religion of the first three centuries AD (Kaizer 2002).

FIGURE 33.4 Banqueting tessera with a crescent and a star. Copenhagen, Ny Carlsberg Glyptotek, I.N. 3263.

© Courtesy of Ny Carlsberg Glyptotek, photograph by Anders Sune Berg.

THE TESSERAE AS WINDOWS TO PALMYRENE RELIGION

While the religious life of Palmyra has been studied mainly through the archaeological remains of sanctuaries, through the epigraphic evidence from the site, and from the representations of the many hundred Palmyrene priests, the tesserae have only recently entered this realm in a more profound way (Kaizer 2002; Raja 2019a; 2021; 2022d). However, it has always been recognized that they were related to the religious sphere. Despite the fact that they cannot be systematically framed in the same way as the funerary representations of priests can, these tesserae give us vivid insights into the lived religion of Palmyra, a religion which was in place on a daily basis and which was shaped by the male elite of the city in terms of its financing. The tesserae remain our best source into understanding the ways in which these individuals, and sometimes the groups that they belonged to, would frame themselves and their choices on these tesserae as they invited others to religious events, which would have included financing a banquet as

FIGURE 33.5 Banqueting tessera with a seal impression depicting a bust of Athena. Copenhagen, Ny Carlsberg Glyptotek, I.N. 3215.

© Courtesy of Ny Carlsberg Glyptotek, photograph by Anders Sune Berg.

well. In this perspective, the tesserae have plenty more to offer us if we want to study Palmyrene religious life and its many facets from an iconographic and lived religion perspective.

Acknowledgements

The author acknowledges the funding received by the Danish National Research Foundation for Centre for Urban Network Evolutions (grant no. 119) as well as the funding received from the Carlsberg Foundation for the various Palmyra projects based at Aarhus University, first and foremost the Palmyra Portrait Project. Furthermore, I thank the ALIPH Foundation as well as the Augustinus Foundation for funding for further Palmyra-related projects.

Bibliography

al-As‘ad, Khaled, Françoise Briquel-Chatonnet, and Jean-Baptiste Yon. 2005. 'The Sacred Banquets at Palmyra and the Functions of the Tesserae: Reflections on the Tokens Found in the Arṣu Temple'. In *A Journey to Palmyra: Collected Essays to Remember Delbert R. Hillers*, edited by Eleonora Cussini, 1–10. Leiden: Brill.

Baird, J., Zena Kamash, and Rubina Raja. 2023. 2023. 'Knowing Palmyra. Mandatory Production of Archaeological Knowledge'. *Journal of Social Archaeology* 23(1): 1–23. doi.org/10.1177/14696053221144013.

Blömer, Michael, Achim Lichtenberger, and Rubina Raja. 2015. *Religious Identities in the Levant from Alexander to Muhammed: Continuity and Change*. Turnhout: Brepols.

Colledge, M. A. R. 1976. *The Art of Palmyra*. London: Thames & Hudson.

Crisà, Antonino, Mairi Gkikaki, and Clare Rowan, eds. 2019. *Tokens: Culture, Connections, Communities*. Royal Numismatic Society. Special Publications 57. London: Royal Numismatic Society.

de Vogüé, Eugène-Melchior. 1868. *Inscriptions sémitiques*. Paris.

du Mesnil du Buisson, Robert. 1944. *Tessères et monnaies de Palmyre*. Paris: Bibliothèque nationale.

du Mesnil du Buisson, Robert. 1962. *Les Tessères et les monnaies de Palmyre*. Paris: Bibliothèque nationale de France.

Ficoroni, Francesco. 1740. *I Piombi antichi*. Rome.

Gnoli, Tommaso. 2016. 'Banqueting in Honour of the Gods: Notes on the Marzeah of Palmyra'. In *The World of Palmyra*, edited by Andreas Kropp and Rubina Raja, 31–41. Copenhagen: Royal Danish Academy of Sciences and Letters.

Ingholt, Harold, Henri Seyrig, and Jean Starcky. 1955. *Recueil des tessères de Palmyre*. Paris: Geuthner.

Kaizer, Ted. 2002. *The Religious Life of Palmyra: A Study of the Social Patterns of Worship in the Roman Period*. Stuttgart: Steiner.

Kaizer, Ted. 2008. 'Man and God at Palmyra: Sacrifice, Lectisternia and Banquets'. In *The Variety of Local Religious Life in the Near East in the Hellenistic and Roman Periods*, edited by Ted Kaizer, 179–191. Leiden: Brill.

Kaizer, Ted, and Rubina Raja. 2019. 'Divine Symbolism on the Tesserae from Palmyra: Considerations about the So-Called "Symbol of Bel" or "Signe de la pluie"'. *Syria* 95: 297–315.

Kubiak-Schneider, Aleksandra, Rubina Raja, Julia Steding, and Jean-Baptiste Yon. Forthcoming. *The Palmyrene Tesserae*. Turnhout: Brepols.

Martens, Marleen. 2015. 'Communal Dining: Making Things Happen'. in *A Companion to the Archaeology of Religion in the Ancient World*, edited by Rubina Raja and Jörg Rüpke, 167–180. London: Wiley Blackwell.

Nielsen, Inge. 2014. *Housing the Chosen: The Architectural Context of Mystery Groups and Religious Associations in the Ancient World*. Brepols: Turnhout.

Nielsen, Inge. 2015. 'The Assembly Rooms of Religious Groups in the Hellenistic and Roman Near East'. In *Religious Identities in the Levant from Alexander to Muhammed: Continuity and Change*, edited by Michael Blömer, Achim Lichtenberger, and Rubina Raja, 47–74. Turnhout: Brepols.

Raja, Rubina. 2015a. 'Cultic Dining and Religious Patterns in Palmyra: The Case of the Palmyrene Banqueting Tesserae'. In *Antike. Architektur. Geschichte: Festschrift für Inge Nielsen zum 65. Geburtstag*, edited by Stephan Faust, Martina Seifert, and Leon Ziemer, 181–200. Gateways: Hamburger Beiträge zur Archäologie und Kulturgeschichte des antiken Mittelmeerraumes 3 Aachen: Shaker.

Raja, Rubina. 2015b. 'Staging "Private" Religion in Roman "Public" Palmyra: The Role of the Religious Dining Tickets (Banqueting Tesserae)'. In *Public and Private in Ancient*

Mediterranean Law and Religion: Historical and Comparative Studies, edited by Jörg Rüpke and Clifford Ando, 165–186. Berlin: de Gruyter.

Raja, Rubina. 2016. 'In and out of Contexts: Explaining Religious Complexity Through the Banqueting Tesserae from Palmyra'. *Religion in the Roman Empire* 2(3): 340–371.

Raja, Rubina. 2019a. 'Religious Banquets in Palmyra and the Palmyrene Banqueting Tesserae'. In *The Road to Palmyra*, edited by Anne Marie Nielsen and Rubina Raja, 221–234. Copenhagen: Ny Carlsberg Glyptotek.

Raja, Rubina, ed. 2019b. *Revisiting the Religious Life of Palmyra*. Contextualizing the Sacred 9. Turnhout: Brepols.

Raja, Rubina. 2020. 'Come and Dine with Us: Invitations to Ritual Dining as Part of Social Strategies in Sacred Spaces in Palmyra'. *Lived Ancient Religion*, edited by Valentino Gasparini, Maik Patzelt, Rubina Raja, Anna-Katharina Rieger, Jörg Rüpke, and Emiliano Urciuoli, 385–404. Berlin: de Gruyter.

Raja, Rubina. 2021. 'Managing the Middle Ground: Priests in Palmyra and Their Iconographies'. In *The Middle East as Middle Ground? Cultural Interaction in the Ancient Middle East Revisited*, edited by Julia Hoffman-Salz, 129–146. Vienna: Holzhausen.

Raja, Rubina. 2022a. *Pearl of the Desert: A History of Palmyra*. Oxford: Oxford University Press.

Raja, Rubina. 2022b. 'Revisiting the Palmyrene Banqueting Tesserae: Conceptualization, Production, Usage, and Meaning of the Palmyrene'. In *The Small Stuff of the Palmyrenes: The Coins and Tesserae from Palmyra*, edited by Rubina Raja, 5–68. Turnhout: Brepols.

Raja, Rubina. ed. 2022c. *The Small Stuff of the Palmyrenes: The Coins and Tesserae from Palmyra*. Studies in Palmyrene Archaeology and History 5. Turnhout: Brepols.

Raja, Rubina. 2022d. 'The Way Your Wear Your Hat. Palmyrene Priests between Local Traditions and Cross-Regional Trends'. *Imperium sine fine? Der romisch-parthische Grenzraum als Konflikt- und Kontaktzone*, edited by Udo Hartmann, Frank Schleicher, and Timo Stickler, 81–118. Stuttgart: Kohlhammer.

Raja, Rubina. Forthcoming. 'Signet Seals with Female Deities on the Palmyrene Tesserae. Iconographic Traditions Between the Mediterranean World and Palmyra'. In *Palmyra and the Mediterranean*, edited by Rubina Raja. Cambridge: Cambridge University Press.

Raja, Rubina, and Eivind Heldaas Seland. 2020. 'Horses and Camels in Palmyrene Art: Iconography, Contexts and Meanings'. *Zeitschrift für Orient-Archäologie* 13: 300–344.

Rostovtzeff, M. 1897. 'Étude sur les plombs antiques'. *Revue numismatique*, 4th ser., 1: 462–493.

Seyrig, Hebri, Robert Amy, and Ernest Will. 1975. *Le temple de Bel á Palmyre: Texte et planches*. Paris: Geuthner.

Simonsen, David. 1889a. *Sculptures et inscriptions de Palmyre à la Glyptothèque de Ny Calsberg*. Copenhagen: Lind.

Simonsen, David. 1889b. *Skulpturer og Indskrifter fra Palmyra i Ny Carlsberg Glyptotek*. Copenhagen: Lind.

Spoer, Hans H. 1905. 'Palmyrene Tesserae'. *Journal of the American Oriental Society* 26: 113–116.

CHAPTER 34

PALMYRENE COINAGE

NATHALIA BREINTOFT KRISTENSEN

PALMYRENE COINAGE: AN INTRODUCTION TO THE TYPES

> The sands of Palmyra are full of little copper coins. After strong winds the people of Palmyra gather them in handfuls. I bought hundreds of them for a few piasters. They are generally adorned with radiated heads, gazelles, fishes, zodiacal signs, and such like emblems. They are probably specimens of the currency with which Zenobia resisted the siege. (Wright 1895, 155–156)

THESE are the famous words of the Irish missionary William Wright, who travelled through Syria in the late nineteenth century. Zenobia's fame was likely what made Wright attribute the coins to her reign. In fact, the coins he describes seem to fit more with the iconography seen on the locally struck coins from Palmyra, minted a century earlier.

The term 'Palmyrene coinage' likely leads one to think of the small locally struck coins that were found in large numbers in the nineteenth century. However, the autonomous coins minted at Antioch and Alexandria between AD 270 and 272 issued by Zenobia in the name of herself and her son Wahballath (also known as Vaballathus or V(h) abalathus) are in a sense also Palmyrene, meaning that there are two types of Palmyrene coinage. Whereas the coins minted in Palmyra were intended for circulation within the city and to supplement the already existing circulation of coins coming from outside; the coins of Zenobia and Wahballath were meant to circulate widely in the Palmyrene territories of Syria and Egypt. In fact, only seven coins with the portrait of Wahballath have been found in Palmyra and none with the portrait of Zenobia (Dunant and Fellman 1975, cat. no. 24; Krzyzanowska 2014, cat. nos. 252–258).

The coinage of Zenobia has long been of interest to scholars because it helps to tell the story of Palmyra's famous queen Zenobia and her revolt against Rome, while the locally struck coins, as is often the case with small change, have been almost ignored in past scholarship due to their small size and poor state of preservation.

The two types of coinage are vastly different, not only in size, denomination, and iconography, but, most importantly, also in the audience they were intended to reach and the message they were supposed to send. The two types of coinage are essentially incomparable and will be treated separately throughout this chapter; both types can inform us of different aspects of Palmyra, its history, and the political landscape the city navigated within.

To better differentiate between the two types and avoid confusion, the locally struck coins of Palmyra will be referred to as 'the Palmyrene coins' or 'Palmyrene coinage' ('Palmyrene small change') throughout this chapter, while the coins of Zenobia will be referred to as that of her and her son Wahballath.

Palmyrene Coinage: Local Small Change

The Palmyrene coins belong to a category of coins sometimes described as 'minute' coins or minimis (Hamburger 1955; Butcher 2023), referencing their small size. The Palmyrene coins, albeit small, vary in size and weight. They measure between 8 and 14.5 mm in diameter and weigh between 0.65 and 2.70 g. No chemical analysis has been undertaken to establish the metal composition of the Palmyrene coins, but it is likely to be a copper-alloy legation.

Past Scholarship and Research

As is the case with many of the 'minute' coins found on excavations or in museum collections, the Palmyrene coins have not received much scholarly attention over the years (see Hamburger 1955). Their small size and poor preservation made them undesirable to pursue in scholarship.

The Palmyrene coins were first treated by Joseph Eckhel (1737–1798), one of the founding fathers of numismatics. He described a single coin in the third volume of his eight-volume work *Doctrina numorum veterum* (Eckhel 1792–1798). A century later, the coins were described again in four separate works, but not in great detail, first by French numismatist Félicien de Saulcy (1874, 59–66). He published a catalogue of an assortment of coins from the Holy Land in 1874, mostly from his own private collection. Among the coins were several attributed to Palmyra. A year after de Saulcy's publication German orientalist Andreas D. Mordtmann (1875, 72–88) published his private collection of Palmyrene coins, seemingly collected on his visits to Palmyra. According to his own account, Mordtmann collected over a thousand Palmyrene coins on his travels, thus giving the same impression as Wright that the coins were truly numerous. Then, in 1895, Wright published his accounts, describing the coins as he found them in the sands of Palmyra. Finally, in 1899, British numismatist Warwick Wroth published seven coins from Palmyra in one of the British Museum's catalogues of Greek coins (*BMC Syria*).

The Palmyrene coins once belonging to de Saulcy are now in the Département monnaies, médailles et antiques at the Bibliothèque nationale in Paris (du Mesnil du Buisson 1944–1962, 714), and the many coins from Mordtmann's collection are now part of the Münzkabinett at Staatliche Museen zu Berlin (not all are available to see in the museum's online catalogue).

It was not until 1944 that the first detailed study of the Palmyrene coins was undertaken. That year the French count Robert du Mesnil du Buisson (1944–1962) published the plates volume to his two-volume work on the Palmyrene tesserae and coins in the Bibliothèque nationale de France. This volume contained photographs and du Mesnil du Buisson's own drawings of the material iconography. Since many of the coins he described were in poor condition, his reconstructive drawings became quite artistic and interpretative (Kristensen 2018; 2021).

Today the majority of the coins attributed to Palmyra are in museum collections, and unfortunately not many of them have a secure provenance, making it problematic to base studies on these coins alone (see Further Reading for a list of museums). Some are correctly identified as Palmyrene, but others are questionable in their attribution, and it appears that 'Palmyrene coins' has become a term to use for small change in general (see Hamburger 1955). Fortunately, modern excavations in Palmyra in recent decades have provided new opportunities to examine the Palmyrene coins and the monetary network they were a part of. The Austrian archaeologist and numismatist Wolfgang Szaivert (2013) examined the Palmyrene coins in a little more detail as part of the German/Austrian-Syrian project in Palmyra taking part in the excavations of the 'Hellenistic city' from 1997 to 2010. He had previously published a short paper on the Palmyrene coins (Szaivert 1987). Nevertheless, it is through the work of Polish archaeologist Aleksandra Krzyzanowska that some of the questions about the Palmyrene coins have been highlighted. She was part of the decades-long Polish excavations of Palmyra, mostly centred around the Camp of Diocletian, and she examined the Palmyrene coins found there (Krzyzanowska 2014). Already in 1976, she published an article on a hoard from Alexandria containing Palmyrene coins (Krzyzanowska 1976). The precise origin of the hoard is debatable. In 1979, she analysed the circulation of coins in Palmyra and included the locally struck coins from the city in her examination (Krzyzanowska 1979). Most importantly, she established a typology for the coins (Krzyzanowska 1982). Other attempts at typologies had already been undertaken by de Saulcy, Mordtmann, and du Mesnil du Buisson. However, they were either extremely rigid, comprised of around fifty different types (du Saulcy 1874; Mordtmann 1875), or were based on a few overall themes (du Mesnil du Buisson 1944–1962), which also turned out to be problematic. Based on Krzyzanowska's (1982) own typology, she later worked on establishing a chronology for the Palmyrene coins, sorting them into different phases (Krzyzanowska 2002).

Dies, Iconography, and Identification

The Palmyrene coins have been repeatedly described as crude and even 'barbarisées' by Krzyzanowska (1982, 445). However, even crudely executed and small in size, the Palmyrene coins show a varied display of imagery predominantly relating to the religious sphere: local gods and goddesses, animals, and attributes connected with the deities. Krzyzanowska (1982) identified eighteen different types (twenty-one if subtypes are counted). Examinations of the types have shown a ratio of 1:1 between the obverse and reverse dies, which is uncommon (Krzyzanowska 1982, 453; Andrade 2022, 129). Very rarely was an obverse die paired with a different reverse die than the types put forth by Krzyzanowska.

At first glance the representations on the Palmyrene coins appear to be unique to Palmyra. The Palmyrene coins do not show the head of the emperor nor is he mentioned in the legends, as was customary on the civic coinage of other cities. Likewise, the city would be identified through legends and the reverse would display symbols associated with the city: local buildings, deities, myths, geographical representations, and language (see Butcher 2004, 216–238; 2005; Howgego 2005). In fact, only a few of the Palmyrene coins bear legends, and the few legends only mention the name of the city in Greek. While the Palmyrene coins were related to the religious sphere, they did not show representations of Palmyrene temples or refer to religious celebrations or commemorations. However, it was common for the 'minute' coins or small change to display a simpler iconography and, instead of representations of the emperor, to display the head of a god or goddess and bear simple legends, if any. In that aspect Palmyra's was no different from other cities' small change. Excavations in Caesarea Marittima have revealed a wide array of 'minute' coins not only minted there but also minted at other cities. However, they all show similar imagery. The well-known coins of Tyre show Tyche with her mural crown on the obverse and a palm tree and a legend identifying the city. Caesarea's own small coins from the second century AD were adorned with the head of Hercules on one side and either a wolf or a boar on the reverse (Hamburger 1955, cat. nos. 35–58). In the third century CE, the coins changed in Caesarea, and they came to show the head of Tyche with a mural crown on the obverse and a galley on the reverse (Hamburger 1955, cat. nos. 59–74), a common motif in many port cities (Butcher 2023).

While it is difficult to precisely identify the gods and goddesses displayed on the Palmyrene coins and the identifications are still debatable, the Palmyrene iconography on the coins was influenced by the imagery seen on civic and 'minute' coins of the Roman East. One type of coin shows a winged Nike next to a scale on the obverse and three male heads on the reverse. This is one of the only types with a legend and also one of the only types where the imagery can be precisely identified (Krzyzanowska 1982). The constellation of the three male heads represents the Triad of Bēl, composed of the lunar god Aglibol with a radiate, Bēl wearing a *kalathos*, and the sun god Yarhibol with a radiate, too. Unfortunately, in most instances, the deities shown on the coins are difficult to identify. Several images depict the head of a goddess wearing a mural crown,

Tyche, or a goddess with a lion. Both images were popular on the civic and 'minute' coins from other cities (e.g., Hamburger 1955; Kristensen 2021). Both Krzyzanowska (1982; 2002) and du Mesnil du Buisson (1944–1962) identified these females as either Tyche or Atargatis. The identification of Atargatis is mainly based on the lion that she is depicted alongside. However, recently, Kaizer (2007, 51–53) has argued that some of these representations should instead be identified as that of Gad, the personification of good fortune and the Aramaic equivalent to Tyche (Drijvers 1976, 20; Kristensen 2021). A relief from Dura-Europos, now at the Yale University Art Gallery (inv. 1938.5343), found at the temple of Atargatis depicts a sitting female, believed to be Atargatis, flanked by two lions. Another relief from Dura-Europos, also at Yale University Art Gallery (inv. 1938.5313) depicts a Palmyrene priest and Gad (identified by an inscription) wearing a mural crown, sitting on a rock next to a lion (in the style of Tyche of Antioch) about to be crowned by Nike which could, however, suggest that the sitting goddess with a lion on one type of Palmyrene coins could be Gad, as argued by Kaizer (2007). Because several goddesses were depicted alongside lions, Atargatis, Cybele, and Allat in Palmyra, any precise identification remains challenging.

Identifications of the male deities are likewise problematic. Baalshamin can be identified on two different types because of his headdress, a *kalathos*, and because he is bearded (Figure 34.1). However, many of the other gods are merely depicted with a radiate (Figure 34.2), a common headdress for male deities in Palmyra, as seen on the famous relief of the Triad of Baalshamin now in the Louvre (inv. AO 19801). A few representations also show a male with horns on his shoulders, and he is sometimes identified as Aglibol (Krzyzanowska 1982; 2002). Secure identifications or not, it is clear that Palmyra chose images that reflected religious aspects of Palmyrene society and were of great importance to the audience exposed to the images. Although Palmyra was indeed inspired by the traditions of the Roman East, the city deliberately chose to interpret these traditions in a local way (Kaizer 2007; Kristensen 2018; 2021).

Period of Minting: When Did Palmyra Start Striking Coins?

The Palmyrene coins have been notoriously difficult to date because they bear no datable markers such as the portrait of the emperor or legends that could refer to a specific event or title of the emperor. Since scholars began describing the Palmyrene coins in their catalogues, the date has been debated. Wright believed them to have been struck in a limited period during the siege in AD 272. De Saulcy thought them to have been minted prior to Hadrian or at least prior to the reign of Caracalla 'qui doivent être antérieures au règne d'Hadrien, et, à plus forte raisan, à celei de Caracalla' (de Saulcy 1874, 60). Du Mesnil du Buisson thought they had been minted in the third century AD as a continuation of the clay tokens, or tesserae, used at religious banquets at the sanctuaries. A similar theory was put forth by Szaivert (2013), who also saw the Palmyrene coins as a type

FIGURE 34.1 Palmyrene coin from Dura-Europos depicting Baalshamin with a *kalathos*. Yale University Art Gallery, New Haven, inv. no. 1938.6000.1336.

Image courtesy of Yale University Art Gallery.

of token with no monetary value. Had this been the case, it is likely that they were found in the drains of the sanctuaries, as has been the case with clay tesserae (Kristensen 2021; see Chapter 33 [Raja], this volume, for the tesserae).

To this day the dating of the coins is still debatable, but Krzyzanowska has made a valiant effort to answer the question. Her typology, presented in 1982, led her to create a chronology for the Palmyrene coinage (Krzyzanowska 2002; 2014). She divided the coins into four phases from the second half of the second century AD (the Antonine period) until the second half of the third century AD, ending shortly before or with the fall of Zenobia and the sack of the city in AD 272/273. The phases were determined based on the quality of the coins and the imagery, in which Krzyzanowska noticed parallels to the coinage of the Severan dynasty (Krzyzanowska 1982; 2002). She noted that the minting quality of the coins declined over time and thus dated the coins of a better quality to the second century and the coins of a lesser quality to the third century. She further noted a type depicting what she argued was Marsyas carrying a sack over one shoulder and a male god standing next to a pyre or altar (Krzyzanowska 1982, 449–450). The identification of Marsyas was also noted by previous scholars (du Mesnil du Buisson 1944–1962, 723–724; Szaivert 1987, 244). The representation of Marsyas was seen on other cities' civic coinage after they received the title of a Roman *colonia* and was believed to imitate a statue of Marsyas on the Forum Romanum (Butcher 2003, 232–233; 2023). Palmyra received this title from either Septimius Severus or Caracalla, leading both Krzyzanowska

FIGURE 34.2 Palmyrene coin from Dura-Europos depicting a male head with a radiate and three ears of corn. Yale University Art Gallery, New Haven, inv. no. 1938.6000.1332.

Image courtesy of Yale University Art Gallery.

and others before her to date this coin type to the Severan period. However, looking at the iconography of the Palmyrene coins, the image of Marsyas seems a very political symbol to place on the otherwise religiously inspired coinage, and the identification is still debatable (Kaizer 2007; Kristensen 2021; 2022). Kaizer has suggested that the minting of coins in Palmyra could have begun as early as the reign of Hadrian and that the city acquired minting rights in connection with his visit to the city in AD 130/131 (Kaizer 2007, 47). Most recently Nathanael Andrade (2022) has undertaken a die study of the Palmyrene coinage. While his examination is still preliminary, he has put forth some valid observations. He has suggested that the coins could have been minted for a short period from around AD 235–272 (Andrade 2022, 130). There are still many factors that remain uncertain, and the dating of the Palmyrene coins continues to need further examination.

Minting and Circulation

Modern excavations have revealed a total of only fifty-four Palmyrene coins (Dunant and Fellmann 1975; Szaivert 2013; Krzyzanowska 2014), but we know from the accounts of Wright and Mordtmann that the coins were found by the thousand in the sand dunes in the city. Many of the coins were likely collected by travellers as small souvenirs, such as Mordtmann and Wright, and one can assume that the Palmyrene coins were minted in a far larger number despite the small number found on excavations.

Andrade's die study indicates that there was not much quality control in the minting process. The Palmyrene minters seem to have used very worn dies or even broken dies for the reverse especially (but there are also signs of wear on the obverse dies) (Andrade 2022, 129). This could also explain the shift in quality that Krzyzanowska (1982; 2002) observed. Instead of a chronological shift in quality, it was simply caused by worn dies and a seemingly careless approach in the minting process (Kristensen 2018; 2021, 122–123; 2022, 115–116; Andrade 2022, 129). Many of the dies were not centred, and there is no consistency in the rotation of the dies (Andrade 2022, 129). It is a possibility that the different types were minted at the same time or very close to each other instead of in chronological phases, as was suggested by Krzyzanowska. However, more studies and examinations are needed before any definitive conclusions can be made.

Twelve Palmyrene coins have been found in Dura-Europos (Bellinger 1949, 86–87) in addition to the Palmyrene coins from the Alexandrian hoard (Krzyzanowska 1976). This suggests a limited circulation of the Palmyrene coinage (Kristensen 2022). The coins only spread within Palmyra and areas that Palmyra had close contact with. Dura-Europos had a strong Palmyrene presence (Dirven 1996; 1999; 2011). The origin of the Alexandrian hoard remains dubious, but if it is genuine, the presence of Palmyrene coins could be explained by Zenobia's short-lived conquest of Egypt. The localized circulation is further substantiated by the lack of legends and distinct iconography. It was easy for Palmyrenes to identify their local currency. It is possible that people visiting the city could have exchanged foreign and larger currencies at the city gate, as is also known from Egypt (see Geissen 2012; for later periods, see Birch et al. 2019). In Caesarea, 'minute' coins from Tyre and Alexandria have been found, albeit the majority are from the Caesarean mint (Hamburger 1955). But, contrary to Caesarea, only the locally struck small change circulated in Palmyra. Almost a third of the total number of coins circulating in Palmyra were the local coinage. A fifth were the provincial imperial coinage minted at Antioch, almost 10 percent were civic issues from other Syrian cities, and around 13 percent were civic coins from other eastern provinces (Kristensen 2018; 2021; 2022). However, this pattern is not exclusive for Palmyra: other cities such as Apamea and Dura-Europos produced very little if any local coins (Butcher 2004; 2023).

COINAGE OF ZENOBIA: A CLAIM TO POWER

In AD 267, Zenobia took over power in Palmyra after her husband Odainath was assassinated. Five years later, by the autumn of AD 270, Zenobia invaded and conquered Egypt, forming a vast Palmyrene kingdom. Shortly after the conquest she began striking coins in Alexandria and Antioch with the portrait of Aurelian and her son Wahballath. After March AD 272, the portrait of Aurelian was removed from the coins and a series of coins with either the portrait of Wahballath or Zenobia was issued. Zenobia claimed the title of *Augusta* and for Wahballath that of *Augustus* in open rebellion against Rome.

The historic accounts of Zenobia and the events leading up to and following her striking coins without the portrait of the emperor have been recounted in several works and will not be further elaborated here (see Hartmann 2001; Estiot 2004; Andrade 2018; Chapter 10 [Hartmann], this volume; Chapter 11 [Andrade], this volume). While Zenobia has fascinated not only modern scholars, but also painters, composers, and authors for centuries, her coinage has not received the full attention that it deserves and has not been incorporated into the historical accounts of the woman herself and the world in which she lived (see Estiot 2004; Bland 2011).

Past Scholarship and Research

The coinage of Zenobia has been described in numerous coin catalogues, albeit the coins have been treated separately. The coins minted at Antioch, also known as *antoniniani* or *radiates*, have been considered part of the Roman Imperial Coinage and have been included in *RIC* (V), while the coins from Alexandria, the tetradrachms, have been considered part of the Roman Provincial Coinage and compiled in different catalogues treating the provincial coinage of Alexandria (e.g., see Vogt 1924; Milne 1971; Emmet 2001). They will likely also be treated as part of volume 10 of the Roman Provincial Coinage series.

Until 1978, scholars doubted the validity of the radiates showing only the portrait of Zenobia since only a single coin had been published in 1890, by Italian numismatist Francesco Gnecchi (1890). However, that year, the British numismatist Robert Carson published six specimens and proved them to be genuine. Krzyzanowska (2003) is still doubtful of Gnecchi's identifications. In 2011, Bland (2011) published a comprehensive article on the Antiochene and Alexandrian coinage of Zenobia and Wahballath, in which he collected a comprehensive catalogue of coins from various museum collections, art dealers, and auction houses.

Archaeologists have long wished to find a coin with the portrait of Zenobia in Palmyra, but so far it has been in vain. In 1960, a bronze tesserae or token was found during excavations in Palmyra (Michalowski 1962, cat. no. 118). The portrait on the token was quickly identified as Zenobia through a partial inscription spelling out ZEN[. . .] (Krzyzanowska 2003). However, a detailed examination of the tesserae years later revealed it to be a coin of Salonina, wife of Gallienus. The legend more likely spelled out SAL[. . .]. Two lead tesserae, one in the Bibliothèque nationale in Paris and one in the National Museum of Damascus, are also believed to depict Zenobia based on their partial inscriptions (du Mesnil du Buisson 1944–1962, 757–758; Hvidberg-Hansen 2002, 76–77). However, the attributions should, like the tesserae from Palmyra, be examined further. Despite the eagerness of archaeologists, no coins with the portraits of Zenobia or Wahballath (alone) have been found in Palmyra, and only a few coins with the image of Aurelian and Wahballath have been uncovered in excavations in the city.

FIGURE 34.3 Double-headed Antoninianus depicting Aurelian and Wahballath. Yale University Art Gallery, New Haven, inv. no. 2001.87.17235.

Image courtesy of Yale University Art Gallery.

The Double-Headed Coins of Aurelian and Wahballath: Legends, Iconography, and Symbolism

The coins with the portraits of Aurelian and Wahballath were minted over a period of about eighteen months; the tetradrachms were struck from the autumn of AD 270 and the radiates from November or December of the same year.

The radiates were issued in far larger numbers from eight different *officinae*. Bland (2011, 143) calculated that between 274 and 910 obverse dies and between 258 and 1,323 reverse dies were used (Bland 2011, 143). A similar study has not been made for the tetradrachms (Bland 2011, 158).

Aurelian is portrayed in the tradition of a Roman emperor on both the radiates and tetradrachms: a mature man with short hair and a beard wearing a radiate crown and a cuirass. The legends identify him as Imperator, Caesar, and Augustus (in Latin on the radiates and in Greek on the tetradrachms). Wahballath is portrayed slightly differently on the coins. On the radiates, Wahballath is seen as a young man with short hair (Figure 34.3), while he has full, mid-length hair on the tetradrachms (Figure 34.4). Otherwise, he is beardless and wears a double headdress composed of a laurate and a diadem as

FIGURE 34.4 Double-headed tetradrachm depicting Aurelian and Wahballath. Yale University Art Gallery, New Haven, inv. no. 2001.87.4173.

Image courtesy of Yale University Art Gallery.

well as a cuirass and paludamentum. The coiffure of Wahballath on the Alexandrian coinage can be seen as an attempt to associate him with the Palmyrene gods wearing military dress: Aglibôl, Yarhibôl, and Malakbêl (Schwentzel 2010, 161–162). It would have been a way for Wahballath to address the Palmyrene soldiers stationed in Egypt. Considering that this type was only struck in Egypt, it could also be suggested that Wahballath wanted to associate himself with the Hellenistic rulers, as his mother also wished for him. Likewise, the double-headdress is considered unprecedented on coin portraits of this period and could be a reflection of Wahballath's eastern origin (Bland 2011, 143). The diadem could also help to assimilate him with the Hellenistic rulers and, in particular, the Ptolemies of Egypt. It has also been proposed that Zenobia sought to associate herself with Cleopatra (Long 1996, 69; Bussi 2003, 265–266; Southern 2008, 93, 116). However, Schwentzel (2010, 165) has rejected the idea of a ruler diadem and instead suggested that it should be seen as a symbol of victory, perhaps their victory over Egypt or maybe even Rome.

The legends on the radiates read: VABALATHVS V(ir) C(larissimus) R(ex) IM(perator) D(ux) R(omanum). On some coins, an H was added to his name: VHABALATHVS. The added H has been suggested to have been yet another emphasis on Wahballath's Palmyrene origin. The added H brings the pronunciation closer to

Aramaic, thus creating a connection to his Syrian origin and flattering the Syrian population (Seyrig 1966, 661; Carson 1978, 223; Schwentzel 2010, 161). This, however, has been rejected by Bland (2011, 146), who merely sees it as a mistake made by the die engravers.

The name Wahballath is Aramaic and means 'gift of Allat'. On the coinage, his name is not translated into Latin but Latinized by adding an 'us', thereby keeping its Palmyrene origin; it was translated into Greek (ΑΘΗΝΟΔΩΡΟΣ, meaning 'the gift of Athena') and placed alongside his Aramaic name on the tetradrachms from Alexandria (Schwentzel 2010, 166). The titles of Wahballath given on the tetradrachms were discussed extensively in the nineteenth century, but, since 1866, Alfred von Sallet's (1866, 16–43) interpretation has been accepted: Ἰούλιος Αὐρήλιος Σεπτίμιος Οὐαβάλλαθος Ἀθηνοδῶρος ὑπατικὸς (or ὕπατος) αὐτοκράτωρ στρατηγὸς Ῥωμαίων. The legend occurs in different versions on the coins. In some instances, the titles are in a different order or some titles have been left out (Hartmann 2001, 250–254; Bland 2011, 156). The titles ὑπατικὸς αὐτοκράτωρ στρατηγὸς Ῥωμαίων may be translated into Latin as 'Consular', 'Imperator', 'Dux Romanum' with the two last titles also occurring on the radiates from Antioch.

The *officina* stamp on the radiates was placed on the side of Aurelian. Usually, the mintmark was placed on the reverse, and it has therefore been argued that Aurelian was placed on the reverse and given an inferior status to Wahballath (Carson 1978, 222; Bland 2011, 142). However, the same occurs on coins struck at the Roman mint of Cyzicus, and this theory has therefore been rejected by others (Long 1996, 64; Southern 2008, 106). On the tetradrachms, there are subtle hints at Wahballath's superior status as, on later coins portraying him and Aurelian, he is seen from behind (normally associated with the senior Augustus). A single type of smaller bronzes with the confronting busts of Wahballath and Aurelian was also struck at Alexandria. Aurelian is placed on the left and Wahballath on the right, indicating Aurelian's seniority (Bland 2011, 157). Only the names of the two are mentioned on this type.

The Single-Headed Coins of Wahballath and Zenobia: Iconography and Symbolism

The single-headed coins of Wahballath and Zenobia were struck in the last few months of the Palmyrene kingdom in AD 272. The minting was begun in March in both mints and continued until May in Antioch and until June in Alexandria. The portrait of Aurelian was removed and Wahballath was declared *Augustus* by his mother, while she took the title of *Augusta* and issued a new coinage with her portrait on it.

The single-headed issues were far fewer in number than the coins of Aurelian and Wahballath, likely because of the brief minting phase. In Antioch, seven of the eight *officinae* struck coins of Wahballath, while only one of the eight *officina* struck coins of Zenobia (Bland 2011, 144–145). The single-headed coins of Wahballath were slightly changed and became almost identical in Antioch and Alexandria. He is shown as a young man with short hair wearing a radiate crown on the coins from Antioch and a laurel wreath on those from Alexandria. He is dressed in a cuirass and a paludamentum. The legend gives him the imperial titles IM(perator) C(aesar) VHABALATHVS AVG(ustus) in Antioch and ΑΥΤ(οκρατόρ) Κ(αίσαρ) ΟΥΑΒΑΛΛΑΘΟΣ ΑΘΗΝΟ(δωρος) CEB(ασος) at Alexandria. The longer hair from the double-headed tetradrachms vanished, but his Palmyrene name continued to be used on the coins. The reverses of the radiates show various standing deities or personifications: Hercules, Venus, Aequitas, Jupiter, or Victoria at Antioch (Bland 2011, 144–145). The tetradrachms show three different reverse types: a radiate bust of Helios or Selene or a standing Hormonoia looking to the left (Bland 2011, 157).

The single-headed coins of Zenobia show a woman with a braid attached on top of her head and wearing a diadem or a stephane. The legend on the radiates gives her name in Latin: Septimia Zenobia Augusta and the equivalent names in Greek on the tetradrachms. The reverses on the radiates show only one image: a standing Juno looking left holding a *patera* and sceptre with a peacock at her feet (Bland 2011, 145), while the reverses on the tetradrachms show the same images as those seen on the single-headed radiates of Wahballath in addition to a walking Elpis (Bland 2011, 157).

The reverses on the single-headed radiates and tetradrachms of Wahballath and Zenobia all followed the designs of 'their Roman predecessors', Gallienus and Claudius II. The reverse type on Zenobia's tetradrachms depicting the goddess Juno with a peacock closely resembles the reverse type of Severina, the wife of Aurelian (Southern 2008, 119). Wahballath's portrait also conformed to the imperial traditions and imitated the portraits of Gallienus, Claudius II, and Aurelian and Zenobia's the portraits of the imperial women of the third century AD, in particular, Salonina, the wife of Gallienus, and Severina.

Schwentzel (2010, 166–167) has suggested that the change was caused by Wahballath and Zenobia's wish to continue the traditions set by 'their' predecessors and better fit in with the imperial traditions of Rome. It is also possible that the imagery and the subsequent change in the iconography was a matter of necessity. If their coinage had to be trusted particularly, as a new dynasty it was necessary to maintain a consistent appearance. They would have been strongly inclined to maintain an imagery consistent with what had preceded them. However, while Zenobia and Wahballath might have felt prone to follow the traditions of 'their predecessors', they still managed to subtly present Hellenistic and Palmyrene symbols and bring forth their own agenda without the validity of the coins being questioned.

Circulation in the Palmyrene Territories

The radiates and tetradrachms of Zenobia and Wahballath have been found in hoards in large numbers, and, while many coins are in museum collections without a known provenance, they can be securely attributed to either the mint at Antioch or Alexandria.

Three hoards consist exclusively of the double-headed radiates: one is from Syria (Hama) (Seyrig 1966), one is from Turkey (Bland 2011), and one is without provenance (Seaby 1972). The Hama hoard also contained a single-headed radiate with the portrait of Wahballath. The coins from the Hama hoard appear to have been unworn by circulation, and Seyrig (1966, 659–662) has argued that the hoard was a reserve from a military treasury meant to be used as payment for the Palmyrene soldiers and as such meant to circulate in areas controlled by the Palmyrene military. He further noted that the double-headed radiates from the hoard differed from those minted at Antioch, suggesting that they had been struck at an emergency mint, possibly at Emesa, after Aurelian had recaptured Antioch and taken control of the city's mint. Bland (2011, 150) also suggests that this was the case with the two other hoards. Two other hoards, both from Syria, also contained a substantial number of double-headed radiates in combination with earlier coins (Evers 1970; Huvelin 1990).

In Egypt, nine hoards containing a total of 534 double-headed tetradrachms and eight single-headed tetradrachms have been found (Milne 1971; Bland 2011, 159–161). The single-headed tetradrachms were found in two different hoards, one specimen in one hoard and seven in the other. Since coins minted in Egypt were only meant to circulate within the province, no tetradrachms of this kind have been found outside of the province (Bland 2011, 159; see also Geissen 2012). The findings of Zenobia's coinage in Syria, Turkey, and Egypt, both double-headed with Aurelian and Wahballath and single-headed coins with Zenobia or Wahballath, reveal that the coinage was meant to circulate in territories under Palmyrene control. The majority of the coins were likely used to pay soldiers in the Palmyrene army and spread across the kingdom through the soldiers, reaching the people now under Palmyrene rule and intended to convince them of Zenobia and Wahballath's legitimate right to rule.

Conclusion

The local Palmyrene coinage and the coinage of Zenobia and Wahballath were meant to reach two very different audiences. The local coinage only circulated locally within the city limits, while the coinage of Zenobia and Wahballath circulated in the recently conquered Palmyrene territories of Turkey, Syria, and Egypt. This difference is clearly reflected in the iconography of the two types.

Palmyra relied on civic coins from other cities but introduced the locally struck coins at a point in time when small change was needed. They were only meant to circulate within the city and be used in the everyday trade taking place in Palmyra. The rare use of legends further substantiates this theory, as the coins were easily recognizable to its citizens. While cities such as Caesarea Maritima also used small change from other cities, it seems that Palmyra restricted the access of other types of small change and only imported civic coinage from other cities. Perhaps because it did not mint larger denominations but could easily follow the demand of small change in the city, the coins depict local deities and animals and attributes connected with them. While some representations seem quite original, such as the Triad of Bēl, others, such as the goddess with a lion or Tyche (or Gad), were clearly inspired by images seen on coins circulating in the Roman East. However, Palmyra still managed to strike a distinct type of local coinage, much more varied than seen elsewhere and one that presented an important part of Palmyrenes' life, that of religion.

On the other hand, the hoard findings of Zenobia and Wahballath's coinage indicate that it reached far into the Palmyrene territories. Likely brought there by soldiers in the Palmyrene army, the coins spread through the soldiers trading in the areas they were stationed and reached ordinary citizens in the conquered areas. The double-headed coins of Aurelian and Wahballath were likely used to show, although it was non-existent, Rome's approval of Zenobia and her conquests. Wahballath was represented differently on the double-headed coins from what Roman tradition would dictate and showed off his eastern origin through the double headdress. Considering he was only depicted with longer curly hair on the Alexandrian coins, he likely wished to associate himself with the Hellenistic rulers of Egypt more than he wished to look like a Palmyrene god. After Wahballath and Zenobia claimed the imperial titles of *Augustus* and *Augusta* and removed Aurelian from the coinage, the iconography conformed completely to Roman tradition, with Wahballath being represented through iconography resembling a Roman emperor and Zenobia in the style of a Roman empress. Gone was the longer hair and the double-headdress seen on the previous coinage. The only Palmyrene thing to remain was Wahballath's (albeit Latinized) Palmyrene name. Even the images on the reverses were copied from the coins of Claudius II, Gallienus, and Aurelian. This alignment with Roman traditions was undoubtedly a way to legitimize their claim to power by presenting a continuation of old traditions.

ABBREVIATIONS

BMC Syria	Wroth, Warwick. 1964. *Catalogue of the Greek Coins of Galatia, Cappadocia, and Syria* (reprint of the 1899 edition). London: British Museum.
RIC V Webb,	Percy H. et al. 1927. *Roman Imperial Coinage*. Vol. 5, pt 1. London: Spink.

BIBLIOGRAPHY

Andrade, Nathanael. 2018. Zenobia: *Shooting Star of Palmyra*. Oxford: Oxford University Press.

Andrade, Nathanael. 2022. 'Palmyra's Small Coins and their Dies: Preliminary Results'. In *The Small Stuff of the Palmyrenes: Coins and Tesserae from Palmyra*, edited by Rubina Raja, 125–144. Turnhout: Brepols.

Bellinger, A. R. 1949. *The Excavations at Dura-Europos: Conducted by Yale University and the French Academy of Inscriptions and Letters, Final Report VI*. New Haven: Yale University Press.

Birch, Tom et al. 2019. 'From nummi minimi to fulūs: Small Change and Wider Issues: Characterising Coinage from Gerasa/Jerash (Late Roman to Umayyad Periods)'. *Journal of Archaeological and Anthropological Science*.

Bland, Roger. 2011. 'The Coinage of Vabalathus and Zenobia from Antioch and Alexandria'. *The Numismatic Chronicle* 171: 133–186.

Bussi, Silvia. 2003. 'Zenobia/Cleopatra: Immagine e Propaganda'. *Rivista italiana di numismatica e scienze affini* 104: 261–268.

Butcher, Kevin. 2003. *Roman Syria and the Near East*. Los Angeles: J. Paul Getty Museum.

Butcher, Kevin. 2004. *Coinage in Roman Syria: Northern Syria, 64 BC–AD 253*. London: Royal Numismatic Society.

Butcher, Kevin. 2005. 'Information, Legitimation, or Self-Legitimation? Popular and Elite Designs on the Coin Types of Syria'. In *Coinage and Identity in the Roman Provinces*, edited by Christopher Howgego, Volker Heuchert, and Andrew Burnett, 143–156. Oxford: Oxford University Press.

Butcher, Kevin. 2023. 'Circuits of Exchange: Palmyrene Coins and Roman Monetary Plurality'. In *Exchange and Reuse in Palmyra: Examining Economy and Circularity*, edited by Nathanael Andrade and Rubina Raja. Turnhout: Brepols.

Carson, R. A. G. 1978. 'Antoniniani of Zenobia'. *Numismatica e Antichità Classiche* 7: 221–228.

de Saulcy, Louis Félicien Joseph Caignart. 1874. *Numismatique de la Terre Sainte, description des monnaies autonomes et impériales de la Palestine et de l'Arabie Pétrée*. Paris.

Dirven, Lucinda. 1996. 'The Nature of the Trade Between Palmyra and Dura-Europos'. *ARAM* 8: 39–54.

Dirven, Lucinda. 1999. *The Palmyrene of Dura-Europos: A Study of Religious Interaction in Roman Syria*. Leiden: Brill.

Dirven, Lucinda. 2011. 'Strangers and Sojourners: The Religious Behaviour of Palmyrenes and Other Foreigners in Dura-Europos'. In *Dura-Europos: Crossroads of Antiquity*, edited by Lisa R. Brody and Gail L. Hoffman, 201–220. Boston: McMullen Museum of Art.

Drijvers, H. J. W. 1976. *The Religion of Palmyra*. Leiden: Brill.

du Mesnil du Buisson, Robert. 1944–1962. *Les tesseres et les monnaies de Palmyre: Un art, une culture et une philosophie grecs dans les moules d'une cité et d'une religion sémitiques; Inventaire des collections du Cabinet des médailles de la Bibliothèque Nationale*, 2 vols. Paris: de Boccard.

Dunant, Christiane, and Rudolf Fellmann. 1975. *Le sanctuaire de Baalshamin à Palmyre*. Vol. 6. Rome: Institut suisse de Rome.

Eckhel, Joseph H. 1792–1798. *Doctrina numorum veterum*. Vol. 3. Vienna: Sumptibus J. Camesina.

Emmet, Keith. 2001. *Alexandrian Coins*. Lodi, WI: Clio's Cabinet.

Estiot, Sylviane. 2004. *Monnaies de l'Empire romain, XII.1 D'Aurélien à Florien (270-276 après J.-C.)*. Poinsignon numismatique. 2 vols. Paris: Bibliothèque nationale de France.

Evers, J. H. 1970. 'Syrische Muntvondst (II)'. *De Geuzen Penning* 20: 56–57.

Geissen, Angelo. 2012. 'The Coinage of Roman Egypt'. In *The Oxford Handbook of Greek and Roman Coinage*, edited by William E. Metcalf, 561–583. Oxford: Oxford University Press.

Gnecchi, Francesco. 1890. 'Appunti di numismatica Romana, VII. Antoniniano di Zenobia'. *RIN* 3: 15–20.

Hamburger, H. 1955. 'Minute Coins from Caesarea'. *Atiqot: Journal of the Israel Department of Antiquities* 51: 115–138.

Hartmann, Udo. 2001. *Das palmyrenische Teilreich*. Stuttgart: Steiner.

Howgego, Christopher. 2005. 'Coinage and Identity in the Roman Provinces'. In *Coinage and Identity in the Roman Provinces*, edited by Christopher Howgego, Volker Heuchert, and Andrew Burnett, 1–17. Oxford: Oxford University Press.

Huvelin, Hélène. 1990. 'L'atelier d'Antioche sous Claude II'. *Numismatica e antichità classiche* 19: 251–271.

Hvidberg-Hansen, Finn O. 2002. *Zenobia: byen Palmyra og dens dronning*. Aarhus: Sfinx.

Kaizer, Ted. 2007. '"Palmyre, cité grecque"? A Question of Coinage'. *KLIO* 89(1): 39–60.

Kristensen, Nathalia B. 2018. 'Coinage and Identity: An Iconographic Study of the Coinage of Palmyra from 312 BCE – 272/273 CE'. Unpublished master's thesis, Aarhus University.

Kristensen, Nathalia B. 2021. 'A Symbol of a City: The Iconography of the Palmyrene Coinage'. In *Individualising the Dead: Attributes in Palmyrene Funerary Sculpture*, edited by Maura K. Heyn and Rubina Raja, 119–130. Turnhout: Brepols.

Kristensen, Nathalia B. 2022. '"Money Makes the World Go Round": Production and Circulation Patterns of the Palmyrene Coinage'. In *The Small Stuff of the Palmyrenes: The Coins and Tesserae of Palmyra*, edited by Rubina Raja, 111–124. Turnhout: Brepols.

Krzyzanowska, Aleksandra. 1976. 'Tresor de monnaies palmyréniennes trouvé à Alexandrie'. In *Actes du 8ème Congrés international de numismatique, New York-Washington, Septembre 1973*, edited by Herbert Adolph Cahn and Georges Le Rider, 327–332. Paris: Association internationale des Numismates professionnels.

Krzyzanowska, Aleksandra. 1979. 'La circulation monétaire à Palmyre d'aprés le materiel provenant des fouilles'. *Wiadomości Numizmatyczne* 3: 44–52.

Krzyzanowska, Aleksandra. 1982. 'Le monnayage de Palmyre'. In *Actes du 9ème Congrès international de numismatique, Berne, septembre, 1979*, edited by Tony Hackens, 445–457. Louvain-la-Neuve: Association internationale des Numismates professionnels.

Krzyzanowska, Aleksandra. 2002. 'Les monnaies de Palmyre: Leur chronologie et leur rôle dans la circulation monétaire e la region'. In *Les monnayages Syriens: Quel apport pour l'histoire du ProcheOrient hellenistique et romain? Actes de la table ronde de Damas, 10–12 novembre 1999*, edited by Frédérique Duyrat and Christian Augé, 167–173. Beirut: Institut français d'archéologie du proche-orient.

Krzyzanowska, Aleksandra. 2003. 'Coins of "Zenobia" in Palmyra'. *Wiadomości Numizmatyczne: Polish Numismatic News* 7: 73–76.

Krzyzanowska, Aleksandra. 2014. 'Monnaies grecques et romaines'. *Studia Palmyreńskie* 13: 13–68.

Long, Jacqueline. 1996. 'Two Sides of a Coin: Aurelian, Vaballathus, and Eastern Frontiers in the Early 270's'. In *Shifting Frontiers in Late Antiquity*, edited by Ralph W. Mathisen and Hagith S. Sivan, 45–71. Aldershot: Variorum.

Michalowski, Kazimierz. 1962. *Palmyre: Fouilles Polonaises 1960*. Warsaw: Pánstwowe Wydawnictwo Naukowe.

Milne, J. G. 1971. *Catalogue of Alexandrian Coins: University of Oxford, Ashmolean Museum*. Oxford: Spink.

Mordtmann, Andreas. David. 1875. *Neue Beiträge zur Kunde Palmyra's*. Munich: Straub.

Seaby. 1972. *Seaby's Coin and Medal Bulletin December 1972*. London: Seaby's Coin and Medal Bulletin.

Schwentzel, Christian-Georges. 2010. 'La propagande de Vaballath et Zénobie d'après le témoignage des monnaies et tessères'. *Rivista italiana di numismatica e scienze affini* 111: 157–172.

Seyrig, Henri. 1966. 'VHABALATHVS AVGVSTVS'. In *Mélanges offerts à Kazimierz Michałowski*, edited by Kazimierz Michałowski and Maria Ludwika Bernhard, 659–662. Warsaw: Państwowe Wydawnictwo Naukowe.

Southern, Pat. 2008. *Empress Zenobia: Palmyra's Rebel Queen*. London: Continuum.

Szaivert, Wolfgang. 1987. 'Die Münzen von Palmyra'. In *Palmyra: Geschichte, Kunst und Kultur der Syrischen Oasenstadt; Einführende Beiträge und Katalog zur Ausstellung*, edited by Erwin Maria Ruprechtsberger, 244–248. Linz: Druck- und Verlagsanstalt Gutenberg.

Szaivert, Wolfgang. 2013. 'Fundmünzen'. In *Palmyras Reichtum durch Weltweiten Handel: Archäologische Untersuchungen im Bereich der Hellenistischen Stadt*. Vol. 2, edited by Andreas Schmidt-Colinet and Waleed al-As'ad, 253–260. Vienna: Holzhausen.

Vogt, Joseph. 1924. *Die Alexandrinischen Münzen: Grundlegung einer Alexandrinischen Kaisergeschichte*. Stuttgart: Kohlhammer.

von Sallet, Alfred. 1866. *Die Fürsten von Palmyra unter Gallienus, Claudius und Aurelian*. Berlin.

Wright, William. 1895. *An Account of Palmyra and Zenobia: With Travels and Adventures in Bashan and the Desert*. London: Darf.

FURTHER READING

American Numismatic Society. Online catalogue, New York City. https://numismatics.org/search/.

Bibliotheque nationale de France, Département des Monnaies, médailles et antiques, online catalogue, Paris. https://catalogue.bnf.fr/index.do.

British Museum, Department of Coins and Medals, online catalogue, London. https://www.britishmuseum.org/collection.

Arthur M. Sackler Museum, online catalogue, Harvard University, Cambridge, Massachusetts, USA. https://harvardartmuseums.org/collections.

Staatliche Museen zu Berlin, Münzkabinett, online catalogue, Berlin, Germany. https://recherche.smb.museum/?language=de&limit=15&sort=relevance&controls=none&collectionKey=MK*.

Yale University Art Gallery, online catalogue, Yale University, New Haven, Connecticut, USA. https://artgallery.yale.edu/collection.

CHAPTER 35

WALL PAINTINGS AND STUCCO WORK IN PALMYRENE FUNERARY HYPOGEA

HÉLÈNE ERISTOV, CLAUDE VIBERT-GUIGUE, AND NICOLE BLANC

STATE OF THE FIELD

UNLIKE sculpted decoration, a wall plaster is fragile; the *a secco* technique on *djousse* (plaster and lime) is very sensitive to humidity and abrasion. In the four necropoleis of Palmyra, only six tombs reveal wall paintings and stucco work; all are located in the south-west necropolis (Tomb of the Three Brothers, of Zabad'ateh and Neša, of Hairan, of 'Atenatan, of Dionysus, of Abd'Astor) and have an inverted T-shaped floor plan (the plan of the tomb of Dionysus is unknown). The decoration covers only one exedra, usually the one on the right side, that in the Tomb of the Three Brothers being an exception (back exedra). Stucco work, however widespread in Palmyra, is present only in the tomb of Abd'Astor (Figure 35.1).

Our knowledge of the Palmyrene tombs is based on descriptions made between 1895 and 1900 by Danish, German, and Russian explorers (Østrup, Sobernheim, and Uspenskij, respectively) and then thanks to the Danish H. Ingholt's archaeological mission in 1924 (Ingholt 1932; 1935; 1938). The recent discovery (2007) of the tomb of Zabad'ateh and Neša by the Directorate of Antiquities has enriched the corpus. In 2011, only two of the six tombs were visible, and the four others were known from brief scientific publications and black-and-white photographs. Apart from some rare colour snapshots of the tomb of Hairan, Kraeling published a photographic catalogue of the Tomb of the Three Brothers (Kraeling 1961–1962). The monuments explored by Ingholt,

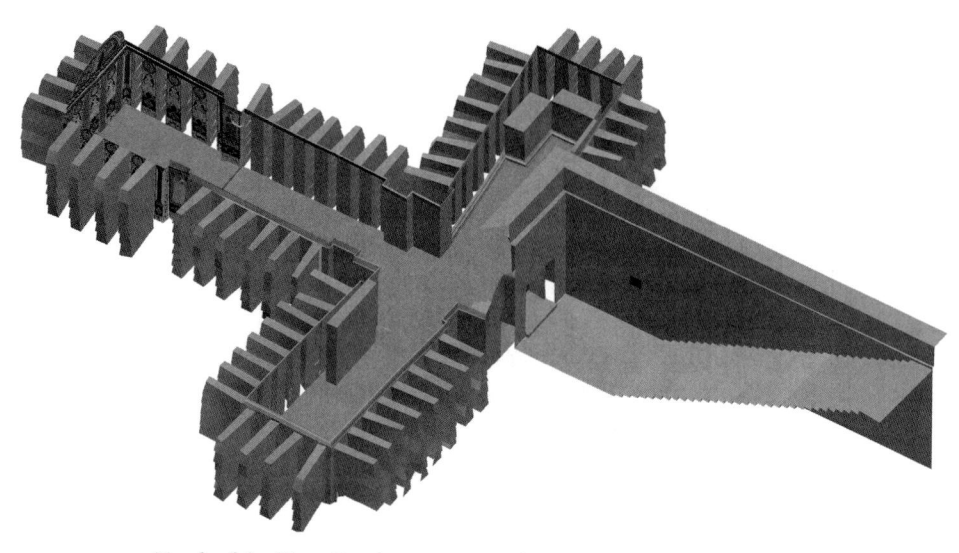

FIGURE 35.1 Tomb of the Three Brothers, topography and location of the painted exedra.
S. Lemeunier, as member of The Three Brothers Tomb (French-Syrian Project) who generated this 3D view.

filled in once again, are no longer precisely localizable and sometimes raise identification problems. Østrup (1894) provided a drawing of a tomb, the description of which seems to match that of the Tomb of the Three Brothers, but he localizes paintings in several exedrae (Sørensen 2014; 2016): Is this nevertheless the same tomb, or a seventh one? See Figure 35.2.

The chronology of the Palmyrene tombs is first based on the foundation dates inscribed on the façade; these dates are followed by dates of successive concessions, as the founders sold some parts of the monument to others, and so forth. The internal decoration is sometimes inscribed: the sepulchre of Malê at the Tomb of the Three Brothers bears the date 142–143, with no indication of whether this concerns the sculpted monument or the exedra. In contrast, in the tomb of 'Atenatan, the painted inscription under a painted medallion gives the date of 149–150. In addition to appearing on the decor, the pictorial technique is also used for some inscriptions, in particular for the property marks of the locations; these texts are painted vertically in red, directly on the spans, and are well-preserved in the Tomb of the Three Brothers (Yon 2019, 134–140).

DESCRIPTION OF THE MONUMENTS

The most complete example of a painted hypogeum is the Tomb of the Three Brothers (Eristov et al. 2019). It is the first presented here, followed by the five other monuments mentioned, in chronological order.

FIGURE 35.2 Tomb of Hairan. Image of the deceased, standing (Palmyra Museum).

By Courtesy of the Palmyra Museum, gift.

THE TOMB OF THE THREE BROTHERS

Discovery and Documentation

The hypogeum of the Tomb of the Three Brothers is located in the south-west necropolis, at the foot of Jebel Muntar. In 1899–1900, a range of inscriptions, photographs, and plans were collected by Moritz Sobernheim and then by Feodor Uspenskij. Josef Strzygowski (1902), followed by Boris Farmakowski (1903), used these elements to describe and analyse the tomb originally called Magharat el-Djedideh. The inscriptions systematically identified by A. Jaussen and R. Savignac (1920) were published by J.-B. Chabot (1922). Th. Wiegand (1932) and J. Cantineau (1936) cleared the tomb entrance, and Ingholt's publication (1932) first identified the site as the 'Tomb of the Three Brothers.'

Dating

The upper register of the lintel inscription at the entrance names the three brothers, Na'am'eîn, Malê, and Ṣa'adaî, 'who have dug and built this cave'; in 160 they sold a part, but one of the brothers had already built a grave in 142–143. Thus, the foundation of the tomb was followed by a series of concessions during that same year (160), and then in 191 and in 241 (Yon 2019, 134–140).

Decor

Although most of the hypogeum has been merely coated with white *djousse*, the walls and vault of the back exedra, on the entrance axis, are entirely covered with painted decor. This entrance opens out beyond an arch adorned with a pattern of secant circles. Both jambs are covered with a design of vine leaf tendrils; at the top, a small circle encloses a *fascinum* (partially visible on the southern jamb): the evil eye—superstitiously believed to cause harm —attacked by a sword, two spikes, and birds' beaks, is threatened by a cock, a snake, a spider, and two scorpions. This apotropaic composition fits naturally in exposed places and where the body is defenceless, as in vestibules, baths, and tombs (Donceel-Voûte 2014, 347–399).

On both sides of the entrance facing the painted exedra, two female figures (height approx. 1.70 m) are identified by their names and attributes rather than by their facial features, which are barely distinguishable. One is Bat'â, daughter of Šim'ôn, dressed in white, holding a child in her arms; she is flanked by a basket and a chest, and a small implement lies at her feet. The other one, Bat'â, daughter of Malê, dressed in red, stands out on a *dorsalium*, along with a chest and a basket. Such full-length representations are unusual; a rare example is, beside the deceased of the tomb of Hairan, for example, the standing figure of the tomb Q7 in Qweilbeh (Jordan) (Barbet and Vibert-Guigue 1988–1994, plate 59). In contrast, there are many examples of small funerary reliefs, most of them dating to before the middle of the second century (Simonsen 1889, 13; Colledge 1976, 66–67).

In the inner corners of the exedra, the Corinthian capitals of the pilasters imitate an architectural elevation. The nine pilasters that separate the spans repeat nearly identical designs: from the bottom up, these are a wildlife painting, a marbleized panel, a winged Victory, and a medallion. Along the tops of the walls, an illusionistic architectural decoration covers the real cornice relief and bears an astragal, a trompe l'œil meander, topped with an egg, dentil, and leaf frieze, and by modillions in perspective.

Along the bases of the walls, clusters of animals are organized in pairs (felines or jackals, and their prey) and groups (birds).

The circular geometric panels are inscribed in a diamond shape, and these sit in rectangles that mimic the marble marquetry (*opus sectile*).

The main figure on each pilaster is a Victory with long black wings, about 1 m tall, in a frontal view, but turned slightly to the left. Her feet rest on a globe enfolded in a bunch of acanthus, and she holds a medallion. Her white chiton, tightened at the chest and at the waist by a pink belt, is rolled up into a green semi-circle repeated above her ankles, and reveals her bare legs and feet. Her chestnut hair is crowned by a schematic wreath of quatrefoil leaves. Her raised arms hold vegetal crowns and medallions (interior diameter 0.42 m), the colours of which recall gilded bronze.

Five effigies of men and four of women are represented against a blue background, in an identical format: a bust with the left hand, the only one visible, at the height of the chest; each has the same rosy skin tone. Turned slightly to the right, the asymmetry of the neckline mitigates the frontal impression. All the men wear a grey-white tunic with lighter drapery over the left shoulder, with a woven ornament (gamma- or H-shaped) that the folds of the drapery transform into a zigzag (Szymaszek 2014 and 2015). Only the man in the middle on the west side wears a *clavus* tunic; he may also be the only one holding a cylindrical red object. On the south side, one of the men stands with a child whose bust appears behind the man's left shoulder and seems to wear a necklace or a bulla. All the women wear a highly conventional garment composed of a light pink chiton covered by transparent drapery, shaped by an asymmetric fold and held by a fibula. Upon a tall, white, cylindrical headdress, a green and light red torsade holds a rectangular grey-black central panel. A transparent white veil covers the headdress and cascades down onto the shoulders. All of them wear jewels: pearl-shaped earrings at the end of a spindle, and most wear two necklaces—one round the neck composed of large pearls, and another, thinner one, probably a jewellery chain holding a large pearl. The gesture of the left hand, turned towards the chest, enhances those jewels, as in sculpted funerary busts. This conventional iconography includes some individuality through some differences in the hairstyles, the possible presence of a short beard, the face shape, the colour of the garment. These would have been more perceptible in antiquity, and the details and their variations could probably identify individuals.

The medallions (*clipeus*) brandished over the heads of the Victories recall the iconography of the Tyche surrounded by winged figures (Schweizer 1931, 224–225), thus the *imago clipeata* worn by the Victory seems to signify the triumph of the deceased upon death. The Tomb of the Three Brothers makes unusual use of the Victory motif, itself common in Palmyrene sculpture, by displaying nine identical Victories (Colledge 1976, 81). However, as far as is known today, the Tomb of the Three Brothers is the only one to present a painted Victory on a globe, wearing the *imago clipeata*. The western lunette (approximately 14 m²), framed with a frieze of laurel and tendrils, is dedicated to an episode from the myth of Achilles. Seeking to forestall his fate, Achilles's mother, Thetis, entrusts him, disguised as a girl, to Lycomedes, king of Skyros. Under the name of Pyrrha, Achilles lives in the gynaeceum and secretly has a child with Deidamia. To unmask the hero and induce him to fight at Troy, Ulysses and the Greeks enter the palace after hiding arms among objects for the girls; the sound of Agyrtes's battle trumpet reveals Achilles's true nature, when he throws off his girl's clothes and takes hold of a spear and shield, to the alarm of his companions and Deidamia's despair. According to Pausanias, the genesis of this theatrical theme dates back to a painting by Polygnotus of Thasos (470 BC), exhibited in Athens: Achilles, wearing women's garments, plays the lyre in the gynaeceum. A century later, Athenion of Maroneus depicts 'Achilles hidden underneath feminine clothes when Ulysses recognizes him' (Pliny, *NH* 35.134). Finally, in the second half of the second century AD, Philostratus Minor includes the ecphrasis of a painting representing the same episode in his *Imagines* (Ghedini 2004b). The literary sources, mostly incomplete, mention this episode in the *Cypria* (Jouan 1966, 202), in a fragmentary poem by Bion of Smyrna, *the Epithalam* of Achilles and Deidamia (Richer 2016), in Ovid's Metamorphoses (13.162), in Seneca's Troades (v. 215), and, above all, in Statius's Achilleid, at the end of the first century AD (Figure 35.3).

FIGURE 35.3 Tomb of the Three Brothers, lunette, Achilles in Skyros.
Cl. Vibert-Guigue, as member of The Three Brothers Tomb (French-Syrian Project) who took this picture.

In the Tomb of the Three Brothers at Palmyra, the number and the disposition of the characters (ten figures in three rows) and the elements of the layout (mirrors, basket, garments) make this work remarkable; the green and vegetal background locate the setting outside, as in the *Imagines* of Philostratus Minor (Ghedini 2004b, 179–190). On the semicircular lunette, the figures are symmetrically distributed on both sides of Achilles: Ulysses, on the left, is symmetrically balanced by the trumpet player (Agyrtes) on the right; Deidamia is balanced by a female figure, dressed in black, perhaps one of her sisters. In the background, the veiled nurse, holding her face in her hand, resembles one of the figures on a beam of the temple of Bēl. The child near Ulysses may be Pyrrhos-Neoptolemus, future hero of the Trojan War, and not, as on Roman sarcophagi, Eros, symbol of the love between Achilles and Deidamia. Several Palmyrene painted inscriptions at the figures' feet, noticed in 2004, transcribe the Greek names of the protagonists in Aramaic (Yon 2019, 139). This iconography is widely depicted in wall paintings and mosaics created between the first and the fourth centuries AD, in numerous variations (Ghedini 2004a). In Palmyra, a mosaic from the house of Achilles represents the scene of the discovery of Achilles on Skyros as a frieze, similar to the Roman sarcophagi (Stern 1977). In the centre of the vault, a pattern of green hexagons encircled in red surrounds a blue medallion showing Ganymede with a Phrygian cap. Practically naked, he wears only a floating white chlamys clasped with a fibula. With his right leg outstretched, one knee on the ground, he gestures fearfully before Zeus as an eagle. His head, slightly turned to the right, mitigates the frontal impression. A well-known story mentioned in the *Iliad*, this myth was very popular in the Graeco-Roman iconographic repertory. Here, the iconographic formula differs from the one of Leochares showing Ganymede carried off in apotheosis (Mansuelli 1950, 32–33). Here we see the abduction, the *Ergreifung* (Sichtermann 1953, 65), and the boy is in the position of a defeated warrior. Six centuries after the mosaic of Morgantina (Sjökvist 1960, 132; Tortorella 2005, 54) (third century BC), the formula survives on the squared *emblema* on a tomb located in Tyre (Chéhab 1975, 373; Wattel-de Croizant 2001, 268). This theme fits all contexts, both domestic and funerary (Santucci 2010; Foucher 1979; Kempter 1980), and all interpretations, from parody (Bruneau 1962) to apotheosis. This amorous abduction may also be interpreted in an eschatological or astrological way, as Ganymede is placed in the sky as the constellation of Aquarius (Wolf 2008, 85).

THE TOMB OF ZABAD'ATEH AND NEŠA, SON OF ḤAṬRAI (AL-AS'AD 2013, 18)

In the tomb Zabad'ateh and Neša, dated AD 130/131, the back exedra is composed of two *arcosolia* or funerary niches. The southern wall has four spans of loculi, and the northern and western ones have one and six, respectively. Some remnants of the mural coating are still visible in some places, especially in the northern *arcosolium*. The *djousse* is roughly spread and very irregular in thickness (approximately 1 cm). The wall surfaces around the *arcosolium* and its internal walls bear figurative designs on a white background.

Northern *arcosolium*: the coated and painted wall (3.80 m long by 2.60 m high, preserved) around the *arcosolium* entrance shows, in the front, two vine plants framing a large ritual vase. Its dark red content was supposed to appear clearly to the diners painted on the back wall of the *arcosolium*.

Each of the three walls of the *arcosolium* (1.84 m wide by 1.70 m deep) is adorned with images of three servants, surrounded by a wide red band, and at the back there is a banquet scene. The state of preservation enhances the outlines of the figures with swatches of the same red colour. However, the outlines of the faces are not clearly distinguishable. The whole complex resembles a *sinopia* (i.e., a preparatory drawing), although once there may also have been white highlights.

Side walls: Three servants in a frontal position float against the white background: the women wear asymmetrical-collared tunics and are barefoot; the men wear rounded-collar tunics with slightly puffed trousers. Their red hair falls over their shoulders. Each of the figures in these two groups of three, displayed alternately on two walls, holds a dish. In one of them, it is possible to see the red contents (liquid?), and the other five hold a green shape, possibly a solid element.

Back wall: Four figures are divided into two couples: on the left are two women, suggested by their whitish skin tone, in a frontal view, and on the right are two men dressed in white, in the banqueter position, holding a cup in their right hands. Although all the women have the same face, the one closest to the centre seems to be more carefully drawn against a light brown background. The mural gives an impression of incompleteness; the restriction of materials and the speed of execution contrast with the luxury of the sculpted banquet details. The men are not wearing toques and the women are apparently veiled, indicating a domestic setting rather than a religious one.

The Tomb of Hairan (Ingholt 1932, 1–14)

In the tomb of Hairan, the inscription on the door lintel states: 'Has done for his honour Hairan, son of Jaddai, son of Haiaran, son of Hantâ, for himself and for his daughters, year 18.' In the right exedra, at the centre of the intrados of the arch, under a garland, is an eagle (wingspan about 1.45 m). The side walls are crowned by a trompe l'oeil cornice with dentils and a black ovolo; beneath, a vine with green leaves and bunch of violet grapes surrounds a man on the left wall and a woman on the right wall. A painted inscription indicates the man's name: Hairan, son of Taimarsous; 1.45 m tall, he stands on a plinth, in the manner of a statue. He wears a black *clavus* chiton, covered with a brown himation, tightened into a knee-length toga. His wife, whose name is not indicated, faces him in the same position; her Greek garment is composed of a green chiton, a brown himation folded up on her waist, and a long veil that covers her head and cascades down to her feet; the only apparent jewel is a fibula that holds the himation on her left shoulder. She makes the typical gesture of funerary reliefs—left hand holding the veil and right hand folded back on the chest.

At the back, above the four niches, against a patterned background of tendrils and leaves, a medallion bears a male bust between two adolescents holding a crown (Ingholt 1932): their Phrygian caps and anaxyrides, and naked winged torsos indicate that they must be interpreted as the Dioscuri (Cumont 2015, 61), protective and psychopomp gods personifying the two hemispheres, supra- and infra-terrestrial, and the season cycle. An inscription gives the date of 149–150.

THE TOMB OF DIONYSUS (INGHOLT 1932, 14–20)

The door of the tomb of Dionysus, which bears no inscription, opens onto two side rooms, of which most of the niches are unfinished, and onto two central rooms, one of them with a painted mural (1.00 × 1.20 m): Dionysus, semi-recumbent, his left arm resting on a pillow and his right arm extended holding a cup, faces the spectator. His diadem and the nimbus, and his almost entire nudity, present him as a divinity. A himation covers his thighs and a part cascades over his left arm. A vine branch surrounding his figure seems to emerge from a large gadroon krater without handles. Some iconographic parallels may be found in Eastern representations of the god (Palmyrene tesserae and Badakshan paterae at the British Museum, London, inv. No. 124086). Concerning the pictorial technique, Ingholt notes that 'like the mural paintings of Hairan and his wife, this one is a drawing executed with a coloured outline, almost entirely in red, even though we can distinguish a kind of yellow shadow beyond the contour lines' (Ingholt 1932, 15). The suggested dating (second half of the third century) is based on stylistic criteria, on the fact that this tomb is unfinished, and thanks to the existence of two Greek painted inscriptions, one from 312 and the other from 333. Therefore, they were inscribed after the fall of Palmyra.

THE TOMB OF 'ATENATAN SON OF ZABD'ATÉ: AXIS EXEDRA AND EXEDRA OF MAQQAI (INGHOLT 1932, 12–14; 1935, 57–140).

Near the tomb of Hairan, the tomb of 'Atenatan, discovered in 1924, bears a bilingual inscription in both Greek and Palmyrene incised in a plaque embedded over the door and carrying the date of March 98. Another inscription indicates that the exedra on the right side of the entrance was built by Julius Aurelius Maqqai in 229. On this exedra, the spandrels on the facade feature two winged Victories in a three-quarters view (Ingholt

1935, 62), each holding a palm and a kind of branch with ribbons; dressed in chitons, the bottoms of which seem to blow in the wind, each stands on a globe. With their allusive and linear design, in an unbalanced and inclined position, they recall the painted Victory on a wood panel from Dura-Europos (Hopkins and Goldman 1979, 106), although, according to Ingholt, 'the jewels of the Victory from Dura underlined the Parthian influence, whereas the Victories from Palmyra are more similar to the usual Greek model' (Ingholt 1935, 62).

On the back wall of the exedra, Ingholt describes an effaced banquet scene, composed of a reclining man with a woman sitting at his left. The tops of the side walls are crowned by a trompe l'œil meander; the irregularity of the exedra led the painter to insert a narrow, triangular area adorned with 'a peopled scroll' motif (i.e., a stem inhabited by bounding deer, bull, masculine bust) between the meander and the ceiling decoration. On the vault, a design of red, blue, and yellow circles and ovals gives a three-dimensional effect by playing with lighter and darker colours inside the circles.

The extrados of the back exedra (Ingholt 1935, 62) features a garland interspersed with quatrefoil flowers. At the edges of the arch, two feminine winged figures, the bodies in a three-quarters position and the faces turned forward, dressed in chitons, hold the two ribbons cascading from the garland in one hand. The state of the mural's preservation makes it impossible to identify what they are standing on.

The Tomb of Abd'Astor (Ingholt 1938, 119–140)

The tomb of Abd'Astor in the south-west necropolis, 40 m west of the tomb of Lisams, was explored in 1924, and it is documented only by Ingholt. Its impressive facade—3.5 m tall—no longer had its inscription *in situ*. Two joined fragments (one found in 1937 near the entrance, the other found in 1925) of a bilingual text—five lines in Palmyrene and two in Greek—indicate that Abd'Astor, son of Nurbel, the doctor, established it for himself and his sons in the year AD 98. This tomb is organized in the classical inverted T-shaped floor plan, with spans of loculi on both sides of the central axis and on the three walls of the back exedra. This symmetry is broken by a square exedra, dug later, opening from the left side of the central axis; its rich decor gives this tomb a particular status in the necropolis (Ingholt 1938, 139, plate L, 2–3). Above three monumental sarcophagi displayed on three sides of a U shape, the bottom of the vault received stucco decoration, different from the simply coated ceiling of the entrance. The blue extrados is adorned by a succession of eggs-and-darts, leaves, astragals, and a half round. On the vault itself, a luxuriant hand-modelled vine scroll on a red background features tendrils with veined leaves and grapes being pecked by birds (Ingholt 1938). A very smooth moulding emphasizes the junction with the back wall. On the lunette, traces of black painting suggest the presence of two Victories holding a medallion with the bust of the deceased (Sørensen 2016, 116, figs. 11–12). The stucco relief enhances the back of the exedra, suggesting a trellis-roofed triclinium accommodating the banquet of the deceased, a widely occurring pattern in

FIGURE 35.4 Tomb of 'Abd'Astor, vault of the exedra.

Ingholt Archive Portrait Project. By Courtesy of Ingholt Archive Portrait Project and Pr. Rubina Raja.

the art of the Levant. Stucco scrollwork is a favourite motif in the vaults of the second century, as exemplified by the hypogeum of Ascia beneath San Sebastiano in Rome (Mielsch 1975, 182–183, K121, plate 88, 2). Here, the beautiful sarcophagi dating from the third century provide the most accurate chronological evidence (Figure 35.4).

CHARACTERISTICS OF PALMYRENE FUNERARY PAINTING: A TENTATIVE APPROACH

Excavated Hypogea and Fictitious Trompe L'oeil (or Illusionism) Architectural Elements

The architecture of the hypogea presented above offers limited space for decor; it is considerably restricted because of the spaces' small dimensions, mainly reserved for burials

(Eristov and Vibert-Guigue 2018). The pilasters between the loculi and the jambs provide narrow vertical spaces that shape the iconography (Three Brothers, Hairan). The arches (extrados and intrados) are suitable for vegetal decoration ('Atenatan, Three Brothers) or symbolic elements (eagle, mask). The vaults or ceilings depict a narrative that includes some figures in a geometric pattern (Three Brothers) or opening on an imaginary fictitious area (Abd'Astor). With regard to the semicircular background of the *arcosolia* and the lunette, these sometimes provide space for figurative scenes (Zabad'ateh and Neša). The exceptional lunette of the tomb of the Three Brothers reveals the painters' mastery of a type of composition known from only a few examples, although it seems to be an innovative solution developed in a funerary context in the Near East around the third century.

Until the third century, the painted decoration in the hypogea employed illusionistic architecture to structure their patterns. In dug hypogea, false columns give the illusion of built architecture and evoke precious materials: porphyry for barrels, gilded bronze for capitals (Three Brothers). The imitations of mouldings (ovolo, astragal, dentils), most of the time quite linear (Hairan, Three Brothers), contrast with the illusionism of the modillions and the meander ('Atenatan, Three Brothers). Stucco mouldings (Abd'Astor) use the same motifs derived from the sculpted repertoire as the cornices of domestic decor (Allag et al. 2010).

Figurative Themes

The figures in the *Palmyrene hypogea* may be divided into portraits or images that are more or less faithful to the deceased, and allegorical or mythological figures. The portraits, usually on medallions or *imagines clipeatae* (Three Brothers, Hairan), are associated with apotheosis and carried by either the Victories or by the Dioscuri; in contrast, the full-length figures welcome the visitor as he enters the exedra (Three Brothers), even if they stand on plinths like statues (Hairan). In any case, they are slightly individualized only by their garments, which also inform us about their status and, perhaps, about their devotion to Romanity. Depictions of banquets portray the deceased couples in the company of servants (Zabad'ateh and Neša) or not (back exedra of the tomb of 'Atenatan).

Among the allegorical or mythological elements, eagles are particularly represented because of their divine and psychopomp associations (see above), but also present are the apotropaic *fascinum*, the Victories, and, more rarely, mythological scenes (Ganymede, Achilles in Skyros), evoking disappearance, abduction, a change in state, and inevitable fate. Beyond their lively and anecdotal character, wild animals and their prey, influenced by the art of the steppes (Schiltz 1994, 56–62), accentuate the oriental character of the tomb of the Three Brothers in a caravan city where exchanges once took place along the Silk Route (Strzygowski 1901, 32).

PALMYRENE ART: BETWEEN EAST AND WEST

Iconography

Graeco-Roman iconography (Achilles in Skyros, Ganymede, *imagines clipeatae*) conveys ideological messages about the concepts of *virtus* and *fortitudo* (Kenner 1970, 146), about the choice (more or less voluntary) of a glorious death rather than a peaceful and obscure life (Ghedini 1997, 83–91), or about the idea of apotheosis. Yet these concepts are also identified in the cultures of the Eastern world. On the one hand, the symbolism of the funerary eagle (Cumont 1917, 52), which probably dates back to Babylonian myths, represents the victorious power of the cosmocrator Bēl-Zeus-Jupiter (Drijvers 1982, 709–733); on the other hand, some episodes of the legend of Achilles enjoyed an early popularity in the Orient, possibly linked with the cult of Achilles as a hero, widespread around the Black Sea since the fourth century BC (Sahin 2005, 413–426). This same duality influenced the iconography of the Victory on a globe, dating back to Actium (Hölscher 1967, 6), and had great popularity until the end of antiquity, even outside funerary contexts (Strzygowski 1901, 25–30), especially in the Near East (bouleuterion of Ashkelon: Fischer 1995, 144; Nabataean temple of Khirbet et-Tannur: McKenzie et al. 2002, 44–83; Starcky 1968, 206–235). The Syrian-Alexandrine form (Schweizer 1931, 224) of Victory holding a medallion or a *clipeus* demonstrates this double interpretation, Western and Eastern, of the same iconographic standard.

Parthian Art?

From the Euphrates to the Ganges, the Parthian sphere of influence affected the Palmyrene so that its Hellenistic art is original in comparison with the Roman Mediterranean. The frontal presentation, in particular, which is considered typically 'Parthian' (Schlumberger 1960; Ingholt 1935, 57–140), prevails in the figures of the deceased as well as in the representation of the mythical figures in the hypogea of Palmyra, although the frontal presentation is softened by slight movements of bodies or heads. From time to time the gesture is more expressive, and the violent movement of Achilles (Three Brothers) may be found in other Eastern examples (Strocka 1977, plate 63; Eristov and Vibert-Guigue 2014, 353–354).

In the Palmyrene hypogea, a more or less Eastern characteristic is evident in the type of clothing depicted and in its treatment: the Greek himation of Hairan contrasts with the Eastern shape of the folds; one of the two full-length representations of the deceased in the Tomb of the Three Brothers is dressed in Eastern fashion, the other as a Roman matron, but both wear the Palmyrene high headdress. This duality is also emphasized in the painted inscriptions, either bilingual ('Atenatan, Abd'Astor) or transliterated (Three

Brothers). Similarly, stucco reliefs in the Graeco-Roman style (Abd'Astor) take advantage of the local tradition of using plaster in domestic and religious architecture (Blanc 2014). Since the Macedonian period, artists and craftsmen carried forward some of the habits and exchanges with the Greek world while including certain pictorial conventions of the Parthians. These coexistences and integrations established an original style (Alabe 2014, 209–216). However, in Hellenized areas of agrarian Syria and in desert cities such as Palmyra or Dura-Europos, local forms contrasted sharply with Hellenized ones, depending on different artistic techniques (Balty 1995, 154; Griesheimer and Kamel 1998, 189).

Technique

The pictorial technique in the *Palmyrene hypogea* is the result of their dug characteristic. The visible irregularity of the rock is covered only by a thin layer of *djousse* (approximately 1 cm), which is a mixture of lime, sand, and plaster (Dandrau 1997; 2005; Abdul Massih 2005; Lucas and Harris 2012). Stucco reliefs, made of lime mortar and calcite powder, are skilfully stamped and modelled (Allag et al. 2010). Some preparatory drawings, incised or painted (Three Brothers), are made before executing the design of a painting *a secco* with pigments in binder (Ingholt 1932, 18–20), which include green earths, red and yellow iron oxide, carbon black, and Egyptian blue; in the Tomb of the Three Brothers, a rare pigment, mimetite, was noticed (Buisson et al. 2014).

This overview of Palmyrene funerary painting remains incomplete because of the small number of Palmyrene hypogea with paintings and stucco that have been explored and published. Nevertheless, beyond certain common features, the variety of situations, social statuses, and dates represented reveals a varied landscape of iconographic choices and cultural references and decorative styles.

BIBLIOGRAPHY

Abdul Massih, Jeanine. 2005. 'Etude ethno-archéologique sur la fabrication du djousse dans la vallée de l'Euphrate: Doura-Europos (Salhiyé) et Deir ez-Zor'. In *Doura-Europos: Études*. Vol. 5, *Paris, 1994–1997*, edited by Pierre Leriche, 199–212. Paris: Geuthner.

Alabe, Françoise. 2014. 'Y a-t-un art parthe à Doura?' In *Art et civilisations de l'Orient hellénisé: Rencontres et échanges culturels d'Alexandre aux Sassanides; Hommage à Daniel Schlumberger*, edited by Pierre Leriche, 209–216. Paris: Picard.

al-As'ad, Waleed. 2013. 'Some Tombs Recently Excavated in Palmyra'. In *Fifty Years of Polish Excavations in Palmyra, 1959–2009: International Conference, Varsovie 6–8 décembre 2010*, edited by Michal Gawlikowski and Grzegorz Majcherek, 15–24. Studia Palmyreńskie 12. Warsaw: Wydawnictwa Uniwersytetu Warszawskiego.

Allag, Claudine, Nicole Blanc, and Klaus Parlasca. 2010. 'Palmyre: Stucs trouvés près de la source Efqa (site de l'hôtel Méridien)'. *Syria* 87: 191–227.

Balty, Janine. 1995. 'Iconographie classique et identités régionales: Les mosaïques romaines de Syrie'. In *Mosaïques antiques du Proche-Orient: Chronologie, iconographie, interprétation*, 154–159. Annales littéraires de l'Université de Besançon 140. Paris: Les belles lettres.

Barbet, Alix, and Claude Vibert-Guigue. 1988–1994. *Les peintures des nécropoles romaines d'Abila et du nord de la Jordanie*. Bibliothèque archéologique et historique 130. Paris: Geuthner.

Blanc, Nicole. 2014. 'Les stucs architecturaux figurés de Palmyre (Syrie): Entre modèle parthe et modèles gréco-romains'. In *Antike Malerei zwischen Lokalstil und Zeitstil: Akten des XI. Internationalen Kolloquiums der AIPMA, 13–17 September 2010 in Ephesos*, edited by Norbert Zimmermann, 337–348. Vienna: Verlag der Österreichischen Akademie der Wissenschaften.

Bruneau, Philippe. 1962. 'Ganymède et l'aigle: Images, caricatures et parodies animales du rapt'. *Bulletin de correspondance Hellénique* 86(1): 193–228.

Buisson, Nathalie, Delphine Burlot, Hélène Eristov, and Myriam Eveno. 2014. 'The Tomb of the Three Brothers in Palmyra: The Use of Mimetite, a Rare Yellow Pigment, in a Rich Decoration'. *Archaeometry* 57(6): 1025–1044.

Cantineau, Jean. 1936. 'Tadmorea: N° 27, Nouvelle inscription du tombeau "des Trois Frères"'. *Syria* 17(4): 354–355.

Chabot, Jean-Baptiste. 1922. *Choix d'inscriptions de Palmyre*. Paris: Imprimerie nationale.

Chéhab, Maurice. 1959. *Mosaïques du Liban*. Bulletin du musée de Beyrouth 14–15. Paris: Librairie d'Amérique et d'Orient Adrien Maisonnneuve.

Colledge, Malcolm A. R. 1976. *The Art of Palmyra*. London: Thames & Hudson.

Cumont, Franz. 1917. *Études syriennes*. Paris: Picard.

Cumont, Franz. 2015. *Recherches sur le symbolisme funéraire des Romains*, edited by Janine Balty and Jean-Charles Balty. Turnhout: Brepols.

Dandrau, Alain. 1997. 'Gypse, plâtre et djousse'. In *Doura-Europos: Études*. Vol. 4, *1991–1993*, edited by Pierre Leriche and Mathilde Gélin, 155–157. Paris: Geuthner.

Dandrau, Alain. 2005. 'Etude pétrographique des enduits peints retrouvés dans le sanctuaire de la rue principale de Doura-Europos'. In *Doura-Europos: Études*. Vol. 5, *1994–1997*, edited by Pierre Leriche, Alain Dandrau, and Mathilde Gélin, 113–118. Paris: Geuthner.

Donceel-Voûte, Pauline. 2014. 'Barrer la route au Malin: une typologie des stratégies utilisées. Images et signes à fonctionnement sécuritaire sur support fixe dans l'Antiquité tardive'. In *The Levant: Crossroads of Late Antiquity; History, Religion and Archaeology*, edited by Ellen Bradshaw Aitken and John M. Fossey, 347–400. McGill University Monographs in Classical Archaeology and History 22. Leiden: Brill.

Drijvers, H. J. W. 1982. 'After Life and Funerary Symbolism in Palmyrene Religion'. In *La soteriologia dei culti orientali nell'Impero romano*, edited by Ugo Bianchi and Maarten J. Vermaseren, 709–733. Études préliminaires aux religions orientales dans l'Empire romain 92. Leiden: Brill.

Eristov, Hélène, and Claude Vibert-Guigue. 2014. 'Iconographie funéraire à Palmyre entre Orient et Occident: Le tombeau des Trois Frères'. In *Antike Malerei zwischen Lokalstil und Zeitstil: Akten des XI. Internationalen Kolloquiums der AIPMA, 13–17 september 2010 in Ephesos*, edited by Norbert Zimmermann, 349–358. Vienna: Verlag der Österreichischen Akademie der Wissenschaften.

Eristov, Hélène, and Claude Vibert-Guigue. 2018. 'Décors muraux au Proche-Orient'. In *Pictores per provincias II – Status quaestionis: Actes du XIII colloque international de l'AIPMA,*

Lausanne, 12–16 septembre 2016, edited by Yves Dubois and Urs Niffeler, 37–54. Antiqua 55. Lausanne: Archäologie Schweiz.

Eristov, Hélène, Claude Vibert-Guigue, et al. 2019. *Le tombeau des Trois Frères à Palmyre.* Bibliothèque archéologique et historique 215. Beirut: Institut français du Proche-Orient.

Farmakowski, Boris. 1903. 'Живопись въ Пальмирѣ'. *Bulletin de l'Institut archéologique russe de Constantinople* 8: 172–198.

Fischer, Moshe. 1995. 'The Basilica of Ascalon: Marble, Imperial Art, and Architecture in Roman Palestine'. In *The Roman and Byzantine Near East: Some Recent Archaeological Research*, edited by John H. Humphrey, 121–150. Journal of Roman Archaeology, Supplementary Series 14. Ann Arbor: Cushing-Malloy.

Foucher, Louis. 1979. 'L'enlèvement de Ganymède figuré sur les mosaïques'. *Antiquités africaines* 14: 155–168.

Ghedini, Francesca. 1997. 'Miti greci nella pittura della prima età imperiale come specchio di un messaggio ideologico: Achille a Sciro'. In *Le Giornate del Castello: Incontri di studio; Pordenone, ottobre–novembre 1996*, 83–91. Quaderni del Museo Archeologico del Friuli Occidentale 1. Udine: Forum.

Ghedini, Francesca. 2004a. 'Achille a Sciro'. In *Le immagini di Filostrato Minore: La prospettiva dello storico dell'arte*, edited by Francesca Ghedini, Isabella Colpo, and Marta Novello, 17–26. Antenor 3. Rome: Quasar.

Ghedini, Francesca. 2004b. 'Filostrato Minore: La prospettiva dello storico dell'arte'. In *Le Immagini di Filostrato Minore: La prospettiva dello storico dell'arte*, edited by Francesca Ghedini, Isabella Colpo, and Marta Novello, 179–190. Antenor 3. Rome: Quasar.

Griesheimer, Marc, and Chehadeh Kamel. 1998. 'Les reliefs funéraires du tombeau du prêtre Rapsonès (Babulin, Syrie du Nord)'. *Syria* 75: 171–192.

Hölscher, Tonio. 1967. *Victoria Romana.* Mainz: von Zabern.

Hopkins, Clark, and Bernard Goldman, eds. 1979. *The Discovery of Dura-Europos.* New Haven, CT: Yale University Press.

Ingholt, Harald. 1932. 'Quelques fresques récemment découvertes à Palmyre'. *Acta archaeologica* 3: 1–20.

Ingholt, Harald. 1935. 'Five Dated Tombs from Palmyra'. *Berytus* 2: 57–140.

Ingholt, Harald. 1938. 'Inscriptions and Sculptures from Palmyra, II'. *Berytus* 5: 93–140.

Jaussen, Antonin, and Raphaël Savignac. 1920. 'Mission épigraphique à Palmyre (juillet 1914)'. *Revue biblique* 29: 359–373.

Jouan, François. 1966. *Euripide et les légendes des chants cypriens.* Paris: Les belles lettres.

Kempter, Gerda. 1980. *Ganymed: Studien zur Typologie, Ikonographie und Iconology.* Cologne: Böhlau.

Kenner, Hedwig. 1970. *Das Phänomen der verkehrten Welt in der griechisch-römischen Antike.* Bonn: Habelt.

Kraeling, Carl Hermann. 1961–1962. 'Color Photographs of the Paintings in the Tomb of the Three Brothers at Palmyra'. *Annales archéologiques de Syrie* 11–12: 13–18.

Lucas, Alfred, and James Rendel Harris. 2012. *Ancient Egyptian Materials and Industries.* 4th ed. North Chelmsford, MA: Courier. 1st ed. London: Edward Arnold, 1926.

McKenzie, Judith S., Sheila Gibson, and Andres T. Reyes. 2002. 'Reconstruction of the Nabataean Temple Complex at Khirbet et-Tannur'. *Palestine Exploration Quarterly* 134: 44–83.

Mansuelli, Guido Achille. 1950. *Ricerche sulla pittura ellenistica.* Bologna: Zuffi.

Mielsch, Harald. 1975. *Römische Stuckreliefs*. Mitteilungen des Deutschen Archäologischen Instituts. Römische Abteilung. Ergänzungsheft 21. Heidelberg: Kerle.

Østrup, Johannes. 1894. *Skiftende Horizonter: Skildringer og iagttagelser fra et ridt gennem ørkenen og Lilleasien*. Copenhagen: Gyldendal.

Richer, Hamidou. 2016. 'L'Épithalame d'Achille et de Déidamie: Entre eidyllion et epyllion'. *Aitia* 6. http://aitia.revues.org/1552.

Sahin, Derya. 2005. 'The *Amisos* Mosaic of Achilles'. In *La mosaïque gréco-romaine*. Vol. 9, *Actes du colloque de l'AIEMA, Rome, 5–10 novembre 2001*, edited by Hélène Morlier, 413–426. Rome: Ecole française de Rome.

Santucci, Anna. 2010. *Monumentum est quod memoriae servandae gratia existat (Ulp. Ad Edict., 11, 7, 42): La tomba del veterano Ammonio nella necropoli nord di Cirene e il suo ciclo pittorico*. Rome: 'l'Erma' di Bretschneider.

Schiltz, Véronique. 1994. *Les Scythes et les nomades des steppes, 8e siècle avant J.-C. – 1er siècle après J.-C*. Paris: Gallimard.

Schlumberger, Daniel. 1960. 'Descendants non méditerranéens de l'art grec'. *Syria* 37: 131–166, 253–318.

Schweizer, Bernhard. 1931. 'Dea Nemesis Regina'. *Jahrbuch des deutsches archäologisches Institut* 46: 175–246.

Sichtermann, Hellmut. 1953. *Ganymed, Mythos und Gestalt in der Antiken Kunst*. Berlin: Mann.

Simonsen, David. 1889. *Skulpturer og Indskrifter fra Palmyra i Ny Carlsberg Glyptothek*. Copenhagen: Linds.

Sjökvist, Erik. 1960. 'Excavations at Morgantina (Serra Orlando) 1959: Preliminary Report IV'. *American Journal of Archaeology* 64: 125–135.

Sørensen, Annette Højen. 2014. 'Revisiting a Painted Tomb in Palmyra'. In *XVIII CIAC: Centro y periferia en el mundo clásico / Centre and Periphery in the Ancient World*. Vol. 2, edited by José M. Alvarez, Trinidad Nogales, and Isabel Rodà, 1227–1230. Mérida: Museo Nacional de Arte Romano.

Sørensen, Annette Højen. 2016. 'Palmyrene Tomb Paintings in Context'. In *The World of Palmyra*, edited by A. Kropp and Rubina Raja, 103–117. Palmyrenske Studier 1. Copenhagen: Det Kongelige Danske Videnskabernes Selskab.

Starcky, Jean. 1968. 'Le temple nabatéen de Khirbet Tannur: À propos d'un livre récent'. *Revue biblique* 75: 206–235.

Stern, Henri. 1977. *Les mosaïques des maisons d'Achille et de Cassiopée à Palmyre*. Paris: Geuthner.

Strocka, Volker Michael. 1977. *Die Wandmalerei der Hanghäuser in Ephesos*. Vienna: Verlag der Österreichischen Akademie der Wissenschaften.

Strzygowski, Josef. 1901. *Orient oder Rom: Beiträge zur Geschichte der spätantiken und frühchristlichen Kunst*. Leipzig: Hinrichs.

Szymaszek, Maciej. 2014. 'The Distribution of Textiles with "Greek Letter" Signs in the Roman World: The Case of the So-Called Gammadia'. In *Textilhandel und -distribution in der Antike*, edited by Kerstin Dross-Krüpe, 189–197. Wiesbaden: Harrassowitz.

Szymaszek. Maciej. 2015. 'On the Interpretation of Textile Finds with Right-Angled or H-Shaped Tapestry Bands'. In *Textiles, Tools and Techniques of the 1st Millennium AD from Egypt and Neighbouring Countries: Proceedings of the 8th Conference of the Research Group 'Textiles from the Nile Valley' Antwerp, 4–6 October 2013*, edited by Antoine De Moor, Cäcilia Fluck, and Petra Linscheid, 168–175. Tielt: Lanoo.

Tortorella, Stefano. 2005. 'Hinc aquila ferebat caelo sublimis idaeum (Petr. Sat. 83,3): Il mito di Ganimede in un emblema da Privernum e in altri mosaici romani'. *Musiva & sectilia* 1: 35–61.

Uspenskij, Feodor. 1902. 'Monuments archéologiques de la Syrie'. *Izvestiya Russkogo Archeologiceskogo Instituta v Konstantinopole* 7: 93–212.

Wattel-de Croizant, Odile. 2001. 'Les 'amours des dieux' sur les mosaïques du Musée national de Beyrouth'. In *La mosaïque gréco-romaine*. Vol. 8, *Actes du VIIIème Colloque international pour l'étude de la mosaïque antique et médiévale, Lausanne, Suisse, 6–11 octobre 1997*, edited by Daniel Paunier and Christophe Schmidt, 265–275. Cahiers d'archéologie romande 85–86. Lausanne: Cahiers d'archéologie.

Wiegand, Theodor, ed. 1932. *Palmyra: Ergebnisse der Expeditionen von 1902 und 1917*. Berlin: Archäologisches Institut des Deutschen Reiches/Abteilung Istanbul.

Wolff, Étienne. 2008. 'Quelques interprétations antiques et médiévales du mythe de Ganymède'. In *Ganymède ou l'échanson: Rapt, ravissement et ivresse poétique*, edited by Véronique Gély, 85–93. Nanterre: Presses universitaires de Paris Nanterre.

Yon, Jean-Baptiste. 2019. 'Inscriptions araméennes'. In *Le tombeau des Trois Frères à Palmyre*, edited by Hélène Eristov and Claude Vibert-Guigue, 134–140. Bibliothèque archéologique et historique. Beirut: Institut français du Proche-Orient.

Zimmermann, Norbert, ed. 2014. *Antike Malerei zwischen Lokalstil und Zeitstil: Akten des XI. Internationalen Kolloquiums der AIPMA, 13–17 September 2010 in Ephesos*. Vienna: Verlag der Österreichischen Akademie der Wissenschaften.

CHAPTER 36

A NOTE ON QUARRIES AND TEXTILES IN PALMYRA

ANDREAS SCHMIDT-COLINET

THE QUARRIES OF PALMYRA

Introduction

The quarries of hard limestone situated about 12–15 km north-east of Palmyra supplied the material for most of the sculptures and buildings of ancient Palmyra. The ancient transport routes between the quarries and ancient Palmyra may be reconstructed from the half-finished or rejected blocks that still lie along these routes today (Schmidt-Colinet 2017, 169, fig. 7). The quarries have been explored, and detailed studies were first made between 1991 and 1993, through a collaborative project between the General Directorate of Antiquities and Museums of Syria and the Damascus branch of the German Archaeological Institute (Schmidt-Colinet 1990; al-Asʿad and Schmidt-Colinet 1993, 576, figs. 8–10; Schmidt-Colinet 1995b; 2005, 86–90; Schmidt-Colinet et al. 2013, 300, 302, 313–314, figs. 7–11; 2016, 341–344, figs. 5–7; Schmidt-Colinet 2017; 2020).

There are three large quarry areas situated close to each other, with many small extraction areas surrounding them. These areas around the quarries give information about the ancient environment and the infrastructure of the lives of people working in or living near the quarries: artificially enlarged caves were used as living quarters by the workers (Schmidt-Colinet 2017, 168–172, fig. 11). The necessary water supply was delivered by a sophisticated system of water channels and cisterns laid out over the entire area (Schmidt-Colinet 2017, 173–174, figs. 12–13).

Most of so-called dragon houses are located near the entrance passages to the quarries (Schmidt-Colinet 2017, 170–177, figs. 14–19). They are constructed of broken or rejected blocks and were used as shelters for guards and for storing equipment (Figure 36.1). Graffiti on the inside walls of these houses reveal names, probably of quarry workers.

FIGURE 36.1 Palmyra, Quarry no. 3, 'Dragon house'.

Photograph by A. Schmidt-Colinet.

Loading ramps are distributed throughout the quarries (Figure 36.2). They allow us to reconstruct the means of transport used, which are also known from sculptured representations: carts with a loading height of about 1 m, pulled by oxen (Wielgosz 1997, 74–75, plate 8; Schmidt-Colinet 2005, 89, fig. 145; 2017, 184, fig. 28).

All phases of quarrying may be observed, from the first quarry grooves (Figure 36.3a) to finished blocks ready for extraction (Figure 36.3b). Unfinished blocks left in the quarries (Schmidt-Colinet 2017, 179–183, figs. 23–26) and the traces of tools on the quarry walls give reliable information about the various methods and techniques used to quarry stone and to produce and manufacture the raw stone blocks. Various quarrying techniques date to between the first and third centuries AD. The traces of the tools testify to a fundamental change in extraction technique and to the introduction of new tools during a certain period. First, the so-called light Greek pick was used, which left straight, parallel marks (Figure 36.4, top; Schmidt-Colinet 2017, 166–167, 177–186; 2020, 54–55, 61, figs. 4–6). Later, the so-called heavy Roman hammer, which left so-called garland strokes (Figure 36.4, bottom) was used for extraction. With the new technique, it was possible to extract larger blocks with less effort and in a shorter time. This can be demonstrated with the columns in particular. With the earlier technique, smaller drums of columns were extracted vertically from the rock; with the new technique, longer column shafts were extracted horizontally (Schmidt-Colinet 2017, 186–189, figs. 30–32; 2020, 55–56, 62–63, figs. 9–17).

FIGURE 36.2 Palmyra, Quarry no. 3, loading ramp.

Photograph by A. Schmidt-Colinet.

As both vertical and horizontal quarrying techniques are evident in the columns fronting the temple of Baalshamin (erected in AD 130), the change in technique must have happened during the first half of the second century AD. Evidently, the change in technique occurred parallel to the building boom in Palmyra during the first half of the second century. That suggests an interdependency and correlation between the mentality of constructing buildings at Palmyra and the development of new methods of quarrying. Also, the different tool marks on the stone give clear hints of an at least rough date of otherwise undated buildings and thus for the chronology of the urban development of ancient Palmyra.

THE TEXTILES OF PALMYRA

Introduction

The more than two thousand textile fragments found in Palmyra—in the 1930s by a French mission (Pfister 1934–1940) and more recently in the 1990s by Syrian, Polish, and German missions—comprise one of the largest groups of antique textiles of proven origin (Schmidt-Colinet et al. 2000. Reviews: Linscheid 2003; Martiniani-Reber 2003;

FIGURE 36.3 Palmyra, different states of quarrying. 3a: Quarry no. 3a, first quarry grooves mark the dimensions of the blocks to be quarried. 3b: Quarry no. 1, quarry state block ready for extraction.

Photographs by A. Schmidt-Colinet.

FIGURE 36.4 Palmyra, Quarry no. 1. Top: parallel tool marks of the 'Greek pick'; bottom: 'garland strokes' of the 'Roman hammer'.

Photograph by A. Schmidt-Colinet.

Thomas 2003; Wild 2002; Yon 2004. Preliminary reports: Schmidt-Colinet 2005, 56–81; Schmidt-Colinet et al. 2013, 301–303, 311, 315, figs. 5, 12; 2016, 341, 344–345, figs. 8–11. Also see Will 1992, 84–86; Sartre 2001, 796, n. 27–29; Sartre-Fauriat and Sartre 2008, 89; Gawlikowski 2010, 67–68; Hildebrandt 2017; 2021). They come from about five hundred different fabrics and were found either as parts of mummy wrappings or as isolated fragments scattered around graves in the upper floors of tower tombs in the Valley of the Tombs. Their exceptional state of preservation is the result of the dry climate in the Syrian Desert and the darkness in the tombs. In general, the textiles may be dated to the first century BC through the second century AD because the tombs where the textiles were found are dated to this period by building inscriptions.

All the Palmyrene textile fragments were cleaned, restored, and studied in a collaboration between the Directorate General of Antiquities and Museums of Syria, and the Damascus branch of the German Archaeological Institute, between 1991 and 1999. Some of the restored textiles were presented to the public in permanent exhibitions in the museums of Damascus and Palmyra (al-As'ad and Schmidt-Colinet 1993, 568–573; Schmidt-Colinet 1995a; Schmidt-Colinet et al. 2000, 6–7, plates 1–10, 98–99; Stauffer 1996; 2005; al-As'ad et al. 2005; Schmidt-Colinet et al. 2013, 301–309, 311, 315, figs. 5, 12; 2016, 341, 344–345, figs. 8–11).

In contrast to other antique textile finds—such as those from Masada (Sheffer and Granger-Taylor 1994), from the Cave of Letters (Yadin 1963), from at-Tar (Fuji and Sakamoto 1987; 1992), or from Mons Claudianus (Bender Jørgensen 2000), the textiles from Palmyra represent only a small part of those commonly used in daily life, for two reasons: first, they were selected specifically for use in a funerary context; second, all were found only in the tombs of the very richest families of that period, which means that they belonged to, and represented, only the upper class, 'les notables de Palmyre' (Yon 2002).

The textiles found reveal an unusual amount of information about the history of Palmyra: about daily life and culture, about various burial customs (mummification) and religion, and about their economy and trade (Stauffer 1996; 2000b; 2005; 2007a; 2007b; 2010).

Two groups of Palmyrene textiles may be distinguished: textiles of local production and fabrics imported from China. The locally produced fabrics (Stauffer 2000a; 2000b) are made of wool, linen, or cotton (Figures 36.5 and 36.6). The fabrics imported from

FIGURE 36.5 Locally produced linen shawl, after restoration, from tower tomb of Yambliq, Museum, Palmyra, inv. no. PAM T. 77.

After Schmidt-Colinet et al. 2000, plate 21b; photograph by A. Schmidt-Colinet.

FIGURE 36.6 Locally produced woollen textile, after restoration, from tower tomb of Elahbel, National Museum, Damascus, inv. no. DAM L 63.

After Schmidt-Colinet et al. 2000, plate 62a, detail; photograph by A. Schmidt-Colinet.

China (Schmidt-Colinet et al. 2000, plates 75–97, VII–VIII) are made of silk. Some of the latter may be dated and attributed to specific imperial workshops owing to the Chinese characters woven into the fabrics (Figure 36.7) (von Falkenhausen 2000; Schmidt-Colinet 2000a; Stauffer 1996; 2007a; Żuchowska 2015; 2016). The textiles produced at Palmyra are generally of outstandingly high quality and have sophisticated designs. Most of them were woven using a tabby weaving technique of the highest standard. Wool, in particular, was dyed before weaving with various colours. The dyestuffs—from plants or animals—were found locally or imported by land and sea routes from as far away as India (Böhmer and Karadag 2000).

The patterns on locally produced textiles also appear on Palmyrene stone sculpture and architectural decoration (Figure 36.8). Apparently, the same patterns were used by

FIGURE 36.7 Chinese silk fabric, after restoration, from tower tomb of Kitot, Museum, Palmyra, inv. no. PAM K 10.

After Schmidt-Colinet et al. 2000, plate VIIIa; photograph by A. Schmidt-Colinet.

textile workshops, sculpture ateliers, and architectural workshops. This makes it possible to reconstruct and determine the distribution of pattern books. And, to a large extent, the typical 'arabesque' architectural decoration of Palmyra may be traced back to patterns of local textiles (Schmidt-Colinet 1996a; 1996b; 2000b; 2005, 54–61, figs. 79–85; 2016; Schmidt-Colinet et al. 2000, 41–46, plates 52–68).

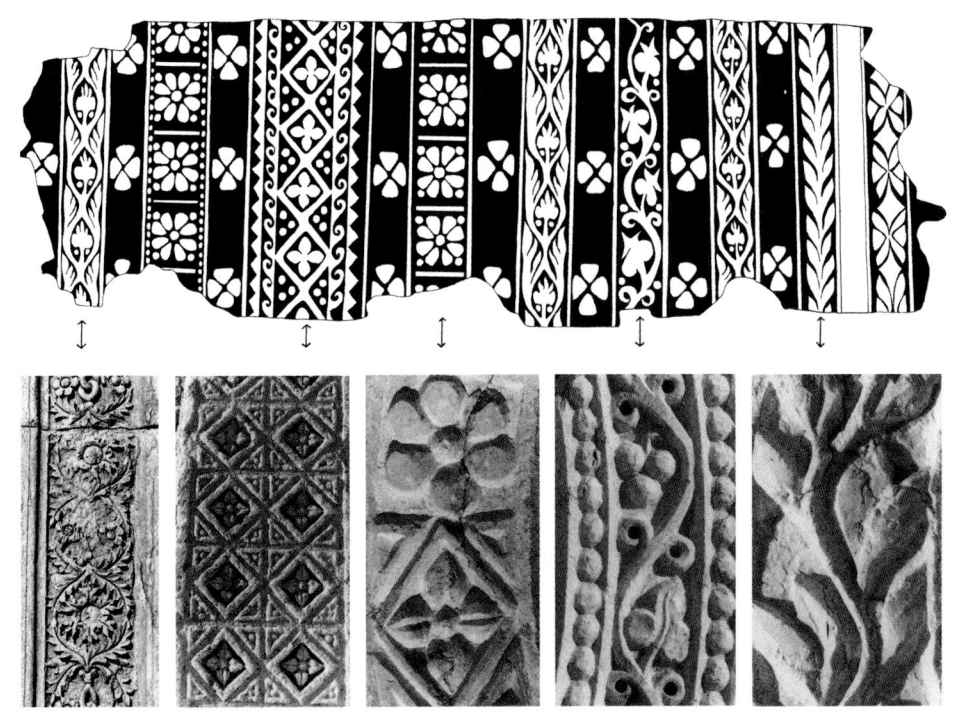

FIGURE 36.8 Examples of textile decoration (above) and architectural decoration (below) from Palmyra.

After Schmidt-Colinet et al. 2013, 311, fig. 5; drawing by A. Stauffer, photographs by A. Schmidt-Colinet.

BIBLIOGRAPHY

al-As'ad, Khaled, Jawdat Chehade, and Andreas Schmidt-Colinet. 2005. 'Die Textilien aus Palmyra. Ein internationales und interdisziplinäres Projekt'. In *Palmyra: Kulturbegegnung im Grentzbereich*, edited by Andreas Schmidt-Colinet, 64–66. Mainz am Rhein: von Zabern.

al-As'ad, Khaled, and Andreas Schmidt-Colinet. 1993. 'Palmyra 1990'. *Syria* 70: 567–576.

Bender Jörgensen, Lise. 2000. 'The Mons Claudianus Textile Project'. In *Archéologie des textiles des origines au Ve siècle: Actes du colloque de Lattes, October 1999*, edited by Dominique Cardon and Michel Feugère, 253–264. Monographies instrumentum 14. Drémil-Lafage: Mergoil.

Böhmer, Harald, and Recep Karadag. 2000. 'Farbanalytische Untersuchungen'. In *Die Textilien aus Palmyra: Neue und alte Funde*, edited by Andreas Schmidt-Colinet, Annemarie Stauffer, and Khaled al-As'ad, 82–93. Damaszener Forschungen 8. Mainz am Rhein: von Zabern.

Fuji, Hideo, and Kazuko Sakamoto. 1987. 'Roman Textiles from at-Tar Caves in Mesopotamia'. *Mesopotamia* 22: 215–233.

Fuji, Hideo, and Kazuko Sakamoto. 1992. 'Cultural Contacts between the East Mediterranean Coastal Area and Mesopotamia in A.D. 1st–3rd Centuries. The Marked Characteristics of the Textiles Unearthed from at-Tar Caves, Iraq'. *Al-Rafidan* 13: 95–103.

Gawlikowski, Michał. 2010. *Palmyra*. Warsaw: Instytut Archeologii.

Hildebrandt, Berit. 2017. 'Silk Production and Trade in the Roman Empire'. In *Silk: Trade and Exchange along the Silk Roads between Rome and China in Antiquity*, edited by Berit Hildebrandt, with Carole Gillis, 34–50. Ancient Textile Series 29. Oxford: Oxbow.

Hildebrandt, Berit. 2021. 'The Terminology of Silks in Texts of the Roman Empire: Qualities, Origins, Products, and Uses'. *ACTA VIA SERICA* 6(2): 117–140.

Linscheid, Petra. 2003. 'Review of *Die Textilien aus Palmyra: Neue und alte Funde*, by Andreas Schmidt-Colinet, Annemarie Stauffer, and Khaled al-As'ad'. *Berytus* 47: 173–176.

Martiniani-Reber, Marielle. 2003. 'Review of *Die Textilien aus Palmyra: Neue und alte Funde*, by Andreas Schmidt-Colinet, Annemarie Stauffer, and Khaled al-As'ad'. *Topoi* 11: 845–848.

Pfister, Rudolf. 1934–1940. *Textiles de Palmyre*. 3 vols. Paris: Les éditions d'art et d'histoire.

Sartre, Maurice. 2001. *D'Alexandre à Zénobie: Histoire du Levant antique, IVe siècle avant J.-C. – IIIe siècle après J.-C.* Paris: Fayard.

Sartre-Fauriat, Annie, and Maurice Sartre. 2008. *Palmyre: La cité des caravanes*. Paris: Gallimard.

Schmidt-Colinet, Andreas. 1990. 'Considerations sur les carrières de Palmyre'. In *Pierre éternelle du Nil au Rhin: Carrières et prefabrication*, edited by Marc Waelkens, 88–92, figs. 1–19. Brussels: Credit Communal.

Schmidt-Colinet, Andreas. 1995a. 'The Textiles from Palmyra'. *Aram* 7: 47–51, figs. 1–5.

Schmidt-Colinet, Andreas. 1995b. 'The Quarries of Palmyra'. *Aram* 7: 53–58, figs. 1–7.

Schmidt-Colinet, Andreas. 1996a. 'East and West in Palmyrene Pattern Books'. *Palmyra and the Silk Road: International Colloquium; Palmyra, 7–11 April 1992, Annales archéologiques arabes syriennes* 42: 417–423, figs. 8–14.

Schmidt-Colinet, Andreas. 1996b. 'Tessuti e decorazione architettonica a Palmira'. *Asia* 7: 20–27.

Schmidt-Colinet, Andreas. 2000a. '"Best Wishes from China". Ancient Textiles from Palmyra: A Glimpse on Globalization in Antiquity'. In *Das Spiel mit der Antike: Zwischen Antikensehnsucht und Alltagsrealität; Festschrift zum 85. Geburtstag von Rupprecht Düll*, edited by Siegrid Düll, 280–289. Möhnesee: Bibliopolis.

Schmidt-Colinet, Andreas. 2000b. 'Ornamentik'. In *Die Textilien aus Palmyra: Neue und alte Funde*, edited by Andreas Schmidt-Colinet, Annemarie Stauffer, and Khaled al-As'ad, 41–47, plates 58–69. Damaszener Forschungen 8. Mainz am Rhein: von Zabern.

Schmidt-Colinet, Andreas, ed. 2005. *Palmyra: Kulturbegegnung im Grenzbereich*. 3rd ed. Mainz am Rhein: von Zabern.

Schmidt-Colinet, Andreas. 2016. 'The Reconstruction and Distribution of Pattern Books in the Roman Empire: Some Archaeological Evidence from Palmyra'. In *Intorno al Papiro di Artemidoro III: I disegni, Atti del Convegno internazionale del 4 febbraio 2011 presso il Gabinetto Disegni e Stampe degli Uffizi, Firenze*, edited by Gianfranco Adornato, 129–46. Milan: LED Edizioni Universitarie.

Schmidt-Colinet, Andreas. 2017. 'Die antiken Steinbrüche von Palmyra: Ein Vorbericht'. *Mitteilungen der Deutschen Orient-Gesellschaft zu Berlin* 149: 159–196.

Schmidt-Colinet, Andreas. 2020. 'A Method to Date Stones, Just Stones: The Quarries of Palmyra'. In *Methods and Models in Ancient History: Essays in Honor of Jørgen Christian Meyer*, edited by Ingvar B. Mæhle, Per Bjarne Ravnå, and Eivind Heldaas Seland, 53–64. Athens: The Norwegian Institute at Athens.

Schmidt-Colinet, Andreas, Khaled al-As'ad, and Waleed al-As'ad. 2013. 'Thirty Years of Syro-German/Austrian Archaeological Research at Palmyra'. In *Fifty Years of Polish Excavations in Palmyra 1959-2009: International Conference Warsaw, 6–8 December 2010*, edited by

Michał Gawlikowski and Grzegorz Majcherek, 299–318. Studia Palmyreńskie 12. Warsaw: Wydawnictwa Uniwersytetu Warszawskiego.

Schmidt-Colinet, Andreas, Khaled al-As'ad, and Waleed al-As'ad. 2016. 'Palmyra: 30 Years of Syro-German/Austrian Archaeological Research (Homs)'. In *A History of Syria in One Hundred Sites*, edited by Youssef Kanjou and Akira Tsuneki, 339–348. Oxford: Archaeopress.

Schmidt-Colinet, Andreas, Annemarie Stauffer, and Khaled al-As'ad. 2000. *Die Textilien aus Palmyra: Neue und alte Funde*. Damaszener Forschungen 8. Mainz am Rhein: von Zabern. With Arabic abstract.

Sheffer, Avigail, and Hero Granger-Taylor. 1994. 'Textiles from Masada: A Preliminary Selection'. In *Masada*. Vol. 4, *The Yigael Yadin Excavations, 1963–1965: Final Reports*, edited by Joseph Aviram, Gideon Foerster, and Ehud Netzer, 149–282, plates 1–8. The Masada Reports. Jerusalem: Israel Exploration Society.

Stauffer, Annemarie. 1996. 'Textiles from Palmyra: Local Production and the Import and Imitation of Chinese Silk Weavings'. *Annales archéologiques arabes syriennes* 42: 425–430, figs. 1–8.

Stauffer, Annemarie. 2000a. 'Material und Technik'. In *Die Textilien aus Palmyra: Neue und alte Funde*, edited by Andreas Schmidt-Colinet, Annemarie Stauffer, and Khaled al-As'ad, 8–40, plates 11–74, 102–104, I–VI, VIIIf. Damaszener Forschungen 8. Mainz am Rhein: von Zabern.

Stauffer, Annemarie. 2000b. 'The Textiles from Palmyra: Technical Analyses and Their Evidence for Archaeological Research'. In *Archéologie des textiles, des origines au Ve siècle: Actes du colloque de Lattes, October 1999*, edited by Dominique Cardon and Michel Feugère, 247–251. Monographies instrumentum 14. Montagnac: Mergoil.

Stauffer, Annemarie. 2005. 'Kleider, Kissen, bunte Tücher. Einheimische Textilproduktion und weltweiter Handel'. In *Palmyra: Kulturbegegnung im Grenzbereich*, 3rd ed., edited by Andreas Schmidt-Colinet, 67–81. Mainz am Rhein: von Zabern.

Stauffer, Annemarie. 2007a. 'Antike chinesische Textilien als Handelsgüter im Westen'. In *Unter der gelben Erde: Die deutsch-chinesische Zusammenarbeit im Kulturgüterschutz; Internationaler Kongress Bonn 2006*, edited by Henriette Pleiger, 189–198. Mainz am Rhein: von Zabern.

Stauffer, Annemarie. 2007b. 'Imports and Exports of Textiles in Roman Syria'. In *Productions et échanges dans la Syrie grecque et romaine: Actes du colloque de Tours, June 2003*, edited by Maurice Sartre, 357–373. Topoi Suppl. 8. Lyon: de Boccard.

Stauffer, Annemarie. 2010. 'Kleidung in Palmyra. Neue Fragen zu alten Funden'. In *Zeitreisen: Syrien – Palmyra – Rom; Festschrift für Andreas Schmidt-Colinet zum 65. Geburtstag*, edited by Beatrix Bastl, Verena Gassner, and Ulrike Muss, 209–218. Vienna: Phoibos.

Thomas, Thelma K. 2003. 'Review of *Die Textilien aus Palmyra: Neue und alte Funde*, by Andreas Schmidt-Colinet, Annemarie Stauffer, and Khaled al-As'ad'. *American Journal of Archaeology* 107: 119–121.

von Falkenhausen, Lothar. 2000. 'Die Seiden mit chinesischen Inschriften'. In *Die Textilien aus Palmyra: Neue und alte Funde*, edited by Andreas Schmidt-Colinet, Annemarie Stauffer, and Khaled al-As'ad, 58–81. Damaszener Forschungen 8. Mainz am Rhein: von Zabern.

Wielgosz, Dagmara. 1997. 'Funeraria Palmyrena'. *Studia Palmyreńskie* 10: 69–77, plates 1–11.

Wild, John P. 2002. 'Review of *Die Textilien aus Palmyra: Neue und alte Funde*, by Andreas Schmidt-Colinet, Annemarie Stauffer, and Khaled al-As'ad'. *Journal of Roman Archaeology* 15: 675–680.

Will, Ernest. 1992. *Les palmyréniens: La Venise des sables (Ier siècle avant–IIIème siècle après J.-C.)*. Paris: Colin.

Yadin, Yigael. 1963. *The Finds from the Bar-Kokhba Period in the Cave of Letters*. Judean Desert Studies 3. Jerusalem: Israel Exploration Society.

Yon, Jean-Baptiste. 2002. *Les notables de Palmyre*. Bibliothèque archéologique et historique 163. Beirut: Institut français d'archéologie du Proche-Orient.

Yon, Jean-Baptiste. 2004. 'Review of *Die Textilien aus Palmyra: Neue und alte Funde*, by Andreas Schmidt-Colinet, Annemarie Stauffer, and Khaled Al-As'ad'. *Syria* 81: 327--329.

Żuchowska, Marta. 2015. '"Grape Picking" Silk from Palmyra: A Han Dynasty Chinese Textile with a Hellenistic Decoration Motif'. *Światowit: Annual of the Institute of Archaeology of the University of Warsaw A; Mediterranean and Non-European Archaeology* 12(53): 143–162.

Żuchowska, Marta. (2016). 'Palmyra and the Chinese Silk Trade'. In *Palmyrena: City, Hinterland and Caravan Trade Between Orient and Occident; Proceedings of the Conference Held in Athens, December 1–3, 2012*, edited by Jørgen Christian Meyer, Eivind H. Seland, and Nils Anfinset, 29–38. Oxford: Archaeopress.

CHAPTER 37

POSTLUDIUM

Palmyra and the Civil War in Syria

ANNIE SARTRE-FAURIAT

THE war that began in Syria in 2011 has spared neither people nor stones. Wherever one looks, the country has been bled, devastated, destroyed. No city, no historical site has escaped a destructive fury unparalleled since World War II. But the catastrophic damage that Syria has experienced since 2011 did not come about only because of fighting between various groups of combatants—it is also the result of deliberate, wanton destruction and looting.

The site of Palmyra is certainly among those in Syria that have suffered most from three plagues of violence which, between 2012 and 2017, annihilated traces of a glorious past and deprived science of new perspectives of knowledge. But the worldwide shock and horror felt in the face of this destruction has introduced a new danger: the desire to rebuild too quickly what was destroyed. Over and above the legitimate longing to see Palmyra once again as it was before the war, many questions arise now about the opportunities for reconstruction, the motives for undertaking them, and what Palmyra would look like in their wake. Modern interactive technologies, which allow us to restore stone and buildings virtually, are certainly one of the ways in which we can retrace the evolution of a monument across the whole course of a long and varied history. But the archaeological site of Palmyra, of which only 20 percent had been excavated before the war, has not yet delivered up all its wealth. Should we not rather devote ourselves to advancing scholarship, science, and the knowledge of the site at every period of its history?

FROM 2012 TO 2015: THE BEGINNING OF THE WAR IN PALMYRA AND THE FIRST DESTRUCTION

From the first outbreak of demonstrations against the Bashar al-Assad's dictatorial regime in March 2011, Palmyra, like other cities, was placed under surveillance.

Roadblocks manned by the army and security services were mounted at the entrance to the city to control access. The presence at the edge of the modern city of a terrible prison in which thousands of prisoners, many of them political opponents, languished raised fears of demonstrations and troubles even before taking into account the well-known antipathy of the Sunni population of Palmyra towards the Alawite regime in Damascus. Before the end of 2011, Palmyra had joined the protest against the regime, and the army occupied not only the modern city but also the archaeological site, which local people were forbidden to enter. The citadel overlooking the city was occupied by the army early in February 2012, and several military installations were established at its foot, especially in the area of the ancient northern necropolis, outside of the late Roman Empire rampart but on a vulnerable archaeological area that required protection.

Upholding such protection was the duty of the Damascus regime—the more so because Palmyra had been declared a World Heritage site by UNESCO in 1980. But Palmyra, no more than any of the rest of Syria's classified World Heritage sites (the old cities of Aleppo and Damascus, the Citadel of Salah al-Din at Sahyun, the Krak des Chevaliers, Bosra, the jebels of northern Syria), was not protected from the possibility of destruction inevitably generated by an armed conflict. This was all the more astonishing given that Syria had undersigned the UNESCO protocols on the preservation of cultural property, including the 1954 protocol signed in The Hague, by which the contracting parties undertook 'to respect cultural property situated within their own territory . . . by refraining from any use of the property and its immediate surroundings or of the appliances in use for its protection for purposes which are likely to expose it to destruction or damage in the event of armed conflict' (UNESCO 1954, Art. 4, 1). 'Cultural property' was clearly defined: 'movable or immovable property of great importance to the cultural heritage of every people, such as monuments of architecture, art or history, whether religious or secular; archaeological sites; groups of buildings which, as a whole, are of historical or artistic interest; works of art; manuscripts, books and other objects of artistic, historical or archaeological interest; as well as scientific collections and important collections of books or archives or of reproductions of the property' (UNESCO 1954, Art. 1a). The protocol concluded with the obligation to furnish 'cultural property under protection with the distinctive emblem: a shield, pointed below, persaltire blue and white' (UNESCO 1954, Art. 16, 1).

In 1999, the original protocol was further strengthened by the introduction of a clause for enhanced protection for 'cultural heritage of the greatest importance for Humanity' (UNESCO 1999, Art. 10a). In such a case, the parties agreed to 'ensure the immunity of cultural property under enhanced protection by refraining from making such property the object of attack or from any use of the property or its immediate surroundings in support of military action' (UNESCO 1999, Art. 12). As we will see, the Syrian combatants made no efforts to comply with the UNESCO World Heritage protocols.

At other sites as well as Palmyra—Aleppo, Bosra, Apamea, or those of the Euphrates Valley, including those classified as World Heritage sites—the Syrian army systematically occupied historic citadels and tells from the beginning of the uprising to secure a dominant position. The military occupation of Palmyra and its surroundings was intended to suppress any uprisings by opponents of the Damascus regime. To do so, the army fired rockets and mortar shells from the citadel or from tanks patrolling in the ruins 'on everything that moved', regardless of the economic consequences (destruction of plantations in the oasis) or the destruction of valuable archeological sites.

The Syrian army's occupation of the site caused vast devastation. To entrench weapons—tanks, rocket launchers, ammunitions depots, trucks—or to cut trenches, the armed forces dug into the ground in the northern necropolis. Antique blocks were removed and relocated to serve as protection and defence for armoured vehicles, and 2-m-high earth berms were ploughed into the archaeological areas, such as that west of the tomb of Marona or in the Valley of the Tombs, thus destroying many layers of these ancient tombs. At the same time, roads allowing military vehicles to access the citadel were laid in several sectors of the site, damaging the late Roman rampart and the funerary towers, and badly shaking the structures of the underground tombs.

Over and above these construction works brutally carried out without regard for the archaeological layers, the monuments of the site also experienced serious attacks from mortars and shells. At the temple of Baalshamin, one of the portico's column drums with its capital and part of the architrave was hit and collapsed. Several parts of the temple of Bēl were also damaged following bombardment during 2013. The wall of the temenos enclosure was affected at several points causing blocks to collapse; to the south-west, the portico on the temenos interior was breached in two places, causing the western architrave and a corner column to crumble, while another column lost its console. The south portico was hit in several places, and five columns were damaged to a greater or lesser extent, resulting in the shaking and shifting of drums, crumbling of shafts, the collapse of a capital, and the destruction of drums threatening the collapse of the whole column. The outer east wall was hit in more than twelve places. Nor was the temple cella spared. In 2013, the wall was hit at seven points on the east side of the exterior wall of the portico, and part of the architrave was broken. Precise reports drawn up on the basis of photographs taken by the Association for the Protection of Syrian Archaeology show that, in addition to the damage to the main temples, all the monuments of the site (the Great Colonnade, the arch, the theatre, the Camp and Wall of Diocletian, the baths) were to a greater or lesser degree impacted by gunfire or bulldozing (APSA2011 2015, 5–39, figs. 3–57). These images earned Ibrahim Moutlak, one of the photographers, his arrest, torture, and murder by the regime's intelligence services in 2013.

This destruction—which, in view of what the site was to undergo after May 2015, seems minimal—was unfortunately accompanied by a great deal of looting.

Since its rediscovery at the end of the seventeenth century, Palmyra has never really been free of the scourge of antiquity theft, and large numbers of objects from the site with dubious provenance figure in the collections of almost all of the world's museums. (More than 3,700 funerary portraits from Palmyra are scattered worldwide in museums, private collections, and the art market. An inventory is in progress, headed by Rubina Raja and funded by the Carlsberg Foundation). In the beginning, it was especially the mummies and the inscriptions that interested travellers who came to Palmyra, as evidenced by the narratives of the French traveller Claude Granger in 1735 or those of the English Robert Wood and James Dawkins in 1751. From the nineteenth century, interest was concentrated on the sculptures, and especially on the funerary busts carved in low relief on limestone plaques that served to conceal the entrances to individual burial niches (loculi) in the tombs. Heads in the round were also removed from the lids of family sarcophagi. Travellers and diplomats stationed in the Middle East were the first 'buyers' of these works, paving the way for a fruitful traffic in which dealers in antiquities based in Beirut or Cairo specialized (Sartre-Fauriat, 2023).

Despite certain precautionary measures taken by the Directorate-General of Antiquities and Museums of Syria (DGAMS) between 2012 and 2014, such as filling in the staircases to the underground tombs, a number of thefts were documented already since 2012. In some cases, the looting was the result of military construction works mentioned above, particularly in the northern necropolis and the Valley of the Tombs. The gutting of the underground funerary structures brought to light unpublished works of sculpture. In the south-eastern and western necropoleis, the Syrian government's attempts at 'protection' have proved derisory, and organized looting has robbed several tombs of their treasures. This was particularly the case with the Artaban hypogeum. Dating from the second half of the second century AD, this was one of the best-preserved hypogea. In November 2014, twenty-two busts and the head of a child were stolen from the tomb (APSA2011 2015, 42–43, figs. 60–61). In the same necropolis, two other hypogea were looted: that of Taybôl (Tomb H), founded in AD 133, was robbed of at least eighteen of its statues and three busts in low-relief that adorned the base of a sarcophagus; and its neighbour, the hypogeum of Bôrefa and Bôhla (Tomb F), dating from AD 128, was also robbed of many of its loculi plaques (APSA2011 2015, 44–46, fig. 63–64; Higuchi and Saito 2001). Discovered in 2001, until 2005 both of these tombs were the subject of superb restorations led by a Syrian-Japanese archaeological team (Saito 2005; 2007, 83–90). Clearly, the bearded, horned satyr that surmounted the entrance to Tomb F to deter violators was not sufficiently frightening to discourage modern-day thieves.

Some of the pieces fortuitously discovered by the army did not, as should have happened, find their way to the museum. In a very few cases, several pieces were found and seized before traffickers could export them to Lebanon or Turkey. In November 2012, sixteen slabs of funeral busts and eleven heads of statues were seized in Homs, north-west of Palmyra; many others were recovered between 2013 and in 2015 in unknown circumstances (APSA2011 2015, 49–53, figs. 67–72).

Many works, unfortunately, had already found their way out of the country, where they are being offered to collectors by smugglers who have not hesitated to use eBay and Facebook to sell their merchandise. Others have been auctioned by less than scrupulous antique dealers incurious about their provenance (for the bust put on sale in Turin, Italy, in July 2013; Sironi 2013, see also Penna 2016) who, to facilitate sales, have produced false certificates of provenance intended to legitimize objects they claim have been on the market for several years. In most cases, these pieces were taken from tombs that had not yet been excavated. Without documentation of the exact source, archaeologists are unable to analyse these antiquities and relate them to their architectural and historical context. And what is the value of an isolated piece to the historian, except for considerations of style?

THE PERIOD 2015 TO 2016: THE MASSIVE DESTRUCTION OF PALMYRA PERPETRATED BY DA'ESH

Already severely tested by fighting in 2012–2015, from May 2015 the site of Palmyra was to experience the most catastrophic blow to a world heritage site that one can imagine.

Rumours had circulated since mid-May 2015 that small bands of Da'esh jihadists had succeeded in taking villages near the oasis—al-Sukhneh and al-Amiriya—as well as several nearby gas fields. But it was on 20 May 2015 that the world learned with shocked amazement that Palmyra, too, had fallen into their hands. The barbaric atrocities committed by these men in Iraq led the world to fear the worst, even more so as the Syrian army withdrew from Palmyra without real combat after progressively evacuating over several days.

Questions remain. How did these twenty-odd pickup trucks, filled with men waving black flags, escape satellite tracking? They were able to cross hundreds of kilometres of desert, coming east from Raqqa with complete impunity. The highly suspect official statement states that no satellites, no aircraft, whether Coalition, Russian, or Syrian, noticed them or tried to slow them. We must wonder: What were both sides thinking as they allowed access to a group whose barbaric methods of dealing with populations and historical heritage were well known? Why did the Damascus army desert the field after a few skirmishes, and why was no attempt made to protect what could be protected? Contrary to statements by the DGAMS, photographs taken after recovery of the site in 2016 show that the museum had not been emptied of its collections prior to occupation. With the authorities apparently unconvinced that the fall of Palmyra was possible, everything was organized too late. Yet, two days before occupying the site, Da'esh spokesmen clearly announced their intentions on their TV channel: 'Now we're going to drive to Palmyra, destroy these heathen monuments, kill people in the theatre as examples, and then it's the turn of those who take care of these idolatrous cultures' (quoted in Schmidt-Colinet and Zederbauer 2017).

There was not long to wait before the fundamentalists' iconoclasm was seen at work. After destroying the marble stelae in the city's Muslim cemeteries, at the end of June they blew up two Islamic mausoleums: that of Mohammad ibn Ali, descendant of a cousin of the Prophet, to the north of the town, and that of the holy man Nizra Abou Baha ed-Dine, in the heart of the oasis and dating from the sixteenth century. With these actions they demonstrated that not even Islamic heritage was immune to their fury.

For a month, we dared to hope that the antiquities would not be affected. Claims surfaced that the people of Palmyra has reached an accord with Da'esh not to attack the ruins. One of the Da'esh commanders affirmed on 27 May 2015: 'Concerning the historic city, we will preserve it and it will not undergo damages, but what we will do is to pulverize the statues that the unbelievers worship. Contrary to what some are saying, we will not touch the monuments with our bulldozers' (audio interview on Radio Alwan, posted on YouTube).

We do not know what led them to change their minds after three months. The barbaric murder of the former Director of Antiquities of the site, Khaled al-As'ad, on 18 August, was the prelude to a full and definitive onslaught on the most beautiful, emblematic, and best-preserved monuments of the ancient city.

On 23 August, the temple of Baalshamin was dynamited. A few days later (perhaps on 27 August), it was the turn of the great temple of Bēl. At the same time perhaps, or in any case by 2 September, seven of the largest and most beautiful funerary towers standing in Valley of the Tombs or on the hill of Belqîs were reduced to dust. We were still struggling to recover from these shocks when the Severan Arch that marks the transition between two portions of the Great Colonnade was bulldozed at the beginning of October. The Da'esh jihadists carefully staged these scenes of destruction and then photographed the introduction of barrels of explosives into the cella of the two temples (Photo ASOR 9/2/ 15).

The archaeological world will never quite be able to sum up the loss to the history of the site and its inhabitants in antiquity that these acts of savagery represent. The balance sheet of monuments destroyed is, simply, frightening.

Of the temple of Baalshamin, nothing is left. The cella was entirely destroyed by the explosion. Only the columns of the porticoes of the enclosure, located some distance from the temple, withstood the blast together with—derisory witness—a small altar in front of the facade. In the temple of Bēl, the cella was also totally destroyed, along with all the columns of the portico. Only the monumental door, although shaken, still stands (Figure 37.1).

Lost are the walls, the columns of the peristyle and all their magnificent sculptures: the historiated beams, the ceilings of the cultic niches, the mouldings of the frames. Also lost are all traces of the later occupations of the temple, first as a church, then as a mosque, in particular the fresco representing the Holy Mother and Child surrounded by angels and saints (Jastrzębowska 2013), the inscriptions in Greek to her glory (*Inscriptions Grecques et Latines de la Syrie* [*IGLS*] XVII, 47), and the inscriptions in Arabic, one of them dated to the thirteenth century (Sauvaget 1931). These two temples of Graeco-Roman appearance were unique testimony to the cultural diversity of the oasis in antiquity. In their architecture, the ancient Palmyrenes showed that, between the first and second century AD, although they were integrated into the Roman Empire, they succeeded in keeping their own traditions while adhering to the dominant culture of the day (Gros 2017). The Graeco-Roman envelope of the sanctuaries did not overpower the particularities of local development and ornamentation connected with local cults and Mesopotamian influences.

FIGURE 37.1 Temple of Bél after 2015.

No less deplorable was the loss of seven of the most beautiful funerary towers, completely pulverized by explosives. In the western necropolis, the Tower of Atenatan, one of the oldest still standing (9 BC) and that of Elahbêl (AD 103) are now only heaps of rubble. The same is true of the tomb towers that stood proudly on the hill of Belqîs: the towers of Kitôt (AD 40), of Iamblicus (AD 83), of the Bene Baa, of Julius Aurelius Bola, and the anonymous Tower 71. All of these towers conserved in various ways the elements that were essential to the understanding of funerary customs and the adoption by the notables of Palmyra of the Graeco-Roman repertory of ornamentation for their houses of eternity. With them have gone exemplars of a unique funerary architecture: sculptures, painted stucco ceilings, property inscriptions, and sarcophagi surmounted by statues of their owners with their families. Over and above the loss to scholarship, without its iconic towers the site will never look as it did or hold the same interest as it formerly had. Its executioners exercised their punishment on both the world that honours the traces of the Graeco-Roman past and the Damascus regime which had made Palmyra a kind of showcase for Syria and the symbol, through the figure of Zenobia, of Syrian Arab nationalism.

The documented damage to the subterranean hypogea consists of brutal acts of looting. In the hypogeum of the Three Brothers in the south-western necropolis, the violations resulted from jihadists using it as a dormitory and dining room. The painted walls in the principal chamber were cemented over and the exedrae obscured by breeze blocks.

The Great Arch, apparently bulldozed mechanically rather than blown up with explosives, may be perhaps one of the few destroyed monuments capable of regaining its former splendour. To the casual visitor, the structure might seem a simple triumphal arch with three arched bays, the middle of which is taller. In reality, it was much more than that. In one respect, it was a masterpiece of imagination on the part of the architects who, after AD 212, accommodated it to the change in orientation of the third section of the Great Colonnade leading to the temple of Bēl, where it was repositioned relative to the second stretch from the Tetrapylon. Examination of the ground plan reveals that this third section is not in alignment with the second and that the bend in the trajectory had to be disguised. The arch achieved this through its form in the shape of a fan, with the eastern section of greater width than the western side, yet creating the illusion that the arch was rectilinear. In other respects, this arch bore an exceptionally important inscription to the history of Palmyra. On the edge of the cornice of a large console on the north side, an inscription commemorated the victory of Hairan and his father Odainat, husband of Zenobia, over the Persians who had come to plunder and destroy the cities of Syria in 259. These two notables of Palmyra had defended Syria for several years; following this victory, which allowed them to pursue the Persian emperor back to Ctesiphon, the two men were decorated with the title of their vanquished adversary, 'king of kings' (Sartre and Sartre 2015, 38–72). What was the fate of this console when the arch collapsed?

Finally, the Great Arch, built in the Severan period under the reign of the Emperor Caracalla or his successors and commissioned by a wealthy inhabitant of the city, is a beautiful example of Syrian decorative art at this time. For their great exuberance, the numerous sculptures that adorned the arch were named 'Syrian Baroque'; the temples of Baalbeck provide further celebrated examples. In Palmyra, the repertory of ornament adopted on the columns, arches, and coffer vaults marries in a unified ensemble elements that are both geometric and floral.

In the arch, we can therefore trace the importance not only of the monuments themselves, but also of the texts and the vocabulary of ornamentation that they preserved, which allow us to reconstruct the history and political and cultural evolution of Palmyra. For this reason, the destruction and looting carried out in the still unpublished tomb interiors of the necropolis constitute an immeasurable loss for historians and art historians.

From 2016 to 2017: Recapture of Palmyra and New Damages

The wave of emotion aroused worldwide as the first acts of destruction of Syria's heritage were announced was unequalled. Hundreds of radio and TV programmes and articles in the world's media were devoted to it. The universal media coverage had barely subsided when a major offensive by the Syrian army, supported by Russian troops, managed to recover Palmyra from the jihadists on 27 March 2016. Furious heavy artillery fire added to the destruction by severely damaging the citadel—a large section of the south wall collapsed, and other parts of the building were also destroyed. This imposing castle is mentioned already in a thirteenth-century Arab chronicle that attributes it to the emir of Homs, al-Malik al-Mujahid Shirkuh, in 1229. Reworked several times in the thirteenth to fourteenth centuries as the walls and towers were enlarged and extended, it was reinforced again at the beginning of the seventeenth century when the Lebanese emir Fakhr ed-Din II took possession of Palmyra. This fortress was intended to command the steppe and the movements of the local tribes.

The museum, situated between the ancient and the modern cities, was also severely hit by gunfire, and a shell went through the roof.

It was clear that, contrary to the Syrian government's assertions and in violation of the UNESCO World Heritage Site conventions (UNESCO 1954, Art. 8, 2), no attempts had been made to secure or protect anything in or around the museum. The devastation that we could see of the largest pieces, such as the family sarcophagi or the Lion of Allat in the museum garden, was dwarfed by the wholesale destruction of loculi plaques, mummies, and small artefacts held in the museum's showcases (textiles, glass, coins, stuccowork).

In the wake of the fighting and the eviction of Da'esh from the site, the museum offered a spectacle of total desolation. All funerary busts on the loculi plaques had been mutilated and deliberately broken, all free-standing statues had been knocked over and broken, the large statue of the goddess Allat in the form of Athena had been decapitated and dismembered, all the showcases had been broken, and the Lion of Allat was knocked over and broken into several pieces.

A quick on-the-ground review of accessible areas of the site confirmed what satellite photos had revealed of the major destruction. (Funeral towers located in a sector still deemed to be riddled with mines were inaccessible; there, remotely flown drones allowed us to visualize the destruction from the height of few metres and thus appreciate the extent and scope of the damage.)

In spite of the new destruction visited on the site, the recapture of Palmyra was hailed as a great victory over terrorism for the regime and for Russian forces. On 5 May, a grand concert was given by the St Petersburg Orchestra, conducted by Valeri Gergiev, in the theatre which, a few months before, had been the stage for mass executions of soldiers by the jihadists. Moscow heralded the concert as 'an extraordinary act of humanity'. Other countries saw it as, at best, a tactless attempt to distract attention from the continued suffering of millions of Syrians' (British Foreign Secretary 2016). At worst, the concert brought to mind musical performances staged in the Nazi concentration camps (interview on LCI on French television). At this same moment, Syrian and Russian planes were bombing the hospitals and neighbourhoods of eastern Aleppo.

The Syrian president's Russians allies, the self-styled 'saviours' and 'liberators' of Palmyra, were soon to discover the limits of the protection afforded to the site. In the days following the recapture of Palmyra, a large military camp was erected in the northern necropolis where the Syrian army had already undertaken destructive building work. Various structures were erected, including a barracks, bakery, hospital, landing strip for helicopters, and various air defence systems. Undoubtedly, soldiers require logistical support for their work in, among other things, demining. But here the question arises: What compelling reason necessitated the erection of a military camp on top of the acknowledged layer of archaeological investigation rather than at distance of 1 km? The desert area around Palmyra offers sufficient space to establish a military camp without prejudicing the archaeological site. For all the denial of the facts by the Russian defence ministry through the propaganda organ *Russia Today* (RT in French, 17 May 2016), the satellite images cannot lie. They show very clearly the location and extent of the camp (supposedly temporary but still in position). One dares not speculate about the damage caused by these works and the incessant coming and going of machines and men. If, as claimed by the Russians, the works were authorized by the Ministry of Culture or other Syrian ministries, this was simply an additional crime against Syria's already mutilated heritage.

Despite the regime and its allies' vaunted assurances of precautionary action in the press, Palmyra was not, in fact, protected. The political exploitation of the recovery of Palmyra from Da'esh came up against its limits when, in December 2016 the army of 'saviours' deserted the area to take up the bombardment of eastern Aleppo. When the Russian army surrendered the site in December 2016, a video posted by Da'esh identified the weapons that had been left on the spot and confiscated them for use (see the video on *Inform Napalm*, 22 December 2016). It did not take long for Da'esh, lying in wait a few kilometres from the site, to return in force to take the oasis on 11 December and engage not only in a new wave of massacres, but also in deliberate fresh destruction. Two monuments that had escaped damage under the previous occupation were deliberately destroyed between 26 December 2016 and 10 January 2017. The Tetrapylon, whose sixteen columns grouped in fours on four high bases at the crossroads of the two main colonnaded streets (only one column was authentic, the others were of pinkish concrete, supposed to imitate the pink granite of the originals, dating from the restoration of the monument in the 1960s), was partially demolished, and the central part of the stage wall of the theatre was destroyed by explosives (Figure 37.2).

The jihadists were driven out once again in March 2017, but Palmyra is still exposed to the threat of possible looting and now to over-hasty decisions to clear the rubble. The problem now confronting us, in the absence of fresh acts of destruction, is that of the restoration and reconstruction of the site.

Should Palmyra Be Rebuilt?

In the aftermath of the recovery of the site in March 2016, the Director-General of the DGAMS stated to the media: 'It will take us five years to restore and rebuild the destroyed buildings of Palmyra.' This statement, given in an emotionally charged climate and with an understandable desire on the part of Syrian authorities to erase the disaster which, through incapacity and neglect, they had helped to bring about, stirred reactions in the world of scholarship. A symposium held in Warsaw in April 2016 and

FIGURE 37.2 Report from [30] showing destroyed CH sites in Palmyra. This map was used as validation for the detected damaged areas.

bringing together all the scholarly specialists on Palmyra—archaeologists, historians, art historians—unanimously signed a statement warning very firmly against haste. They considered that, above all, it was necessary, in the immediate future, 'to limit oneself to an inventory, to consolidate what is in danger of collapse, to collect all the information necessary for subsequent restoration work, scientifically prepared and documented.' They concluded that 'no restoration or untimely reconstruction can be envisaged of the kind that some media have echoed in recent days, which could irreparably damage the authenticity of the site.'

Above all, before any work is undertaken, we must first be absolutely sure that the fighting is over and that new combat will not break out on the historical site. Of the tasks that we face, the least difficult will be to learn from failures of recent years in this area and to place the site under surveillance to prevent further damage. Assessment of the damage requires that nothing can be cleared in haste. On the contrary, a precise registration must be undertaken of all the blocks on the ground and a selection made of those that are capable of reuse. Indeed, the chances of restoration—still more of reconstruction—depend on the percentage of authentic blocks registered. This phase of the work will take well over five years.

Many other parameters also need to be taken into account. In particular, the technical skill of those to whom the worksite will be entrusted must be assured. Above all, there must be a clear definition of objectives, for what, and for whom. Russian scholars who have at no time ever excavated or participated in the study of the Palmyra site can be heard today capitalizing on their status as 'victors' and the credit they hold with the Damascus regime to expect that they will be awarded the restoration of the site. (The permanent exhibition at the Hermitage Museum in St Petersburg, since 1901, of the so-called 'Tariff of Palmyra' is due to a gift by the Sultan Abdulhamid II to a Russian traveller, the Prince Simon Abamelek Lazareff who, in 1891, had discovered in Palmyra the four slabs on which the text was inscribed.) In the past two years, two agreements were concluded between the Russians and the Syrians. The first was with the Hermitage Museum in Saint Petersburg in November 2019 for the restoration of antiques from Syria and particularly from Palmyra. The second was with the Association for the Stone Industry in November 2020 for the restoration of the Great Arch. Recently, Russian and Syrian teams have cleared the area of the Efqa spring where the water seems to flow again, and a complete study of the Great Arch has been carried out, with the view to its reconstruction (Bulletin no. 13 of the Russian Academy of Sciences, Institute for the History of Material ci-ulture, St Petersburg, 2022). The phrase 'Do not do a Disneyland' or 'a Palmyraland' is frequently heard and sometimes ridiculed, but lying behind these expressions is the fear of an unsuitable reconstruction pushed through to bring tourists back to the area without any regards for the site's value and authenticity. Syria's economic situation naturally requires the maximization of resources, and the notorious events at Palmyra cause many to fear the influx of large numbers of visitors to the site whose primary interest is not cultural. Do we want to make Palmyra into a pseudo-archaeological theme park, of the kind we already know in the Middle East? The examples of Jerash or Umm al-Jimal, with a Roman operetta army manoeuvring in the ruins, are not models that we should follow. We dare not imagine how Palmyra would look with its temples and towers reconstructed with materials that are too new, too white, and mechanically cut (or, even worse, made of concrete), as has already happened with the exterior wall of the theatre. One of the beauties of the monuments of Palmyra was the patina of their stones, which only time can bring. Considering the consequences, it might be better to leave the ruins in peace to bear witness to human barbarity and to imagine other methods of reconstruction.

Some museums already use animated exhibits, but today there are better, more modern interactive techniques that use 3-D glasses or iPads to allow the viewer to virtually walk around a site and see the monuments in three dimensions in their environment—both exterior and interior—and to follow their development step by step and their alteration over time. Of course, we must also be vigilant and cautious when faced with an onslaught of propositions from private specialists in 3-D visualization technology who want to seize quickly on the project. We are not immune to outlandish projects that, aiming at economic profit or worldwide notoriety, risk being insufficiently respectful of scholarly and scientific objectivity. We saw this with the purported reconstitution of the Great Arch of Palmyra in London, which respected neither the proportions nor the ornamentation of the monument. The 'New Palmyra Project', drawing on the work of Bassel Khartabil, the young Syrian computer scientist who developed an open-source 3-D reconstruction of the ancient city before his execution in a regime prison in 2015, could serve as model in the case of an eventual reconstruction, but it must be based on more reliable documentation than incidental images captured in an unsystematic way.

Such a technological solution is perfectly possible if we are prepared to use the abundant and precise scholarly documentation that we already possess on the destroyed monuments. These include the archives of the work carried out at the temple of Bēl by the architect Robert Amy and jointly published with Henri Seyrig and Ernest Will (1968/1975). Robert Amy's archives in the Institute for Research on Antique Architecture (IRAA) in Aix-en-Provence contain more than six hundred documents (photos, plans, drawings, precise measures) that, together, constitute our memory of the temple and its excavation. If we decide, one day, to restore the temple, these will be of enormous assistance (Binninger 2017). The same is true of the temple of Baalshamin, which was the subject of a thorough scholarly study by Swiss archaeologists. Paul Collart, who led the project, bequeathed his very complete documentation to the University of Lausanne (Michel 2017).

The option of virtual reconstitution offers an additional advantage. The monuments can be shown at all stages of their construction and through their evolution over time. If we were to rebuild, then what monument in time would we privilege? Would we re-build the temple of Bēl as it was when it was completed at the end of the second century AD, or as it was in 2012? The temple was a church, then a mosque, for longer than it was a pagan temple: Why hide these evolutions, which left their powerful traces in the form of frescos and inscriptions in the cella of the temple? And, using this method, we could even bring to life the medieval village that occupied the temenos of the temple from the twelfth century until 1930, when it was evacuated to make way for the excavation and restoration of the temple.

There is also another perspective of fundamental importance that must be taken into account before any restoration or reconstruction of the destroyed monuments of Palmyra can be contemplated: the continuation of scientific research at the site. We know that the temple of Bēl was built upon an older temple, erected on the levelled tell of the second-millennium BC settlement. We know almost nothing of this earlier temple (except for some fragments identified in the foundations of the newer temple) and nothing either of human occupation during the second-millennium BC. Better know-ledge of this would allow to us to improve our documentation of the ancient history of the oasis. Before we think of rebuilding the temple, is it not more urgent to survey the site and excavate these lower levels?

Furthermore, by 2012, only 20 percent of the site had been excavated. Vast areas re-main buried in which essential historical information may yet be intact. The results re-vealed by the only two surveys carried out in the Hellenistic part of the city by a team of archaeologists led by Andreas Schmidt-Colinet between 1998 and 2010 are proof of this. The results of this partial excavation indicate that this large area south of the wadi al-Suraysir contains a wealth of information about the period before Rome's presence in the East, a period in which Palmyra was also a prosperous city, as evidenced by the anal-ysis of the buildings and artefacts revealed (Schmidt-Colinet and al-As'ad 2013). There is still so much to learn about Palmyra. Science must take precedence over profit and over spectacle.

The question posed by these unexplored areas is their integrity after eight years of warfare, during which no care was taken to prevent the repeated incursion of military machinery or looting. In these conditions, what will we find, and in what state? So much is gone, and, even if we somehow recover it, much of the historical knowledge of the site is forever lost.

It is clear therefore that there is no simple answer to the recovery of Palmyra. What we do know, however, is that nothing would be worse than rushing to rebuild the site for reasons of economy and politics. Finally, in a country so totally ruined, where millions of people are in urgent need of housing, infrastructure, industry, and commerce so that life can begin again, is it reasonable to commit so much money and so much energy in the coming years to rebuilding the antique ruins, important as they were?

What we thought was unthinkable in our time—the deliberate destruction of an ancient site fundamental to our history, the monumental witness to a glorious past and an original civilization—nevertheless took place. To our incredulity was added stupefaction, anger, and rage at our helplessness in the face of the destructive madness of a few radicalized fanatics. The Syrian civil war has laid waste to a site that belonged to all humanity. Let us then make sure that what is left is carefully protected and that it will not be damaged further in the name of profit.

Bibliography

Amy, Robert, Henri Seyrig, and Ernest Will. 1968/1975. *Le temple de Bêl à Palmyre.* Vol. 1, *Textes et planches*; vol. 2, *Album.* Bibliothèque archéologique et historique 83. Paris: Geuthner.

APSA2011. 2015. *Palmyra: Heritage Adrift; Detailed Report on All Damage Done to the Archaeological Site between February 2012 and June 2015.* By Cheikhmous Ali. https://en.unesco.org/syrian-observatory/sites/syrian-observatory/files/reports/APSA_Palmyra_Heritage_Adrift_Report_2012-20151.pdf.

British Foreign Secretary. 2016. 'Russia's Valery Gergiev Conducts Concert in Palmyra Ruins'. *BBC News*, 5 May. https://www.bbc.com/news/world-middle-east-36211449.

Binninger, Sophie. 2017. 'Le temple de Bêl à Palmyre. Étude préliminaire des archives produites par Robert Amy (fonds IRAA)'. In *Les archives au secours des temples détruits de Palmyre*, edited by Pierre Ducret, Pierre Gros, and Michel Zinck, 45–72. Paris: Académie des inscriptions et belles-lettres.

Gros, Pierre. 2017. 'Les choix formels et ornementaux des concepteurs du temple de Bêl: Une relecture à partir des recherches récentes'. In *Les archives au secours des temples détruits de Palmyre*, edited by Pierre Ducret, Pierre Gros, and Michel Zinck, 95–133. Paris: Académie des inscriptions et belles-lettres.

Higuchi, Takayasu, and Kiyohide Saito. 2001. *Tomb F: Tomb of BWLH and BWRP; Southeast Necropolis Palmyra Syria.* Vol. 2. Nara: Nara Research Center for Silk Roadology, University of Nara.

Jastrzębowska, Elżbieta. 2013. 'La christianisation de Palmyre: L'exemple du temple de Bel'. *Studia Palmyrenski* 12: 177–191.

Michel, Patrick Maxime. 2017. 'Le sanctuaire de Baalshamin à Palmyre dans les archives de Paul Collart à l'Université de Lausanne'. In *Les archives au secours des temples détruits de Palmyre*, edited by Pierre Ducret, Pierre Gros, and Michel Zinck, 11–25. Paris: Académie des inscriptions et belles-lettres.

Penna, Noemi. 2016. 'Il collezionista di San Mauro: ho comprato un pezzo di Palmira non so come sia arrivato a Parigi'. *La Stampa*, 6 April 2016. https://www.lastampa.it/torino/2016/04/04/news/il-collezionista-di-san-mauro-ho-comprato-un-pezzo-di-palmira-non-so-come-sia-arrivato-a-parigi-1.36588927.

Saito, Kiyohide. 2005. 'Excavation of Tomb H at the Southeast Necropolis in Palmyra 2004'. In *Reconstruction of the Ancient Orient in 2004: Proceedings of the 12th Annual Meeting of Excavation in West Asia*, edited by Directorate-General of Antiquities and Museums, 83–90. Damascus: Dar al-Marqaz al-Shaqafyieh. In Japanese.

Saito, Kyiohide. 2007. 'Tomb H (Tomb of TYBL)'. In *Southeast Necropolis, Palmyra, Syria, Nara-Palmyra Archaeological Mission: Directorate of Palmyra Antiquities and Museums*, edited by Directorate-General of Antiquities and Museums. Damascus: Dar al-Marqaz al-Shaqafyieh, August 2007.

Sartre-Fauriat, Annie. 2023. 'Palmyre, pillage d'un site d'hier à aujourd'hui'. In *Life in Palmyra, Life for Palmyra: Conference Dedicated to the Memory of Khaled al Asa'ad (1934–2015), Varsovie 21–22 avril 2016*, edited by Dagmara Wielgosz and Marta Żuchowska, 437–450. Warsaw: Uniwersytet Warszawski.

Sartre Annie. 2021. *Aventuriers, voyageurs et savants: À la découverte archéologique de la Syrie (XVIIᵉ-XXIᵉ siècle)*. Paris, CNRS éditions.

Sartre, Annie, and Maurice Sartre. 2015. *Zénobie: De Palmyre à Rome*. Paris: Perrin.

Sartre, Annie, and Maurice Sartre. 2016. *Palmyre, vérités et légendes*. Paris, Perrin.

Sauvaget, Jean. 1931. 'Inscriptions arabes du temple de bel à Palmyre'. *Syria* 12: 143–153.

Schmidt-Colinet, Andreas, and Walid al-As'ad, eds. 2013. *Palmyras Reichtum durch weltweiten Handel: Archäologische Untersuchungen im Bereich der hellenistischen Stadt*. Vienna: Verlag Holzhausen.

Schmidt-Colinet, Andreas and Andrea Zederbauer. 2017. '"We Should Do Nothing!" On the History, Destruction and Rebuilding of Palmyra'. Eurozine. http://www.eurozine.com/we-should-do-nothing-on-the-history-destruction-and-rebuilding-of-palmyra/.

Sironi, Francesca. 2013. 'Rubato in Siria, venduto in Italia'. *L'Espresso*, 1 July 2013. http://espresso.repubblica.it/internazionale/2013/07/01/news/rubato-in-siria-venduto-in-italia-1.56168.

UNESCO. 1954. *Convention for the Protection of Cultural Property in the Event of Armed Conflict*. The Hague: UNESCO.

UNESCO. 1999. *Second Protocol (1999) to the 1954 Hague Convention for the Protection of Cultural Property in the Event of Armed Conflict*. The Hague: UNESCO.

INDEX

Figures are indicated by *f* following the page number